# IRRIṮITJA
# KUWARRI
# TJUNGU

—

# PAST &
# PRESENT
# TOGETHER

 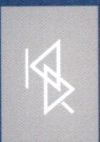

*Mirrinytjanyirriku*—for those who came before and left these powerful paintings, and to the Purple House, which has shown the power of art to keep people on Country.

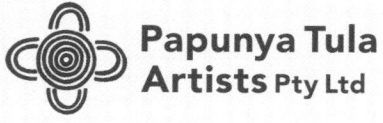  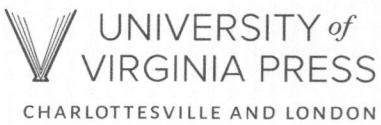

Published by the Kluge-Ruhe Aboriginal Art Collection of the University of Virginia

Distributed by the University of Virginia Press, Charlottesville

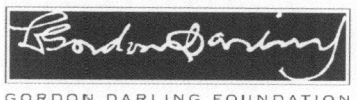

GORDON DARLING FOUNDATION

Publication Sponsor: The Gordon Darling Foundation made possible by Creative Partnerships
Australia through the Australian Cultural Fund and UVA Alumni Association

# Irrititja Kuwarri Tjungu | Past & Present Together

## Fifty Years of Papunya Tula Artists

EDITED BY Fred Myers AND Henry Skerritt

WITH CONTRIBUTIONS BY

John Kean

Steve Martin

Elizabeth Marks Nakamarra

Narlie Nelson Nakamarra

Eileen Napaltjarri

Charlotte Phillipus Napurrula

Punata Stockman Nungurrayi

Rachel Paltridge

Hetti Perkins

Cara Pinchbeck

Margo Smith

Marina Strocchi

Paul Sweeney

Morris Jackson Tjampitjinpa

Joseph Jurra Tjapaltjarri

Bobby West Tjupurrula

Jodie Napurrula Ward

PUBLISHED ON THE OCCASION OF THE EXHIBITION

*Irrititja Kuwarri Tjungu | Past and Present Together:*
*Fifty Years of Papunya Tula Artists*

CURATED BY HENRY SKERRITT

Kluge-Ruhe Aboriginal Art Collection of the University of Virginia
PART 1: 1971—1995 on view June 24, 2021—February 27, 2022
PART 2: 1996—2021 on view March 17, 2022—February 26, 2023

The Embassy of Australia, Washington, DC
March—September, 2023

*Irrititja Kuwarri Tjungu* is presented by the Kluge-Ruhe Aboriginal Art Collection of
the University of Virginia in partnership with Papunya Tula Artists. It is sponsored by
Robert and Molly Hardie and the H7 Foundation, the Gordon Darling Foundation made
possible by Creative Partnerships Australia through the Australian Cultural Fund,
Stephen and Agatha Luczo, the Embassy of Australia, the UVA Parents Fund, the Institute
of Humanities and Global Cultures, the Mapping Indigenous Worlds Lab,
the UVA Department of Art and the Vice Provost for the Arts.

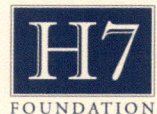
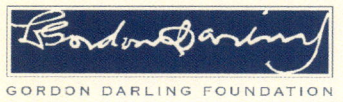
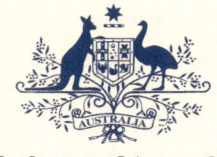

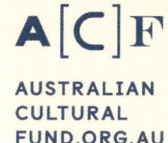
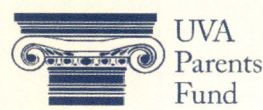
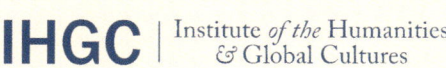

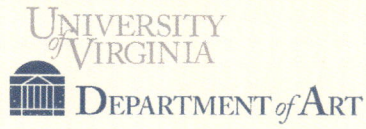
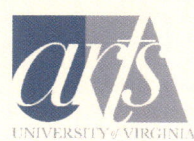
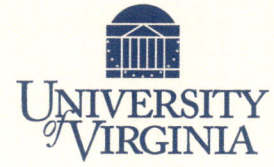

# CONTENTS

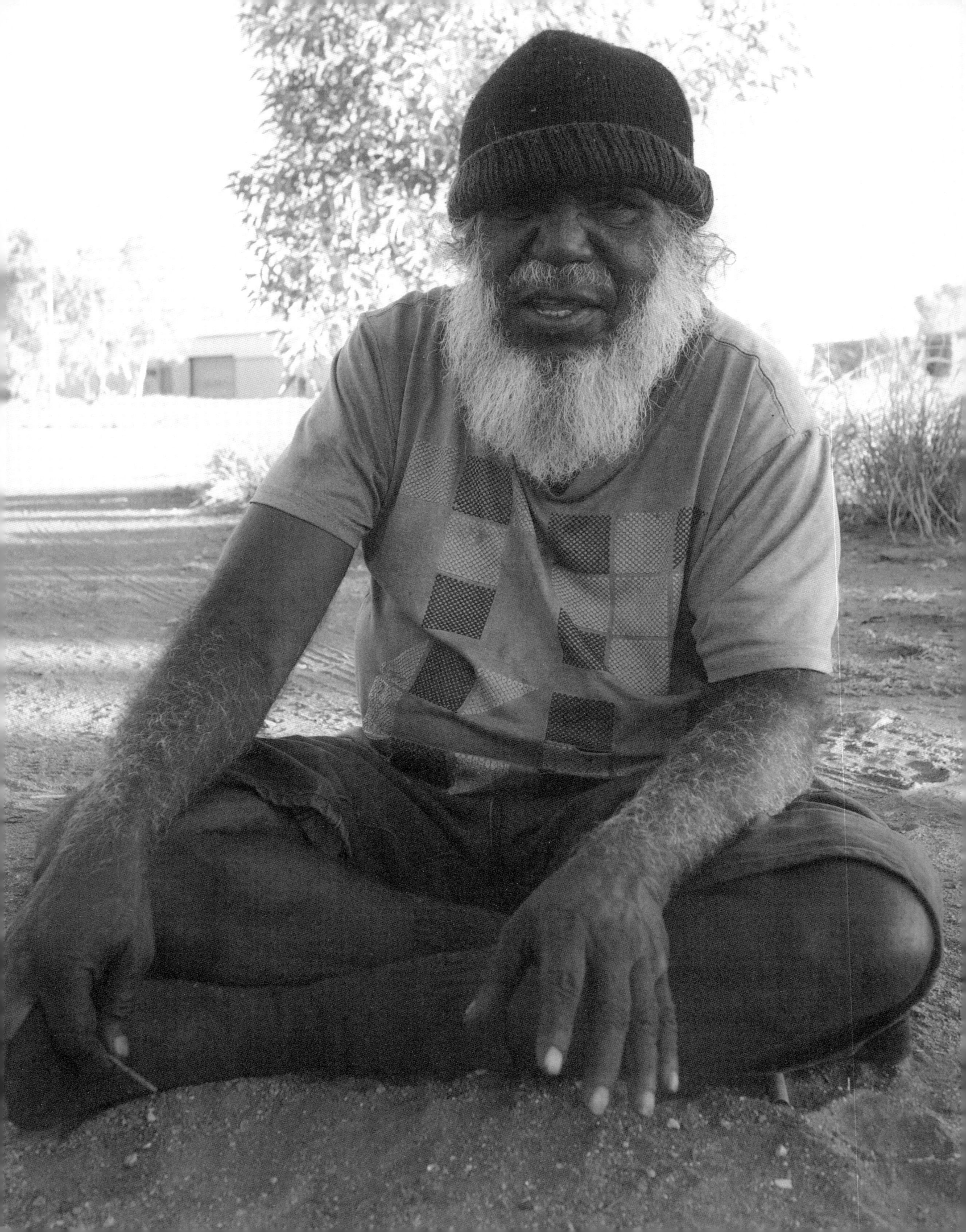

# PALYA | WELCOME

**This is for all the people in America looking at the pictures, all the canvases.**

*Kulila* [listen], this is our Tjukurrpa [Dreaming], *martupura* [important] Tjukurrpa from the old people, men and women. The Tingarri came from the bush a long time ago, and that's why we started painting. Painting makes everyone think about the old people. The company is good for the old painters. They like it. They say, "I want to paint him, *martupura*."

—JOSEPH JURRA TJAPALTJARRI

Joseph Jurra Tjapaltjarri
at Walungurru (Kintore),
December 2014. Photo by
Matt Frost.

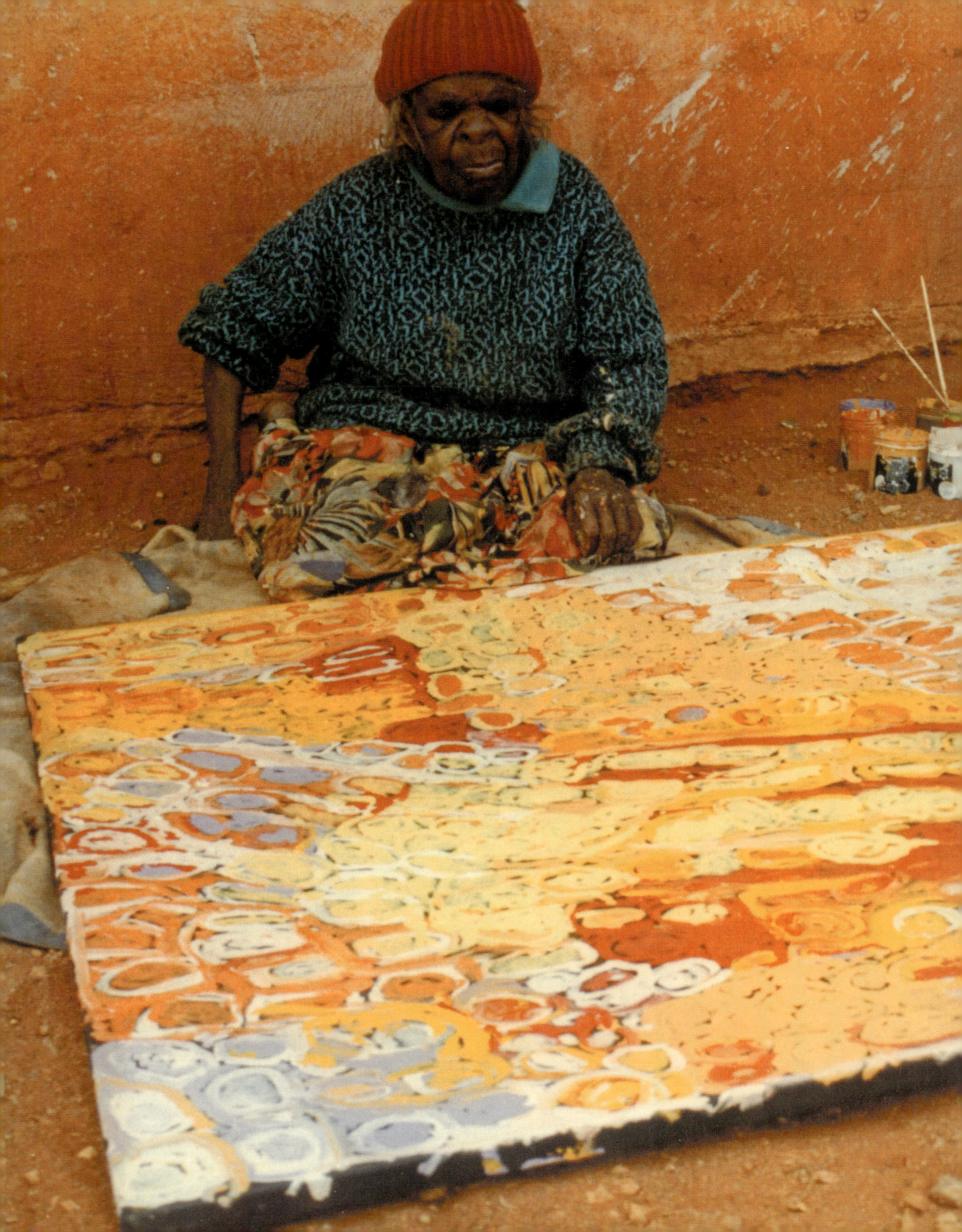

# Director's Foreword

This is a very special moment for the Kluge-Ruhe Aboriginal Art Collection. Around the same time that Papunya Tula Artists celebrates its fiftieth anniversary as a company, Kluge-Ruhe will celebrate its twenty-fifth year at the University of Virginia. More than signifying perseverance in the rapidly changing art world, these anniversaries provide us with an opportunity to reflect and to see how far we have come.

When I think about the fifty-year history of Papunya Tula Artists, four very different yet representative paintings come to mind. The first is *Pintupi Design* (1971, plate 1), the cover image chosen for this book, an unattributed early work painted on an irregular sheet of concretized fiber board. A printed floral design peeks through spaces where the thickly applied gold and pink pigments have chipped away. What are these materials? A piece of wallboard that was stripped from an abandoned trailer? Paint consisting of white acrylic mixed with red desert sand?

Even though the painter's name and the story of this painting are not known to us, this humble work reveals much about his urge to record important knowledge using whatever materials were at hand. It carries us back to Papunya where, in 1971, the materials available

to artists could not keep up with the demand. Paintings in Kluge-Ruhe's collection attest to the artists' use of any number of surfaces, from tiles to orange crates to car-door panels. Paints likewise ranged from watercolor to tempera to acrylic, with homemade pigments derived from crushed ochres and, yes, even sand, when needed. Lack of quality materials was not sufficient to diminish the enthusiasm of Papunya's early painters, who worked feverishly to document their extensive knowledge of country and Tjukurrpa (Dreaming). And, as if one side of this small board were not sufficient to contain the grandness of the story being represented, the artist also painted the other side. This raw and vivid painting looks as if it were manifested from little more than its maker's own will and knowledge. Professor Fred Myers says Pintupi men often remarked "Tjukurrtjanu *mularrarringu*" (from the Dreaming, it became real), when discussing their artworks; this painting captures that concept exactly.

My first experience of Papunya Tula Artists was in 1991, when I arrived in Mparntwe (Alice Springs) as a graduate student. Desert paintings were riding an international wave of high visibility and success following the exhibition *Dreamings: The Art of Aboriginal Australia* at New York's Asia

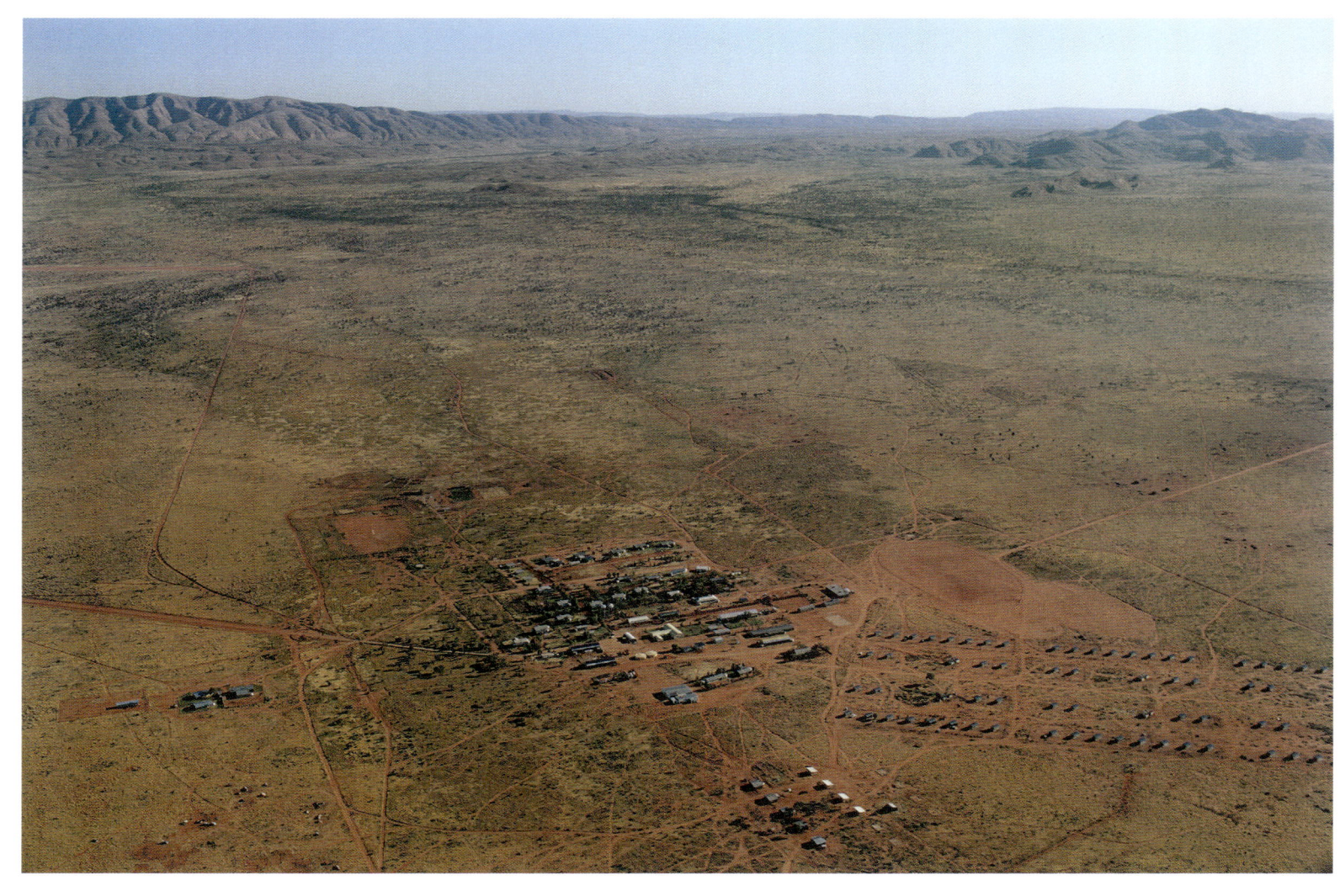

Papunya, 1972. Photo by Michael Jensen.

Society Galleries in 1988. Indigenous artists and their works increasingly traveled to exhibitions around the world, including a number of commercial shows at John Weber Gallery in New York. John W. Kluge was among the notable Americans who began collecting Aboriginal Australian art at this time. Papunya Tula Artists represented the hallmark of quality, and the canvases the company's artists produced in that period were enormous. The painting that comes to mind from this period is William Sandy Tjapaltjarri's splendid *Bush Tucker Dreaming at Wingellina* (1988, plate 42), which graced the cover of one of Weber's catalogs.

What I have always loved about this work is the way it effortlessly straddles differing aesthetic worlds. At first glance, it appears to be two paintings jostling to occupy the same space. By focusing intently on one of the roundels, the viewer can coax them into interacting, so that one layer appears to float on top while the other recedes to the background, and then, into switching places through a classic figure-ground reversal. The curvature of the jagged lines separating the two layers gives the interior form a slightly concave or convex appearance, depending on your perspective. Yet look again and realize these are not lines—they are seedpods of a bush bean called *walkapiri* (*Rhyncharrhena linearis*). Though not a particularly relished food, *walkapiri* has therapeutic qualities, such as preventing scurvy. Noticing these organic forms awakens me to the artist's intention and focus. In this painting, Sandy demonstrates Indigenous ways of knowing and seeing that personalize his relationship to Country and the nourishing resources it provides.

Returning to Mparntwe in 1996 as John Kluge's curator of Aboriginal art, I stopped in at Papunya Tula Artists' Todd Street location. Daphne Williams and Janis Stanton probed me to discover more about Kluge's enigmatic collection, recalling his memorable visit to the Papunya Tula gallery in 1989. As if letting me in on a tightly held secret, they unfurled a roll of canvases and awaited my reaction. This was a collection of the first paintings by women from Walungurru (Kintore) and Kiwirrkurra, who were on the precipice of emerging as stars. What I saw dazzled me with its passion and immediacy. Their male counterparts were, at this time, exploring a kind of minimalism characterized by concentric rectangles and line work that imbued their works with more contemplative tones. The women, on the other hand, seemed to be zinging paint at their canvases with unbridled urgency. As my eyes danced across one canvas after another, Daphne announced they had been consigned to Utopia Art Sydney. By the time I returned to the United States and contacted gallery director Christopher Hodges, only a few small works remained, and we swiftly acquired them for the Kluge collection. I still regret not having tried a bit harder to purchase the lot!

One need only look at Inyuwa Nampitjinpa's *Women's Dreaming at Pangkupirri* (1996, plate 62) juxtaposed with William Sandy's work to marvel at the shift. While diminutive in comparison, Inyuwa Nampitjinpa's painting packs a punch. The dots, which had become synonymous with desert painting, are more like dabs, overlapping one another with no apparent definition. White mounds, representing a place where a group of ancestral women ground tiny seeds to make dense cakes, seem to hover above the painting's gold surface, as if they will momentarily take flight. Are they the grind stones or the seed cakes, or possibly the women themselves? Or all three, simultaneously, exemplifying the multiple layers of meaning in ancestral stories? Paintings like this one fairly ring with the sounds that accompany women's work, the companionable chatter, fading into whispers when talk turns to sensitive subjects or gossip, and songs recounting deeds of the old people who enlivened the Country.

The final work that speaks to me about the history of Papunya Tula painting is the *Fiftieth Anniversary Suite* commissioned for *Irrititja Kuwarri Tjungu*, acquired by Kluge-Ruhe's great friends Richard Klingler and Jane Slatter and loaned to the museum for the second part of the exhibition. This selection of fifty works by contemporary artists includes paintings by Warlimpirrnga Tjapaltjarri and Yukultji Napangati, two of the company's most esteemed artists, who have each earned solo exhibitions at New York's Salon 94 and garnered international attention. They are also members of the "Pintupi Nine," who pursued a hunter-gatherer lifestyle until 1984 when they joined their relatives at Kiwirrkurra. Their paintings hang side by side with works by descendants of the original Papunya painting men, such as Bobby West Tjupurrula (son of Freddy West Tjakamarra) and Eileen Napaltjarri (daughter of Charlie Wartuma Tjungurrayi). The relatively small, 24 × 21⅝–inch canvases that compose this historic commission are hardly a departure for Papunya Tula. Even the most storied artists produced works of varying sizes. What makes this work unique is the collective knowledge embodied in this montage, spanning the

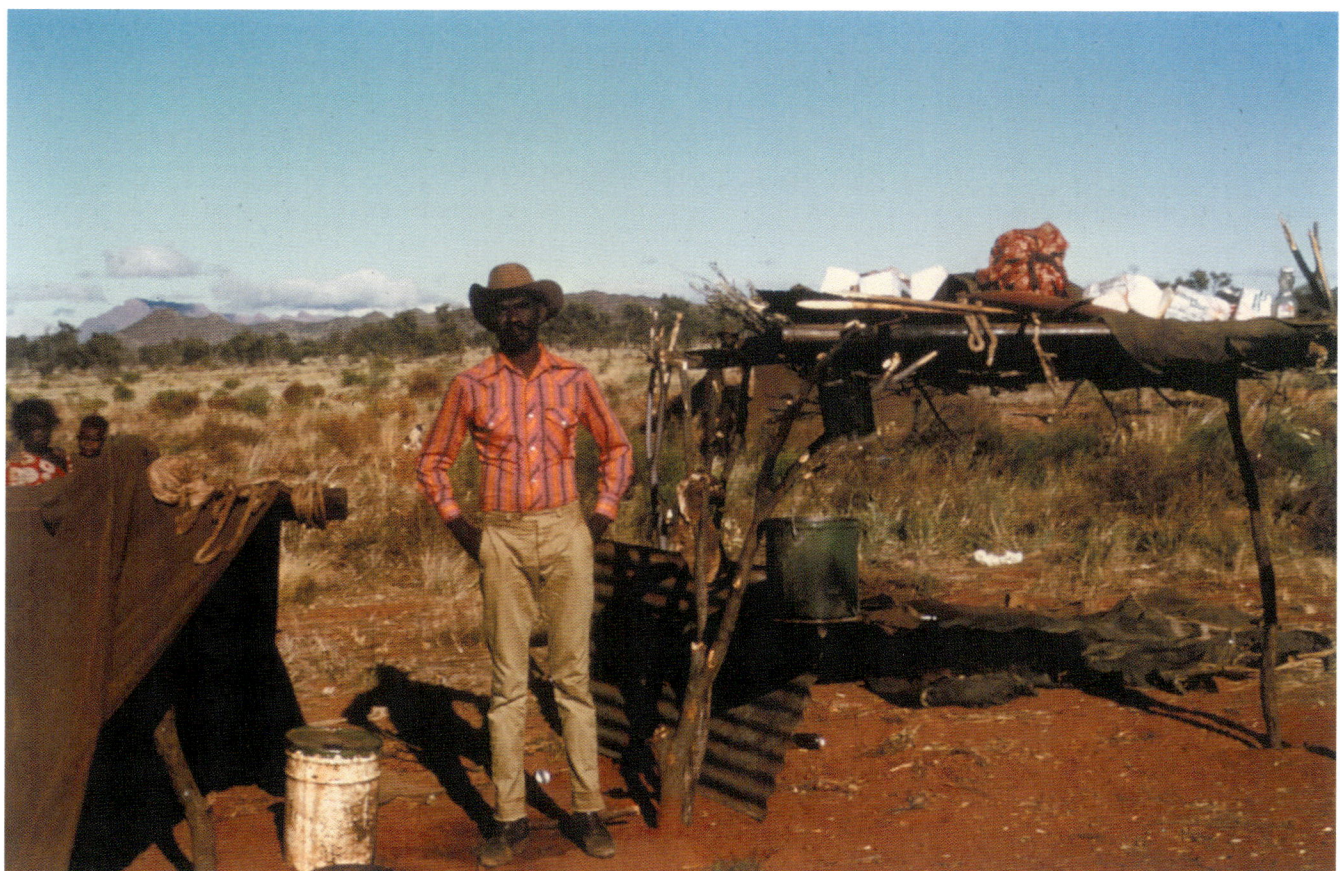

Timmy Payungu
Tjapangati at Yayayi, 19
Photo by Fred Myers.

lifeways of desert people from time immemorial to the remarkable past half-century and the life of the company.

In celebrating Papunya Tula Artists, we reflect on a story of resilience and cultural survival, of creativity, innovation and success and, above all else, of community. At the heart of this project are the artists and their descendants, as well as Papunya Tula's management staff, all of whom graciously welcomed yet another anniversary exhibition. Along with them, in ever-expanding circles of support and encouragement, stand the people, both Indigenous and non-Indigenous, spanning the globe who have connected and collaborated with Papunya Tula Artists over the years. They are the anthropologists, art historians, researchers, curators, gallerists, artists, art managers, and collectors who share a role in Papunya Tula "becoming real"—or, more aptly, in realizing its potential and changing Indigenous Australian art forever.

There are many people to thank for contributing their substantial effort, knowledge and skill to this project, beginning with the artists and descendants of Papunya Tula Artists Pty Ltd and company manager Paul Sweeney.

Fred Myers, Silver Professor of Anthropology at New York University, a longtime friend and colleague, collaborated with Kluge-Ruhe's dedicated and talented curator, Henry Skerritt, to research the works in the collection, develop the exhibition and edit this catalog. By going back to his field notes, Myers identified the stories behind many works that were previously undocumented. He and Skerritt uncovered new information almost daily, and their energy and enthusiasm is apparent in every aspect of this project.

John Kean undertook significant field research on behalf of Kluge-Ruhe, enabling us to communicate with artists and their descendants to verify new and existing information. We are particularly grateful to Elizabeth Marks Nakamarra, Candy Nelson Nakamarra, Narlie Nelson Nakamarra, Pamela Tolson Nakamarra, Isobel Major Nampitjinpa, Jeannie Bruno Nampitjinpa, Janie Karpa Nangala, Katarra Butler Napaltjarri, Eileen Napaltjarri, Glenys Gibbs Napaltjarri, Nanyuma Napangati, Charlotte Phillipus Napurrula, Rubilee Napurrula, Aileen Napurrula Rowe, Clara Napurrula Rowe and Punata Stockman Nungurrayi, along with Peter Cole, Martin Hagan, Peter Leura, Mike Tjakamarra, Dennis

Nelson Tjakamarra, Johnny Jack Tjampitjinpa, Aubrey Tjangala, Ray James Tjangala, Joseph Jurra Tjapaltjarri, Matthew Tjapangati, Tony Eggley Tjungurrayi, Bundy Rowe Tjupurrula, Bobby West Tjupurrula, Matthew West Tjupurrula and Mike Warangula for participating in this project. We so appreciated Kean's extraordinary photographs taken on his epic journey through the Australian desert and posted on social media. As we tracked his progress, we felt ever closer to the Country depicted in Papunya Tula artworks.

Other essayists and contributors to the catalog include Hetti Perkins, Cara Pinchbeck, Marina Strocchi and Steve Martin, each of whom provides a unique and insightful perspective on Papunya Tula Artists through their different personal experiences of the company and its artists. Contributors of photography, much of which has never been published, include Christopher Anderson, Peter Carroll, Greg Castillo, Tom Cogill, Matt Frost, Juno Gemes, Neil Greentree, Don Hadden, Christopher Hodges of Utopia Art Sydney, Michael Jensen, Emeritus Professor Vincent Megaw AM, Adam Reich, Dennis Schulz, Greg Weight and Marcia Weinstein. Additional images were graciously supplied by Tracey Dall at the Art Gallery of South Australia, Alissa Friedman and Ross Godick at Salon 94, Clare Gidwitz and Rob McKeever at Gagosian Gallery, Crispin Gutteridge and Claire Kurzmann at Deutscher and Hackett, Blair Hartzell at the Luczo Collection, Julie Harvey at Harvey Arts Projects, Tim Klingender at Sotheby's, Jude Fowler Smith at the Art Gallery of New South Wales, Andrew Weislogel and Andrea Potochniak from the Herbert F. Johnson Museum of Art at Cornell University, and Stephen Williamson at Araluen Art Centre. We are grateful to Aboriginal Artists Agency Ltd and Anthony Wallis for clearing copyrights to reproduce Papunya Tula Artists' artworks.

Lenders to the exhibition have enabled us to tell a fuller story of Papunya Tula art, and we are particularly thankful to the Embassy of Australia, Richard Klingler and Jane Slatter, Agatha and Stephen Luczo, Steve Martin and Anne Stringfield, John and Barbara Wilkerson, and the family of James and Elaine Wolfensohn.

Kluge-Ruhe's brilliant team includes Collections Manager Nicole Wade and Education and Programs Manager Lauren Maupin, who contributed significantly to the development and implementation of the exhibition, catalog and programs. This exhibition enabled us to undertake conservation on a number of early Papunya paintings in Kluge-Ruhe's collection, and we thank Scott Nolley for his skillful work on them. We also want to acknowledge the hard work of students and interns at the University of Virginia who contributed to this project, namely Alexis Baker, Ana Gonzalez, Alden Myers, Emmy Monaghan, Eleanore Neumann and Lee Woods.

The following people offered advice and assistance throughout the project for which we are truly appreciative: Rebecca Allen, Jennifer Biddle, John Carty, Françoise Dussart, Wayne Eager, Jason Gibson, Faye Ginsburg, Winston Green, Dick Kimber and Margaret Friedel, Alec O'Halloran, Damien Miller, Laura Nix, Rachel Paltridge, Sarita Quinlivan, June Ross and Luke Scholes.

We are tremendously grateful to our generous partners, who recognized the virtue of this project and supported the exhibition and catalog. Funding from the Gordon Darling Foundation was made possible by Creative Partnerships Australia through the Australian Cultural Fund and UVA Alumni Association. Our champions were Molly and Robert Hardie and the H7 Foundation, Agatha and Stephen Luczo and the Embassy of Australia. Their support enabled us to scale up the project to include many more artists and artworks in both the exhibition and catalog. At the University of Virginia, we thank UVA Parents Fund, the Institute for the Humanities and Global Cultures, the Mapping Indigenous Worlds Lab, the Department of Art and the Vice Provost for the Arts for their sponsorship. The University of Virginia Press has been amazing in sharing their knowledge and contacts with us and promoting the catalog to broad and receptive audiences. We are also thankful for the remarkable skills of designer Lindsay Starr and editor Kristin Swan.

If we return to that first modest painting, it is almost inconceivable that its maker could have imagined the fifty-year endeavor set in motion by his hand. Through this exhibition and catalog, *Irrititja Kuwarri Tjungu | Past and Present Together: Fifty Years of Papunya Tula Artists* celebrates and extends the remarkable legacy of the founding artists of Papunya Tula.

**MARGO SMITH AM**
Director, Kluge-Ruhe Aboriginal Art Collection
of the University of Virginia

NEXT SPREAD
Papunya, 2004. Photo by Claire Leimbach.

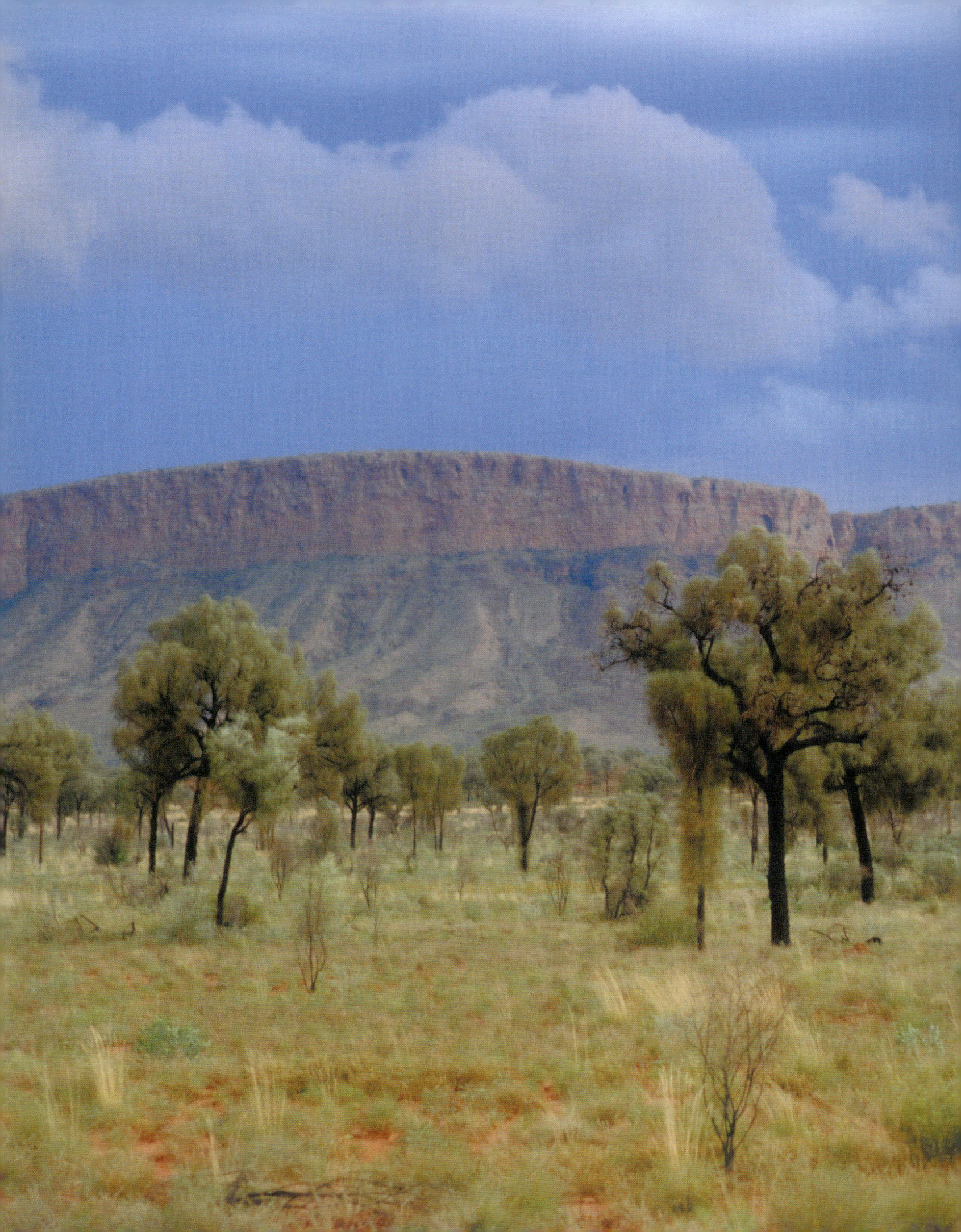

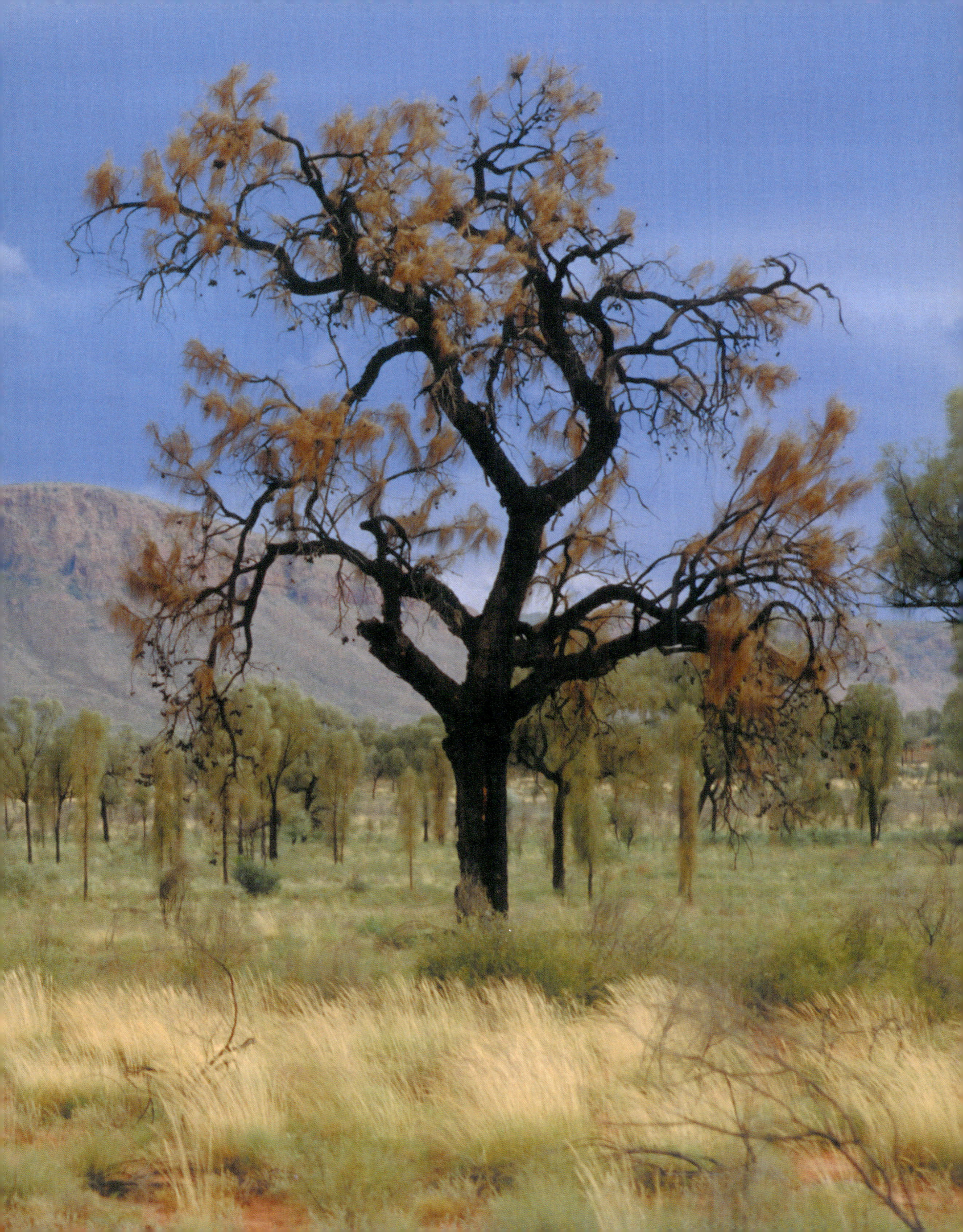

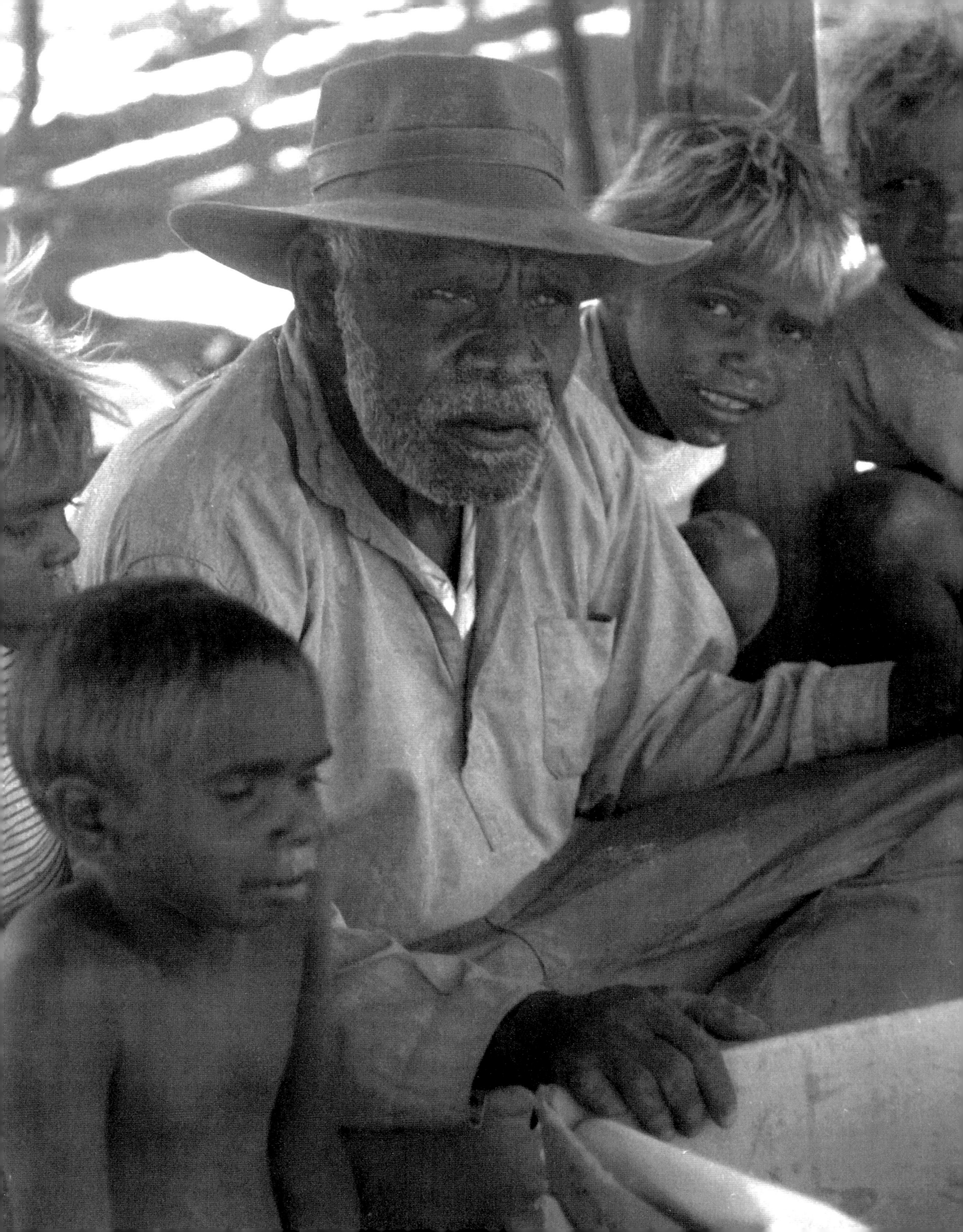

# Irriṯiṯja Kuwarri Tjungu | Past and Present Together

HENRY SKERRITT

Fifty years ago, a painting movement emerged from Australia's Central Desert. It arose with such force and conviction that one could be forgiven for thinking it had existed forever, as though etched from the earth by the slow passage of time and the seasons. And yet, as Hetti Perkins and Hannah Fink have noted, it was equally the result of more recent forces: "Forged in the aftershock of colonization, the Papunya painting movement is as much a product of historical circumstances as the ancient traditions on which it draws."[1] This conclusion was delivered in the catalog to the exhibition *Papunya Tula: Genesis and Genius* (2000), the last major exhibition to attempt, in Perkins's words, to map the "topography" of the movement's history.[2] Two decades later, *Irriṯiṯja Kuwarri Tjungu | Past and Present Together: Fifty Years of Papunya Tula Artists* is an attempt to rechart and extend this terrain, revisiting one of the foundational narratives of Australian art history.

## A HISTORY OF PASTS

The founding of Papunya Tula Artists is one of the best-known tales in Australian art. Vivien Johnson notes, "It has been told and retold so often that it almost has the force of a Dreaming narrative itself."[3] Like any mythos, it has

accumulated mystery, obfuscation and misinformation that the passing of time has not alleviated. Even pinning down a precise date to celebrate is difficult. The most stable date is November 16, 1972, when the company was officially incorporated, but this milestone is more bureaucratic than art historical, the endpoint in a protracted process of negotiations and paperwork. And, in any case, the company did not come into full effect until June 1973, by which stage the most iconic works of the early movement had already been painted, and many of the company's founders had left Papunya for new settlements to the west.

Perhaps a better date to commemorate is the meeting at Charles Creek in Mparntwe (Alice Springs) around May 1972, when Charlie Wartuma Tjungurrayi gave the company its name, blurting it out "as if he'd known all his life."[4] But even this moment is mired in cross-cultural confusion. While Geoffrey Bardon describes the name as referring to "two hills not far from Papunya," it seems likely it was a mishearing of the word *tjarla*, referring to the Honey Ant ancestor, whose travels pass through Papunya.[5]

Another candidate is the moment in late July 1971 when a team of men, led by Kaapa Tjampitjinpa and under the direction of Tom Onion Tjapangati and Mick Wallangkarri Tjapangati, commenced a thirty-foot mural of the Honey

Tutama Tjapangati with school children
at Yayayi, 1974. Photo by Fred Myers.

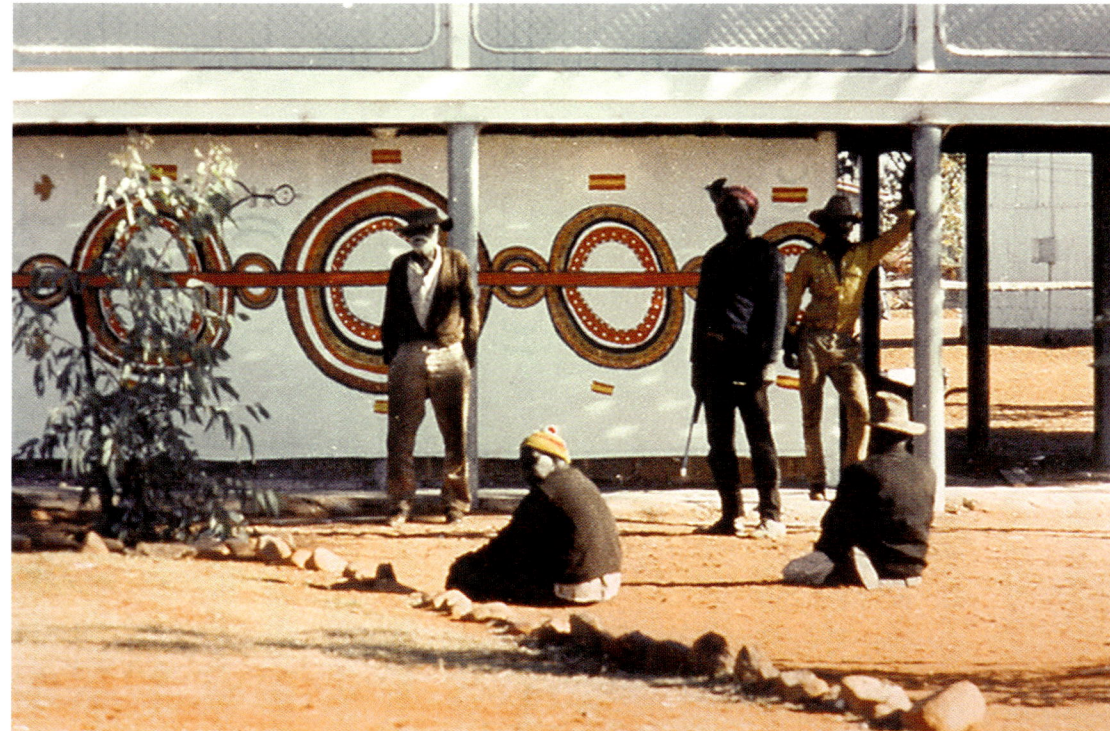

FIG. 1.1

Tom Onion Tjapangati, Nosepeg Tjungkarta Tjupurrula, Jack Long Phillipus Tjakamarra and two unidentified men with the Honey Ant Mural at Papunya, 1971. Photo by Geoffrey Bardon.

Ant's travels on the wall of the Papunya Special School (fig. 1.1). The Honey Ant mural was a powerful public announcement of the nascent painting movement and aroused considerable interest in the community. But the mural had its own fits and starts, requiring multiple revisions before all the stakeholders were satisfied in its appropriateness for public view. Moreover, the decision to paint the mural was almost certainly inspired by the recent opening of the nearby Yuendumu Men's Museum, which featured murals by senior men, including Paddy Japaljarri Stewart, who also contributed to the Papunya mural.[6]

A more commonly cited starting point is the arrival at Papunya in February 1971 of the schoolteacher Geoffrey Bardon. According to this version of events, after encouraging his students to explore their Indigenous mark-making traditions, Bardon befriended a group of Aboriginal men, providing them with space and encouragement to paint their designs with acrylic on board. This narrative has tended to dominate popular accounts of the early movement, in part because Bardon was its chief chronicler.[7] Amid the casual racism of Australian society, it was undoubtedly easier to accept a hero named Geoff than one named Tjangala, Tjapaltjarri, Tjapangati or Tjungurrayi.

It cannot be disputed that Bardon's advocacy played a vital role in the emergence of the painting movement at Papunya. Recent scholarship has, however, dislodged the singularity of his role. Rather than downplay Bardon's importance, scholars such as Luke Scholes and Vivien Johnson have revealed the complexity of the historical moment and the clear-eyed determination of the artists themselves.[8] Scholes's diligent archival research has shown how integral artists such as Tim Leura Tjapaltjarri were in maintaining the company in the face of Bardon's increasingly erratic behavior and extended absences from Papunya. The birth of Papunya Tula Artists emerges more as a team effort, led by a committed group of artists with a network of supporters in government, museums and art galleries.[9]

Johnson's account stresses the pivotal role of the artist Kaapa Tjampitjinpa, who was already painting with acrylic on board prior to Bardon's arrival at Papunya.[10] Around August 1971, Kaapa consigned several works to the Mparntwe District Welfare Officer Jack Cooke, who nominated one, *Men's Ceremony for the Kangaroo, Gulgardi* (1971, fig. 1.2), for the Caltex Art Award in Mparntwe. Painted on a battered piece of board, possibly once a cupboard door, the work was an unlikely winner. In her announcement speech, the judge Jo Caddy exclaimed: "This old man is a true artist. He took what he found, an old piece of waste lumber he located in a rubbish tip and the dregs of some paint he found lying around the settlement and made art out of it."[11] Kaapa's win was definitely a watershed moment, stirring interest in the potential of a new painting moment among both the Mparntwe art scene and the residents of Papunya. But the urgency to paint clearly extended beyond Kaapa. We can see this in contemporaneous works by Tutama Tjapangati (plate 2), Timmy Payungu Tjapangati (plate 5) and numerous others produced by unidentified artists at Papunya (plates 1, 4). By the early months of 1971, whether painting on discarded building materials, fruit crates, cardboard or linoleum tiles, artists at Papunya were using anything and everything at hand to force their paintings into the world.

The success of Papunya Tula Artists was the result of a perfect storm. John Kean, art adviser at Papunya from 1977 to 1979, describes it like this: "Papunya Tula painting was generated by the impact of Indigenous culture with European aspirations and aesthetics. It is the shiniest of the shards from this collision of cultures."[12] This is a beautiful metaphor, but I am not sure that "shards" is entirely appropriate, indicating, as it does, a level of brokenness or fragmentation. Perhaps a better metaphor for the serendipity of Papunya Tula is a celestial one: the worlds aligned in such perfect balance that an entirely new constellation of stars was born.

It is fitting that one of the first works in this exhibition—just as it was in *Genesis and Genius*—is Tutama Tjapangati's *Stars at Night Twinkling* (1971, plate 2). It is painted on a fragile piece of cardboard possibly salvaged from the interior of a car door. Bardon collected this painting in June 1971, the same month he began commissioning works from the painters at Papunya. His original photograph of the work shows that it was already water damaged when he acquired it, suggesting that it could have been painted some weeks or months earlier. We cannot know if Bardon's title or description of the work is accurate, but he was clearly enamored by what he saw as the painting's "rapturous understanding of a most beautiful concept."[13] It awoke in Bardon a realization of the multiple layers of meaning embedded in the iconography of these paintings. A circle could be a star, a campsite, the fires of the ancestors and more: it could depict events in the past, present and future.

To reflect on fifty years of Papunya Tula Artists is to realize that there is no single history of the company, but instead many histories that sweep and curl around one another. This makes the comparison to a Dreaming narrative even more apt. Like the many ancestral narratives that crisscross the desert, these histories are distinct but overlapping; at key points they intersect, but then diverge, continuing on their way, leaving an indelible trail of wonder and creation in their wake.

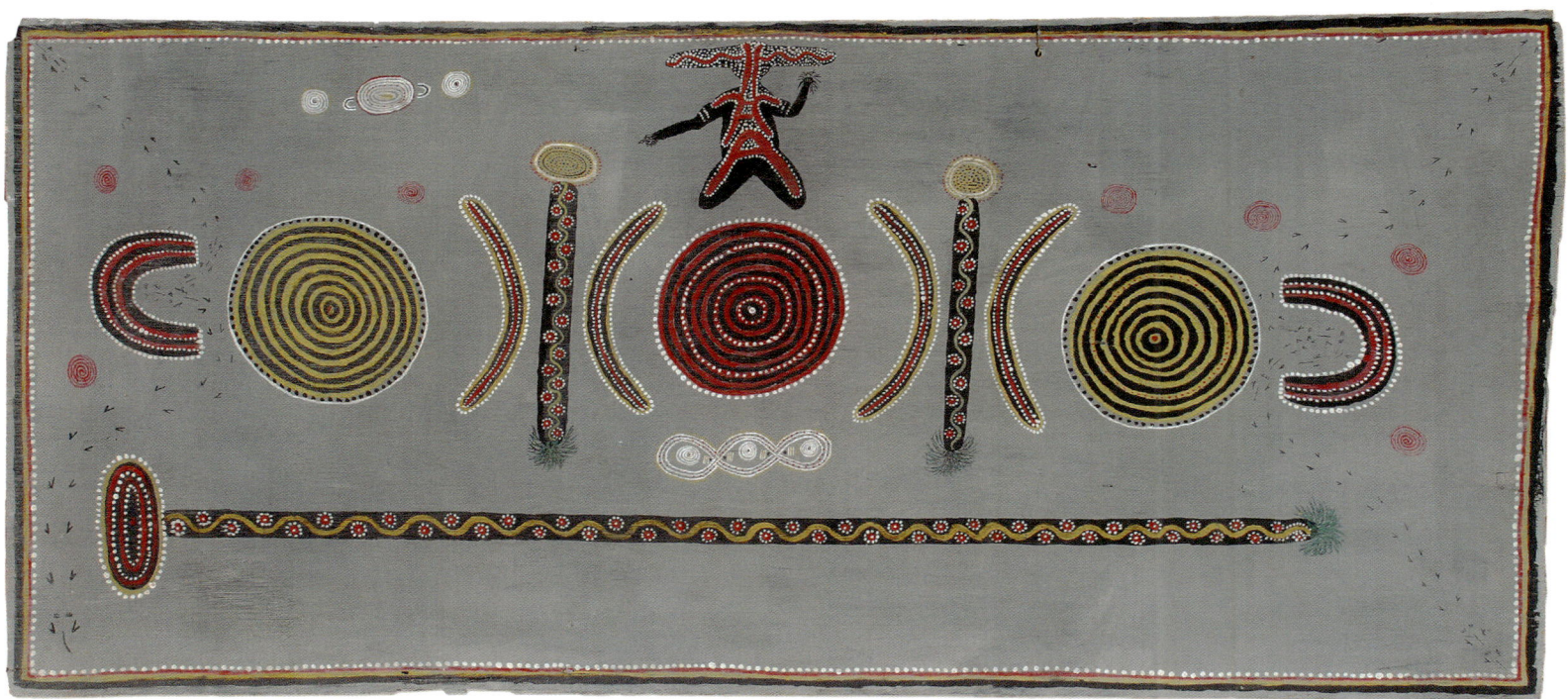

FIG. 1.2

Kaapa Tjampitjinpa, *Men's Ceremony for the Kangaroo Gulgardi*, 1971, gouache on plywood 24 × 54 in. (61 ×137 cm). Araluen Art Collection, Joint winner of the 1971 Caltex Art Award, Acquired by the Central Australian Art Society.

## A HISTORY OF PRESENTS

The title for this book and exhibition was conceived by Joseph Jurra Tjapaltjarri. Like all good titles, it has an elegant simplicity that belies its conceptual depth. Survey exhibitions have traditionally been opportunities to examine the trajectory of an artist or movement. Through the process of anachronism (in which objects that exist in the present are cast as representations of the past), the survey exhibition lays out a chronology of the past to account for the present within a universe of alternate possibilities. This approach reflects the temporal logic that underpins the modern museum.[14] Past, present and future are not so much "together" as bound sequentially in the fleeting narrative of progress. Today, most scholars are prepared to concede that this is far from a natural or inevitable temporal condition. The persistence of Indigenous ways of being and their markedly different approaches to time has been central to dislodging the hegemony of progressive time.[15] The battle for Indigenous peoples' rights to "temporal sovereignty" has become a key ethical concern in efforts to seek an equitable coevality or, put more literally, to assert their right to exist in the present.[16]

In Australia, it is through art that Indigenous Australians' right to coevality has been most visibly staked. The international success of Aboriginal art has been the single most effective tool in making mainstream Australians aware of the unbreakable ties between Aboriginal people and their land, along with the ancestral connections, or "Dreamings," that underpin this worldview. For Pintupi speakers, the correct term for this worldview is Tjukurrpa, alternately spelled Jukurrpa for Warlpiri, Tjukurpa for Pitjantjatjara and Altyerr for Anmatyerr people. Tjukurrpa is the creation epoch, when powerful ancestral beings shaped the earth, creating its natural features, people and law. It is also the narratives, songs and ceremonies about these events that ensure the continuing essence of the ancestors in the land. Fred Myers notes, "If the Dreaming can be said to transcend the present in this fashion, the fact that the landscape is a series of stories allows it, also, to transcend the immediate."[17] Tjukurrpa exists in its own temporal frame: it is neither an eternal present nor an eternal past, but rather a constant state of past and present together: *irritja kuwarri tjungu*. Or, as Bobby West Tjupurrula explains, "Tjukurrpa isn't written, it's not just drawing or painting, Tjukurrpa is places. . . . Tjukurrpa is everything, Tjukurrpa doesn't move; we live there all the time."[18]

In 1971, this might have seemed an esoteric proposition. Today, however, globalization, the internet and the mass movement of information, goods and people across national borders (whether voluntarily or through the forces of political and environmental displacement) have made us acutely aware of the proximity of difference. Terry Smith argues that this has ushered in a new epoch of *contemporaneity*, replacing modernity as the dominant ordering principle of our time.[19] He notes that the very etymology of the word "contemporary," which comes from the Latin *con-* (together with) and *tempor-* (time), denotes the sharing of time with others that is implicit in the recognition of the multiple temporalities that operate in our present.[20]

Smith has been the most prominent theorist of contemporary art to champion Indigenous Australian artists. Indeed, living in a world in which ancestral presence is a constant animating force in daily life should make Aboriginal artists exemplars of contemporaneity.[21] By this rationale, Ian McLean has even argued that Aboriginal artists "invented the idea of contemporary art."[22] And yet, as McLean concedes, this does not guarantee a seat at the table of the contemporary art world.[23] Until very recently, indigenous artists, globally, have had relatively little traction in that world, more often being consigned to the lesser categories of "primitive," "ethnographic" or "tribal" art. And yet, among such artists who have broken the code of contemporary art world success, a remarkably high proportion have come from Papunya Tula Artists. It might not feel this way to the artists, managers, fieldworkers and supporters who have poured their energy into the company over the last fifty years, but from the outside it appears as though Papunya Tula has had an uncanny aptitude for being in the right place at the right time, preempting art world fashions and changing zeitgeists with remarkable consistency. The heroic mythology surrounding the company has not hindered this success, but nor can it entirely account for it.

## A HISTORY OF PLACES

At Papunya in 1971, many histories collided. While triumphant narratives might privilege one over the other, hindsight reveals that it was the chemistry of their coming together that catalyzed the moment. Even the Honey Ant ancestor, who was chosen for the school mural because its travels pass through Papunya, belongs to a bigger story. Papunya has come to dominate accounts of this Tjukurrpa in much the same way that it has come to dominate art historical accounts of desert painting. But, like all Tjukurrpa, it is multinodal, spreading outward and connecting people and places across time and space.

The Australian government established Papunya in 1959 to provide room for an increasing population of Aboriginal people leaving the desert. The reasons for this displacement were complicated: drought, environmental change and the encroaching pastoral industry had made it difficult for Aboriginal people to live traditionally on Country. The conservative government led by Robert Menzies was determined to centralize and assimilate Aboriginal people, but was also wary of a mass influx to towns like Alice Springs and Darwin. There is a heart-breaking honesty in one Pintupi spokesman's assessment, recorded by Myers: "They came in because they were hungry. They didn't know that they could not go back."[24]

Papunya drew together people from a disparate range of language groups: Luritja, Pintupi, Anmatyerr, Warlpiri and Kukatja. Some had considerable experience of white Australians—whether through exposure to missionaries at Ikuntji (Haasts Bluff) or Ntaria (Hermannsburg) or through their involvement with the cattle industry. For others, it represented their first encounter with the colonizers. This was particularly the case for the Pintupi— the people from the West—who were being relocated to Papunya in ever greater numbers by Welfare Patrols around Wilkinkarra (Lake Mackay), Kaakurutintjinya (Lake Macdonald) and Puntutjarrpa (Jupiter Well). It was also a space of Aboriginal cosmopolitanism, as people from across the vast desert region found themselves living in close quarters. Painting offered a way of asserting legitimacy and authority: of explaining who you were and where you came from, amidst this chaotic mélange of strangers.

Quentin Sprague rightly notes that this "'transactional environment' prompted the radical local reimagining that allowed the imposed frame of Western modernity to be re-fashioned in the modulated light of localized perspectives."[25] In taking up painting, the men at Papunya appropriated not only the modern materials of acrylic paint and canvas, but the very concept of 'high art,' using it as the battle ground for a last ditch attempt to assert their sovereignty. It is a sentiment perfectly captured in Bardon's own assessment: "The glory, as I came to under-stand, surged forth in the immense, almost desperate creativity of people seeking only to be themselves."[26] This might explain some of the urgency with which the men at Papunya wished to display their Tjukurrpa to both Bardon and their peers.

## A HISTORY OF TIMES

Like the Honey Ant, the story of Papunya is also connected to wider narratives. The emergence of painting in 1971 fits squarely within a timeline of Indigenous Australian activism that includes, but is not limited to, the Yirrkala Bark Petition (1963), the Gurindji Strike (1966), the Consti-tutional Referendum (1967), the Aboriginal Tent Embassy (1972), the founding of the Aboriginal Arts Board (1973), the Woodward Royal Commission into Aboriginal Land Rights (1973) and the passing of the Northern Territory Aboriginal Land Rights Act (1976). It also coincided with a critical juncture in the history of art, when the dominance of late modernism was being radically usurped by a range of new socially engaged and conceptual art practices. This was fortuitous timing: desert painting appealed to both sides of this critical divide. On the one hand, these visually brilliant works with their affinities to late-modernist abstraction appeased those hoping that these desert prophets could resuscitate the formalist tradition.[27] This has particularly been the case for collectors, who have continued to lavish praise on the "transcendence" of Papu-nya Tula paintings, elevating its most abstract practition-ers as evidence of the universality of abstract painting.

On the other hand, Papunya Tula has been a mag-net for artists, poets and critics seeking more visceral, spiritual or philosophical experiences outside of the canon of Euro-American art and culture. Artists such as Marina Abramović and Ulay, Sol LeWitt, Tim Johnson, Imants Tillers and John Wolseley all looked to the desert to find kindred spirits. Most were driven by intellectual curiosity, camaraderie or a spirit of social justice; others by opportunism and cultural cachet. Rather than seeing desert painting as the salvation of modernist abstraction, these artists saw it as a vibrant alternative. Writing in 1989 for *Art & Text*, Australia's most ostentatiously cutting-edge art magazine, Nicholas Baume celebrated the artists of Papunya Tula as the country's leading conceptualists: "The lingering desire to look beyond the painted surface to its conceptual base is gratified by Aboriginal art. It pro-duces a language of symbols just waiting to be made ver-bal. It not only caters to conceptual taste, but the social integration of its ideas makes the attempts of Conceptual art look amateur."[28] Baume interpreted the icons of desert paintings as being a visual language, reading the paint-ings as a form of ancestral cartography: elaborate maps documenting sacred sites and the creation narratives associated with them. This was encouraged by the early marketing of the works. Beginning with Bardon—who was, no doubt, influenced by the pioneering writings of anthropologist Nancy Munn[29]—it became accepted practice to accompany every painting with a certificate and schematic diagram identifying each iconographic element.

But the nature of this "language of symbols" is far from straightforward. For a start, the graphic system is decidedly multivalent: any individual icon can hold several different (and frequently simultaneous) meanings. As Myers explains, "extragraphic knowledge is often necessary to interpret the representation. . . . Ambiguity (or multivocality) constitutes part of their aesthetic force."[30] In a ceremonial context, the precise meaning of these icons would be explained and negotiated according to the particular knowledge or custodial interests of the various participants.

Moreover, Baume's analysis came at a moment when the dynamics within Papunya Tula Artists had shifted decisively westward. Included in *Irrititja Kuwarri Tjungu* are two paintings that perfectly preempt this divergence: Uta Uta Tjangala's *Tingarri Men at Warnmanpanya* (1973, plate 96) and Clifford Possum Tjapaltjarri's *Paths of the Ancestors* (1973, plate 21). Both were commissioned by Peter Fannin, the schoolteacher who took over the operations of Papunya Tula after Bardon's departure. In 1973, Fannin began distributing larger sheets of particle board to the artists as part of a commission from the newly formed Aboriginal Arts Board. The board's director, Bob Edwards, wanted larger, more imposing works for the exhibition *Art of Aboriginal Australia*, which toured thirteen museums in Canada from 1974 to 1976.[31] These chipboard paintings marked the start of an expansion in the scale and international prominence of Papunya Tula Artists works.

The year 1973 also marked a more local milestone. Since the mid-1960s, the Pintupi had agitated for the recognition of their unique and separate identity, and the Northern Territory government had made several unsuccessful efforts to relocate the Pintupi before the establishment of a permanent settlement at Yayayi in 1973.[32] That June, Uta Uta and two hundred of his Pintupi kin left Papunya for Yayayi, inaugurating the Pintupi homelands movement that would culminate in the founding of communities at Walungurru (Kintore) in 1981 and Kiwirrkurra in 1983.[33] Uta Uta painted *Tingarri Men at Warnmanpanya* at Yayayi toward the end of 1973.[34] Its classic Tingarri design of radiating concentric circles—painted with a clear enthusiasm for the ceremonial connections underpinning it, as indicated by the presence of partially obscured

sacred boards—heralds a new era in which the focus of Papunya Tula Artists would shift increasingly away from Papunya to the Western Desert.[35]

Painted while the artist was visiting Papunya, Clifford Possum's *Paths of the Ancestors* represents an equally significant but divergent history and an extraordinary moment in his artistic development. Using the expanse afforded by the larger chip-board, Clifford Possum conceived a new vision of desert painting uniquely tailored to explaining Indigenous cosmology to outside audiences. While most early Papunya paintings focus on a single ceremony or site, *Paths of the Ancestors* is the first of what would become a series of encyclopedic "map" paintings that detail multiple ancestral narratives, showing their connections across vast areas of Country. With the introduction of canvas, Clifford would expand these maps to monumental scale, bringing him international acclaim.

By 1988, the "map" paintings of Clifford Possum and fellow Papunya painter Michael Jagamara Nelson (plate 28) would be the most widely recognized style of Aboriginal paintings. This represented a high point for those painters who remained in the orbit of Papunya. Global interest reached a zenith in 1988 when the exhibition *Dreamings: The Art of Aboriginal Australia* opened at the Asia Society Galleries in New York (fig. 1.3).[36] Michael Nelson, Clifford Possum and Bill Stockman Tjapaltjarri all traveled to New York for the exhibition, where they were feted by the news media.[37] In the same year, Clifford Possum was given a solo exhibition at the Institute of Contemporary Arts in London, while Michael Nelson's *Possum and Wallaby Dreaming* (1985) was used as the basis for a mosaic on the forecourt of the new Australian Parliament House (fig. 1.4). In hindsight, this fame would be fleeting, with the "map" style of Clifford Possum and Michael Nelson soon being eclipsed by the more abstract "Tingarri" paintings from Walungurru and Kiwirrkurra. In December 1989, the Pintupi artist Yanatjarri No. III Tjakamarra was given the first New York gallery solo exhibition, at John Weber Gallery.[38] It was the second exhibition of Papunya Tula Artists at Weber's renowned gallery in less than six months, illustrating the unexpected frequency with which desert painting could be seen in the United States at the time. From the earlier exhibition, the Metropolitan Museum of Art, New York, acquired its first desert painting, Yanatjarri's *Tingari Cycle Dreaming at Paratjakutti* (1989).[39] To date, the Met has acquired five works by artists from Papunya Tula, all of them by Pintupi painters.[40]

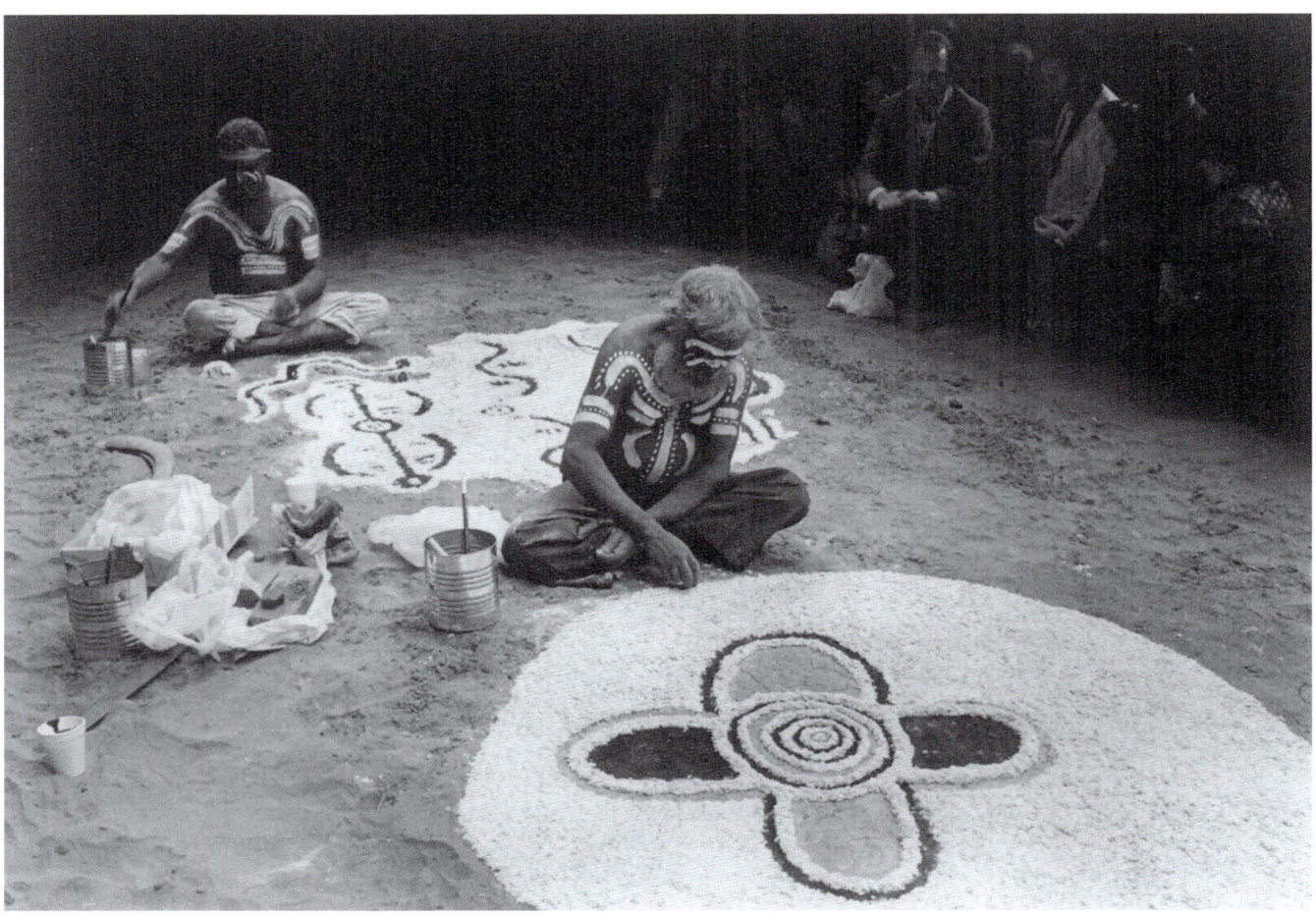

FIG. 1.3

Michael Jagamara Nelson and Bill Stockman Tjapaltjarri creating a sand sculpture at the Asia Society Galleries, New York, for the exhibition *Dreamings: The Art of Aboriginal Australia*, November 1988. Photo by Marcia Weinstein.

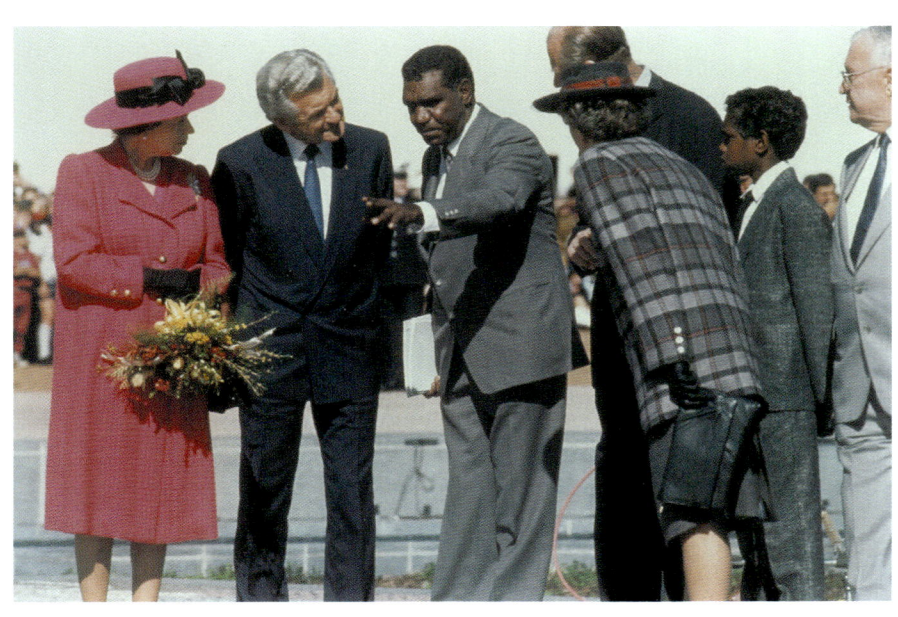

FIG. 1.4

Queen Elizabeth II, Prime Minister Bob Hawke, Michael Jagamara Nelson, Prince Philip, Hazel Hawke, Jonathan Jupurrurla Nelson and William McIntosh at the opening of the Australian Parliament House, Canberra, 1988. Photo courtesy of the National Archives of Australia.

## A HISTORY OF ABSTRACTION

By the 1990s, abstraction, not traditional iconographies, seemed to dominate desert painting. While this tendency is most famously associated with the work of Emily Kame Kngwarreye from Utopia, artists from Papunya Tula were integral to this shift.[41] By the late 1980s, the Warlpiri artist Maxie Tjampitjinpa had almost completely abandoned any iconic references in his paintings (plates 25, 26). Dragging his brush over the surface of the canvas, he created a stippling effect that artists across the desert would imitate—to varying degrees of success. At the time, Maxie's style was powerfully original and evocative, conjuring images of rising flames, burning ashes and wisping smoke. He conveyed, in easily understandable visual cues, the physical sensation of the great Tjukurrpa bushfire at Warlukurlangu, whose ancestral resonances had been famously chronicled in the more iconographic work of artists such as Clifford Possum (plate 24) and Tim Leura (plate 23).

But the abstraction of Maxie Tjampitjinpa is markedly different in tenor and tone from that of his Pintupi contemporaries, such as Simon Tjakamarra (plate 72) or Ronnie Tjampitjinpa (plates 59, 98–100, 132). Despite removing any iconographic elements that might identify the particular location or Tjukurrpa of their paintings, the lexicon of forms in these images retains a clear pedigree with those carved into shields, pearl shells and other ceremonial objects (fig. 1.5). Comparing Warlimpirrnga Tjapaltjarri's *Tingarri at Tjulnga* (1993, plate 103) with his later *Maruwa* (2013, plate 105) sheds light on the clear thread that connects the epic abstractions of George Tjungurrayi (plate 104), Doreen Reid Nakamarra (plate 90) and Yukultji Napangati (plate 91) with their traditional source materials.

While the market influences that encouraged abstraction across desert communities might have been singular, its local manifestations were diverse, reflecting different geographic, social and art historical reference points. The movement of artists, for familial or ceremonial reasons, complicates these narratives further. At Warlayirti Artists, the art center founded at Wirrimanu (Balgo) in 1985, the artists favored bright colors, looser brushwork and more organic compositions. Having witnessed the different styles of paintings being produced across the two art centers, artists such as Dini Campbell Tjampitjinpa (fig. 1.6; plate 83) and Patrick Tjungurrayi (plates 82, 109) developed their own styles that softened the rigidity of

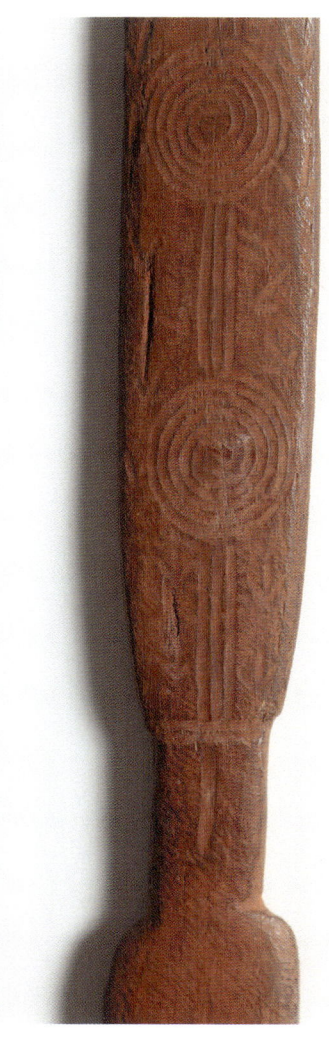

FIG. 1.5

Unidentified Central Desert artist, incised spear thrower showing tracks of the bush turkey (*Ardeotis australis*) (detail), before 1968, natural pigments, string and resin on wood, 37½ × 2 × 1 in. (95 × 5 × 2.5 cm). Kluge-Ruhe Aboriginal Art Collection, The Edward L. Ruhe Collection, Gift of John W. Kluge, 1997, 1993.0004.222.

Papunya painting with free-flowing forms and lively color combinations.[42] Marina Strocchi's firsthand account of the emergence of women's painting at Papunya Tula shows the close familial relationships between artists at Walungurru and Ikuntji, which led to the looser, more gestural styles of artists such as Tjunkiya Napaltjarri (plates 50, 51, 127), Tatali Nangala (plate 63) and Makinti Napanangka (plates 64–67, 137). Their explosion onto the scene in 1996 inaugurated a new chapter in the history of Papunya Tula Artists, reviving the movement at a critical moment when many felt it had run its course.

Though much more work is needed to tease out these individual but entangled histories, it is clear that if these works represent a "language of symbols just waiting to be made verbal," as John Carty writes, that language has become increasingly difficult to translate. "Today the abstract, expressive forms on canvas continue to index the Dreaming, and the Country that artists are entitled to paint," Carty continues, "but they do so in ways that require different kinds of analysis and interpretation."[43]

Already, this demand has been met with a wealth of substantive critical thinking, as art historians, sociologists and philosophers have pondered the cross-cultural dynamics of desert painting.[44] Following from Howard Morphy's crucial insights into the aesthetics of Yolŋu bark painting, scholars such as Jennifer Biddle, Françoise Dussart and John Carty have offered significant insights into the nature of desert painting as an enactment of Tjukurrpa and its revelation as a haptic, sensory and phenomenal presence.[45] It would be unfair to summarize in a single paragraph the nuance of such thinkers, whose work has added substantially to the discourse around Aboriginal art while challenging accepted ideas around abstract painting. Unfortunately, the idea that Aboriginal aesthetics can be reduced to a generalized system of "ancestral presencing" has become mainstreamed through commercial gallery catalogs, sales brochures and fluff pieces to such a degree that, in the hands of lesser thinkers, it is often used to justify a weak universal aestheticism. This runs counter to the remarkable diversity of Aboriginal art and cultures and ignores the profound challenge that these paintings pose to the ideology of modernist aesthetics. Moreover, it elides the complexity of the relationship between Tjukurrpa and its reproduction in both Country and paint.

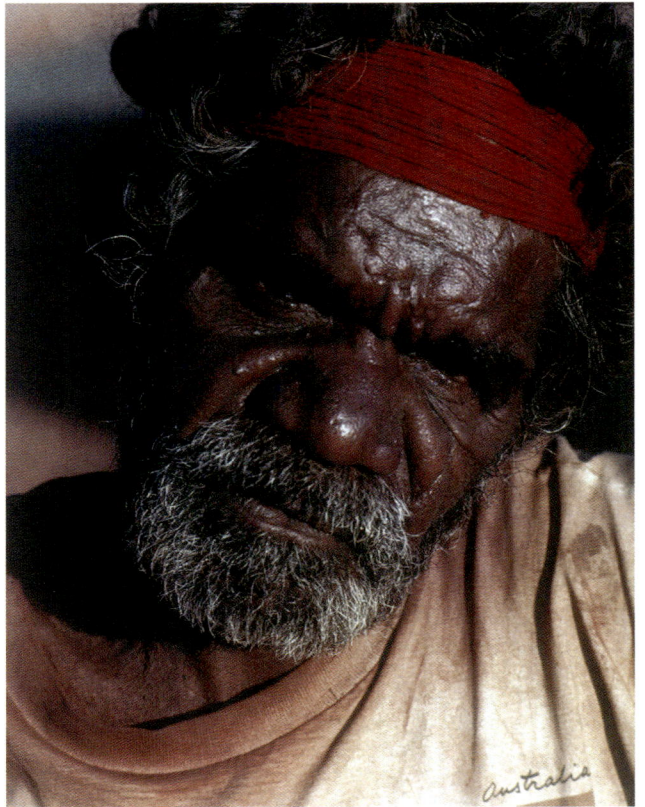

FIG. 1.6

Dini Campbell Tjampitjinpa.
Photo by Dennis Schulz.

## A HISTORY OF REVELATION

According to Myers, the Pintupi cosmos is divided into two contrasting spheres: that which is *yuti* (visible) and that which is Tjukurrpa. The first of these categories, he argues, is phenomenal, the latter noumenal; one can be grasped with the senses, the other is "outside human affairs and constitutes an enduring primary reality." As everything in the Pintupi world is said to have originated in the Tjukurrpa, a third term is needed to describe the passage between these two states—Tjukurrtjanu *mularrarringu*—meaning, literally, "from the Dreaming, it becomes real." Thus, the visible and the Dreaming are inextricably linked, just as the stories in Pintupi paintings are said to be both Tjukurrtjanu (from the Dreaming) and *yutinu* (revealed).[46]

The analogy of the passage from Tjukurrpa to *yuti* is helpful in considering the development of the Papunya painting movement—in which once-secret designs of ceremony and ritual were recalibrated into the new, self-contained and secular aesthetic of acrylic on board. In ceremony, the meaning of decorated objects such as shields or *tjurunga* are not autonomously visual, but generated in conjunction with a series of other systems of meaning production that include song, dance, performance or ritual. The first problem of acrylic painting was how to distill this complex accumulation of meanings into the autonomous zone of the two-dimensional picture plane.

The second, more culturally specific problem was how to display this information in a way that did not contravene the strict hierarchies of secrecy and revelation. The early painters at Papunya generated considerable controversy over some of their choices of images and motifs, which were deemed to transgress what could be safely seen by uninitiated members of the extended desert community. Critical opinions on the reasons for such transgressions are divided. Myers mounts a convincing argument that the artists were simply over eager to explore the possibilities of this new medium, while Kean suggests that it was partly due to the pioneering artist Kaapa Tjampitjinpa's personality as a maverick prepared to transgress social mores.[47] But perhaps a simpler answer might lie in the idiomatic conception of these works. In ceremony, the rules of revelation and concealment—of precisely what and how designs could be represented—were always negotiated in advance among the ceremonial leaders; content reflected consensus. In contrast, as curator Judith Ryan explains, the Papunya artists all worked "independently, and not collaborating with others, as customary ritual required."[48] As the new painting was not governed by ceremonial rules, there was no firm consensus on the boundaries of representation. Thus, Myers notes, the art market allowed artists to paint with both greater frequency and less oversight than in the traditional ceremonial context, creating the ideal conditions for an inventive new artistic virtuosity.[49]

Although drawing on a preexisting iconographic lexicon, the paintings' poetics were similarly fluid. "The early paintings are," argues Ryan, "a series of discrete aesthetic experiments with line, color and pictorial space that enabled the painters to analyze and objectify the tangible elements of myth and ritual, using a shared visual language and hermeneutics of meaning."[50] The evocation of hermeneutics—a term derived from the practice of interpreting biblical texts—is a useful one. These paintings must be considered as part of a great and long religious tradition. But what is the text that is being interpreted? It is, of course, Tjukurrpa, both the earth itself, which is mimetic of ancestral actions, and the record of these actions in song and sacred objects.[51] Philosopher Robyn Ferrell has argued that Tjukurrpa "gives the lead to its translation, and indeed it *is* its translation since the whole effect is to represent an order."[52] Paintings are thus a double degree of interpretation, translating Tjukurrpa into a form that Ferrell summarizes as "aesthetic contours comprehensible to others."[53] The plural of "others" is important here; despite how desert painting is often written about, its audiences cannot and should not be reduced to exclusively non-Indigenous outsiders.

Most artists (regardless of their background) are cognizant of the fact that their works might have multiple audiences. This was, no doubt, the case for the early painters at Papunya. In the privacy of the Men's Painting Room, they were clearly painting for one another, showing off their knowledge in a glorious process of one-upmanship. But they were also painting for outside audiences: Bardon, gallerists such as Pat Hogan and collectors who would purchase their paintings. Even those artists least experienced with white Australians would have been acutely aware of this audience's almost-complete ignorance of their works' sacred content. For a brief moment, it might have seemed that their paintings could transfer without controversy from one context to the next. While a level of naiveté might be expected—after all, they were embarking on something that had not been done before—it feels inadequate to explain the revelations within early Papunya paintings.

A better explanation can be found in one of the key insights of Myers's foundational ethnography *Pintupi Country, Pintupi Self*, in which he describes the enormous emphasis placed on personal autonomy within Pintupi society. Social advancement is effected by knowledge and the taking on of responsibility: "Dangerous knowledge and sacred objects provide men with the opportunity to demonstrate their quality through autonomy."[54] Before the radical disruption and dislocation caused by the white invasion, knowledge of Tjukurrpa was held by senior people and traded in ceremony. Knowledge of these ancestral mysteries—which was both one's ancestral birthright but also represented the authority that comes with initiation and ceremony—was the most dramatic assertion of an artist's standing. The hermeneutics described by Ryan was thus a direct result of the "coming together" of men from different language groups and personal experience at Papunya. In the secluded atmosphere of the Men's Painting Room that Ian McLean has described as akin to a men's social club, the men were painting not just for Bardon, but for one another, with all the bravado and machismo one might expect.[55] They were sharing their knowledge, impressing their authority upon one another, and piecing together places and events in epic narratives that cross the desert, linking each verse in complex and lengthy songlines.

Through painting and its subsequent mass reproduction, knowledge was, for the first time, centralized. The seriousness with which the founding painters at Papunya took this venture might be compared to that of the theologians who gathered at the Council of Rome in 382 to establish the Christian canon. And these paintings have, in every conceivable sense, become canonical. As John Kean notes in his essay in this volume, they are now held as vital records among the painters' descendants. In subsequent generations, it has become common to hear artists declare their motivation as being the preservation of important knowledge for future generations. But like all religious traditions, the practice of hermeneutics contains a high degree of subjectivity, opening the canon to reinterpretation and remodeling by the most articulate, intelligent or charismatic individuals.

It is not enough, then, to suggest that the founding artists were only trying to convey an "aesthetic contour," nor to generalize their formal progress as being simply a refinement of ancestral sensations. Rather, wherever possible within the bounds of cultural protocol and sensitivity, it is essential that we pay attention to the particular ideas that these artists were trying to convey. Generalized aesthetic theories have often failed to interrogate the *specific* content of individual works, with the result that the numerous, competing and entangled stories that define the history of Papunya Tula Artists are lost in a haze that obscures the profound individuality of the artists and the scale of their artistic, theological and intellectual achievements.

Despite the depth of scholarship on Papunya Tula Artists and desert painters more generally, there remain enormous gaps in our knowledge. Working on this exhibition has often felt like piecing together a jigsaw made of a million grains of sand, with much information on individual works either partial, inaccurate or absent altogether. Why is this so? The first reason is clearly the language barrier, which means that the names of places or ancestors have often been misheard or mistranscribed. There has also been considerable confusion over similar narratives. For instance, there are multiple unique, unrelated narratives involving Kungka Kutjarra (Two Women), which are easily conflated.[56] Moreover, prior to the digitization and online publication of numerous artworks, there was a severe lack of access to images, with only a limited number of paintings reproduced in books or journals. Finally, most of the early literature was either penned or influenced by Bardon. The publication of his posthumous magnum opus *Papunya: A Place Made after the Story* provided easy access to a trove of early paintings (as have subsequent exhibitions, such as *Tjukurrtjanu* and *Tjungunutja*). Unfortunately, *A Place Made after the Story* is also riddled with inaccuracies, in part a consequence of the difficulty of its completion in the final months of Bardon's life. In some cases, the titles and attributions given in the book even differ from the handwritten documentation Bardon made contemporaneously with the paintings themselves. More significantly, however, it does not seem that Bardon fully realized the precise geographic specificity of the paintings, in which each one refers to particular ancestral sites. This can be seen in his grouping of works according to broad themes such as "Water Dreamings," "Bush Tucker Stories" or "Ritual Dance Dreamings."

Once in print, many incorrect details have become widely circulated and reproduced, due to the relatively limited amount of information circulating. One might think this would signal the death knell for an art movement, but in some senses it has been hugely advantageous among Western audiences for Papunya Tula Artists. Art lovers, collector, curators and art historians have been able to completely elide the cultural details, allowing space for creative thinking around the aesthetic and social histories and affording freedom to bask solely in the aesthetic glory of the work.[57]

## A HISTORY OF MAPPING

In compiling this book and exhibition, instead of taking a chronological approach, we were guided by place, kinship and Tjukurrpa, inspired by Dick Kimber's call to curate a "cultural topography of the Western Desert."[58] We have attempted, wherever possible, to sequence the works in accordance with their position along the routes of ancestral travels. Thus, the reader can travel alongside Yina, the Old Man, as he moves from Tjurrpungkuntja (plate 45) to Ngurrapalangu (plate 46) before arriving at Yumari (plates 50–52) where his narrative intersects with the travels of a group of ancestral women (plate 44). This might sound like an overly ethnographic approach, but in many ways it is fundamentally art historical, revealing key insights on the development of style, motif and aesthetics by the comparison of multiple representations of the same (or related) subjects across multiple generations of artists.

This curatorial approach shows that what has frequently been cast as the straightforward progress of desert painters from iconic representation to abstraction is a more complicated one, in which the founding artists of Papunya Tula, through their process of standardization and hermeneutics, created forms of visual shorthand. This is not an unusual process in the movement toward abstraction, as artists gradually refine and reduce their personal iconography, including obtuse references to their own work (or that of others) in ways not necessarily recognizable in isolation.[59] Comparing multiple representations of the same narrative or site, painted at different times or by different artists, can bring some of this shorthand into focus. Take, for instance, Shorty Lungkarta Tjungurrayi's *Rumiya Tjukurrpa (Goanna Dreaming at Wantarritja)* (1980, plate 44), which for many years went under the highly generalized title *Patterns in the Sand*. Comparing this work to other depictions of *Rumiya Tjukurrpa* created by the artist, as well as those by his daughter Pamela Morgan Napaltjarri and granddaughter Debra Nangala, shows not only the process of reduction in the work of Shorty Lungkarta (fig. 1.7), but also how these elements retained their referential potential among subsequent generations. The central circle with radiating arcs that connects Shorty Lungkarta's 1972 *Goanna Love Story* (fig 1.8) with his 1980 version continues to refer to the same Tjukurrpa, despite the removal of more clearly identifiable icons.

Another example is Mick Namarari Tjapaltjarri's *Muruntji* (1972, plate 58), which was initially given the infantilizing title *Family Bush Tucker Dreaming*. According to Bardon's original documentation:

> The story is one of domestic happiness where, in accordance with Aboriginal custom, each member of the family has his or her own fire. They are warm in the night's coolness, sitting inside windbreaks and eating bush raisins, yams and witchetty grubs, and body paint indicates that they are celebrating a bush tucker ritual. The undulating band and pattern represents the earth where the grubs are found, the grubs being shown by simple curves.[60]

In the corpus of early Papunya paintings, such an innocuous subject would be unique almost to the point of unbelievability. Indeed, when asked for permission to reproduce the image in 1991, Mick Namarari described it as being Muruntji, a site associated with the ancestral Snake Woman, Kutungu. Rather than a scene of family bliss, this would suggest that it is a painting of a group of boys who, after playing near the site, found Kutungu asleep and raped her.[61] Mick Namarari described the undulating bands as representing the digging stick with which Kutungu later killed the boys in revenge, surrounded by U-shapes representing women. While this might seem a

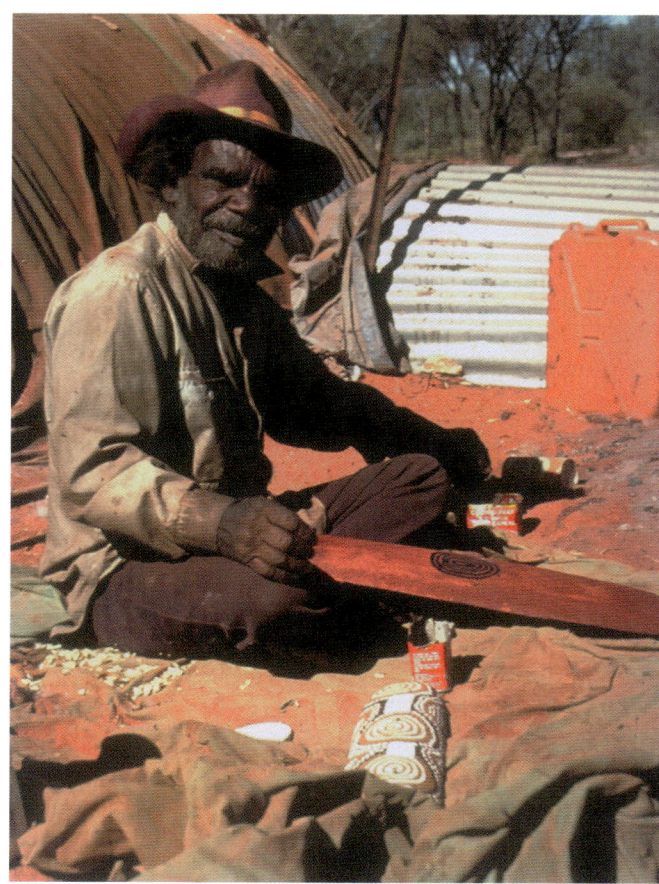

FIG. 1.7

Shorty Lungkarta Tjungurrayi at Yinyilingki, 1979. Photo by Fred Myers.

FIG. 1.8

Shorty Lungkarta Tjungurrayi, *Goanna Love Story*, 1972, synthetic polymer paint on composition board, 24⅞ × 18⅞ in. (63 × 48 cm). Papunya Community School Collection.

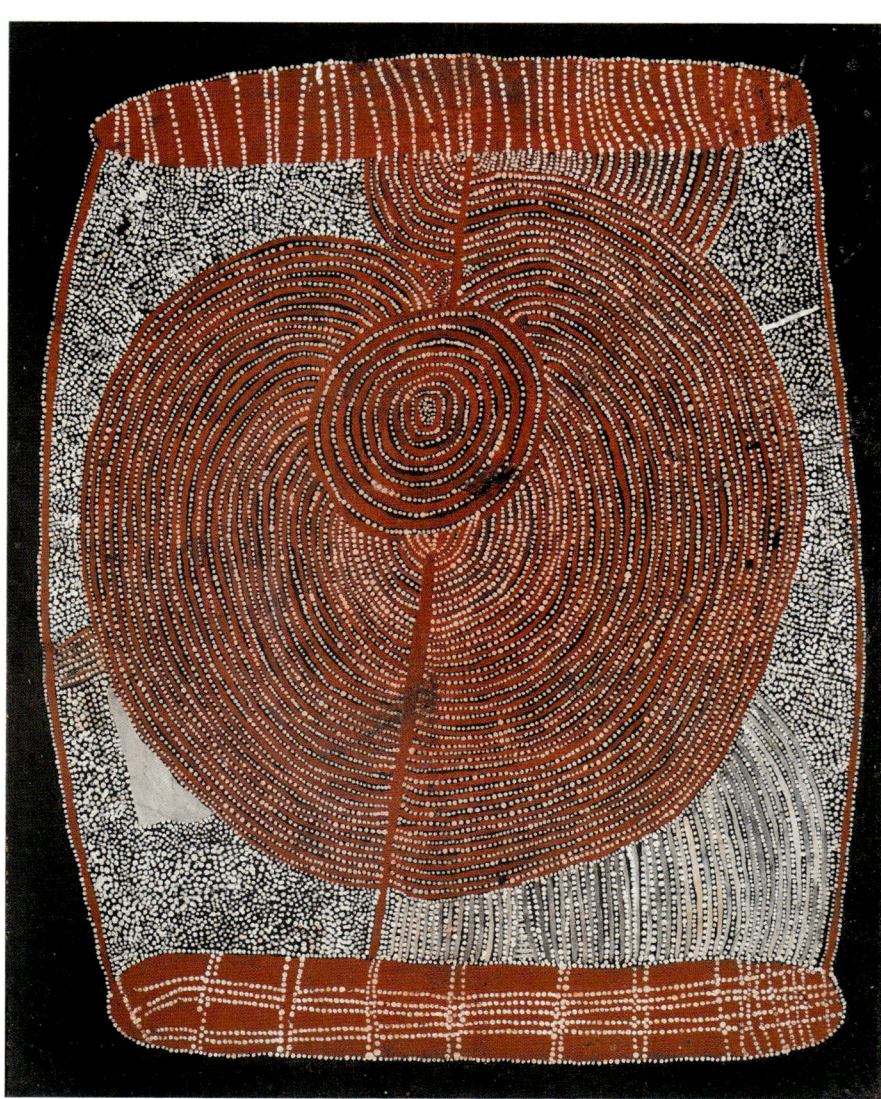

relatively minor distinction, it dramatically changes the meaning of a painting like *Family Bush Tucker* from one of bliss to terror. Comparing this image to other works by Mick Namarari, such as two of his earliest known paintings, *Sandhill and Clouds* (1971) and *Snake Dreaming* (1971), begs the question as to whether these paintings might also relate to Muruntji.[62] Might the same also be true for other works by the artist, such *Naughty Boys Dreaming* (1971) or *Untitled (Travelling Dreaming)* (1972), whose outward whimsy might disguise more violent undercurrents?[63]

This also raises the question, How could Bardon have gotten the subject so wrong? One obvious reason is that humor and horror are decidedly culturally specific phenomena. But another possibility is that these works were painted at a time when Bardon was requesting "children's stories" from the artists of Papunya Tula after controversy over a selection of early paintings exhibited at the Yuendumu sports carnival in August 1972. A group of Indigenous men had complained that those works revealed secret, sacred aspects of men's law.[64] In response to the "embarrassment" this caused, Bardon asked the men to paint children's stories devoid of secret, sacred ceremonial content. "I used to tell them I wanted *chichichukachuk* paintings; children's stories and family stories."[65] Bardon himself noted the difficulty of explaining this concept cross-culturally and was surprised to find the painters continued painting "powerful," "dangerous" and "taboo" stories.[66] He attributed this to a mixture of irresponsibility and ignorance: "They just liked to paint powerful stories. They didn't know enough about the outside world to fully grasp the implications."[67]

But perhaps there is a simpler explanation. Surveying many of the so-called children's stories painted by Pintupi artists such as Mick Namarari, Uta Uta Tjangala and Charlie Wartuma Tjungurrayi, it seems possible that they interpreted Bardon's request as asking them to paint Tjukurrpa *about* children. As seen in Mick Namarari's *Muruntji* or Uta Uta's *Tjitji Kutjarra (Two Boys at Yawarankunya)* (1971, plate 43), these are not necessarily family-friendly tales. This opens the possibility that Namarari's 1972 *Untitled* (formerly *A Children's Story*) (plate 60) might also depict Muruntji; the sinuous lines certainly have a snakelike feel. There are several sites at Muruntji, including caves and numerous rockholes, which might explain Mick Namarari's segmentation of the board into discrete areas. The top right quadrant is similar to other forms that he used to evoke caves (see, for instance,

*Mitukatjirri* [1971–72, plate 78]), and might represent the cave where Kutungu was raped. The central circles could indicate *manguri*, the padded head rings women use to carry coolamons, indicating Kutungu's presence at the site. This analysis is speculative, but shows the wealth of information still to be uncovered by interpretation that takes into account iconography, geography and personal style. Without scholars doing so, these paintings will remain enigmas, what the artists aimed to communicate lost to the sands of time.

The optical shimmer in the work of George Tjungurrayi (plate 104) or Warlimpirrnga Tjapaltjarri (plate 103) is more than just an individual's artistic interpretation of ancestral presence. They are the response to a specific place (Wilkinkarra) from a specific cultural vantage point, informed by ancient visual traditions but produced within a cultural and artistic milieu in which certain painterly signs have become instantly associated with these places.[68] Their unique manifestations are the signs of their individuality and genius, of which there is ample evidence in this exhibition.

## A HISTORY OF NAMES

Because desert languages are oral traditions, their adaptation in written form has been fraught with miscomprehension and mistranscription. This has particularly been the case in the art movement, where the names of artists, places and ancestors have often been recorded by fieldworkers and art advisors with relatively limited training in linguistics. In this volume, we have tried wherever possible to correct the spelling of the ancestral and place names. In particular, we have attempted to return the site-specificity of the paintings to their titles—for example, changing Mick Namarari's *Men's Corroboree* to *Mitukatjirri*. We have done this to honor the artists' communicative intentions and remove terms that might be misleading, inaccurate or trivializing.

In the case of artists' names, we have opted for the most recognized spelling in order to avoid confusion, acknowledging that many of the artists have built celebrated careers under these "professional" names. The only exceptions to this rule are where we have received specific guidance from family members of an artist. At the request of Charlotte Phillipus Napurrula, we refer to her father as Jack Long Phillipus Tjakamarra. Likewise, at the request of Winston Green, we refer to his grandfather as Yanatjarri No. III Tjakamarra.

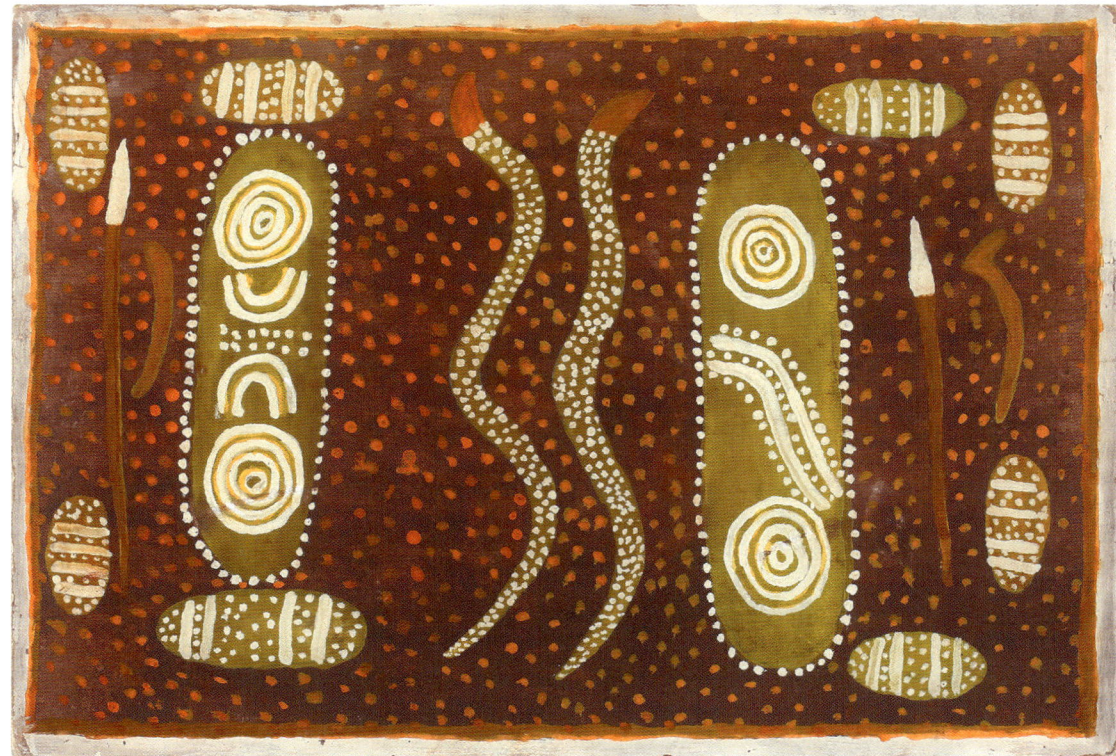

FIG. 1.9
Mick Wallangkarri Tjakamarra, *Meeting of the Snake Men*, 1975, synthetic polymer paint and natural pigments on watercolor board, 14⅞ × 21⅜ in. (37.8 × 54.3 cm). Kluge-Ruhe Aboriginal Art Collection, purchased with funds provided by Sharon Hirschland in honor of Roger Hirschland, 2019, 2019.0005.001.

## A HISTORY OF MEDIUM

While the history of Papunya Tula Artists can be described through the processes of hermeneutics and enunciation, attention must also be paid to the medium of its products' delivery. The often-used moniker the "acrylic painting movement" elides a more complex narrative. The early works described previously were executed with whatever paints and scrap materials the artists could find. Some were drawn with pencil on paper and others on watercolor board acquired through the Arunta Art Gallery and Bookshop, which supplied many of the painters' relatives who worked in the watercolor tradition initiated by Albert Namatjira (for instance, Mick Wallangkarri's *Meeting of the Snake Men* [1975, fig. 1.9]).

Bardon professionalized the men's practice, getting them to paint on Masonite boards in standardized sizes. He also asked them to work with "traditional earth colors of red and yellow ochre," playing into stereotypes of "authentic" Aboriginal art. During his long absences, however, a wider range of colors crept into the artists' works, often to brilliant effect. In the top right corner of *Tjitji Kutjarra (Two Boys at Yawarankunya)*, Uta Uta lends the sacred objects a flashing brilliance by the subtle addition of hot-pink dotting. This same hot-pink poster paint turns up in the lower half of Mick Namarari's masterpiece

*Mitukatjirri*. The artist uses the matte translucence of yellow, pink and orange poster paints to create a contrast between the internal space of the cave and the explosive energy of the ceremonial performance alluded to in the forms above, which he renders in the thicker and more opaque acrylic paints provided by Bardon.

Mick Namarari (fig. 1.10) was the first artist provided with a canvas by Bardon, in mid-1972. It was, Bardon later recalled, a canvas that he had intended for his own use. He was convinced to give it to Mick Namarari, who used it to paint *Yam Spirit Dreaming for Children* (1972).[69] Until 1973, however, Masonite remained the most common substrate for Papunya Tula painters. This would begin to change in 1973, when Peter Fannin started distributing canvas boards to the artists. Canvas boards are made from canvas stretched over and glued to a cardboard backing. They are usually considered a cheaper alternative to canvas, used by students or for preparatory sketches. While Fannin was trying to professionalize the artists' practices, the company was in a precarious financial position, unable to invest in more costly materials. Canvas board did, however, have two significant advantages over Masonite: as a primed canvas surface, it was better suited to holding paint and maintaining the color of the pigments—hence the clarity of color in works such as Yanatjarri's *Untitled* (possibly *Wati Kutjarra at Pakarangaranya*, 1973, plate 81) or Charlie Mutju Egalie Tjapaltjarri's *Wallaby Dreaming in the Sandhills at Tjunti* (1977, plate 32).

Finally, in 1974, the move to canvas facilitated Papunya Tula Artists' ascension onto the global stage. This was only possible as a result of commissions from the Aboriginal Arts Board (AAB), whose director, Bob Edwards, was a strong supporter of the company, visiting the artists on numerous occasions.[70] With Edwards's encouragement, Fannin began distributing canvases to the artists. Dinny Nolan Tjampitjinpa's *Men's Ceremony* (c. 1974, plate 15) is among this first group of canvases. Painting on canvas was different from painting on board: canvas absorbs more paint, allowing for differing levels of translucency and opacity, which Dinny Nolan skillfully exploited to create areas of shimmering depth in this early work.

For much of the 1970s, the AAB would be the principal purchaser of Papunya Tula paintings, helping keep the company afloat while building its reputation overseas.[71] Although canvases were a significant outright investment for the company, they were far easier to ship than boards. Once removed from their wooden stretcher bars, multiple canvases could be rolled into a single tube, and they were less likely to suffer the fate of chipped paint or frayed corners. Most importantly, they allowed for a grand expansion in scale, as can be seen in Kaapa Tjampitjinpa's *Dreaming at Mikantji* (1975, plate 17), commissioned by the Aboriginal Arts Board for the exhibition *Art of the First Australians*, which toured the United States and Japan from 1976 to 1978. One of ten monumental paintings created for the exhibition, the commission heralded a new era of large-scale canvas paintings from Papunya.

Whether intentional or not, canvas also resulted in a further standardizing of sizes, as the stretcher bars would be reused for multiple works. Combined with the recognizable "house" palette, size parity would allow for epic, serial installations in which works by different artists could sit seamlessly side by side in grids that accentuated their modernity. This was used to particular effect by gallerists such as Gabrielle Pizzi, whose annual Papunya Tula exhibitions would feature a lineup of 6 × 8–foot canvases in austere rows to rival installations of Agnes Martin's painting. By the 1980s, the artists of Papunya Tula were using premium acrylic paints and working on the finest Belgian linen, creating a professional standard that was hard to match.[72]

## A HISTORY OF TOGETHERNESS

Any attempt to survey the five-decade history of Papunya Tula Artists is bound to be partial. Despite our best efforts, the lack of space and available works has meant that many significant artists are not represented here, among them George Tjampu Tjapaltjarri, Pinta Pinta Tjapanangka, Kanya Tjapangati, Pirrmangka Napanangka and Kawayi Nampitjinpa.

With the exception of the *Fiftieth Anniversary Suite* of fifty new works commissioned for this exhibition (plates 106–55), all the works in *Irriṯitja Kuwarri Tjungu* are drawn from American collections. While this means that none of the masterworks from Australian collections are included, it invites a different line of inquiry, allowing us to examine the pivotal role that the relationship between Papunya Tula Artists and the United States has played in shaping the movement's profile in Australia and internationally. It also allows for the showcasing of works that have rarely been seen over the past five decades.

The expanded scale of canvas painting allowed Papunya Tula Artists to take on the world. It might seem strange that the fiftieth anniversary of the company is being celebrated in the United States, but in many ways,

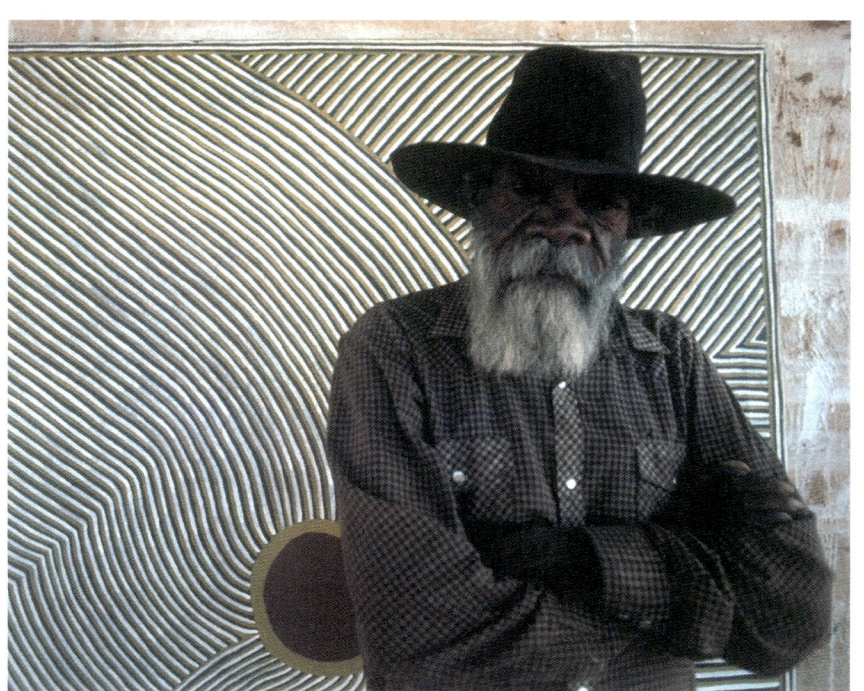

FIG. 1.10

Mick Namarari Tjapaltjarri at Walungurru (Kintore) with his work *Ninu (Bandicoot) at Kutju* (1993), acquired by the National Gallery of Victoria in 2002. Photo by Dennis Schulz.

this country is integral to the history of Papunya Tula. Many of the works in *Irritjitja Kuwarri Tjungu* were commissioned for earlier exhibitions in the United States and Canada, and these commissions provided the impetus for the increased scale and grandeur of Papunya painting in mid-1970s.

Such international exhibitions were central to establishing Papunya Tula Artists as the gold standard of Aboriginal Australian art. This was most dramatically illustrated by the 1988 exhibition *Dreamings: The Art of Aboriginal Australia*, which brought a heightened level of international attention to Aboriginal art. According to one of the exhibition's curators, Christopher Anderson, the initial response from Daphne Williams, manager at Papunya Tula Artists, to the exhibition proposal was muted.[73] However, when *Dreamings* opened in New York, Papunya Tula Artists were the undeniable stars. At the entrance of the exhibition, Tim Leura and Clifford Possum's *Spirit Dreaming through Napperby Country* (1980) held pride of place, while Michael Jagamara Nelson's *Five Stories* (1984) became the iconic emblem of the exhibition by its reproduction on the cover of the widely distributed exhibition catalog. Shorty Lungkarta's *Rumiya Tjukurrpa* was also among the eighteen works from Papunya Tula included in the exhibition.

Eleanore Neumann notes that "*Dreamings* catalyzed the collecting of Indigenous Australian art in the United States."[74] For a brief moment, the United States became the epicenter of private collecting, with Richard Kelton and billionaire John W. Kluge both acquiring works with a budget and fervor beyond the reach of most Australians. This coincided with increased gallery representation in the United States. In October 1988, Carol Lopes opened CAZ Gallery in West Hollywood, and the following year, John Weber Gallery held its two New York exhibitions.[75]

Within a few short months after seeing *Dreamings*, Kluge had headed to Australia, where he acquired sixteen works directly from Papunya Tula Artists, including Yanatjarri No. III's *Artist's Country near Kulkurta* (1988, plate 71). On his return, Kluge built upon this collection with works from CAZ Gallery, including Bill Stockman's unusually colorful *Ngatitjirri Tjukurrpa (Budgerigar Dreaming)* (1988, plate 19) and Kenny Williams Tjampitjinpa's *Hill Site of Karilywarra* (1988, plate 87), as well as from Gallery Gabrielle Pizzi in Melbourne, where he acquired important works by Don Tjungurrayi (plate 20), Mick Namarari (plate 40) and Yanatjarri No. III Tjakamarra (plate 56). When *Papunya Tula: Contemporary Paintings from Australia's Western Desert* opened in May 1989 at John Weber Gallery, Kluge acquired the majority of the exhibition, including centerpiece works by Clifford Possum Tjapaltjarri (plate 22), Michael Jagamara Nelson (plate 28) and Timmy Payungu Tjapangati (plate 95).

After building a formidable collection of contemporary works from Papunya Tula Artists, Kluge soon turned his attention to the movement's history. By good fortune, this coincided with the decision by philanthropist Margaret Carnegie to sell her extensive collection of early works, including some of the very first works produced at Papunya in 1971, such as Tutama Tjapangati's *Stars at Night Twinkling* as well as later works including Shorty Lungkarta's *Rumiya Tjukurrpa*, which Kluge had no doubt seen in *Dreamings*.[76] Kluge's timing was doubly fortunate in that it predated the Sotheby's June 1997 auction of "Important Aboriginal Art," in which, led by Johnny Warangkula Tjupurrula's masterpiece *Water Dreaming at Kalipinypa* (1972, plate 10), the early paintings from Papunya suddenly became prime fetish items of the Aboriginal art market.[77] By this stage, Kluge was already in the process of donating the majority of his collection to the University of Virginia, supplementing his initial gift with a further donation of sixteen early works from Papunya in 2008. Kluge's collection would form the basis of the Kluge-Ruhe Aboriginal Art Collection, creating a permanent center for Aboriginal art in North America. To date, the collection holds over two hundred works from Papunya Tula Artists.

Beyond simply acquiring paintings, American collectors have played a significant role through sharing their works with the public, helping to promote desert painting in the United States. *Irritjitja Kuwarri Tjungu* features works from several of these collectors: Richard Klingler and Jane Slatter, Stephen and Agatha Luczo, Steve Martin and Anne Stringfield, John and Barbara Wilkerson and James and Elaine Wolfensohn, but many others have also made their collections available to museums in Australia and the United States over the years.[78] More recently, the Miami-based collectors Debra and Dennis Scholl included the work of the Papunya Tula artists Warlimpirrnga Tjapaltjarri, Yukultji Napangati and Wintjiya Napaltjarri in the touring exhibitions drawn from their collections *No Boundaries* (2014) and *Marking the Infinite* (2016), both organized by the Nevada Museum of Art.[79] In 2012, the Scholls had seen and subsequently acquired two major works by Warlimpirrnga Tjapaltjarri, which had been included in *documenta 13*, curated by Carolyn

Cristov-Bakargiev. Through their contemporary art world connections, the Scholls convinced gallery director Alissa Friedman to give Warlimpirrnga a solo exhibition at the prestigious gallery Salon 94 in the Bowery, New York, to coincide with the opening of *No Boundaries* at the Perez Art Museum in Miami in 2015.

Like Michael Nelson and Bill Stockman before him, Warlimpirrnga traveled to New York, where the press were captivated by his zingy abstract paintings and his family's story of leaving the desert in 1984.[80] His exhibition received rave reviews in the *New York Times*, the *New Yorker* and the *Wall Street Journal*.[81] Roberta Smith, who 27 years earlier had been underwhelmed with the desert acrylic paintings in *Dreamings*, which she dismissed as resembling "nothing so much as a solo show of a moderately talented abstract painter of the 70's,"[82] was converted by "the elaborately topographical patterns" of Warlimpirrnga's paintings. "It's always thrilling," Smith declared, "when examples of a given art form make you think this is the best (fill in the blank) I've ever seen."[83] Staring boldly from the front page of the arts section of the *New York Times* (see fig. 8.1), Warlimpirrnga's imposing visage caught the attention of actor and art collector Steve Martin, who rode his bicycle to the Bowery and acquired the first of what would quickly become

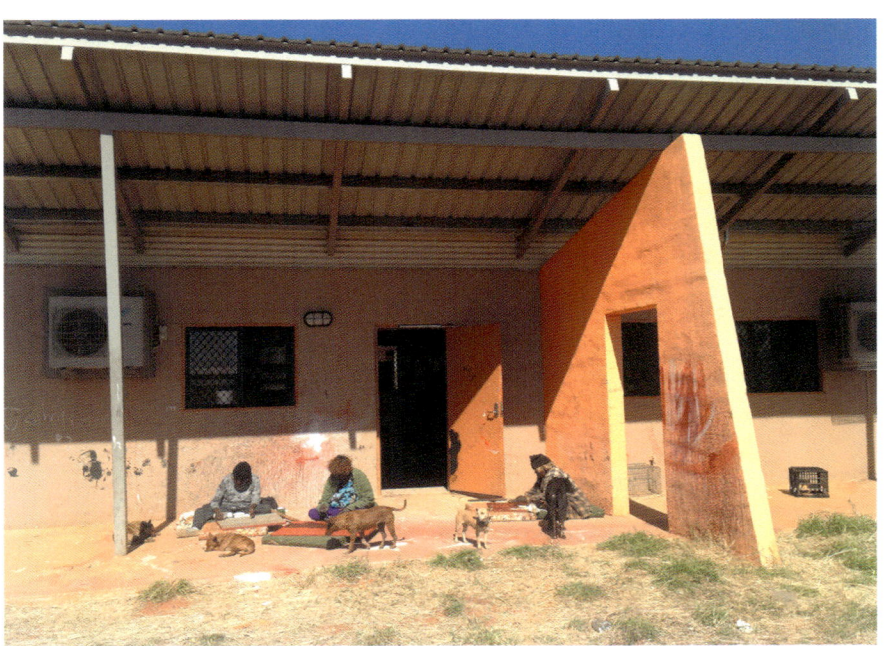

FIG. 1.11

Mantua Nangala, Yukultji Napangati and Nanyuma Napangati working at the Papunya Tula Artists studio in Kiwirrkurra, 2015. Photo by Henry Skerritt.

a major collection of Aboriginal paintings, the bulk of which were created by artists from Papunya Tula. In 2019, Martin would leverage his own art world connections to showcase his growing collection at Gagosian Gallery in New York.[84] And so, the success of Papunya Tula Artists continues, like the radiating concentric circle of a Tingarri painting, spiraling outward in a pulse that connects a diverse range of people across time and space.[85]

## A HISTORY OF BUSINESS WORTH CELEBRATING

The five-decade history of Papunya Tula Artists has been anything but a clear and inevitable progression toward success. The company overcame moments of financial peril in the 1970s, '80s and '90s before emerging as one of Australia's most successful Indigenous-owned businesses. As the market for Aboriginal art grew, the company faced the increasing challenge of private dealers enticing artists to paint outside the company, often using inferior materials and without the strict quality control of Papunya Tula. And yet, despite all the challenges, the company has survived, thanks in large part to the dogged determination of its artists and staff. From Geoffrey Bardon and Peter Fannin, through Dick Kimber, Janet Wilson-Holt, John Kean, Andrew Crocker, Daphne Williams, Faye Bell and Paul Sweeney, it has been led by a dedicated series of managers, supported by fieldworkers on the ground such as Wayne Eager, Luke Scholes, Sarita Quinlivan, Vanessa Merlino, Grant Rundell and Matt Frost,[86] along with countless others whose assistance and encouragement in the studios at Walungurru and Kiwirrkurra (fig. 1.11) have helped artists realize their unique visions.[87]

As the first Aboriginal-owned arts organization in Australia, Papunya Tula Artists established a model that would be emulated across the country in subsequent decades. Yet Papunya Tula is markedly different from the community art centers that proceeded it. At the time of its foundation, allies in the Welfare Branch of the Northern Territory Government, as well as those in the Aboriginal Arts Board, sought to ensure that the artists would never lose control of their company. Rather than being established along the loose lines of a cooperative, therefore, Papunya Tula formed as a proprietary limited company with Aboriginal directors and shareholders. Today, the company has fifty shareholders and is run by a board of directors whose current chair is Yukultji Napangati. Each year, shareholders attend an annual

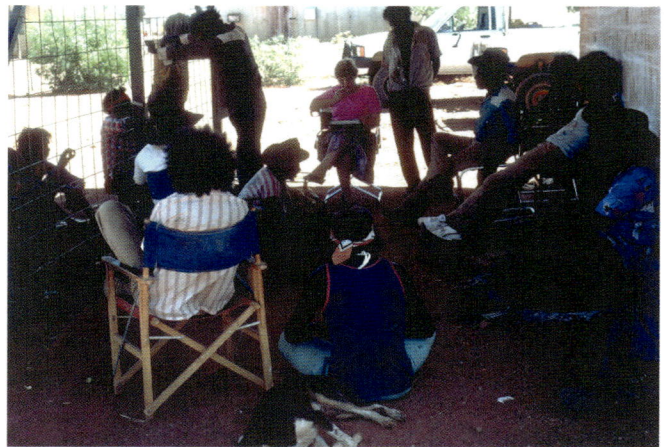

**FIG. 1.12**

Papunya Tula Artists Annual General Meeting, Walungurru, 1988. Photo by Fred Myers.

general meeting to learn about the state of the company and discuss matters of finances, dividends and community investments (fig. 1.12). Since 1987, Papunya Tula Artists has operated its own gallery in central Mparntwe. Like any capitalist structure, this business model has its own in-built inequalities, but it has provided a remarkable level of stability against the fluctuations of personalities or the dominance of particular family groups. In his essay in this volume, Paul Sweeney points to the ways in which the profits of the company have allowed for community development in the Western Desert, including supporting remote dialysis services and funding a public swimming pool at Walungurru. As Bobby West Tjupurrula notes, "Papunya Tula has never failed, it's still going. It is always there to help."[87] As we reflect back on five decades of Papunya Tula Artists, many mysteries remain in our understanding of the art, artists and history of the company. Its survival, against all odds, is a mystery worth celebrating.

## NOTES

This essay would have been impossible without many hours of patient conversations with Fred Myers, who never once sighed at my inability to untangle the many snakes, goannas or *kungka* than move through the desert, nor laughed at my unflappable inability to pronounce Ilingawurrngawurrnga.

1. Hetti Perkins and Hannah Fink, *Papunya Tula: Genesis and Genius* (Sydney: Art Gallery of New South Wales, 2000), 185.
2. See the interview with Perkins in this volume, "The Stories I Can Tell," p. 77.
3. Vivien Johnson, *Lives of the Papunya Tula Artists* (Alice Springs, NT: IAD Press, 2008), 124.
4. Geoffrey Bardon, *Papunya Tula: Art of the Western Desert* (Melbourne: McPhee Gribble, 1991), 36. Bardon cites the date as June 1972, but communications uncovered by Luke Scholes show that the name was in use by early May. Luke Scholes, "Unmasking the Myth: The Emergence of Papunya Painting," in *Tjungunutja: From Having Come Together*, ed. Luke Scholes (Darwin, NT: Museum and Art Gallery of the Northern Territory, 2017), 145.
5. See John Kean's text in this volume, "Tjarla | The Honey Ant," p. 106.
6. See Scholes, "Unmasking the Myth," 130.
7. See, for instance, Geoffrey Bardon, *Aboriginal Art of the Western Desert* (Adelaide: Rigby, 1979); Geoffrey Bardon, *Papunya Tula: Art of the Western Desert* (Melbourne: McPhee Gribble, 1991); and Geoffrey Bardon and James Bardon, *Papunya: A Place Made after the Story: The Beginnings of the Western Desert Painting Movement* (Carlton, VIC: Melbourne University Publishing, 2004).
8. See, for instance, Scholes, "Unmasking the Myth," and Vivien Johnson, *Once Upon a Time in Papunya* (Sydney: University of New South Wales Press, 2010).
9. See Scholes, "Unmasking the Myth." For further accounts of the extensive networks behind the success of Papunya Tula Artists, see Fred Myers, "The Wizards of Oz? Nation, State and the Making of Aboriginal Fine Art," in *The Empire of Things*, ed. Fred Myers (Santa Fe: SAR Press, 2001), 165–206.
10. Bardon himself noted this fact in *Papunya Tula: Art of the Western Desert*, 108.
11. Johnson, *Once Upon a Time in Papunya*, 12.
12. John Kean, "Papunya, Place and Time," in *Papunya Painting: Out of the Desert*, ed. Vivien Johnson (Canberra: National Museum of Australia, 2007), 7.
13. Bardon and Bardon, *Papunya: A Place Made after the Story*, 105.
14. See, for instance, Tony Bennett, *The Birth of the Museum: History, Theory, Politics* (New York: Routledge, 1995). For a discussion of the impact of this temporal frame on Indigenous peoples' engagement with the museum, see Henry Skerritt, "When Time's Arrows Collide: Historical Critique in Indigenous Contemporary Art" (Ph.D. diss., University of Pittsburgh, 2017).
15. See, for instance, James Clifford, *Returns: Becoming Indigenous in the Twenty-First Century* (Cambridge, MA: Harvard University Press, 2013); and Jeffrey Sissons, *First Peoples: Indigenous Cultures and Their Futures* (Chicago: University of Chicago Press, 2005).

16. An early and influential articulation of this idea can be found in Johannes Fabian, *Time and the Other: How Anthropology Makes Its Object* (New York: Columbia University Press, 1983). Fabian's thinking has since been taken up by numerous scholars, most prominently Mark Rifkin, *Beyond Settler Time: Temporal Sovereignty and Indigenous Self-Determination* (Durham, NC: Duke University Press, 2017).

17. Fred Myers, *Pintupi Country, Pintupi Self: Sentiment, Place, and Politics among Western Desert Aborigines* (Washington, DC: Smithsonian Institution Press, 1986), 49.

18. Sid Anderson, Long Jack Phillipus Tjakamarra, Michael Nelson Jagamara AM, Joseph Jurrah Tjapaltjarri, Bobby West Tjupurrula and Desmond Phillipus Tjupurrula with Luke Scholes, "*Tjungunutja* (from Having Come Together)" in *Tjungunutja: From Having Come Together*, ed. Luke Scholes (Darwin, NT: Museum and Art Gallery of the Northern Territory, 2017), 117.

19. According to Smith, "Contemporaneity consists precisely in the acceleration, ubiquity, and constancy of radical disjunctures of perception, of mismatching ways of seeing and valuing the same world." Terry Smith, *Architecture of the Aftermath* (Chicago: University of Chicago Press, 2006), 9.

20. Terry Smith, "Contemporary, Contemporaneity," *Keywords Project* (University of Pittsburgh), accessed June 2021, http://keywords.pitt.edu/pdfs/contemporary_and _contemporaneity.pdf.

21. The complex strata of times that coincide in contemporary desert painting are expertly described in David Brooks and Darren Jorgensen, *Wanarn Painters of Place and Time: Old Age Travels in the Tjukurrpa* (Crawley: University of Western Australia Press, 2015), 46–47.

22. Ian McLean, *How Aborigines Invented the Idea of Contemporary Art* (Brisbane and Sydney: IMA and Power Publications, 2011).

23. Ian McLean, "'Surviving the Contemporary': What Indigenous Artists Want, and How to Get It," *Contemporary Visual Art and Culture Broadsheet* 42, no. 3 (2013): 167–73.

24. Quoted in Myers, *Pintupi Country, Pintupi Self*, 25.

25. Quentin Sprague, "Collaborators: Third Party Transactions in Indigenous Contemporary Art," in *Double Desire: Transculturation and Indigenous Contemporary Art*, ed. Ian McLean (Newcastle-upon-Tyne, England: Cambridge Scholars Publishing, 2014), 73.

26. Geoffrey Bardon, "The Gift that Time Gave: Papunya Early and Late, 1971–72 and 1980," in *Mythscapes: Aboriginal Art of the Desert*, ed. Judith Ryan (Melbourne: National Gallery of Victoria, 1989), 13.

27. See McLean, *How Aborigines Invented the Idea of Contemporary Art*, 43–47.

28. Nicholas Baume, "The Interpretation of Dreaming: The Australian Aboriginal Acrylic Movement," *Art & Text* 47, no. 1 (Winter, 1989): 112.

29. See the widely circulated essay by Nancy Munn, "Visual Categories: An Approach to the Study of Representational Systems," *American Anthropologist* 68 (1966): 936–50. She would expand upon these ideas in the seminal book Nancy Munn, *Walbiri Iconography: Graphic Representation and Cultural Symbolism in a Central Australian Society* (Ithaca, NY: Cornell University Press, 1973).

30. Fred Myers, *Painting Culture: The Making of an Aboriginal High Art* (Durham, NC: Duke University Press, 2002), 34.

31. Rothmans of Pall Mall Canada Limited, *Art of Aboriginal Australia* (Vancouver: Rothmans of Pall Mall Canada, 1974). Uta Uta's work was included in the exhibition, but Clifford Possum's was sold to Peter Brokensha, a close friend of Bob Edwards, who in 1970 founded the Argyle Art Centre in Sydney and was an early supporter of the Papunya artists.

32. See Fred Myers, "History, Memory and the Politics of Self-Determination at an Early Outstation," in *Experiments in Self-Determination: Histories of the Outstation Movement in Australia*, ed. Nicolas Peterson and Fred Myers (Canberra, ACT: Australian National University Press, 2016): 81–104.

33. See "Go West | The Pintupi Return Home" in this volume, p. 158.

34. Fred Myers documented the painting at Yayayi on December 2, 1973.

35. For more on this transition, see Paul Sweeney's essay in this volume, "Art of Resilience: The Importance of Papunya Tula Artists in Australia's Western Desert."

36. Peter Sutton, ed., *Dreamings: The Art of Aboriginal Australia* (New York: G. Braziller, 1988). *Dreamings* was shown at the Asia Society Galleries, New York, October 6–December 31, 1988, before traveling to the David and Alfred Smart Gallery, University of Chicago, January 26–March 19, 1989; Los Angeles County Museum of Natural History, May 13–August 5, 1989; Museum of Victoria, Melbourne, September–December 1989; and South Australian Museum, Adelaide, February–April 1990.

37. See Lucia Colombari, "1988: The Scintilating Arrival of Aboriginal Australian Art in the U.S.," in *Beyond Dreamings: The Rise of Indigenous Australian Art in the United States*, ed. Henry Skerritt (Charlottesville: Kluge-Ruhe Aboriginal Art Collection of the University of Virginia, 2019), 14–15.

38. John W. Kluge acquired the work *Women's Dreaming near Kiwirrkurra* (1989, plate 93) from this exhibition.

39. Yanatjarri No. III Tjakamarra, *Tingari Cycle Dreaming at Paratjakutti*, 1989, synthetic polymer paint on canvas, 59 × 71 in. (150 × 180 cm), Metropolitan Museum of Art, New York, Purchase, Aust Art Gift, 1989, 1989.315.

40. The Papunya Tula artists currently represented in the Metropolitan Museum of Art are Doreen Reid Nakamarra, Wintjiya Napaltjarri, Yanatjarri No. III Tjakamarra and Yukultji Napangati.

41. See John Carty, "Rethinking Western Desert Abstraction," in *Crossing Cultures: The Owen and Wagner Collection of Contemporary Aboriginal Australian Art at the Hood Museum of Art*, ed. Stephen Gilchrist (Hanover, NH: Hood Museum of Art, Dartmouth College, 2012), 105–18.

42. See John Carty, *Patrick Tjungurrayi: Beyond Borders* (Crawley: University of Western Australia Press, 2015).

43. John Carty, "Creating Country: Abstraction, Economics and the Social Life of Style in Balgo Art" (Ph.D. diss., Australian National University, 2011).

44. These include John Carty, Una Rey, Quentin Sprague, Robyn Ferrell, Jennifer Biddle and Darren Jorgensen, among others.

45. See, for instance, Howard Morphy, *Ancestral Connections: Art and an Aboriginal System of Knowledge* (Chicago: University of Chicago Press, 1991); Françoise Dussart, "A Body Painting in Translation," in *Rethinking Visual Anthropology*, ed. Howard Morphy and Marcus Banks (New Haven, CT: Yale University Press, 1999), 186–202; Jennifer Biddle, *Breasts Bodies Canvas: Central Desert Art as Experience* (Sydney: University of New South Wales Press, 2007); and Carty, "Rethinking Western Desert Abstraction."

46. Myers, *Pintupi Country, Pintupi Self*, 48–52.

47. Fred Myers, "Intrigue of the Archive, Enigma of the Object," in *Tjukurrtjanu: Origins of Western Desert Art*, ed. Judith Ryan and Philip Batty (Melbourne: National Gallery of Victoria, 2011), 30–31; and John Kean, "Catch a Fire," in Ryan and Batty, *Tjukurrtjanu*, 48–50.

48. Judith Ryan, "Aesthetic Splendour, Cultural Power and Wisdom: Early Papunya Painting," in Ryan and Batty, *Tjukurrtjanu*, 18.

49. See Fred Myers, "Truth, Beauty and Pintupi Painting," *Visual Anthropology* 2, no. 2 (January 1989): 163–95.

50. Ryan, "Aesthetic Splendour, Cultural Power and Wisdom," 18.

51. For a further discussion of this system of mimesis, see Henry Skerritt, "A Stitch in Time: How Aboriginal Australian Artists Are Reweaving Our World," in *Everywhen: The Eternal Present in Indigenous Art from Australia*, ed. Stephen Gilchrist (Cambridge, MA: Harvard University Press, 2016), 16–27.

52. Robyn Ferrell, *Sacred Exchanges: Images in Global Context* (New York: Columbia University Press, 2018), 144.

53. Ferrell, *Sacred Exchanges*, 144.

54. Myers, *Pintupi Country, Pintupi Self*, 245.

55. Ian McLean, *Rattling Spears: A History of Indigenous Australian Art* (London: Reaktion, 2016), 132–33.

56. See "Kungka Kutjarra | Two Women" in this volume, p. 184.

57. This is much harder to do with the artists of Arnhem Land, for example, whose work has been much more insistently figurative, clan based, and presented by articulate cosmopolitans from Wandjuk Marika OBE to Djambawa Marawili AM.

58. Richard G. Kimber, "Tjukurrpa Trails: A Cultural Topography of the Western Desert," in Perkins and Fink, *Genesis and Genius*, 269–73.

59. This was one of the key insights of John Richardson's three-volume biography of Pablo Picasso. I have made a similar argument in relation to the Yolŋu artist Noŋirrnga Marawili. See John Richardson, *A Life of Picasso* (New York: Random House, 1991, 2006, 2007); and Henry Skerritt, "The Country Speaks through Her," in *Noŋirrnga Marawili: From My Heart and Mind*, ed. Cara Pinchbeck (Sydney: Art Gallery of New South Wales, 2018), 34–45.

60. Bardon, *Papunya Tula: Art of the Western Desert*, 88.

61. See "Kutungu | The Snake Woman" in this volume, p. 174.

62. Mick Namarari Tjapaltjarri, *Sandhills and Clouds*, 1971, synthetic polymer paint on chipboard, 18½ × 9⅞ in. (47 × 25 cm), Museum and Art Gallery of the Northern Territory, Darwin, WAL 1; and Mick Namarari Tjapaltjarri, *Snake Dreaming*, 1971, synthetic polymer paint on chipboard, 21⁹⁄₁₆ × 10 in. (55 × 25 cm), Museum and Art Gallery of the Northern Territory, Darwin, WAL 15.

63. Mick Namarari Tjapaltjarri, *Naughty Boys Dreaming*, 1971, synthetic polymer paint on composition board, 18⅛ × 36 in. (46 × 92 cm), National Gallery of Australia, Purchased 1993–1996, 93.180; and Mick Namarari Tjapaltjarri, *Untitled (Travelling Dreaming)*, 1971, synthetic polymer paint on compressed fiber board, 32½ × 28 in. (83 × 71 cm), Museum and Art Gallery of the Northern Territory, Darwin, WAL 127.

64. See Richard G. Kimber, "Politics of the Secret in the Contemporary Western Desert," in *Politics of the Secret*, Oceania Monographs, no. 45, ed. Christopher Anderson (Sydney: University of Sydney, 1995), 123–42.

65. Geoffrey Bardon, quoted in Ulli Beier, "Geoff Bardon and the Beginnings of Papunya Tula Art," in *Long Water: Aboriginal Art and Literature 1988*, ed. Uli Beier and Colin Johnson (North Sydney: Aboriginal Artists Agency, 1988), 96. The correct Pintupi term is *tjitji tjukutjuku* (literally "children little").

66. Bardon, quoted in Beier, "Geoff Bardon and the Beginnings of Papunya Tula Art," 96.

67. Bardon, quoted in Beier, "Geoff Bardon and the Beginnings of Papunya Tula Art," 96.

68. This is brilliantly argued in Fred Myers, "Emplacement and Displacement: Perceiving the Landscape through Aboriginal Australian Acrylic Painting," *Ethnos* 78, no. 4 (2013): 435–63.

69. The resulting painting is now in the collection of the National Gallery of Victoria: Mick Namarari Tjapaltjarri, *Yam Spirit Dreaming for Children*, 1972, synthetic polymer paint on canvas, 30 × 24 in. (76 × 61 cm), National Gallery of Victoria, Melbourne, Purchased through the Art Foundation of Victoria with the assistance of North Broken Hill Ltd,

Fellow, 1987, O.52-1987. It is unclear whether Bardon was persuaded by Namarari to part with the canvas, or whether he was simply swayed by the artist's prodigious output at the time. See Bardon and Bardon, *Papunya: A Place Made after the Story*, 493. It is worth speculating whether this work also relates to Muruntji, with the figures bearing clear resemblance to those in Mick Namarari's painting of the same year *Muruntji* (formerly known as *Family Bush Tucker Dreaming*, plate 58).

70. See Fred Myers, "Painting at Yayayi, 1974," in *Papunya Painting: Out of the Desert*, ed. Vivien Johnson (Canberra, ACT: National Museum of Australia, 2007).

71. See Kate Khan, "Looking Back: The Story of a Collection. The Papunya Permanent Collection of Early Western Desert Paintings at the Australian Museum," *Technical Reports of the Australian Museum, Online* 25 (2016): 11–12.

72. On occasion, Papunya Tula artists have also worked on paper, as well as producing limited-edition etchings with printmaker Dian Darmansjah.

73. Christopher Anderson, personal correspondence with the author, January 26, 2021.

74. Eleanore Neumann, "Making Their Own Mark: Collecting Indigenous Australian Art in the U.S. since *Dreamings*," in *Beyond Dreamings: The Rise of Indigenous Australian Art in the United States*, ed. Henry Skerritt (Charlottesville: Kluge-Ruhe Aboriginal Art Collection of the University of Virginia, 2019), 29.

75. *Papunya Tula: Contemporary Paintings from Australia's Western Desert* was held at John Weber Gallery, May 25–June 17, 1989. It was followed by a solo exhibition of Yanatjarri No. III Tjakamarra in December 1989. Since 2009, Papunya Tula Artists has maintained representation in the United States through Harvey Arts Projects in Sun Valley, Idaho.

76. See Paul Taylor, "ART; Primitive Dreams Are Hitting the Big Time," *New York Times*, May 21, 1989; and Fred Myers, "Collecting Aboriginal Art in the Australian Nation: Two Case Studies," *Visual Anthropology Review* 21, no. 1–2 (March 2005): 116–37.

77. See Roger Benjamin, "The Fetish for Papunya Tula Boards," in *Icons of the Desert: Early Aboriginal Painting from Papunya* (Ithaca, NY: Herbert F. Johnson Museum of Art, Cornell University, 2009), 21–49.

78. These include Robert Kaplan and Margaret Levi, Will Owen and Harvey Wagner, Robert and Eva Shaye, Harold Burch, Martha Hesse and Robert Dolan, May and Victor Lam and the late Richard Kelton. See Eleanore Neumann, "Making Their Own Mark."

79. See Henry Skerritt, ed., *No Boundaries: Aboriginal Australian Contemporary Abstract Painting* (Reno and New York: Nevada Museum of Art and Prestel Publishing, 2014); and Henry Skerritt, ed., *Marking the Infinite: Contemporary Women Artists from Aboriginal Australia* (Reno and New York: Nevada Museum of Art and Prestel Publishing, 2016).

80. On this, see Fred Myers, "Locating Ethnographic Practice: Romance, Reality, and Politics in the Outback," *American Ethnologist* 15 (1988): 609–24.

81. See Randy Kennedy, "A World Away from His Shimmering Desert Sands," *New York Times*, September 19, 2015; Ralph Gardner Jr., "Out of the Outback, into the Big City," *Wall Street Journal*, September 23, 2015; "*Warlimpirrnga Tjapaltjarri*," *New Yorker*, October 5, 2015, 18; and Roberta Smith, "Warlimpirrnga Tjapaltjarri's Aboriginal Dreamtime Paintings," *New York Times*, October 16, 2015. For a fuller analysis of Warlimpirrnga's exhibition, see Terry Smith, "The Bowery in Two Contemporary Differential Systems," in *Brooklyn Rail*, December 2015, http://brooklynrail.org/2015/12/art/the-bowery-in-two-contemporary-differential-systems.

82. Roberta Smith, "Review/Art; From Alien to Familiar," *New York Times*, December 16, 1988.

83. Smith, "Warlimpirrnga Tjapaltjarri's Aboriginal Dreamtime Paintings."

84. *Desert Painters of Australia: Works from the Kluge-Ruhe Aboriginal Art Collection of the University of Virginia and the Collection of Steve Martin and Anne Stringfield*, Gagosian Gallery, 976 Madison Avenue, New York, May 3–July 3, 2019.

85. A final, often-overlooked factor in the strong US connections with Papunya Tula has been the presence in the United States of Fred Myers, Silver Professor of Anthropology at New York University. After living with the Pintupi at Yayayi, Myers has played an important role as interpreter and intermediary for visiting artists, as well as consulting with museums such as Kluge-Ruhe, where, in 2008, he curated the exhibition *Virtuosity: The Evolution of Painting at Papunya Tula*. In 2009, he played a major role consulting on the exhibition *Icons of the Desert: Early Aboriginal Paintings from Papunya* at the Herbert F. Johnson Museum of Art at Cornell University.

86. This list is only a partial one. In its fifty-year history, Papunya Tula Artists has had over sixty employees. Ben Danks, Janis Stanton and Jenny Taylor also served in assistant managerial roles, and a significant contribtuion was made in the field by Tim Dilworth, Ben Currie, Matt Cotter, Grant Rundell, Bryony Nicholson, Riley Davison and Haley King, among many others.

87. For an insightful account of the role of Papunya Tula field officers, see Luke Scholes, "Field Notes," in *Unique Perspectives: Papunya Tula Artists and the Alice Springs Community*, ed. Stephen Williamson (Alice Springs, NT: Araluen Art Centre and Papunya Tula Artists, 2012), 82–83.

88. See Bobby West Tjupurrula's text in this volume, "A Really Good Celebration," p. 95.

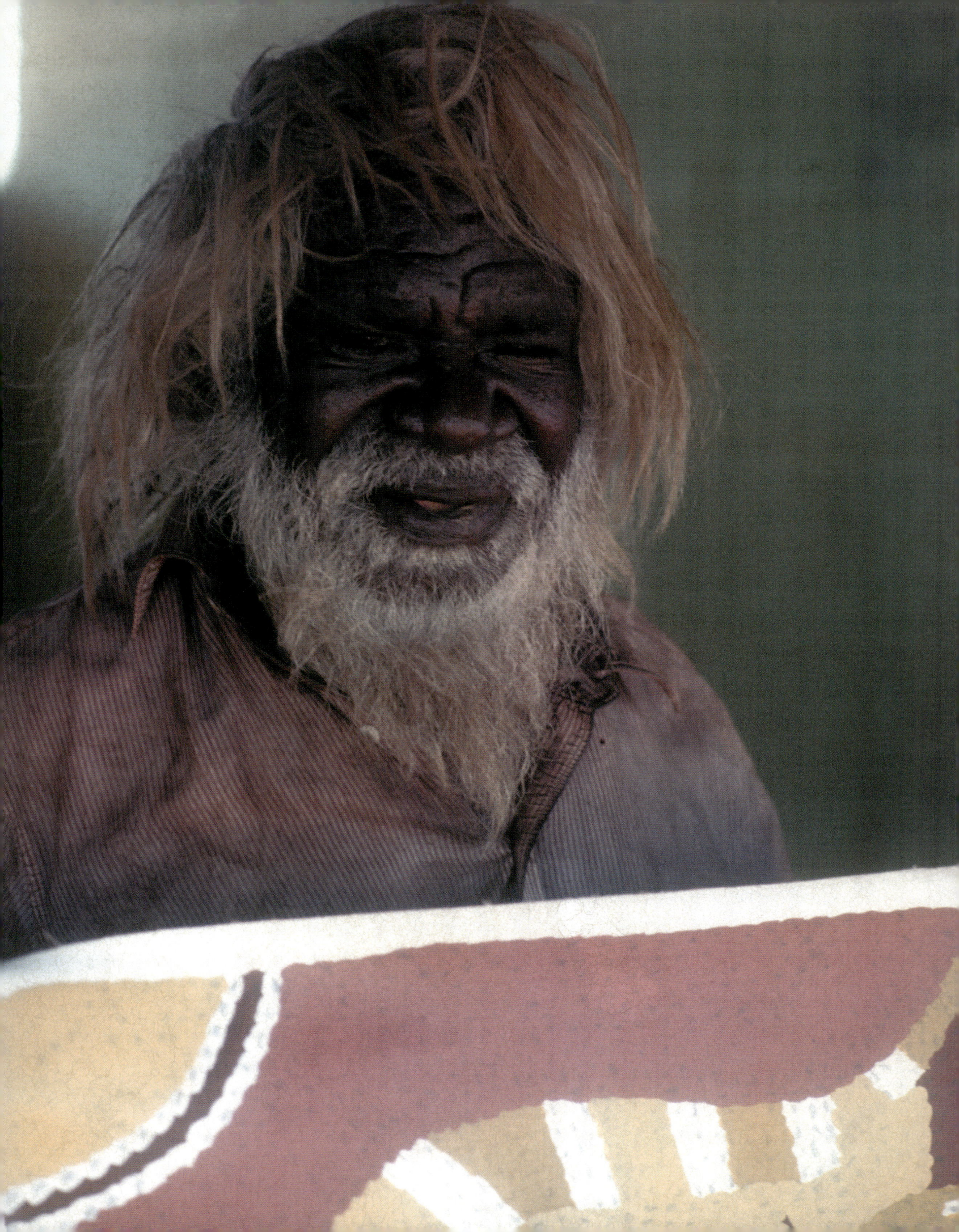

# IT BLEW UP LIKE A BALLOON

They started painting at the school, drawing on the walls. That's where all the children saw them, and we said, "Eh, that's interesting what they are doing." And they were telling a story. We used to stand and look. I used to think, "How clever are these old men."

That's when they started to do painting on box or board. There was not a place to do painting, so they used to paint there in the town hall. They were thinking, "We can make paintings for money for food." My dad, Bill Stockman Tjapaltjarri, used to say, "I can make money from painting so my kids can go to school." The white people were looking and thinking, "How clever, those old people."

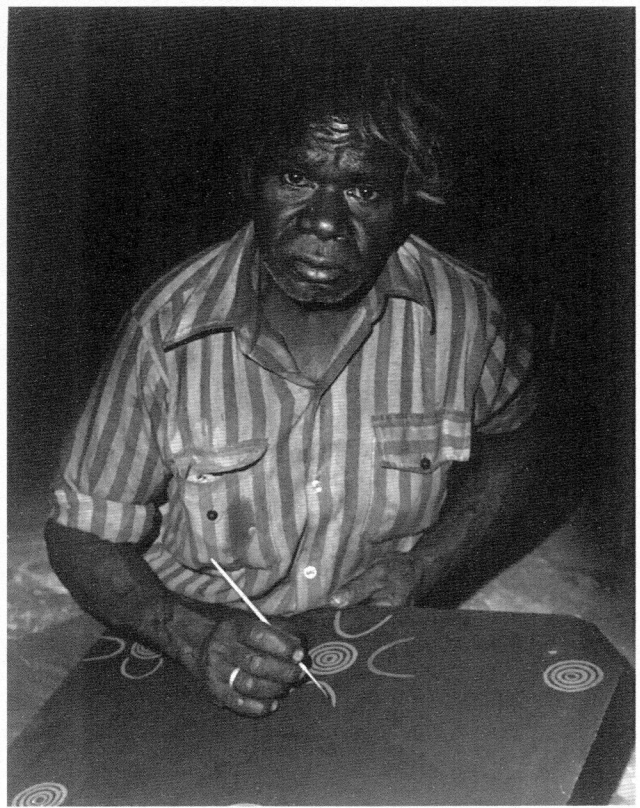

But these old men had a picture in their mind from Country and ceremony, and they were starting to think about how they were going to do that new form of painting. Pintupi had their Tjukurrpa (Dreaming) and Anmatyerr had their Tjukurrpa. My father and all the Anmatyerr—Tim Leura Tjapaltjarri, Clifford Possum Tjapaltjarri, Kaapa Tjampitjinpa and Dinny Nolan Tjampitjinpa—they had a different style. They started the style of painting that we are now doing. Our people learned from them and were happy.

Looking back is a good surprise: at how they started and how we are still doing it. Now the new generation are starting to come up. Like us, my sister and two brothers— we started by looking, watching our father. We used to sit on the side. We used to watch him and hear him telling stories about the painting. And he would say, "All this belongs to you, you'll be taking over from those older men who first painted at Papunya Tula."

My father used to say, "Hey *kungka* (young women), you've got to learn how to paint your *ngurra* (home) country, your Tjukurrpa." They (the Anmatyerr men) were encouraging their wives, "*Nyuuntulpa ngurra* painting (paint your country)." From there, it blew up like a balloon. They started small, and from small they blew up. From Australia to the United States, overseas, like a balloon.

— PUNATA STOCKMAN NUNGURRAYI

FACING

Bill Stockman Tjapaltjarri, Watiyawanu, 1994. Photo by Dennis Schulz.

Bill Stockman Tjapaltjarri at Papunya, 1972. Photo by Allan Scott.

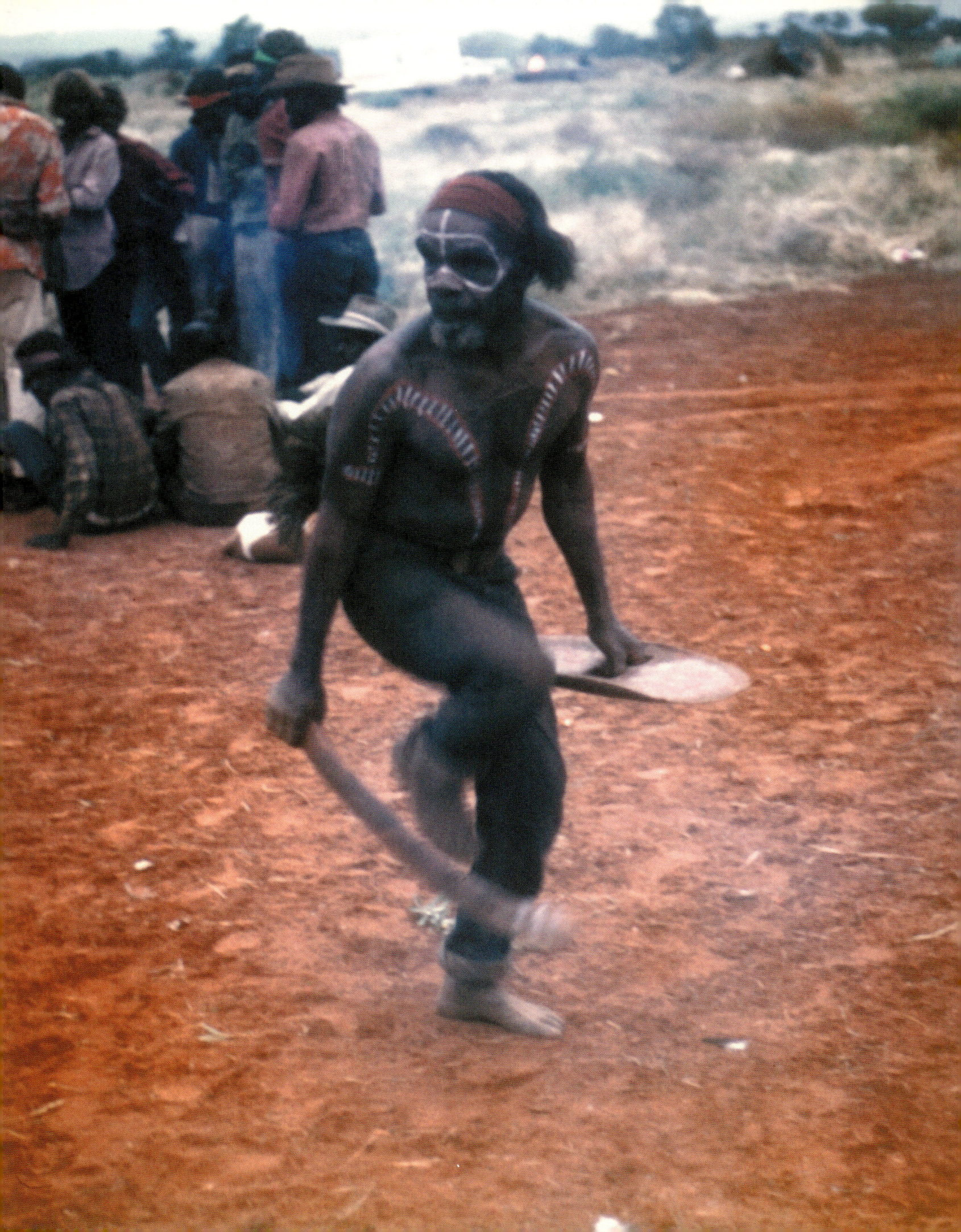

# The Goannas Are Dancing

## The Generation and the Generations of Papunya Painting

**FRED MYERS**

In 1988, the landmark exhibition *Dreamings: The Art of Aboriginal Australia* made Indigenous Australian art visible in the United States.[1] It opened in New York at the Asia Society Galleries (fig. 2.1), where it drew the interest of the wealthy collector John W. Kluge, catalyzing his collecting of work by Indigenous artists from central and northern Australia.[2] Kluge's acquisitions—which would ultimately form the core holdings of the Kluge-Ruhe Aboriginal Art Collection of the University of Virginia—included an extensive collection of acrylic paintings from Papunya Tula Artists, a cooperative that began at a remote government settlement where Indigenous people from diverse language groups had been relocated from their homelands. Beginning in the 1970s, their work transformed the appreciation of Aboriginal art for Australian and international audiences and inspired a movement in acrylic painting on two-dimensional surfaces, which spread to communities across the Central and Western Deserts. The exhibition *Irrititja Kuwarri Tjungu | Past and Present Together: Fifty Years of Papunya Tula Artists* at Kluge-Ruhe chronicles this rich history of artistic innovation from its genesis to the present.

As the founding center of this proliferating movement, the Papunya Tula Artists company has long inspired great interest among scholars, critics and general audiences about the origins and innovations of acrylic painting in Indigenous Australia. I understand these paintings as transformations of a range of preexisting ritual and secular iconographic and performative practices into two-dimensional works in (often) new media. The exhibition at the Asia Society Galleries offered a huge range of Indigenous art practices, from bark painting and sculpture to acrylic works. The similarly broad, Indigenously curated *Aratjara: Art of the First Australians* exhibition followed in Europe in 1993–94.[3] Papunya Tula Artists earned a singular exhibition celebrating its first twenty-five years with *Papunya Tula: Genesis and Genius* (2000), curated by Hetti Perkins at the Art Gallery of New South Wales in Sydney.[4] Not so long after, in the United States, *Icons of the Desert* (2009) presented the private collection of John and Barbara Wilkerson, highlighting the early work of Papunya Tula artists. *Icons* included an exquisite set of the small paintings, rendered on a variety of surfaces, regarded by many as what I remember

Shorty Lungkarta performing a public ceremony at Yayayi, 1974. Photo by Fred Myers.

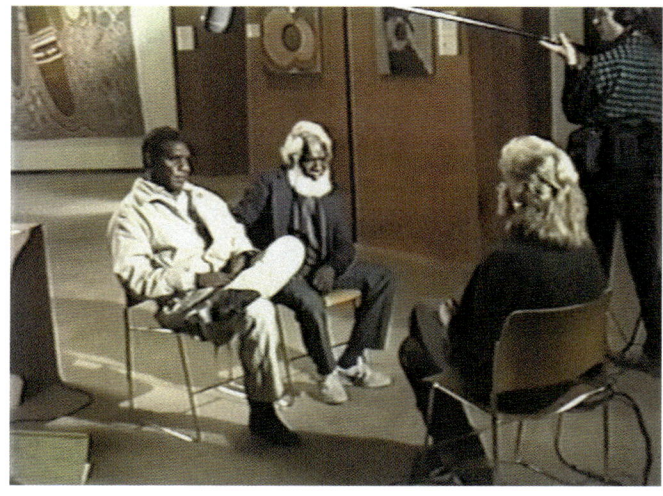

FIG. 2.1

Michael Jagamara Nelson and
Bill Stockman Tjapaltjarri being
interviewed by Joanna Simon for
the MacNeil/Lehrer NewsHour
(PBS), New York, January 1989.

Australian historian Dick Kimber having called the "jewels" of the acrylic painting movement.[5] The term is appropriate, since so much of this work is small in scale, involving the "fine detail" that Kimber has described as characteristic of the early Papunya Tula style. In this vein, one of the highlights of the Kluge-Ruhe collection is Mick Namarari Tjapaltjarri's brilliant bifurcated *Mitukatjirri* (1971–72, plate 78), an image of the great ceremony at the cave of Mitukatjirri. This site is mythologically and geographically associated with the nearby place known as Ilingawurrngawurrnga. Depicted in Turkey Tolson Tjupurrula's *Straightening Spears at Ilingawurrngawurrnga* (1993, plate 79), the latter takes its name from a word in a song cycle enunciated by the Tingarri ancestral beings as they came to that place.[6]

There was a reason that *Icons of the Desert* focused on early Papunya paintings. In 1971–72, a new practice of painting and forms emerged at Papunya. Using the new medium of acrylic paint rather than traditional pigments—applied to rectangular, flat surfaces rather than bodies or objects—the painters drew upon the iconography, ritual practices and decorative forms of their ceremonial life, and the mythological traditions invested in the sacred places they knew as their *ngurra* (Country). The new practice of painting attempted to transform this

wide array of knowledge, imagination and embodied experience—musical, performative, visually exuberant, multidimensional and restricted to initiates—into a two-dimensional painted surface.[7] This remarkable period was brilliantly explored in the recent exhibition *Tjungunutja: From Having Come Together* at the Museum and Art Gallery of the Northern Territory in 2017.[8] The early paintings show the excitement and intensity of that new experience for the Papunya Tula painters as well as their dramatic engagement with the problem of presenting their knowledge in novel forms and materials. This first engagement heralded the emergence of virtuoso creativity and commitment that continues to inspire viewers.

The fact that these "jewels" are somewhat mysterious to most audiences, and are often exhibited with only shreds of description suggesting what their meaning might be to the painters, is part of their fascination. What were the artists doing when they began this work? What did they think they were doing? We simply do not know as much as we would like to know. Geoffrey Bardon, the now-famous schoolteacher whose collaboration with the painters was essential to the emergence of Papunya Tula, was there with them, providing materials and encouragement.[9] So, at times, was Pat Hogan, the gallery owner at the Stuart Art Centre in Mparntwe (Alice Springs), who documented some of the paintings in Bardon's absence. But the early documentation is more typically tantalizing than it is definitive. The limited language skills and cultural knowledge of Bardon and Hogan, neither of whom spoke Pintupi, Warlpiri or Anmatyerr, make their records a puzzle. Is Mick Namarari's *Mitukatjirri* indeed concerned with the great Tingarri ceremony at the cave of Mitukatjirri, as we believe it is? Sometimes the mysteries are solvable, sometimes not. The recent scholarly contributions of Luke Scholes and John Kean, following the earlier efforts of Vivien Johnson,[10] have dramatically enhanced our understanding of many of these early works and our appreciation of their artistry.

In general, Australians have had many opportunities to see substantial numbers of these early Papunya works: they are collected and exhibited in all of the major public galleries and explored in surveys and retrospective exhibitions. Like any exhibition, *Irrititja Kuwarri Tjungu* cannot represent the entirety of possibilities and relationships posed in the paintings of the period. Nonetheless, this collection of works, exhibited in two parts over two years, is more comprehensive, both representatively and perhaps aesthetically, than any other previously circulated in the United States. It allows viewers to appreciate the originality, range and vitality of the Papunya Tula Artists' work over the company's fifty-year history. Every viewer and participant will, no doubt, have their own distinctive interests sparked by these paintings, although, in the United States, I doubt they will speak to the spirit of reconciliation or recognition of what Indigenous Australians call Country as they have done, at times, in Australia. And they may not speak to the tensions inherent in the insistence on Indigenous possession of their Country. They should—such tensions are no less acute in the Americas. In this era where concerns about decolonization are being strongly expressed throughout the art world and in the academy, the paintings speak powerfully, insistently and loudly, from the past to the present.

As a witness to some of the early period, for me, these works have the power of enunciation. They project the conviction I heard from the early Papunya Tula painters who formed the cooperative at the end of an assimilation-oriented period in Australia's Indigenous policy. The paintings were and are an assertion that their culture was valuable; an anchor of the profound cultural legacy they embodied, these works are worthy of deep respect and recognition. Moreover, these paintings asserted Indigenous presence in and custodianship of the country,

anticipating the critiques that postcolonial theory would begin to raise in the 1980s.[11]

When I lived with Pintupi people at various times in the 1970s and 1980s—as an anthropologist at the outstation Yayayi (35 miles west of Papunya), and later in other communities—they explained to me that their paintings were Tjukurrtjanu (from the Dreaming) and not something made up, or mere pretty pictures. They were powerful, "like gold," "dangerous" or "dear" and were connected with the painters' *ngurra*, the Country they held as part of their ancestral estates, of Tjukurrpa, which we commonly translate as "the Dreaming."

The early and middle periods of Papunya Tula painting convey an extraordinary intensity of feeling, attachment and vital creativity. The works represent the power of Tjukurrpa. They do so as stories of the activities of beings whom we may choose to call, loosely, ancestors (as progenitors) and as a visible presence of the signs of those ancestors, who gave the world its shapes and meanings. Like other such representations familiar to the men who were initially the painters here,[12] the paintings simultaneously reveal and conceal. The painters were sharing knowledge of their country with viewers but also withholding facts, information and features that are restricted to initiated Pintupi men.[13] This is one of the aesthetic dimensions of ritual performance, but in painting—and even sometimes in ritual—too much may be revealed, with dangerous or unfortunate consequences. Some of the early paintings—joyous in their depiction of the power of Tjukurrpa and its ceremonial/ritual objects—were later thought to be showing too much, to have transgressed the protocols of revelation. But their energy and excitement continue to be expressed in contemporary work from Papunya Tula Artists. When the acclaimed Pintupi painter Warlimpirrnga Tjapaltjarri visited New York for a gallery exhibition in 2015, his enthusiasm, his eagerness to share the ancestral story that motivated his visualization of Tjukurrpa power, matched the visual energy of his large, optically overwhelming paintings.

The very survival of and continued interest in Papunya Tula Artists' paintings demonstrates the ability of these Indigenous people to bring their way of seeing and their own protocols of imagery into contemporary spaces. The painters see it as the expected recognition of the power and the truth of Tjukurrpa, but the movement of this work into the contact zone of contemporary art has not been straightforward. Aboriginal people in other nearby desert communities, related through shared traditions, expressed concern about the revelation of certain iconography they had in common with the painters from Papunya. By 1973, when I arrived, the painters of Papunya Tula Artists had already restricted themselves to those portions of the mythological cycle that were acceptable for uninitiated people to see. What, then, of the paintings from the earlier period that had already entered into the world of commoditization, bought, sold and exhibited as "art"?

One could say that these images by artists of Papunya Tula have continued to bear the traces, indexically and iconically, of their standing in the local Indigenous regime of value. The signs themselves—the circles and lines, the very marks used—are valued, dear, said to "come from the Dreaming," are part of it, or indices, handed down intergenerationally as proof of Tjukurrpa. At the same time, they represent, or are icons of, Tjukurrpa events and places through forms that communicate through similarity of shape—circles for hills, fire and water, sinuous lines for the paths of snakes and so on. Strict rules of authorship, kinship and gender articulate rights to represent, reproduce or communicate what are intergenerational forms of knowledge and heritage. The paintings continue to embody forms of collective identity and the shared traditions of extended groups of people. And, certainly, the restrictions on new conditions of circulation, since those early works raised objections, have shaped the formal practice of painting farther toward abstraction and ambiguity, as painters masked or omitted the more esoteric and secret elements of the ancestral traditions.

Still, the older paintings have remained in the marketplace, selling for high prices at auction and becoming much-prized objects for the major public galleries in Adelaide, Melbourne, Sydney and Canberra. In spite of their capacity to objectify Indigenous points of view as cultural heritage, they have, as objects for sale, escaped local control by belonging to others. However, this is not a settled business; their power is not containable in commodity form, with the traces of inalienable identity and heritage they bear often overriding the forms of ownership transacted in the market.

Many of the early paintings have been published in catalogs and exhibited, even reproduced as postcards and on calendars. Yet, by 2006, the contemporary generation of artists had begun expressing opinions ranging from concern about to objections to the exhibition of such images to uninitiated people. These very paintings had been made and sold as commodities, and their sale, as

reported by Bardon, was jubilantly seen as a measure of success. How, then, is a curator or collector to approach such proposed restrictions on the right to see and to exhibit works already purchased at such high prices?

Unusually for a nongovernmental institution, the organizers of *Irrititja Kuwarri Tjungu* took the step of developing a protocol of consultation that respects Indigenous frameworks of custodianship and cultural property. The staff of Kluge-Ruhe made efforts to have the images shown to the descendants and relatives of the original painters in order to ensure that the museum had permission to display them. This seems appropriate for a heritage that has a foot in the two distinctive worlds of contemporary art and Indigenous culture. Those paintings deemed to be restricted, inappropriate to show to uninitiated viewers, were thus excluded from the exhibition.

The continued availability of the early paintings is, nonetheless, important to understanding the work that came later, even in showing—through their continued accessibility to at least some acceptable or initiated viewers—what came to be regarded as inappropriate. Taken together, these paintings, enhanced by the growing scholarship about them, make evident the different kinds of sensibilities that the painters possessed. In the course of preparing this catalog, I have been encouraged by the possibilities of using the archive(s) of works to interrogate the intentions and practices of the artists. Having spent a lifetime engaged with the project of understanding, I want to insist on the importance of viewers—Indigenous and non-Indigenous—considering these works as the complex product of knowledge of Country, ceremony, story and artistic skill and preferences.

One constant is that the power of Tjukurrpa is manifestly everywhere in these works. A brilliant painting in this exhibition attributed to Uta Uta Tjangala, *Old Man Dreaming at Yumari* (1973, plate 47), may bear an iconic resemblance (in shape) to the X-shaped rockhole at Yumari, as some others of his paintings of Yumari do. However, I believe it also transposes the figures I once saw engraved on an overpainted oval-shaped wooden board left behind in a truck driven by Andrew Crocker, manager of Papunya Tula Artists in 1981. For us, it has to be enough that the possibly sacred markings traced covertly are pure indices of their power, held in the mind of the painter, and the few notes to accompany it simply tease us as viewers who lack deep cultural knowledge and have only the experience of the revelation. Another painting of Uta Uta's, *Ngurrapalangunya* (c. 1971–2, plate 46), which many of us might have expected to be restricted from exhibition because of the depiction of what appeared to be sacred objects, was approved for display by the artist's oldest son, Morris Jackson Tjampitjinpa.

On the other hand, the paintings of the Anmatyerr artist Kaapa Tjampitjinpa may be a different matter. Kaapa always claimed he was not showing anything that could not be seen by others. But his untitled painting of 1971 in the Kluge-Ruhe collection is now regarded as inappropriate to show, while his later painting *Dreaming at Mikantji* (1975, plate 17) avoids traces of the ritual forms he often used in earlier paintings. For Kaapa, the power of Tjukurrpa seems invested in the formal, symmetrical organization of the picture space, following the symmetrical organization of ceremonial practice. The 1971 painting is, very nearly, a formal presentation of the ceremony itself, but I think the painting is not meant as "ethnography," simply illustrative of ceremony for viewers. Instead, the image is understood as bearing the imprint of the ancestor, an extension expressing the ancestor's power to impose form on the world.[14] While Kaapa was confident of his authority to expose this to audiences, his descendants are less certain about whether it should be viewed in Australia.[15] But we have one more way in which Kaapa and other painters, in their own ways, seek to communicate esoteric ancestral knowledge to us.

There are, in this exhibition, examples of many ways in which the painters have sought to offer their knowledge, or to communicate the mystery of it, to us. A number of the paintings by different artists contain evidence, not easily discerned by some viewers, of shared ritual responsibilities and knowledge. Charlie Wartuma (also known as Charlie Tjaruru) Tjungurrayi's painting of *Travels of an Old Man to Yumari* (1980, plate 48) represents his shared relationship to the same story painted by his "brother-in-law"[16] and close kin Uta Uta. The site is also painted by their shared female relative Tjunkiya Napaltjarri in *Women's Ceremonies at Yumari* (1996, plate 50). Other paintings of the Yina (Old Man) cycle—held jointly by a number of Pintupi painters—such as Wartuma's *Old Man's Dreaming at Tjurrpungkuntjanya* (1974, plate 45), have more explicitly represented the erect penis identified with the "Old Man," a lascivious trickster, on his movements westward across Pintupi country, leaving behind the marks of his activities at various named places. But it is important to recognize that these artists are painting parts of the same story, the same "songline," the same Tjukurrpa. This is their right and expression of their relationships to one another.

In these stories, there is also entertainment, along with explorations of moral frailty. The phallic properties of the Old Man Tjukurrpa, for example, are prominent in narrative and performance, invariably humorous indicators of excessive sexuality. These features are evident in ceremonies and in visual representations. This Yina is said to have traveled westward, and sometimes his testicles left his body and traveled separately; other times, his penis left its mark on the landscape. Famously, the Old Man committed the serious transgression of having sex with his *yumari* (mother-in-law), which resulted in his subsequently suffering an attack of ants on his phallus and fleeing further west. At another level, of societal integration, the repeated painting of parts of the story by different artists is evidence that the men and women are all "from one Country," reflecting their shared custodianship. As an historiographic note, in some of the very earliest documentations of these paintings, the artists identified them as "medicine stories." The term medicine refers to the power of sorcery carried by this ancestral figure as he crossed the country, east to west. The paintings are surely not of exactly the same portions as the story, but much information has obviously been lost in translation and documentation, so we cannot really know how the individual artists arrived at their own iconographies.

Johnny Warangkula Tjupurrula's paintings, in their extraordinary style of "over-dotting" (applying dots over the depicted shaped throughout the painting) and shading of colors, are known especially for the intense representation of particular places in his Country. He often painted Kalipinypa, with its caves and watercourses running through the site. The varied texturing, with circles representing caves connected by the different lines of water paths, and various representations of bush tucker (foods) from the area, communicates a profound sense of place. Of course, rain and lightning are forms of ancestral power, emanating from Warangkula's Country and informing his own identity. In his paintings, Warangkula depicts the forms of the Country, revealing and concealing associated sacred objects. The focus of this work, as Kimber remarked, may well be the "prolific growth of locally occurring plants after good rains," especially the *kampurarrpa* (wild raisin).[17] Warangkula's depictions of Kalipinypa are images of nurturance: the bounty that the country provides for its people (see plates 9, 10).

Papunya Tula paintings from later periods allow us to see the stylistic innovations, the creativity, and generational and gendered reinterpretations of painting practice and storytelling within the company. These changes also reflect the separation of artists into geographically separated communities over time, as distinctive styles and approaches to work came to characterize the different communities. Many of the Pintupi painters moved westward away from Papunya, differentiating their work from that made in Papunya by many of the Warlpiri, Anmatyerr and Luritja painters (the eastern mob).[18]

The more recent paintings look different—in both their generational and geographical divisions—but one should not think the defining ontology has shifted.[19] For example, in generational terms, Ronnie Tjampitjinpa's *Tingarritjarra* (1989, plate 99) and Simon Tjakamarra's *Tingarri Camp at Pillintjinya* (1988, plate 72) continue to exhibit relationships to ancestral initiation events being performed in ceremonial camps for young men—events I often witnessed in the Yayayi community in the early 1970s. Actors decorated for ceremonies could be seen with white *wamulu* (bush cotton) body decoration in concentric circles on their stomachs and backs, connected over their shoulders and sides, preparing to reenact in living present the performances as they are understood to have been enacted in Tjukurrpa. In the body decoration itself, the circles commonly represent camps or places (*ngurra*) where the ancestral initiates sat down. But the overall decoration of these paintings with dotting has a further effect in indicating the power of Tjukurrpa through the visual patterning and optical effect of foreground and background.[20]

Whereas many early paintings had features the painters identified directly (iconographically, as it were) with features of the landscape or particular ceremonial actions, the informational specificity of the place is muted in these later paintings, perhaps in accord with the sense of restriction on explicit sacred images. Instead, they emphasize the optical effect of foreground/background or the effect of the multiplicity of circles indicating the multitude of novices and men applying decorations to one another's backs. The circles are at once the circular designs on the bodies and also the men themselves. It is the aggregation, the multitudes gathered by ancestral figures, that constitutes one aesthetic articulation of Tjukurrpa power. More immediately, perhaps, the foreground/background organization performs the visual effect of Tjukurrpa, of the flash of ancestral power or the flash of body decorations as performers enacting the ancestral events move into the strobe-like light of the night-time fires (fig. 2.2).[21]

Turkey Tolson Tjupurrula's brilliant (literally) and justly famous *Straightening Spears at Ilingawurrngawurrnga* illustrates this artistic move. This is demonstrated immediately in juxtaposing Tolson's painting with a work from two decades earlier, Shorty Lungkarta Tjungurrayi's *Tingarri Ceremony at Ilingawurrngawurrnga* (1974, fig. 2.3), marking the stylistic transition in representations of the same story. I saw the latter being painted in June 1974 (fig. 2.4) and know how it related to the ancestral events

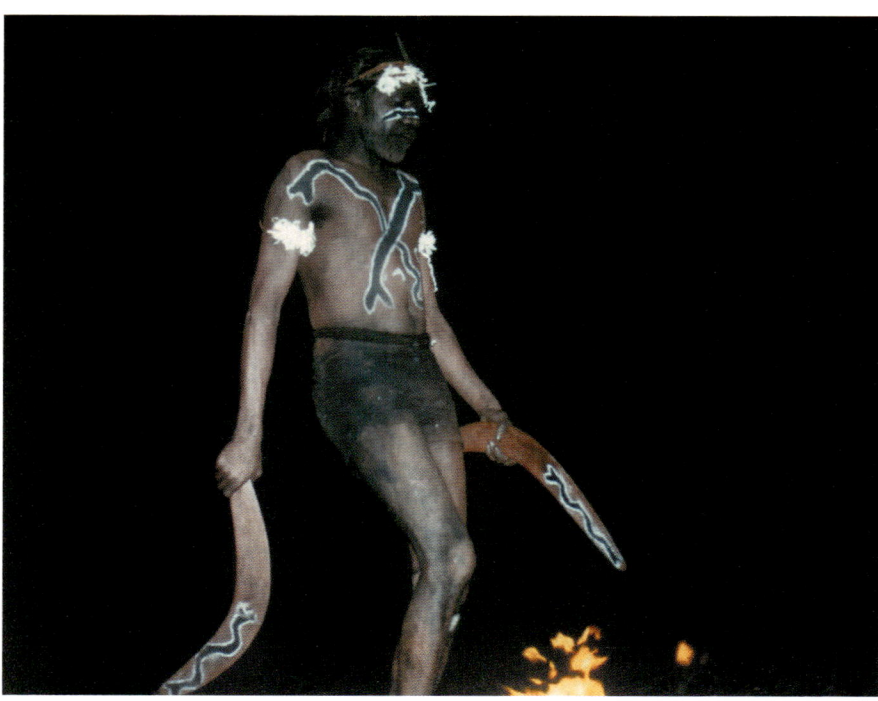

FIG. 2.2

Illuminated by firelight, Jeffrey James Tjangala dances in a Rain Dreaming Ceremony at Yayayi, 1974. Photo by Fred Myers.

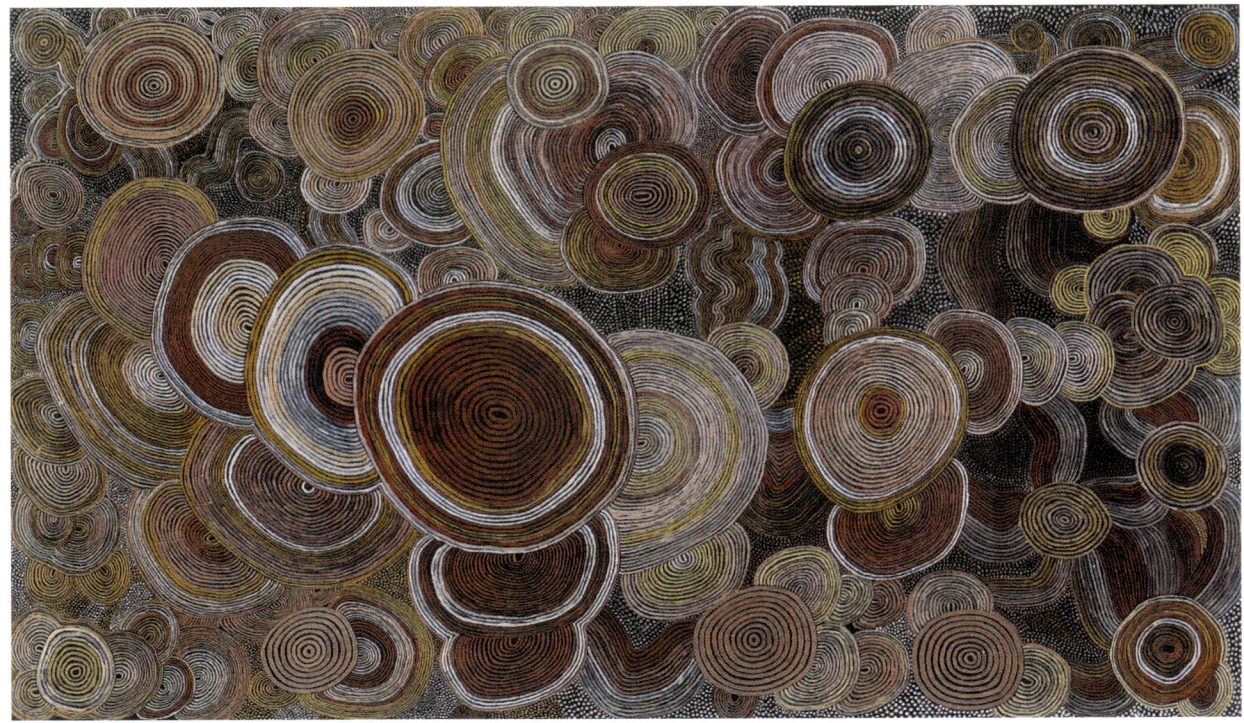

FIG. 2.3

Shorty Lungkarta Tjungurrayi, *Tingarri Ceremony at Ilingawurrngawurrnga*, 1974, synthetic polymer paint on canvas, 66⅜ × 40⅛ in. (169 × 102 cm). Collection of John and Barbara Wilkerson.

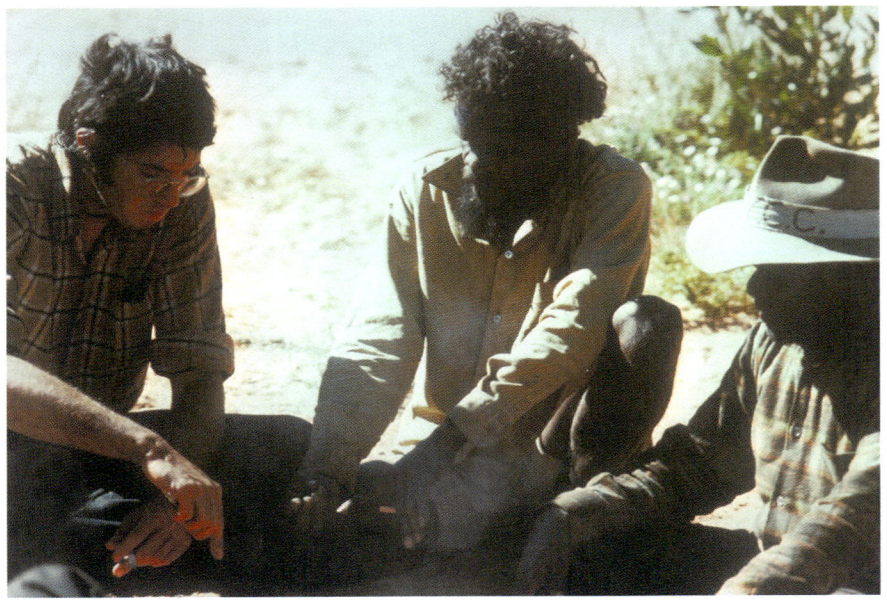

FIG. 2.4

Fred Myers with Yanatjarri No. III Tjakamarra and Shorty Bruno Tjangala at Yayayi, 1974. Photo by Es Giddy.

being performed in the initiates' camp in the Yayayi community. While Lungkarta's *Ilingawurrngawurrnga* derives a particular force from the numerous repeated semicircles on semicircles representing novices and men, in Tolson's painting, the story and Tingarri men are represented through the repetition of spears, all lined up in parallel across the surface. However, Tolson's emphasis on the dotting itself produces a visual sense of intensity to mark the immensity of the activity of the Tingarri ancestors. Yanatjarri No. III Tjakamarra's paintings of this later period, such as *Women's Dreaming near Kiwirrkurra* (1989, plate 93), use a more muted palette of dotting in which depictions of ritual object/features are embedded in and less differentiated from the background, positioning them more as emerging from the ground.

In such ways, the men's paintings show a general stylistic evolution from the 1970s to 1990s, moving to relatively conventionalized forms, depicting relatively abstractly the features of Tjukurrpa events that they chose to emphasize, with more attention to overall visual effect and less specific information about particular ancestral stories. This was consonant with the realization of the need to restrict much ritual and sacred information from public circulation. Nonetheless, works in the new medium of acrylic painting derive their forms from the engraved decoration of traditional ceremonial objects, such as pearl shells, spear throwers or shields, as exemplified in the photograph of Timmy Payungu incising a design in his shield and in a completed shield in the Kluge-Ruhe collection (figs. 2.5, 2.6).[22] Ronnie Tjampitjinpa, for example, abstracted a rectilinear form that might be used in an object representing the ancestral Tingarri story in *Ralyanya* (1999, plate 100). The rectangle is an alternative to the circle-line-dot motif within Pintupi ceremonial design, and Ronnie extended it even further in later works organized around concentric rectangles.[23] This can be seen in paintings such as *Tjilkamata Ancestor Traveling East from Tarkulnga* (1988, plate 98), but also in the small work *Walungurru* (2020, plate 129) by his son Aubrey Tjangala.

From the works of a second generation of painters, including Ronnie Tjampitjinpa and Simon Tjakamarra, but especially in Ronnie's virtuosic range of experimentation across various paintings, one can see a line of change leading to the celebrated, highly abstract works of Charlie Ward Tjakamarra, George Ward Tjungurrayi, George Tjungurrayi and, ultimately, Warlimpirrnga, along with his close female relative Yukultji Napangati and their fellow Kiwirrkurra resident Doreen Reid Nakamarra, too early deceased. It is not hard to see how Warlimpirrnga's painting *Maruwa* (2013, plate 105) draws on the same form that Ronnie developed: the concentric rectangle. Because they use abstract forms, these images are not restricted from being viewed by outsiders.

*Maruwa* depicts a claypan, a large but temporary water source one finds after rains, where Warlimpirrnga's family often camped. He was famously part of the group known as the "Pintupi Nine," the last Western Desert small family group to leave life in the desert, in 1984, to join their families in more permanent settlement communities.[24] Maruwa and other claypans and water sources in the area near Wilkinkarra (Lake Mackay) have remained central to Warlimpirrnga's identity and sense of himself. These are the places whose stories he paints and for which he has the rights to do so. What we see in his paintings is possibly the light reflected off the surface of this water, moved by the wind, but certainly its ancestral form in the rectilinear designs, recalling the Tingarri ancestral beings whose activities made this. We can see the key design form also in other works in the exhibition, such as Nyilyari Tjapangati's *Wilkinkarra* (2017, plate 152). The abstracted rectilinear marks used in Warlimpirrnga's acrylic paintings reference the engraved rectangular markings on sacred objects that index (link to), even as they conceal, the power of ancestral creation. It works

through the optical effect of the figure-ground construction but also in the rectilinear form itself. A Pintupi man would recognize this, but Warlimpirrnga would not say so publicly.

If the first two periods of creativity are generational, one might regard the third period of "reinvention" to be the work of women painters in the 1990s and on, discussed in detail in the essays by Marina Strocchi and Cara Pinchbeck in this volume. The women whose paintings appear in this exhibition were sometimes the wives of the first generation of men who painted, sometimes their offspring. Some of these paintings, such as Pansy Napangardi's *Kungka Kutjarra (Two Women) at Winpirri* (1988, plate 54), represent a movement that opened to a few women at a time when Papunya Tula came to be divided between the original community of Papunya and the breakaway Pintupi

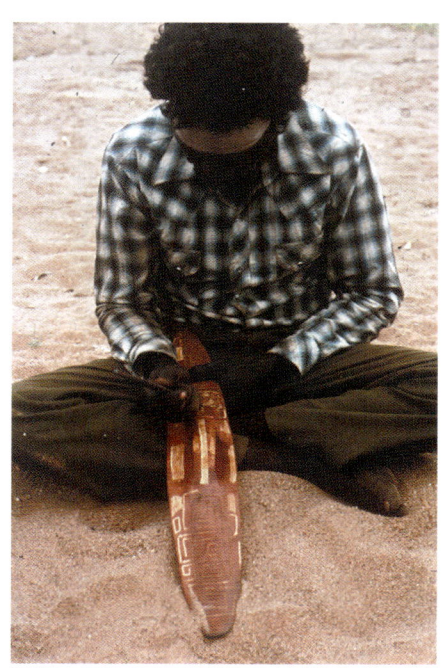

ABOVE | FIG. 2.5

Timmy Payungu Tjapangati at Yayayi, c. 1975. Photo by Fred Myers.

RIGHT | FIG. 2.6

Unidentified artist, incised parrying shield, before 1968, natural pigments on wood, 28.5 × 10 in. (72 × 25 cm). Kluge-Ruhe Aboriginal Art Collection, The Edward L. Ruhe Collection. Gift of John W. Kluge, 1997, 1993.0004.717.

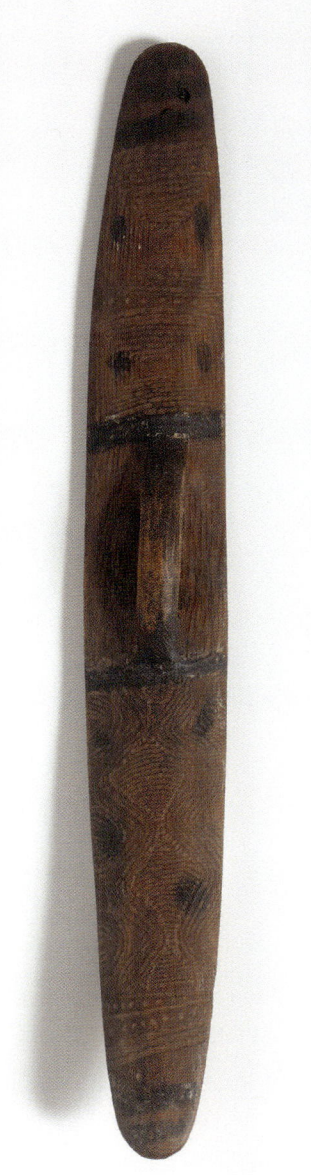

community at Walungurru (Kintore) in 1981. At Papunya, the Warlpiri artist Michael Jagamara Nelson continued to paint with great success, and within the more iconographically explicit tradition. However, the painters in the two communities were no longer so closely in contact. Inspired by the uptake of painting among their female relatives at Ikuntji (Haasts Bluff), the Pintupi women at Walungurru were guided by workshops with Strocchi, an artist.

These middle-aged and older women, active and knowledgeable in women's ceremonial life, brought a fresh and different perspective to the painting movement, starting anew to engage with canvas and acrylics as the men had done two decades earlier. This exhibition includes five of the earliest paintings by some of these women, as well as some stunning accomplishments in the work of Wintjiya Napaltjarri, Naata Nungurrayi and Makinti Napanangka. For example, Wintjiya's 2001 painting of *wartunuma* (flying termites; plate 53) in black and white suggests both an aspect of their flight, as they leave through an exit in a cave, and the hard earth "pavement" these insects leave on the ground. These artist's paintings are informed by their particular set of ancestral stories and ceremonies related to places that were the purview of women, but they are distinctive for their expressiveness with paint—more like the application of traditional pigments on women's bodies and breasts for ceremony. One subject for further inquiry is whether the history and traditional sources of Pintupi women's paintings differ from the histories of women artists at Utopia (such as Emily Kame Kngwarreye), Yuendumu or Lajamanu. Nonetheless, in each community, such women have painted the stories of the Tjukurrpa places they have inherited from their parents—as in Naata Nungurrayi's *Karilywarra* (2010, plate 88) or Tjunkiya Napaltjarri's *Yumari* (2009, plate 127)—emphasizing both the bounty of the country as exploited by female ancestors and the features of the landscape left behind.

Second-generation artists and women at both Papunya and Walungurru continue to work their effects on those who view their paintings, as the first painters of Papunya Tula sought to do. The innovations in these works, as distinctive expressions of creativity, are compelling reductions of the complex phenomenon of ancestral presence into two dimensions. Together, these paintings bring recognition to those who made them and, through them, reflect the profound powers of their cultural worlds.

At the same time, we must recognize the mystery of the Papunya Tula paintings, and I want to communicate the texture of what it takes—in composing an exhibition like *Irrititja Kuwarri Tjungu*—to grapple with these works, armed with only partial information that is sometimes spotty and uneven. Here lies the puzzle for those of us trying to grasp the knowledge behind the images, to understand what these Indigenous men and women were doing, and especially at the moments when they first engaged with the medium, in putting marks on two-dimensional surfaces for outsiders. Beyond the deciphering of meaning, authorship, too, can be questioned. The archival record and qualities of an image itself may raise issues about its history and of who recorded it, with the credibility or adequacy of the documentation and documenter becoming part of the histories of the work, drawing attention to the relationships—the networks and institutions—in which objects are embedded and circulated.

But the incompleteness of the archive is part of its appeal, inviting us to seek knowledge wherever we can find it: in the associations, perhaps, that the *panpanparlala* (crested bellbird) might have for Pintupi people; or the seasonality of goanna mating and fertility (see fig. 1.8), which might be communicated in painting what Shorty Lungkarta referred to as "goanna dance time," when the lizards would rise out of their burrows to feed on the *wartunuma*. Detective work is a necessity in coming to terms with any single painting, as well. To understand its specificity, one must see its alternatives, its possibilities in a series and the choices the painter may have made. For example, the differences between the works of Uta Uta, on the one hand, and those of his junior Yanatjarri, on the other, might be difficult to discern. And yet, one might observe that the younger man was more focused on the control of secret knowledge, its hidden nature and selective revelation, and on his people's possession of it. In the works of the older painter, the sense of performance, the haptic quality of movement in the play and politics of ceremony, can be more marked.

If the artists could have told us what they were thinking, what they were communicating, directly, perhaps they would have done so. There might not have been anyone who could understand them, in any case. And we do not truly know how much their works can be understood as the consequence of individual intention or practice. But if we can understand more of what is in a given painting, what its relationship to the artist was, and if we can consider it within a range of their works (an oeuvre, as it were), we surely will understand it better.[25]

## NOTES

I am grateful to Jennifer Biddle, Faye Ginsburg, John Kean, and Henry Skerritt for their incisive and generous comments and insights on earlier drafts.

1. Peter Sutton, ed., *Dreamings: The Art of Aboriginal Australia* (New York: G. Braziller, 1988).
2. Following its presentation at the Asia Society (October 6–December 31, 1988), *Dreamings* traveled to the David and Alfred Smart Gallery, University of Chicago (January 26–March 19, 1989); Los Angeles County Museum of Natural History (May 13–August 5, 1989); Museum of Victoria, Melbourne (September–December 1989); and the South Australian Museum, Adelaide (February–April 1990).
3. Gary Lee and Bernhard Lüthi, *Aratjara: Art of the First Australians: Traditional and Contemporary Works by Aboriginal and Torres Strait Islander Artists* (Cologne: DuMont, 1993). The exhibition venues included the Kunstsammlung Nordrhein-Westfalen, Düsseldorf (April 24–July 4, 1993); the Hayward Gallery, London (July 23–October 10, 1993); Louisiana Museum of Modern Art, Humblebaek, Denmark (February 11–May 23, 1994); and the National Gallery of Victoria, Melbourne (June 23–August 15, 1994).
4. Hetti Perkins and Hannah Fink, eds. *Papunya Tula: Genesis and Genius* (Sydney: Art Gallery of New South Wales, 2000).
5. I cannot recall where I heard this from Kimber, but Roger Benjamin used the same phrasing in the exhibition's catalog when he wrote that "it is not every day that a new kind of beauty is born to the world," and that the most potent of the early paintings possess a kind of ritual authority, an aura, that adds to "the visual power that these small jewel-like works project." Roger Benjamin, "The Fetish for Papunya Boards," in *Icons of the Desert: Early Aboriginal Paintings from Papunya*, ed. Roger Benjamin and Andrew C. Weislogel (Ithaca, NY: Cornell University Press and the Herbert F. Johnson Museum of Art, 2009), 23, 25.
6. For a discussion of Pintupi concepts of Tjukurrpa (the Dreaming) and its relation to place, ancestral action, and song, as well as the category of ceremonies and stories known as Tingarri, see Fred Myers, *Pintupi Country, Pintupi Self: Sentiment, Place, and Politics among Western Desert Aborigines* (Berkeley: University of California Press, 1986). The use of "the Dreaming" as the English translation of a fundamental Aboriginal concept was deployed and popularized by the anthropologist W. E. H. Stanner (1953) in a famous essay, "The Dreaming (1953)," republished in Stanner, *White Man Got No Dreaming: Essays, 1938–1973* (Canberra, ACT: Australian National University Press, 1979), 23–40. But see below for examples of the Pintupi framework.
7. The painters, in the early period, did not anticipate that their works might come back to the community where uninitiated people might see them. They also thought that outsiders would not know what they were seeing, so believed they would not be revealing anything significant through their paintings.
8. Luke Scholes, ed., *Tjungunutja: From Having Come Together* (Darwin, NT: Museum and Art Gallery of the Northern Territory, 2017).
9. It was Bardon who initiated the formation of the "company," named Papunya Tula at the painters' choice, by creating a limited liability corporation of which the artists were the shareholders.
10. Luke Scholes, "Unmasking the Myth: The Emergence of Papunya Painting," in Scholes, *Tjungunutja*, 126–31; John Kean, "Dot, Circle and Frame: How Kaapa Tjampitjinpa, Tim Leura, Clifford Possum and Johnny Warangkula Created Papunya Tula Art" (PhD diss., University of Melbourne, 2020), http://minerva-access.unimelb.edu.au/handle/11343/242476; Vivien Johnson, *Once Upon a Time in Papunya* (Sydney: University of New South Wales Press, 2010).
11. For brevity, I am only alluding here to the role painting has had in the context of land rights and in catalyzing Aboriginal-owned and determined on-Country art collectives, of which Papunya Tula was a first and a model.
12. Because of a combination of androcentric views of Indigenous religion, male art advisers, and economic limitations, it was men principally who painted for Papunya Tula in the early years (see below and essays in this volume by Marina Strocchi, "Family Connections: Walungurru Women in Action," and Cara Pinchbeck, "Following Kungka Kutjarra").
13. I have discussed the issue of secrecy and restriction in Aboriginal painting in earlier essays as a problem, presented in the desert communities, of showing some ritual imagery or stories to uninitiated persons. See, for example, Fred Myers, "Showing Too Much or Too Little: Predicaments of Painting Indigenous Presence in Central Australia," in *Performing Indigeneity: Global Histories and Contemporary Experiences*, ed. Laura R. Graham and H. Glenn Penny (Lincoln: University of Nebraska Press, 2014), 351–89. The most important discussion of the historical situation is R. G. Kimber, "Politics of the Secret in Contemporary Western Desert Art," in *Politics of the Secret*, ed. Christopher Anderson, Oceania Monographs 45 (Sydney: Sydney University Press, 1995), 123–42.
14. Jennifer Biddle has eloquently and repeatedly made this point; see, for example, Biddle, *Breasts, Bodies, Canvas: Central Desert Art as Experience* (Sydney: University of New South Wales Press, 2007).

15. The artists have often been less concerned about exhibitions outside of Australia, anticipating that such displays will not be viewed by uninitiated members of their own communities and judging that outsiders will not really know what they are seeing. Nonetheless, they prefer steps be taken to maintain the protocol of restriction.

16. Without getting too complicated here, I just note that the English term "brother-in-law" is a translation of the Pintupi word *marutju*, which refers to a relationship between men who may marry one another's sisters. It is a relationship of respect and close cooperation. Uta Uta and Tjungurrayi were, in this respect, lifelong close affinal relatives.

17. The quotation is from notes provided by Dick Kimber in 1997, published in Perkins and Fink, *Papunya Tula: Genesis and Genius*, 281. See also Kimber's notes in *Sotheby's Aboriginal Art* catalog, June 2000, 58.

18. As a document of the first moment of separation, the movement of many Pintupi to the outstation community of Yayayi in 1973, the film *Remembering Yayayi* (dir. Pip Deveson, Ian Dunlop and Fred Myers, 2014) offers a view of the painters, their discussions with the art adviser and their relationship with the other members of the Papunya Tula community in Papunya.

19. For a more extended discussion of this point, see my article, "Emplacement and Displacement: Perceiving the Landscape through Aboriginal Australian Acrylic Painting," *Ethnos* 78, no. 4 (2013): 435–63, http://doi.org/10.1080/00141844.2012.726635.

20. Dotting is a technique used in men's ceremonial decoration on bodies and objects, and is referred to by a secret name. Its use in acrylic painting carries the resonance of this profound significance.

21. The "flash" is a desired effect not only in Arnhem Land art, as Morphy has shown (see Howard Morphy, "From Dull to Brilliant: The Aesthetics of Spiritual Power among the Yolŋu," *Man* 24, no. 1 [1989]: 21–40); it seems the same is true also in the Papunya area, as noted by Ian Green, "Make Im Flash, Poor Bugger: Talking about Men's Painting in Papunya, 1988," in *The Inspired Dream*, ed. Margaret West (Brisbane: Queensland Art Gallery, 1988), 41–47.

22. For both men and women, it seems, the initial use of what was restricted information followed from an expectation that outsiders would not understand its sacred meanings. The subsequent decision to limit the inadvertent revelation of spiritual knowledge, Jennifer Biddle suggests, came as intercultural exchange—rather than trading in traditional objects with non-Indigenous audiences—became a central reason for painting (personal communication with the author). For a sense of the unsettled nature of these exchanges and the destabilized meanings of painting and revelation, see Fred Myers, "Unsettled Business: Acrylic Painting, Tradition and Indigenous Being," *Visual Anthropology* 17, no. 3–4 (2004): 247–71.

23. An excellent account of the circle-line and rectilinear (square) forms in desert art can be found in T. G. H. Strehlow, "The Art of the Circle, Line and Square," in *Australian Aboriginal Art*, ed. Ronald M. Berndt (Sydney: Ure Smith, 1964), 44–59. I have discussed the rectilinear in Pintupi art previously, in relation to the work of Anatjarri (Yanyatjarri) Tjakamarra, in Fred Myers, *Painting Culture: The Making of an Aboriginal High Art* (Durham, NC: Duke University Press, 2002); and in Fred Myers, "Aesthetics and Practice: a Local Art History of Pintupi Painting," in *The Art of Place: Dialogues with the Kluge-Ruhe Collection of Australian Aboriginal Art*, ed. Howard Morphy and Margo Smith Boles (Seattle: University of Washington Press, 1999), 219–59.

24. The well-known women artists Yalti Napangati, Yukultji Napangati and Tamayinya Tjapangati were also part of the nine, and have works in the *Papunya Tula Fiftieth Anniversary Suite* (plates 106–55).

25. For these concluding comments, I have drawn heavily on an essay I wrote in 2011, but which has had limited attention. See Fred Myers, "Intrigue of the Archive, Enigma of the Object," in *Tjukurrtjanu: Origins of Western Desert Art*, ed. Judith Ryan and Philip Batty (Melbourne: National Gallery of Victoria, 2011), 29–42.

# THAT'S HOW WE LEARNED

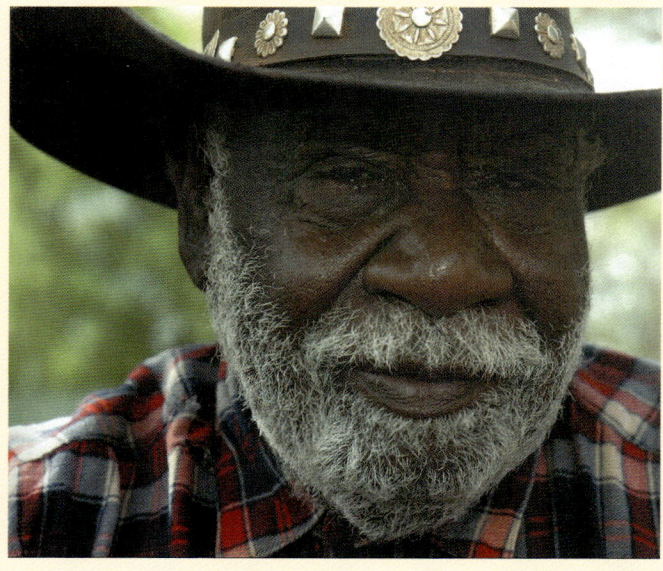

I am thinking that all the Western Desert people, all the original artists, should be celebrated. All the old people. I was thinking that we should remember those old people with an exhibition.

My father, Jack Long Phillipus Tjakamarra, was a really good painter. He used to do painting among all the old people at the Town Hall. When they split up [when the Pintupi moved to Yayayi] he would paint at home with the family. That's how we learned, by sitting down, watching his hand, doing the painting. Good memories, of my father looking at the painting and thinking about them. The ideas were really strong. Strong like everyone else. All the Anangu were really strong back then.

—CHARLOTTE PHILLIPUS NAPURRULA

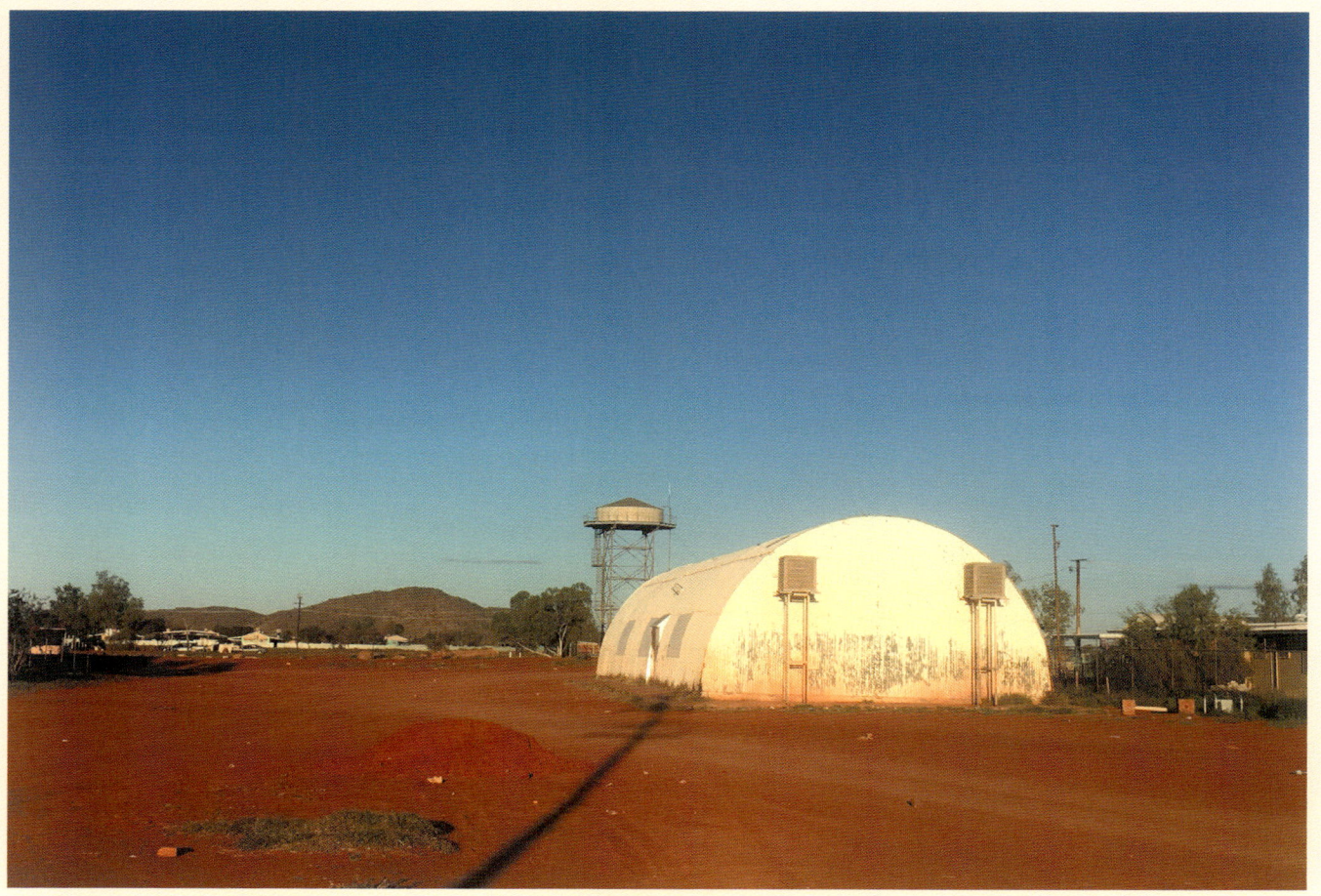

TOP

Jack Long Phillipus Tjakamarra at Mparntwe (Alice Springs), May 2005. Photo by John Donegan.

BOTTOM

Papunya Town Hall and Men's Painting Room with Warumpi (Honey Ant Hill) in background, 2016. Photo by John Kean.

# IT'S LIKE MY FATHER TOLD ME

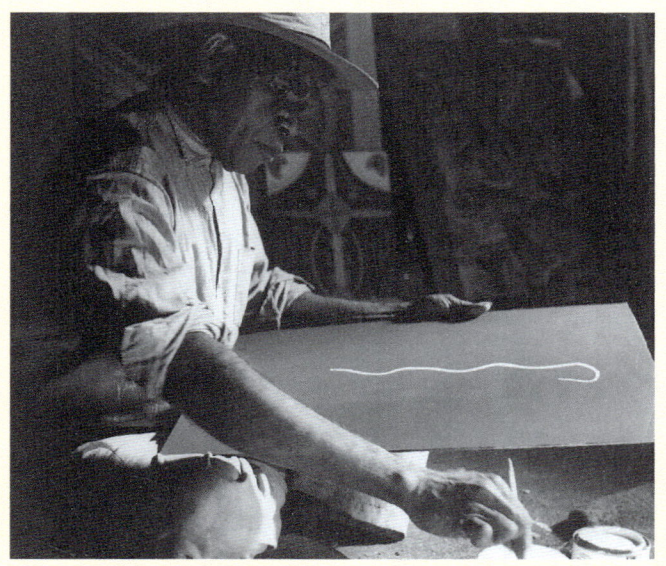

It's like this. My father told me, "When I am gone, you have to carry on. You are going to paint Kalipinypa and Ilpili."

Anmatyerr, Luritja, Warlpiri, and Pintupi people, *nyinapayi ngaangka*. They sat down here for a long time. They all went to the canteen, *ngurrpa tjuta*. They had not experienced settlement life before. *Maaniku ngurrpa*. They knew nothing of money. After that, it was one-pound and five-pound notes—old money.[1]

I used to *paayilpayi* [assertively tell someone to leave] all the school teacher mob. I would tell them, "Those old men are working over there, painting, you want to look at them, but you shouldn't because they are working." I kept my eyes open!

—NARLIE NELSON NAKAMARRA

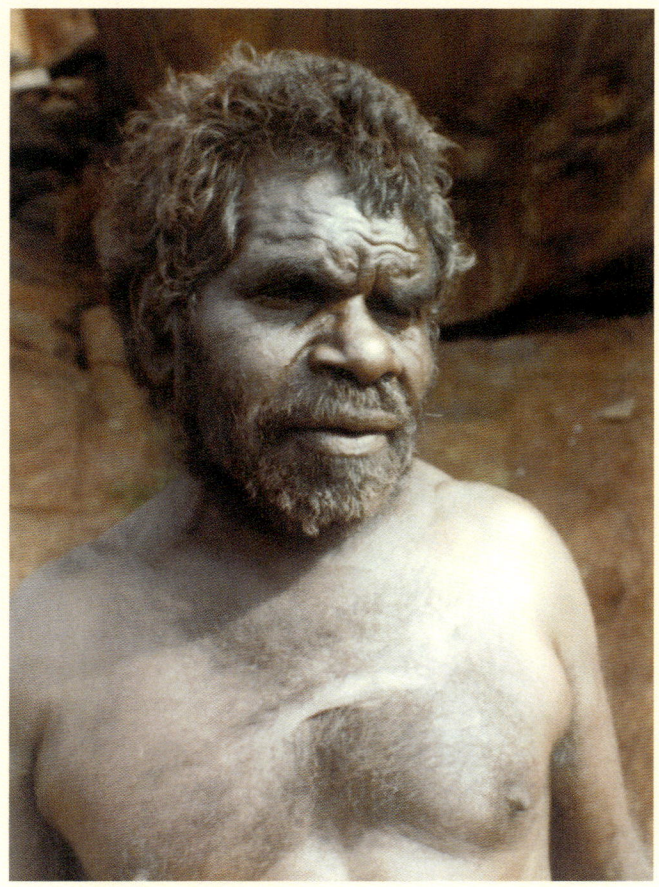

**TOP**

Johnny Warangkula Tjupurrula at Papunya, 1972. Photo by Allan Scott.

**BOTTOM**

Johnny Warangkula Tjupurrula at Tjikarri, 1978. Photo by Phillip Batty.

1. That is, notes from before the introduction of decimal currency to Australia in 1966.

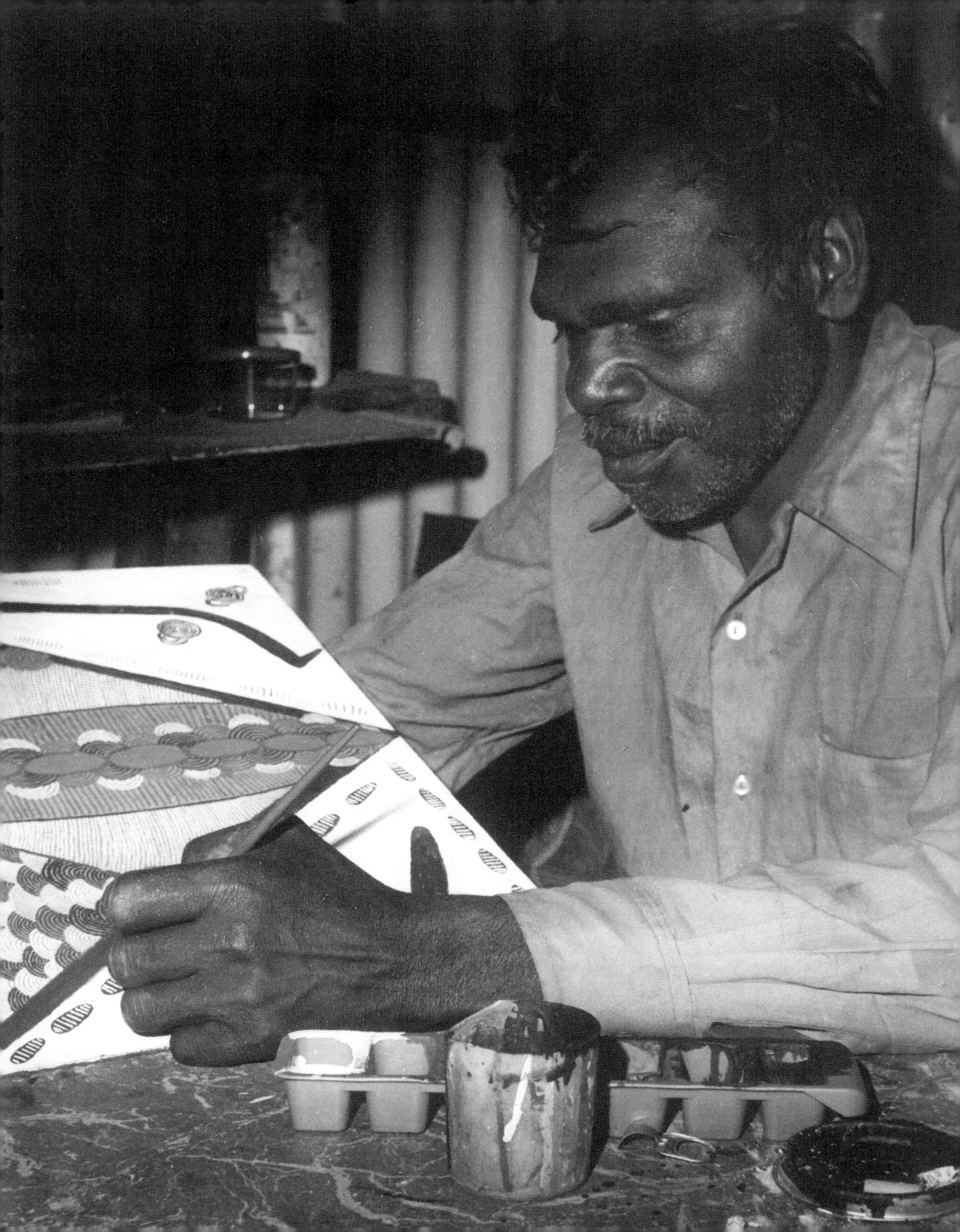

# East to West

## The Diversity of Papunya Tula Art

**JOHN KEAN**

Collectively, the Papunya Tula Artists have brought about the most radical transformation in Australian Art since the arrival of the Port Jackson Painter on the first fleet of English vessels in 1788.[1] Ample evidence supports this grand claim, from the influence that Papunya painting has exerted on both Indigenous and non-Indigenous painting in Australia to the international acclaim the movement has garnered. Most significant is the degree to which desert visuality—introduced to the broader public through Papunya artists' painting—has permeated the national consciousness. Fifty years after the inception of painting at Papunya in 1971, contemporary desert painting has spread—as Jack Long Phillipus Tjakamarra proclaimed, "like a bushfire"—outward and across the continent's arid heartlands, where thousands of Indigenous artists in a constellation of small communities practice related styles of painting.[2] From school art projects to Michael Jagamara Nelson's *Possum and Wallaby Dreaming* mosaic on the forecourt of Parliament House in the nation's capital, the reach of the iconography popularized by Papunya Tula painting extends everywhere. Elements of the "dot and circle" vocabulary have penetrated the national vernacular. The Papunya Tula Artists' logo itself is an icon that is now understood to represent a meeting of minds and the convergence of individuals—to represent community (see fig. 3.7).

Yet the success of Papunya Tula Artists, the extent of their collective influence, masks the range of distinctive practices among the company's founders (fig. 3.1). They were a diverse and eccentric band, drawn from distinct cultural groups. The men who assembled in the dusty streets of Papunya were brought together through the contingencies of history and government policy, not through the magnetism of a united vision. The convergence of these gifted individuals whose creativity was ignited in the midst of an otherwise-diabolical intercultural cultural collision is, without doubt, remarkable.[3] Nonetheless, the fact of this movement's emergence does not indicate that the founding artists were compelled to paint by a single shared purpose, nor does it mean that the paintings produced at Papunya can be understood as constituting a single school. Importantly, the intent of particular artists is lost when the breadth of their vision is reconstituted as a unitary cultural monolith. To that end, this essay will examine a selection of approaches taken by the company's original artists to dispel any assumptions of homogeneity.

Tim Leura Tjapaltjarri painting at a table, 1972. Photo by Allan Scott.

While the phenomenon of Papunya Tula art is best understood through the lens of diversity, several compelling stylistic conventions were developed communally in the Men's Painting Room, a makeshift studio operating at one end of a Nissan Hut from November 1971 until late 1973.[4] Before contrasting the distinctive approaches developed by the artists of Central Australia with those of the Western Desert artists, and examining the nuanced approach of those artists who bridge the two, I will describe some key conventions that unite them. I will then examine the works of a few artists at a more granular level, so the voices of individual artists can be heard.

## THE VISUAL LEXICON OF CENTRAL AUSTRALIA AND THE WESTERN DESERT

Most paintings produced in the first few years at Papunya use customary iconography, comprising a limited number of signs. Unlike the representational conventions of European art, which for several centuries aimed to configure images of people or objects as they "appear," many signs in Australian Indigenous iconography refer to traces that are read from the earth: the footprints of people; the tracks of game and the scrapes, burrows and excreta produced as animals rest and forage; the waterholes and caves marking sites where ancestors emerged from the land or reentered it. Put most simply, the iconography, semantics and spatial relationships of desert art relate to tracking, whether following the tell-tale imprints of snakes, kangaroos and possums, or tracing the paths of totemic ancestors across landforms created by their actions. The same lexicon is used in both secular and sacred realms. Everyday events are recounted with signs drawn in a cleared sweep of sand (fig. 3.2) or as totemic icons, including in the composition of expansive ritual ground paintings created on hardened earth.[5] Whereas the European tradition coheres around the depiction of the world through perspectival representation, desert iconography can be understood as a language of imaginative reconstruction.

Papunya paintings refer to the integrated realms of ceremony and Country. For example, Charlie Mutju Egalie Tjapaltjarri's *Ceremony Dancing* (1972, plate 33) emphasizes the paths of dancers in an ampersand on ritual ground, while *Wallaby Dreaming in the Sandhills at Tjunti* (1977, plate 32), by the same artist, evokes the passage of Warru, the Black-Flanked Rock Wallaby ancestor, across the artist's Country via three water places (concentric circles). While the first example refers to the traces left by performance

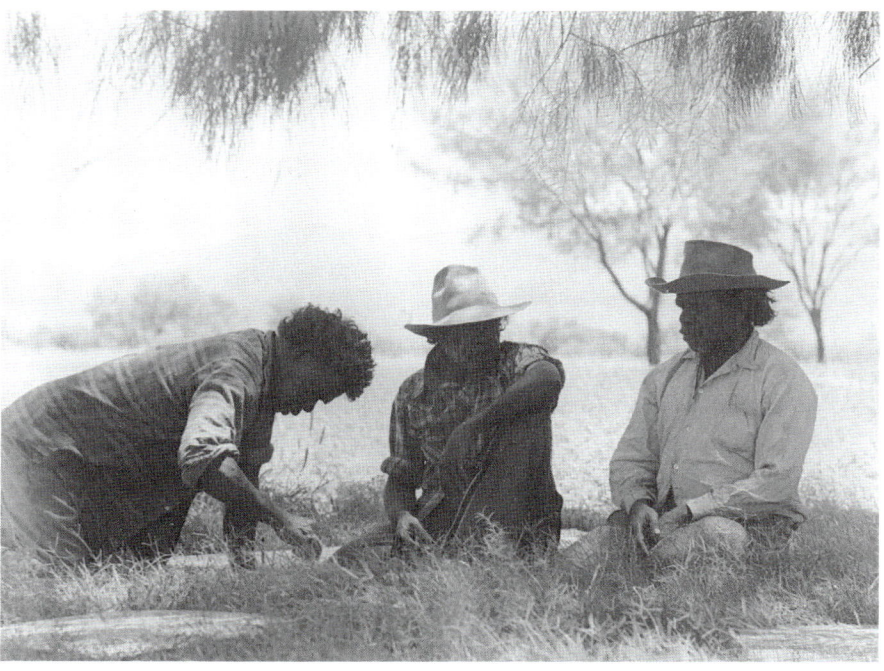

FIG. 3.1

Mick Namarari Tjapaltjarri (center), with Limpi Putungka Tjapangati (left) and Eddie Edimintja Tjapangati near Ikuntji (Haasts Bluff), mid-1970s. Photographer unknown

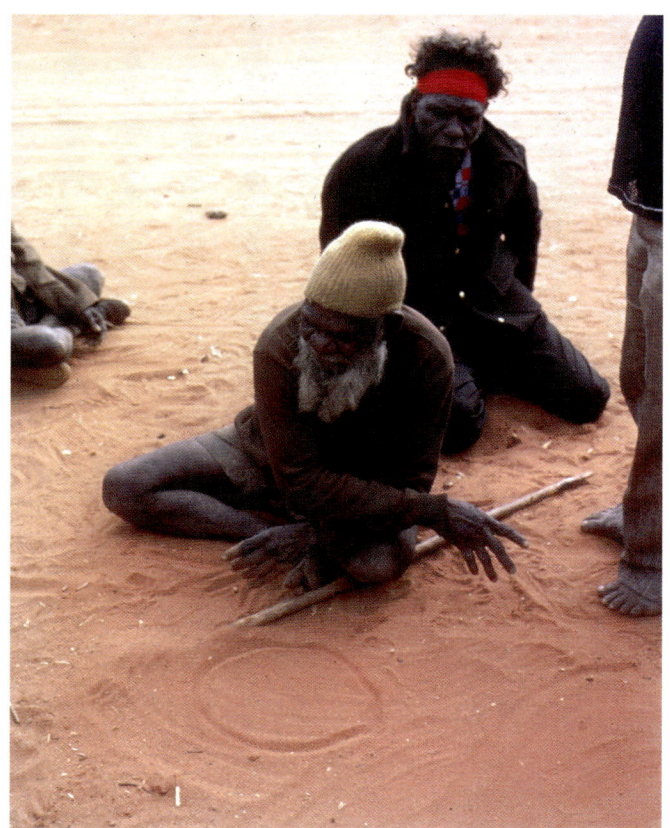

FIG. 3.2

Nosepeg Tjungkarta Tjupurrula drawing a circle in the sand, planning the return to Country, at Papunya, 1981. Seated behind, listening, is Yala Yala Gibbs Tjungurrayi. Photo by Fred Myers.

of ceremony (and *assumes* the Country to which that ritual refers), the second refers more clearly to the features of place, describing the path and rate of movement of Warru, hopping though sparse vegetation dotted across the red earth of parallel sandhills. Both ceremony and Country have their source in the actions of the Tjukurrpa ancestors, and, in the minds of the artists, these realms are bound and indivisible.

During the initial burst of painting at Papunya, most artists emphasized iconographic motifs associated with religious epics, delineating ancestral travel paths, or songlines, and detailing ceremonial objects associated with the sites through which ancestral beings traveled, as in Uta Uta Tjangala's *Ngurrapalangunya* (c. 1971–72, plate 46). In such works, dots were used sparingly to emphasize signs or objects, or to establish a ground over which ancestors moved. It was only later, in the second half of 1972, that the dots were more subtly articulated, as in Tim

Leura Tjapaltjarri's *Yam Spirit Dreaming* (1972, plate 12). During this period, the ongoing conventions of Papunya Tula painting crystallized through cultural exchange in the shared space of the Men's Painting Room (see figs. 3.5, 3.6), where artists speaking different languages worked cheek by jowl, learning from one another's songlines and exchanging approaches, artist to artist. Bobby West Tjupurrula, who was initiated into manhood during this period, insists that this moment of intense intercultural exchange extended from the men's painting spaces to ceremonial camps outside the settlement. Here, under a canopy of stars, Pintupi, Luritja, Warlpiri and Anmatyerr men shared their post-initiatory ceremonies to substantiate and extend the exchange commenced in the Men's Painting Room.[6] While accepting West's contextualization of the painting movement within the more encompassing realm of ceremonial exchange, the consensus around certain stylistic conventions formed somewhat mysteriously in the seclusion of the Men's Painting Room. Critically, it was the marriage of iconography and embellishment, foreground and background, content and form, that resulted in a durable yet infinitely malleable practice.

Kaapa Tjampitjinpa was a leader in the development of these stylistic conventions, and his *Dreaming at Mikantji* (1975, plate 17) exemplifies the use of dots as a dynamic composition element in Papunya Tula painting. Significantly, this work was included in *Art of First Australians* (1976), the first touring exhibition to emphasize the continuity between traditional artifacts and contemporary painting on canvas.[7] The integration of background and foreground, so effectively achieved in works such as Limpi Putungka Tjapangati's *Yalka and Maku Tjukurrpa (Bush Onion and Witchetty Grub Dreaming)* (1980, plate 41), was not wholly unprecedented. Putungka's painting can be compared with a prescient 1948 watercolor on the same theme attributed to Albert Namatjira, *Untitled (Yalka)* (fig. 3.3). Painted more than three decades apart, the paintings by Putungka and Namatjira are based on the same central iconography but use distinctive approaches to dotting to enliven their surfaces.

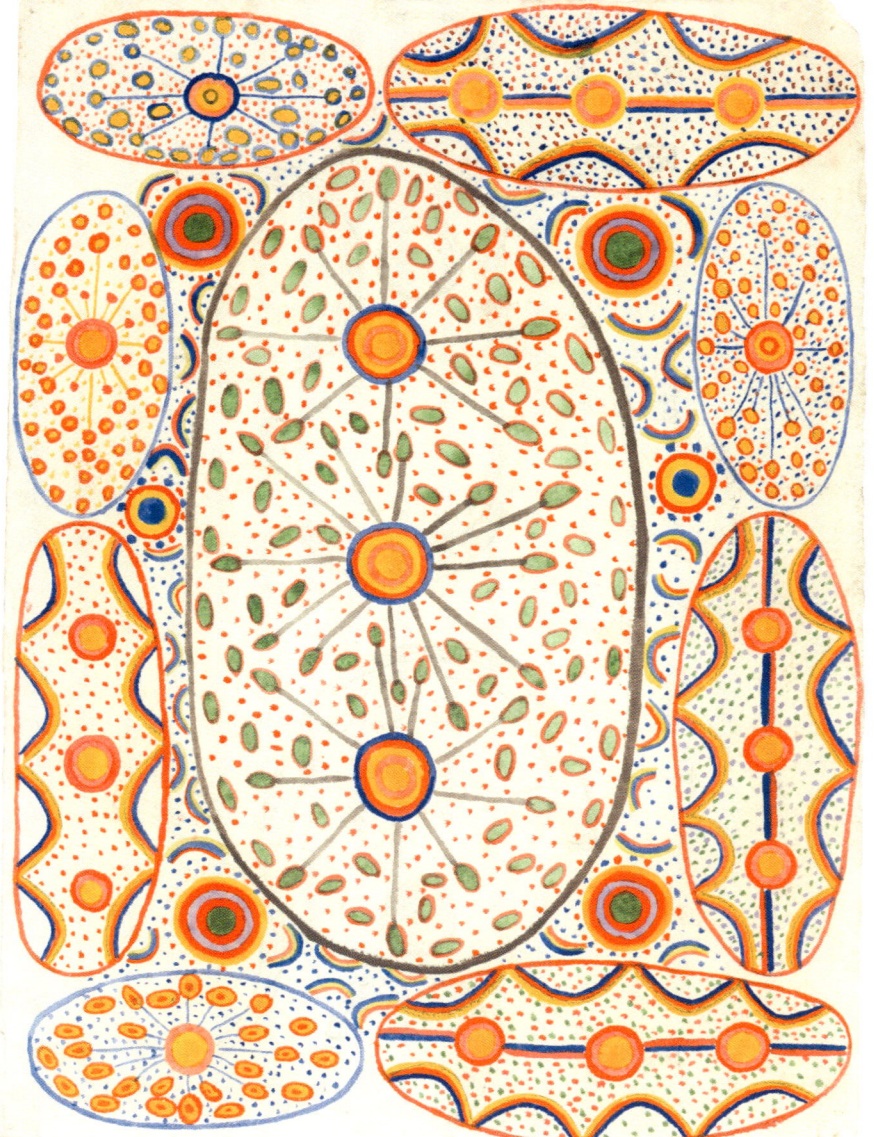

FIG. 3.3

Attributed to Albert Namatjira, *Untitled (Yalka)*, 1948, watercolor and pencil on paper, 15½ × 11¼ in. (39 × 29 cm). Art Gallery of South Australia, Gift of Emeritus Professor Anne Edwards AO, Andrew Gwinnett, Lipman Karas, Andrea Helen Katsaros, Thomas Mansfield, Dick Whitington QC and Peter Wilson through the Art Gallery of South Australia Foundation Collectors Club, 2016.

## JOHNNY WARANGKULA'S EXPERIMENTATION IN THE MEN'S PAINTING ROOM

The defining conventions of Papunya Tula Art can also be traced to the breakthroughs of several individuals. Johnny Warangkula Tjupurrula, whom I regard as the inventor of the articulate dot, was among the most influential innovators. A Pintupi man whose family had relied on Kalipinypa, a permanent waterhole far to the west of Papunya, Warangkula identified with Winpa, the Lightning ancestor who "sang up" the elements of an ancestral storm at that site. The force of Warangkula's paintings emanates directly from his ancestral identification with Winpa, expressed overtly as a dancer in ceremony, when singing verses of the lightning man or when painting images of Winpa's creation of the original storm at Kalipinypa with contemporary media.

Warangkula's breakthrough came in late 1971 / early 1972 while tracing the sinuous icons of lightning and running water in his first large-scale board, *Rain, Lightning and Stars at Night* (fig. 3.4). The artist's hand was freed when working at scale; his inconsistent dotting, which had jarred in smaller works, suddenly started to sparkle. Each patch of dots is painted rapidly, with the tip of the brush, or obliquely to create an irregular edge. Warangkula's miscellany of textures and supple lines draped with skeins of dots suddenly stretched and breathed. Fortuitously, his inventions coincided with a particularly wet period when, as a rainmaker, he was galvanized by downpours that hammered on the corrugated iron roof of the Men's Painting Room. Warangkula created two of the most poetic paintings in *Irrititja Kuwarri Tjungu | Past and Present Together*, *Kalipinypa* (1972, plate 9) and *Water Dreaming at Kalipinypa* (1972, plate 10), during this wet period, and the surface of each board shimmers with refracted light and electrical energy.

Photographs taken by Michael Jensen in August 1972 show Warangkula painting *Water Dreaming at Kalipinypa* (figs. 3.5, 3.6). Significantly, a pair of boomerangs is laid out formally, close at hand, in several of these images. Warangkula clapped the boomerangs, used as instruments, as he sung verses to conjure the power of the Lightning ancestor Winpa at intervals while painting.[8] In addition to the words of such songs, Warangkula drew on the visual kinship between rain clouds emerging on the horizon, prismatic light refracted through raindrops

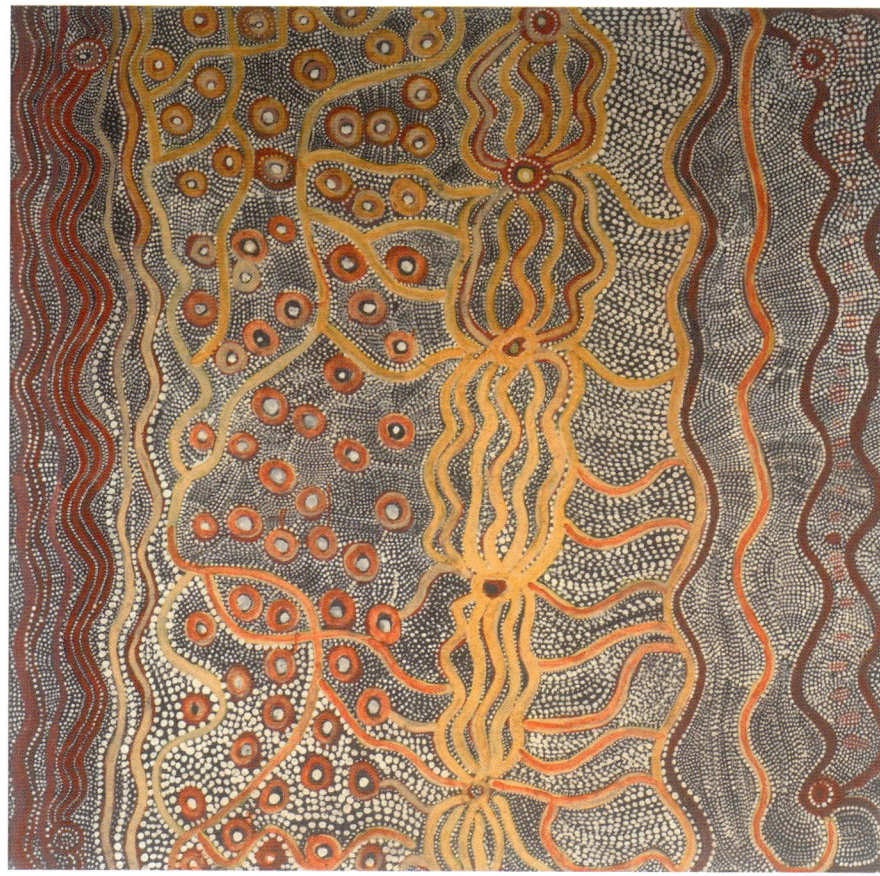

FIG. 3.4

Johnny Warangkula Tjupurrula, *Rain, Lightning and Stars at Night*, 1971, synthetic polymer paint on compressed fiber board, 36 × 35¹⁵⁄₁₆ in. (92 × 91 cm). Museum and Art Gallery of the Northern Territory, Darwin, WAL 39.

and the spectrum array of a rainbow. Rainmakers like Warangkula, along with Walter Tjampitjinpa and Kaapa Tjampitjinpa, activate the affinity between these phenomena to conjure the elements of a storm: clouds, lightning, rain, hail and running water. As is the case with the nacre of pearl shells used in rainmaking rituals, the refracted light in Warangkula's painting becomes unpredictable and transient. His work is characterized by spontaneous experimentation, through which the shimmer of living light, an essential quality of Indigenous aesthetics, is manifest, as it is in the manipulation of meteorological phenomena in ceremony.[9]

## MOVING BACK WEST—THE PINTUPI

The stylistic developments did not stop in 1973, when artists abandoned the shared space of the Men's Painting Room to work in smaller groups in the shade of trees or behind windbreaks at outstations, far from the administrative center at Papunya. The contingency of history that had brought these diverse artists together—most particularly the policy of assimilation, which assumed Aboriginal people should be trained in the ways of European culture—was starting to shatter. A new policy of self-determination began to gain traction, especially after the election of the reformist government of Gough Whitlam in December 1972.[10] Having been forced to live as virtual refugees on a fringe of the Papunya settlement, many Pintupi longed to return to their country in the Gibson Desert, two hundred and fifty miles to the west. They moved first to Yayayi, an outstation just thirty miles west of Papunya, where the painting men established a bush studio in the dappled shade of river red gum trees on the bank of a large creek. Although limited by the scale of the available canvas boards, artists such as Uta Uta Tjangala, Shorty Lungkarta Tjungurrayi and Yanatjarri No. III Tjakamarra painted with extraordinary confidence, reducing their compositions to dynamic, often-symmetrical geometric forms that were amplified by boldly patterned dotted infill,[11] as in Yanatjarri's *Untitled* (possibly *Wati Kutjarra at Pakarangaranya*) (1973, plate 81). Having contributed to the development of the conventions of Papunya Tula painting, where the dot was harnessed to carry the affective power of Tjukurrpa (the Dreaming), the Pintupi artists continued to distill their imagery. Whereas Johnny Warangkula had suffused his inherited iconography in a veil of dots, other Pintupi artists employed the

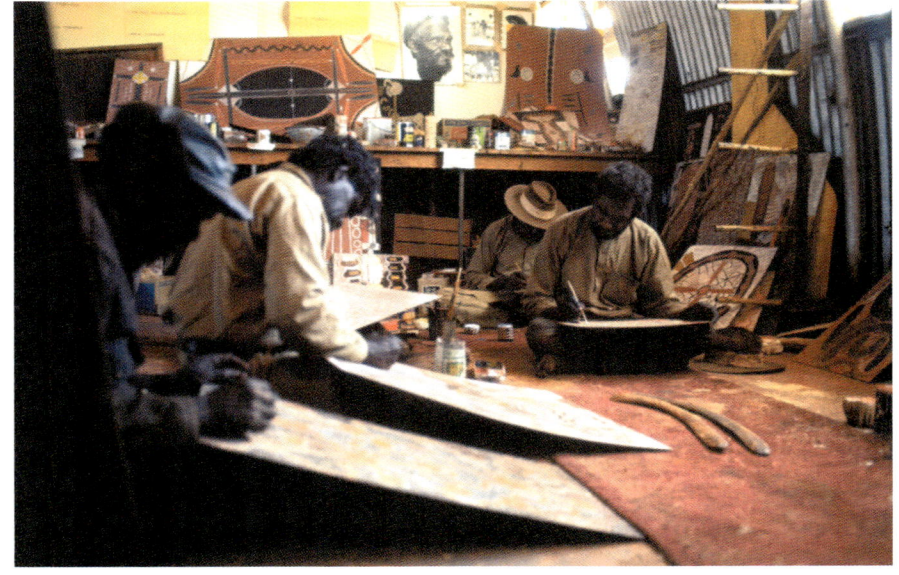

TOP | FIG. 3.5

Charlie Wartuma Tjungurrayi, Johnny Warangkula Tjupurrula, Walter Tjampitjinpa, and Kaapa Tjampitjinpa in the Men's Painting Room at Papunya, August 1972. Photo by Michael Jensen.

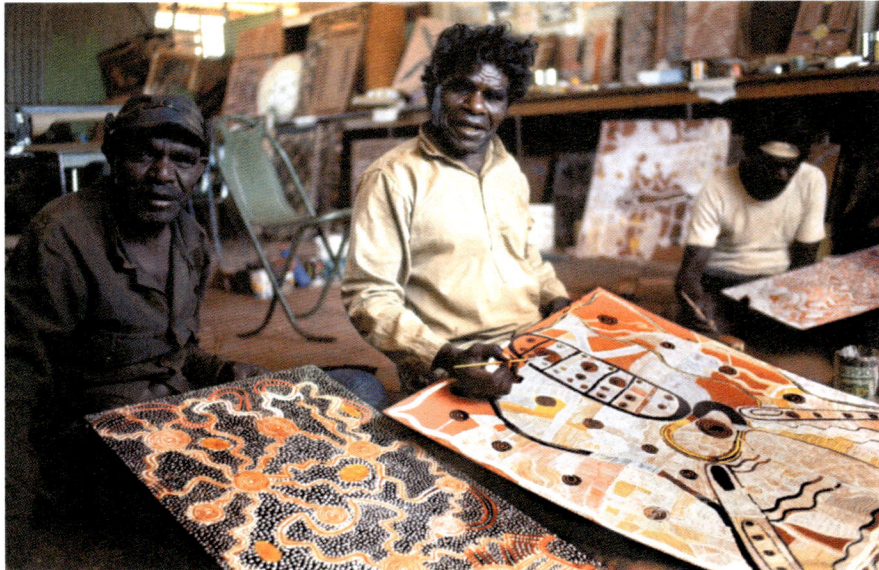

BOTTOM | FIG. 3.6

Charlie Wartuma Tjungurrayi and Johnny Warangkula Tjupurrula with *Water Dreaming at Kalipinypa* (plate 10), August 1972. Photo by Michael Jensen.

same irreducible element to create bands of optically charged dots that amplify the kinetic energy of their compositions. Just as the repeating, marginally irregular lines appear to shift on the surface of Bridget Riley's Op Art "events," the closely aligned, yet slightly varied dots of these early Pintupi paintings create a visual disturbance that activates the surface. Unlike Riley's abstract constructions, however, the optical effects of Pintupi art refer to Tjukurrpa; the shimmering discloses the latent power of the ancestors, redolent at distant sites where the artists lived and were initiated into manhood.[12]

The essential form of Pintupi painting coalesced at Yayayi and nearby outstations from 1973 to 1981, yet these outstations were merely staging posts for an eventual return to Country. It was further west, at Walungurru (Kintore) and Kiwirrkurra, communities established in the early 1980s, where the Pintupi artists could paint at scale with greater freedom.[13] Based on their own Country, they could effect a more complete separation from the Anmatyerr, Warlpiri and Luritja artists with whom they had established contemporary desert art in the early 1970s. Meanwhile, armed with the same suite of materials and sharing some of the technical approaches, artists who remained in the east took contemporary desert painting in a very different direction.[14]

## "PAINTING AND SING-EM-UP MOB": THE ANMATYERR ARTISTS

From the outset, the Anmatyerr artists Kaapa Tjampitjinpa, Bill Stockman Tjapaltjarri, Tim Leura Tjapaltjarri and Clifford Possum Tjapaltjarri were keenly interested in the formal possibilities of acrylic paints to express songs and ceremony. Such was their enthusiasm that Johnny Jack Tjampitjinpa remembers the Anmatyerr artists as the "Painting and sing-em-up mob."[15] Whereas the Pintupi had lived in the bush with little or no contact with non-Aboriginal people, the Anmatyerr painters had grown into manhood on cattle stations, their Country having been occupied by pastoralists in the years preceding their birth. Denied autonomy over their lands, the Anmatyerr had come to an uncomfortable accommodation with the occupying pastoralists.[16] Leura, Stockman and Possum were skilled horsemen who rode alongside gnarled white "bosses" and fresh-faced jackaroos and, in the process, became acutely aware of the value of their labor.[17] Whereas traditional cultural practices were suppressed on most missions, the pastoralists, hard as they

were, did not interfere with customary ceremonial life. In fact, the Anmatyerr stockmen sensed that some whitefellas whom they met were deeply interested in Aboriginal culture.

Kaapa, Tim Leura, Bill Stockman and Clifford Possum recognized that they could earn good money as artists, selling their carvings to schoolteachers, station managers and at mission stores.[18] Leura and Possum, in particular, were gifted carvers who honed their skills making distinctive, life-size polychrome snakes and goannas. Just as significantly, they were closely related to Arrernte painters, including Albert Namatjira, who had created a popular school of watercolor landscape painting at the Finke River Mission at Hermannsburg, sixty miles southwest from Papunya. Inventive, and aware of the conventions of representational art and photography, the Anmatyerr were critical to the development of Papunya Tula art, a genre they tailored to the cross-cultural market.[19]

Kaapa proved to be the most enterprising of the Anmatyerr and was the first to achieve public acclaim for the freshness of his vision and the precision of his compositions. Gregarious and assertive, he was a mimic and trickster who challenged the conventions of his own society as squarely as he did the government officials who sought to control his restless spirit.[20] In May 2021, in preparation for the *Irrititja Kuwarri Tjungu* exhibition, the Kluge-Ruhe Aboriginal Art Collection and Papunya Tula Artists commissioned me to consult with various artists and their descendants on which works might be included. When I showed contemporary Anmatyerr elders a reproduction of one of Kaapa's early paintings, they drew breath. These works remain contentious and, as the curators had anticipated, the elders asked that we exclude the work from the exhibition, as it depicted secret objects from the restricted realm of men's ritual. Tim Leura was Kaapa's cousin and a close artistic collaborator, especially in 1972, when they worked on adjacent tables in the Men's Painting Room.[21] Like Kaapa, Leura also produced early works that are now regarded as too revealing. However, their experimentation was not limited to the explicit representation of ceremony; together, Kaapa and Leura established the taut compositional geometry, exemplified in Tim Leura's *Honey Ant Dreaming* (1973, plate 7), upon which many Papunya Tula paintings have been based.[22]

Tim Leura's pictorial interests soon extended beyond those pursued by Kaapa—or any of the other founding Papunya Tula artists. Liberated by the potential of acrylic paint to mimic qualities observed in nature, Leura sought to give form to the liminal: a metaphysical realm of crepuscular light, the glow of ritual fires and the unseen world of Honey Ant ancestors suspended in darkness under the surface of the earth. Having observed water-color artists, Leura thinned his paints to achieve transparency, allowing the medium to find its own way through the warp and weft of the canvas. Sometimes, as is the case with *Women Sitting around a Fire at Sunset* (c. 1973–74, plate 23), he applied layers of paint wet on wet to encourage the accidental mixture of colors and textures. The poetic intent in Leura's paintings—how they relate to the verses of ancestral songlines—is a deep pool, yet to be plumbed.[23]

Whereas Tim Leura was fascinated by intangible phenomena, his younger brother Clifford Possum felt compelled to investigate how customary iconography could be articulated to describe space, in all its dimensions. The extent of Possum's technical skill and his particular aptitude for spatial extrapolation became evident in a series of commanding "map" paintings, most of which he produced in the late 1970s. Painted in September 1973, the aptly named *Paths of the Ancestors* (plate 21) is the most significant precursor to that remarkable series. The painting was among a group of identically sized works by a variety of artists, commissioned by the Aboriginal Arts Board. Although based on inherited iconography, Possum's map paintings go beyond anything that was produced by other Papunya-based artists in the first years of the movement. Rather than depicting a single songline, site or ceremony, Possum's map paintings are encyclopedic representations of Country at a synoptic scale, inspired, perhaps, by his familiarity with the topographic maps unrolled by pastoralists. Individual songlines, indicated by the tracks of various totemic ancestors, are shown passing through a series of sites across huge estates. In turn, the trails of the ancestors are embedded within a matrix of dotted patterns to represent the major topographic and vegetative associations of the Country over which the ancestral heroes traveled. Possum's map series are unmatched in both geographic scope and intellectual rigor.[24]

Tim Leura and Clifford Possum had worked closely with Johnny Warangkula in the Men's Painting Room. Encouraged by his improvisations, the brothers used the dot to represent specific topographic, vegetative or atmospheric phenomena. In contrast to their relatives, the Arrernte watercolorists, who painted the land in an elevation, according to picturesque conventions, Leura and Possum applied their carefully modulated hues to a scrupulously flattened picture plane. By the mid-1980s, Possum's conceptual sophistication had made him the first superstar of the painting movement. *Rain Dreaming at Mount Denison* (1989, plate 22) is a fine example of his mid-career acuity, epitomizing Possum's capacity for pre-planning and impeccable precision.[25] Possum intercuts the codified representation of ceremony and Country with deftness on the same picture plane, each element clearly defined and expertly resolved. The central panel of *Rain Dreaming* features the ceremonial incarnation of the Water/Rain ancestors, while the mosaic of background dots shows the effect of the original downpour on the adjacent land, the color of each patch representing a different food plant growing in response to the rain. Tracks are embedded in the earth and the ancestral Emu is imagined pecking at emergent bush fruits as it traverses the moistened country.

## CROSSING THE COLONIAL FRONTIER

Between the eastern/Anmatyerr and western/Pintupi extremes of Papunya Tula painting is the distinctive approach taken by artists whose Country lay between the MacDonnell Ranges and the Gibson Desert. Whereas the western Pintupi (from the Gibson Desert) had their first substantial exposure to non-Indigenous people in the late 1950s and early 1960s, their eastern neighbors sustained a much longer period of contact. This group, whom I will refer to as eastern Pintupi, camped on the fringes of Hermannsburg mission and near the Ikuntji (Haasts Bluff) ration station before moving to Papunya during the construction of the new government settlement in the late 1950s. These immigrants maintained a semitraditional, hunter-gatherer lifestyle in Kukatja country, ranging back into their own desert homelands when opportunity and the seasons allowed. Living around the farthest outpost of European governance, the eastern Pintupi continued to move to and fro, across the colonial frontier.[26]

Three of Papunya Tula's founding artists, Charlie Wartuma Tjungurrayi, Johnny Warangkula and Mick Namarari Tjapaltjarri (see fig. 3.1) were boys when their families left their Country to travel east toward Hermannsburg in the early 1930s. They returned to their own Country as "doggers," earning cash hunting dingoes for their "scalps," redeemed for £1 each at the station or, more purposefully, collected in larger groups for ceremony.[27] Despite their lack of formal education, Warangkula, Namarari and Wartuma were familiar with printed media, mostly through cowboy cartoons and biblical illustrations of the Holy Land circulated at Ikuntji and Papunya. I contend that, on occasion, the imagery and framing of their work shows the influence of Western media.[28]

Mick Namarari appears to have been particularly interested in figuration; *Muruntji* (1972, plate 58), for instance, includes fully resolved individuals painted on the same pictorial plane as a range of customary abstracted icons. While their outline sometimes relates

to schematic figures painted on rock shelters in the Western Desert, Namarari's figures also borrow from transcultural media.[29] For example, it was customary to present human figures frontally, but the men in *Ceremony at Tjilka* (1973, plate 36) appear in profile, suggesting Namarari's exposure to the European media in which figures are presented from various angles.

Although Warangkula, Namarari and Wartuma were closely related to their western Pintupi neighbors, they painted with considerably more freedom. On occasion, Namarari and Wartuma painted conventional "site path" configurations, composed of sets of concentric circles (sites) linked by straight or sinuous lines (pathways),

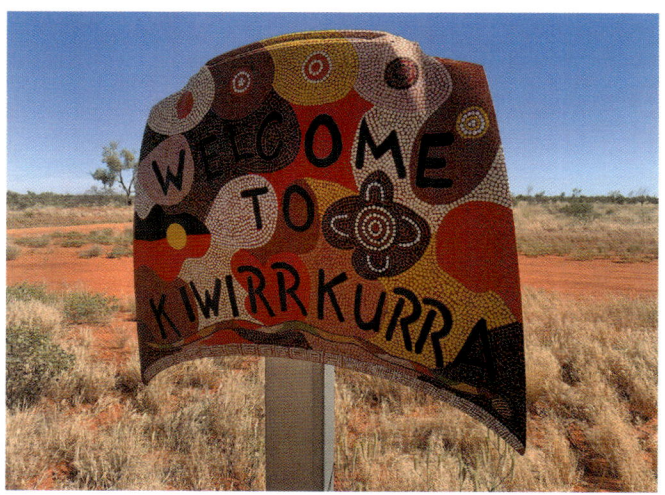

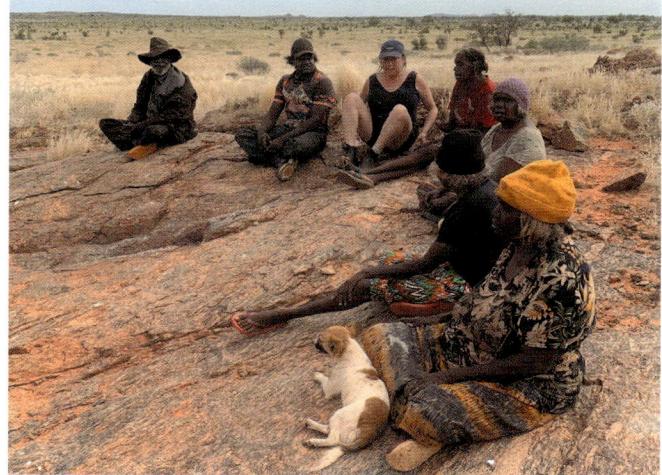

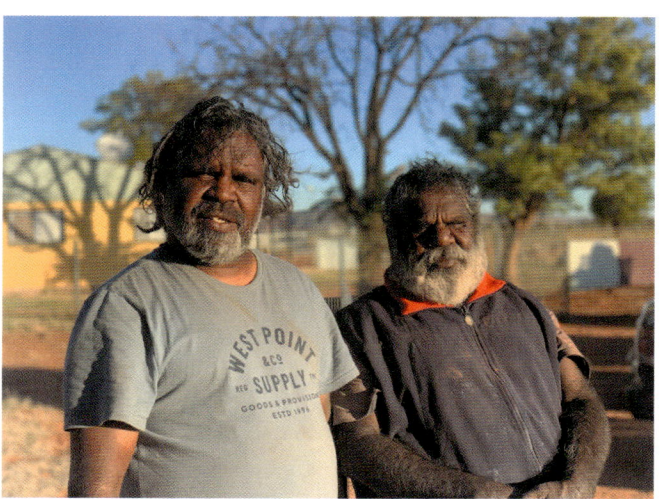

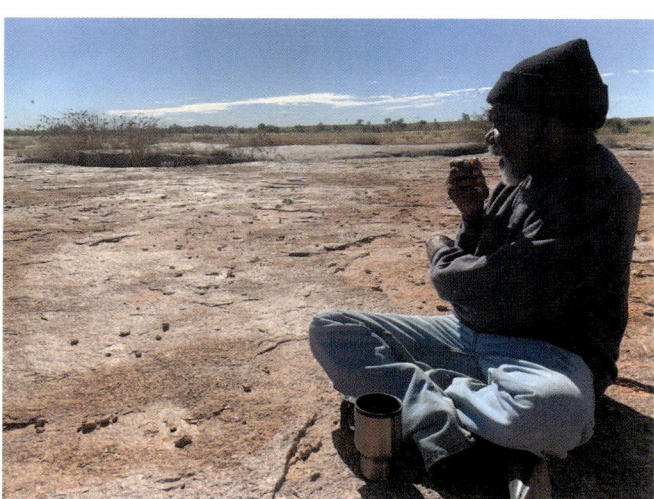

TOP LEFT | FIG. 3.7

Welcome to Kiwirrkurra sign, featuring the "meeting place" icon, on the turnoff from the Gary Junction Road, May 2021. Photo by John Kean.

BOTTOM LEFT | FIG. 3.8

Tony Eggley Tjungurrayi, son of Charlie Mutju Egalie Tjapaltjarri, and Mike Tjakamarra at Watiyawanu consulting for *Irrititja Kuwarri Tjungu*, May 2021. Photo by John Kean.

TOP RIGHT | FIG. 3.9

Yuwalki family and Papunya Tula fieldworker Paloma Pizzarro at Muni Muni on the Kungka Kutjarra (Two Women) songline, May 2021. Photo by John Kean.

BOTTOM RIGHT | FIG. 3.10

Matthew Pinta Tjapangati, son of Pinta Pinta Tjapanangka, at Yumari, May 2021. Photo by John Kean.

similar to those produced by Yala Yala Tjungurrayi or Freddy West Tjakamarra. But they also created more painterly works, in which figures and representations of Country emerge from playful experimentation. It is difficult to be certain whether their approach reflects a higher number of naturalistic signs within their inherited iconography, or if their spontaneity arose from experiencing a more protracted period of contact with Western ideas and transcultural media. It is tempting to think that their eccentricity arises from their unique and formative experiences, crossing the frontier between the constraints and novelty of colonial governance and the patterns of customary lifeways. Whatever determined their approach, these Pintupi-speaking artists constitute a discernable yet highly individualistic cluster.[30] Despite differences in their individual styles, the work of these border crossers is united by a boldness of line, sinuous in the case of Namarari (plate 78) and Warangkula (plate 9) and broad and unashamedly direct in that of Wartuma (plate 45). There is candor in the works of these artists; their paintings are internally animated, each artist creating worlds inspired by their rich identification with places whose deeper meaning they were inducted into as young men, and to which they made considerable effort to return at intervals throughout their lives. Their paintings express the indomitable spirit of each individual, maintaining a sense of playfulness in a radically changing world.

## CONCLUSION

Even now, half a century after Kaapa Tjampitjinpa salvaged building materials to create the first of his revolutionary boards, understanding the scope and influence of the founding Papunya Tula Artists is a challenge for art historians. Unlike many twentieth-century art movements that ran their course, Papunya Tula Artists persists as a contemporary force. Moreover, a host of Indigenous artists, working at a remote Aboriginal communities scattered across Australia's desert heartlands, continue to paint with passion in a style that can be traced to Papunya. Taken as a whole, the desert art movement confounds simple classification, as it continues to expand and diversify.

The period from the winter solstice of 1971 through the southern spring of 1972 was the *annus mirabilis* of Australian desert art, when the Men's Painting Room at Papunya became a laboratory from which new forms of expression emerged to become a globally recognized

phenomenon. The unlikely atelier, whose architectural form has more in common with WWII military facilities than it does with most artists' studios, holds many mysteries. The songs that were sung in the space were never recorded, and even the attribution of some of the approximately one thousand works produced in the Men's Painting Room remains uncertain.[31] With the exception of Ronnie Tjampitjinpa, the men who painted in that space have now passed into the Dreaming.[32] There remain a few photographs showing some of the artists at work, and there are several descriptions of how the nascent artists arranged themselves in this crowded space. The Men's Painting Room, however, was effectively a proscribed ritual area from which, according to custom, most—including the artists' wives and children—were excluded. As a consequence, there are only a handful of living witnesses to what transpired in that cloistered room. The detailed discussions, conducted in Anmatyerr, Warlpiri, Luritja and Pintupi languages, about what was to be painted and what should be concealed have vanished with the artists.

Yet works produced in the Men's Painting Room continue to enter the public realm—recovered from cupboards and walls at distant locations. They are analyzed by anthropologists, gallerists and art historians within the context of what is known of the beginnings of Papunya Tula art. Because the paintings were produced in seclusion, then exported to Australian state and territory capitals or included in traveling exhibitions that were later disassembled and dispersed, the rediscovery of each early Papunya painting can be a revelation, especially for the children of the artists, descendants who were not afforded even a glimpse of these revolutionary works before they were transported from the desert. Major exhibitions, such as *Irrititja Kuwarri Tjungu*, create an opportunity for communities to encounter and discuss previously unsighted paintings. I was fortunate to take images of potential works for this exhibition to the communities where the founding artists lived. It was a joy to share recollections of the visionary artists with their families, many of whom I have known for over forty years (figs. 3.7–3.10). The travel took me over thousands of miles of unsealed roads to Laramba (Napperby), Papunya, Ikuntji, Yamunturrngu (Mt Liebig), Walungurru and Kiwirrkurra, along with visits to several families in Mparntwe (Alice Springs). The absence of the founding artists is keenly felt at each settlement, where turning the pages of the exhibition folder was accompanied by melancholy and grief—"finished, poor thing," "deadfella, that one," "my uncle, he's gone." As well as establishing a movement that is central to Anangu identity today, the founding painters included in *Irrititja Kuwarri Tjungu* were the leaders of the communities where their descendants now live. The original Papunya Tula artists have transformed, in a very real sense, to become ancestral heroes.

Alongside the celebration of their collective achievement, the founding Papunya Tula artists demand attention as individuals and distinctive creative thinkers. Tim Leura and Clifford Possum, for instance, explored nuanced conceptual realms beyond those reached by their peers—or by any of the artists who have followed in their footsteps. Uta Uta Tjangala and Shorty Lungkarta painted with such assurance that the palpable performative authority of their works is rarely matched. Others, like Mick Namarari and Johnny Warangkula, reveal ecological secrets of the desert landscape, its animals and its seasonal extremes, with intimacy and precision. Namarari and Warangkula can take us into cryptic sites, such as Marnpi and Kalipinypa, and in doing so communicate the mysteries at the core of their own being. The diverse and singular achievements of these artists transcend and exceed the movement they helped to found.

Nonetheless, it is undeniable that the Papunya Tula Artists, as a collective, have exerted remarkable influence. Visitors to major Australian art museums will discover extensive collections of delicate boards, painted at Papunya in the early 1970s, exhibited en masse to encapsulate the moment when the compass of Australian art history began to shift from the seaboard to the desert. Dazzling architectonic canvases by the same artists, or their close relatives, created from the mid-1970s to the present day, complement these earlier Papunya boards.[33] The paintings produced at Papunya, Yayayi, Walungurru and Kiwirrkurra have long been established as essential monuments of Australian art.

Despite their shared origins, Papunya Tula paintings possess an essential diversity as vast as the land itself, from visions of totemic landscapes painted by the Anmatyerr artists to the thrumming abstraction of Pintupi compositions. Born of Country and educated in ceremony, the founding artists of Papunya Tula lived as hunter-gatherers, stockmen and doggers, many knowing life on both sides of the colonial frontier. They converged for a miraculous moment in the 1970s to realize a world that, without their vision, would have remained hidden.

## NOTES

1. Works by the anonymous Port Jackson Painter(s) were created during the initial English colonization in the Sydney area. While they were naïve in style, these were the first examples of the European landscape, portraiture and natural history genres produced on the continent.

2. See Luke Scholes, "Long Jack Phillipus Tjakamarra," in *Tjukurrtjanu: Origins of Western Desert Art*, ed. Judith Ryan and Philip Batty (Melbourne: National Gallery of Victoria, 2011), 315–16. While in previous publications I refer to the artist as Long Jack Phillipus, at the request of the artist's daughter, Charlotte Phillipus Napurrula, he is identified as Jack Long Phillipus in this volume.

3. Philip Batty et al., *Colliding Worlds: First Contact in the Western Desert 1932–1984* (Melbourne: Museum Victoria Publishing, 2006).

4. Geoffrey Bardon and James Bardon, *Papunya: A Place Made after the Story: The Beginnings of the Western Desert Painting Movement* (Carlton, VIC: Melbourne University Publishing, 2004), 27–34; Luke Scholes, "Unmasking the Myth: The Emergence of Papunya Painting," in *Tjungunutja: From Having Come Together*, ed. Luke Scholes (Darwin, NT: Museum and Art Gallery of the Northern Territory, 2017), 138–60.

5. For analysis of vernacular narratives, see Jennifer Green, *Drawn from the Ground: Sound, Sign and Inscription in Central Australian Sand Stories* (Cambridge: Cambridge University Press), 2014. For an overview of ground paintings, see Richard G. Kimber, "Mosaics You Can Move," in *Hemisphere* 21, no. 1 (1977); 2–7; 29–30. For a discussion of visual semiotics in desert art, see Nancy Munn, "Visual Categories: An Approach to the Study of Representational Systems," *American Anthropologist* 68 (1966): 936–50.

6. Bobby West Tjupurrula, in Scholes, *Tjungunutja*, 117–18.

7. Aboriginal Arts Board, *Art of the First Australians: An Exhibition of Aboriginal Painting, Sculpture and Artefacts of the Past Two Hundred Years* (Sydney: Australia Council, 1976), 47–56. For more on the continuity between traditional objects and painting practice, see Fred Myers's essay in this volume, "The Goannas Are Dancing: The Generation and Generations of Papunya Painting."

8. Although I was not in the room when this work was created, I observed Warangkula singing while painting on numerous occasions from 1977 to 1979.

9. John Kean, "Dot, Circle and Frame: How Kaapa Tjampitjinpa, Tim Leura, Clifford Possum and Johnny Warangkula Created Papunya Tula Art" (Ph.D. diss., University of Melbourne, 2020), 177–98.

10. For a discussion of assimilation and self-determination, see Peter Thorley, "Outstations through Art: Acrylic Painting, Self-Determination and the History of the Homelands Movement in the Pintupi-Ngaanyatjarra Lands," in *Experiments in Self-Determination: Histories of the Outstation Movement in Australia*, ed. Nicolas Peterson and Fred Myers (Canberra, ACT: Australian National University Press, 2016), 135–56.

11. Fred Myers, *Painting Culture: The Making of an Aboriginal High Art* (Durham, NC: Duke University Press, 2002), 80–189.

12. For a broader discussion of "shimmer" in Indigenous Australia, see Howard Morphy, "From Dull to Brilliant: The Aesthetics of Spiritual Power among the Yolŋu," *Man* 24, no.1 (1989): 21–40.

13. For on the developments at Walungurru and Kiwirrkurra, see Paul Sweeney's essay in this volume, "Art of Resilience: The Importance of Papunya Tula Artists in Australia's Western Desert."

14. Vivien Johnson, *Streets of Papunya: The Re-invention of Papunya Painting* (Sydney: New South Publishing, 2015), 108–29.

15. Johnny Jack Tjampitjinpa, cited in Jason Gibson, "Painting and Sing-em-up Mob: The Anmatyerr Painters," in *Out of the Boxes and into the Desert*, no.16 (Crawley, WA: Berndt Museum of Anthropology, 2019), 21.

16. Jason Gibson, *Ceremony Men: Making Ethnography and the Return of the Strehlow Collection* (Albany: State University of New York Press, 2020), 47–57.

17. Vivien Johnson, *Clifford Possum Tjapaltjarri* (Adelaide: Art Gallery of South Australia, 2003), 35–39.

18. Richard G. Kimber, "Recollections of Papunya Tula 1971–80," in *Papunya Tula: Genesis and Genius* (Sydney: Art Gallery of New South Wales, 2000), 210.

19. Jason Gibson and John Kean, "'New Possum Found!' Photographic Influences on Anmatyerr Art," *emaj* 9 (May 2016), DOI: 10.38030/emaj.2016.9.1.

20. Vivien Johnson, *Once Upon a Time in Papunya* (Sydney: University of New South Wales Press, 2010), 11–28.

21. Bardon and Bardon, *Papunya: A Place Made after the Story*, 27–29.

22. Kean, "Dot, Circle and Frame," 149–76.

23. Kean, "Dot, Circle and Frame," 216–35.

24. John Kean, "Clifford Possum," in *Paths of the Ancestors* (Melbourne: D'lan Contemporary, 2000), 8–15.

25. Vivien Johnson, *Clifford Possum Tjapaltjarri* (Adelaide: Art Gallery of South Australia, 2003), 163–91.

26. The Haasts Bluff Aboriginal Reserve was created in 1941 to enable people from the Western Desert to maintain a semi-traditional lifestyle, away from "corrupting" non-Indigenous influences. For an extended discussion of this period, see Kean, "Dot, Circle and Frame," 61–89.

27. John Kean, "Johnny Warangula Tjupurrula: History, Landscape and La Niña 1974," in *Indigenous Archives: The Making and Unmaking of Aboriginal Art*, ed. Darren Jorgensen and Ian McLean (Perth: University of Western Australia Publishing, 2017), 131–34.

28. By "framing," I mean the way in which the image is composed and cropped. Kean, "Dot, Circle and Frame," 97–98; 131–34.

29. John Kean, "Framing Papunya Painting: Form, Style and Representation, 1971—72," in Scholes, *Tjungunutja*, 173–94.

30. The cluster of three artists could be expanded to include Walter Tjampitjinpa, also Charlie Mutju Egalie Tjapaltjarri and Jack Long Phillipus Tjakamarra from the north, and Limpi Putungka Tjapangati and Mick Wallangkarri Tjakamarra from the east.

31. Desmond Phillipus Tjupurrula, quoted in Scholes, *Tjungunutja*, 120.

32. At the time of writing, Tjampitjinpa is a resident of Hetti Perkins Home for the Aged, Mparntwe (Alice Springs).

33. In particular, the installations at the National Gallery of Australia, Art Gallery South Australia, Queensland Art Gallery and National Gallery Victoria.

NEXT SPREAD

Artists in front of *Kaakurutintjinya, the Nangala Canvas* for the Haasts Bluff / Kintore Canvas Project after the Walungurru painting camp, outside the Ngintaka Women's Centre, June 1994. From left: Nyurapayia Nampitijinpa "Mrs Bennett" (seated), Linda Napurrula (behind), Inyuwa Nampitjinpa, Ningura Napurrula, Katarra Nampitjinpa, Pantjiya Nungurrayi, Tjunkiya Napaltjarri, Wintjiya Napaltjarri, Tatali Nangala (behind), Josephine Napurrula, Narputta Nangala, Anmanari Napanangka, Mantua Napanangka, Loline Nungurrayi, Makinti Napanangka (seated in front). Photo by Marina Strocchi.

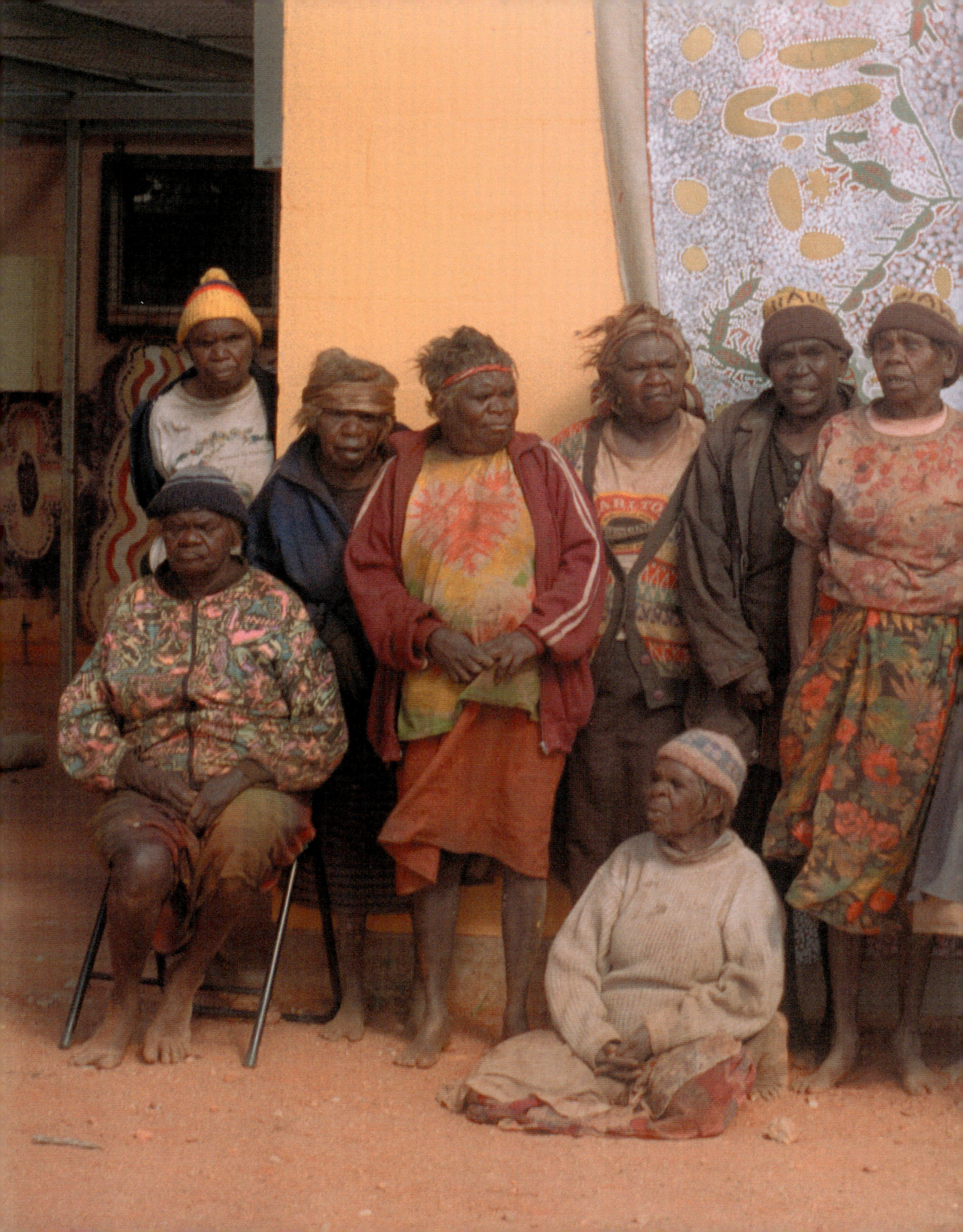

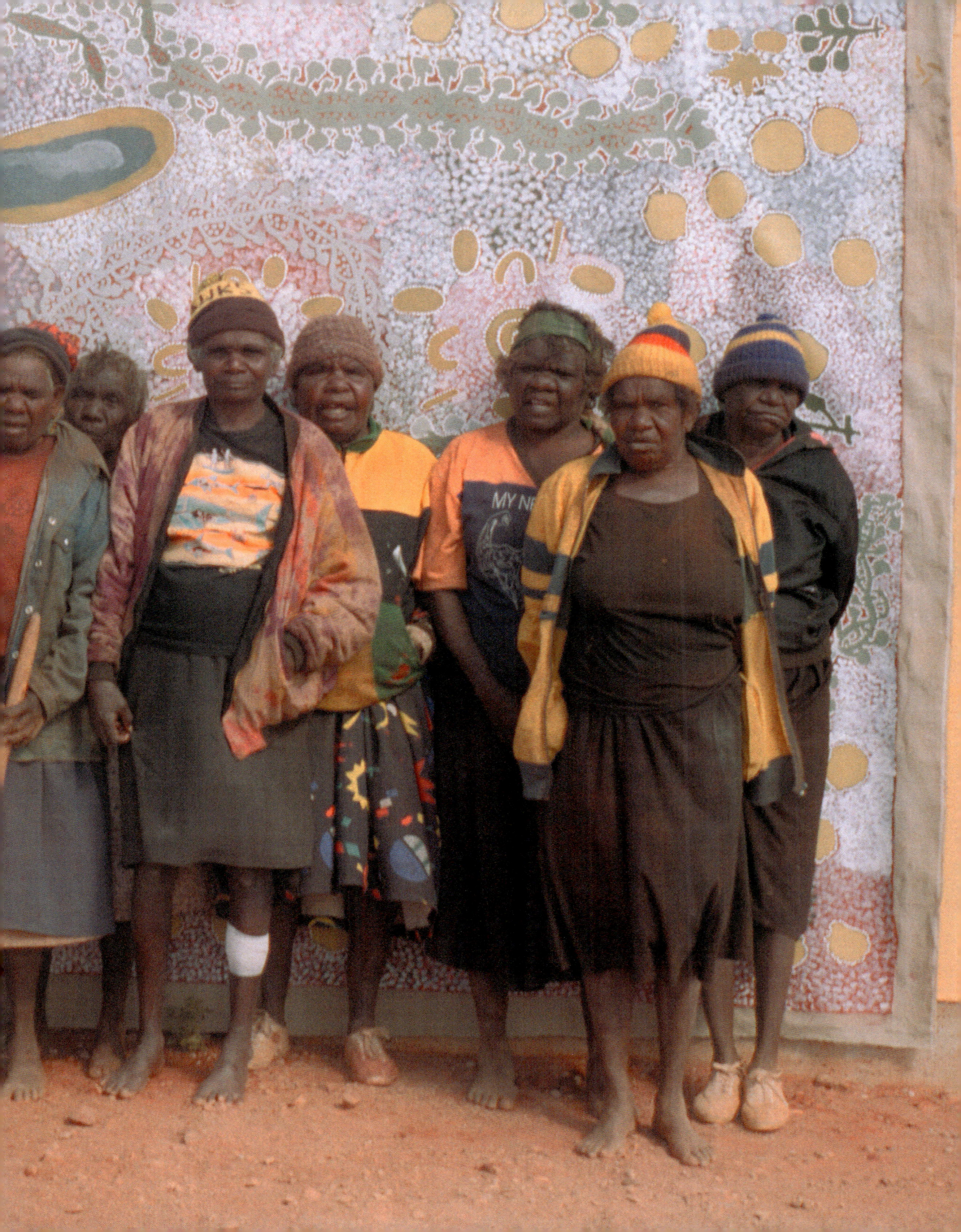

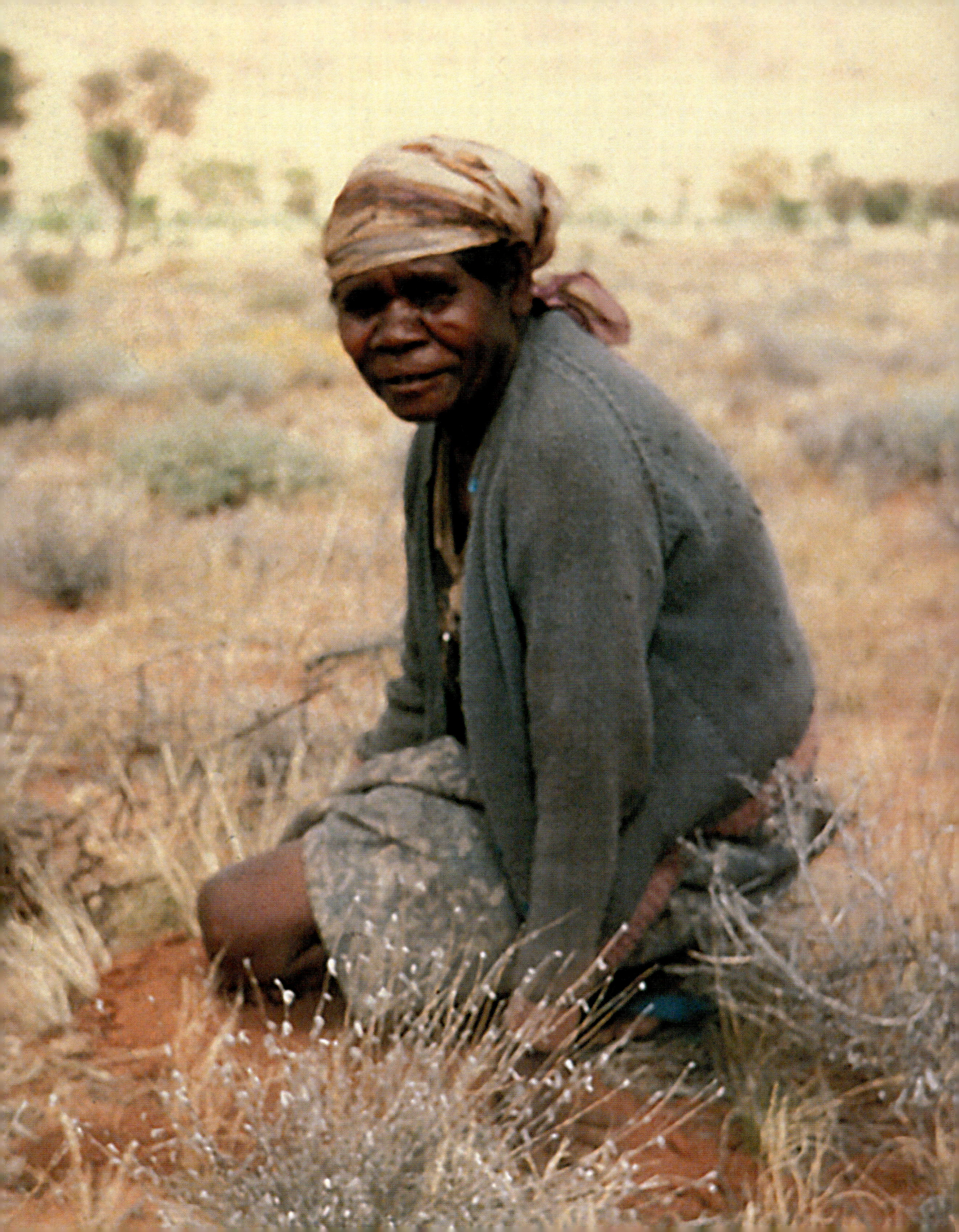

# Family Connections

## *Walungurru Women in Action*

### MARINA STROCCHI

I first visited Ikuntji (Haasts Bluff), a small, First Nations community three-hours' drive west of Mparntwe (Alice Springs), in January 1992. By August, Daisy Napaltjarri Jugadai and her sister, Ester, had secured a contract for me to work at a new, unused building, which was known as the Women's Centre. My job description was never defined; I was hired on a temporary wage from the community council with funds originally earmarked to employ an electrician. My partner, Wayne Eager, a painter, accompanied me on this trip. I had been working in Melbourne as a community-based artist and printmaker, and we both had experience in arts organizations and shared an interest in art from all epochs and cultures. The women and men of Ikuntji wanted to develop skills and needed the kind of logistical support that Papunya Tula Artists supplied artists in Papunya, Kiwirrkurra, and Walungurru. Once we set up the phone and bought some white goods, effectively establishing the center at Ikuntji, painting immediately became the main focus and had its own momentum. It was the one activity that everyone tried, and those who were particularly interested painted daily. Unlike the Papunya Tula company, there was no "money up front." Artists were paid only when their work was sold, which meant that anyone painting was doing so because they enjoyed the process; there was not a quid pro quo relationship with the work. Despite a keen interest in monitoring sales, at that point the act of painting was primary.

Papunya Tula Artists had ceased making field trips to Ikuntji in 1986, and Gideon Tjupurrula was the only Papunya Tula artist still living there in the early 1990s. The women who started painting at Ikuntji in 1992 were largely doing so for the first time. Gideon recommended painting immediately, and Long Tom Tjapanangka started within a year. There was sporadic interest from other men, too. There were also a few watercolor artists in the community, cowboys who had honed their skills in snatched moments while mustering cattle.

In December 1992, Magdalena Napaltjarri Multa and others informed me that I was going to Walungurru (Kintore) soon to dance. Magdalena and her husband, Joe Multa Tjakamarra, and their family took me on the four-hour drive further west to attend a ceremony for a family member, and Magdalena told me that I had to meet two old women when I got there. She referred to them as "the Napaltjarris."

Tjunkiya Napaltjarri at Walungurru
(Kintore), 1981. Photo by Bette Clark.

Soon after my arrival at Walungurru, the Napaltjar-ris—Tjunkiya and Wintjiya—showed me murals painted on the outside walls of the tiny Ngintaka Women's Centre (see figs. 5.1–5.4).[1] These murals were the paintings that I had dreamed of seeing: intense, bold, spontaneous and raw; they had qualities I had seen in some early Papunya Tula boards, the Yuendumu doors and the early Balgo work, and that I would later see in cave paintings in the south.[2] They had been done by the Napaltjarris and a group of older women who held their ancient cultural practices close and readily sang and danced, sharing their knowledge with openness and generosity. By my next visit, the murals had been painted over out of respect for one of the muralists, who had died.

It was common then for family members to assist their male relatives to finish paintings without being credited on the work. This included women, who often did the "infill" work with the artist. The main Tjukurrpa (Dreaming) design was done by the male artist, who "owned" the Tjukurrpa, while the painting and infill work was seen as secondary. There were some women on the Papunya Tula books at this time, doing their own paintings. However, these women lived at Papunya or Wati-yawanu (Mount Liebig).[3] In 1992, to my knowledge, Linda Syddick Napaltjarri was the only woman at Walungurru painting for Papunya Tula Artists.

One of the many people I met on this trip was Mantua Napanangka (fig. 4.1). Over the course of her several visits to Ikuntji, we became friends, and she told me she wanted me to come and work at Walungurru. Mantua was born in the 1940s at the Haasts Bluff Reserve. Established in 1940 by the Australian government, the reserve was created to secure land for displaced people and reduce the movement of desert people into the township of Mparntwe. Pastoral leases and prevailing racist attitudes had pushed Aboriginal people off their lands, disrupting their traditional ways of living. By 1950, over a thousand people from across the Central Desert were living at Ikuntji and searching for family and a sense of security.

Walungurru had a strong group of elders who had grown up *nikkity* (naked)[4] in the bush, with a deep connection to cultural practices and the land. Living on their Country with the knowledge of their ancestors made Walungurru a relatively cohesive community. The family connections through the Central Desert region are ancient and crisscross in every direction. The Walungurru women visited Ikuntji and saw that their family were

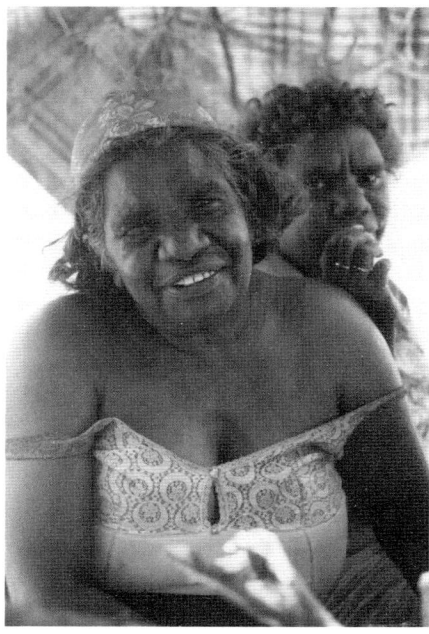

FIG. 4.1

Mantua Napanangka with Daisy Napaltjarri at New Store, 1992. Photo by Marina Strocchi.

painting. Tjunkiya and Wintjiya's son (they were co-wives) Turkey Tolson Tjupurrula, the chairperson of Papunya Tula, lived at Walungurru. Tjunkiya's daughter Mitjili Napurrula (married to Long Tom Tjapanangka) lived at Ikuntji and was painting. Tatali Nangala was married to Charlie Wartuma Tjungurrayi, a prominent Papunya Tula painter. After a death in the family, Tatali came to Ikuntji for an extended stay with her sister Narputta Nangala. She also wanted to paint and did a painting at the Ikuntji Women's Centre on this visit. Another friend and relative from Walungurru, Nyurapayia Nampitjinpa, also known as "Mrs. Bennett," told me that she wanted to paint, too. Her husband, John John Tjapangati ("Mr. Bennett"), had been a Papunya Tula painter in the past and started again in 1996.

We would see these Walungurru women at cultural events or sports festivals, and I got regular requests to "bring big canvas" to Walungurru. The women wanted to paint. The Ikuntji artists had become known locally as "winners." The artists were working toward a group exhibition at Gallery Gabrielle Pizzi, the leading art gallery for Indigenous Australian artists at the time, and had planned a trip to attend the opening in Melbourne in early 1994.

In April 1993, the Walungurru, Papunya and Wati-yawanu women met in Mparntwe with the Ikuntji women and me during a protest against the sale of take-away liquor at Glen Helen. The women from Walungurru told us that they would come to Ikuntji to ceremonially "sing" open the Women's Centre, and they invited women from

Papunya and Watiyawanu to join as well (fig. 4.2). The event happened organically, lasting for four days, from April 24 to 27. The men killed a cow to help with catering, and about fifty women were driven home in the cattle truck used for transporting people at that time.

In 1992, there were fewer art centers in the desert than exist today, and some in the arts community did not imagine that the Aboriginal painting movement would develop to the point that is has today. There was a lot of what I called "tourist art" and trinkets in the shops

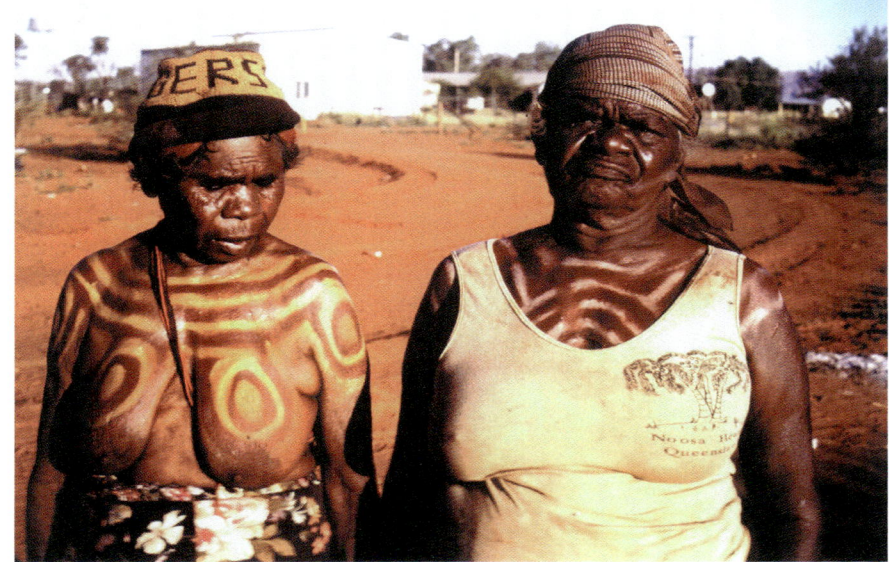

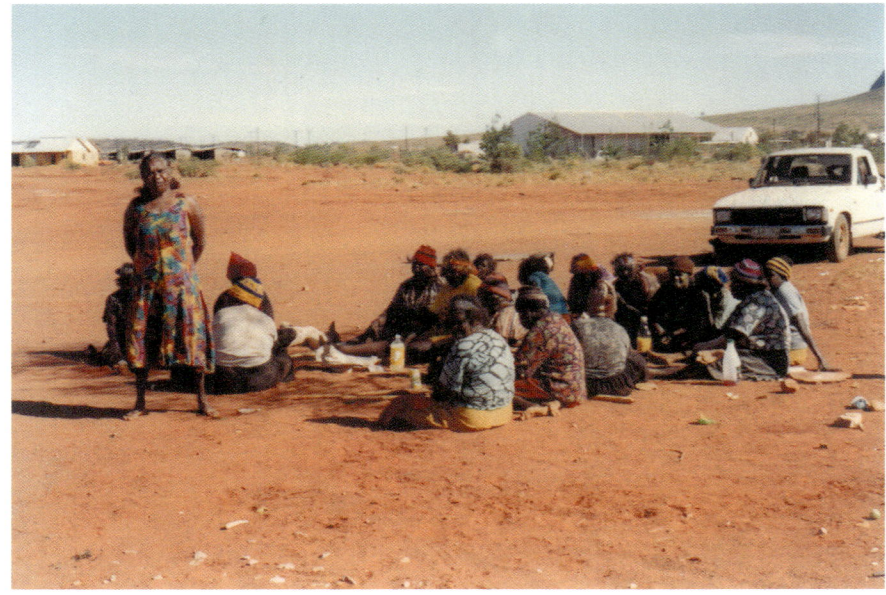

Tjunkiya Napaltjarri and Nyurapayia Nampitjinpa ("Mrs. Bennett") at Ikuntji (Haasts Bluff) in April 1993 after the ceremony to open the Ikuntji Women's Centre. Photo by Marina Strocchi.

Mantua Napapangka (standing) during a meeting at Walungurru, mid-1993. Photo by Marina Strocchi.

in Mparntwe. This work was decorative and craft based, which had its place, as it created work for a lot of people. A representative from Desart, the association representing desert art centers, suggested that there were "enough dot paintings" and I should get "them" to do *punu* (poker-worked sculpture).[5] I was not encouraged to develop painting, yet painting was what people were doing at Ikuntji and it was what the women from Walungurru wanted to do. At Ikuntji, they started painting as soon as we had the materials, and they became known as painters. Mantua, the Napaltjarris and Mrs. Bennett had tried unsuccessfully to get assistance to paint in the past. They recognized that I could provide the opportunity for which they had been waiting.

In September 1993, I went with Narputta Nangala, Mitjili Napurrula and Tjungupi Napaltjarri from Ikuntji to Kintore Sports Carnival. We had a meeting with a large group of women gathered under a lone tree at a place slightly out of the main traffic, not far from the football oval. The women launched into storytelling (fig. 4.3). They were discussing the Tjukurrpa to be painted, who was going to do what stories and how people were going to be grouped. They wanted "big canvas, really big canvas." The Walungurru women reminded me that they had danced for the Ikuntji Women's Centre opening and that the deal was that we would provide "big canvas" for them in return. At this meeting, Makinti Napanangka performed a mesmerizing solo dance with a *nulla nulla* (digging stick) to the accompaniment of the singers.[6]

Before we returned to Ikuntji to work out the logistics of a painting project, the women took us to Putjanya, a women's rockhole in the Kintore Range (fig. 4.4), where more dancing and more discussion ensued. The dance at Putjanya had been performed there for so many thousands of years that the friction of bare feet and *nulla nullas* had worn shiny tracks into the granite. Close to the waterhole were indentations in the rock, worn down after centuries of grinding *wangunu* (woollybutt grass seeds) to make bush damper (bread) in the outdoor kitchens of the past. On hearing their ancient stories and seeing this tangible link to the past, I was deeply moved by the significance of what was being shared with me, and I felt compelled to ensure that these women got what they wanted.

Over the first two years of my work at Ikuntji, I heard from people from outside the communities suggesting that the Pintupi men did not want the Pintupi women to paint. My experience led me to believe that this was not

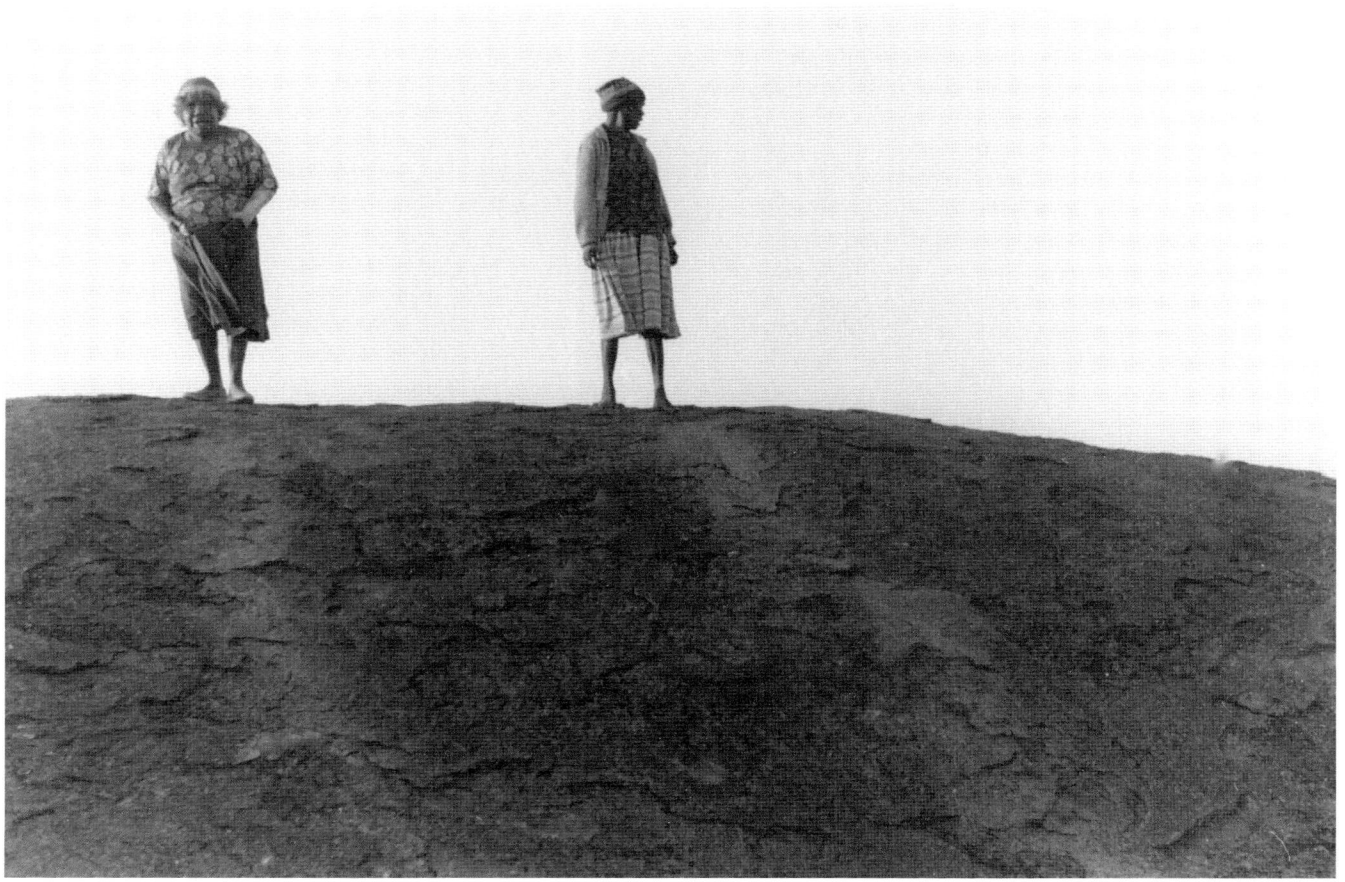

FIG. 4.4

Narputta Nangala and Tjunkiya Napaltjarri at Putjanya, 1993. Photo by Marina Strocchi.

true. Daphne Williams, longtime manager of Papunya Tula, quoted her predecessor Andrew Crocker's parting advice in September 1981, warning her about the women at Umbhangara outstation: "Don't start them off Daphne, you'll never contain it."[7] This was certainly true once the women began painting in earnest at Walungurru. In this era, Papunya Tula Artists only had a small group of men painting, and it was known as a men's company. But the concern about adding women painters—or any new men painters—was largely financial: the company paid for paintings as they were finished, before they were sold, making expansion a fiscal gamble.[8]

## A TURNING POINT FOR WOMEN'S PAINTING

At Ikuntji, we discussed the requests for assistance from the Walungurru women and decided that we should help them. They were family, and they had shown a keen interest to paint. It could be described as a cultural need, a modern take on cultural maintenance, which preoccupied these particular women. They had asked for help from their family. I approached John Wagner from the Aboriginal Development Unit of the Education

Department, and he agreed to fund the Walungurru women's painting project. The department was also funding my position at Ikuntji. (The Ikuntji Women's Centre was eventually funded as an art center through the Aboriginal and Torres Strait Islander Commission [ATSIC], and so the name was subsequently changed to the Ikuntji Art Centre late in 1994.) By June 1994, I had secured letters of support from Faye Bell, the manager of Papunya Tula Artists, the Kintore Community Council and the Haasts Bluff Community Council. Narputta Nangala, Eunice Napanangka and I packed our swags and the painting materials into the back of my pickup truck and headed west for Walungurru.

We organized a one-week women's painting workshop at Walungurru in 1994, which led to a two-week painting workshop at Ikuntji in 1995. At the time, we knew that the workshops were important but could not have imagined the explosion of women's painting they would catalyze. Hetti Perkins has argued that they "heralded perhaps the most radical shift in the Papunya Tula corpus," as women took the reins to "paint" a new chapter in the history of the company.[9] When we arrived at Walungurru for the first part of the project, the Kintore school principal told me that I "would never get the women to paint without paying them money." Money had not been mentioned as we planned the project, so his comment caught me off guard. I organized a pre-workshop meeting with the women to let them know that I did not have any cash handouts, that this was just a painting workshop. I was reassured that there was no expectation for money; they just wanted to paint. The women gathered at Walungurru to discuss the plans and decided to make camp on the other side of the Women's Mountain, Ngampagna. Vehicles from the police and Health Department were commandeered to help us get there, and on arrival, we cleared a camp, made windbreaks, secured camp sheets and rolled out the linen canvases.

We were at the campsite for five days. There were hours of animated discussion (all filmed) that seemed to be about who was to work on which linen and with whom, with the women splitting up according to skin groups and Tjukurrpa. I had prepared five linens for the week: three that were 3 meters square, and two smaller 1.5 × 3–meter canvases. A calmness came over the camp once everyone had settled into painting. The women were absorbed in singing and painting from dawn to dusk, working and reworking areas; each song cycle specific to the painting being worked on.

Yuyuya Nampitjinpa had spoken to her brother Ronnie Tjampitjinpa, a renowned Papunya Tula artist, to get permission to paint Ngurrapalangu. During a supply run into Walungurru, I stopped for a cup of tea with the local doctor and his wife, and Ronnie joined us. He proudly told me of his positive discussion with Yuyuya

regarding the Nampitjinpas' painting of the site Ngurra-palangu. It was Yuyuya's country through her late father, Minpuru, and his brother, Uta Uta Tjangala, who was also a prominent Papunya Tula artist (see plate 43). Inyuwa Nampitjinpa, who was recovering from eye surgery at the time, sat with the Nampitjinpas but did not paint, although she would later establish a formidable reputation as an artist for Papunya Tula. Inkitjili Nampitjinpa, who was Mantua's mother and Alice Nampitjinpa's older sister, also camped with us but did not paint, though she started later with both Papunya Tula and Ikuntji Art Centre. The Nampitjinpa painting started with an enormous "swamp," a flat, black shape surrounded by some figures representing the family and motifs representing vegetation (fig. 4.5).[10] It was heavily layered with additions and subtractions made until the last hours. The swamp was lost beneath the finished painting, but it was there, underlying the work. Even though it was not visible, the knowledge of it was there, and the artists referred to it as being there.

Tatali and Narputta were the leaders of the Nangala painting. Tjunkiya and Wintjiya were the leaders of the Napaltjarri canvas (fig. 4.6). Though Wintjiya's eyesight prohibited her from painting at that time, she sat on the edge of the linen issuing authoritative instructions. Makinti Napanangka grabbed a big brush in the first hour and was keen to start painting. She was diminutive and very determined. She sat in the middle of a linen and painted a row of circles representing the salt lake Kaakurutintjinya. She was considered too old to paint, and her efforts were not taken seriously by the other women, but time was on her side. She painted with diminished eyesight for the first three years of her career, finally having her cataracts removed in 1999. Her daily routine of painting led to a phenomenal body of work and international recognition. The women were awake at the crack of dawn, setting the fires, boiling billycans to make tea, singing, dancing and mixing up paint. "Work 'em up, work 'em up," Narputta called out like a coach. It was remarkable to watch the canvases develop. Narputta and Eunice acted as the bosses, helping with ideas and solutions; they showed the other women the "feathering" technique that helped to unify these collaborative works.

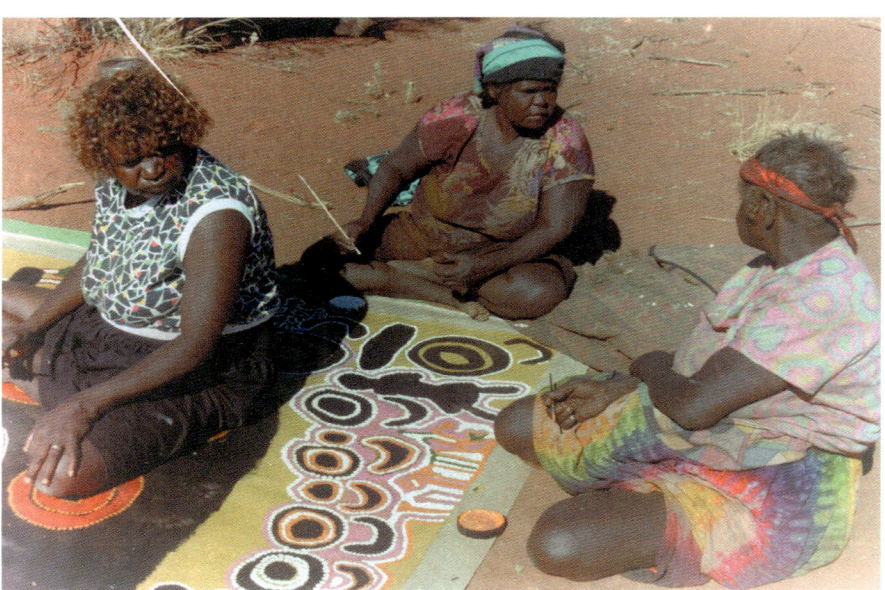

FIG. 4.5

Yuyuya Nampitjinpa, Kayi Kayi Nampitjinpa and Nyurapayia Nampitjinpa at the Walungurru (Kintore) painting camp, 1994. Photo By Marina Strocchi.

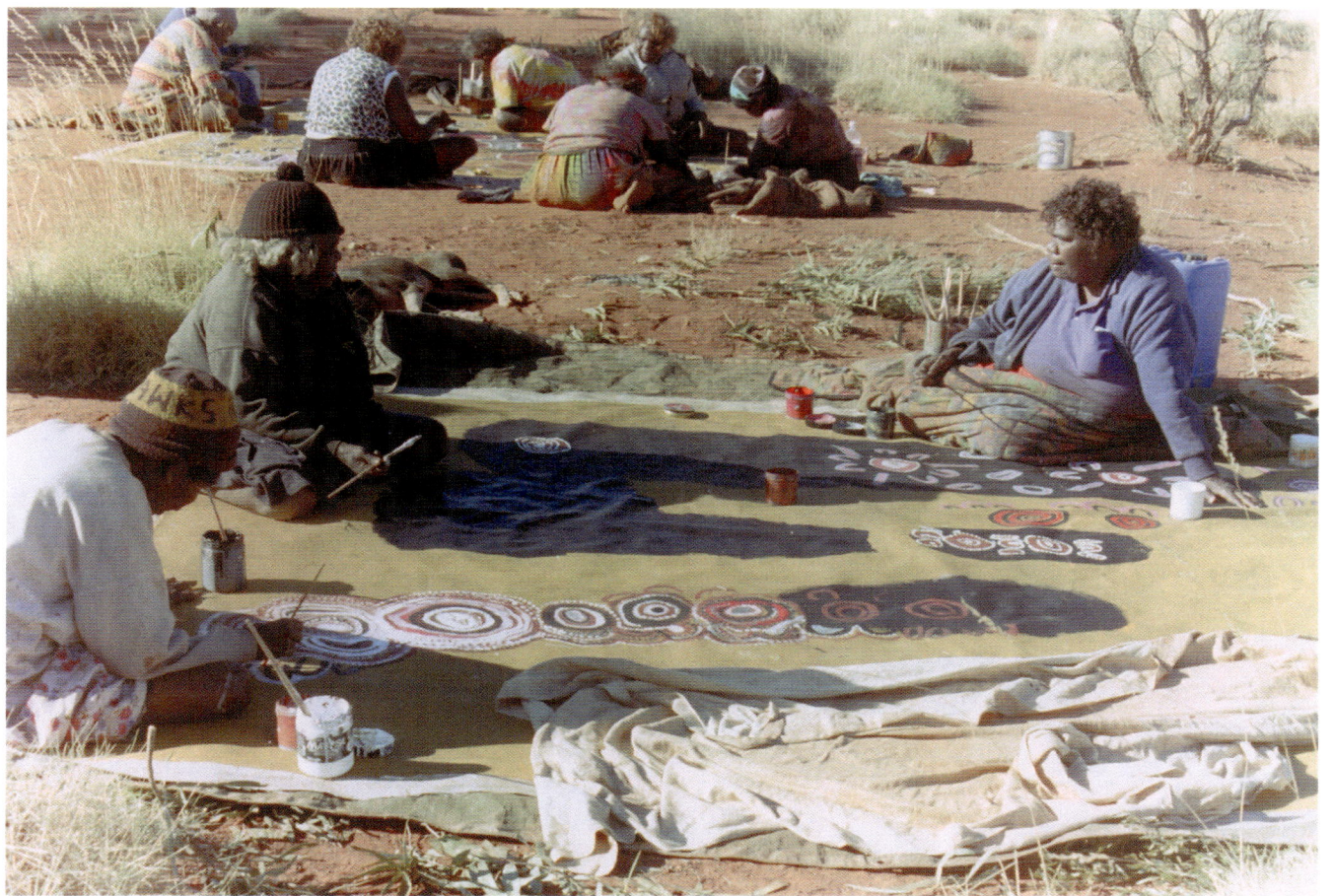

FIG. 4.6

Tjunkiya Naplatjarri (left) works on the Napaltjarri canvas, while the Nampitjinpas work in the background at the Walungurru (Kintore) painting camp 1994. Photo by Marina Strocchi.

Individuals were unbothered if someone else painted over their work with a big brush. Up to eight people at a time were working on any painting. The paintings were resolved on the last day when they magically became unified—strong works sharing a visual softness with the surrounding vegetation and dawn and dusk light.

After a full week at the Women's Centre Outstation Bush Camp, as it became known, we rolled our swags and canvases and returned to Walungurru. Rather than take the paintings to Mparntwe to "change" them for cash, as the women had discussed, I suggested that we try to have an exhibition so that a wider audience could see them. I stressed that museums and art galleries would be interested in these works.

We photographed the works in the dusty Walungurru wind. During a break, Turkey Tolson came and sat down next to me. A man of few words, he said, "Canvas palya," meaning, "Good paintings." That exchange gave the project an endorsement from the person who had the most authority to do so. We had the support of the men from Walungurru—they had made that clear. After we rolled up the five linens, I placed them in the roof cavity of the

Ngintaka Women's Centre, where the sacred ceremonial objects were kept. The women were to guard them closely and wait for a response from the outside world. Judith Ryan from the National Gallery of Victoria was immediately interested in the works. Another swift response came from Doreen Mellor at Tandanya National Aboriginal Cultural Institute in Adelaide, who suggested a big exhibition the following year, so we planned the second painting camp for April 1995, this time at Ikuntji, to prepare more works.

Not long after the Walungurru painting camp, Tjunkiya, Wintjiya, Pinta Pinta Tjapanangka and Benny Tjapaltjarri traveled to Mparntwe on an army plane for eye surgery to have their advanced cataracts removed. It was still winter, and they came back clad in retro 1970s, double-breasted vinyl jackets and wraparound sunglasses, looking like a Pintupi version of the Mod Squad. They were rejuvenated, and it was a moment of great joy in the community. They were strong, older individuals with a second lease on life and could now paint for the rest of their active days.

Ten months later, it was the Walungurru women's turn to visit Ikuntji for a two-week painting camp. Riley Major Tjangala, the brother of Narputta and Tatali Nangala, kindly drove the women to Ikuntji in the football team's new bus, and they made camp at the back of the Women's Centre; the swags were lined up with little fires in between. The intention of the second half of the project was to create smaller paintings by individuals.

One night, I filmed Nyurapayia putting the finishing touches to a 1.5 × 3–meter work that Makinti had also worked on, declaring, "*Yuwa* [Yes], finished." At nine o'clock the following morning, I arrived to find the whole canvas reworked and wet, "Finished properly." While at Ikuntji, Nyurapayia pulled a small, neatly folded, grubby canvas from her handbag. She unfolded it to reveal a four-foot squarish, roughly painted cacophony of colossal witchetty grubs, lizards, snakes and honey ants on the cheap cotton duck canvas sold in community stores. It had been over-painted many times with low-grade paints. I cleaned it up and sold it to the schoolteachers on her behalf.

We were missing three women, who would come to be known as the "*ninu* mob," as they had gone off for five days with the Conservation Department to look for *ninu* (bilby), an endangered marsupial bandicoot. After this trip, they arrived at Ikuntji in the late evening and joined in the singing and dancing. They woke up the next day to go hunting for sand goannas, came back and painted late into the night. This was impressive stamina for women in their seventies. Tjunkiya and Wintjiya Napaltjarri were making the most of their eyesight after the cataract surgery and did a three-meter-long, collaborative work, as well as a number of smaller paintings (see fig 5.5). Most of the women involved with this project were doing the first

paintings of their Tjukurrpa. They were middle aged to elderly at the time, with husbands, brothers or sons who were, or had been, Papunya Tula artists. They were active "dancing women," hunting and gathering bush tucker as often as they could, and they were always ready to launch into Tjukurrpa.

During the workshop at Ikuntji, the washing machine and shower were in constant use. We had supplies of washing powder, soap and towels, and our guests made good use of the amenities. Such resources were scarce at Walungurru. There was a festive atmosphere. The electric hotplates on the stove became fry pans, and the oven became a barbecue. It was mayhem. The energy and enthusiasm to paint was inspiring to me then, and over the years it never waned. Painting was a way for people to keep the Tjukurrpa first and foremost in their daily lives. Painting, singing and telling Tjukurrpa stories became the daily trifecta. Catastrophes occur regularly in the lives of this group of First Nations people. There is a therapeutic benefit of getting into the zone of the work. The act of painting helps people process trauma; it creates mental space to step back and have a moment of reprieve. The income generated from paintings is much needed and welcomed, but the social value of painting, often done in a communal setting, supplements the gross shortfall in mental health services.

The exhibition of works from the painting camps was booked for June 1995 at Tandanya. Altogether, there were forty-four works, including sixteen works on paper and the five big linens from the Walungurru camp.[11] The trip to Adelaide was more mayhem, fifteen women and one child. We took over the ground floor of the Adelaide Backpackers hostel. Fresh fruit was laid out every morning: oranges, bananas and apples from the markets nearby. The women squirreled it all away under their beanies, in their brassieres, in skirt pockets and handbags. Back in the dorm, there were more stashes under pillows and at the bottom of the bedclothes and under mattresses. They wanted to take the caretaker back to Walungurru with them, as he had been so kind and accommodating.

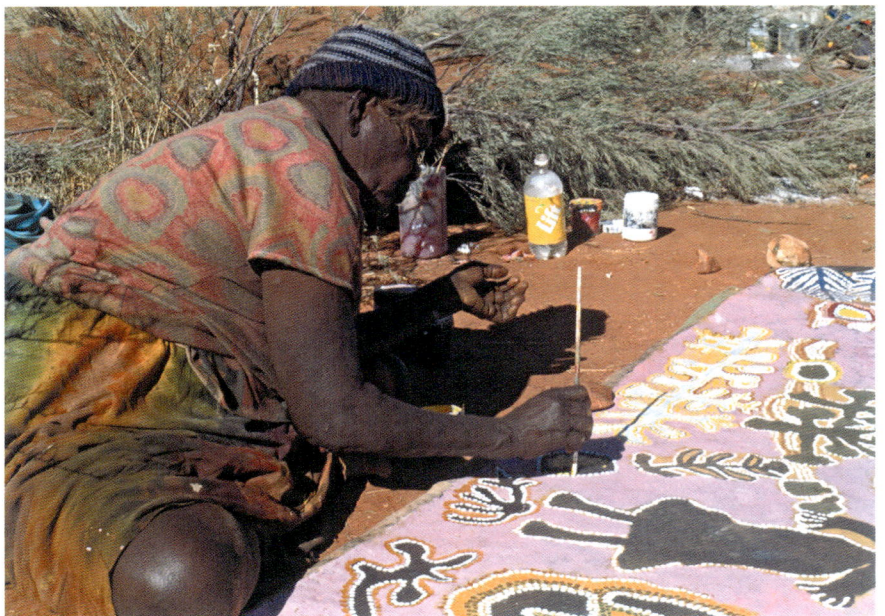

FIG. 4.7

Nyurapayia Nampitjinpa ("Mrs. Bennett") painting on the Ngurrapalangu canvas for the Haasts Bluff / Kintore Canvas Project, Walungurru painting workshop, June 1994. Photo by Marina Strocchi.

They spent the day of the opening preparing, which entailed hours of singing and body painting in front of the main paintings, honoring these works with the songs and dances that are associated with the Tjukurrpa represented in them. The women danced for their Tjukurrpa in groups of three, while the singers sat off to the side. Some singers danced, too. Little Alkalita, the young child traveling with us, was brought into the dancing as well.

For our return trip, we had forty-seven pieces of luggage that needed their own bus. At the check-in, the flight attendant started to speak about excess baggage but had second thoughts and hurried us on and out of the way.

All the paintings from the 1994 workshop sold to major collections, either from the Tandanya exhibition or shortly afterward. The Kelton Foundation USA purchased *Kaaku-rutintjinya* by Tatali Nangala, Narputta Nangala, Loline Nungurrayi and Pantjia Nungurrayi. The Campbelltown Regional Gallery bought the other *Kaakurutintjinya* by Makinti Napanangka, Eunice Napanangka and Narputta Nangala. The National Gallery of Victoria purchased one of the large canvases by the Napaltjarris from the exhibition and later received *Ngurrapalangu* as a gift from a private donor; the other large work went to the University of Tasmania. I had kept a roll of the painters who had worked on all the collaborative works and divided up the payments for distribution through the Ikuntji Art Centre. The women from that project now rank among the leading women painters from Papunya Tula Artists.

Mantua's friendly pressure made this project happen, and it was just in time. Tragically, not long after the Adelaide exhibition, we got bad news from Walungurru. Mantua had died of heart attack after hearing that her daughter, Maureen, was in intensive care in Adelaide. Maureen had traveled to Adelaide to accompany her nephew, Mantua's grandson, who was returning for a prosthesis after having a leg amputated the year before. Maureen died in ICU, and someone else was sent to bring back the boy.

Ten months after the exhibition, in April 1996, Papunya Tula Artists began providing the women of Walungurru with painting materials.[12] The exhibition had proven that there was a wide and deep interest in their work, which was sophisticated and evolved both culturally and aesthetically. This decision to expand may have been crucial to the continuation of the company, as many of the original male painters had died, were ailing or were also painting "privately."[13] This era was a time of change all around. Papunya Tula Artists were also reengaging men who had stopped painting and encouraging new talent, both men and women. At this time, the record-breaking sales of the early boards focused art world interest on the art from this area. The communities in the Anangu Pitjantjajara Yankunytjatjara Lands and the Western Desert, where *punu*, batik and decorative painting had predominated in the past, began to take painting more seriously.

Wayne Eager was hired as a fieldworker with Paul Sweeney (who had commenced field work in October 1995). At the request of Daphne Williams, as part of his duties, Wayne was tasked with engaging the women at Walungurru, whom he knew well by now. This led to the question of women painting at Kiwirrkurra, fulfilling Andrew Crocker's prediction that once the women got started painting, there would be no stopping them. Wayne remembers that Daphne instructed him to speak to Brandy Tjungurrayi or Kanya Tjapangati (two senior cultural men and Papunya Tula artists) to see what they thought of women painting at Kiwirrkurra. Kanya didn't answer immediately but came into the art shed the next morning and said yes, it was good for the women to paint, but did it mean that the men would have to stop?[14] Not at all.

## NOTES

1. Ngintaka, or *perentie* (monitor lizard), refers to the ancestral being who was active at one of the hills in the location of the community.

2. In 1984, a group of Warlpiri elders painted the doors of the Yuendumu School to prevent vandalism and encourage respect for traditional culture. See Philip Jones with Warlukurlangu Artists, *Behind the Doors: An Art History from Yuendumu* (Adelaide: South Australian Museum in association with Wakefield Press, 2014). Around the same time, a group of men and women at Wirrimanu (Balgo) also began painting their Tjukurrpa on canvas. See Jacqueline Healy, *Warlayirti: The Art of Balgo* (Melbourne: RMIT Gallery, 2014); and John Carty, "Style in Balgo Art," Ph.D. thesis (Canberra: Australian National University, 2011). The painting movements that emerged at both Yuendumu and Balgo were characterized by their use of bright color and looser brushwork than the more austere paintings being produced by artists at Papunya Tula at that time.

3. These included Daisy Leura Nakamarra, Fabrianne Peterson Nampitjinpa, Gladys Napanangka, Eunice Napangardi, Pansy Napangardi, and Narpula Scobie Napurrula.

4. People often used this term to define the time before contact. Some alternatives include "before flour and oranges," "before trousers" and "before whitefellas."

5. *Punu* means "wood" in Pitjantjatjara; it also refers to intricate hot-poker-work designs on wooden sculptures.

6. A *nulla nulla* is a long, straight stick made from mulga wood used in a ceremonial context, as a walking stick, a tool or a weapon. They are known as *kuturu* or *wana* in Pintupi.

7. Andrew Crocker, quoted in Daphne Williams and Hetti Perkins, "Company Business: Daphne Williams and the Papunya Tula Artists Company," in *Papunya Tula: Genesis and Genius*, ed. Hetti Perkins and Hannah Fink (Sydney: Art Gallery of New South Wales, 2000), 227.

8. For an extended discussion of the economic complexities of the desert painting movement, see Fred Myers, *Painting Culture: The Making of an Aboriginal High Art* (Durham, NC: Duke University Press, 2002).

9. Hetti Perkins, "A Gift from the Heart," in *Marking the Infinite: Contemporary Women Artists from Aboriginal Australia*, ed. Henry F. Skerritt (Reno and Munich: Nevada Museum of Art and Prestel, 2016), 22–23.

10. The term "swamp" refers to a temporary, extended, open body of water, often a claypan. This is one of the main geographic features of Ngurrapalangu.

11. *Minyma Tjukurrpa: Kintore / Haasts Bluff Canvas Project*, June 10–August 13, 1995, Tandanya National Aboriginal Cultural Institute, Adelaide. See Marina Strocchi, *Minyma Tjukurrpa: Kintore / Haast's Bluff Canvas Project* (Adelaide: Tandanya National Aboriginal Cultural Institute, 1995). The complete list of women who painted in one or both workshops and whose work was exhibited at Tandanya includes: Alice Nampitjinpa, Katarra Nampitjinpa, Kayi Kayi Nampitjinpa, Nyurapayia Nampitjinpa ("Mrs. Bennett"), Yuyuya Nampitjinpa, Narputta Nangala, Sharon Nangala, Tatali Nangala, Eileen Napaltjarri, Tjunkiya Napaltjarri, Wintjiya Napaltjarri, Anmanari Napanangka, Eunice Napanangka, Makinti Napanangka, Mantua Napanangka, Josephine Napurrula, Mitjili Napurrula, Ningurra Napurrula, Loline Nungurrayi, and Pantjiya Nungurrayi.

12. They became registered Papunya Tula painters, which meant that their works were catalogued and they were looked after by the company. The artists signed paperwork for this process. Sometime in the months prior to Wayne Eager commencing as a fieldworker, Jennifer Taylor (who, at the time, was joint manager of Papunya Tula with Janis Stanton) handed out some 8 × 10–inch canvas boards to some women at Walungurru, which were not catalogued.

13. This term refers to paintings done by the artists outside of their relationship to Papunya Tula, for sale to private dealers or other buyers.

14. Kanya's concerns were economic rather than cultural. As Papunya Tula was providing so few canvases to artists at that time, he did not think it would be possible for everyone to paint. The market for Aboriginal paintings had declined following the 1987 financial crash. In addition, the company had suffered serious financial losses from the fallout of a bad gallery relationship in the United States. Daphne Williams responded with a management strategy of consolidation, keeping production low and under tight control. It was only following Sotheby's 1997 Melbourne auction of "Important Aboriginal Art," when early boards from Papunya began setting record prices, that the market for Papunya Tula paintings returned to its former strength.

# THE MARRAPINTI WOMEN'S CAMP

Our Women's Camp at Marrapinti was very special, I loved it. Marrapinti was my grandmother's Tjukurrpa. It's Tjukurrpa for women only.

Lots of people came—from the health service, the Ngaanyatjarra Pitjantjatjara Yankunytjatjara council, rangers and the ladies from Kiwirrkurra. We camped around the fire, right in the cave at the ancestral Women's site at Marrapinti. We had old people there with us teaching us, telling us about the songlines, teaching us singing and telling us stories.

I cried the first time I heard Mantua Nangala telling me a story about my grandmothers and other old ladies, and how they lived in the past. Passing onto the young ones so we can keep carrying on Tjukurrpa, stories from our elders and from our past.

We were also doing activities, like making sandals for the *tjina* [foot] from the *taliwanti* plant [*Crotolaria cunninghamii*], so they could walk around on the hot sand. We were learning about our traditional culture and hunting skills, learning Tjukurrpa, stories from our ancestors. It's good to have young people with the elders. They are passing stories on to us so we can keep passing them on to the younger generations. High-school girls were there and young mothers, too, with the old people showing us how they lived in the past.

This Tjukurrpa is only for the women. It's the story of the young women having a ceremony with that nose bone (also called *marrapinti*), as they are changing from girls to proper women. That's the Tjukurrpa for Marrapinti. Women travel to Marrapinti [plates 89, 90], then after that ceremony they go to Ngaminya to make the *kampurarrpa* [wild raisin] balls [plates 92, 93], then all the way to Wirrulnga [plate 94] to have their babies, then east to the rocks where they smoke the babies, then they go all the way to the lake [Wilkinkarra, plate 95].

I know this story. My mother and my grandmother used to tell me, when I was little. Nanu, my mother's mother. She left me when I was six years old. But she told me that story. But now my mother's teaching me, and the other ladies. So, it's time for me to keep the culture and keep learning more and more so I can pass it on.

Dancing was very special. I was so happy. I did my special dance for my grandmother. It was the first time for me. I was crying, and I felt so proud. Mantua passed the dance on to me, because we are same skin [Nangala/Napurrula]. My heart felt so special the first time I did it. After I did it, I slept, and in that dream the old ladies came to me. I saw Monica Nangala's mother and my grandmothers. They came to me in my sleep and told me, "It's your turn. It's yours now. You keep it, the culture, you can keep passing it on." And I cried when I saw them.

Next day, I wanted to talk to the elders. I spoke to Mantua first and I told her how I saw the old ladies, and I spoke to Monica about seeing her mother. I cried, and they all felt so happy when I told them about my dream. They believed me and they were so happy, they were all in tears. Because of that, everyone had to dance.

We enjoyed our trip. Dancing was *palya lingku* [really good]. There was so much laughter and fun, just the girls having fun. *Yuwa* [yes]. We all had a big smile. Getting embarrassed, but we all did it. It is very special, and I know that it was special to all the ladies, all the *minyma tjuta*. Tjukurrpa goes to all the women in other communities.

My mum, Yukultji Napangati, paints the Marrapinti story [plates 91, 120]. And I've started painting it too. I tell the story for Marrapinti because of my grandmothers—that's their Tjukurrpa, that's their Dreaming. It's just for the women.

—JODIE NAPURRULA WARD IN CONVERSATION
WITH RACHEL PALTRIDGE

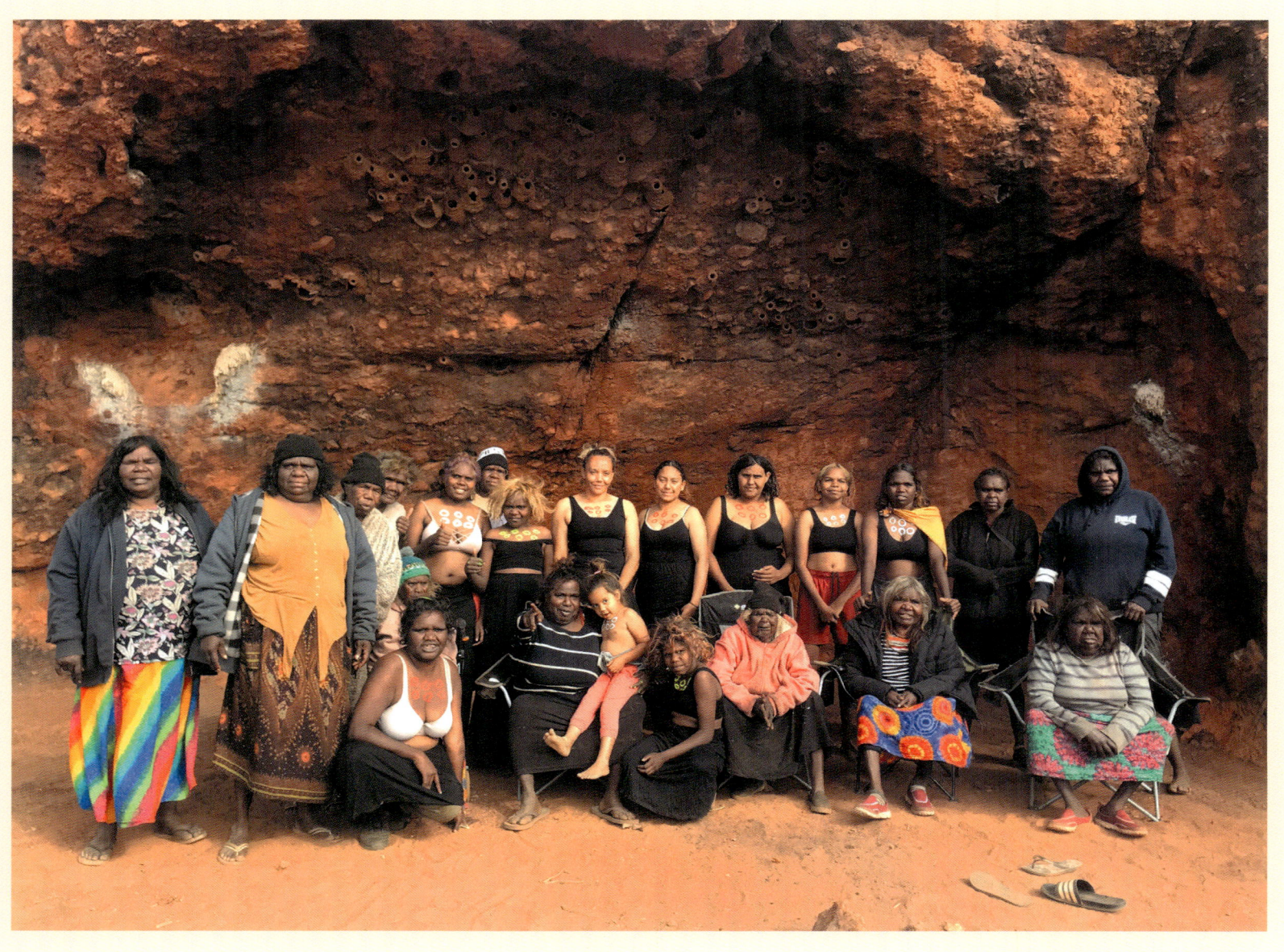

Kiwirrkurra Women's Culture and Health Camp at Marrapinti, May 2021. Photo by Rachel Paltridge, courtesy of the Tjamu Tjamu Aboriginal Corporation.

The Kiwirrkurra Indigenous Protected Area program supports Kiwirrkurra people to look after Country, culture and community. Rangers work hard to manage fire and feral animals to promote and protect their bush foods, water sources and threatened species. Also integral to the program is mapping cultural sites, recording Tjukurrpa stories and ensuring that traditional skills and knowledge are being preserved and passed on to younger generations, in part through separate men's and women's culture camps held each year.

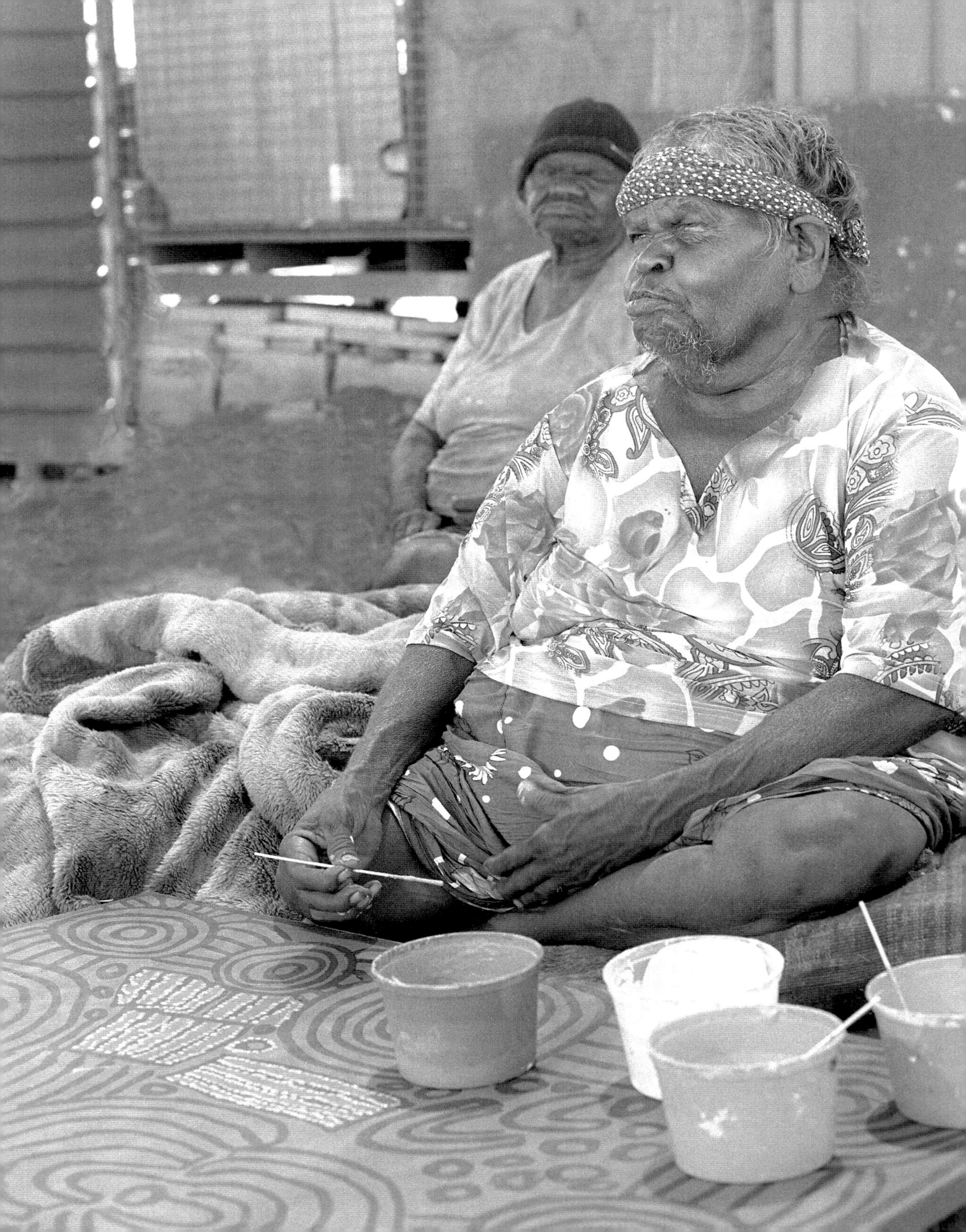

# Following
# Kungka Kutjarra

CARA PINCHBECK

The small community of Walungurru (Kintore) is nestled between two hills—together known as Puli Kutjarra. The smaller of these is known by locals as the Women's Mountain, not simply because it is an important site for women's ceremonies, but also in reference to the Kungka Kutjarra—two ancestral women who traveled across Country in the Tjukurrpa (Dreaming) and remain as an animating presence within the landscape.[1] These women are integral to the past, present and future—to the cyclical understandings of time that inform Aboriginal worldviews. Kungka Kutjarra are of particular importance to women, and knowledge of their travels and actions informs understandings of Country. While there are areas of the Women's Mountain where men are permitted to visit—and it has long been the subject of many male Pintupi artists such as Charlie Wartuma Tjungurrayi, Turkey Tolson Tjupurrula and Shorty Lungkarta Tjungurrayi—women hold responsibility for the mountain. In 1994, the Women's Mountain was chosen as the site for Pintupi women to gather and paint, giving rise to an explosion of new painters whose work would define Papunya Tula Artists over the next two decades.[2]

For these artists, painting is not some whimsical form of expression. It is deeply rooted in the interconnected nature of people and place, and a responsibility to uphold one's cultural inheritance and knowledge. For women to come together to paint alongside the Kungka Kutjarra Tjukurrpa sites was pertinent; it lay culturally appropriate foundations for what has become a phenomenal painting movement. This movement did not miraculously materialize. It was very much informed by the lives of the older generation of women painters and their family connections, particularly to men who had begun painting for Papunya Tula Artists some two decades earlier. And within the movement, there are diverse forms of personal expression as artists have refined and established distinct styles and as the younger generation has sought its own approach. Consideration of the lives and experiences of select individuals among the Pintupi women painters provides nuanced insight into this movement and the dynamic paintings that are at its core.

Tatali Nangala played a vital role in the 1994 workshop at Walungurru and began painting for Papunya Tula Artists in May 1996. She was a senior leader who, at the time,

Walangkura Napanangka (Uta Uta's Widow) with Nyurapayia Nampitjinpa (in back) at Walungurru, 2007. Photo by Greg Weight.

held ceremonial responsibilities due to her close cultural ties to the area. Tatali was born at the Kungka Kutjarra rockhole at the Women's Mountain and spent her early years living on Country, learning of and retracing the travels of the women who gave her birth site its name, and following in the footsteps of generations of her family. In painting *Kungka Kutjarra Tjukurrpa* (*Two Women Dreaming*) (1996, plate 63), Tatali pays homage to this site and these women, enlivening their presence through a cluster of vibrant roundels that oscillate on the canvas. The work confidently captures a Tjukurrpa of extreme personal importance through energized visual qualities, highlighting that these women are not something of the past: they remain as a sentient presence within the landscape.

While this painting is among Tatali's earliest works, art had been very much a part of her life for the preceding two decades. Her husband was the renowned artist Charlie Wartuma Tjungurrayi, who painted consistently from 1971 to 1999. As a young woman, Tatali walked hundreds of miles eastward with her family from their home Country around Walungurru to Ikuntji (Haasts Bluff), a ration depot run by missionaries where many of their Pintupi relatives had taken up residence. It was here that she married Wartuma, a Pintupi man who had long engaged with non-Aboriginal people. They started a family at Ikuntji, where six of their seven children were born, including the now well-known artist Eileen Napaltjarri.[3]

Along with other Pintupi, Tatali, Wartuma and their young family moved further north to Papunya following its establishment in 1959. Many had wanted to remain at Ikuntji, but a lack of permanent fresh water and will from the government to provide such a necessary resource made this difficult. Papunya was a government settlement designed with the intention of centralizing and assimilating Aboriginal people from the surrounding regions. Compliance to European norms was central to the settlement's operations in its early years. Children were not permitted to speak their own languages at school, and daily life was punctuated by meals in a communal canteen. This dining experience would have been in stark contrast to Eileen's memories of "getting *purrarra* (honey ants) and *katati* (witchetty grubs)" with her parents.[4] The government control that was exerted over Indigenous people's lives at Papunya no doubt contributed to her father, Wartuma, famously stating, "If I don't paint this story some whitefella might come and steal my country."[5]

Wartuma was an integral member of the group of men who began painting at Papunya in 1971 and was a founding member of the Papunya Tula Artists company. His cross-cultural experience saw him take a central role in many negotiations as he and his peers employed painting as a means of maintaining culture, remembering Tjukurrpa and allaying their longing for home.[6] Tatali observed these events and the subsequent outpouring of painting activity that became central to the lives of many in Papunya and then at the community of Walungurru, as families were able to return to their home Country after the new settlement's establishment in 1981.

Like her female peers, alongside whom she began painting in the 1990s, Tatali would have been aware of the agency that came with being an artist. Her husband was honored with a retrospective exhibition that toured to four Australian states in 1986. He had traveled to England and Hong Kong in 1982 with Andrew Crocker, then serving as the Papunya Tula manager, and performed *Nightsea Crossing / Conjunction* with Marina Abramović, Ulay and Ngawang Soepa Lueyar at Sonesta Koepelzaa, Amsterdam in 1983. While few of his fellow artists traveled so extensively, numerous men at Walungurru forged successful artistic careers and were provided with a variety of opportunities following increased market interest in their works beginning in the mid-1980s.

In the early 1990s, Tatali saw her sister, Narputta Nangala, painting when visiting her in Ikuntji. Women at Ikuntji had begun painting sporadically throughout the 1980s, and in August of 1992, their dream of having their own art center was realized with the establishment of Ikuntji Women's Centre. While it had a wide-ranging remit, it became known as a place where women could paint. A large cultural event marked the official opening of the center in April 1993, and given the close family ties between the communities, Tatali and other women from Walungurru traveled to Ikuntji to join in four days and nights of celebratory singing and dancing. Marina Strocchi, the former manager of the center, has recalled that the Walungurru women felt their involvement required reciprocity in the form of large canvasses on which they could paint.[7]

Some painting was already evident in Walungurru in 1992, with a small mural present on the wall of the Ngintaka Women's Centre (figs. 5.1–5.4). In seeing this, one cannot help but be reminded of the mural painted by men on the wall of Papunya School in 1971, which

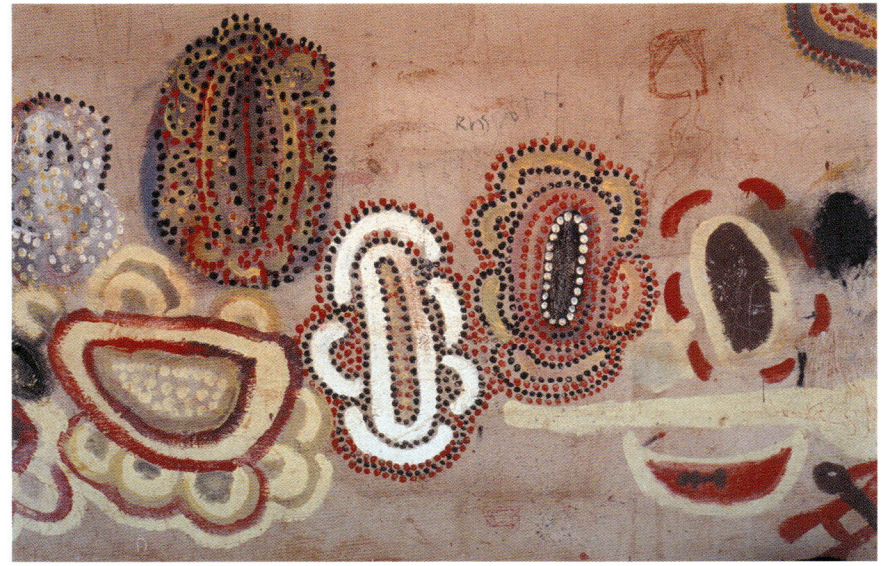

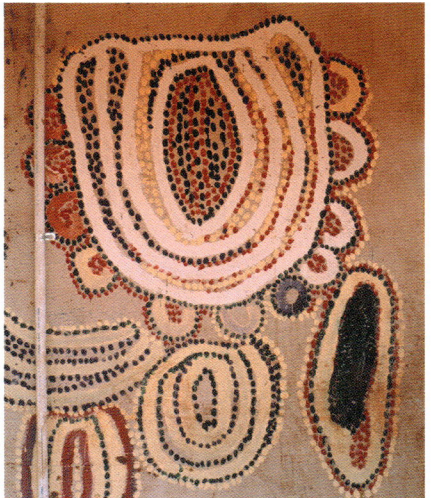
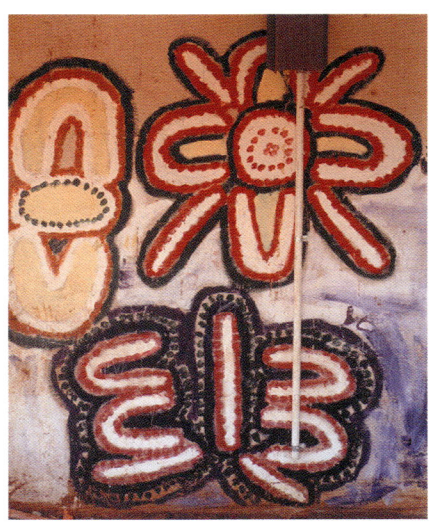

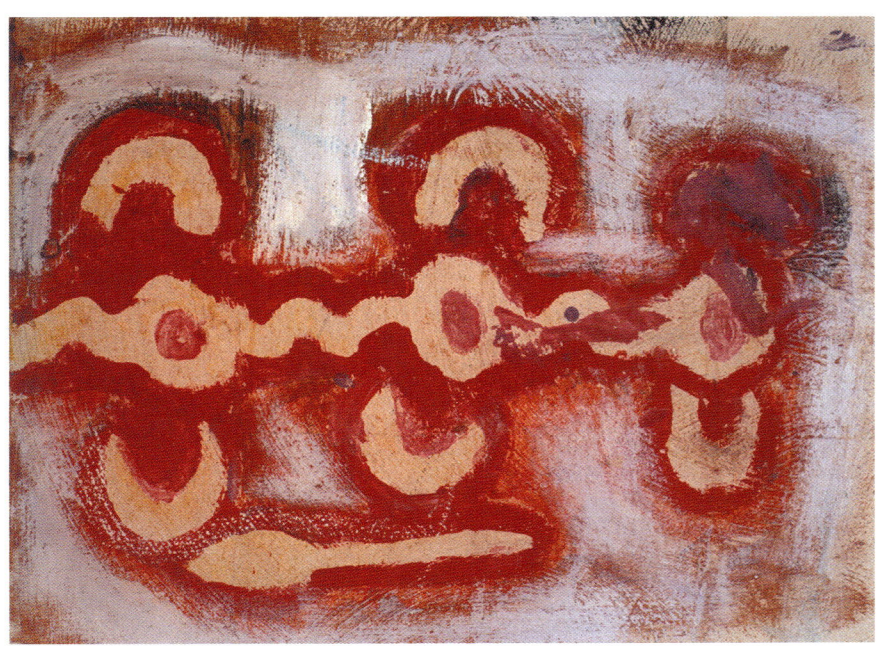

FIGS. 5.1–5.4

Murals at the Ngintaka Women's Centre, Walungurru (Kintore), December 1992. Photos by Marina Strocchi.

was a strident expression of identity within an institution actively suppressing Aboriginal culture. Women in Walungurru also desired self-determination, and while the Women's Centre had encouraged women to paint in the early 1990s, it was not until they themselves initiated a painting workshop in 1994, with Strocchi's assistance, that painting began in earnest.

Camped at the Women's Mountain in the winter of 1994, senior women from Walungurru joined with women from Ikuntji Women's Centre to collaborate on several large canvases that captured the women's shared Tjukurrpa (see p. 50). The location provided the necessary cultural context, and the project was so successful that Tandanya National Aboriginal Cultural Institute in Adelaide expressed interest in displaying the works as part of a larger group. This led to a second workshop at Ikuntji, in 1995 (fig. 5.5), and the works from both artist camps formed the exhibition *Minyma Tjukurrpa: Kintore / Haasts Bluff Canvas Project* in June 1995. The women traveled halfway across the country to Adelaide for the exhibition: the first time they had traveled outside of central Australia. As they had done at the opening of the Ikuntji Women's Centre, Tatali and her peers sang and danced at the exhibition opening, celebrating culture and the opportunities that painting was providing.

In response to the quality of the works and the strength of the exhibition, Papunya Tula Artists began to provide canvases to the women living in Walungurru in early 1996. A burst of activity followed as Tatali and other artists including Inyuwa Nampitjinpa, Nyurapayia Nampitjinpa and Tjunkiya Napaltjarri created punchy, small-scale works. In comparison to most works being painted by their male peers at this time, these paintings were generally gestural, colorful, and laden with paint. The immediacy with which they were painted created a palpable sense of joy and excitement on the surface, as if the women were frantically expelling built-up creative energy. The women made it clear that they had no desire to emulate their male peers: they were presenting their own imagery in their own way.

In November 1996, Papunya Tula Artists held its first exhibition of women painters outside of Mparntwe (Alice Springs), at the commercial gallery Utopia Art Sydney. It was from this exhibition that John W. Kluge acquired the works by Tatali, Nyurapayia, and Nowee included in *Irritja Kuwarri Tjungu | Past and Present Together: Fifty Years of Papunya Tula Artists*. The exhibition sold out, with many of the paintings acquired by major institutions, including the Art Gallery of New South Wales, which purchased sixteen

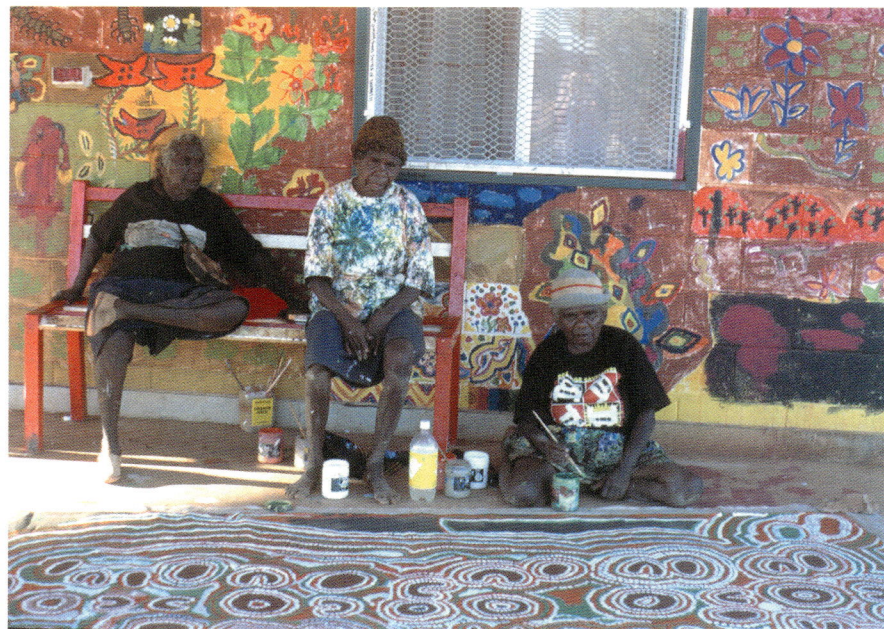

FIG. 5.5

Tatali Nangala, Tjunkiya Napaltjarri and Wintjiya Napaltjarri outside the Ikuntji Women's Centre at Ikuntji (Haasts Bluff) in April 1995 at the second painting camp for Haasts Bluff / Kintore Canvas Project. Photo by Marina Strocchi.

works from the exhibition, including a large collaborative painting by the sisters Wintjiya and Tjunkiya Napaltjarri.[8]

Like Tatali, Tjunkiya had spent her early years on Country to the north of Walungurru, moving to Ikuntji and Papunya before returning to Walungurru when she was in her fifties.[9] Her children were born at Ikuntji, and, during a visit there in 1994, she painted her first works at the Women's Centre where her daughter Mitjili Napurrula had begun painting the previous year. This initial foray into painting led to inspired works when Tjunkiya began painting for Papunya Tula Artists in May 1996. Tjunkiya often painted alongside her sister, Wintjiya Napaltjarri, and both were already known to Papunya Tula, having previously made small craft items for the company (and other markets).[10]

From her earliest works, Tjunkiya hinted at what would become her signature approach, employing a limited color palette to explore the potential of contrast. In *Women's Ceremonies at Yumari* (1996, plate 50) vibrant red is set against vivid white, with the juxtaposition intensified through generously applied white dots that merge to form textural fields. In later works, following an operation to remove her cataracts, Tjunkiya further developed this technique, scratching lines into her thick fields of paint to create a distinct surface finish. She also established her preferred color combination, saturating the canvas with a thick coat of oranges delicately highlighted with whites along the slivers of black background that are left exposed, to create the detail within the composition (for

instance, in *Rockhole Site of Yumari* [2008, plate 51]). In most paintings, this elegant linework references the site of Yumari, with its rockholes captured in circular form and its sandhills in linear splices. Tjunkiya's mother was the sister of Uta Uta Tjangala, and she would often visit Yumari with her parents. In offering constant iterations of this one location, her painting functioned as a means of reminiscing and countering the passing of time, as she stated, "When I paint, I feel happy, I don't feel sick, I don't feel any pain. I feel strong and healthy, like I'm a young girl again."[11]

By the end of 1996, Tjunkiya's works had been included in numerous exhibitions, and in 2000, she was recognized with a solo exhibition at William Mora Galleries in Melbourne. A year earlier, in a somewhat meteoritic rise to fame, her colleague Inyuwa Nampitjinpa had a solo exhibition at Gallery Gabrielle Pizzi in Melbourne. Inyuwa had played a supervisory role at the 1994 painting workshop, ensuring that cultural content was appropriately included.[12] Her husband, Tutama Tjapangati, had played a similar role in the early days of the men's painting movement at Papunya. Tutama ceased painting in the mid-1980s due to poor eyesight, and Inyuwa began painting in earnest in 1997 following eye surgery. With renewed vision, she created bold compositions in which globular forms reminiscent of rockholes and water sources float in a sea of color. The density of Inyuwa's paint and the stippled manner in which it was applied was in stark contrast to the technique employed by

Tutama, yet compositional and stylistic similarities are evident in their works and can be appreciated in Inyuwa's *Travels of Kutungu from Papunnga to Muruntji* (1999, plate 55) and Tutama's *Stars at Night Twinkling* (1971, plate 2). Just as one may wonder what Tutama's paintings may have been if he had retained his eyesight, one wonders how Inyuwa's practice may have developed if she had begun painting earlier.

Since the early 1980s, a small number of women at Watiyawanu (Mount Liebig) and Papunya had painted for Papunya Tula Artists. However, the company's limited resources and tenuous finances restricted the more widespread involvement of women from other communities. The circumstances in which the organization was established also contributed to the dearth of women artists. The founding artists were all men, and many early works included significant cultural content accessible only to initiated men. While this approach shifted as the public nature of open display became more widely appreciated, the notion of painting being "men's business" largely remained.[13]

Pansy Napangardi (fig. 5.6) was among the few women to paint for Papunya Tula Artists in the early 1980s, joining the company in 1983 after working independently in Mparntwe for several years.[14] By the end of the decade, she was widely recognized, winning the National Aboriginal Art Award in 1989 after a solo exhibition at the Sydney Opera House in 1988 organized through the erstwhile Centre for Aboriginal Artists. Pansy's paintings are distinct from those made in later years by female Pintupi artists at Walungurru and more stylistically similar to the work of male Warlpiri, Luritja and Anmatyerr artists who began painting in the 1970s at Papunya and were at the height of their careers by the late 1980s. This is not surprising given Pansy's Luritja and Warlpiri cultural inheritance and the time period in which she was painting. Refined and highly composed, Pansy's works often feature a layering technique akin to that mastered by Kaapa Tjampitjinpa in the mid-1970s, with a defined background and middle ground overlaid with graphic elements in the foreground. This can be seen in *Kungka Kutjarra (Two Women) at Winpirri* (1988, plate 54), where the tendency toward symmetry espoused by Clifford Possum Tjapaltjarri and Michael Nelson Tjakamarra in the late 1980s is also evident. Pansy's hallmark use of dots of circles within the background design can be fully appreciated in this work, with circular forms emerging within the blocks of color on the outside edges. Her use of multicolored dotting creates areas of light and shade unique among artists of this period.

Pansy's grandparents told her of her Tjukurrpa and how to depict them through sand drawings. They taught her further details about her mother's Luritja inheritance.[15] Notably, this also included a Kungka Kutjarra Tjukurrpa—albeit one featuring different women from those in the Pintupi version. In this songline, the two women are pursued by a lustful old man who chases them from Kampurarrnga to Winpirri before they continue their journey south, in a travel-line that connects women from the Central Desert with those of the Anangu Pitjantjatjara Yankunytjatjara lands some five hundred miles away. The intergenerational exchange of such knowledge ensures that culture and the codified modes in which it is presented are maintained. The widespread references to Kungka Kutjarra by artists from different cultural affiliations also speaks to the intrinsic connections that exist between distinct, but neighboring, groups of people, each of which holds responsibility for aspects of expansive Tjukurrpa.

During their travels, ancestral women undertook various creative activities. In *Lupulnga* (2001, plate 64), Makinti Napanangka (fig. 5.7) draws attention to their

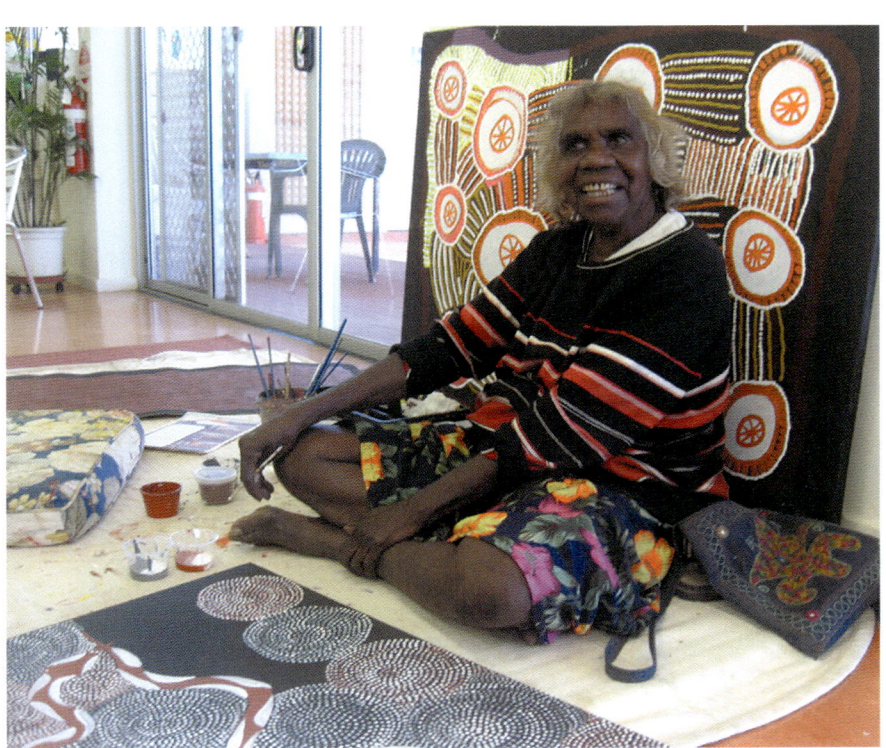

FIG. 5.6

Pansy Napangardi working at the Iltja Ntjarra (Many Hands) Art Centre in Mparntwe (Alice Springs), 2007. Photo by Margo Smith.

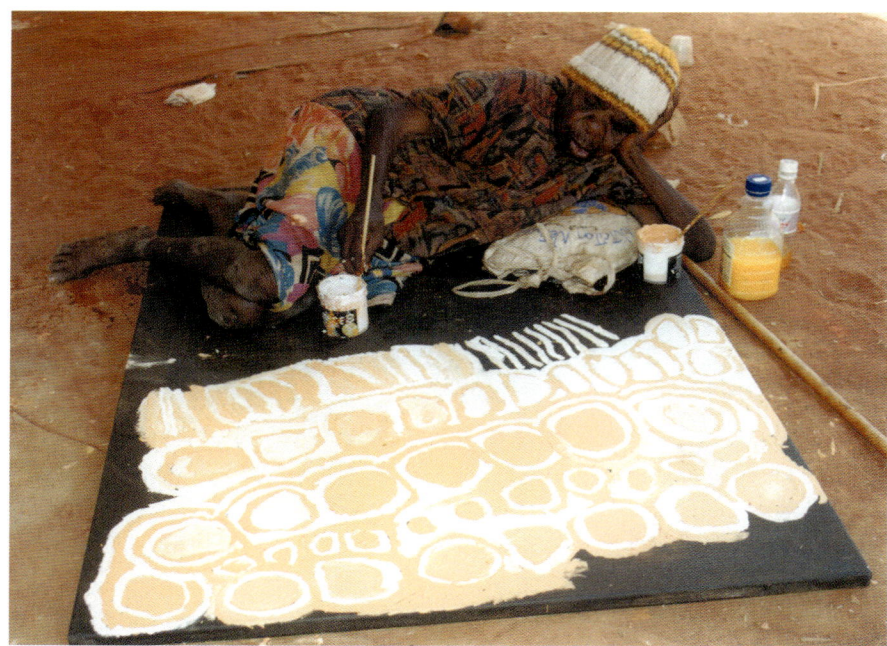

FIG. 5.7

Makinti Napanangka at Walungurru, 1997. Photo by Paul Sweeney.

actions at her birth site to the south of Walungurru. Through bands of color that sweep across the canvases, Makinti emulates the form of spun-hair string, which the women made at this site, while capturing a sense of the movement of the *nyimparra* (hairstring skirts) the women wear while dancing within ceremony. Makinti imbued her works with a luminosity that enhances the musicality implied by her gestural, rhythmic mark making. Encompassing the entire composition, her arcs of color are simple but compelling, their shifting curves and reverberations providing cadence within an uplifting melodic score. The celebratory nature of culture is obvious in the work, both in the use of brilliant color and in the tactile way it is applied, which is reminiscent of ochre being painted onto the body for ceremony. Enlivening the canvas, this technique bears similarities to the work of Tatali, Makinti's cousin, alongside whom she often painted. Both were among the select group of female artists featured in the major retrospective *Papunya Tula: Genesis and Genius* at the Art Gallery of New South Wales, Sydney, in 2000.[16] Following this, Makinti received numerous accolades, and her work was included in major exhibitions, among them the 2012 Biennale of Sydney at the Museum of Contemporary Art. In 2011, she was posthumously appointed a Member of the Order of Australia, for "service to the arts as a contemporary Indigenous artist, to women painters of the Western Desert Art movement, and to the community of the Northern Territory."[17]

The clarity of Makinti's distilled visual expression contrasts with that of her fellow artist Naata Nungurrayi. Naata joined the group of women painting at Walungurru in June 1996. Hailing from further west than many of the other women at Walungurru, Naata became known for assertive depictions of her Country around Karilywarra (in the Pollock Hills), busy with detail and dominated by orange. In *Karilywarra* (2010, plate 88) clusters of roundels and bands of lines are interspersed within a veil of color to create a patchwork of forms reminiscent of an aerial view of Country. Her shifts in color are loose and her linework freewheeling, although it is often partially masked by expressive dotting. Naata's works are devoid of symmetry and she avoids repetition, both within individual works and across her practice. While many of her peers have developed a singular style within which they explore subtle shifts, Naata has celebrated change, confidently painting distinct works that provide insight into the vitality of Country with its radiating heat, shifting sandhills, partially hidden rockholes and variation within vegetation across vast areas. Naata does not offer stylized views of sites, but instead paints atmospheric works that capture the physical reality and personality of Country, as intimately known through her lived experience underscored by deep cultural knowledge. Naata was among the few women artists to have a large-scale work included in *Papunya Tula: Genesis and Genius*, and was further distinguished when a selection of

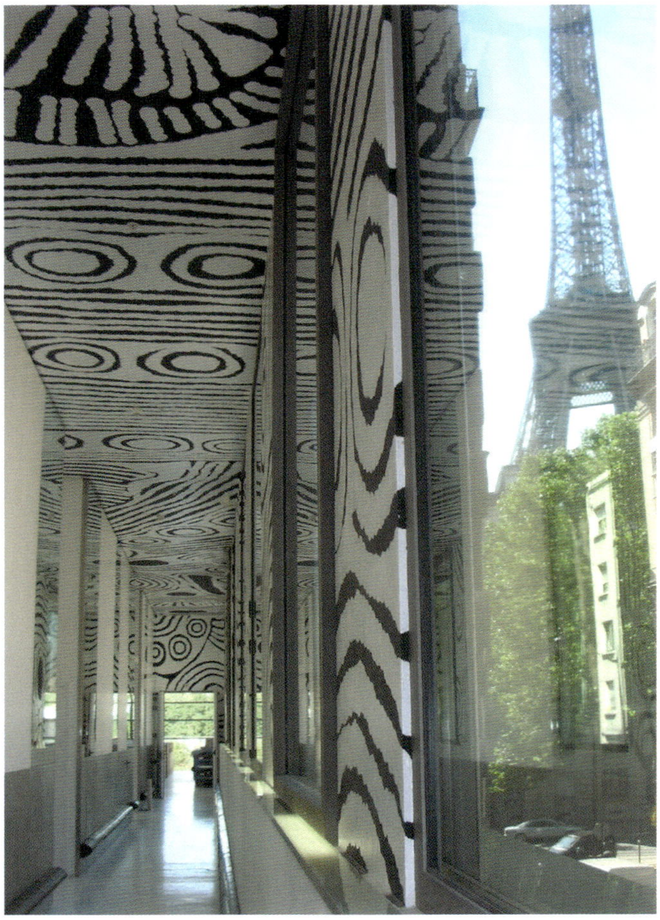

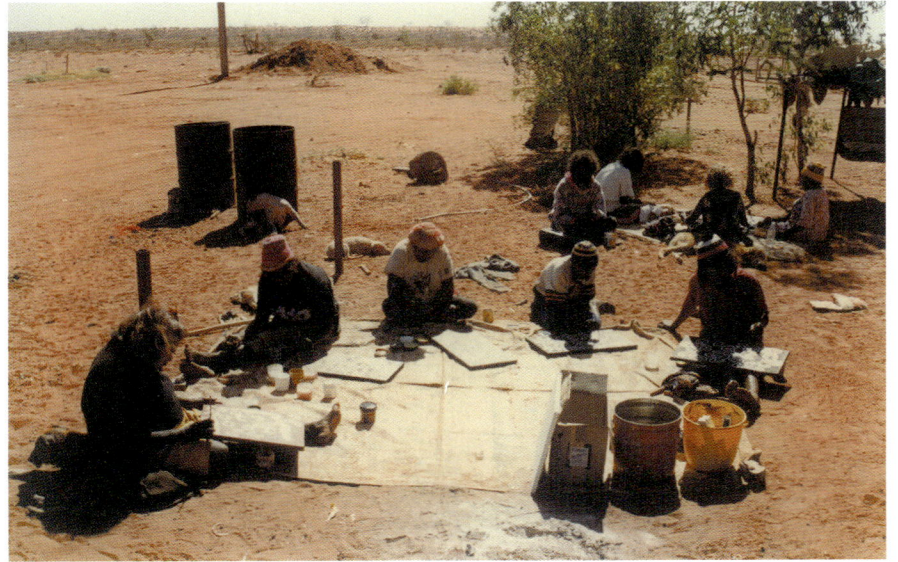

FIG. 5.8

Ningura Napurrula's work installed at the university building of the Musée du quai Branly, Paris, 2006. Photo by Paul Sweeney.

her works was included in *unDisclosed: The Second National Indigenous Art Triennial* at the National Gallery of Australia, Canberra, in 2012.[18]

In 2006, Ningura Napurrula gained international attention when she was one of eight Aboriginal artists whose works were built into the fabric of the Musée du quai Branly in Paris as part of the Australian Indigenous Art Commission (fig 5.8). The organic geometry that forms a dramatic image on an entire ceiling of the museum's administration building is drawn from a work Ningura completed in 2000, only five years after beginning to paint her own works. Ningura was married to Yala Yala Gibbs Tjungurrayi, one of the founding members of Papunya Tula Artists, and she began painting by assisting him with the dotted infilling of his backgrounds. While she took part in the second women's painting workshop in 1995, she became more prolific following the death of her husband in 1998.[19] Ningura quickly refined her individual approach, creating works with decisive black details set within vivid white. Occasionally, Ningura employs ochre red in addition to black, but this does not alter her technique of forming striking details through the overlay of white dots, which are so close together that they form a textural field of brilliant impasto. This approach can also be appreciated in the graphic works of Wintjiya Napaltjarri and Nancy Nungurrayi (see plates 53, 89).

While Makinti, Tatali, Tjunkiya, Naata and Ningura all painted at Walungurru, women were also active at Kiwirrkurra (fig. 5.9). In the early 2000s, as the individual styles of artists became prominent, the differentiation between approaches within each of the locations became more evident. Women at Kiwirrkurra began to excel at a form of refined simplicity, with hypnotic compositions based on the repetition of restrained elements across the entire work.[20] This technique had been developed by artists such as Mick Namarari Tjapaltjarri and Turkey Tolson Tjupurrula in the late 1990s, and numerous men employed a similar approach in subsequent years, reducing the complexity of their designs while limiting the range of colors used to create intensifying optical effects.

Doreen Reid Nakamarra was among the younger group of artists who began painting in 1996 and, over time, perfected this trend toward minimalism. *Rockhole Site of Marrapinti* (2006, plate 90) epitomizes Doreen's work, with zigzagging bands of dotted lines meandering across the canvas, energizing the surface and bringing Country to life as ridges and valleys seem to emerge and recede in mesmerizing expanses. This dynamism

FIG. 5.9

Women painting at Kiwirrkurra, 1996. Photo by Paul Sweeney.

reflects the geography of Marrapinti, a cave and creek bed surrounded by sandhills, as well as referring to the bone nose-piercings that go by the same name. These piercings were created at Marrapinti in the Tjukurrpa and are worn by men and women following their transition to adulthood. The elegant sophistication of these works led to international opportunities for Doreen Reid, who was included in the Moscow Biennale of Contemporary Art in 2009, the same year she traveled to New York to see her works displayed as part of the important exhibition *Nganana Tjungurringanyi Tjukurrpa Nintintjakitja: We Are Here Sharing Our Dreaming* at New York University (see fig. 6.5). In 2012, she was posthumously included alongside Warlimpirrnga Tjapaltjarri in *documenta 13* in Kassel, Germany. The impact of her success is reflected in the subsequent acquisition of her work by the Metropolitan Museum of Art, New York.

Yukultji Napangati traveled to New York with Doreen Reid in 2009 and returned in 2019 for a solo exhibition of her works at Salon 94 in the Bowery.[21] This was momentous for Yukultji and followed on the success of her brother Warlimpirrnga Tjapaltjarri's solo show at the same gallery in 2015. Both artists work in a style closely aligned to that of Doreen Reid, with minimal colors, evenly and methodically painted for shimmering effect (see plates 91, 120; 103, 105, 148). Yukultji's works often reference Yunarla, a location to the west of Kiwirrkurra where women camped in the distant past and collected the edible roots of the *yunarla* (bush banana or silky pear vine, *Marsdenia Australis*). The swathes of lines in Yukultji's works represent the sandhills surrounding this location, which run in an east–west direction, as well as the underground tubers of the plant. Devoid of a horizon line, the landscape in Yukultji's paintings is all encompassing, with subtle optical shifts providing an impression of movement within the undulating lines, reminiscent of desert haze. Yukultji's paintings do not seek to explain this landscape but provide a sense of its immensity and importance.

Yukultji began painting in 1996 alongside her mothers and sisters, a familial approach whereby painting activity could be accompanied by conversation and song. Communal gathering during which painting occurs has been central to Papunya Tula Artists since its earliest days, and while the names of some individual artists now loom large in the art world, this sense of community and the importance of family connections remains. Among the works in the *Papunya Tula Fiftieth Anniversary Suite* (plates 106–55), an exciting and diverse group of works that provide a snapshot of current practice, is a bold painting by Eileen Napaltjarri. As the daughter of Wartuma and Tatali, Eileen is part of an artistic dynasty. She often sat alongside her parents as they painted, and while she completed her first painting in 1996, Eileen did not paint regularly until 1999, the year her mother died.[22] Since then, Eileen has continued her parents' legacy, creating paintings that merge elements from their respective practices. In *Tjitururrnga* (2020, plate 145), Eileen zooms in to provide a macro view that seems to extend beyond the edges of the canvas. The vibrancy of color and luminous use of white is reminiscent of her mother's works, while the subject depicted is her father's conception site. Located to the west of Walungurru, Tjitururrnga is a soakage water site that sits within rocky hills, known for a profusion of *jitjara* (desert yam from *Ipomoea costata*). Men and women traveled to this site in the distant past, and subsequent generations have followed in their footsteps. Eileen's reverberating lines capture the life-sustaining nature of this location as a burst of energy that vibrates across Country.

This sense of energy rippling out from one location seems pertinent, given the role played by the painting camp that took place at the Women's Mountain in 1994. This camp provided an opportunity for women to come together, work collaboratively and paint. From these small beginnings behind a significant mountain in a remote community, the works of women artists of Papunya Tula have filtered out across the world, capturing attention and commanding admiration. The success of these works lies in their strong cultural foundations in following the Kungka Kutjarra and other Tjukurrpa, and in the ability of each artist to translate inherited knowledge into captivating visual form. Painting now provides immense opportunities to many women as well as men and, through the collective model of Papunya Tula Artists, this success supports the next generation who will inherit, and visualize, the future.

## NOTES

1. These ancestral women are interchangeably referred to as Kungka Kutjarra and Minyma Kutjarra, the first referring more generically to women of all ages (although often used for younger women), the latter being used more specifically for older women.

2. For a firsthand account of this gathering, and one that followed in 1995, see Marina Strocchi's essay in this volume, "Family Connections: Walungurru Women in Action."

3. Biographical details are informed by Vivien Johnson, *Lives of the Papunya Tula Artists* (Alice Springs, NT: IAD Press, 2008), 295.

4. Johnson, *Lives of the Papunya Tula Artists*, 297.

5. Charlie Tarawa or Wartuma Tjungurrayi, quoted in *Charlie Tjaruru Tjungurrayi: A Retrospective, 1970–1986* (Orange, NSW: Orange City Council, 1987), n.p.

6. This can be clearly seen in the film *Remembering Yayayi* (dir. Pip Deveson, Ian Dunlop and Fred Myers, 2014), as Charlie Wartuma negotiates with art adviser Peter Fannin and members of the Aboriginal Arts Board.

7. Marina Strocchi, in excerpt for "Family Connections: The Rise of Aboriginal Women Painting in the Desert," Kluge-Ruhe Aboriginal Art Collection of the University of Virginia website, accessed March 30, 2020, http://kluge-ruhe.org/event/family-connections. See also Kiernan Finnane, "From First Canvas to National Collections in Three Years," *Artlink*, December 1997, http://www.artlink.com.au/articles/2820/from-first-canvas-to-national-collections-in-three.

8. *Papunya Women* was held at Utopia Art, Sydney, November 16–December 14, 1996.

9. Biographical details are informed by Johnson, *Lives of the Papunya Tula Artists*, 305.

10. Hetti Perkins, "Mitjili Napurrula," in *Tradition Today: Indigenous Art in Australia*, ed. Julie Donaldson and Theresa Wilsteed, rev. ed. (Sydney: Art Gallery of New South Wales, 2013), 110.

11. Tjunkiya Napaltjarri, quoted in "Tjunkiya Napaltjarri: A New Way" exhibition page, Papunya Tula Artists website, 2008, http://papunyatula.com.au/tjunkiya-napaltjarri-a-new-way.

12. Vivien Johnson, "Inyuwa Nampitjinpa," in Donaldson and Wilsteed, *Tradition Today*, 106.

13. Vivien Johnson provides an overview of women painting for Papunya Tula in Johnson, "Seeing Is Believing: A Brief History of Papunya Tula Artists, 1971–2000," in *Papunya Tula: Genesis and Genius*, ed. Hetti Perkins and Hannah Fink (Sydney: Art Gallery of New South Wales, 2000), 187–97; and Johnson, *Lives of the Papunya Tula Artists*, 267–71.

14. Johnson, *Lives of the Papunya Tula Artists*, 190–91.

15. Johnson, *Lives of the Papunya Tula Artists*, 190.

16. Perkins and Fink, *Papunya Tula: Genesis and Genius*.

17. The Queen's Birthday 2011 Honours List, Department of Prime Minister and Cabinet, Australian Government, accessed March 30, 2020, http://honours.pmc.gov.au/honours/awards/1144297.

18. National Indigenous Art Triennial, *unDisclosed: The Second National Indigenous Art Triennial* (Canberra, ACT: National Gallery of Australia, 2012).

19. Biographical details are drawn from Vivien Johnson, "Ningura Napurrula," in Donaldson and Wilsteed, *Tradition Today*, 112.

20. See, for instance, Luke Scholes, "Kiwirrkurra Women: The Shifting Shape of Western Desert Painting," *Art and Australia* 3 (Autumn 2009): 498–505.

21. For critical discussion of Yukultji's success, see Matthew Knot, "Yukultji Napangati's Shimmering Outback Images Shine in New York," *Sydney Morning Herald*, January 28, 2019, http://www.smh.com.au/world/north-america/yukultji-napangati-s-shimmering-outback-images-shine-in-new-york-20190124-p50t9w.html; and Will Heinrich, "What to See in New York Art Galleries Right Now," *New York Times*, March 1, 2019, http://www.nytimes.com/2019/03/01/arts/design/what-to-see-in-new-york-art-galleries-right-now.html.

22. Johnson, *Lives of the Papunya Tula Artists*, 297.

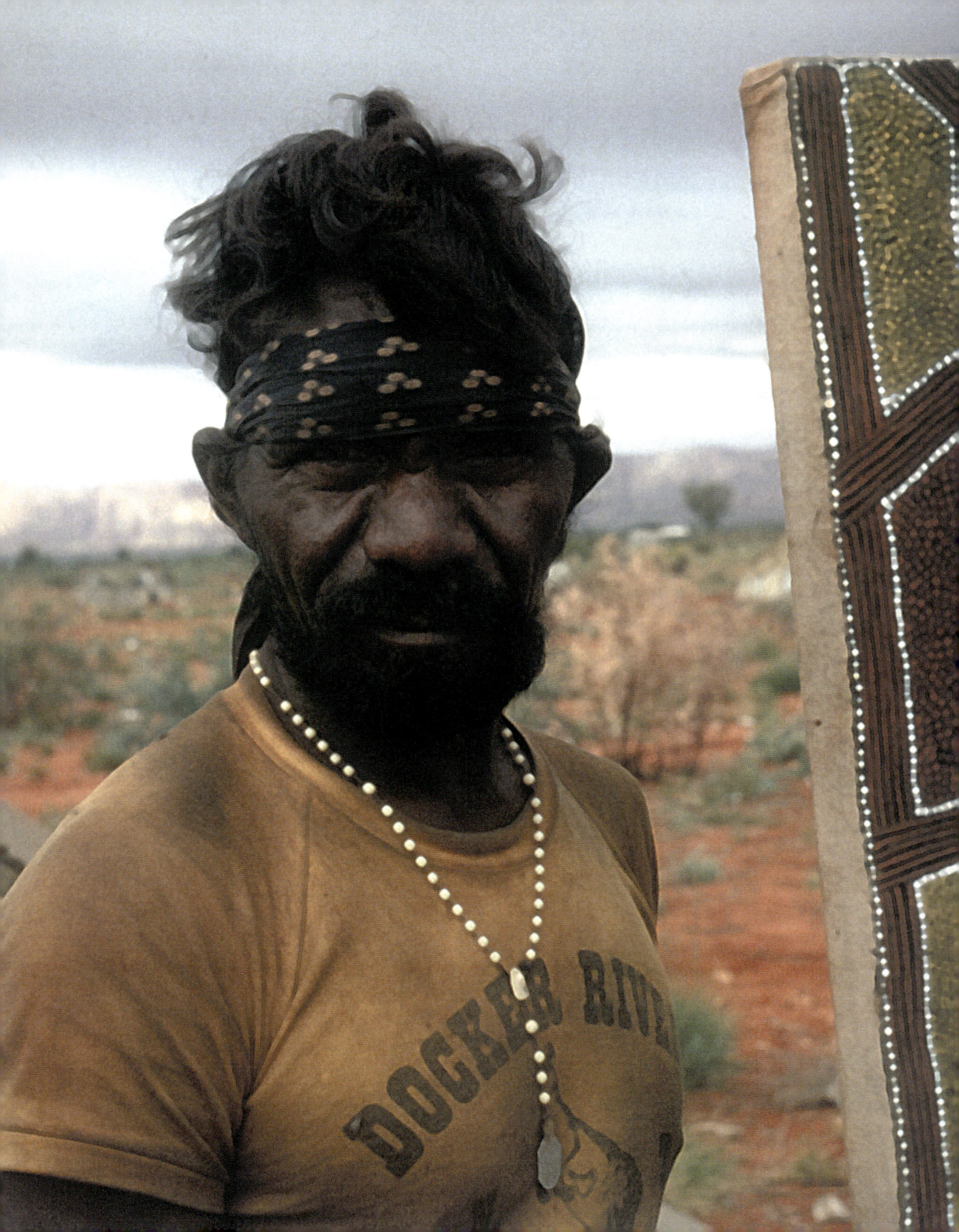

# Stories I Can Tell

## HETTI PERKINS IN CONVERSATION WITH
## FRED MYERS AND HENRY SKERRITT

To coincide with the Sydney Olympic Games in 2000, the Art Gallery of New South Wales held the exhibition *Papunya Tula: Genesis and Genius*. While there had been several smaller attempts at chronicling the emergence of Papunya Tula Artists, *Genesis and Genius* was the first major institutional survey of the movement. The exhibition was curated by Hetti Perkins, an Arrernte and Kalkadoon woman who had been employed as the curator of Aboriginal and Torres Strait Islander Art at the gallery since 1998. Drawing works from public institutions and private collections around the world, *Genesis and Genius* marked a key moment in the historiography of Papunya Tula Artists. Bobby West Tjupurrula, Kenny Williams Tjampitjinpa, Charlie Tjapangati and Warlimpirrnga Tjapaltjarri, along with Papunya Tula staff members Daphne Williams (manager) and Paul Sweeney (assistant manager), traveled to Sydney for the installation and opening of the exhibition and created a ground work of sand and *wamulu* (vegetable down) in the gallery (fig. 6.1; see fig. 6.3). The exhibition's opening coincided with the dramatic opening of the Olympic Arts Festival in Sydney.

**FRED MYERS (FM):** We wanted to start by getting you to describe your history of involvement with Papunya Tula Artists. When did you first become involved with the company? You've brought such a broad background to Papunya Tula, because you came from a bigger assortment of Indigenous art. We thought that should be recognized: while you've been doing a lot with Papunya Tula, you came from the Aboriginal Artists Gallery and Boomalli. So, working with Papunya Tula, was it a choice?

**HETTI PERKINS (HP):** When I work with any artists in my capacity as a curator or as a friend, colleague or even relation, one of the things that I remember very vividly is my childhood, my early years, and how that has influenced the way that I see the world. I've been very fortunate with my father, Charles Perkins, being an activist; growing up in Sydney and living at the Foundation for Aboriginal Affairs when I was young; and, in Canberra, for instance, being at the Tent Embassy when that was being established, and attending all the marches and protests (fig. 6.2).[1]

A lot of those things inform my sense of myself in Australia and, by association, of my people in Australia. It's a

Timmy Payungu Tjapangati at West Camp, near Papunya, c. 1981. Photo by J. V. S. Megaw.

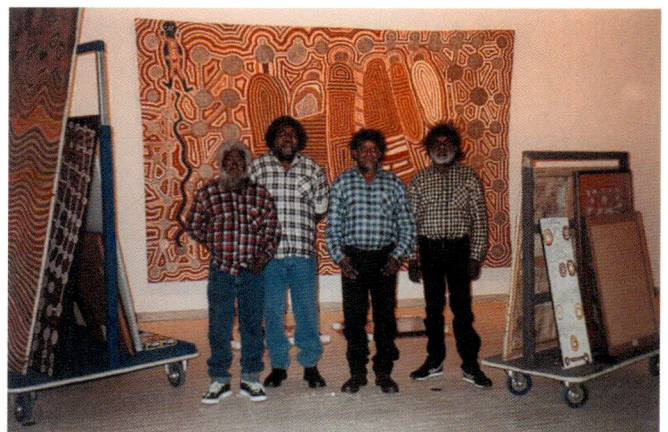

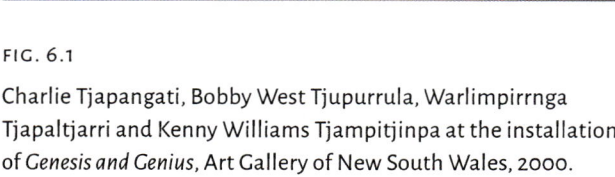

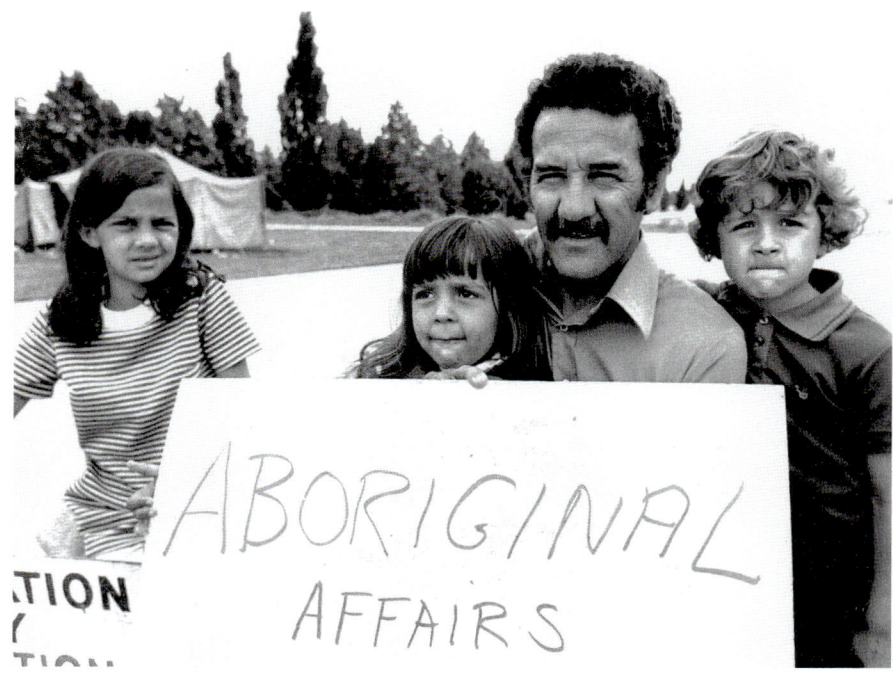

FIG. 6.1

Charlie Tjapangati, Bobby West Tjupurrula, Warlimpirrnga
Tjapaltjarri and Kenny Williams Tjampitjinpa at the installation
of *Genesis and Genius*, Art Gallery of New South Wales, 2000.
Photo by Fred Myers.

FIG. 6.2

Assistant Secretary of the Department of Aboriginal Affairs Charles
Perkins protests on the lawns outside Parliament House in Canberra
with his children, Hetti (9), Rachel (4) and Adam (6), November 18,
1974. Photo by Ernest McLintock.

really interesting point in history that we are at, in that
very soon we will have no Aboriginal people in Australia
who have living memory of what life was like before white
people came to this country. It strikes me that we are at
the cusp of a fundamental change in Australia. That's
something that very much informs my work and some of
the urgency I feel around the work that I do.

Another experience that was a very pivotal moment
in my childhood was going to Papunya in the early seventies, traveling with Dad and my family. We went to
Yuendumu and Papunya, and other communities, but I
vividly remember Papunya and Yuendumu because they
were slightly bigger communities. I remember seeing the
housing—if you could call it housing—that people were
living in. I don't know what you'd call them really—gal-
vanized sheds and "lean-tos" or "humpies." Seeing those
conditions, which Geoffrey Bardon described so cinemat-
ically, was something that had a very deep impact on me
as a child. And living in Canberra with the Tent Embassy
and being an observer as well as a participant—but, of
course, a very young one—in that activism with the Tent
Embassy and all the demonstrations was something
that created the political foundations for my future life.

When we were living in Mparntwe (Alice Springs) and on
trips back, Dad would often take me to Papunya Tula when
he dropped in to say "hi" to Daphne Williams, as he had a
great deal of respect for her.

Mum (Eileen Perkins) also had a gallery in the garage
downstairs from our house, the Aboriginal Heritage Gallery. In Canberra, which, of course, is the political capital,
there was no gallery, no museum. And Mum felt strongly
that diplomats, as well as the local community, Aboriginal
people who moved to Canberra to work in the Department
of Aboriginal Affairs—as well as visitors to Canberra—
needed a place to come and see and experience Aboriginal
art. A lot of things, such as early paintings by the pioneer
artists of Papunya Tula, came into that gallery, along with
bark paintings and all of the beautiful things that were
being made in the seventies. You can imagine—it was
incredible. I spent a lot of time in that gallery. I've just been
super lucky, and I feel like I've had these desert paintings as
part of my life from a very young age.

One thing that happened, on the way to actually
getting a job as a curator, I drove down to Melbourne in
the mid-1980s with some friends. I happened to go to the
National Gallery of Victoria, because I've always been

interested in the arts just generally. I wanted to be an artist, actually. Thank God that dream wasn't realized—dream for me, nightmare for everyone else! But I went to the National Gallery, looked at their collections and happened upon a stunning display of Papunya Tula paintings.

I was so blown away by it that I took photos of every single work and wrote down every single extended exhibition label. And then I put them all into a photograph album and made my own little catalog, this album, so I could see the works all the time. And then when I came to curate *Genesis and Genius* decades later, I found it. And I remember bringing it into the Art Gallery of New South Wales and showing it to Cara Pinchbeck and Jonathan Jones and Ken Watson.

**FM:** Was there a special fund dedicated to doing something at the art gallery for the Olympics?

**HP:** Yes, I think there must've been. They were throwing money at everyone to do something special for the Olympics. I think there was money to support it, because it probably wouldn't have happened otherwise—because Aboriginal exhibitions generally are free, not ticketed. So, it's very hard to get that major temporary exhibition space, that real estate.

**HENRY SKERRITT (HS):** When you were going out to Walungurru (Kintore) or Kiwirrkurra, you were obviously talking to people about the exhibition. What was the general response from the community about doing a show like *Genesis and Genius*?

**HP:** Obviously those things can be very tricky, because you're dealing with artists, and everybody—not everybody, but quite a few artists—thinks they're "number one." With *Genesis and Genius*, it was a case of just going back and forth, talking to Daphne Williams and Paul Sweeney about different works and going out to Walungurru and then to Kiwirrkurra. It was quite difficult, obviously, because there's such a vast history, just such a vast amount of work. To try to navigate a path through, that was very difficult. The way we curated it with Paul and Daphne was that we collected as many images as we could. I went up to Mparntwe on a few trips, and we just looked through all of them. Really, it was just a case of going, "Well, that's obvious, that's obvious, that's obvious, that's obvious," you know? And then there were a couple of times . . . You know that lovely Timmy Payungu?[2] That

was actually just leaning up against the wall, in the stockroom at the back in the old store. As I'm poking my nose in where it doesn't belong as usual, I pulled it out, and I was like, "This is amazing." We got that for the Art Gallery of New South Wales.

It was a bit of a random way of curating the show, but I feel that there comes a point where you just have to be ruthless. It's one person's view of how it should be, but you can't have everyone's view. Every single person would do it a different way.

And you can get tied up in these things by being representative: that there has to be one work by everyone and all of that sort of stuff. That's where I don't know how well the democratic process works for curating. When we were working on it—with Cara Pinchbeck and Jonathan Jones and Hannah Fink, who did a brilliant job in editing the catalog and also just being part of the family—it was great. And with you Fred, and John Kean, and so many other knowledgeable people around, it was very much a collaborative venture.

But I realized, at some point, that at the end of the day, the buck has to stop with someone. And so, to get it done, someone just has to be the person. And I thought, well, I'll just have to charge through. And I did feel that we didn't obviously represent some artists as well as we could have. But one way I thought about it was that we were representing the topography of the day. At that time, thanks to Tim Klingender,[3] interest in and prices for the early boards were really going through the roof, and the "Warlpiri moment" had sort of been and gone, while women artists were really coming to the fore. The Pintupi artists were coming back, and their style was something that people really wanted to tap into. It was like, "This is how I think the topography of that history looks now," and that's just what we did. But I tried not to dominate it with all my favorites.

It was great to sit down with Daphne and Paul, because for them, of course, it's so much more than a job. It was wonderful for them to guide me in terms of which works they thought should be included, and to hear them share all the funny yarns along the way about different people and their stories. Obviously, Daphne just had a wealth of stories, particularly about some of her favorite artists and how they looked after her when she was making those trips out to Kintore. That was a real pleasure, just being able to talk about those stories, as well as look at incredible paintings. Honestly, it was all you could do to stay in your seat.

And, of course, I'd been buying for the Art Gallery of New South Wales, very actively collecting Papunya Tula works. The gallery had acquired works from the *Painted Dreams* exhibition from Vivien and Tim Johnson's collection,[4] and other works had also come into the collection. I had to deaccession a few things that were acquired by people prior to my work there. We were constantly frustrated that we couldn't sort of compete with the big end of town that were buying all the early boards from auction; it was quite frustrating, watching those works leaving the country. But then, of course, it was really wonderful to be able to have collections like the Kluge-Ruhe Aboriginal Art Collection of the University of Virginia to lend them back. Then they could come back to Australia for these types of shows. We were also happy to focus on the contemporary works of living artists.

**FM:** In terms of getting the men's and women's paintings from Kintore and Kiwirrkurra, and the tie-in with the Western Desert Dialysis Project,[5] how did that come to fruition? First of all, the fundraising of that project produced these amazing works and brought together a history of people who were collecting. It is a very unusual thing for an Indigenous art movement to have their followers just jump in the game and say, "Here we are, we want you to keep going."

**HP:** I remember a couple of times when I went to Mparntwe and sat down with Daphne and Paul, looking through things. Timmy Payungu Tjapangati was there.[6] He came in after dialysis. This was in the late nineties, and he hadn't seen a dietician, and he hadn't even seen a proper renal specialist. There was no nephrologist in Mparntwe hospital; there was just nothing, none of those services, even though the region had one of the highest incidences of renal failure in the world. And people like him were just brought in from places like Walungurru, and then, once they'd done their dialysis, they were told, "Off you go." No sandwich, no food, nothing to support people and no accommodation, no services, nothing offered to these patients. It was hardly surprising that the overwhelming majority of people were choosing to not have dialysis, to stay on community and just die. We were just losing this generation, this vital generation of people, because they didn't want to bring their family into town, because that causes all sorts of problems. They'd just take it on the chin and stay out bush and slowly die, a bad way to die.

My father was a kidney-transplant recipient, and he was very fortunate. And when he was in hospital in Sydney, when his kidneys first failed, in the ward with him was a Warlpiri man. I don't know how he ended up in that hospital, and Dad doesn't say in his book.[7] He just remembers this poor fella being in this big city and being seriously ill and not speaking English. So, when I was in Mparntwe, Timmy Payungu would come in, and I remembered that Dad couldn't eat certain foods, and I realized Timmy hadn't seen anyone to talk to him about that.

So that was what Papunya Tula was as well. People would walk from the hospital, come to the gallery in Mparntwe, and literally just lie down on the floor in the office and be made comfortable. They'd set up a little bed for them, give them sandwich, a cup of tea and really look after people and find them a place to stay. They were running this social service outside of the hospital service, treating people with respect and dignity.

And they were doing it with a lot of humor. I was trying to do some research around one of the paintings—I think it was one of Timmy's paintings, probably that one I pulled out. Paul was documenting it. And as weak as Timmy was, having just come from dialysis, I have this vivid memory of him lying there on the office floor and just giving Paul so much grief, because Paul was speaking to him in Pintupi. I think, at one point, Paul was saying, "So is this that place, west side?" And Timmy was like, "Uhmmm. You say it." And then Paul would try and say the site name and Timmy would roll around on the ground laughing. And that kind of humor is something else that I really think of—people coming in and out of the office and joking. That kind of playful talk and all that sort of stuff, those funny moments. Because you're doing this work, you have access to these special moments.

We did the Western Desert Dialysis Appeal for the Purple House in 2000. That was amazing. Smithy Zimran[8] was really the driving force of that. And Daphne had seen too many people suffer and die from renal failure, so we definitely wanted to acknowledge that.

I think that's one of the significant things about Papunya Tula, the artists and the company. I don't think it's been really shouted from the rooftops as much as it should be, but it's an incredible success story in Aboriginal Australia in terms of self-determination. And as we know, that has been due not just to the artists, but also to the stewardship of people who have been its managers and supporters over the years and who have been dedicated to the work and to the story. People were very receptive to loaning works for the exhibition, and then I think it was Tim Klingender and Paul who said we should do a fundraiser. I had this idea that the gallery needed to give something back, that whenever we did a major show, we should do something to reciprocate the generosity of communities for being involved. So, we did the Western Desert Dialysis Appeal. We held a fundraiser auction that centered on four collaborative canvases: two women's canvases, two men's canvases each from both Kiwirrkurra and from Walungurru. What's interesting about that fundraiser is that, like everything with Papunya Tula, they paid the artists in full for those works. It wasn't a donation from the artists; they got paid, but Papunya Tula, the company, just gave the works entirely over to the auction.

I was there while the artists were painting them. That was just amazing for me. I remember particularly Turkey Tolson Tjupurrula—what an amazing person he was—saying, "Nakamarra" [referring to my "skin," or subsection category in the kinship system], signaling for me to fetch notebooks, recorders, to put the recorder on while they were singing the painting. Like, "Come into the men's room, put that recorder on, and then bugger off." Just totally appropriate [given my status as a woman]. Then, of course, I spent most of my time in the chaos of the women's painting room, with kids and dogs everywhere, both at Kintore and Kiwirrkurra—which was just a wonderful privilege, watching these works come to life.

Of course, there was no way I was getting into the men's painting room at Kiwirrkurra, which was fine. But I remember at the end of the one day, I was allowed in to have a look and see how it was going. And I think it was Charlie Ward Tjakamarra, who came in in his very (as I have heard) typical way he did things, and who did that amazing, pivotal roundel in the center. Well, I won't mention names, but one of the whitefellas (support staff) there had a heart attack. He was like, "He's ruining it, he's ruining it. Stop him, stop him!" And I said, "You can't do that." Then, when they all left, it was amazing! It just made the painting pop.

It was fun. We camped out at Kiwirrkurra. It was a really precious time for me, to have that kind of experience. And I think that, particularly, going to Kiwirrkurra and Kintore over the years was great for me to see how this homeland or outstation movement had developed from what I'd seen at Papunya in the early days. To compare it to what I had seen thirty years before was just really validating. And I was struck by how people had overcome that considerable adversity and had been able to get back

home and build these very successful enterprises and communities and all of the things that they'd been able to achieve.

My father passed away during *Genesis and Genius*, just before we held that fundraiser. I think it was about a week after he passed, and he was the patron of it, patron of the fundraiser. Dad didn't live to see the auction. He was very involved, and that's when he said, "We're not just saving lives, we're saving a way of life." In some ways, *Genesis and Genius* helped me when I needed the most help personally. And when I go out there, people are so very kind. "*Kuunyi*," they say, and they pat you, "*Kuunyi*, sorry, sorry." When people say, "Oh, you did this amazing show," or whatever, I feel like, "One, it wasn't just me that did it. And two, it did more for me, really." It really got me through quite a tough time. And I felt very supported by all that mob. I knew that they were thinking of me, and I could feel that support. So, I'm very grateful for that experience.

FM: The exhibition really had a kind of explosive forward energy. I thought it was very expressive of the way in which Pintupi think about their world, of all their fellow travelers and their network of people they expected to be there. And they respected them, too, as contributors to the enterprise. I thought it was amazing how they gathered so many people around them so gracefully.

HP: One of the things that we've always struggled with—and I've tried to say to galleries—is that our people are the audience for this work, as well as the producers of the work. This is something we need to work on, we need to try and be much better in the way that we engage our communities as the audience.

Obviously, as much as you do it for your own community and the artists' community, it was also really pitched at a non-Indigenous audience, because there's still a long way to go. Coming off the back of the Australian Bicentennial, international collectors were starting to twig onto Western Desert art and also Emily Kame Kngwarreye's work, and then the success of Sotheby's auctions of early desert works and so on. But then, as a result of that, all the "sharks" came out, and the "carpetbagging" industry was creating this inner turmoil in the industry. As prices went through the roof, so did unethical operations. With *Genesis and Genius*, we were trying to bring it back to how amazing this art movement is and what it's about and what it has achieved. Without all of the hype, the humbug that was happening around it.

That's why I called it *Genesis and Genius*. First, I love a bit of alliteration. But also, in response to this trend in public galleries of having exhibitions that mythologized things, calling them "masters" and so on. I wanted to get some of that language into the title, to try to bring that level of appreciation and put some kind of marker on the show that would resonate with certain audiences: the kind of people who love "masters" and French Impressionists and things like that. And then "Genesis" was obviously talking about religion, this kind of religious or spiritual belief that predates other ones, as well as alluding to the extraordinary beginnings of the movement. It was a very pointed term. The title was a very deliberate and purposeful one, and it was very hard to get it through the trustees. There was a lot of resistance to calling the show that. They were like, "Genius? Really?" I was like, "Yes, really." I'm finding it very hard to explain why they resisted it. But I think that there was and still is a place for Aboriginal art, and the vernacular is expected to stay very much within that. You can't pull it out of there and give it associations that put it on par with the best art in mainstream art movements and mainstream religious beliefs. Anyway, I just had a tantrum.

And then we had the opportunity to invite artists to Sydney, and the public programs and things like that were very much community directed. They wanted people to come to Sydney and to be there while these works were uncrated and brought out and all of that sort of stuff. That was entirely up to Papunya Tula to decide: who would come and what they would be happy to do. Then, of course, they did that beautiful painting, that ground work with all the *wamulu* [decorative vegetable down] and everything (fig. 6.3). Wasn't it wonderful, Fred, when the crates were being opened and the works were lifted out of the crates after they'd been acclimatizing? It was like Pandora's box. It was a beautiful thing.

**HS:** You had artists come for the uncrating and, presumably, the installation as well?

**HP:** And to create the sand drawing installation. Fred was there, of course, Warlimpirrnga. Kenny Williams Tjampitjinpa and Bobby West Tjupurrula and Charlie Tjapangati. We picked them up from the airport and put them in a big, posh hotel. And we got a stretch limousine to pick them up. We tried to think of every detail. On the night of the opening, we picked them up an hour or so before the opening and got the limo to drive them around Sydney, like the rock stars that they are. It was for the artists, but also for Daphne, to recognize all that she had done for the artists (fig. 6.4). I was also struck by what you, Fred, said in your book how you felt welcomed. And we really tried to do that at *Genesis and Genius*. We went to the Bangarra [Aboriginal dance performance at the Olympic Arts Festival opening] thing and all that sort of stuff. And that's the way it should be, and if you felt welcomed, then we'd got a tick on that job.

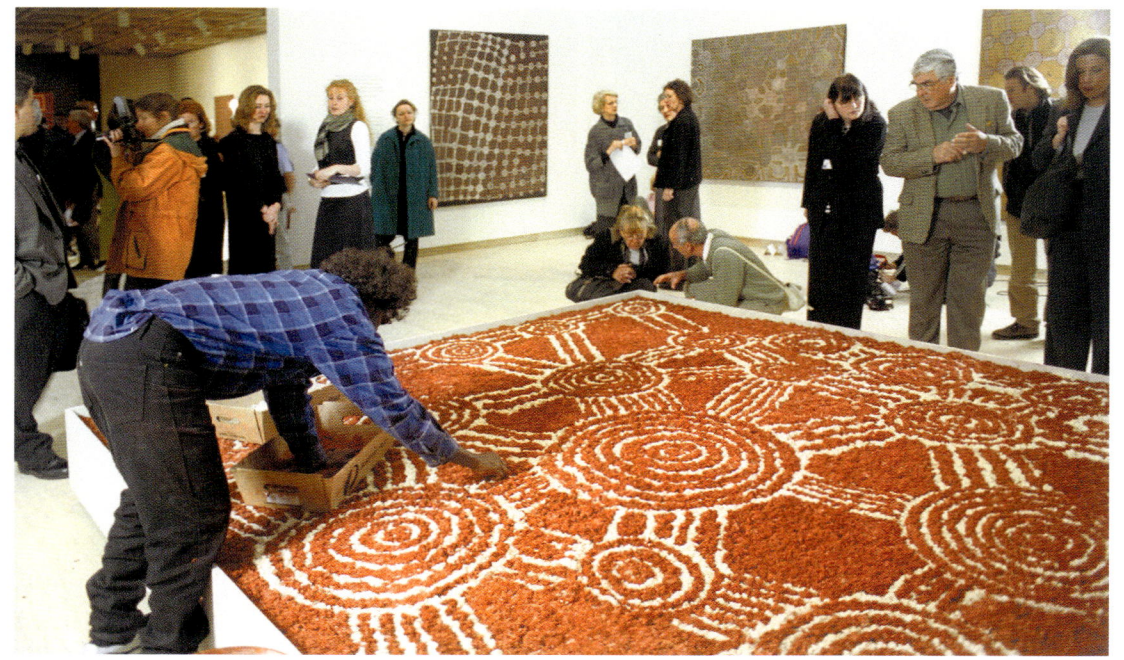

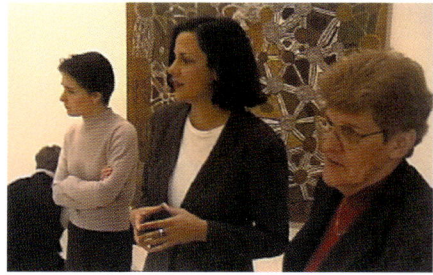

LEFT | FIG. 6.3

Warlimpirrnga Tjapaltjarri working on the ground work for *Papunya Tula: Genesis and Genius*, Art Gallery of New South Wales, 2000. Photo by Jenni Carter for the Art Gallery of New South Wales.

ABOVE | FIG. 6.4

Cara Pinchbeck, Hetti Perkins and Daphne Williams at the opening of *Papunya Tula: Genesis and Genius*, Art Gallery of New South Wales, 2000. Photo by Fred Myers.

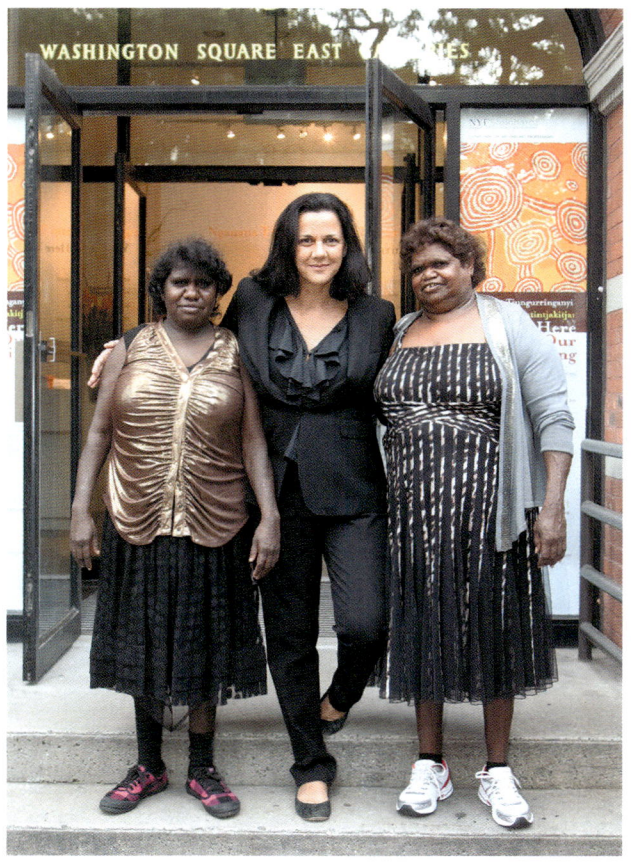

FIG. 6.5

Yukultji Napangati, Hetti Perkins and Doreen Reid Nakamarra at the opening of *Nganana Tjungurringanyi Tjukurrpa Nintintjakitja: We Are Here Sharing Our Dreaming* at 80 Washington Square East Galleries, New York University, 2009. Photo by Paul Sweeney.

FM: I thought that was actually one of the most remarkable experiences of my life. It was magical, totally magical, magical, at the *Genesis and Genius* events. You even got the Warumpi Band [which originated at Papunya, using Pintupi-Luritja lyrics and familiar to the artists, but also iconic for self-determined Indigeneity in Australia, coming out of the remote communities in Central Australia] to play?

HP: Yeah, the Warumpi Band played in the Great Hall at the gallery. We set up a stage in there, and it was so much fun. We had the best time, and George Rrurrambu [the lead singer, now deceased] got us all dancing. It was a really good time. And that's what we wanted, to have an event that the artists would enjoy. Have a car for them and all of that stuff, because it is stressful enough, and they made that beautiful painting, that ground work, and

being there, they supported us all the way through it. We really wanted to give them a nice sort of party, but it was so much fun. George was just on fire, wasn't he, singing? We really loved it.

FM: I think what you were saying about the personality of each of these people that we experienced . . . It flows into their paintings, but they're bigger, there's just so much personality that people have, humor and a range of these things, and they're very generous, offering it to the people they engage with.

HP: Absolutely. I think that people have a level of kindness and compassion, and respect, but also a kind of authority. Approaching an exhibition like *Genesis and Genius*, you feel like you need to—what's the word?—*genuflect* the whole time, which is as it should be. The opportunity to have that kind of contact with individuals is such a privilege. That was really the motivation for doing *Art+Soul* [two groundbreaking series on Indigenous art and artists across Australia made with Indigenous filmmakers Warwick Thornton and Steven McGregor for the ABC]: to try to share that with other people, just having an opportunity for our communities to show what really goes on there.

FM: I have to say, I loved that part in *Art+Soul* when you're sitting there with Doreen Reid Nakamarra, who doesn't talk much anyway. You could have been sitting there for a very long time, just kind of connecting in that sort of friendship way. There was a nice, long, long shot of that.

HP: I think there is a term for it in poetry. There's a word, *caesura*, the pause in poetry. And I think that is something that I had to learn to do. I learned from watching Dad. Say, for instance, when going out to Papunya in the early 1970s, you couldn't be like, "Oh my God, this is terrible," because that was shameful for people. You had to pay them respect. You've just got to sit down there and just organically make connections. I spent a lot of time with Nakamarra. And one of my most special moments was in New York in 2009, just walking over to the gallery for the exhibition *Nganana Tjungurringanyi Tjukurrpa Nintintjakitja*[9] with Yukultji Napangati and Doreen (fig. 6.5), and Doreen just took my hand. Just so lovely to just walk with her, holding hands and to be able to, I guess in some ways, offer a little bit of comfort, like, "You're a blackfella like me. We're in this big city together." Because I've always felt that I live in a world that is not so much in two worlds. I really live in one world. I mean, Sydney. I'm away from my Country. And every now and then I like to think, actually, that I can be helpful for people, to be able to use my experiences, to be able to broker or help people when they have to come into this world. I can be a little bit of a helper or an ambassador. And that feels like it's some compensation to me, if that makes sense.

**FM:** Yes, it does. With Doreen and that visit in New York, I think that you were a bridge for her, for support and comfort. You were from, in a way, her Country. And she could share the experience with you, because I don't think people like to have it only to themselves. I think that they want to be there with somebody. And she was a remarkably empathetic person.

I've been having this conversation with Henry where we have gone down a rabbit hole on every painting when the information seems wrong. Sometimes, I happened to be able to construct what it was, and maybe I even documented it [provided the original documentation with the painter], but the thing is that people don't actually know what's in the painting. And if you know something about what is in the painting, you can see what they've done, like what makes them artists, right? Of course, it's beautiful, and they have a great sense of color and balance and all of these things, but there's more there. When you sit and you talk to people, as you would do with any artist, in theory, you would need to know more about why they're doing it and what they think they're doing. That takes a lot more knowledge than most people have been willing to invest.

**HP:** I think the point I was trying to make about *Genesis and Genius*, and what we tried to do with the exhibition, was that we tried not to have too many titles in the show. We wanted people to look at the work. We just had numbers [rather than descriptive wall labels], and then we had a room sheet [identifying the works]. You could grab a sheet, but otherwise it was just you and the pictures—particularly in the room with the early boards. Because people walk up and read a label and move on. We really wanted to take that out and make people look at the pictures. Our guiding philosophy was that these artists are making these pictures for a reason: for you to look at them and to feel them and hear them, as well as see them.

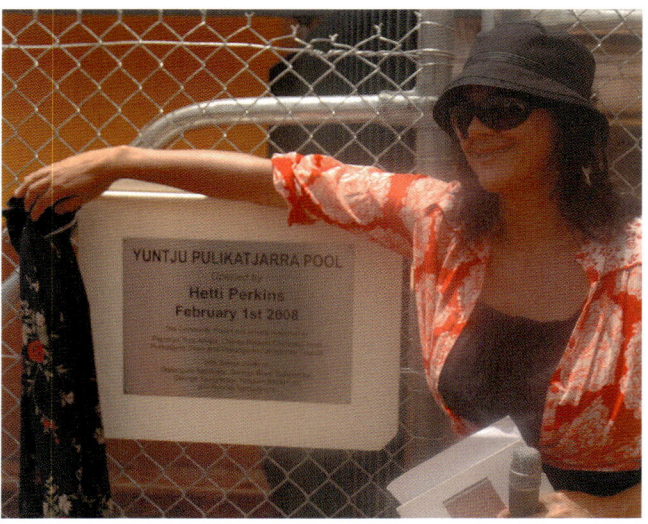

FIG. 6.6

Hetti Perkins opening the Kintore Swimming Pool, February 2008. Photo by Paul Sweeney.

Because it was on for the Olympics, we got a host of people coming through. The actor Kenneth Branagh came, and we spent probably about two hours in the show. As we walked, we had the most interesting talk. He said, "Oh, I see you don't put up any labels. I really like that. Why have you done that?" I was explaining to him that we wanted people to respond to the work, and he said that there's a line, one of his favorite lines in Hamlet: "You would pluck out the heart of my mystery." Isn't that a beautiful way of putting it? It really focuses on the way people often write about Aboriginal art; it's almost like it's about everything except the work. And like you're saying, Fred, when you understand the work, you understand what it's doing and saying and what the artist is saying to you. It's a much more interesting way of engaging with the art.

I remember, immediately after the opening of the swimming pool at Walungurru (fig. 6.6), for which the gallery also held a fundraiser, I went back to the art center to get out of the sun and have a minute to myself, and I saw Matthew West Tjupurrula. And I said to him, "This dust! Today we're opening this pool and it's so dusty and everything." And he said, "Oh, it's those Kungka Kutjarra [referring to the Kungka Kutjarra Tjukurrpa identified with Walungurru]. They are pounding their *wana* [digging sticks]. They're happy for this thing and happy that water has come here. They're pounding their sticks. That's what the dust is."

**FM:** What it seems like you're saying is that without the mediation and the work of curators who are committed to and who appreciate the work, it doesn't get out there—it's not magic. I mean, it's really about histories of exhibition. It's about people trusting you, or somebody like you who has worked with them or been an ally for years. That has been a huge thing for the success of Papunya Tula.

HP: Yeah, absolutely. It's hard. It is. It is. And it's sort of breaking down those walls that everyone talks about. But that is the great flip side of this. I think what you were saying is that that show really had to cut a line through the dross, the mythologizing of "songlines" and "spirituality" and so on. We wanted to show that these are actually concrete works made by people who have their own histories and stories. They are not just generic stories, but they are their own, as you can see in their work. Because everybody's work is different. That's the part that really

materializes in the paintings—that they're all different. I think people have underestimated what the effect of a good show is, that you see that there are personalities, that there are distinctive engagements and so on. That's a huge thing for people to recognize. Like I said, the people, the artists and the people who have been part of that story—it's an incredible story. At heart, it's a story of fifty years of an Aboriginal business that has thrived despite the odds, considerable odds. Today, it's not without its complications. And that kind of returning to something over and over, like Johnny Warangkula Tjupurrula painting Kalipinypa again and again (plates 9, 10), but in myriad ways and all the colors and seasons—just that passion. It's really amazing. Just extraordinary people, extraordinary stories.

## NOTES

1. The Aboriginal Tent Embassy was established in 1972 to protest for Indigenous Australian Land Rights. It has since become a permanent occupation, located on the lawn opposite the old Parliament House building in Canberra.
2. Timmy Payungu Tjapangati, *Untitled*, 1998, synthetic polymer paint on canvas, 60 × 48 in. (152 × 122 cm). Art Gallery of New South Wales, Mollie Gowing Acquisition fund for Contemporary Aboriginal Art, 2000, 215.2000.
3. Klingender was the founder of Sotheby's Aboriginal Art Department and a major international promoter of the secondary market for Indigenous art.
4. Art Gallery of New South Wales, *Painted Dreams: Western Desert Paintings from the Johnson Collection* (Sydney: Art Gallery of New South Wales, 1995).
5. The Western Desert Dialysis project was developed through the initiative of the Pintupi communities of Kintore and Kiwirrkurra with support from Papunya Tula Artists, the Art Gallery of New South Wales and Sotheby's to provide dialysis care on Country and in culturally suitable settings for these communities and, subsequently, many more. It is now known as Purple House, taking its name from the color of the first headquarters in Alice Springs. See Paul Sweeney's essay in this volume, "Art of Resilience: The Importance of Papunya Tula Artists in Australia's Western Desert," for more details.
6. Perkins notes, "I'm using people's names because it's just us—rather than avoiding mentioning the names of people who have passed away, as one would do in community."
7. Charles Perkins, *A Bastard Like Me* (Sydney: Ure Smith, 1975).
8. Smithy Zimran, or Smithy Tjampitjinpa Zimran, a leading figure of Pintupi living at Walungurru and Administrator of the Kintore Community Health Service, died from kidney disease in 2000 in Mparntwe (Alice Springs).
9. *Nganana Tjungurringanyi Tjukurrpa Nintintjakitja: We Are Here Sharing Our Dreaming*, 80 Washington Square East Galleries, New York University, September 23–26, 2009.

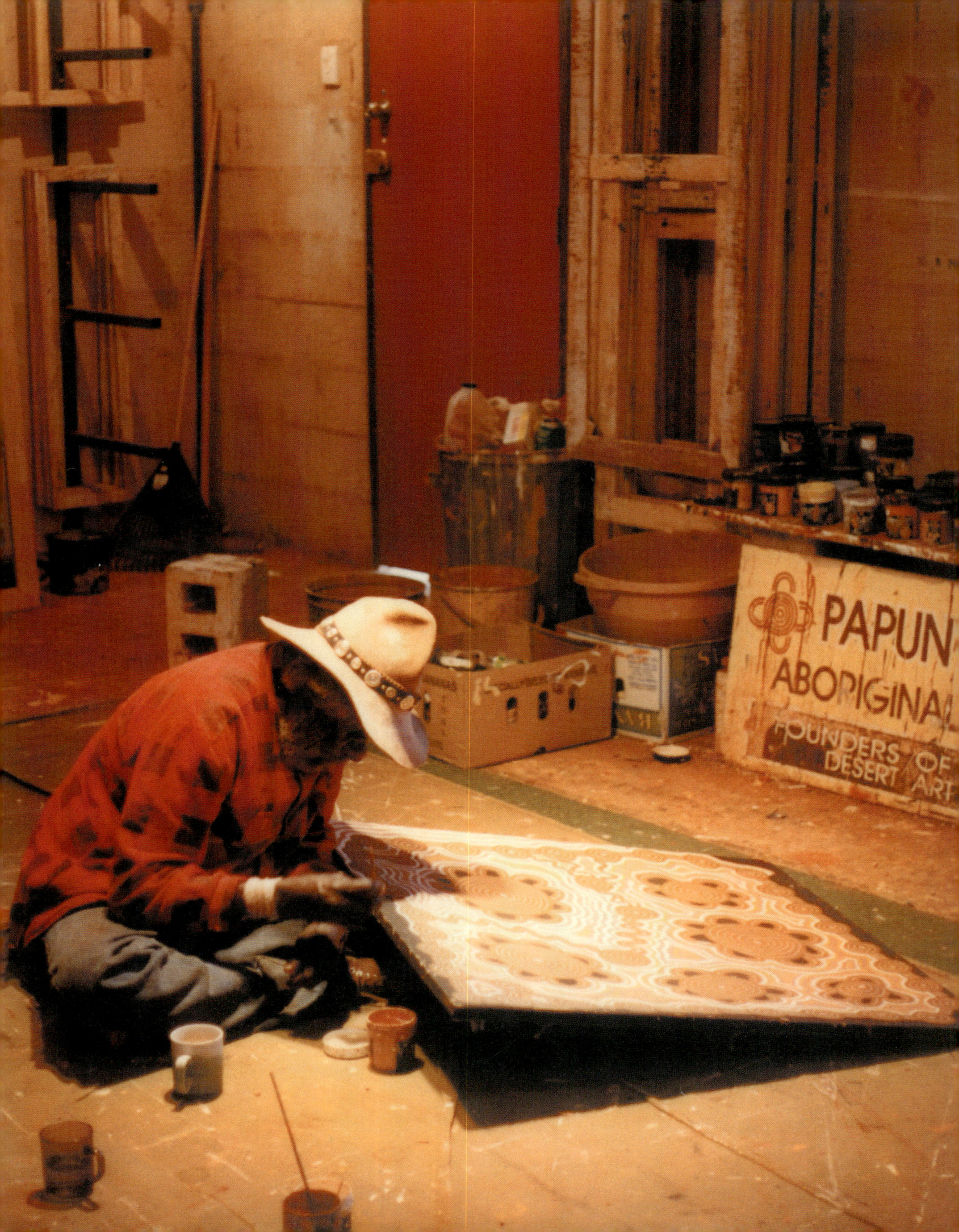

# Art of Resilience

## *The Importance of Papunya Tula Artists in Australia's Western Desert*

**PAUL SWEENEY**

When it comes to art movements, a lot can happen in a short time. Just imagine, then, what could happen in fifty years! The Western Desert Art Movement is no ordinary art movement, and the layered and complex backstory of the Papunya Tula collective's origins—of the artists and their personal histories—is, quite simply, incredible. The first paintings at Papunya, a settlement of Indigenous people relocated from their homelands by the Australian government, were created in 1971. The establishment of Australia's first-ever Aboriginal-owned and -directed artists company, Papunya Tula Artists Pty Ltd, followed only a year later. What followed since has been nothing short of epic. Like a theatrical performance, the story of the company has been one of drama, tragedy and triumph. A story of survival, of adaptation and reinvention. And, above all, one of resilience.

Papunya Tula Artists was founded by Aboriginal men, predominately from the Pintupi, Luritja and Anmatyerr language groups to the west and northwest of Mparntwe (Alice Springs). These men felt compelled to paint their cultures, using modern materials like acrylic paint, in an attempt to illustrate and affirm their identity and place, both individually and collectively, in a rapidly changing social landscape.

Many factors fueled this urge, but none more so than the artists' displacement from their ancestral homelands as the result of government policies of centralization and assimilation. People living a fully traditional nomadic life, some up to three hundred miles west of Papunya in the most remote reaches of the Gibson and Great Sandy Deserts, were met by government welfare patrols and brought into the Papunya settlement.

By the late 1960s, the population of Papunya had grown to more than one thousand people, a scenario completely foreign to community members who had previously spent their lives hunting and gathering on familiar Country in small family groups. Social conflicts, access to alcohol and severe illness as a result of overcrowding soon ravaged the community. Yet before this backdrop of oppressive and failing government policy, something truly remarkable took place when residents of the settlement created the first paintings there.

Amid the language and cultural void between the Aboriginal and non-Aboriginal people of Papunya and its authorities, painting soon provided an opportunity for the men to illustrate their true identity, to display visually

Willy Tjungurrayi working at the Papunya
Tula Artists Walungurru (Kintore) studio,
1997. Photo by Paul Sweeney.

their knowledge, customs and, most importantly, ownership of the land. Creating and selling their art also meant they could generate an income and cultivate a growing sense of self-determination. Against the dysfunction and hardship of being forced to adopt and live a European lifestyle, the men had pushed back through their art, making a clear and unmistakable statement of who they were. Significantly, for the Pintupi men from west of Papunya, painting also created a platform for them to lobby government authorities to establish additional settlements in their homelands. While living at Papunya, these men and their families were hundreds of miles from their Country, so finding a way to return soon became a matter of urgency. As the art movement gathered momentum, so, too, did the homeland movement. These two forces were inextricably linked; by the early 1980s, permanent settlements at Kiwirrkurra and Walungurru (Kintore) had been realized, and the Pintupi people had returned home.

The two additional communities stretched the company's then-limited resources. Its small staff were required to travel up to a thousand miles round trip, now servicing artists and shareholders from Papunya and Walungurru in the Northern Territory to Kiwirrkurra, eighty miles across the border in Western Australia. Initially, studio and staff accommodation in the two new communities was nonexistent. Daphne Williams, one of the company's longest-serving employees, who worked as both field officer and company manager for over twenty years, would sleep

on the back of the company's four-wheel drive Toyota while on field trips to Walungurru and Kiwirrkurra in the early eighties. On one occasion, a mischievous youngster tried to steal the company vehicle at night while Daphne was asleep in the back! The preparation of materials and the stretching and priming of canvases—some as tall as twelve feet—were done under the shade of a tree by the nearby community football oval. Some of the iconic works of the late 1970s and early 1980s by the likes of Uta Uta Tjangala (fig. 7.1), Shorty Lungkarta Tjungurrayi and Willy Tjungurrayi were painted before the company even owned a proper studio. Works now considered priceless masterpieces housed in museums around the world were stretched, primed, created and cataloged without the luxury of ever being under a roof. They literally came directly off the surface of the land.

## ART AS AN ECONOMY

The importance of Papunya Tula Artists to the people of the Western Desert was apparent from the minute it was formed, but once Walungurru and Kiwirrkurra had been established, the company took on even greater significance. Not only was the opportunity to paint and earn money open to shareholders and established artists, but the studio and its facilities were soon made available to almost anyone who wanted to try their hand. At Walungurru and Kiwirrkurra, the company and the production

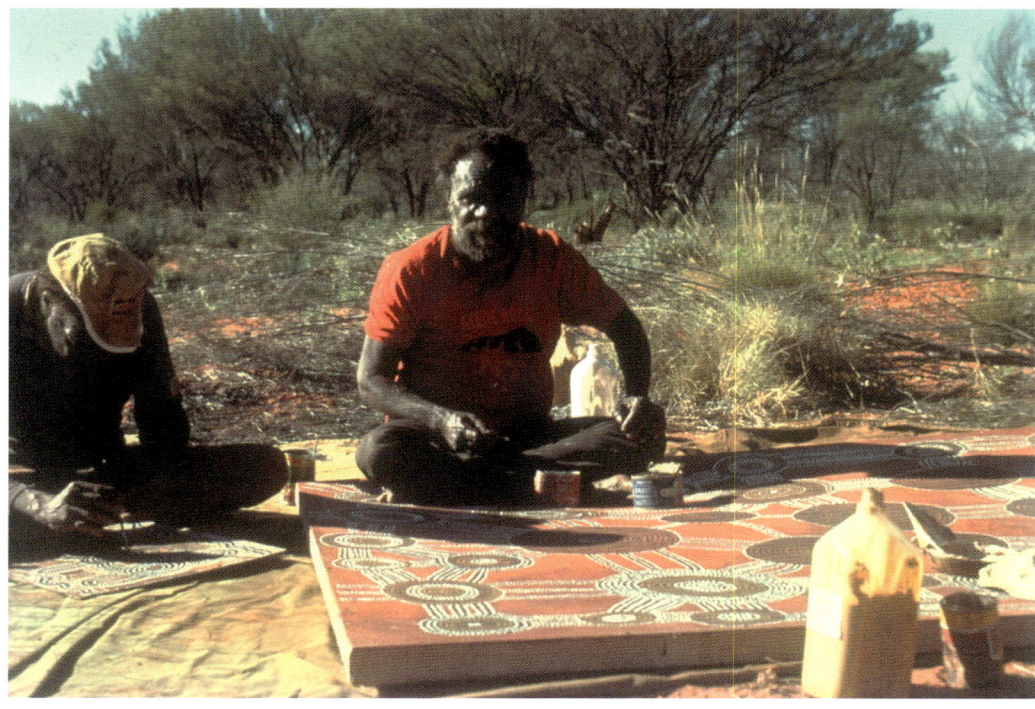

FIG. 7.1
Charlie Tjapangati (left) and Uta Uta Tjangala painting outside at Walungurru (Kintore), 1979. Photo by Fred Myers.

of art immediately became the most significant form of employment within the community, which remains true to this day. At times, there would be up to eighty practicing artists working across the two communities, matching those employed by the schools, clinics, community offices and essential services combined. On any single day in Walungurru, with a population of less than four hundred people, there could be as many as thirty or more artists working either in the studio or on their home verandas. In the smaller setting of Kiwirrkurra, with around two hundred community members, a similar number of artists could be found painting.

Papunya Tula Artists employs a small team of fieldworkers who are, for the most part, permanent members of the Walungurru and Kiwirrkurra communities (fig. 7.2). Aside from intermittent short trips back to Mparntwe to deliver completed works and stock up on art materials, they commit their time to liaising with the artists, cataloging the paintings and maintaining the studios. They assemble and prepare the raw materials of art making to a stage where all the artists need to do is sit down and begin painting. Remote art center work is hectic, and the bush studios operate at a frenetic pace. A typical day in the life of a fieldworker could involve almost anything imaginable and, quite often, have absolutely nothing to do with the creation of fine art. If someone needs something done that will in some way result in them producing a great work, then it is up to the fieldworker to assist

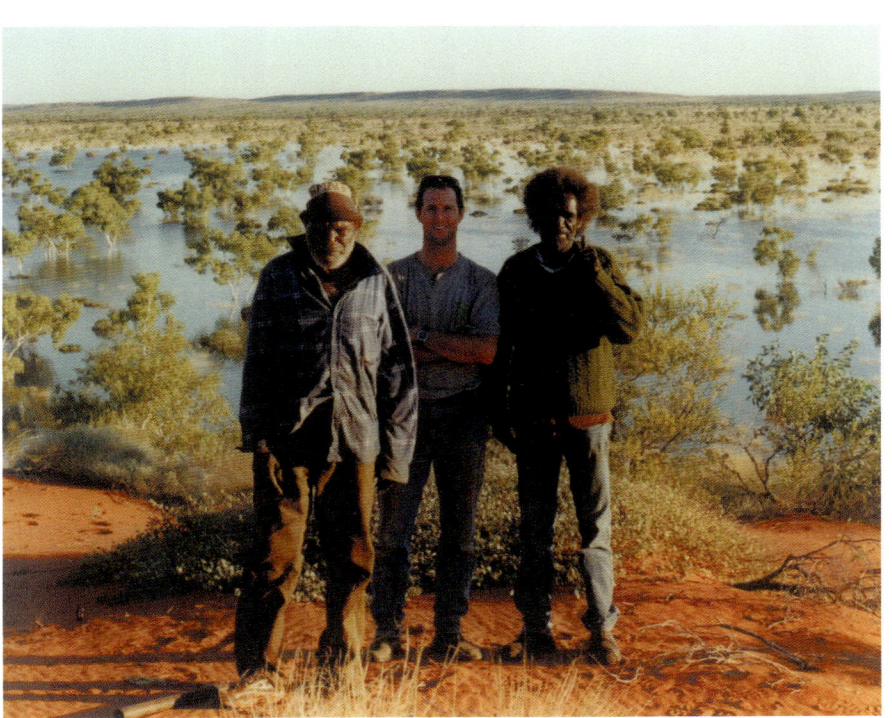

them. No job description accurately reflects this position, where tasks ranging from the rescuing of a lost dog to the towing of a broken-down car are run of the mill. Artists in the studio are often overrun by needy children and bickering dogs, while those painting at home on porches are at the mercy of the desert elements and gusts of dusty wind. Yet somehow, despite this challenging environment, works of great beauty continually emerge, carefully and precisely painted despite the surrounding chaos.

One of the great benefits for the artists of Papunya Tula is the company's ability to offer immediate payment for completed works. This is a best-case scenario for people living hand to mouth and heavily reliant on daily trips to the community store for food and supplies. Cashflow is paramount in remote desert settlements, and from its first days, Papunya Tula Artists has been able to provide a payment and financial support system that has successfully met the social and cultural expectations of its members. It is an arrangement that would please any practicing artist, anywhere, but for Western Desert painters the company's guarantee of instant cash in return for completed works offers a unique form of financial security. In addition, company shareholders receive an annual dividend, which today totals in excess of AU$150,000. Each year, a total well in excess of AU$1 million is returned directly into the artists' hands and the Pintupi community. Aside from the government's social support system, Papunya Tula Artists is easily the greatest economic driver in the region.

Throughout its history, Papunya Tula Artists has maintained a grassroots and community-oriented philosophy. It has remained inclusive and supportive, committed to the fostering of emerging new talent and the long-term investment needed to develop artists' careers. But not every company artist goes on to reach international acclaim. In many cases, the company has commissioned paintings from people who never achieved commercial viability, ultimately selling their works at a loss, sometimes over a period of years. Nonetheless, Papunya Tula has created an opportunity for community members to engage with a form of self-employment, generating valuable income for them and their families in the form of dividends paid to shareholders (descendants of the

**FIG. 7.2**

Johnny Yungut Tjupurrula, Paul Sweeney (then serving as a Papunya Tula fieldworker) and Kanya Tjapangati at Yumari, 2001. Photographer unknown.

founding artists), and also uses its profits to fund vital community services. In the economic environment of a remote Aboriginal community, where the cost of living is drastically higher than that enjoyed by most Australians, any chance to supplement government support is a step toward a better standard of living.

## ART TO IMPROVE HEALTH

Without doubt, the most alarming and distressing reality facing Western Desert people since European contact has been their tragically shortened life expectancy. As a result of shifting from traditional hunting and gathering to adopting a Western diet, coupled with a less active lifestyle, the Aboriginal community's health has deteriorated dramatically. Along with the introduction of processed food came the ready availability of alcohol, which alone has left a legacy of sorrow and destruction. Cars speeding long distances along dirt roads have also caused a great number of deaths, including many well-known Papunya Tula painters.

Since the establishment of the company, a majority of its shareholders and artists have been senior members of the community. Painting remains predominately an older person's occupation, with most artists at least in their sixties. A modest number of artists between the ages of thirty and fifty currently work for the company, but with popular culture's ever-increasing influence on and distraction of younger generations, senior community members continue to be the company's main contributors. Given the average age of those who turn up to the studio each day, it is no surprise that almost every artist carries some kind of injury or illness. This goes well beyond the simple aches and pains of old age, though, and in many cases involves serious and complex chronic illnesses that artists have endured for many years. The most publicized of these is the alarming rate of kidney disease.

Renal failure first arrived among Western Desert people in the early 1990s. Initially, only a small number were diagnosed and required regular dialysis, but that figure rose quickly, and within a few years many more patients were suffering the same fate. Among the ranks of Papunya Tula, Timmy Payungu Tjapangati, Maxie Tjampitjinpa, Mick Namarari Tjapaltjarri and Yala Yala Gibbs Tjungurrayi all suffered kidney failure and died between 1997 and 2000. These were not only important senior men of their communities, but also giants of the Papunya Tula movement. To date, a staggering

twenty-four painters from Walungurru and Kiwirrkurra have succumbed to the same debilitating illness, with numbers only set to continue rising.

One positive development to come from the epidemic of kidney disease, however, was the creation of the Purple House, an organization that delivers renal dialysis to patients through clinics in eighteen remote Aboriginal communities. The effects of renal failure cannot be reversed, and the best treatment one can hope for is being able to receive dialysis in one's own community. Prior

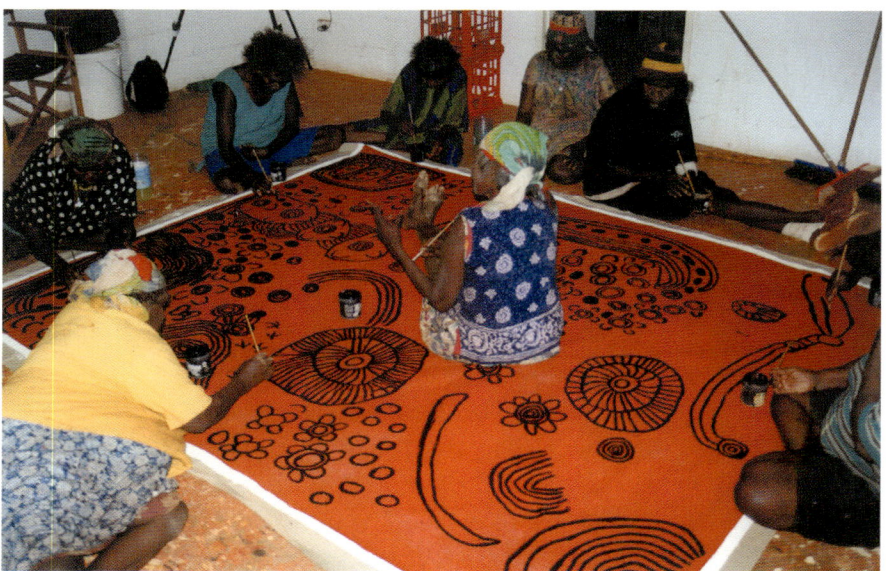

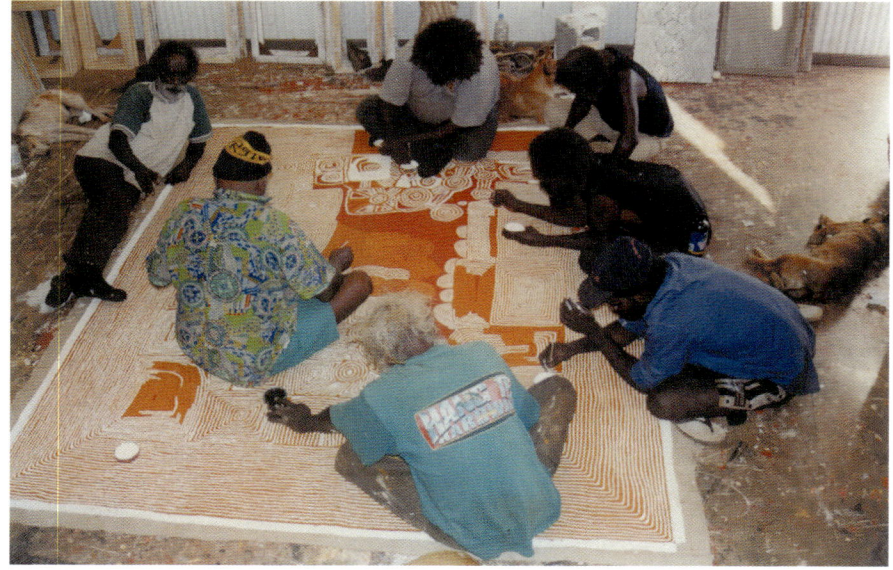

TOP | FIG. 7.3

At work on the Walungurru (Kintore) women's collaborative painting for the Western Desert Dialysis Appeal, 1999. Photo by Paul Sweeney.

BOTTOM | FIG. 7.4

At work on the Kiwirrkurra men's collaborative painting for the Western Desert Dialysis Appeal, 1999. Photo by Paul Sweeney.

to the establishment of the Purple House, patients from remote communities were forced to permanently relocate to Mparntwe—for some, hundreds of miles from their homes—to receive treatment, leaving behind their friends, families and connection to their Country. This had such a terrible impact on the patients and their communities that some sufferers even decided against moving for treatment and instead remained at home to die.

At a time when the Australian government refused to recognize the importance of treating Aboriginal patients from remote communities on their own land, Papunya Tula Artists and its network of committed supporters took on the responsibility to establish local treatment services for those suffering renal failure. News of the growing health crisis filtered through Papunya Tula to its audience, which raised money to establish a pilot program to dialyze Pintupi people on their own Country. Collectors, gallery owners and industry figures banded together and donated works of art to be auctioned at a gala event on November 11, 2000, in the foyer of the Art Gallery of New South Wales. The highlight of the thirty-five artworks up for auction was a group of four large-scale collaborative works by the men and women painters of Walungurru and Kiwirrkurra (figs. 7.3–7.4). The event raised over AU$1 million, with the four Papunya Tula collaborative paintings collectively fetching over AU$600,000.

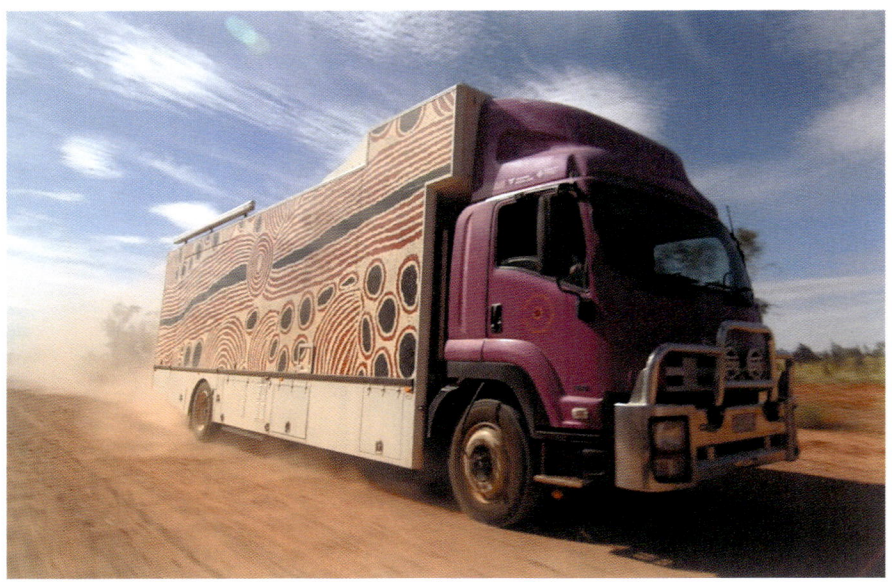

The Purple Truck is a self-contained dialysis unit on wheels. Established in 2012 with the help of Medicines Australia, Papunya Tula Artists and Fresenius, it gives patients with end-stage renal failure the chance to return home for family, cultural or sorry business.

This remarkable result became a shining example of the artists' ability to fund their own response to a serious community problem. By their own means, they were able to bring about a positive outcome from a situation that was threatening the cultural stability of their communities. As Sarah Brown AM, chief executive officer of the Purple House, noted:

In 2000, Papunya Tula Artists Pty Ltd had a clear vision of the needs of their communities. The right to remain on country, with family was central to this vision. They were not frightened by Western medical technology, they saw only the imperative to look after family members, to "hold them close."

The independent money that they raised through the Western Desert Dialysis Appeal gave them power; power to take charge of their own health care and to develop a model of care which was to become the envy of others. This action has not just changed the future of Pintupi communities, but through their generosity and compassion helped many thousands of Aboriginal and non-Aboriginal people across remote Australia. They have shown there is a different/better way to offer healthcare embedded with cultural priorities, the responsibilities of looking after family and country.

When government departments and bureaucrats said dialysis on country was an impossibility, Papunya Tula Artists, its shareholders and many friends pushed on, assured that they could find a way to do this. And the rest . . . is history! [fig. 7.5]

Five years later, another fundraising event, modeled on the dialysis auction, took place at the same venue in Sydney, this time with the goal of constructing a swimming pool in the center of Walungurru, just 100 yards west of the art center. Research has shown that access to swimming pools provides numerous benefits to the health of young Indigenous people, and, importantly, reduces the risk of future renal failure through a lower incidence of chronic skin-related infections. The pool would also represent a valuable resource for a community desperately in need of sporting and recreational infrastructure. When the idea to construct such a facility to help prevent health issues emerged, Papunya Tula Artists once again rose to the challenge. The company donated five large, solo works that collectively raised AU$583,000 of the AU$902,000 auction profits.

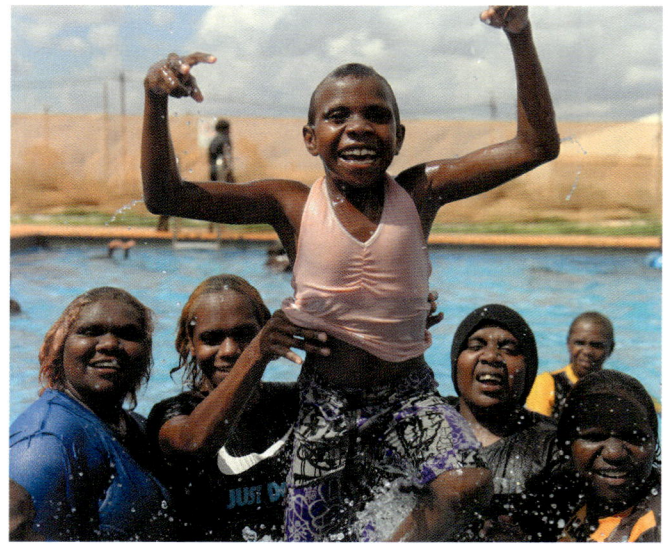

FIG. 7.6

Walungurru (Kintore) Pool opening,
February 2008. Photo by Paul Sweeney.

On February 14, 2008, Hetti Perkins, then curator of Aboriginal and Torres Strait Islander art at the Art Gallery of New South Wales, who led the project from the beginning, officially opened the pool (fig. 7.6). Once again, the power of art had spoken, and rather than relying on government handouts, the artists and their company had asserted themselves to fund a major project that would not have happened otherwise. The township of Walungurru now had its own remote dialysis clinic and town pool largely funded by the community.

## ART FOR SELF-EMPOWERMENT

Throughout its journey, Papunya Tula Artists has proven itself to be far more than a simple art center and retail gallery. In response to local needs, it has become a major source of funding and support for almost every aspect of community life. When the summer months arrive, so, too, does the "business," a colloquial term for the initiation

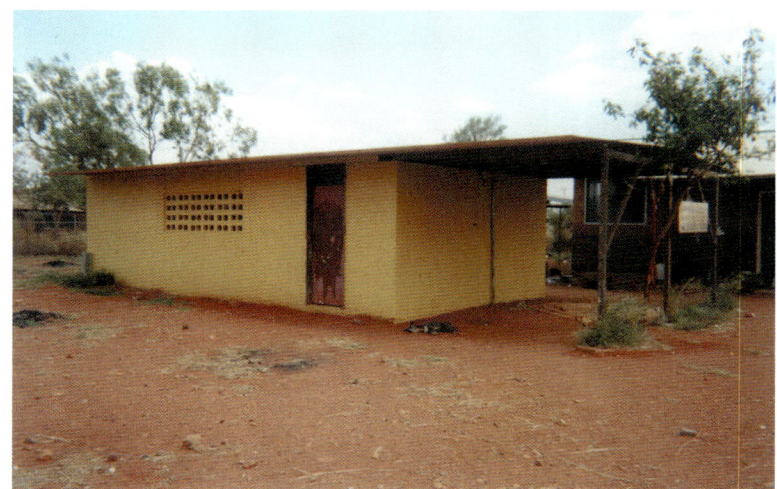

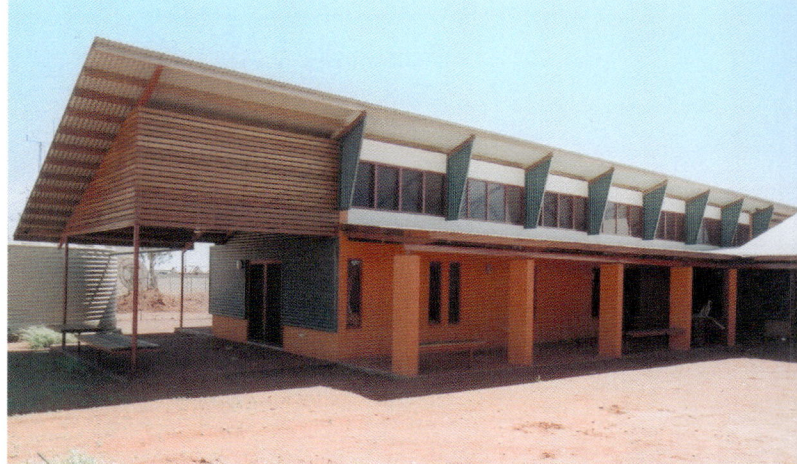

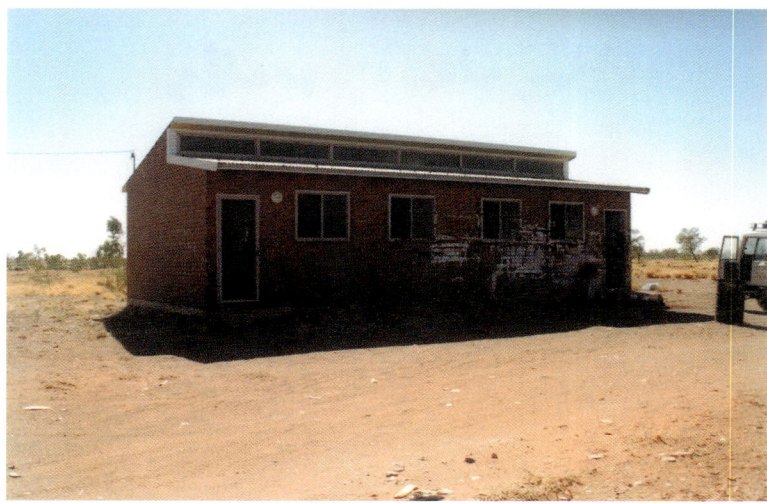

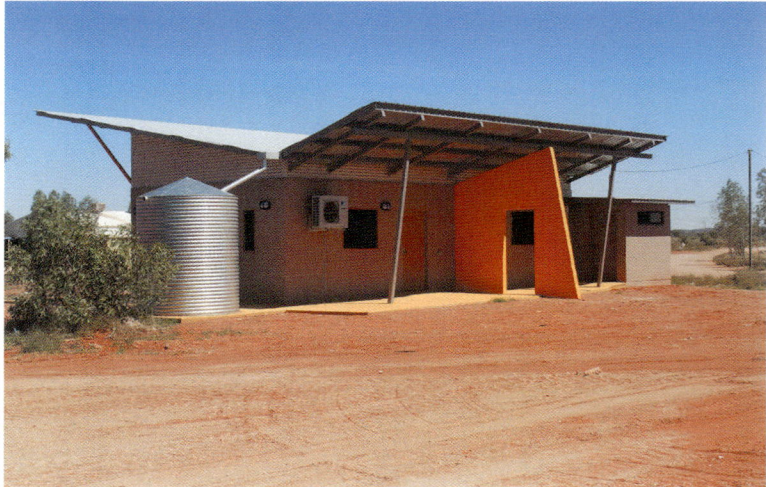

ceremonies of young men. This can often involve large groups of men, women and children traveling long distances to neighboring communities for weeks at a time. The company has always prioritized these events as essential cultural maintenance, and in doing so commits many thousands of dollars annually to fuel cars and provide food and supplies for the participants. Elders charged with the responsibility of guiding the proceedings become the point of contact for cash deposits and purchase orders, as caravans of vehicles loaded with people snake their way across the desert, collecting more and more people as they go. The obligatory ceremonial exchange of trailer loads of food and blankets that takes place between participating communities and family groups is complex and costly. Once again, the company empowers artists to fund important community events as a direct result of the profits generated from the sales of their artwork.

Papunya Tula has also independently undertaken and funded the construction of new studios and housing. Local architects in Mparntwe designed purpose-built studios and staff accommodation at both Walungurru and Kiwirrkurra (figs. 7.8–7.11), and, since 2007, the company has invested over AU$2 million in major infrastructure without requesting a single dollar from the Australian government. Beyond these significant financial assets, though, lies something of far greater value: a sense of pride, ownership and self-determination. Buildings, dialysis units, the swimming pool and the ability to fund ceremonies, funerals, sporting carnivals and more have all been made possible through the creation of art and can be traced back to those first works done in Papunya fifty years ago. After the unimaginable shock of first encountering Europeans, then being relocated to a central community at a vast distance from their homelands, Aboriginal people found their voice in the act of painting, which provided them with the power to direct their own lives and return to their own Country.

Today, Papunya Tula Artists remains the financial cornerstone of the two Pintupi communities and their respective studios in Walungurru and Kiwirrkurra, the central hubs of activity. Beyond these desert communities, the Aboriginal art movement, spearheaded by Papunya Tula Artists, has reached out globally, with the company now firmly established as an international brand. Artists have traveled in support of exhibitions and, while meeting with admirers to talk about their art, have expanded their own lives and experiences, returning home to their desert settlements with stories of altered time zones, exotic food and crowded cities. Despite what goes on elsewhere in the world, the Western Desert painters remain unfazed. Their universe is that which is immediately around them. The ancestors and spirits that created and rule their land are of greatest value to them and lie embedded within each and every artwork they create. The artists' drive to keep their ancestral stories alive remains resolute and unwavering, guaranteeing their company's future.

TOP LEFT AND RIGHT
FIGS. 7.8, 7.9
Papunya Tula Artists studio at Walungurru (Kintore), 2002 and 2007. Photos by Paul Sweeney.

BOTTOM LEFT AND RIGHT
FIGS. 7.10, 7.11
Papunya Tula Artists studio at Kiwirrkurra, 1997 and 2010. Photos by Paul Sweeney.

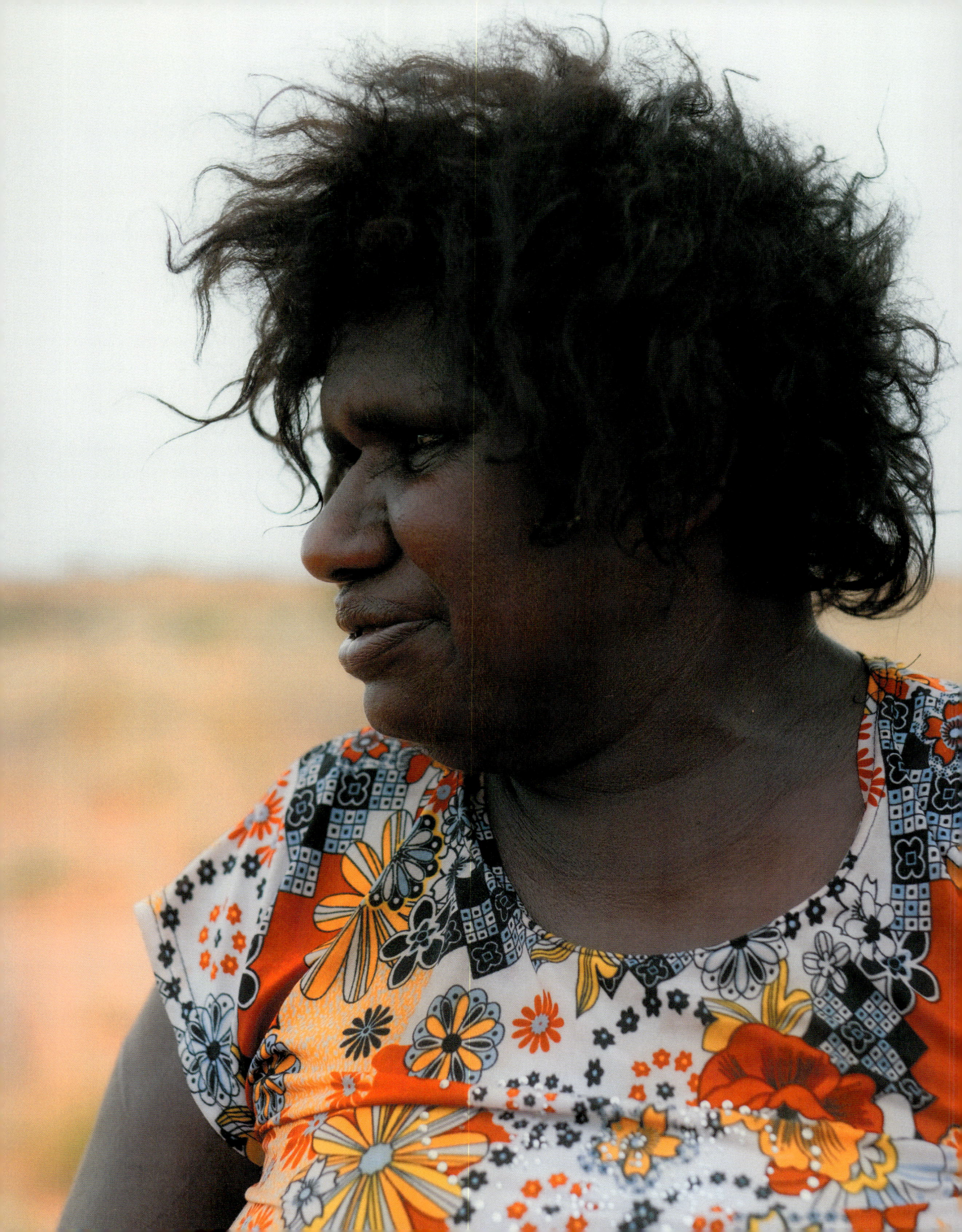

# Adventures in Art Comeuppance

**STEVE MARTIN**

I've had a fantasy that a contestant would fall ill on *Jeopardy*, and I would be invited to be the emergency replacement. In my fantasy, the questions are all art flashcards, and I get them all right, from Bronzino to Pablo Picasso. Then, because everyone is so amazed, I am taken from behind my lectern and, with more flashcards, asked to identify various movements from the Hudson River School, to Fluxus, to Suprematism, on through Futurism and beyond.

The audience, now on its feet for the Final Jeopardy question—under the rubric of "American Still-Life Painting"—considers an image of a pile of books and a few copper coins. They wait breathlessly as the *Jeopardy* countdown theme music ends. I, pausing for effect, say, "Who is John Peto?"

There is another pause. The host looks concerned. The answer was supposed to be William Harnett. "The judges are checking . . ."

Then: "You are correct! The painting was misattributed to Harnett but it's actually by Peto!" I am carried out of the studio, borne in the arms of the jubilant audience, who shout, "Good eye, Steve! Good eye!"

So, imagine my surprise when I opened the *New York Times* arts section six years ago and saw Warlimpirrnga Tjapaltjarri standing mightily beside works taller than he is (fig. 8.1), works in a style I had never seen before, works vibrating with life, works from a curious place called Papunya Tula, an artists' enterprise wholly outside my fifty-plus years of art knowledge osmosis. One question about it on my fantasy *Jeopardy* and I would have been drubbed out in the first round.

A few taps on a tablet brought the world of Papunya Tula Artists closer, and a little effort helped me understand—a bit—what was going on in the paintings. I ordered books, and they started arriving by the boxload. I thumbed through them, read closely, and immersed myself in this perplexing yet inviting art. A few purchases later, the cavalry arrived in the form of advice from dealers, scholars, collectors and curators. I learned a few hard lessons about correct provenance and its necessity, and, as usual, the rewards of the enterprise were not only an introduction to great, new-to-me art, but also the connection to people willing to share their own devotion and knowledge (fig. 8.2).

Yukultji Napangati near Kiwirrkurra, 2014.
Photo by Matt Frost.

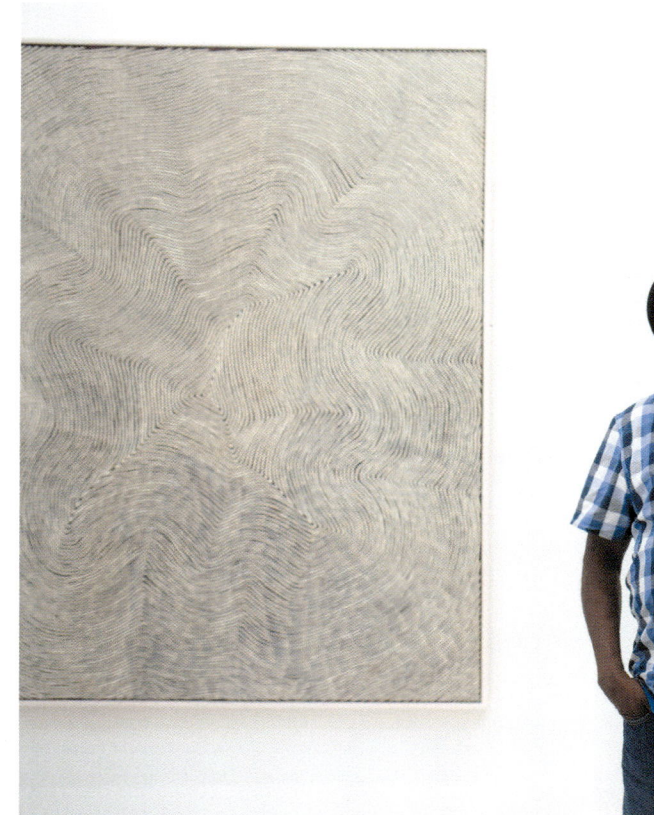
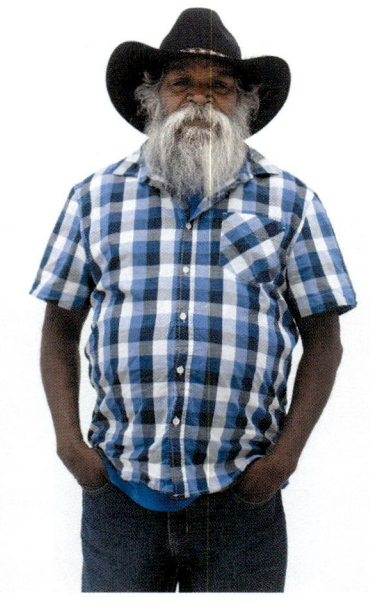
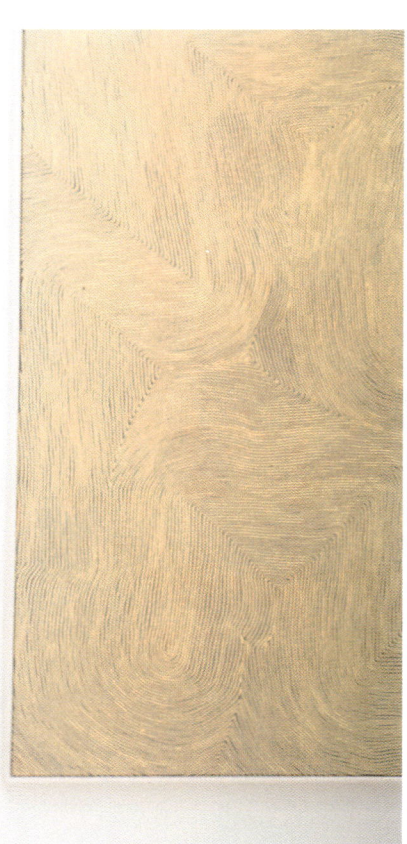

FIG. 8.1

Warlimpirrnga Tjapaltjarri at his exhibition
*Maparntjarra*, Salon 94, New York, September 2015.
Photo by Karsten Moran.

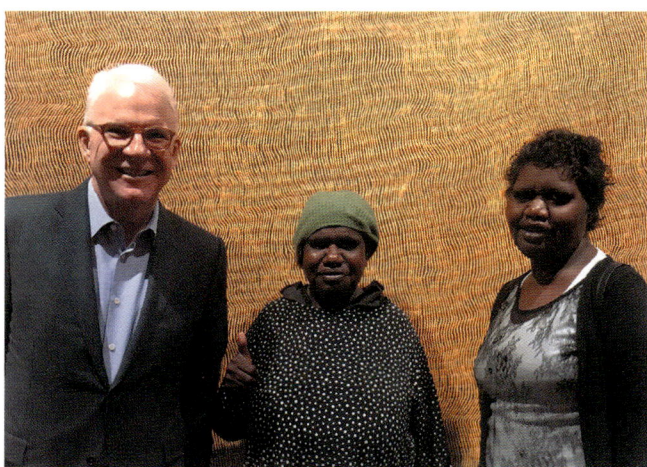

FIG. 8.2

Steve Martin, Yukultji Napangati and Jodie
Napurrula Ward at Salon 94, New York, January 2018.
Photo by Paul Sweeney.

Internet sleuthing continued to offer an abundance of images, all springing from the same cultural source. It was challenging to sort them out. Soon, a few walls in our apartment were hung with a few pieces, and I found myself lingering before them as I would in front of an Edward Hopper.

I was in Australia—before the pandemic—and visited many major museums hosting Aboriginal art. I was able to browse the stacks of the Holmes à Court Gallery's collection in Perth and left entranced. Who the hell is Rover Thomas? I learned quickly, after I was set back on my heels. On returning the United States, I was astounded by the Kluge-Ruhe Aboriginal Art Collection, a King Tut's cache of Indigenous Australian treasures in the unlikely setting of the University of Virginia. Unlikely, but why not? I never considered the art as something exotic from another culture. Was I supposed to? I always saw it as art that vied for a high position in the international contemporary art scene.

I have replaced my *Jeopardy* fantasy with a new one: I envision this art hanging in a museum next to canonical paintings, mixing in casually with the Mark Rothkos, Jackson Pollocks, and Agnes Martins. It is assigned no special category, no footnotes or asterisks. Just art that holds its own alongside renowned art that, too, is considered wonderful.

Good eye, Steve, good eye!

# A REALLY GOOD CELEBRATION

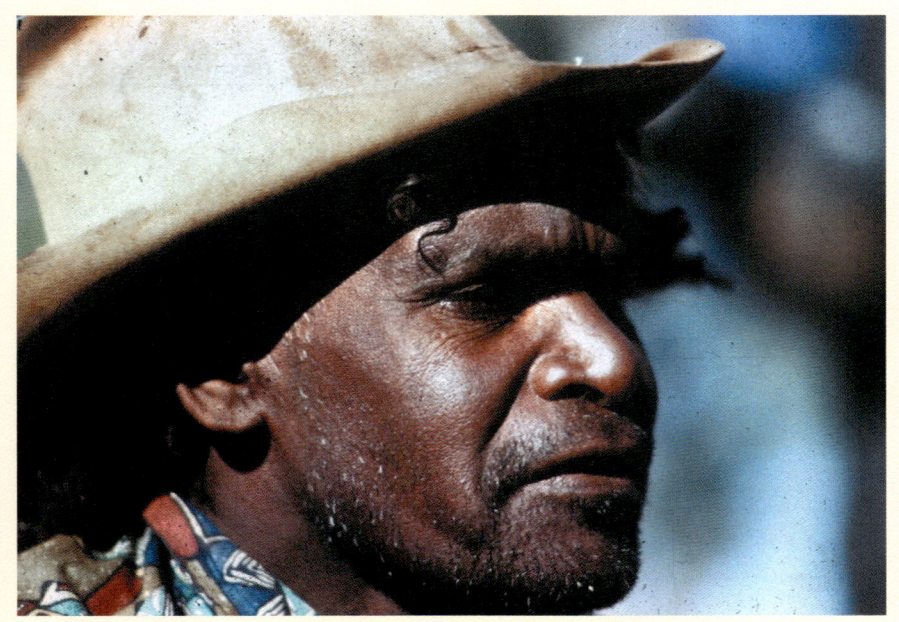

Old people started working and made it, and this company is still going for a long time, for fifty years now. It's been going on for a long time. You look at other companies and they don't do that—only Papunya Tula Artists. It's *martupura* (important) for A̱nangu, Pintupi and Luritja. When we're stuck in Fitzroy Crossing, Halls Creek and Jigalong, we always ring up Papunya Tula, and there's money there all the time, supporting everyone, including the Purple House. We've got something there, you know, always. The company is there working for people, all the time. It's going to be a really good celebration for A̱nangu tjurtangku (all the Aboriginal people). All around Australia and in the museum in America, which is a good thing, because Papunya Tula has never failed, it's still going. It is always there to help with fuel and tucker and for Sorry Business. Very important for A̱nangu. *Martupura*!

—BOBBY WEST TJUPURRULA

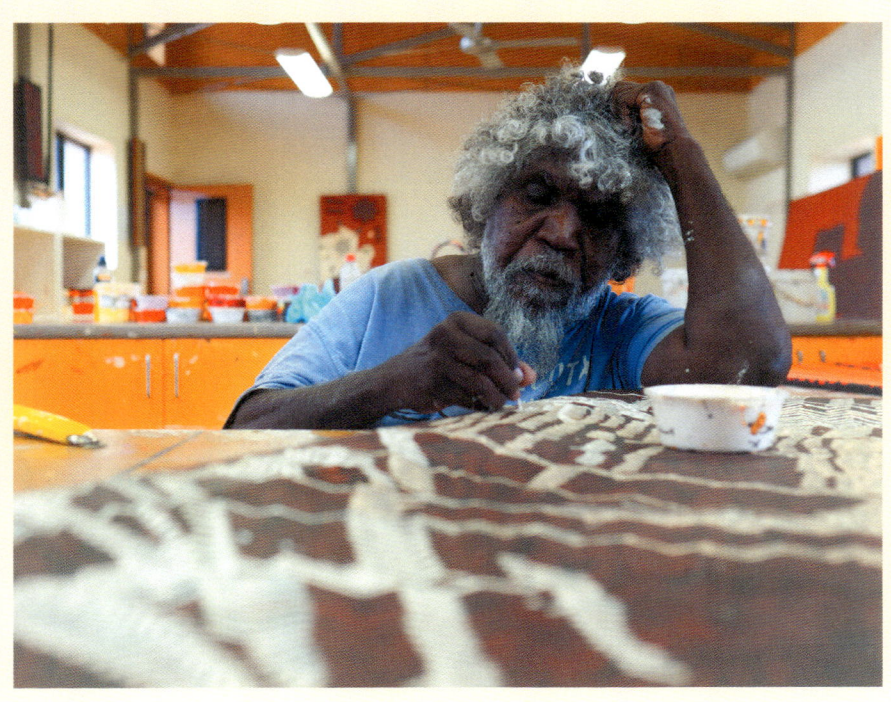

TOP

Freddy West Tjakamarra at Yayayi, 1974. Photo by Es Giddy.

BOTTOM

Bobby West Tjupurrula in Kiwirrkurra, 2015. Photo by Matt Frost.

NEXT SPREAD

Ngaminya. Photo by Matt Frost.

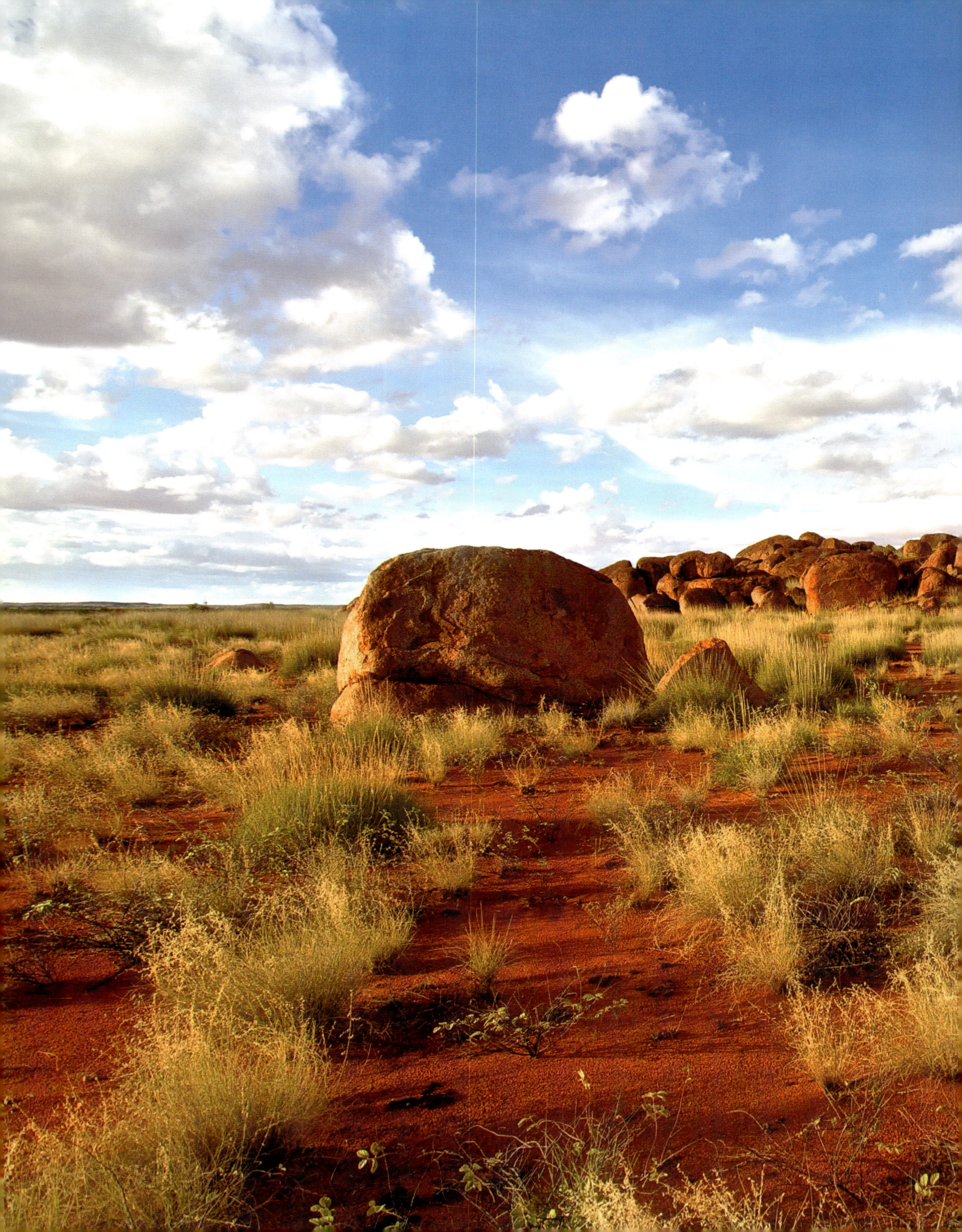

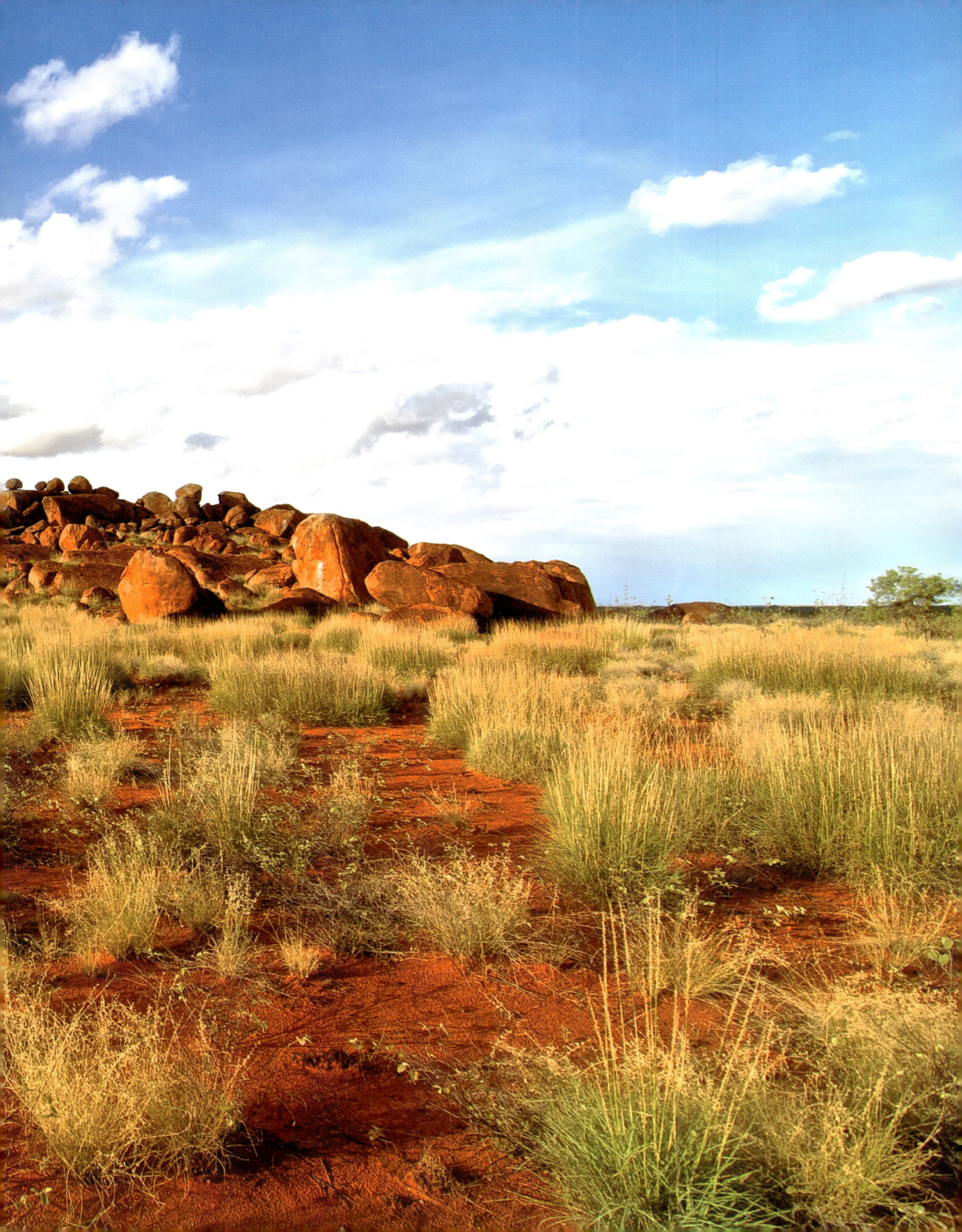

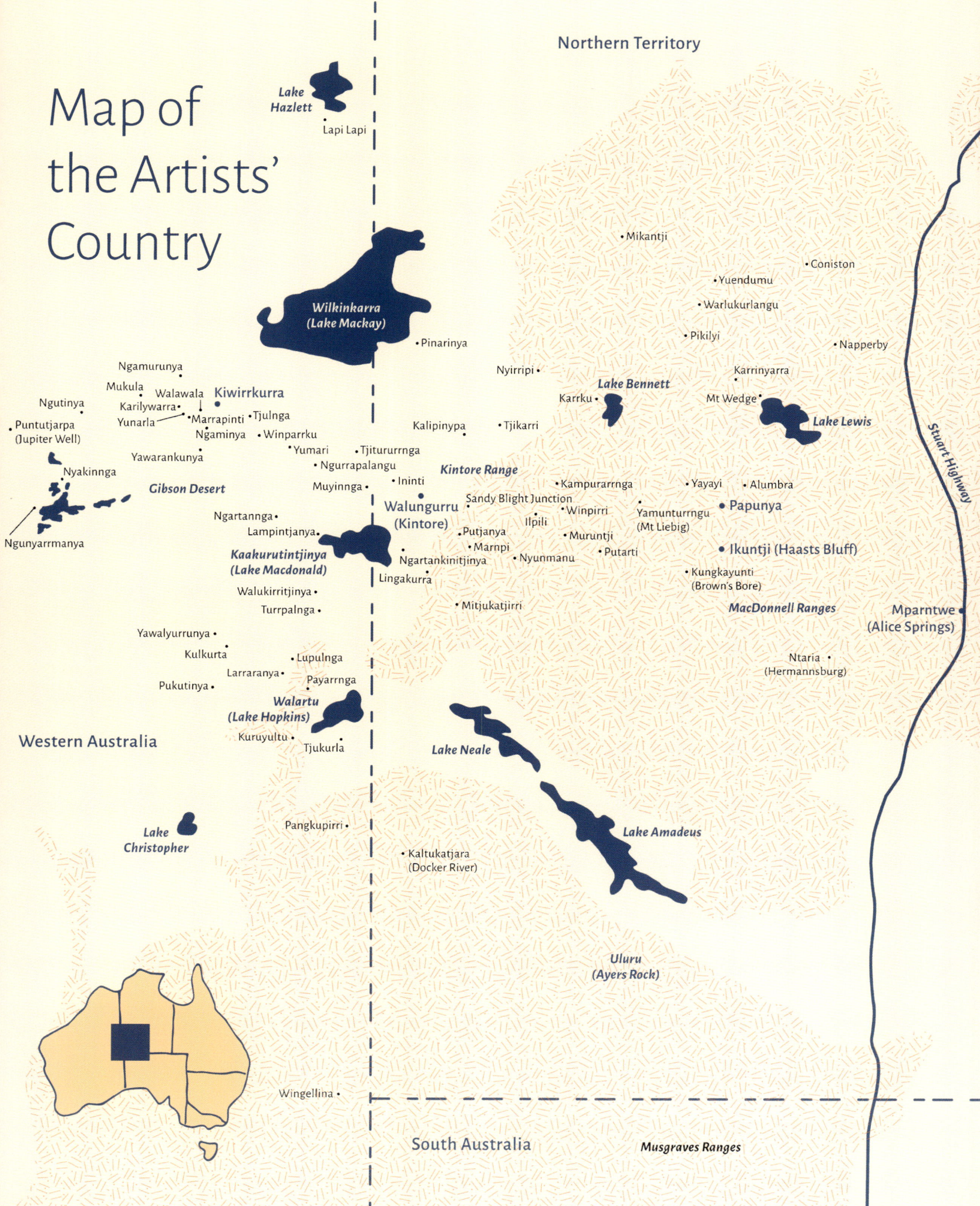

# Map of the Artists' Country

**Northern Territory**

Lake Hazlett
• Lapi Lapi

Wilkinkarra
(Lake Mackay)

• Pinarinya

• Mikantji

• Coniston

• Yuendumu

• Warlukurlangu

• Pikilyi

• Napperby

Ngamurunya •
Mukula •          • Walawala      Kiwirrkurra
Ngutinya •    Karilywarra •          ↓
• Puntutjarpa    Yunarla •   • Marrapinti   • Tjulnga
(Jupiter Well)       Ngaminya •   • Winparrku
Yawarankunya •
Nyakinnga •

• Nyirripi          Karrinyarra •
Karrku •          Mt Wedge •   Lake Lewis
Lake Bennett

• Kalipinypa      • Tjikarri

• Yumari
• Ngurrapalangu      • Tjitururrnga
Muyinnga •      • Ininti    **Kintore Range**      • Kampurarrnga   • Yayayi   • Alumbra
Sandy Blight Junction      • Papunya
Ngartannga •      Walungurru       • Winpirri   Yamunturrngu
(Kintore)   Putjanya •   Ilpili •   (Mt Liebig)
Lampintjanya •      • Marnpi      • Muruntji   • Ikuntji (Haasts Bluff)
**Kaakurutintjinya**      Ngartankinitjinya •   • Nyunmanu   • Putarti
(Lake Macdonald)      Lingakurra •      • Kungkayunti
(Brown's Bore)
Walukirritjinya •
Turrpalnga •      • Mitjukatjirri      **MacDonnell Ranges**      **Mparntwe**
(Alice Springs)

**Gibson Desert**

N; Ngunyarrmanya

Yawalyurrunya •
• Kulkurta      • Lupulnga
Larraranya •      • Payarrnga
Pukutinya •      **Walartu**
(Lake Hopkins)
Kuruyultu •   • Tjukurla

Ntaria •
(Hermannsburg)

Lake Neale

Lake Amadeus

**Western Australia**

Lake
Christopher      • Pangkupirri

• Kaltukatjara
(Docker River)

Uluru
(Ayers Rock)

• Wingellina

**South Australia**      **Musgraves Ranges**

**Stuart Highway**

# PLATES

# BEGINNINGS

In 1971, a small group of Aboriginal artists from Australia's Central Desert changed the face of global art history. The town of Papunya was established by the Australian Government in 1959 to provide room for the increasing population of Aboriginal people leaving the desert for access to water and infrastructure. Aboriginal people were caught between worlds. The government expected them to assimilate to modern culture, but white Australians were fearful of an influx of so-called uncivilized Aboriginal people to towns such as Mparntwe (Alice Springs). At the same time, changing environmental and social conditions made it impossible for them to stay on their traditional homelands.

By the 1970s, the population of Papunya, built to accommodate only four hundred people, had swelled to over one thousand. Aboriginal people from a five-hundred-mile radius and a disparate range of language groups—Luritja, Pintupi, Anmatyerr, Warlpiri, and Kukatja—were living in cramped conditions amid horrific poverty and disease. Geoffrey Bardon describes a devastating scene of despair, violence and hatred: "an unsewered, undrained garbage-strewn death camp in all but name."[1] Some residents had considerable experience of white Australians, whether through exposure to missionaries at Ikuntji (Haasts Bluff) or Ntaria

(Hermannsburg), or through their involvement with the cattle industry. For others, Papunya represented their first encounter with the colonizers. It was the site of more than just a clash between Aboriginal and Western cultures; it was also a space of Aboriginal cosmopolitanism, replete with its own potential and problems. In this atmosphere, painting offered a way of asserting legitimacy and authority—of explaining who you were and were you came from, amidst this chaotic mélange of strangers.

Using ancient designs rarely seen by outsiders, a small group of men began painting on whatever materials they could find. Motivated by their desire to preserve and share their cultural knowledge, the painters illustrated their connection to the Tjukurrpa (Dreaming). In July 1971, encouraged by the newly arrived schoolteacher Geoffrey Bardon, the men created a mural on the local school wall that defiantly announced the arrival of a new artistic renaissance. They painted the story of the Honey Ant ancestor. The following year, they founded their own company: Papunya Tula Artists Pty Ltd, the first Aboriginal-owned artistic enterprise in Australia. The movement quickly grew into a potent medium for effecting economic and social justice. From humble beginnings, a multimillion-dollar industry would emerge, transforming the world of contemporary art and creating a powerful voice for Indigenous artists.

1. Geoffrey Bardon, quoted in Paul Carter, *The Interpretation of Dreams, in Dark Writing: Geography, Performance, Design* (Honolulu: University of Hawai'i Press, 2009), 104–5.

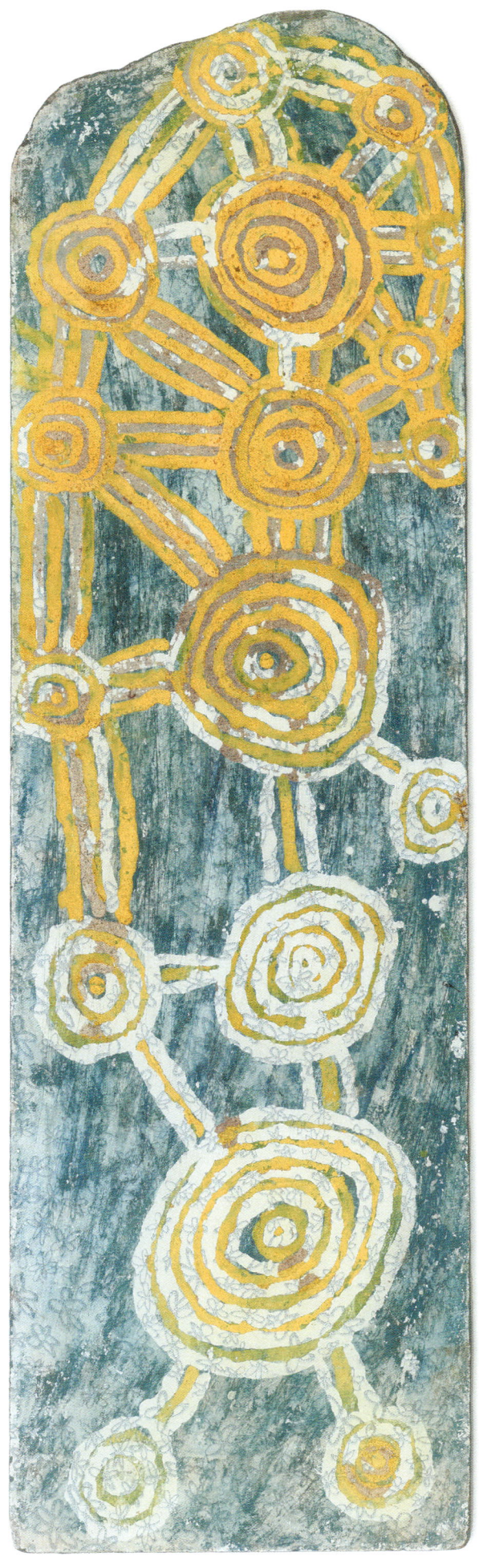
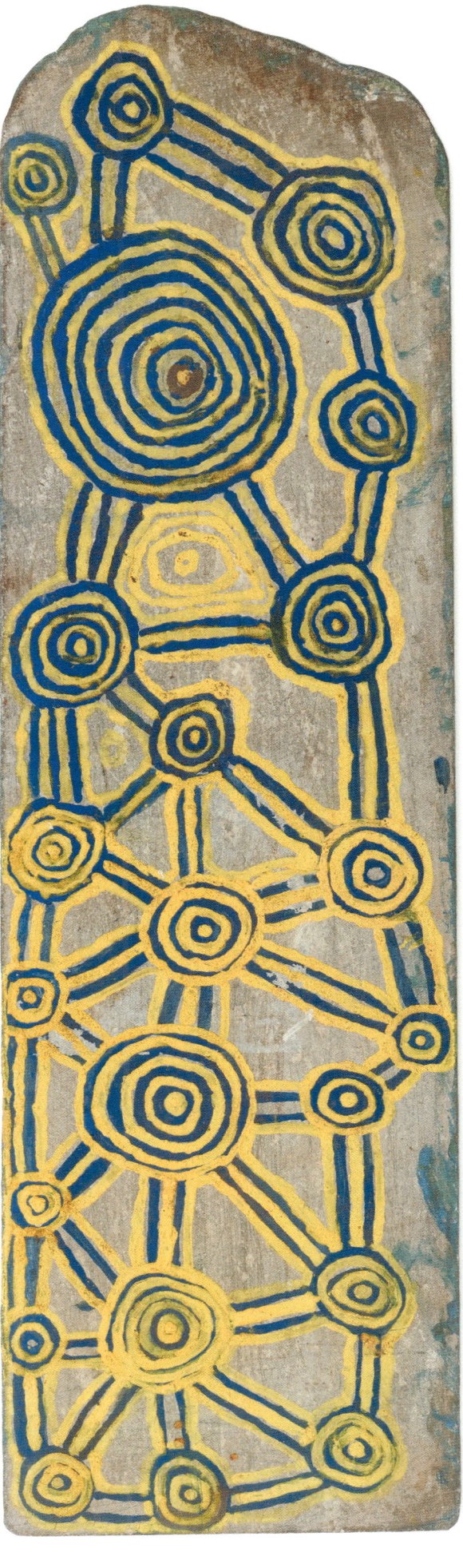

PLATE 1

Unidentified artist
*Pintupi Design* (front
and back), 1971

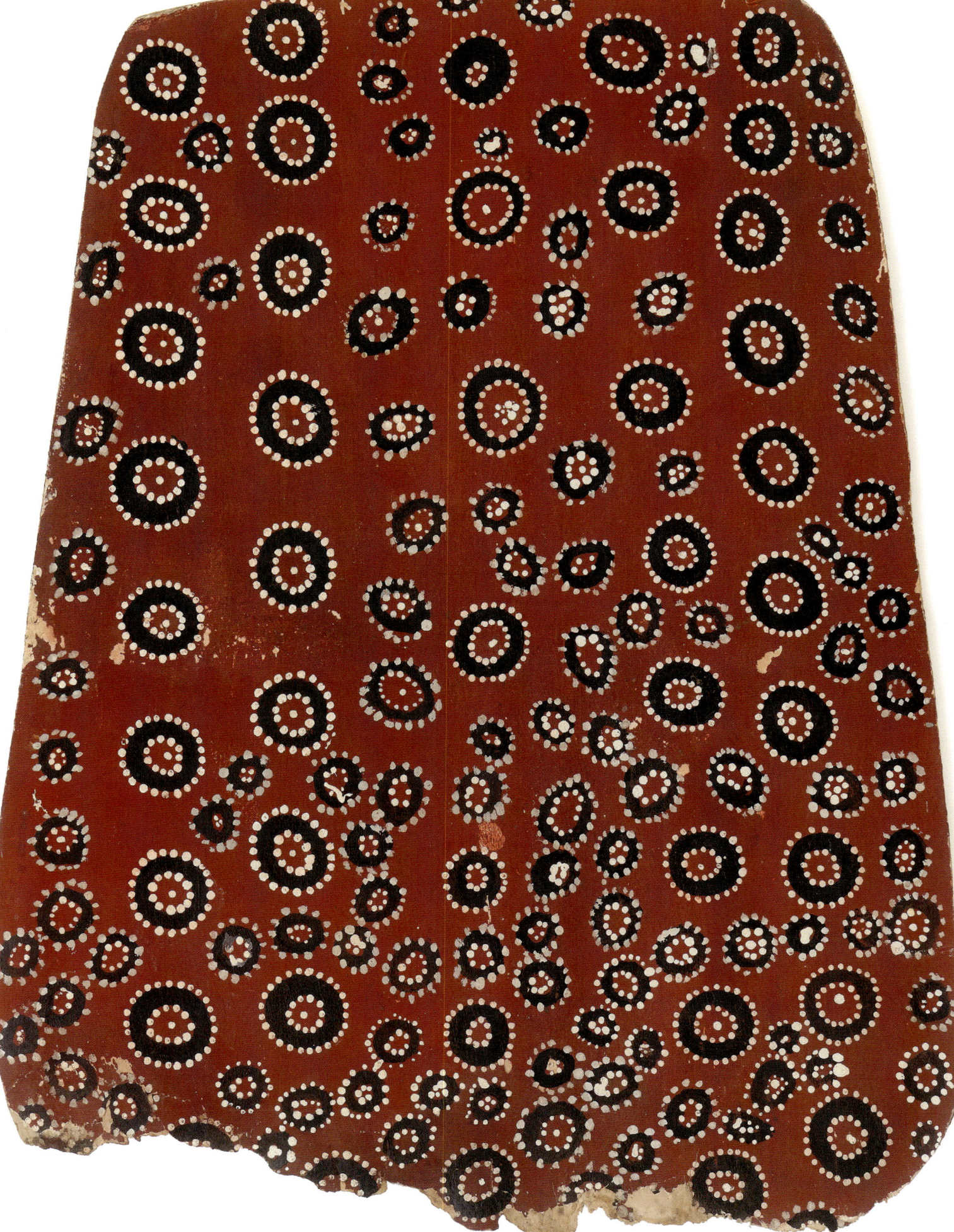

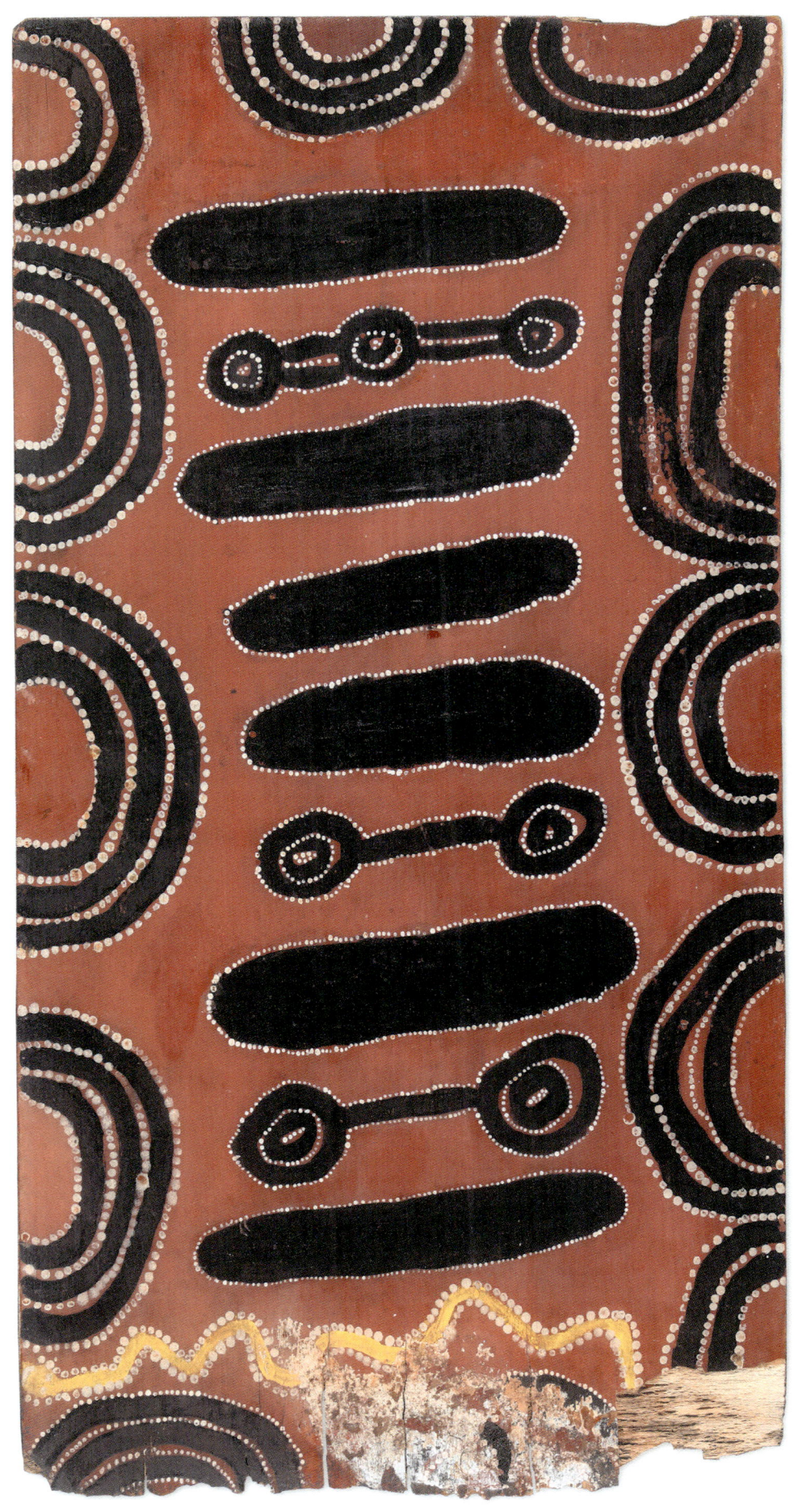

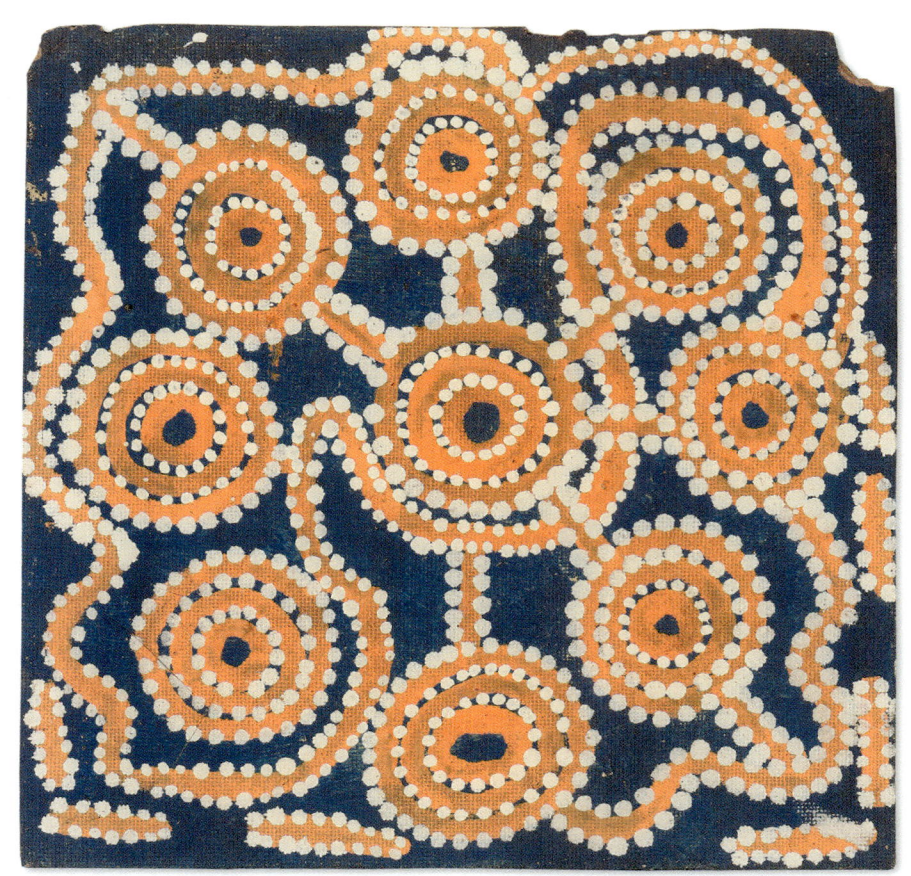

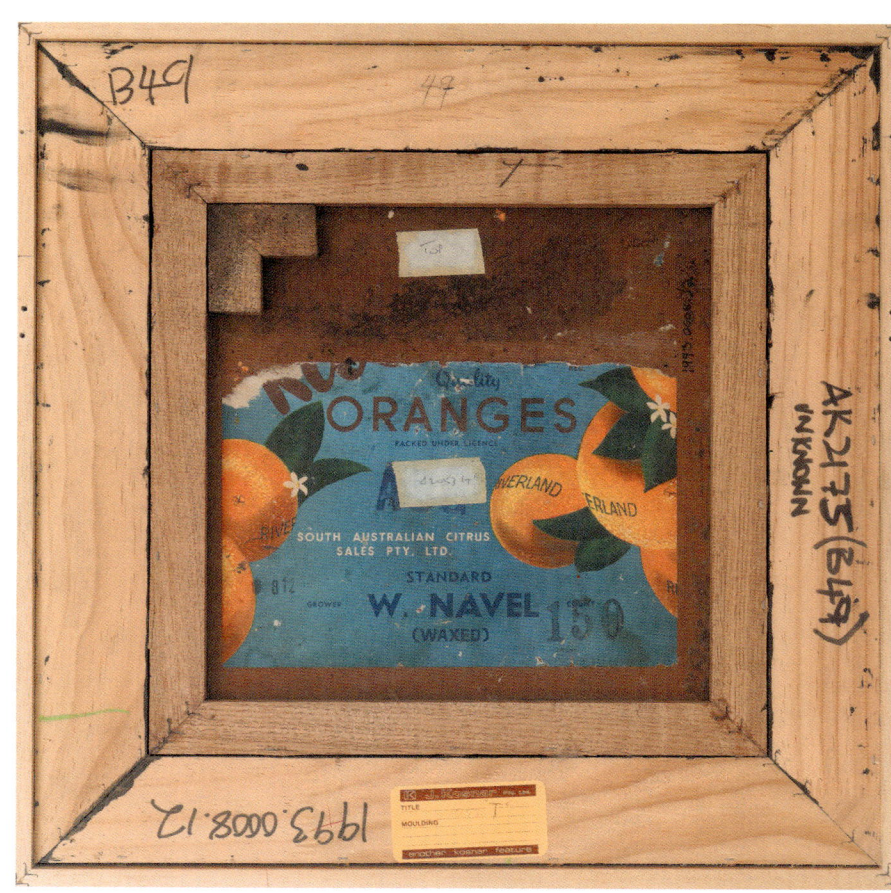

PLATE 4

Unidentified artist
*Dreaming Story* (front and back), 1971

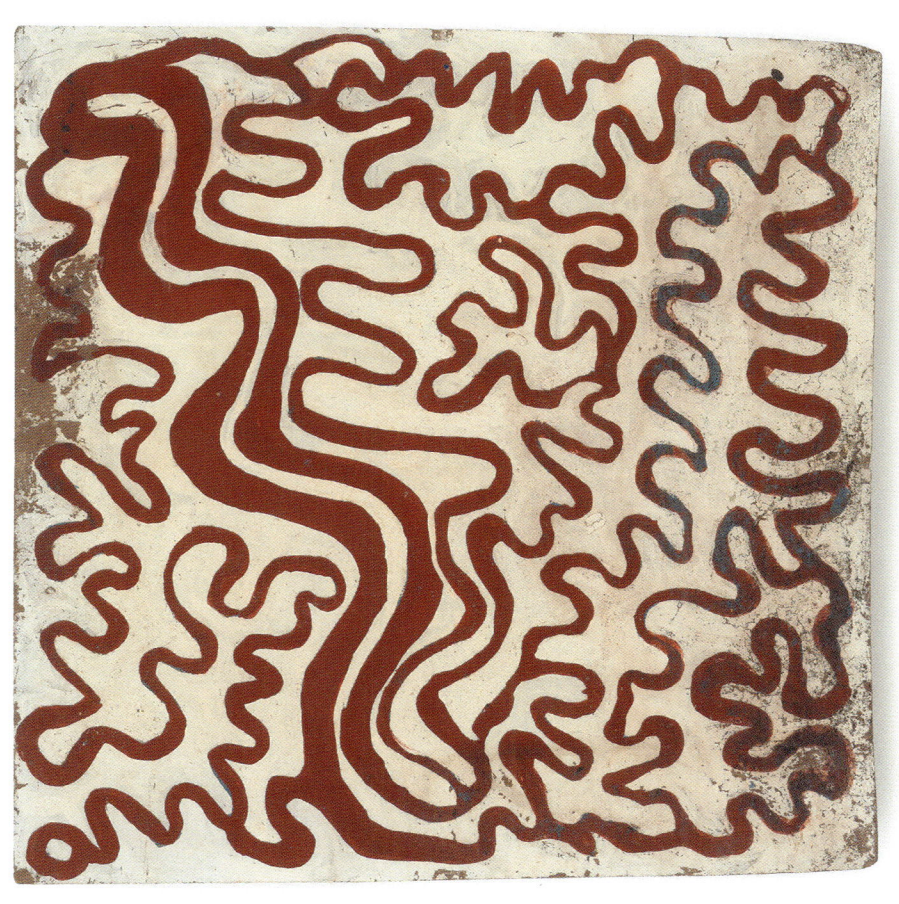

PLATE 5

Timmy Payungu Tjapangati (attr.)
*Ngapa Tjukurrpa (Storm Dreaming)*, 1971

# TJARLA

—

# HONEY ANT

Papunya rests on the Tropic of Capricorn in Honey Ant Country. Beginning in October each year, monsoonal storms scud across the plain from the Tanami Desert. Below the ground, *tjarla* (honey ants) hang suspended in the darkness of underground chambers.[1] Unmoving, they wait to be fed by worker ants that bring exudate from the branches of mulga trees, under which the colonies reside—living larders. The chambers of the *tjarla* are invisible from the surface, but well known to Aboriginal people, who follow the cryptic traces of worker ants across the ground to tiny holes that plummet three feet into the earth. From this cool place, numerous smaller tunnels radiate to reach further chambers in which more honey ants cling, a handful in each chamber, their abdomens distended with sweet nectar.

Honey ants are important to the people of Central Australia. Not only do they provide a rare source of sweetness but, more significantly, their interconnected chambers exemplify important aspects of Indigenous ontology. The subterranean honey ant colonies epitomize the notions of community and connectedness at the heart of Aboriginal belief. Their underground presence gives force to the concept of the earth as the original life giver.[2]

Unsurprisingly, *tjarla* feature in the spiritual and ceremonial lives of Central Australian people, their cultural significance surpassing their size or the lowly status accorded invertebrates in European culture. In the harsh, desiccated environment of Central Australia, their liquid sweetness, while hard won, signifies the bounty of the land.

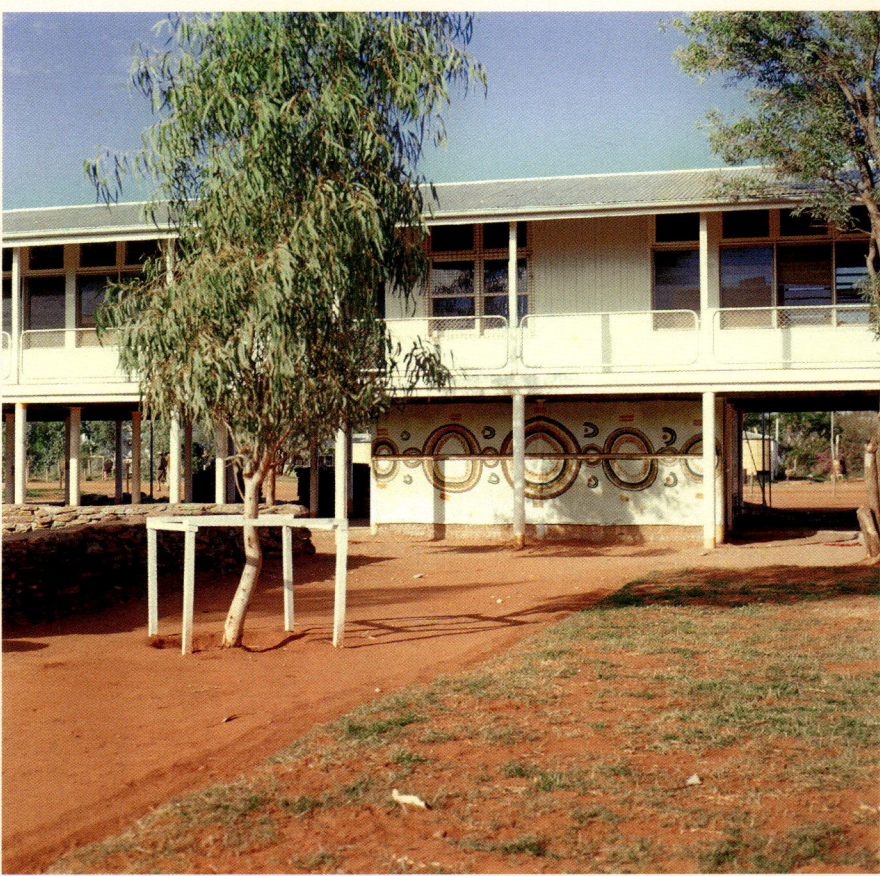

*The Honey Ant Mural at Papunya, 1971. Photo by Allan Scott.*

Papunya has always been a site for the celebration of Honey Ant ancestors. The innumerable children conceived in the vicinity of Papunya are recognized as having ancestral connection to these eternal honey ant forebears. Papunya is Honey Ant country.

Like the hub of a great wheel, Papunya is considered to be at the center where Honey Ant songlines, like spokes from distant lands, converge—from Tatata in Pintupi country to the west; from Yuendumu in Warlpiri/Anmatyerr country in the north; from Akwerrperl (Korbula) in Anmatyerr country and Ngkwarlerlanem ("where the honey is") in Alyawarr country to the northeast; from Lyapa, in Northern Arrernte country to the east; even as far as Utnadata ("the catkins on mulga trees") in Lower Arrernte country, a site better known as Oodnadatta, in South Australia, six hundred miles southeast of Papunya.

—JOHN KEAN

1. *Tjarla* is just one name used for the species *Camponotus inflatus*. Other names used at Papunya include *ngari, tiwirrpa, purrarra, yirrampa* and *tjuupi*. Kenneth C. Hansen and Lesley E. Hansen, *Pintupi/Luritja Dictionary*, 3rd ed. (Alice Springs, NT: IAD Press, 1992), 81.
2. Nadine Amadio and Richard G. Kimber, *Wildbird Dreaming: Aboriginal Art from the Central Deserts of Australia* (Melbourne: Greenhouse Publication, 1988), 67.

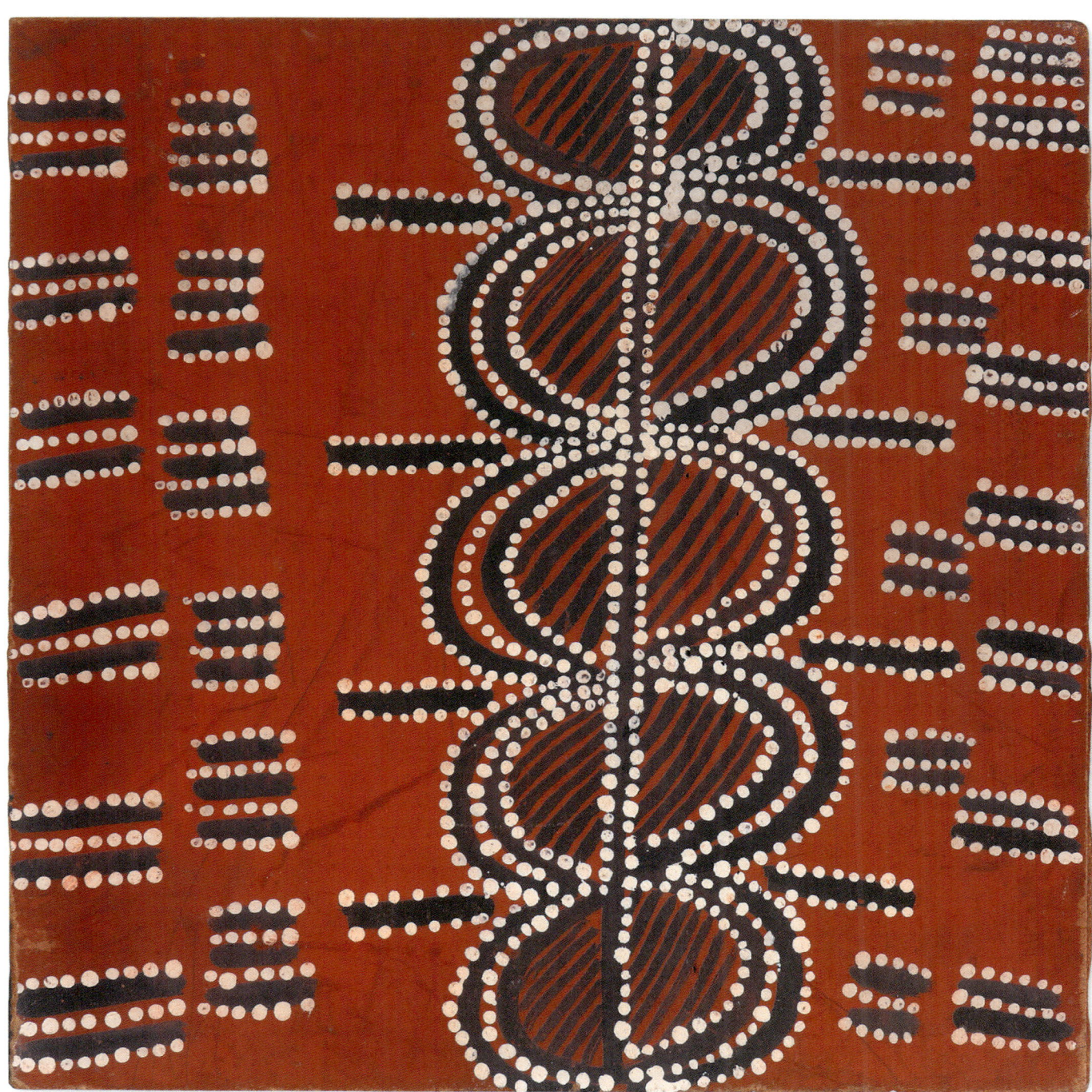

PLATE 6

Mick Wallangkarri Tjakamarra
*Honey Ant Travels*, 1971

PLATE 7

Tim Leura Tjapaltjarri
*Honey Ant Dreaming*, 1973

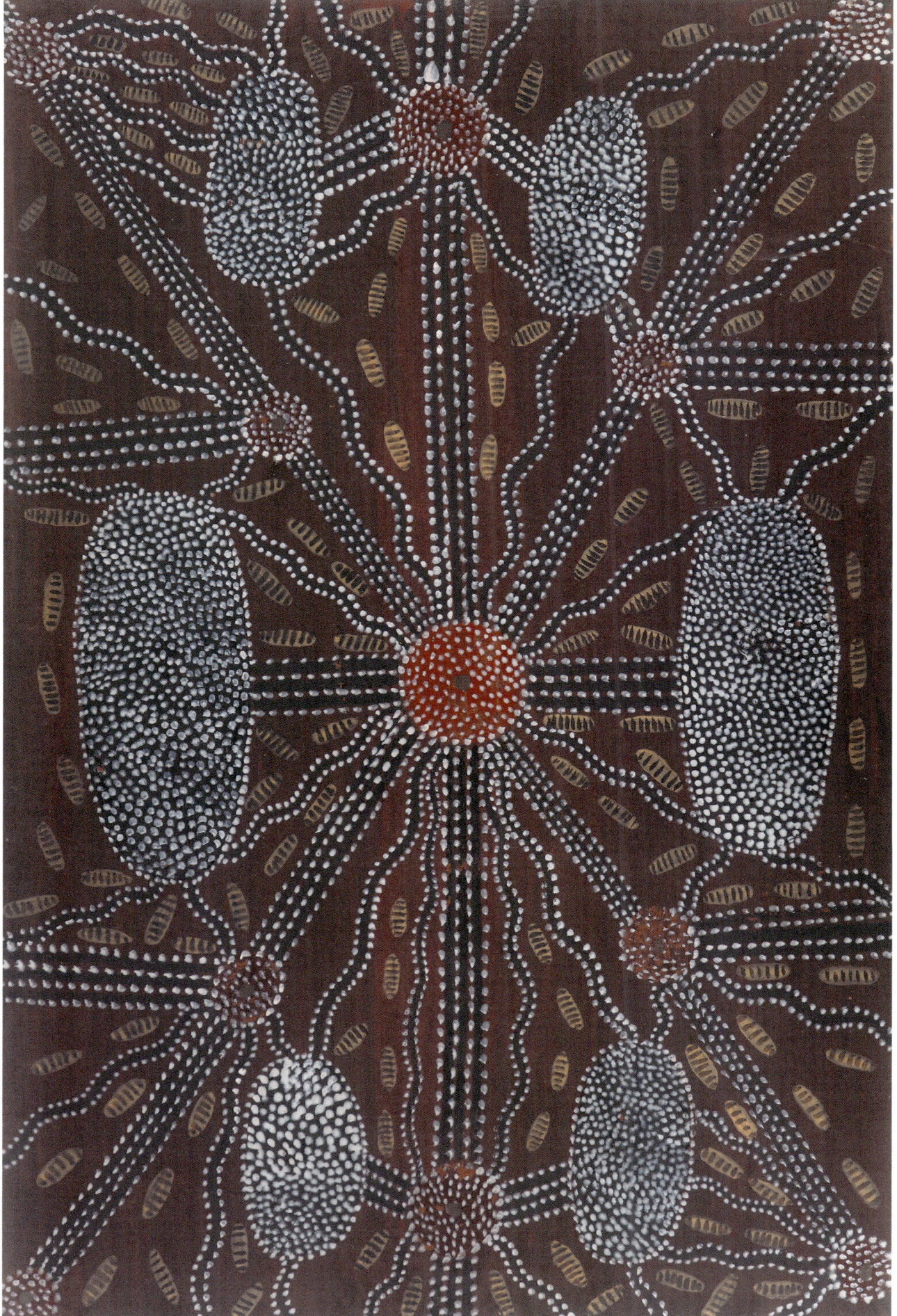

# NGAPA TJUKURRPA

## STORM DREAMING

In the Tjukurrpa, two old men sat, each at his own camp, hundreds of miles apart. They sang into existence all the different elements of a storm: lightning, thunder, clouds, wind, rain and hail. When all the elements had amassed, they were sent off on a destructive path across the land. Descendants of these original rainmakers, and those associated with important sites along the storm's path, have the knowledge and power to make rain by recreating the song of the original rainmakers.

They're making rain, Tjampitjinpa, Tjangala, they're singing. Tjakamarra, Tjupurrula too. After one week you'll see 'im cloud. [From] no cloud you'll see 'im cloud. Every way lightning, then big wind, from song. Start 'im rain now, rain e'll come out.

One of the original storms was created at Kalipinypa (plates 8–10, 144), a deep well in Pintupi country. It traveled over the land to Watulpunya, where it coincided with another great storm coming from Irralyingilya in Alyawarr country to the east. The two storm ancestors traveled together to Mirrawarri (which means mirage), where they fought violently. As the two storms moved across the land, they carried with them the bird Kirrkalanji (Peregrine falcon). They went through Mikantji, up to Kulpuluntu in Warlpiri country and on to Gurindji lands, continuing until they reached the sea.

(Then they) bin turn back again, come right back to Mikanji. Altogether, whole lot. Everything all here long Mikantji. That Tjangala, Tjampitjimpa, all finish now, Tjakamarra, Tjupurrula and all.

After their epic journey, all the storm ancestors seeped into the earth at Mikantji leaving the many soakages that now mark the site (plate 17). Intalykunyia (the black-headed python) also came to Mikantji and entered the ground with the Storm ancestors. He would reemerge later and travel back to the east. As he moved, he grew bigger and bigger until he eventually became the huge and dangerous Wanampi (Water Snake) that is said to live near Atywerl (Twenty Mile Bore) on Napperby Station.

— KAAPA TJAMPITJINPA AND JOHN KEAN

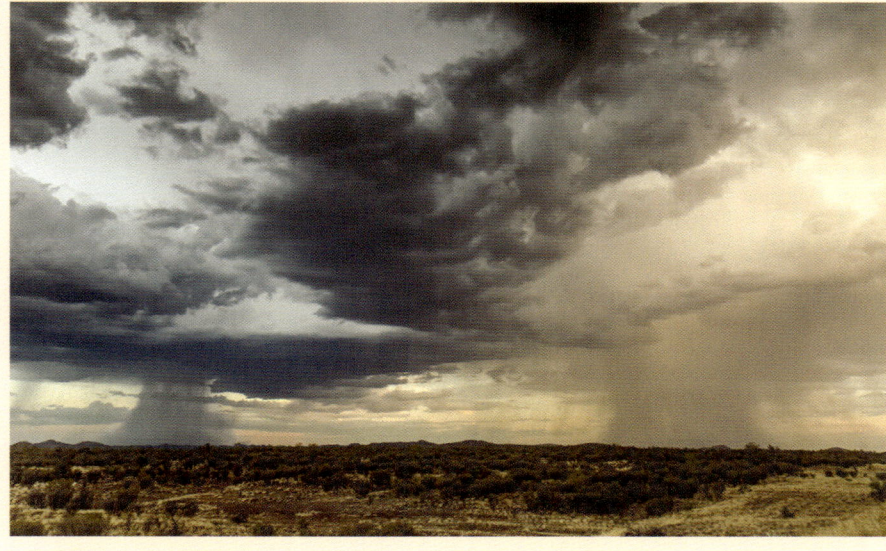

Two storms colliding, Mparntwe (Alice Springs), November 2014. Photo by Peter Carroll.

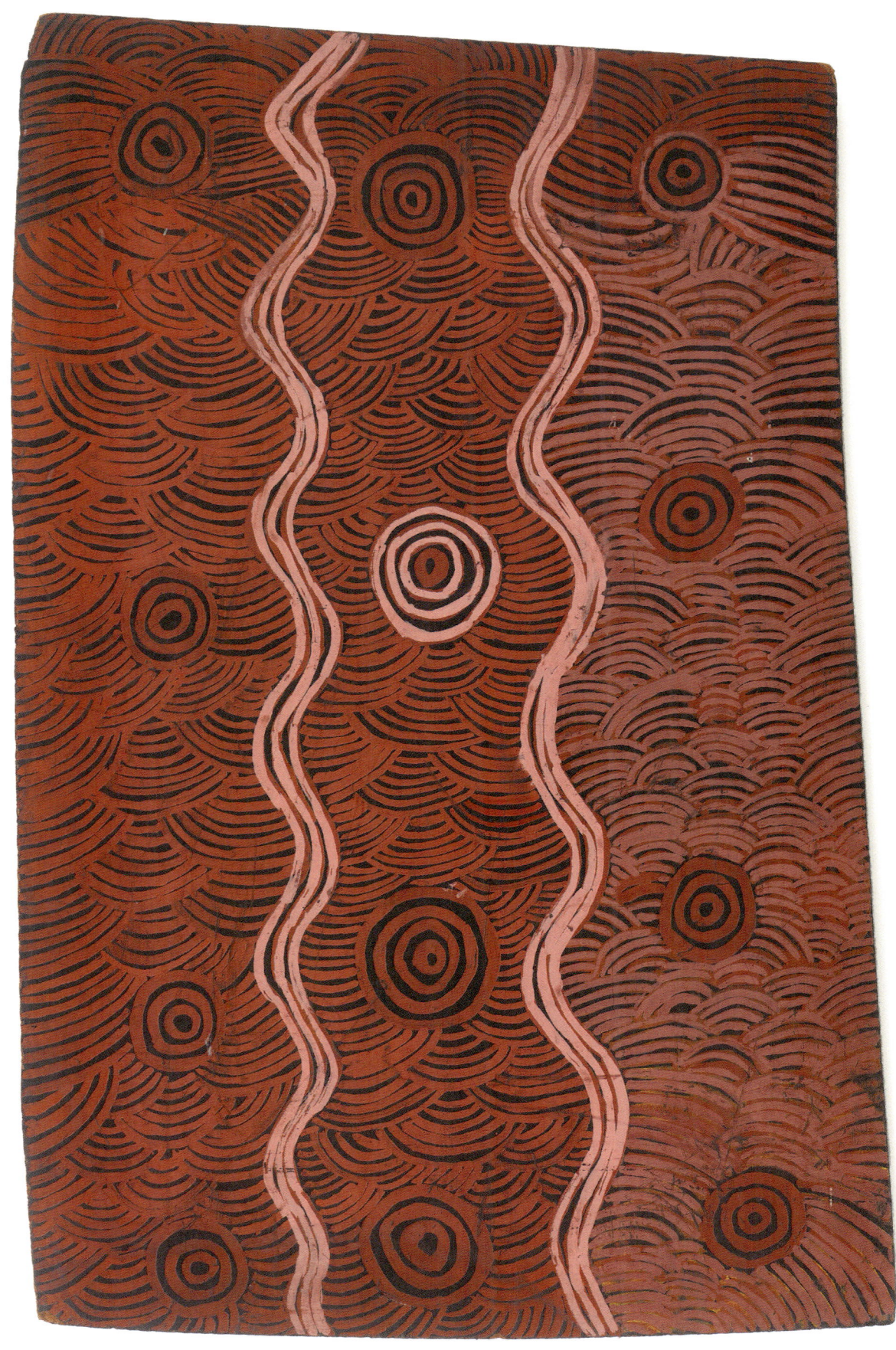

PLATE 8

Walter Tjampitjinpa

*Kalipinypa*, 1972

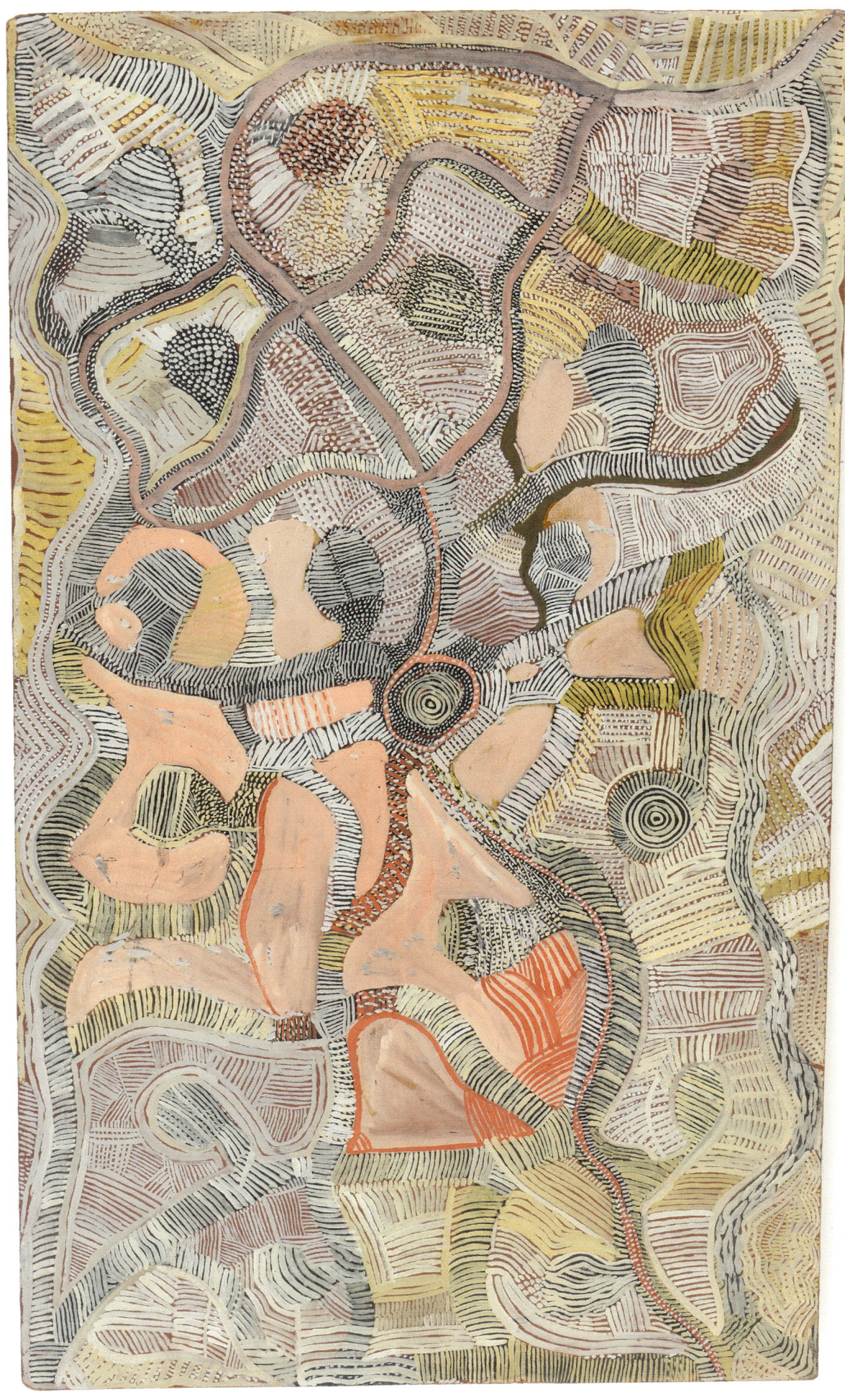

PLATE 9

Johnny Warangkula Tjupurrula
*Kalipinypa*, 1972

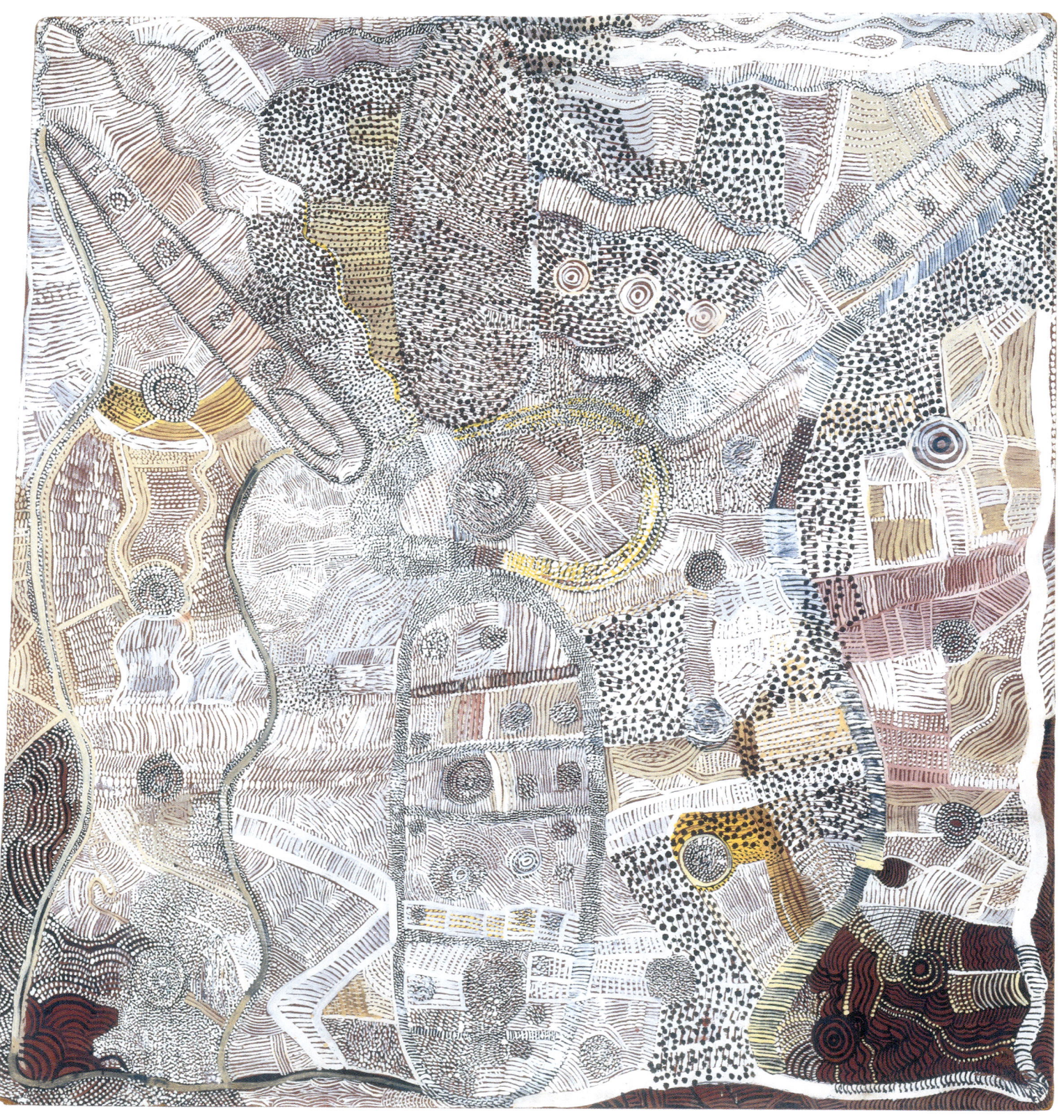

PLATE 10

Johnny Warangkula Tjupurrula
*Water Dreaming at Kalipinypa*, 1972

PLATE 11

Johnny Warangkula Tjupurrula
*Yala Tjukurrpa (Desert Yam Dreaming)*,
c. 1971

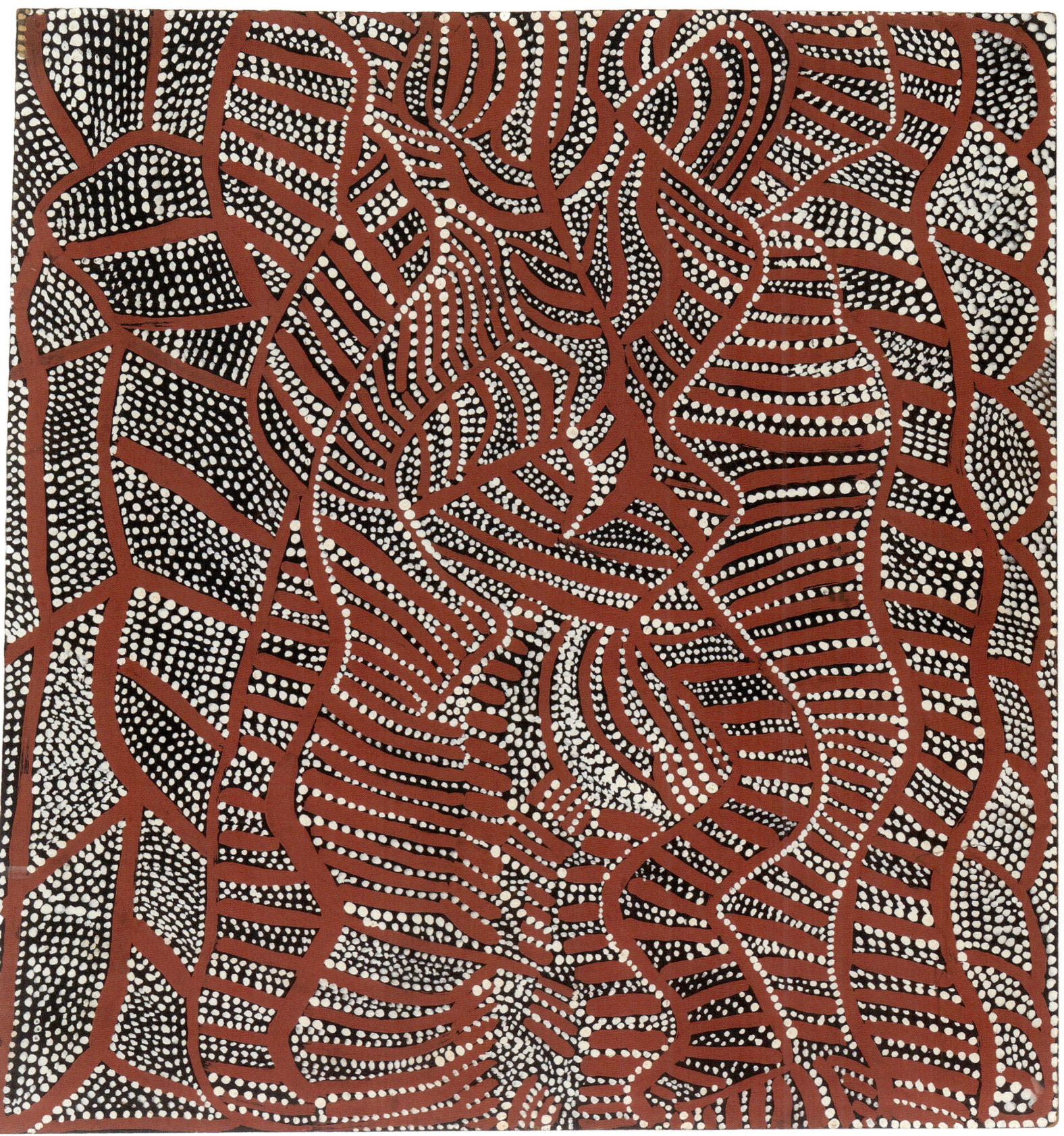

PLATE 12

Tim Leura Tjapaltjarri
*Yam Spirit Dreaming*, 1972

The *yala* (desert yam, *Ipomoea costata*) is an important source of food and moisture in the desert. Visible as a looping, vinelike shrub, the plant's growth above ground is mirrored below the earth with radiating roots producing large tubers that retain their moisture long after rain. *Yala* are located via telltale cracks in the earth created by the plant's tubers as they swell. The *yala* tubers are then harvested with robust digging sticks. The succulent tubers can sustain travelers on extended marches across otherwise-waterless ground. *Yala* is strongly identified with masculinity and men's Law. The travels of Yala ancestors across a vast swathe of country are celebrated at various sites where ceremonies are performed to ensure the health, abundance and expansion of the species. The plants are conceived as radiating from each of these totemic centers to spread across the country. *Yala*'s vigorous radial growth provides a perfect illustration of the widespread Indigenous concept that ritual observation at particular totemic sites ensures the maintenance of that species across the broader landscape. Thus, the influence of Water ancestors, featured in paintings by Johnny Warangkula (plates 9, 10) and Clifford Possum (plate 22), extends from the sites they depict along songlines and into adjacent areas where floodwaters create ideal conditions for the emergence of further totemic food plants, including *yala*.

In *Yam Spirit Dreaming*, Tim Leura Tjapaltjarri subtly integrates human presence, suggesting the intertwined connection between people and the ecological wellbeing of their country. The sinuous lines that emanate from the center of the work simultaneously denote the underground roots of the original plant (with its associated tubers) and the principal path taken by the ancestral Yala to and from this site. The Yala ancestor shares both human and vegetable attributes, and at different stages of his travel, either human or vegetative characteristics come to the fore. The shape-shifting outlines of tubers emphasize the anthropomorphic forms of *yala*, terminating in a virtual community of mandrake-like figures, men hunting, women carrying coolamons and objects that suggest the typical ovoid form of sacred objects. Tim Leura would continue to examine the tension between symmetry and the infinite variability of natural forms throughout his career.

—JOHN KEAN

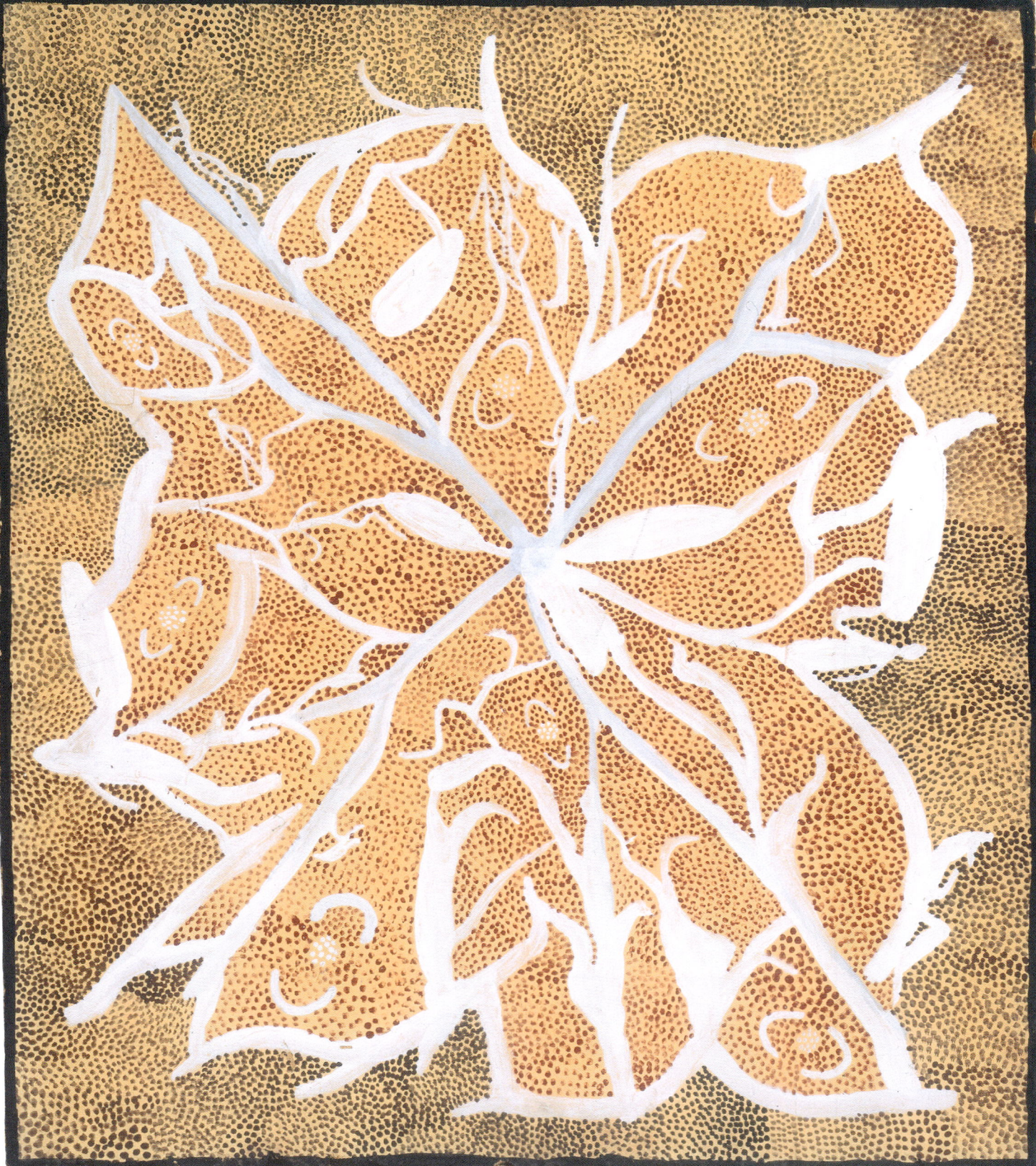

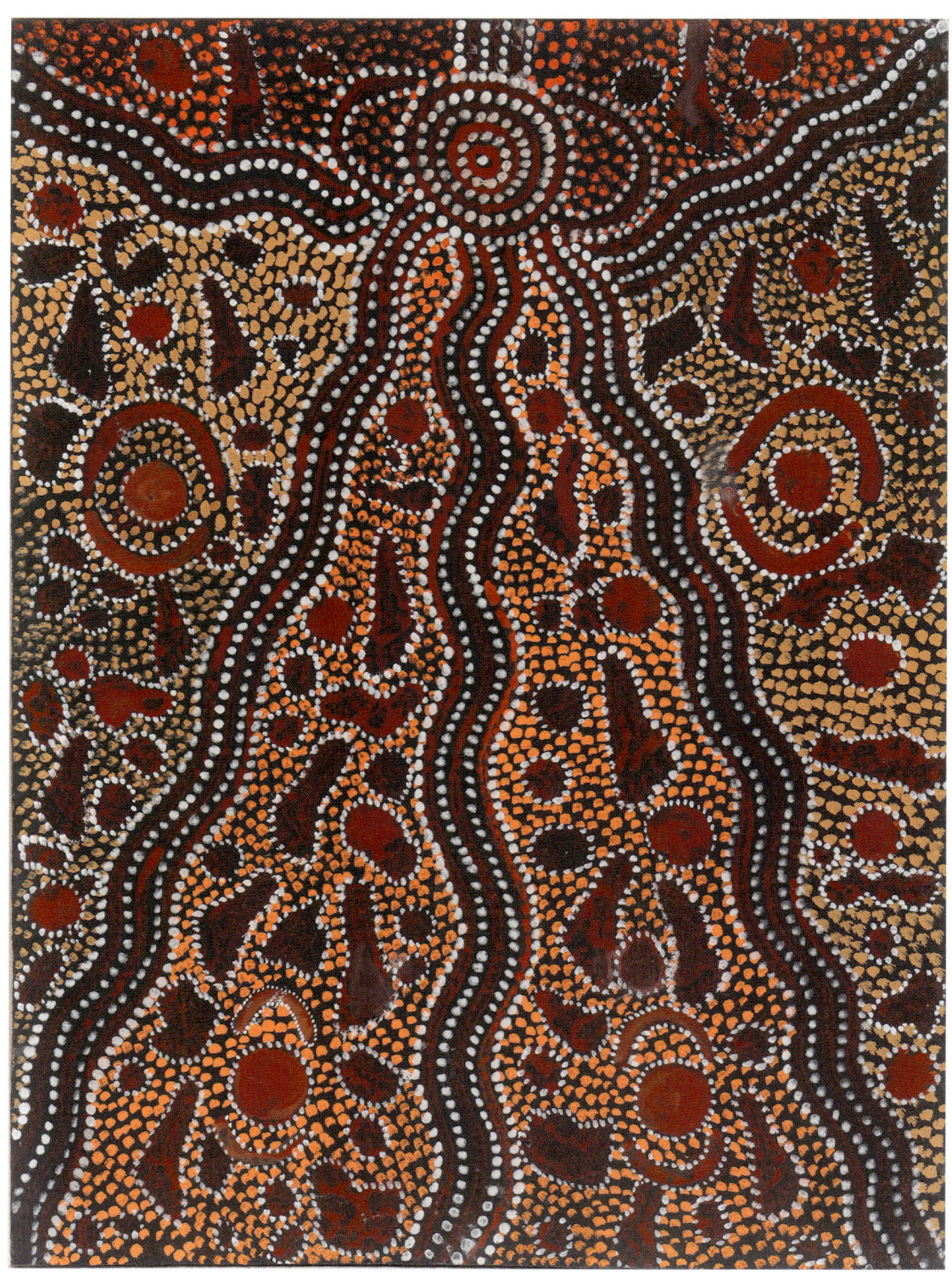

PLATE 13

Tim Leura Tjapaltjarri
*Water Dreaming*, 1975

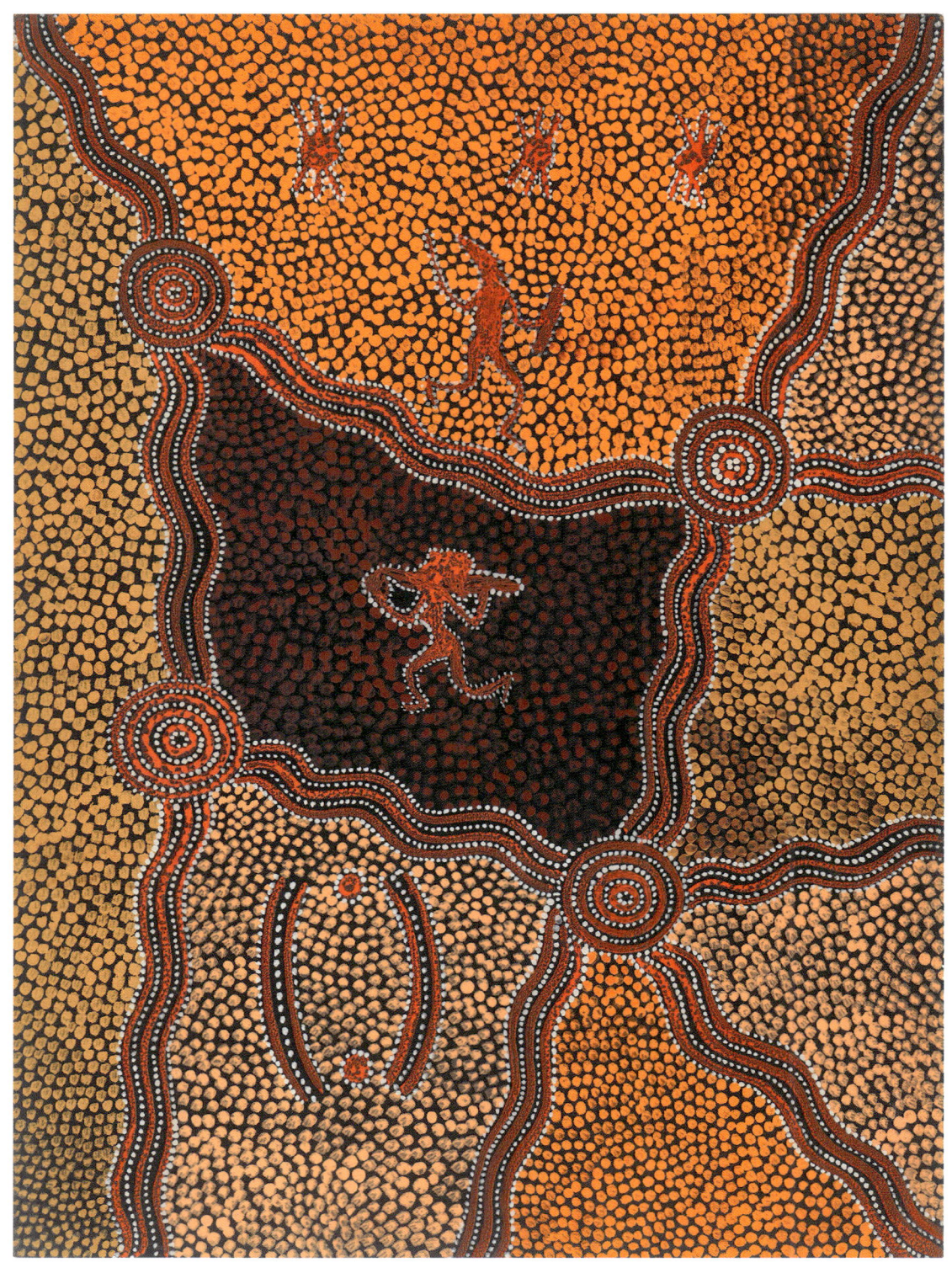

PLATE 14

Tim Leura Tjapaltjarri
*An Old Person's Dreaming*, 1975

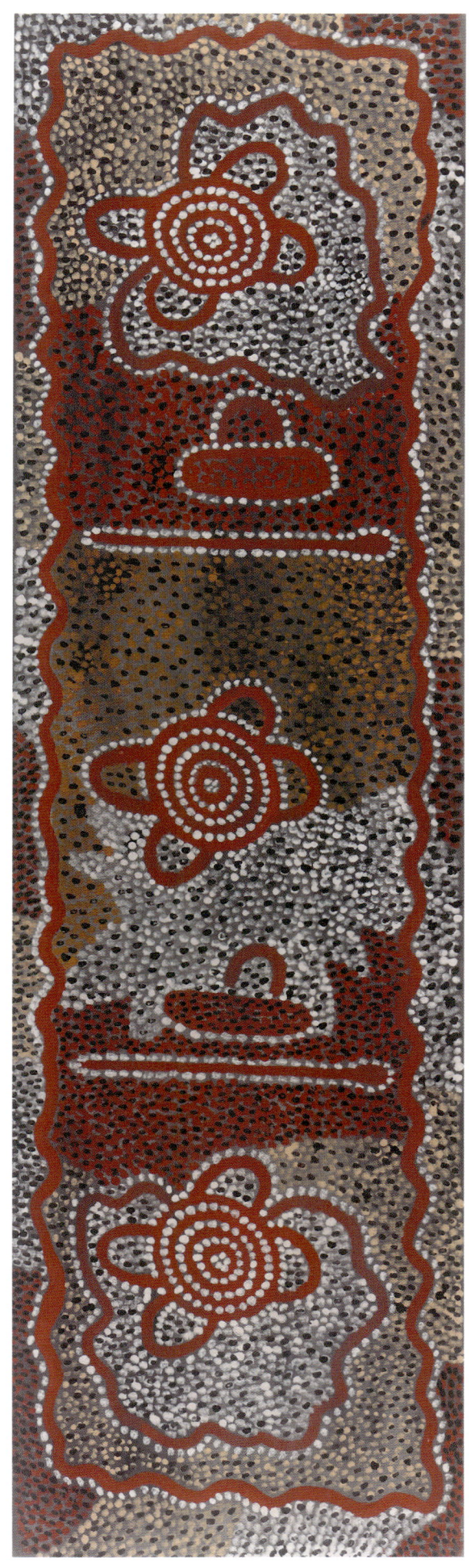

PLATE 15

Dinny Nolan Tjampitjinpa
*Men's Ceremony*, C. 1974

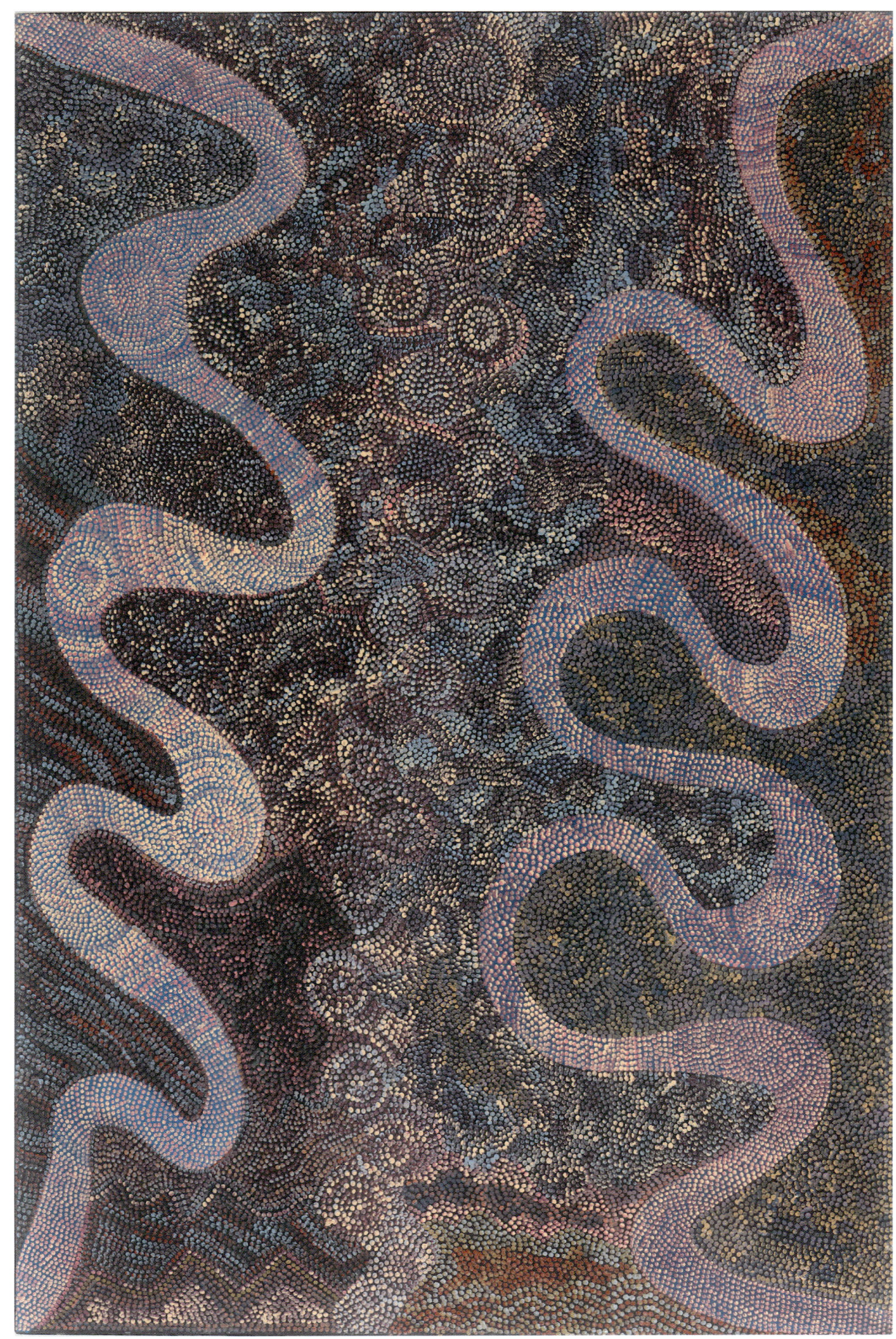

PLATE 16

Pansy Napangardi
*Men's Dreaming at Ilpili,*
1991

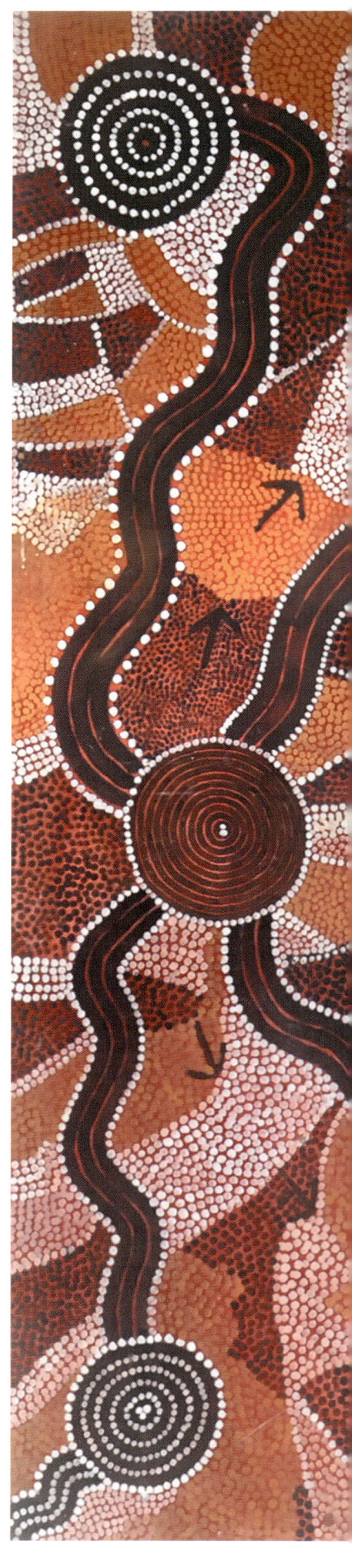

PLATE 17

Kaapa Tjampitjinpa
*Dreaming at Mikantji*, 1975

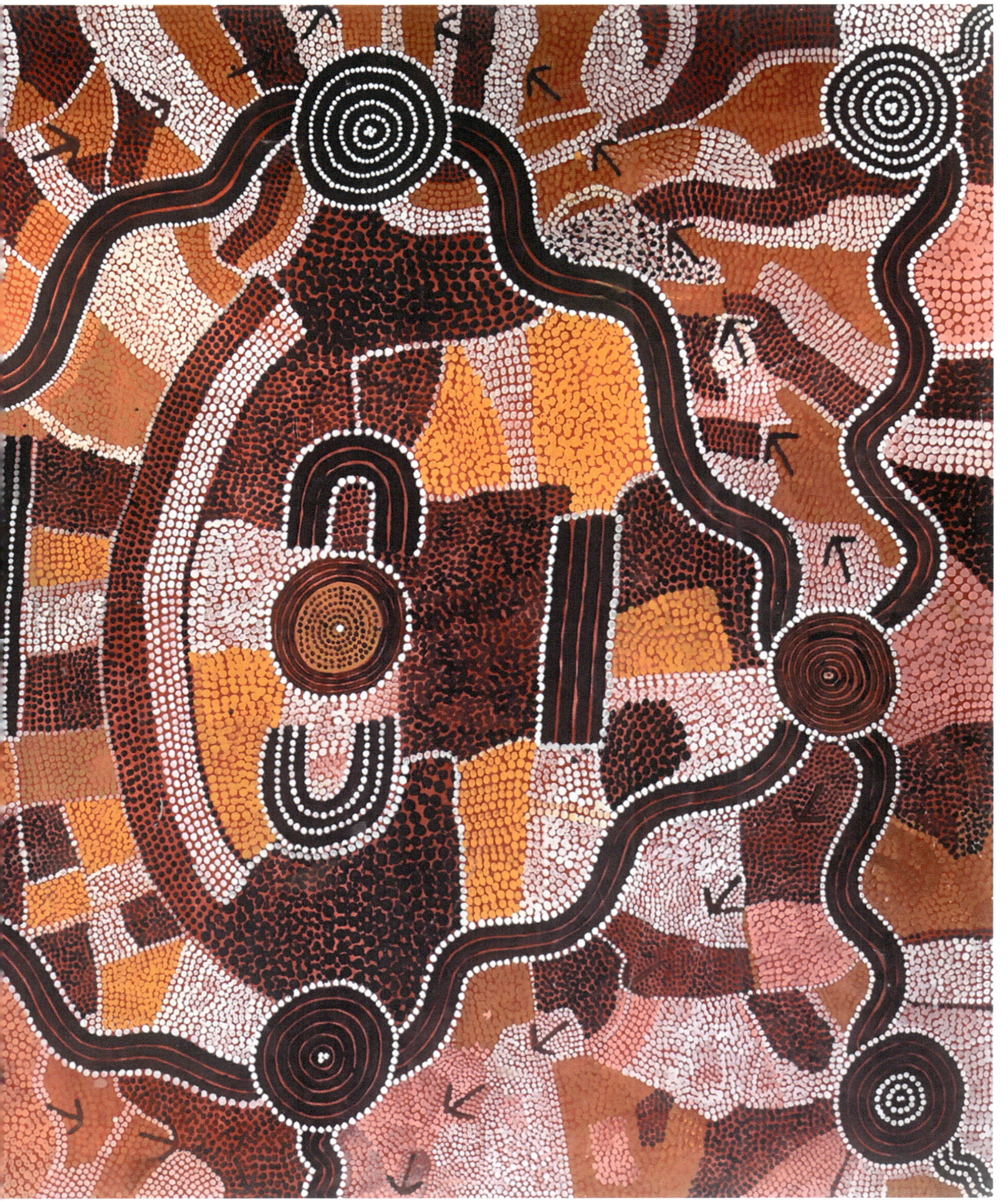

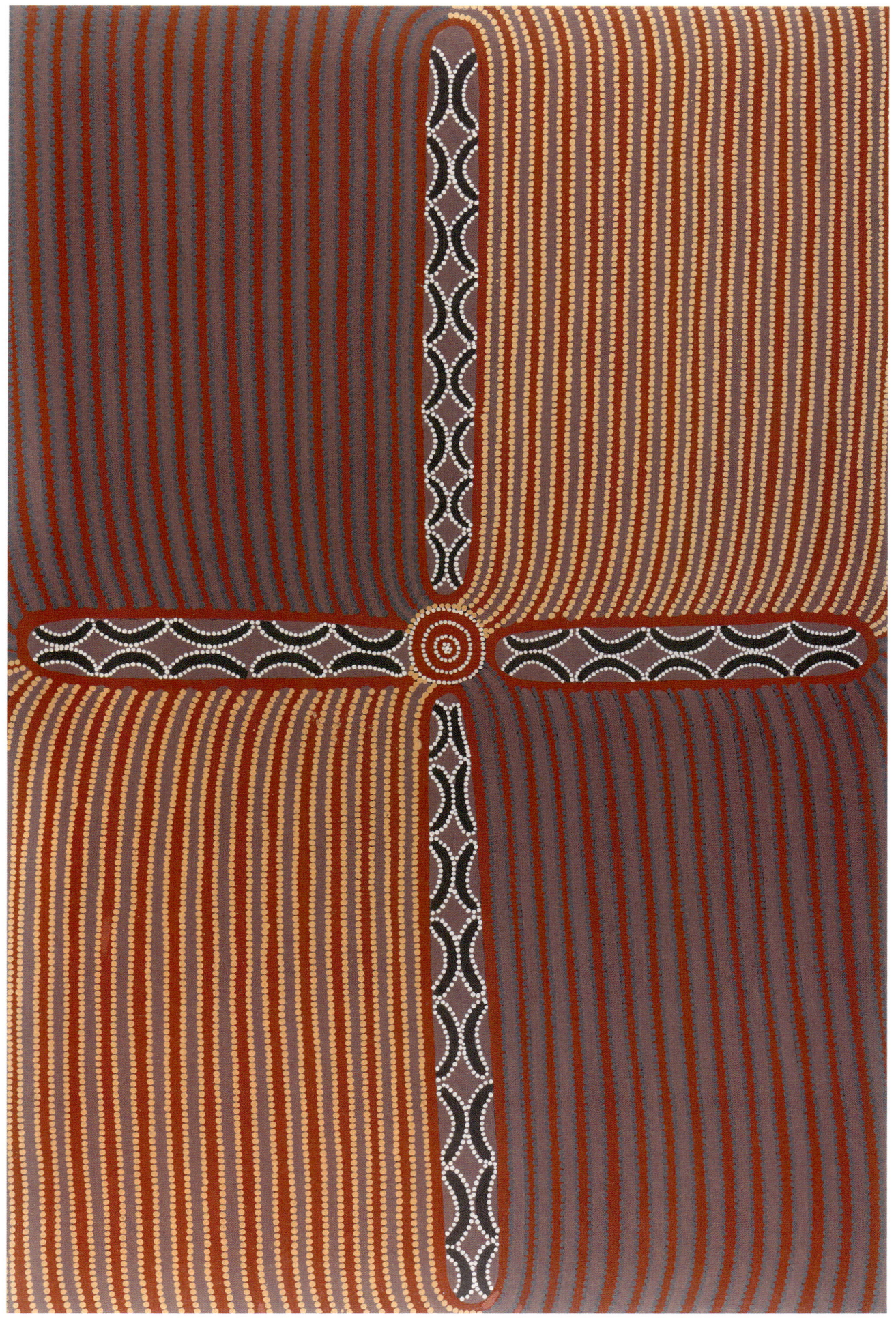

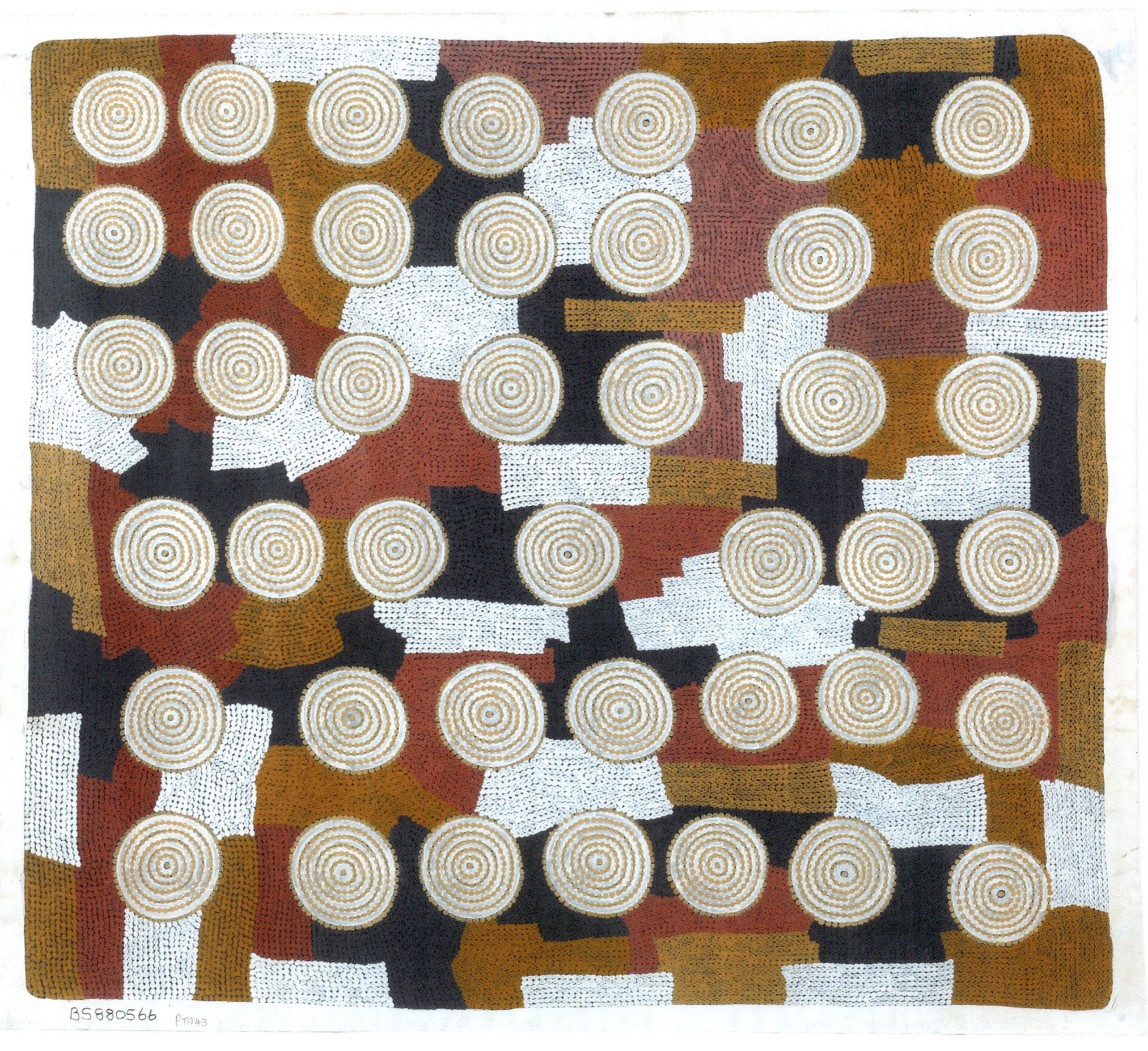

BS880566 PTA43

FACING | PLATE 18

Paddy Carroll Tjungurrayi
*Pupulu Jukurrpa (Lizard Dreaming)*
*at Tali Tali*, 1990

PLATE 19

Bill Stockman Tjapaltjarri
*Ngatitjirri Tjukurrpa (Budgerigar*
*Dreaming)*, 1988

125

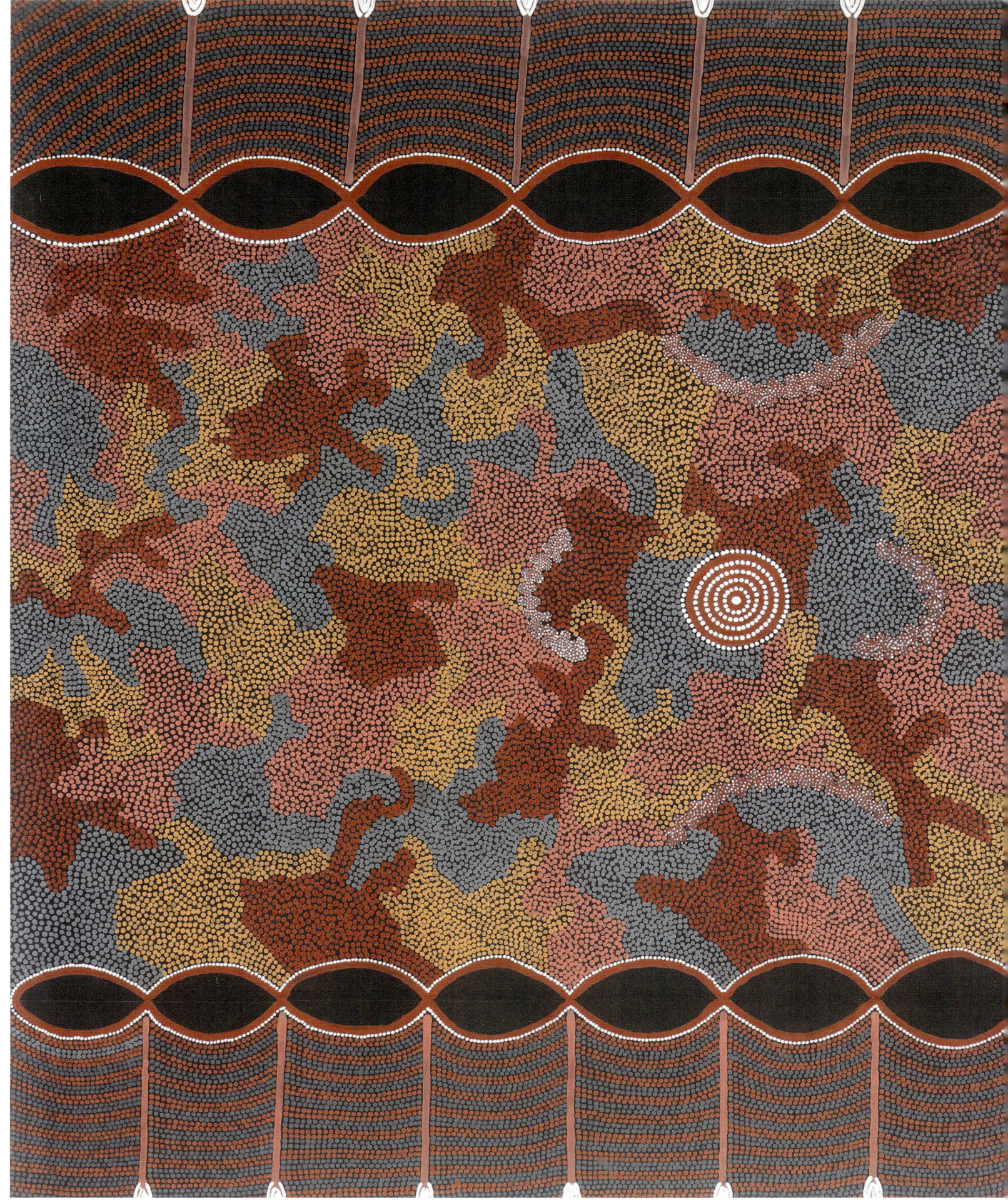

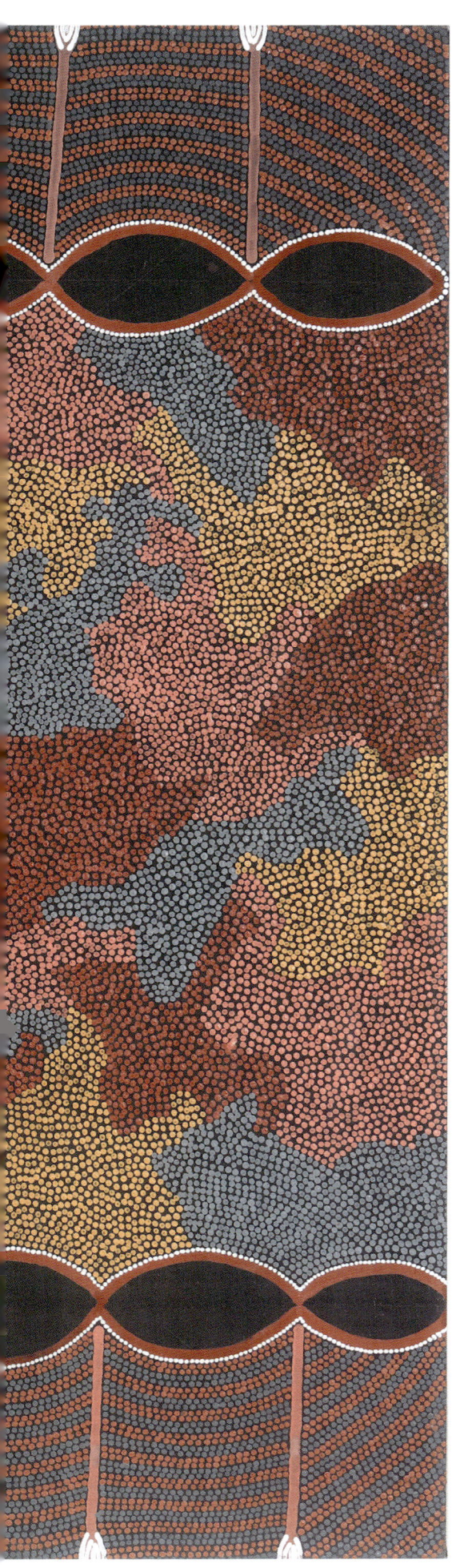

PLATE 20

Don Tjungurrayi
*Yantjipirri*, 1985

PLATE 21

Clifford Possum Tjapaltjarri
*Paths of the Ancestors*, 1973

Clifford Possum Tjapaltjarri learned of the extended songlines that
link distant ancestral estates while working as a stockman, herding
cattle on horseback around Central Australia, as well as through his
participation in exacting ceremonies. Painted in September 1973, *Paths
of the Ancestors* is an exceptional and innovative precursor to his later
series of "map paintings," such as *Warlugulong* (1977) in the National
Gallery of Australia.

    Rather than being a depiction of a single totemic site or ceremony,
Clifford Possum's map paintings are encyclopedic representations of
Country. Individual songlines, indicated by the tracks of the respective
totemic ancestors, are shown passing through a series of sites across
huge estates. In turn, the trails of the ancestors are embedded within
a matrix of dotted patterns to represent the major geological features
and vegetative associations of the country over which the ancestral
heroes traveled.

    A highly original and innovative artist, Clifford Possum was
uniquely able to communicate his Anmatyerr worldview in paint. *Paths
of the Ancestors* depicts nine songlines traversing his Country to show
their connections in time and space, as well as their geological and
botanical impact on the earth. Individual songlines are indicated by
the tracks of ancestral beings, such as Rrpwamper (Brushtail Possum
ancestor, *Trichosurus vulpecular*), Arley (Emu ancestor) and Antwerrkenh
(Black-Headed Python ancestor, *Aspidites melanocehalus*). He also maps
the travels of dancing women, deadly assassins tracking their target,
and raging bushfires sweeping the land. Whereas other Anmatyerr
artists featured icons associated with a single songline as they might
appear in a ritual, Clifford Possum revealed many songlines in geographic relationship to one another. This approach would be taken up
by other artists, such as Yanatjarri No. III Tjakamarra (plate 56) and
Michael Jagamara Nelson (plates 27, 28).

—JOHN KEAN

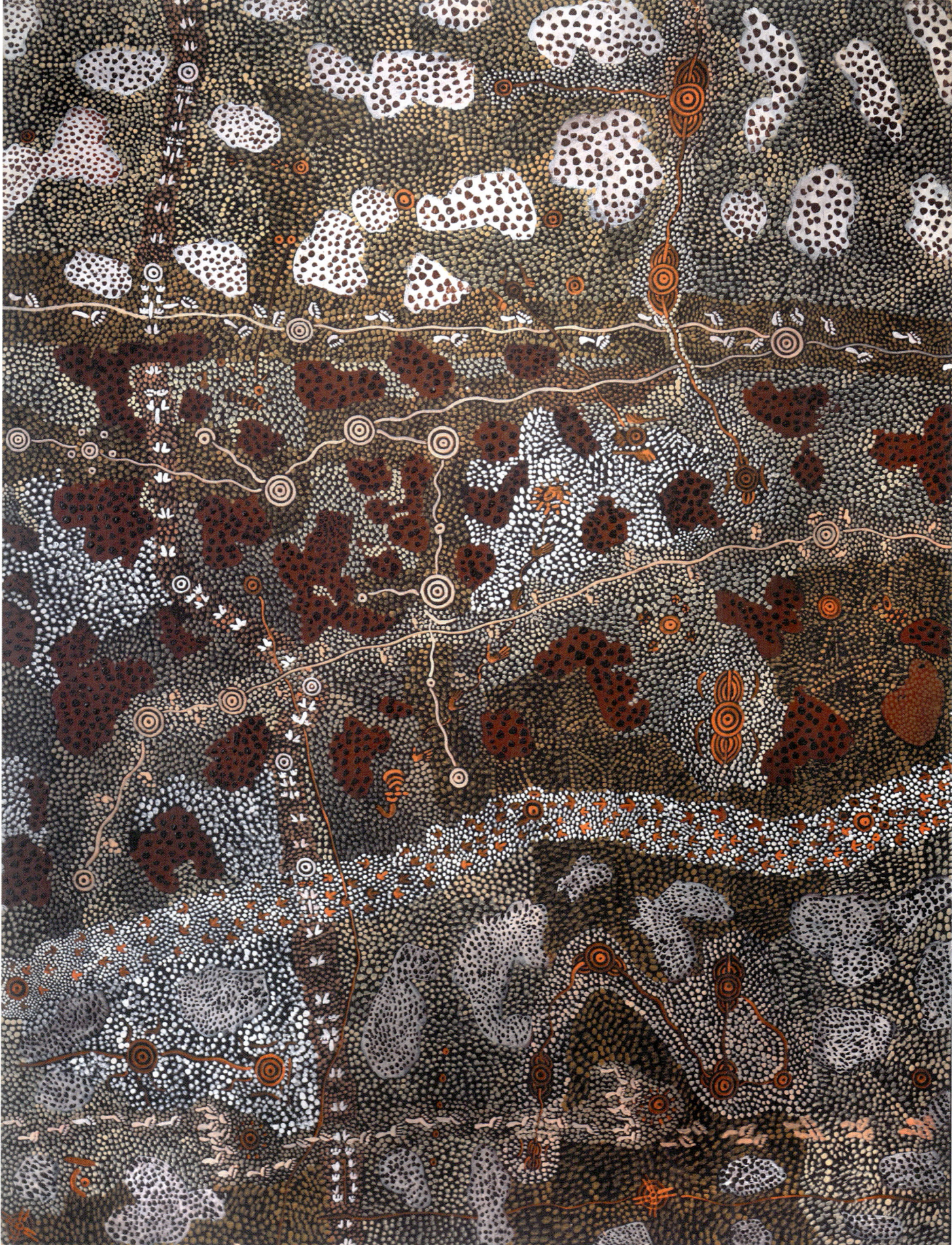

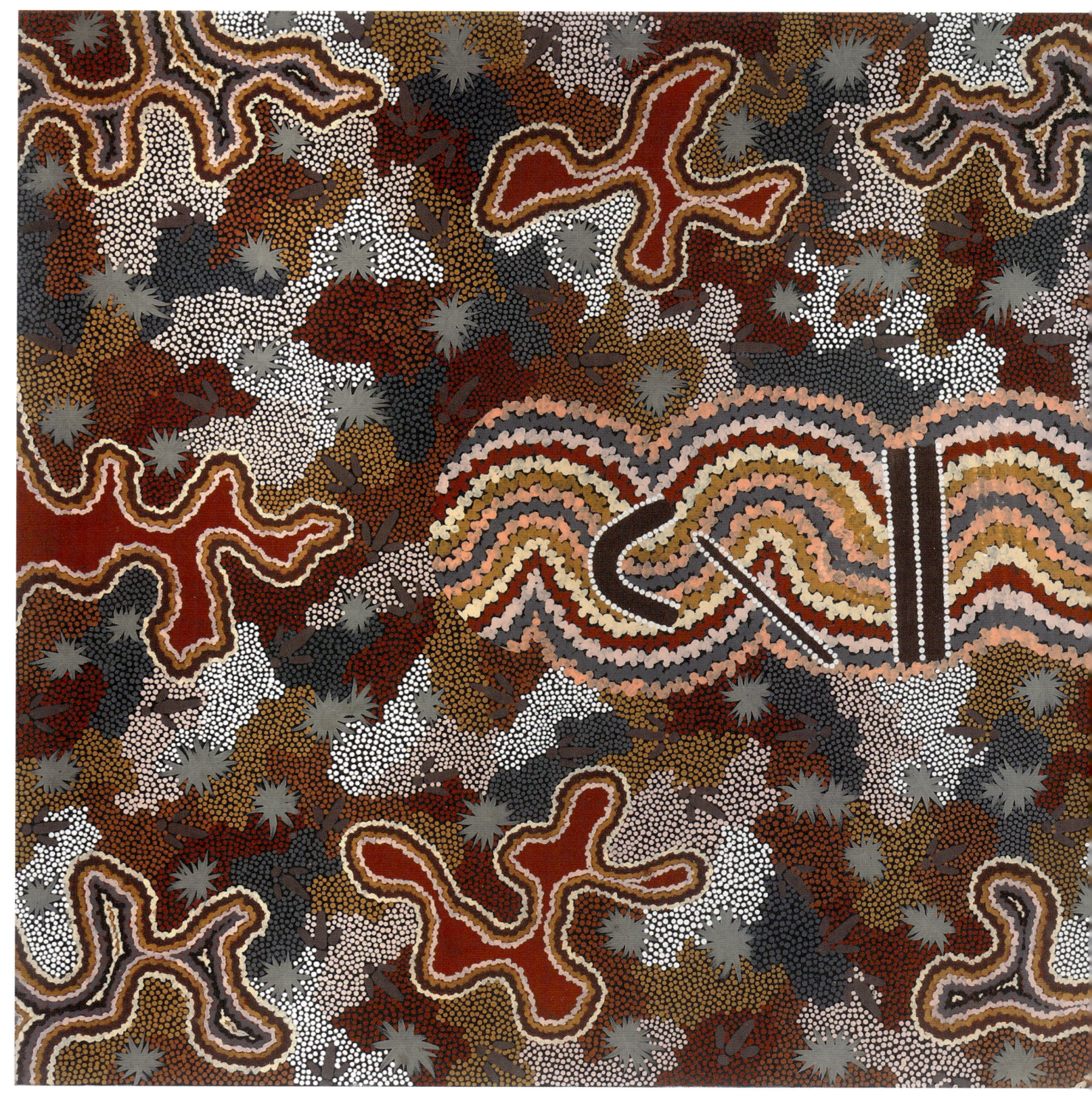

PLATE 22

Clifford Possum Tjapaltjarri
*Rain Dreaming at Mount Denison*, 1989

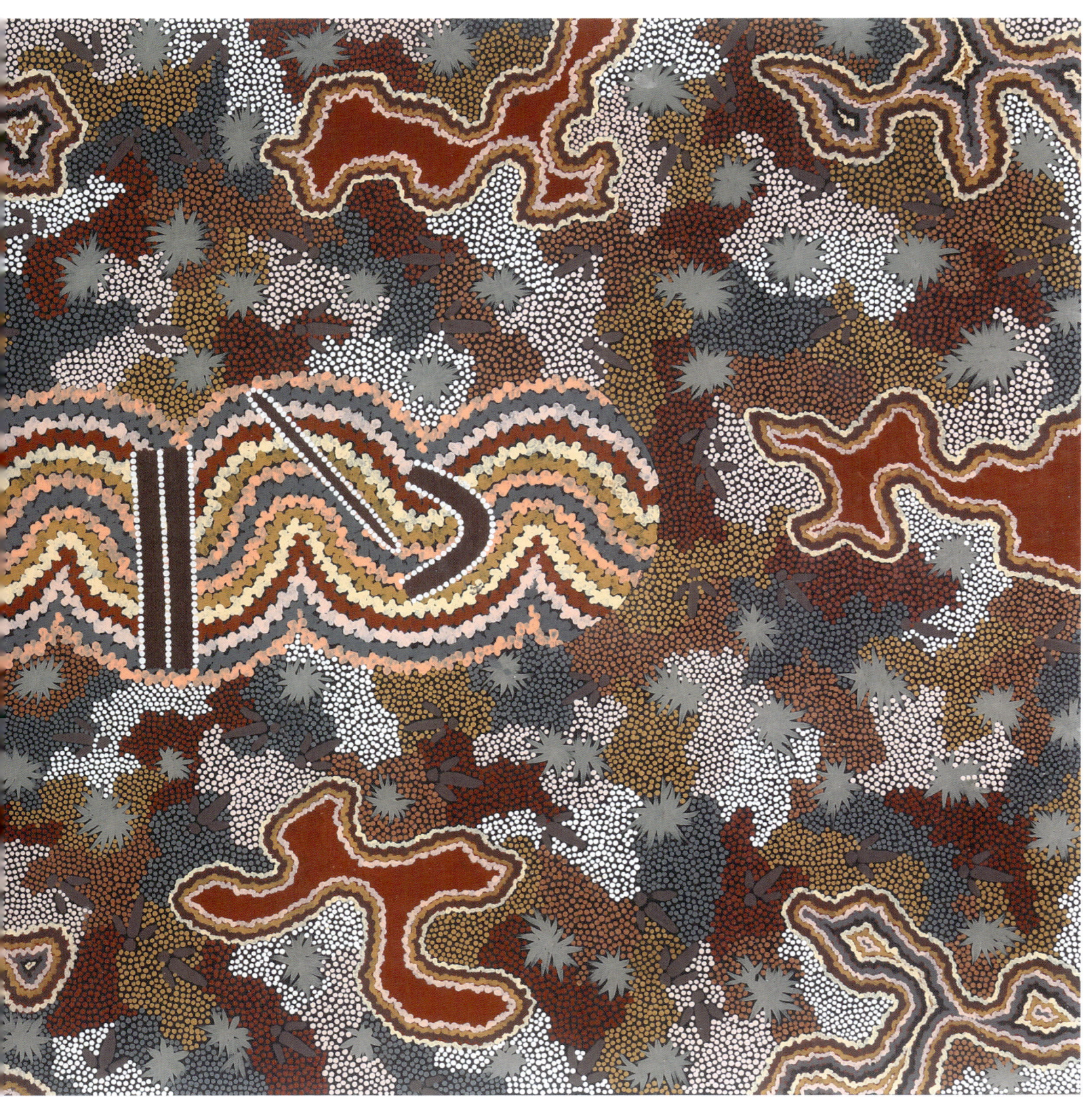

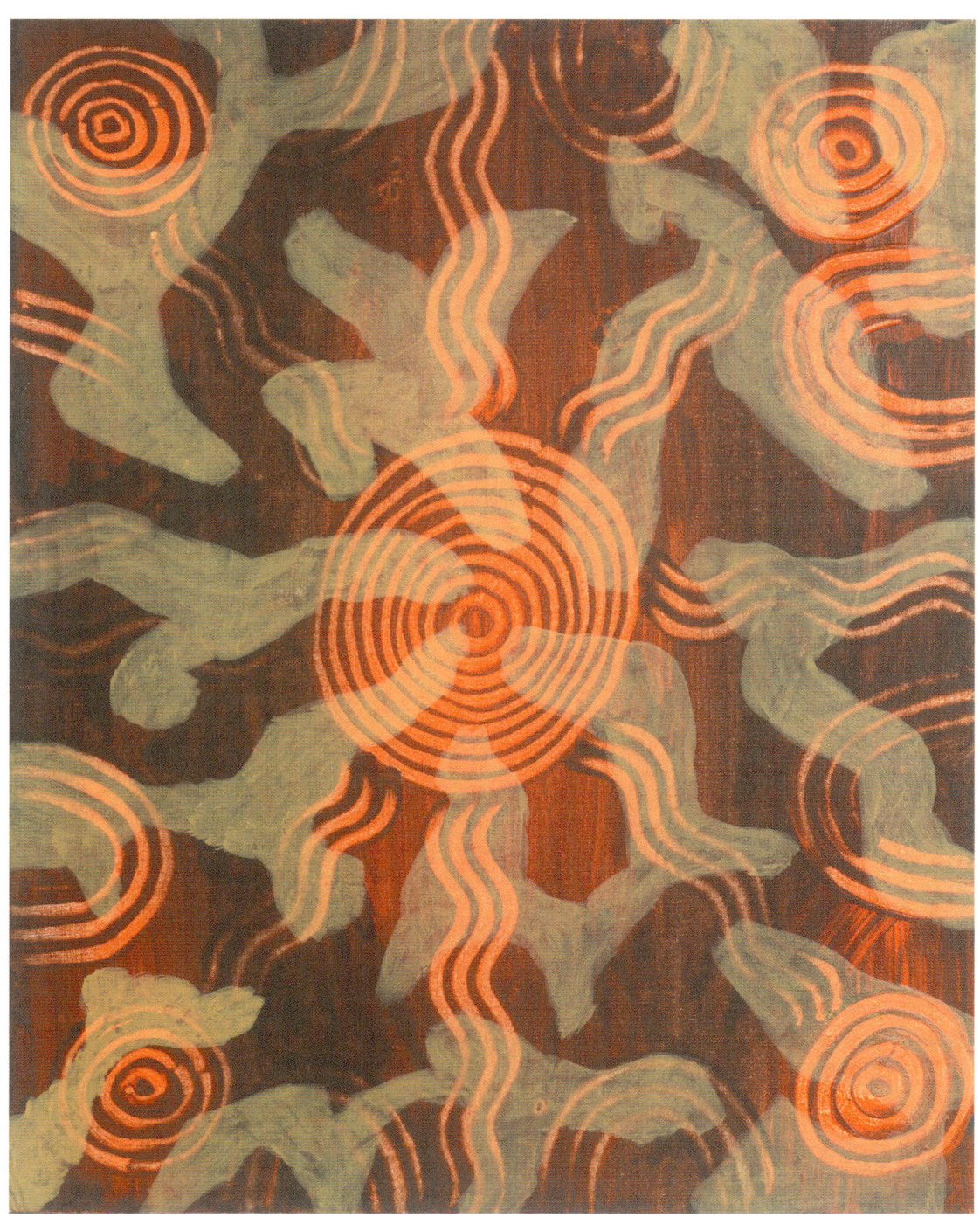

PLATE 23

Tim Leura Tjapaltjarri
*Women Sitting around the Fire at Sunset,*
C. 1973—74

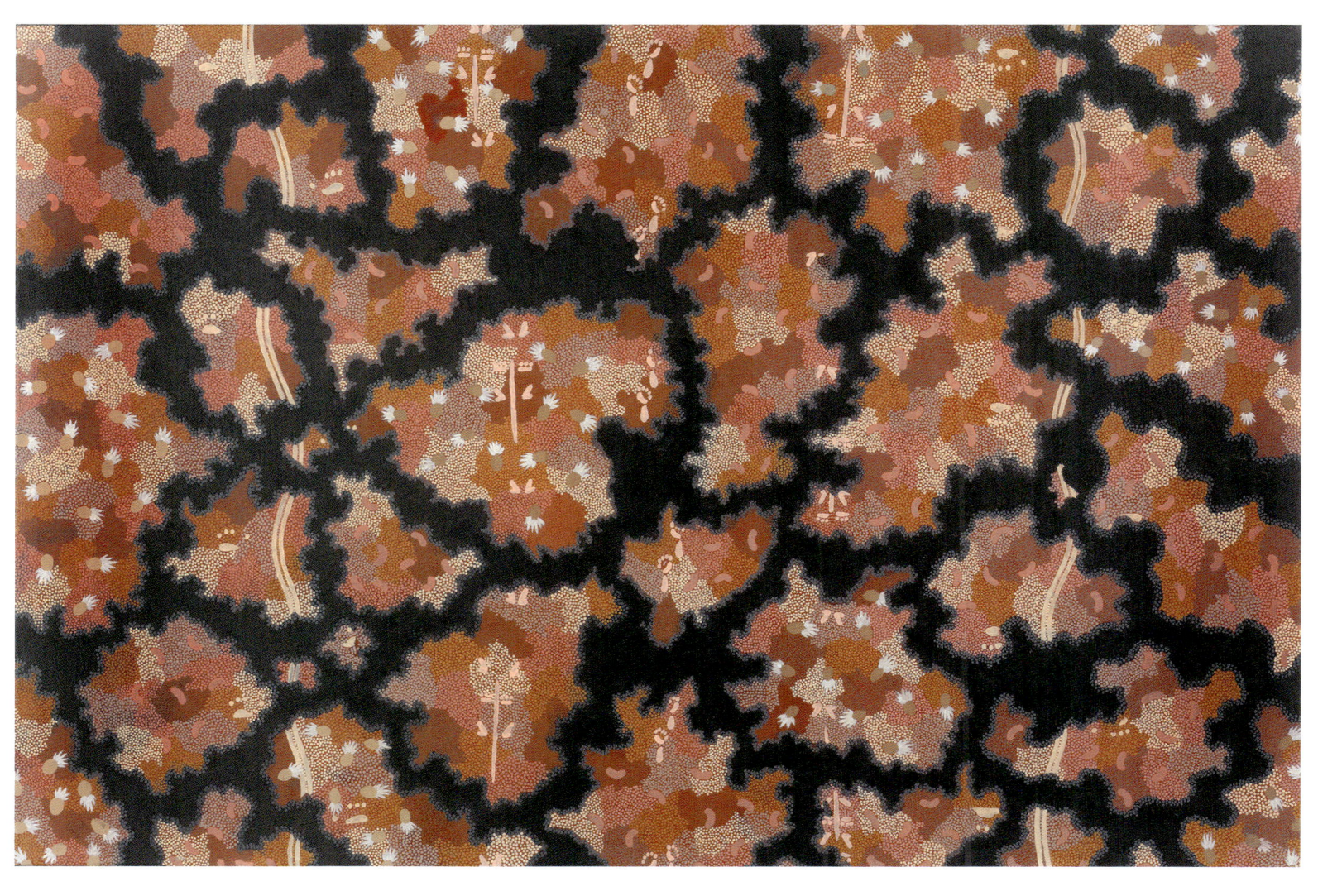

PLATE 24

Clifford Possum Tjapaltjarri
*Bushfire Dreaming,* c. 1986

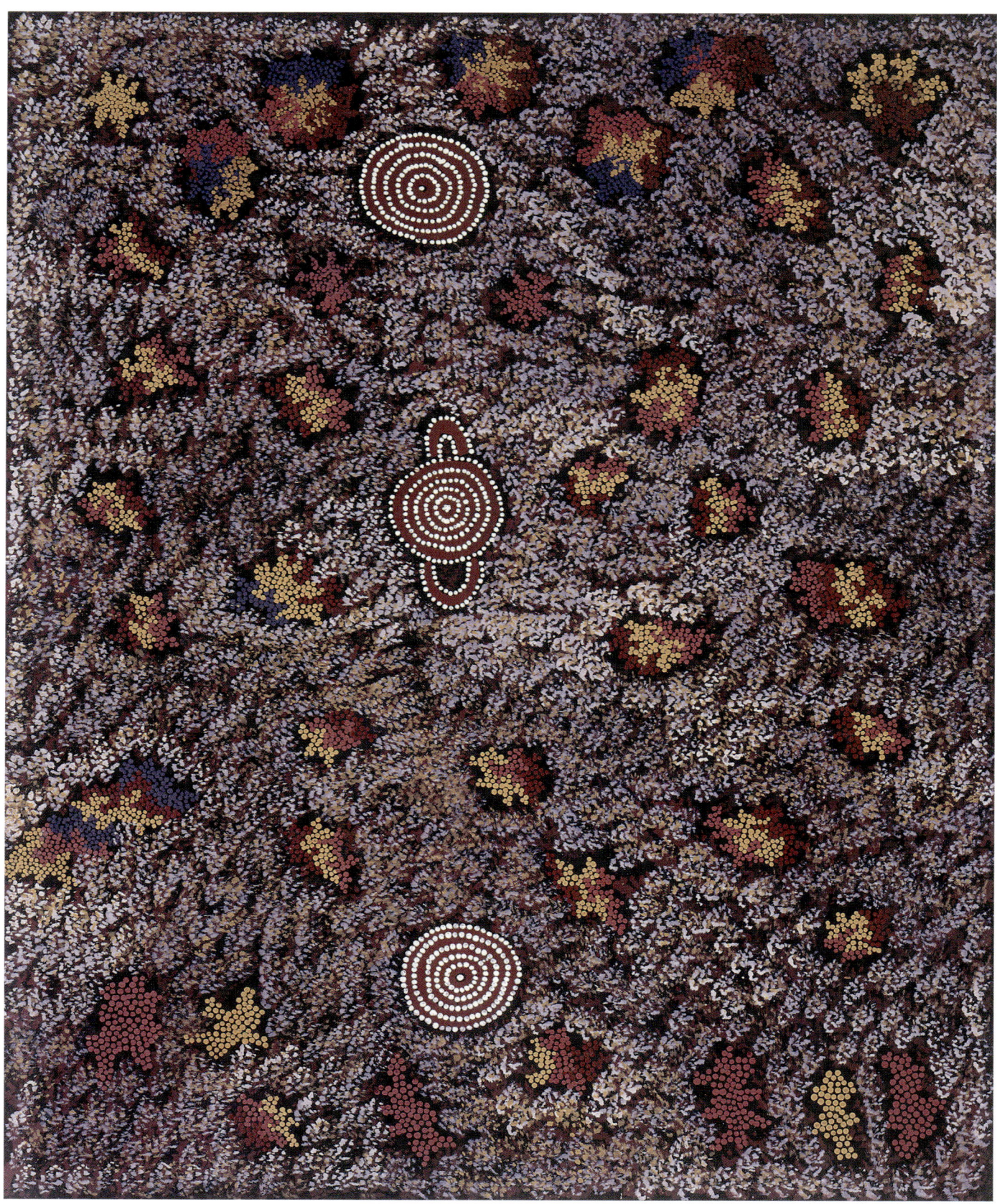

PLATE 25

Maxie Tjampitjinpa
*Bushfire at Warlukurlangu*, 1988

PLATE 26

Maxie Tjampitjinpa
*Evening Bushfire Dreaming*, 1991

PLATE 27

Michael Jagamara Nelson
*Pikilyi*, 1990

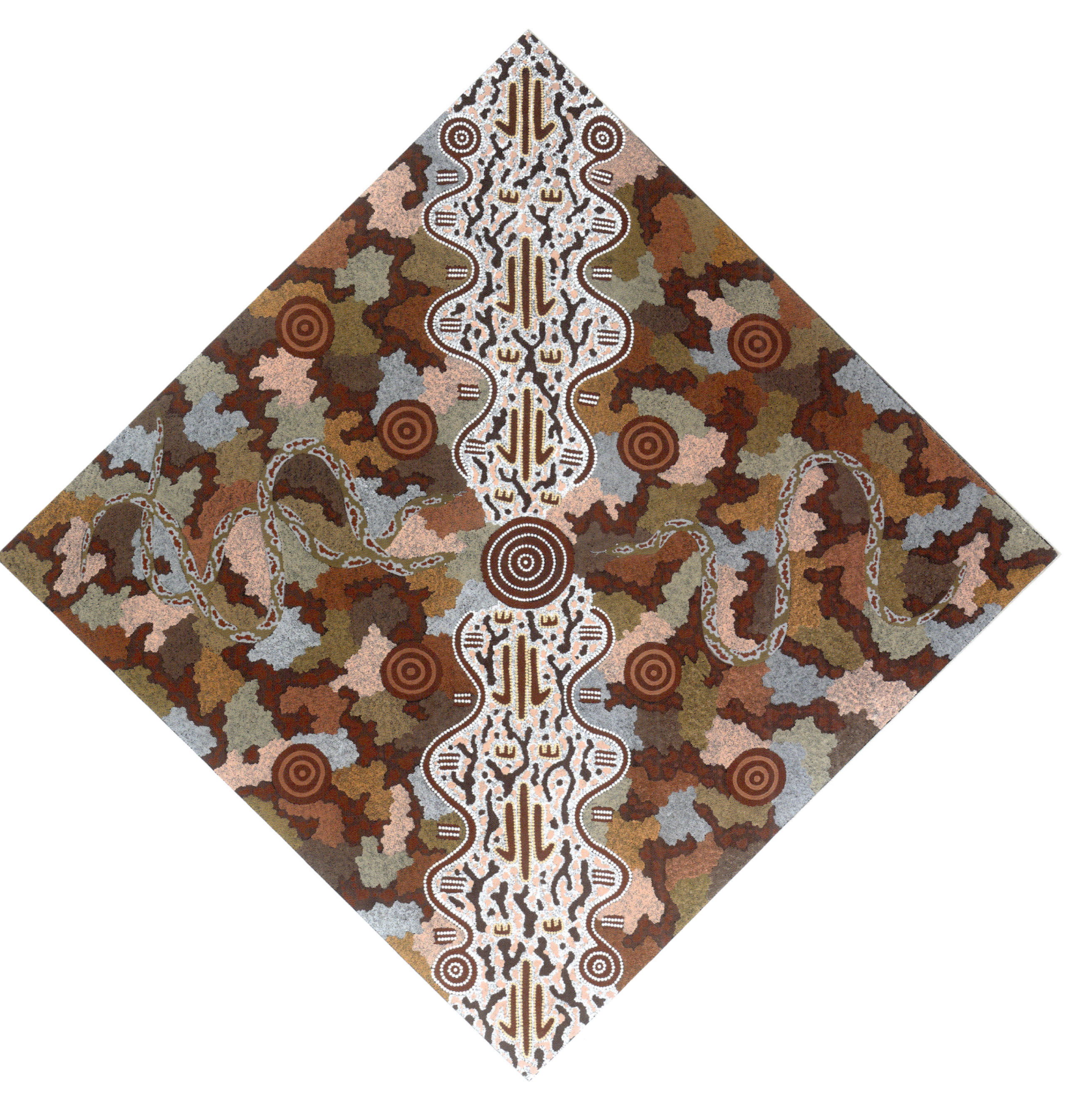

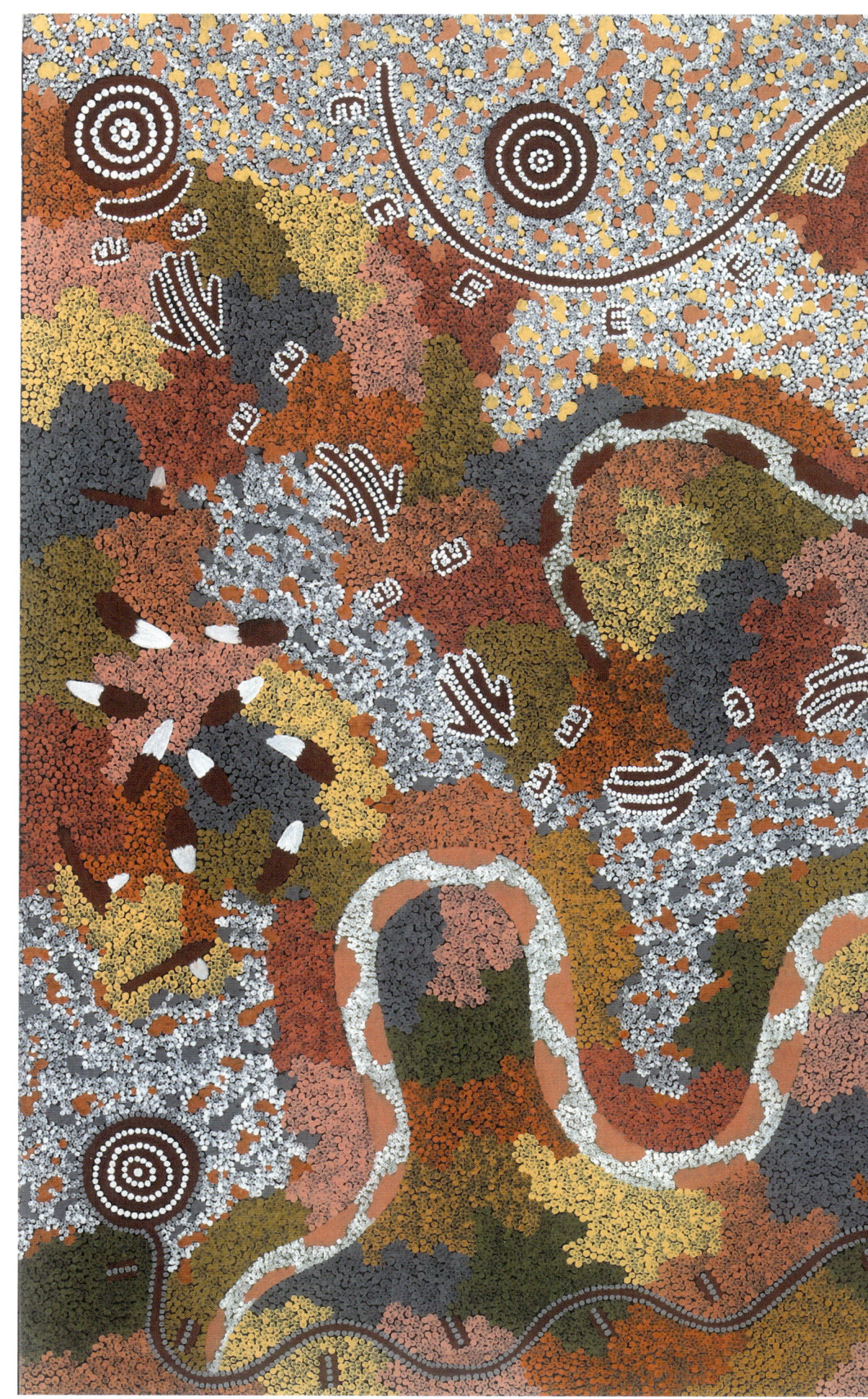

PLATE 28

Michael Jagamara Nelson
*Four Stories at Pikilyi*, 1988

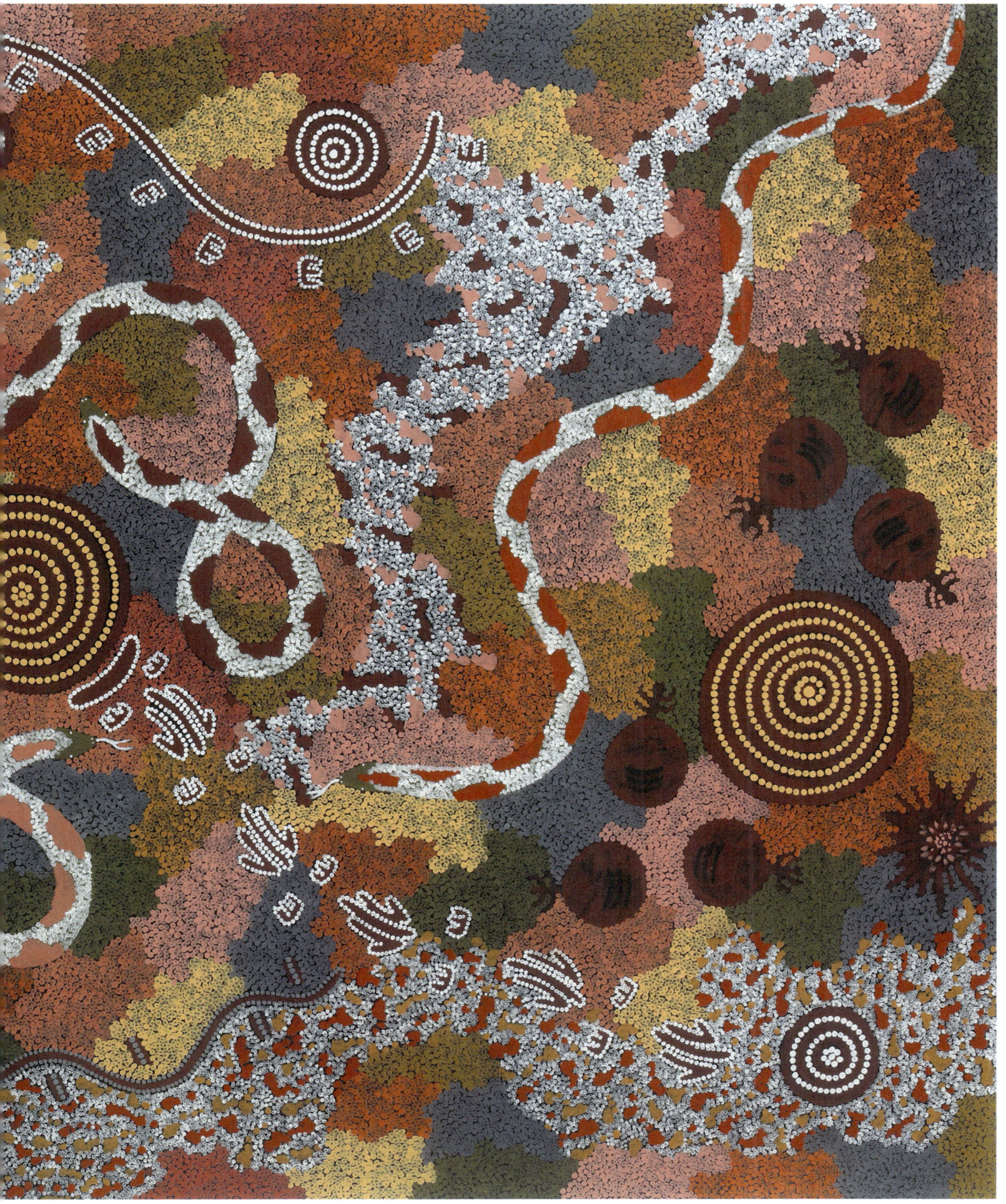

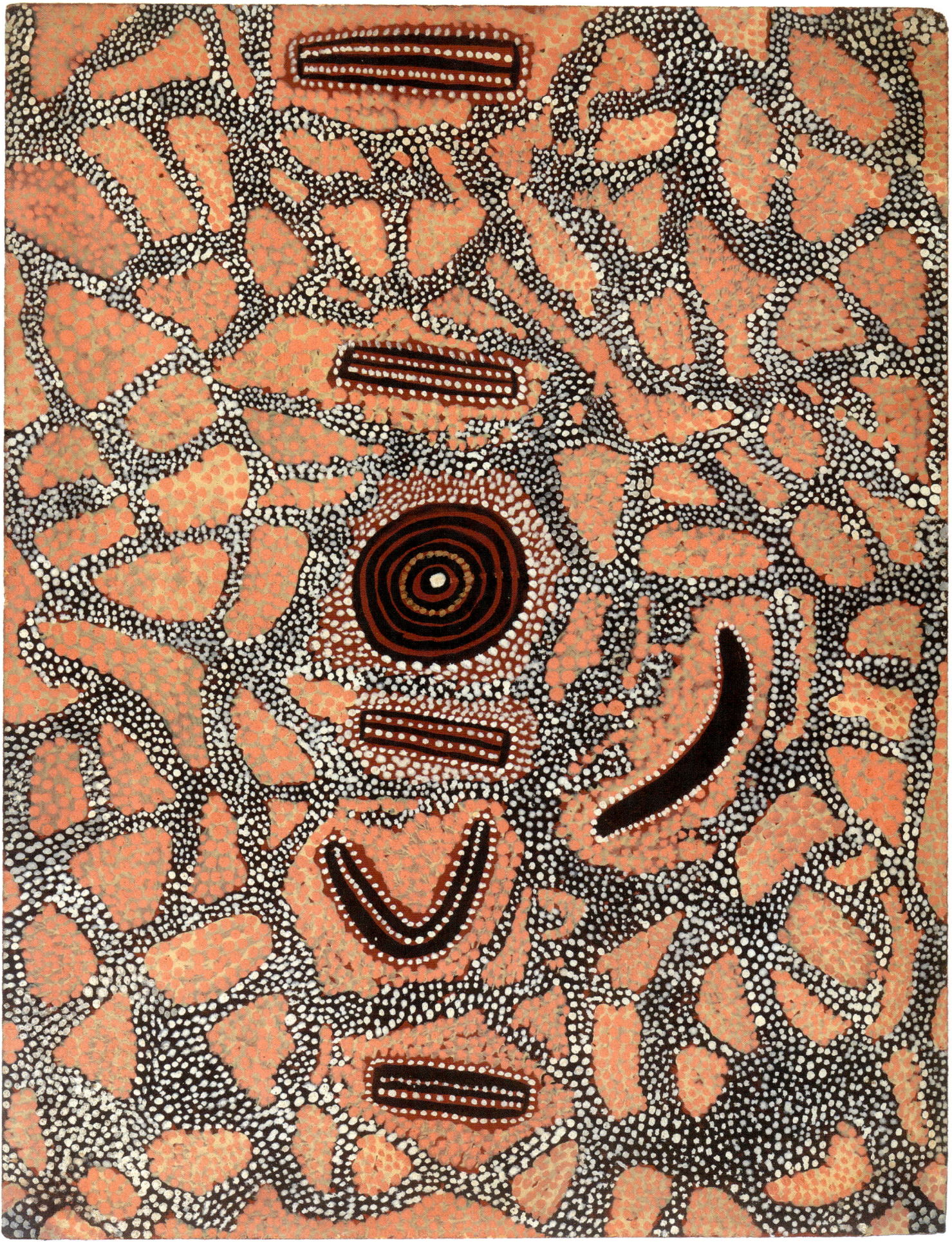

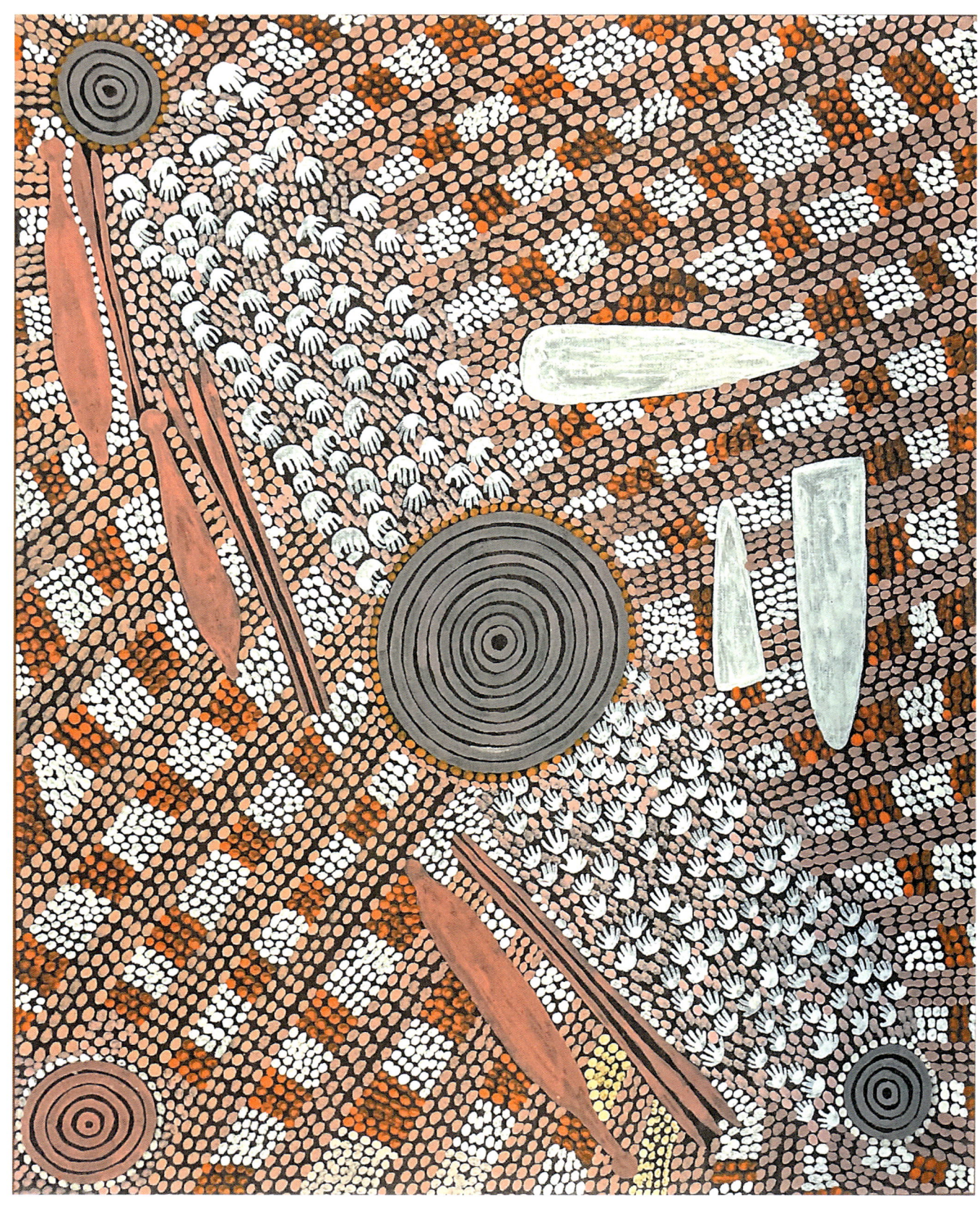

FACING | PLATE 29

Jack Long Phillipus Tjakamarra
*Wayuta (Possum Ancestor) at Ngamurunya*, 1973

PLATE 30

Yanatjarri No. III Tjakamarra
*Wapintjanya*, 1975

141

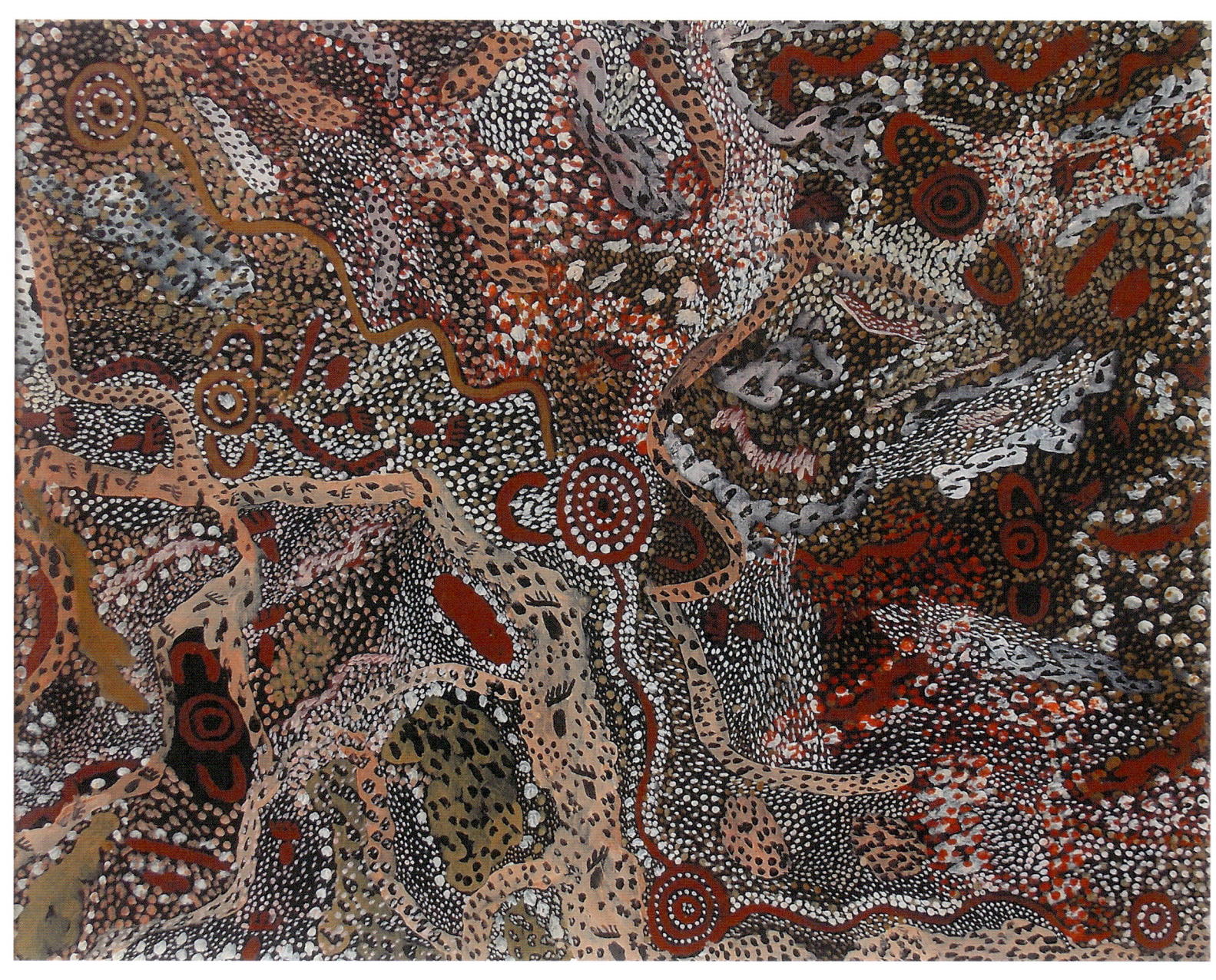

PLATE 31

Johnny Warangkula Tjupurrula
*Tjikarri*, 1974

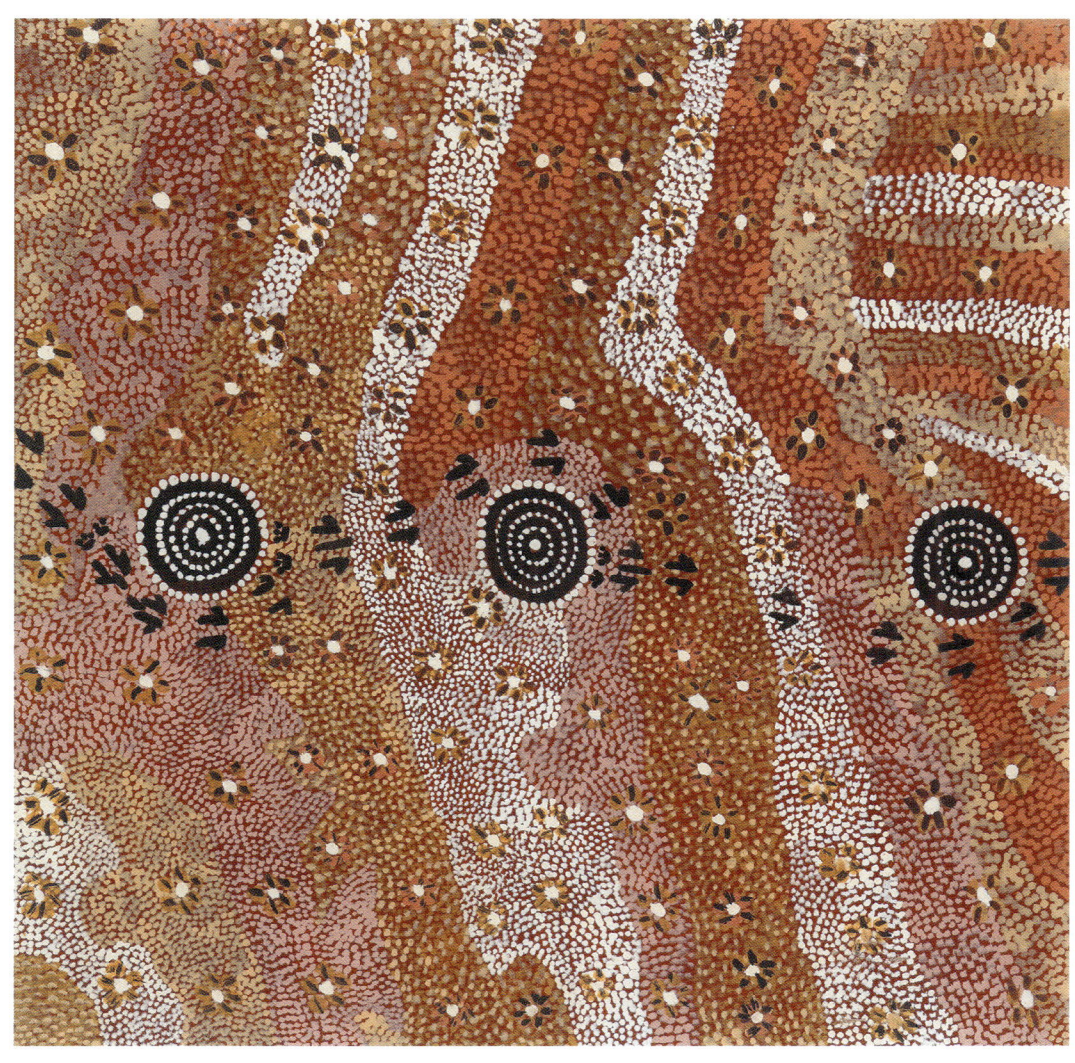

PLATE 32

Charlie Mutju Egalie Tjapaltjarri
*Wallaby Dreaming in the Sandhills at Tjunti*, 1977

PLATE 33

Charlie Mutju Egalie Tjapaltjarri
*Ceremony Dancing*, 1972

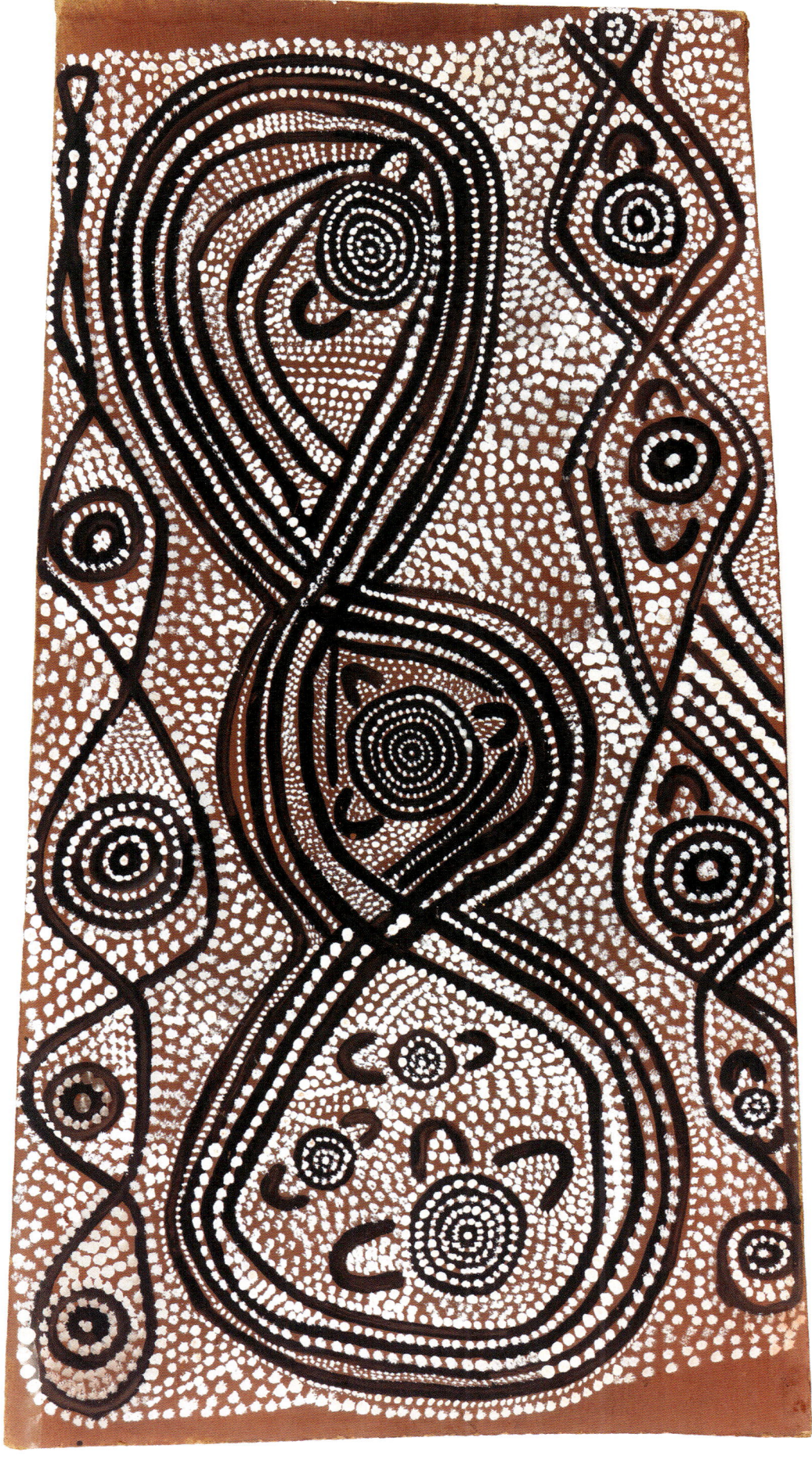

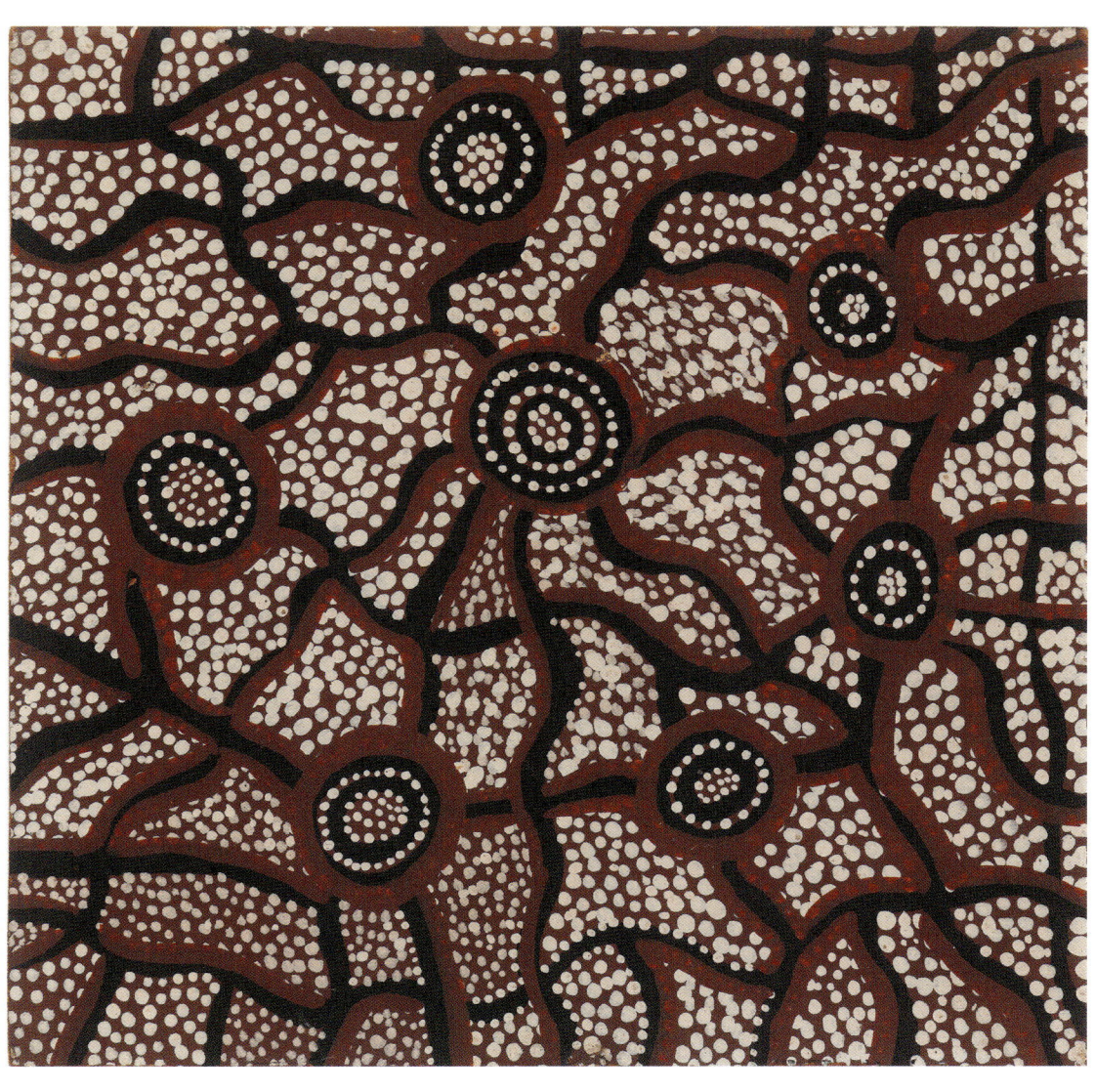

PLATE 34

Charlie Wartuma Tjungurrayi
*Frost at Tjitururrnga*, 1971

Tjitururrnga is over there [pointing to the northwestern horizon].
It's level with Mantarti. It's a rockhole Tjilpi Tjuta dancing, old
woman dancing. My son was dancing, they were teaching him.
*Wati minyma* mix [old men and women in combination]. *Ngayuku
tjamuku ngurra* [my grandfather's home]. Singing and dancing.

——EILEEN NAPALTJARRI

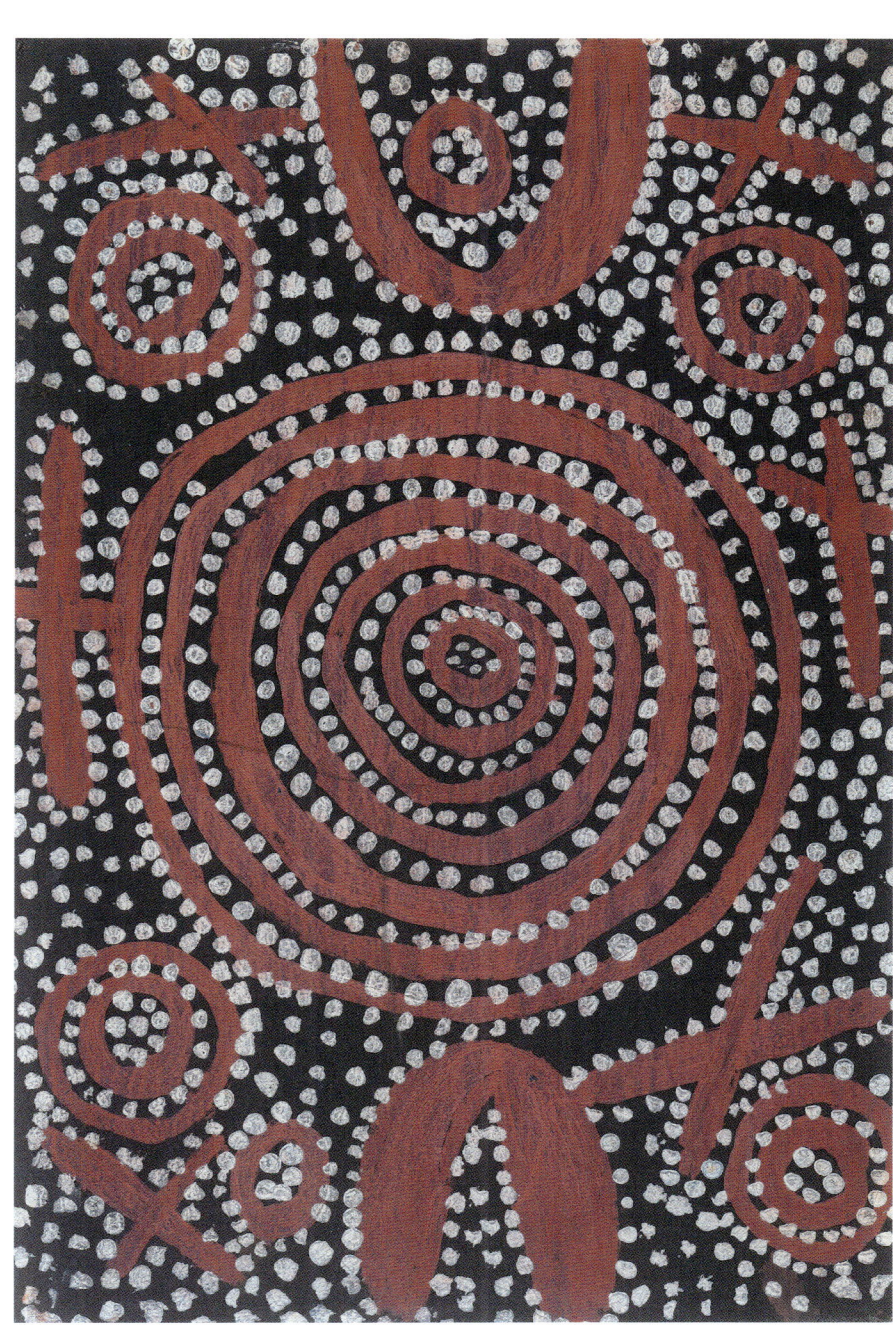

PLATE 35

Charlie Wartuma Tjungurrayi

*Untitled* (probably *Tjitururrnga*), 1972

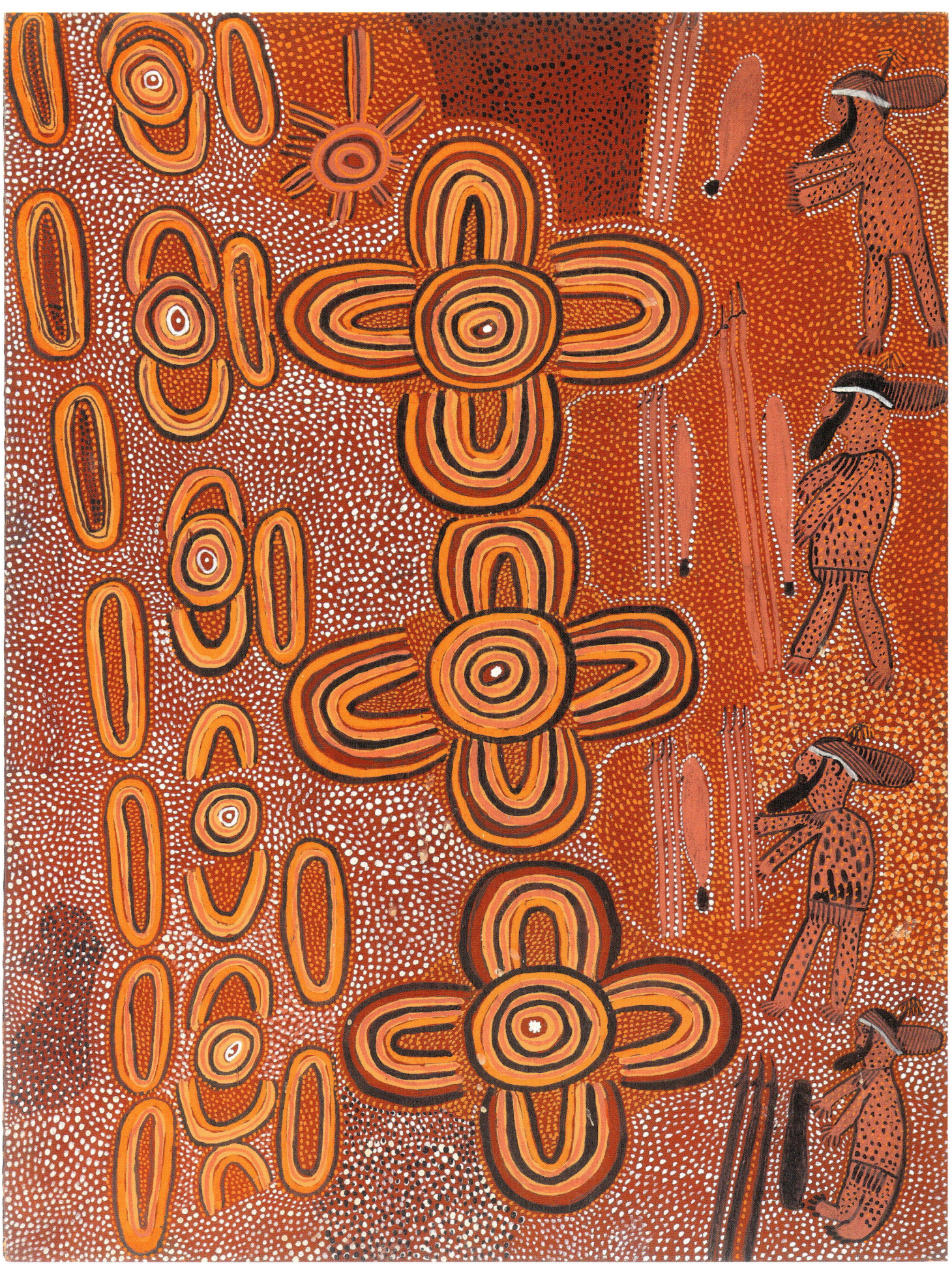

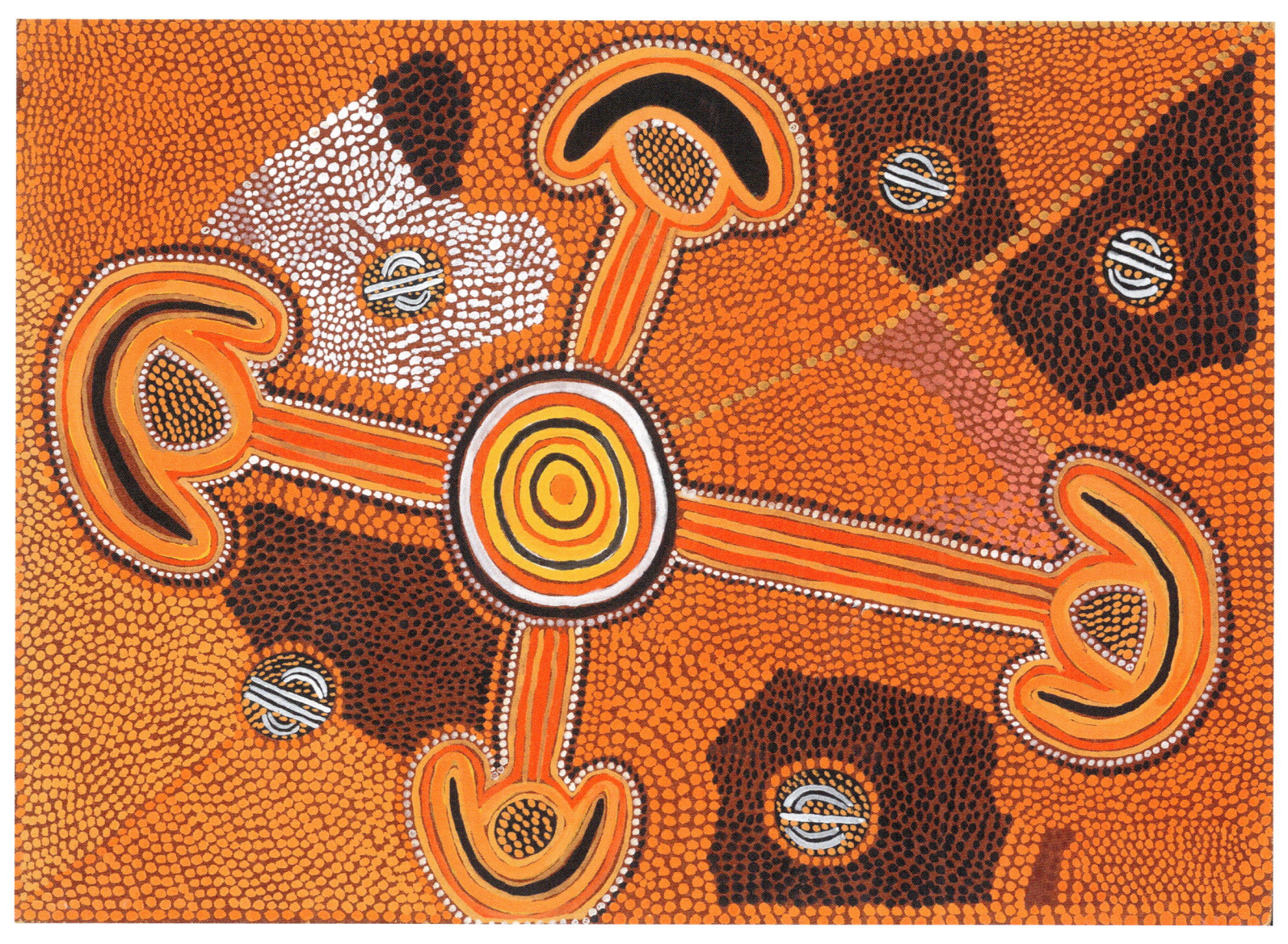

FACING | PLATE 36

Mick Namarari Tjapaltjarri
*Ceremony at Tjilka*, 1973

My husband's country that one. I remember him telling stories for
that country. He used to talk about Tjilka, his country before he
moved to Walungurru and Nyunman. Maybe early days traveling
from Tjilka.

—ELIZABETH MARKS NAKAMARRA

PLATE 37

Mick Namarari Tjapaltjarri
*Family Moon Dreaming*, 1977

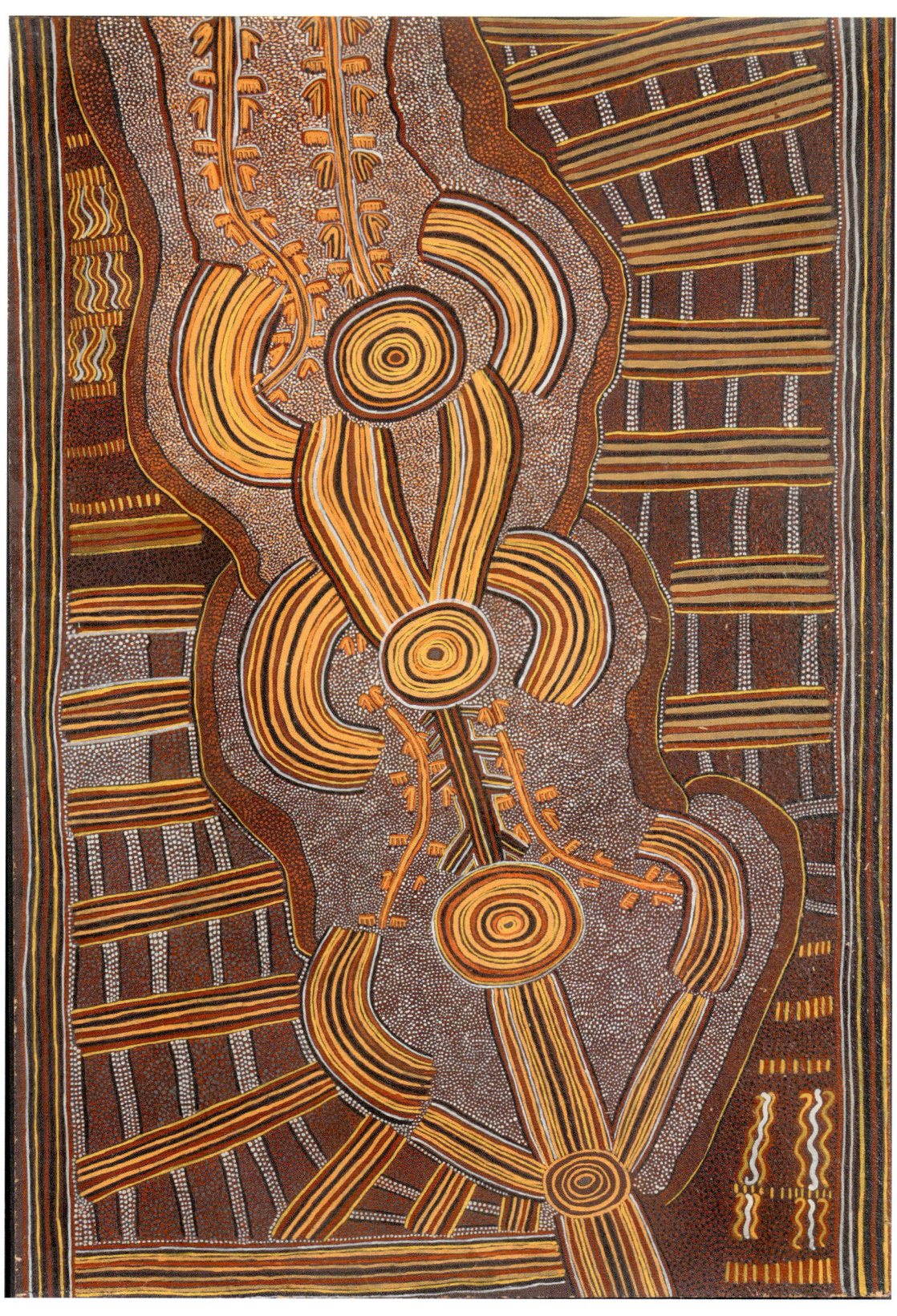

PLATE 38

Mick Namarari Tjapaltjarri
*Kangaroo Ancestor at Walukirritji,* 1973

Mick Namarari Tjapaltjarri
*Two Wallabies at Marnpi,* 1989

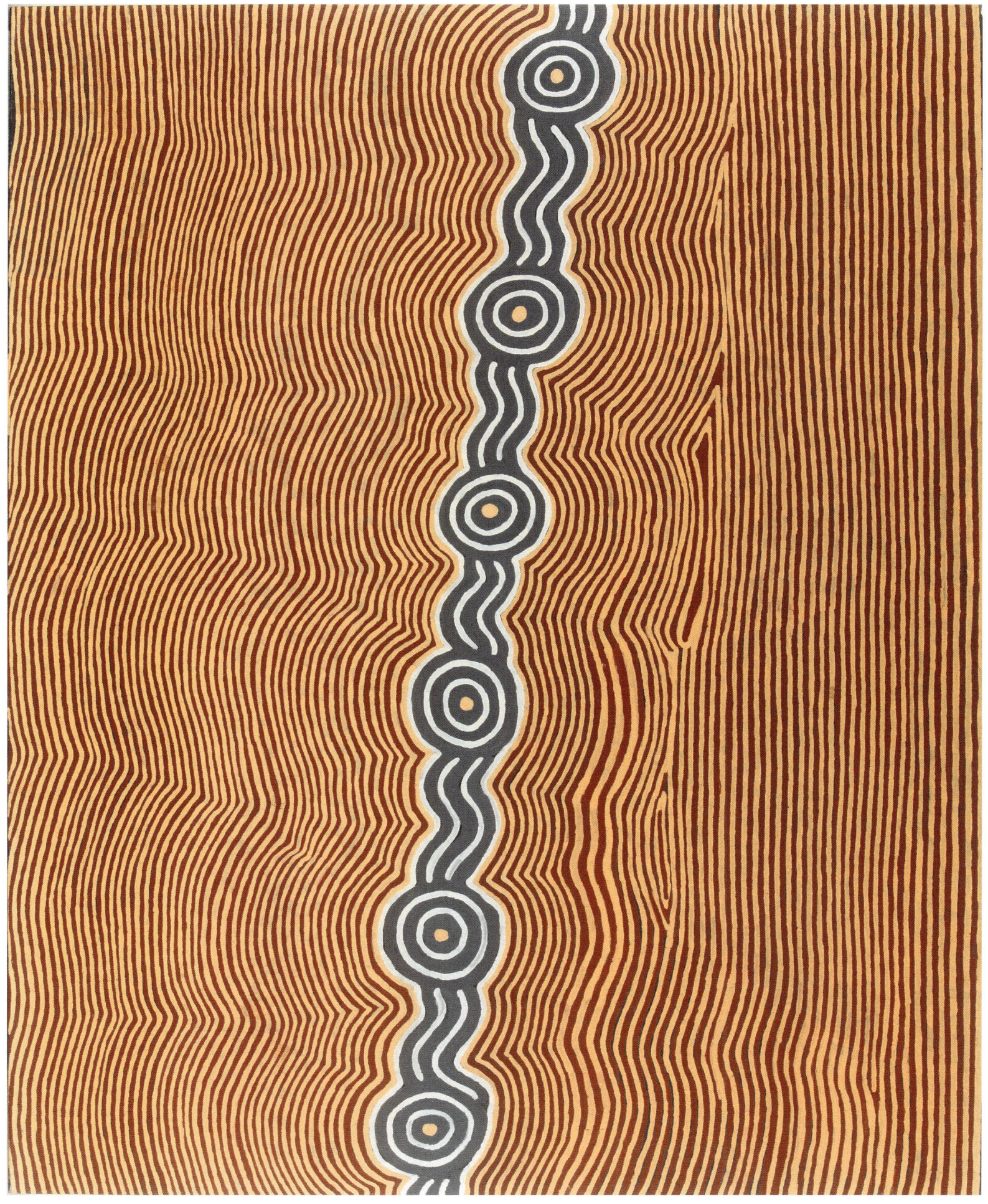

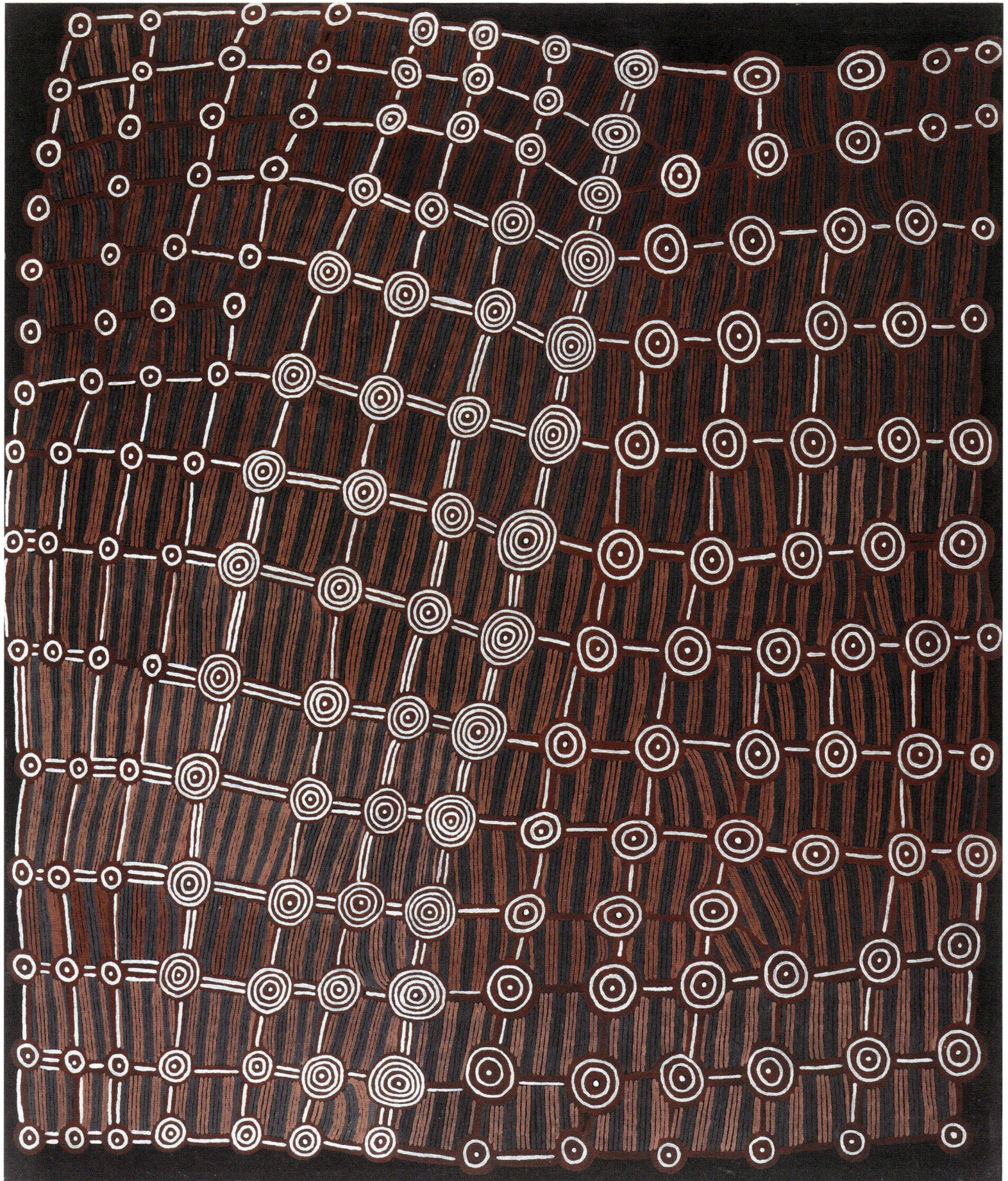

PLATE 40

Mick Namarari Tjapaltjarri
*Wallaby Dreaming at Tjunginpa*, 1990

Limpi Putungka Tjapangati
*Yalka and Maku Tjukurrpa (Bush Onion and
Witchetty Grub Dreaming)*, 1980

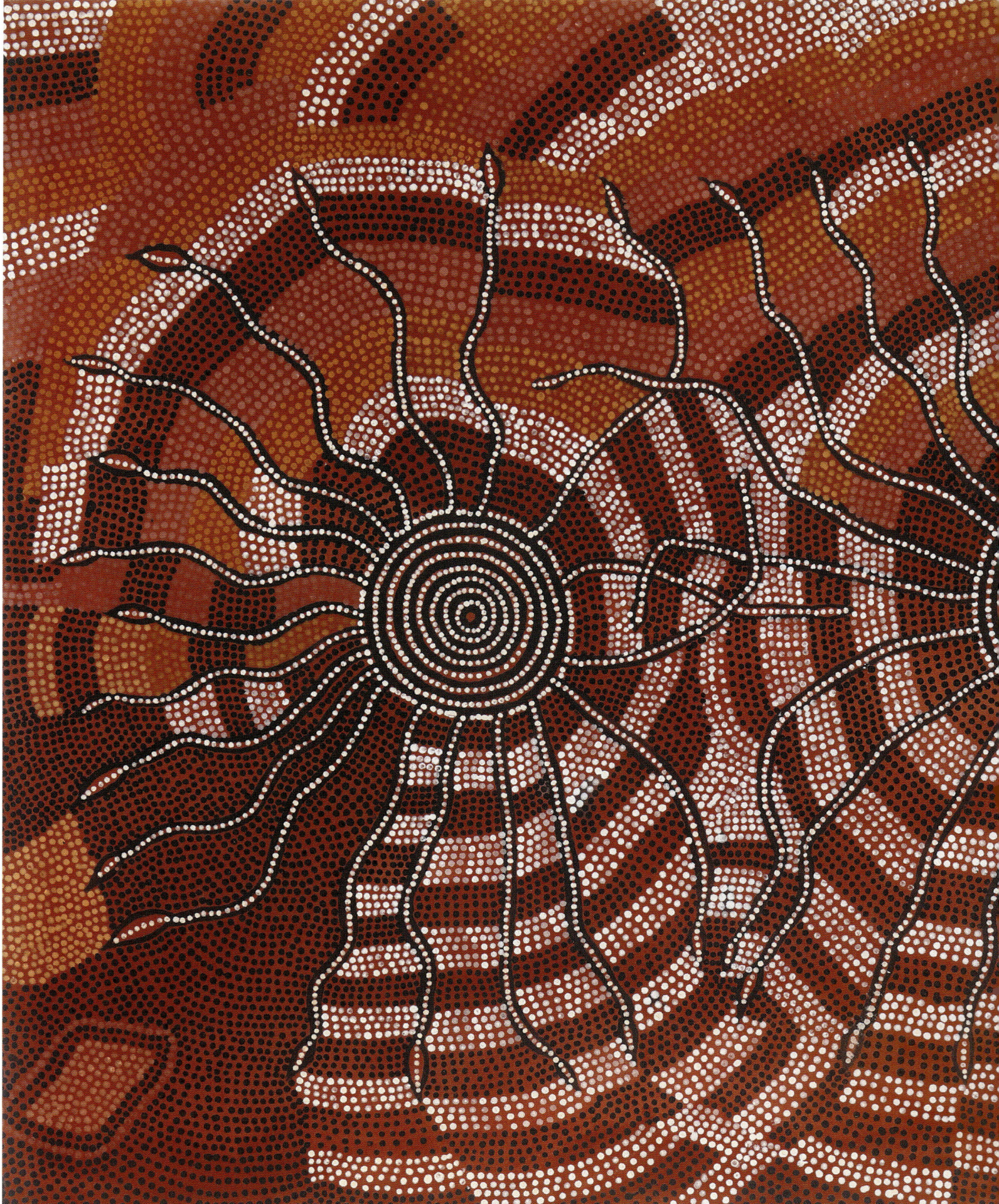

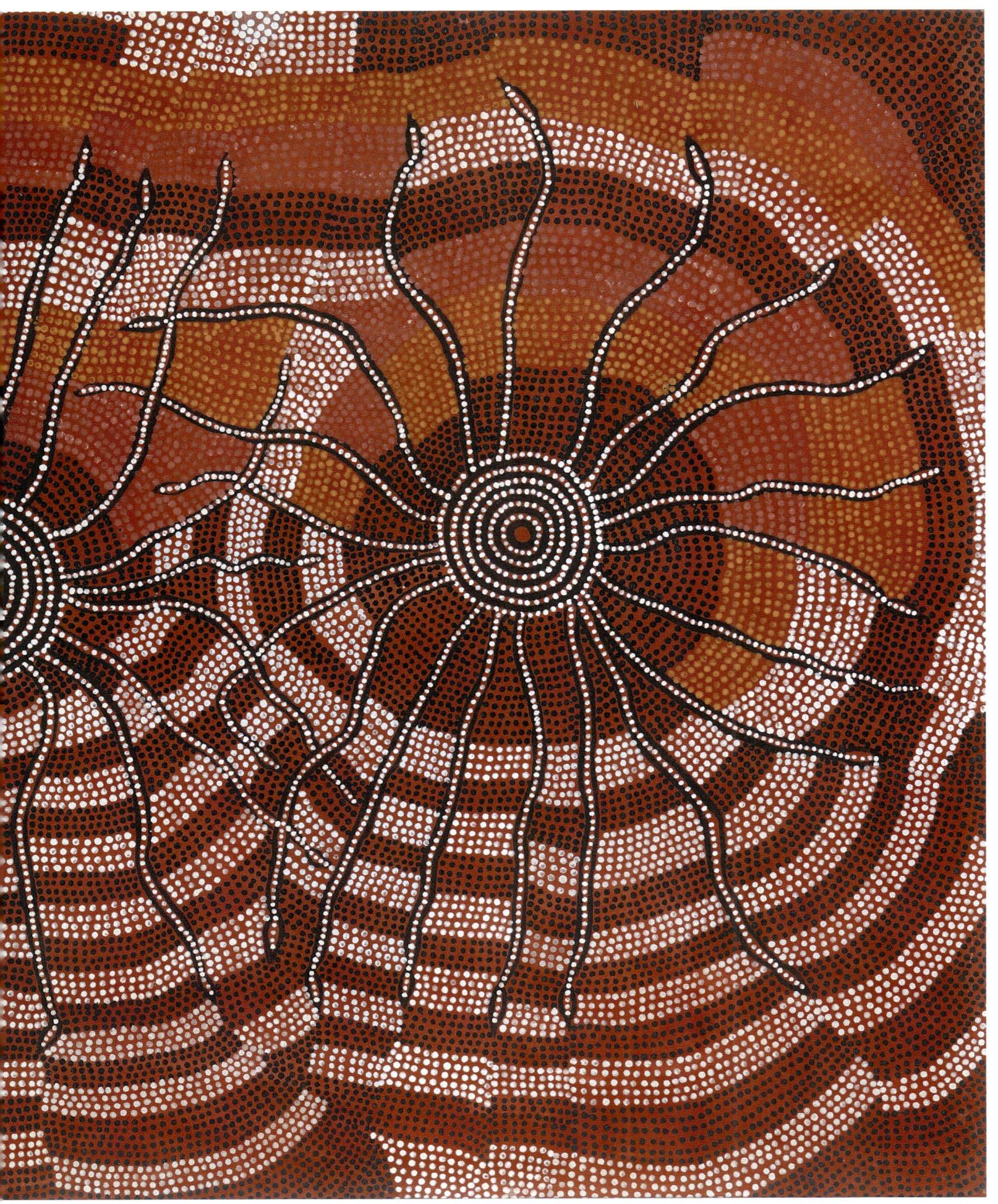

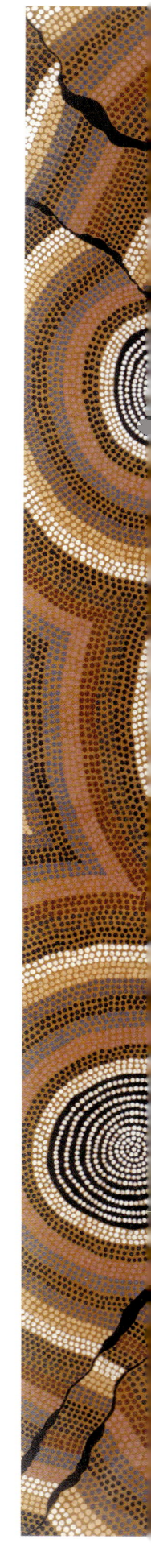

PLATE 42

William Sandy Tjapaltjarri
*Bush Tucker Dreaming at Wingellina*, 1988

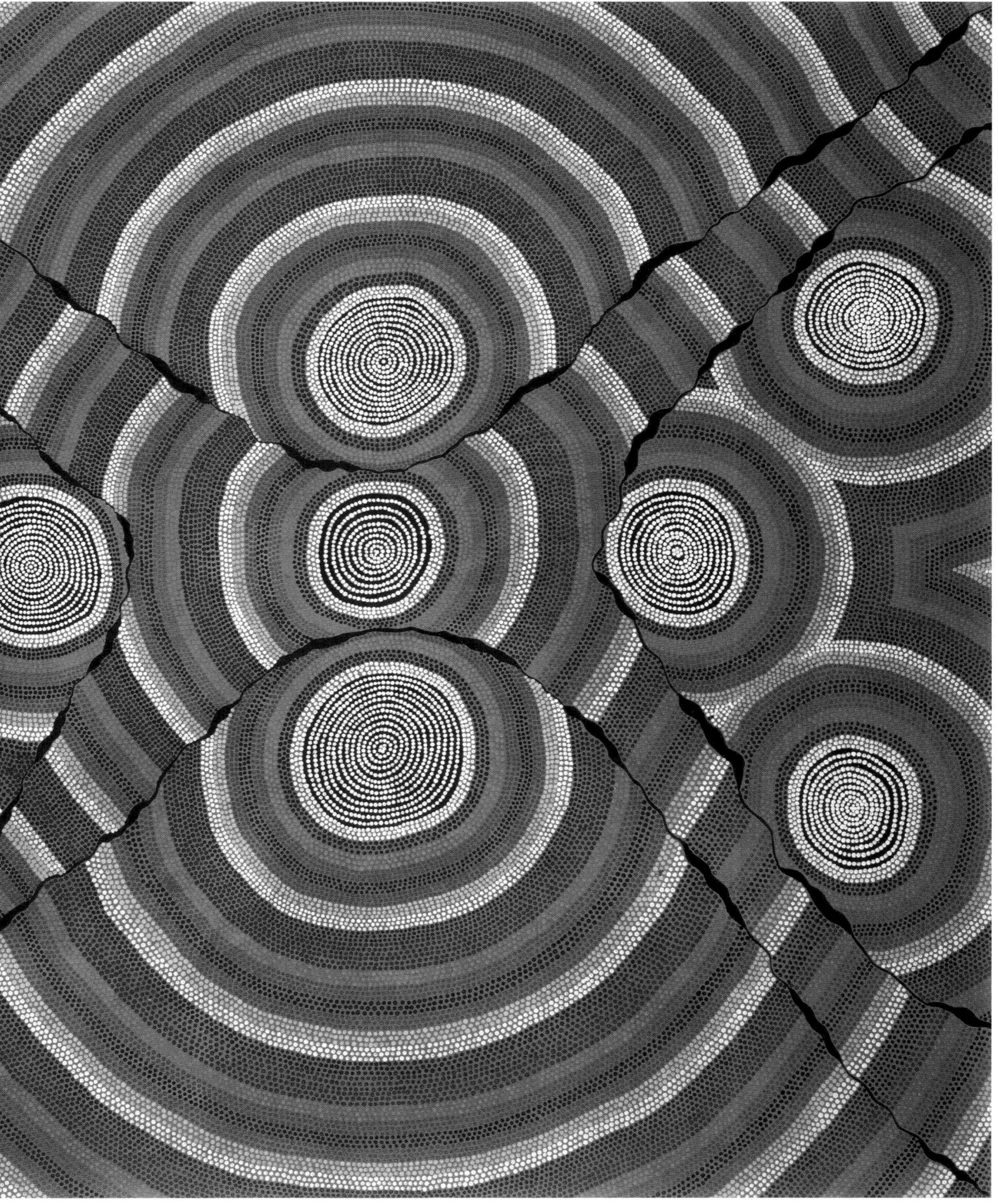

# GO WEST

—

## THE PINTUPI RETURN HOME

Throughout the 1960s, government patrols in the far Western Desert brought an increasing number of Pintupi people from their traditional Country in the west, near Wilkinkarra (Lake Mackay) and Lake Macdonald to the new settlement of Papunya. These included many men and women who would form the heart of the Papunya painting movement over the next five decades, including Timmy Payungu Tjapangati, Uta Uta Tjangala, Inyuwa Nampitjinpa and Naata Nungurrayi. As overcrowding, disease and social dysfunction set in at Papunya, Pintupi agitated for the recognition of their unique group identity. Beginning in 1967, the Welfare Branch of the Northern Territory Government made efforts to help the Pintupi move to their own community, separate from Papunya. Shifting political attitudes, catalyzed by the election of the progressive Whitlam government and the rise of civil rights movements across the world, created the right conditions for Pintupi to return to their homelands. In June 1973, two hundred Pintupi moved west to the new settlement of Yayayi, twenty-five miles from Papunya. By 1976, forty percent of Papunya residents had relocated to outstations. In 1981, a permanent settlement was established at Walungurru (Kintore), and then another at Kiwirrkurra in 1983. Inspired by their renewed connection to Country, Pintupi artists began to develop their own unique style of painting by experimenting more with abstraction and zingy optical effects. This great return required the Papunya Tula company to serve artists across a vast stretch of the remote Western Desert. The company, which had been formed from disparate groups "coming together" in Papunya, was now stretched to its limits. By the mid-1990s, Papunya Tula Artists had shifted its focus almost entirely from Papunya to new studios at Walungurru and Kiwirrkurra, which would quickly become the epicenters of the movement.

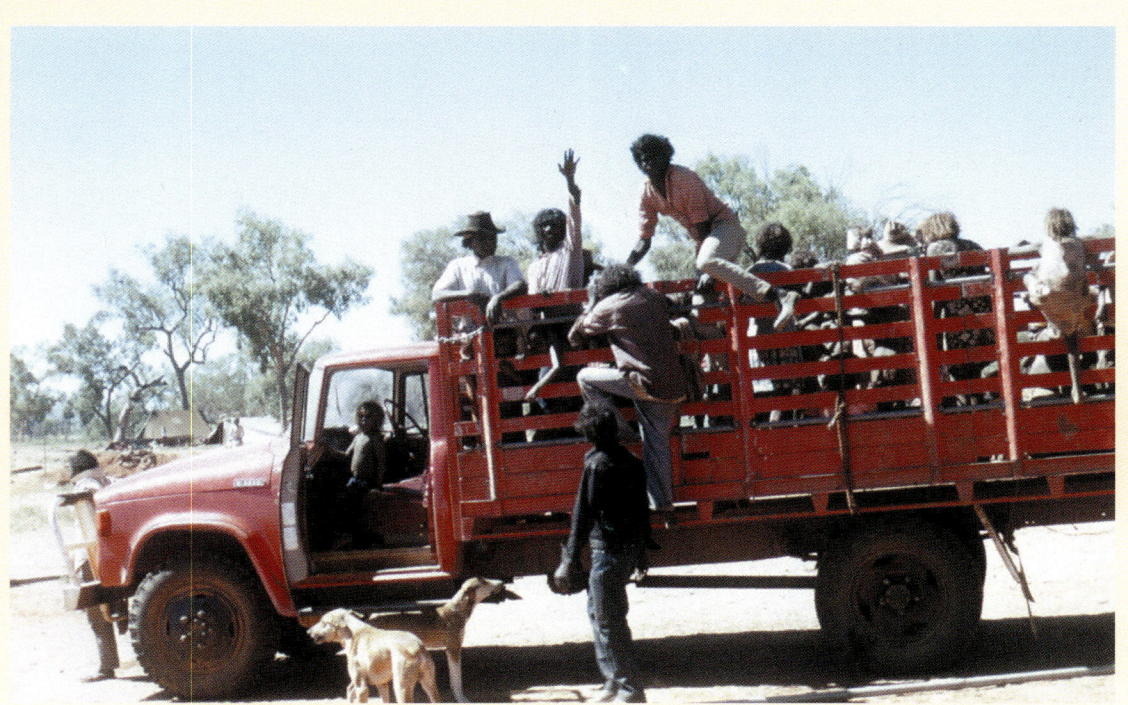

Freddy West Tjakamarra and Jeffrey James Tjangala stand at the front of the truck purchased by the Yayayi community with support from the Department of Aboriginal Affairs, 1973. Photo by Fred Myers.

FACING | PLATE 43

Uta Uta Tjangala
*Tjitji Kutjarra (Two Boys at Yawarankunya)*, 1971

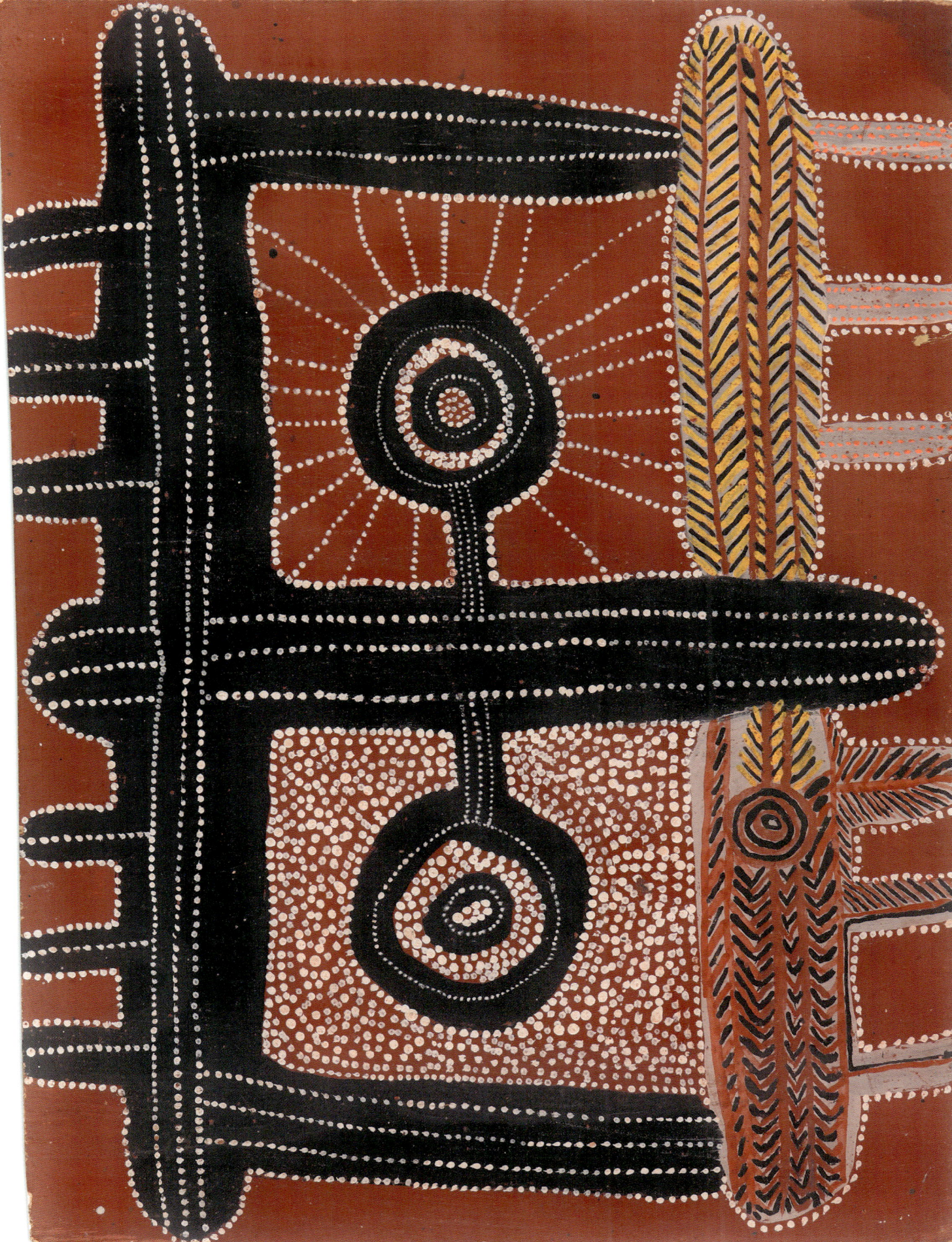

PLATE 44

Shorty Lungkarta Tjungurrayi
*Rumiya Tjukurrpa (Goanna Dreaming at Wantarritja)*
(formerly *Patterns in the Sand*), 1980

This painting was included in the exhibition *Dreamings: The Art of Aboriginal Australia* at the Asia Society in New York in 1988. While curators assigned it the title *Patterns in the Sand*, in their description they cited the work as belonging to the series of paintings by Shorty Lungkarta Tjungurrayi that were often titled *Goanna Love Story*. These works have enchanted viewers but have also remained relatively mysterious. Some of the confusion, no doubt, emanates from the linguistic mismatch between the artist and his interlocutors. Shorty Lungkarta painted numerous versions of Tjukurrpa stories involving the sand goanna, known as *rumiya* to many eastern Pintupi speakers. These stories are geographically located in his Country, in places he identified as Wantarritjanya—where the male goanna lifted himself into a prostrate position, attempting to entice the female into sex, calling her to him and leaving his marks in the ground; then moved on, following her into the ground, into a cave (or rock shelter); and eventually arrived at Piltjartanya, southeast of Walungurru, where the two goannas grew tired and turned into water snakes.

The story references the seasonal cycle of goannas mating in the spring, when they come out of their burrows and "dance," eating the plentiful *wartunuma* (flying termites) of the season. Lungkarta often referred to the desert spring as "goanna dance time." This is also the season when Pintupi people would move out of the permanent water-holes after the rains came. It is a "goanna love story," but much more. In some documentation that Shorty Lungkarta's own children have offered, as the goannas turn into two snakes, the male and female represent complementary principles of cooperation—the male snake searching at night for the female who, travels during the day.[1]

1. Thanks to Jeff Hulcombe for his insights and
   documentation on this Tjukurrpa.

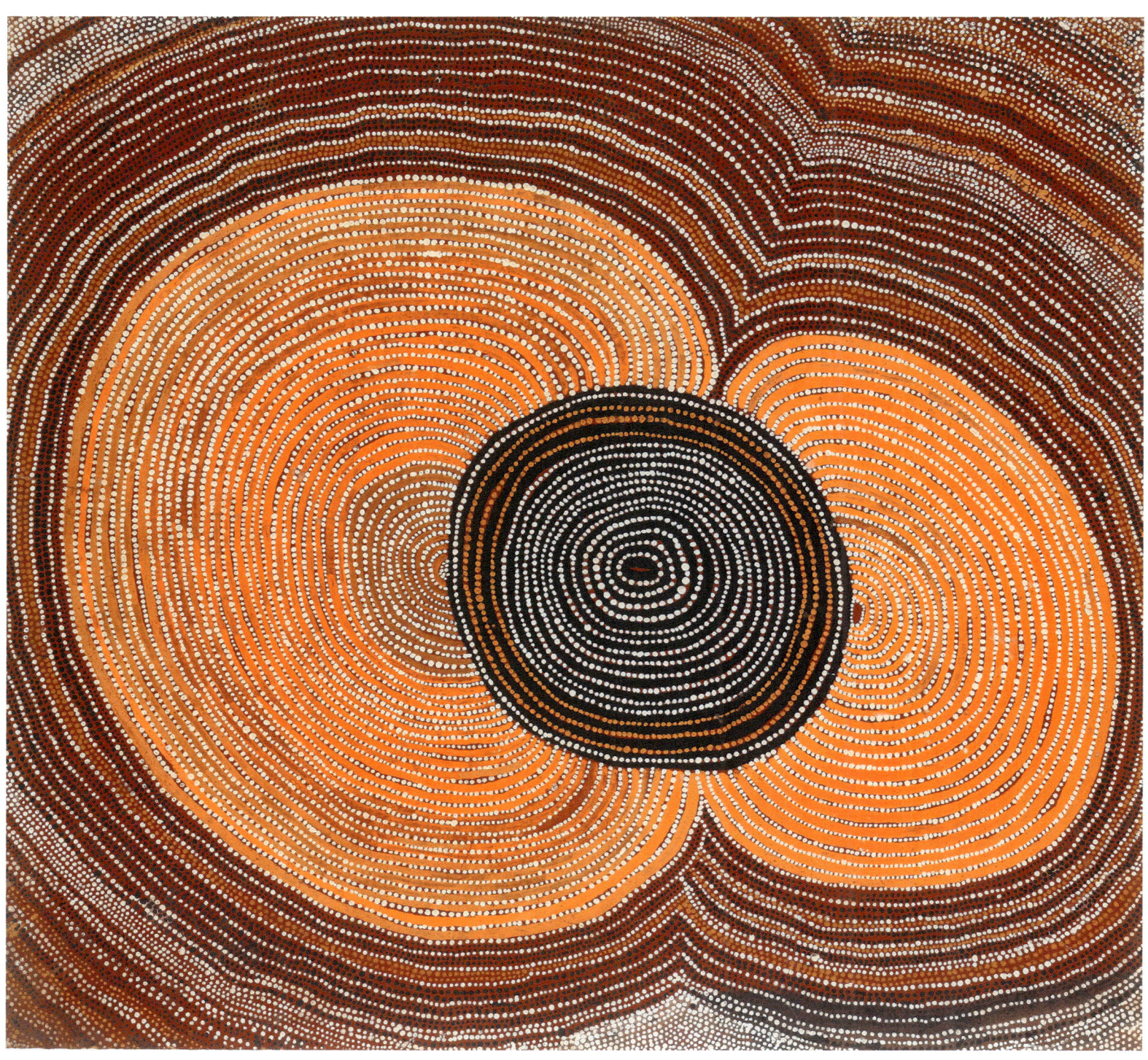

# YINA TJUKURRPA

## OLD MAN DREAMING

The ancestral travels of the trickster Yina (the "Old Man") track a path from Kampurarrnga through Ngurrapalangu and Yumari and on westward, traversing precisely the traditional route that Pintupi would traverse across the desert plains.

Yina's exploits are reenacted in both painting and ceremony, particularly those involving his genitals, which frequently separate from his body and take on a life of their own. In Charlie Wartuma Tjungurrayi's painting *Old Man's Dreaming at Tjurrpungkuntjanya* (1974, plate 45), the artist depicts a rocky rise where Yina's testicles raced ahead by the side of Yina's path. Considerable humor is found in Yina's calling for his penis and testicles, which are variously bitten by ants or trodden on by dogs before turning to gold at Nyuntjulnga. For all the levity, however, Yina is also a frightening figure and the bearer of powerful sorcery.

At the beginning of his journey, Yina intersects with the Kungka Kutjarra (Two Women, depicted by Pansy Napangardi, plate 54) and lustfully pursues them before they escape his advances and head south. At Yumari—whose name literally translates as "mother-in-law place"—Yina breaks a sacred taboo and copulates with a woman who in desert kinship terms would be considered his mother-in-law. For this transgression, his penis is attacked by a swarm of ants.

Many women artists also paint Yumari, particularly Tjunkiya Napaltjarri and Yuyuya Nampitjinpa (plates 126, 127). Their paintings tell of the travel of a group of ancestral women who stop at Yumari to collect *kampurarrpa* (desert raisin) and perform ceremonies before continuing on to Pinari and, finally, Kalipinypa. It was one of these women who separated from the group and had intercourse with Yina at Yumari.

There are many distinctive sites on Yina's path, including an X-shaped rockhole at Yumari where he lay down before arising in the night to have sex with his mother-in-law. To the south of Yumari are a series of "standing rocks" called Tilirrangarranya (literally, "light the fire and stand") where Yina stood by the fire and decorated himself the following morning. Suffering great pain from the ant bites on his penis, Yina fled westward, leaving many marks on the landscape, such as the limestone ridge of Yarrpalangunya, before disappearing in the far-western reaches of the desert.

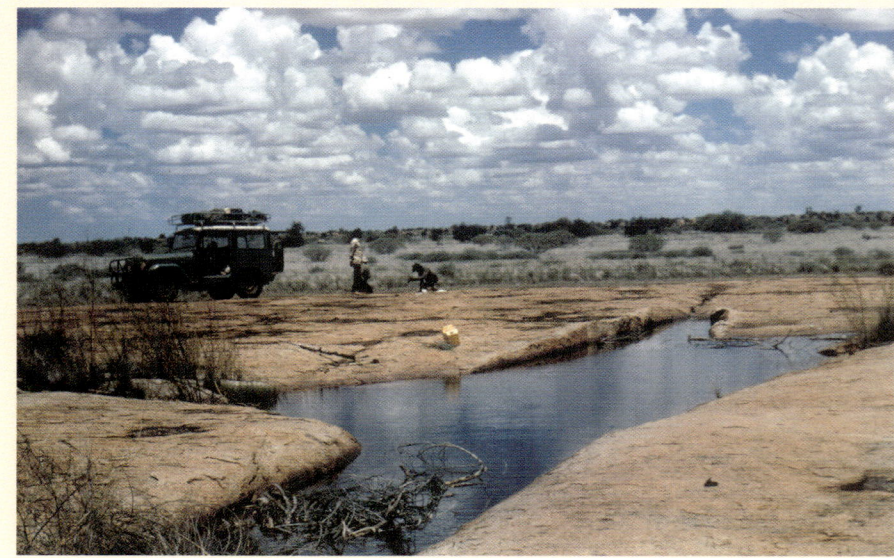

Yumari rockhole, 1974. Photo by R. G. (Dick) Kimber.

FACING | PLATE 45

Charlie Wartuma Tjungurrayi
*Old Man's Dreaming at Tjurrpungkuntjanya*, 1974

162

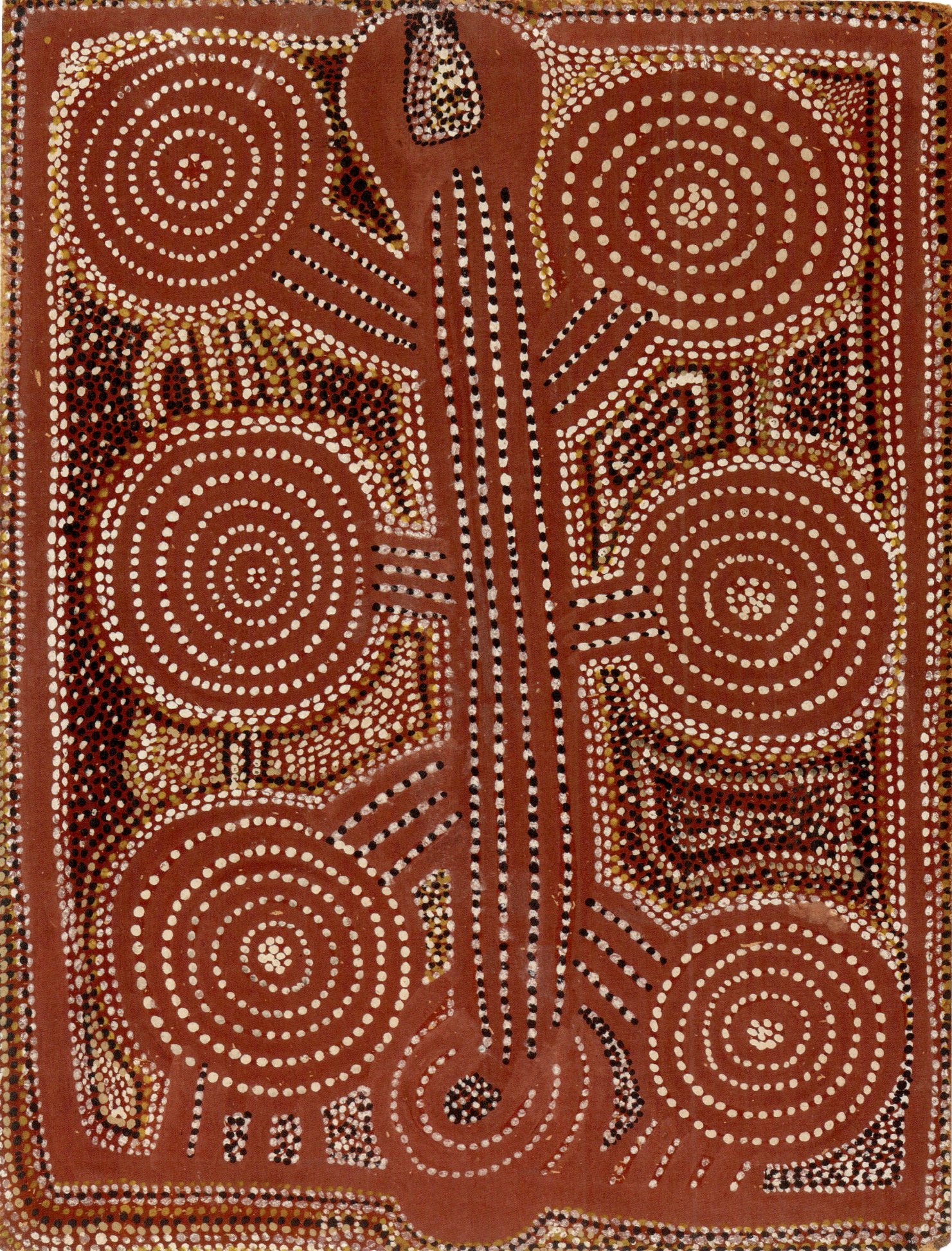

# Ngurrapalangu

My father was like a teacher. He was the one who taught the other men all about Ngurrapalangu. This man here, my father. He was showing them what he knew, sharing his knowledge, and then he passed away. All these people, they knew my father could sing all the songs right through.

— MORRIS JACKSON TJAMPITJINPA

Ngurrapalangu is a hill and claypan site to the west of Walungurru (Kintore). Uta Uta Tjangala described the place as Tjuntamurtuku *ngurra* (the place of the ancestor Tjuntamurtu, or "Short Legs"). It was a highly significant site for the artist, as it was where his spirit was conceived in his mother's womb. After rainfall, the claypans at Ngurrapalangu bloom with a succulent known as *mungilpa (Tecticornia verrucose)* whose seeds are ground into cakes and eaten. The artist's mother ate these seedcakes at the time of his conception, linking him to the ancestor Tjuntamurtu. Uta Uta returned to the theme of Tjuntamurtu many times throughout his career, and it has been suggested that they represent self-portraits of the artist as ancestor.[1]

In the Tjukurrpa, Tjuntamurtu was frightened by the approach of the dangerous and powerful Yina (the Old Man). He crawled deep inside a cave at Ngurrapalangu and frantically tossed out sacred objects stored there to make room for himself. These sacred objects became the hill called Wintalynga. The oblong feature on the left of this work represents the hill, but also the sacred board that created it. A field of objects extends outward from the hill/board, sometimes clearly representing sacred objects and sometimes, more ambiguously, the claypans themselves. Until recently, this painting was considered restricted due to its overt references to ceremonial objects. In 2018, it was approved for exhibition by the artist's son Morris Jackson Tjampitjinpa.

1. See, for instance, Fred Myers, "Aesthetics and Practice: A Local Art History of Pintupi Painting," in *Art from the Land: Dialogues with the Kluge-Ruhe Collection of Australian Aboriginal Art*, ed. Howard Morphy and Margo Smith (Charlottesville: University of Virginia Press, 1999), 251–52; and John Carty and Alison French, "Art of Central Australia: Refigured Ground," in *The Cambridge Companion to Australian Art*, ed. Jaynie Anderson (Port Melbourne: Cambridge University Press, 2011), 137–40.

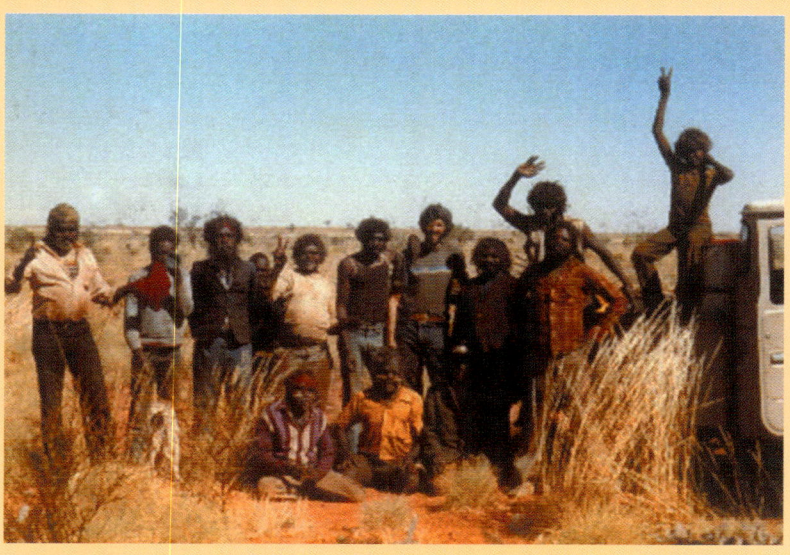

Pinta Pinta Tjapanangka and Uta Uta Tjangala (seated), Yumpurlurru Tjungurrayi and John Tjakamarra in back (second and third from left), Martin Tjampitjinpa, Itiminyi Tjapaltjarri, Fred Myers, Joe Tjakamarra and Ronnie Tjampitjinpa at Ngurrapalangu, 1981. Photo by Andrew Crocker.

FACING | PLATE 46

Uta Uta Tjangala
*Ngurrapalangunya*,
c. 1971–72

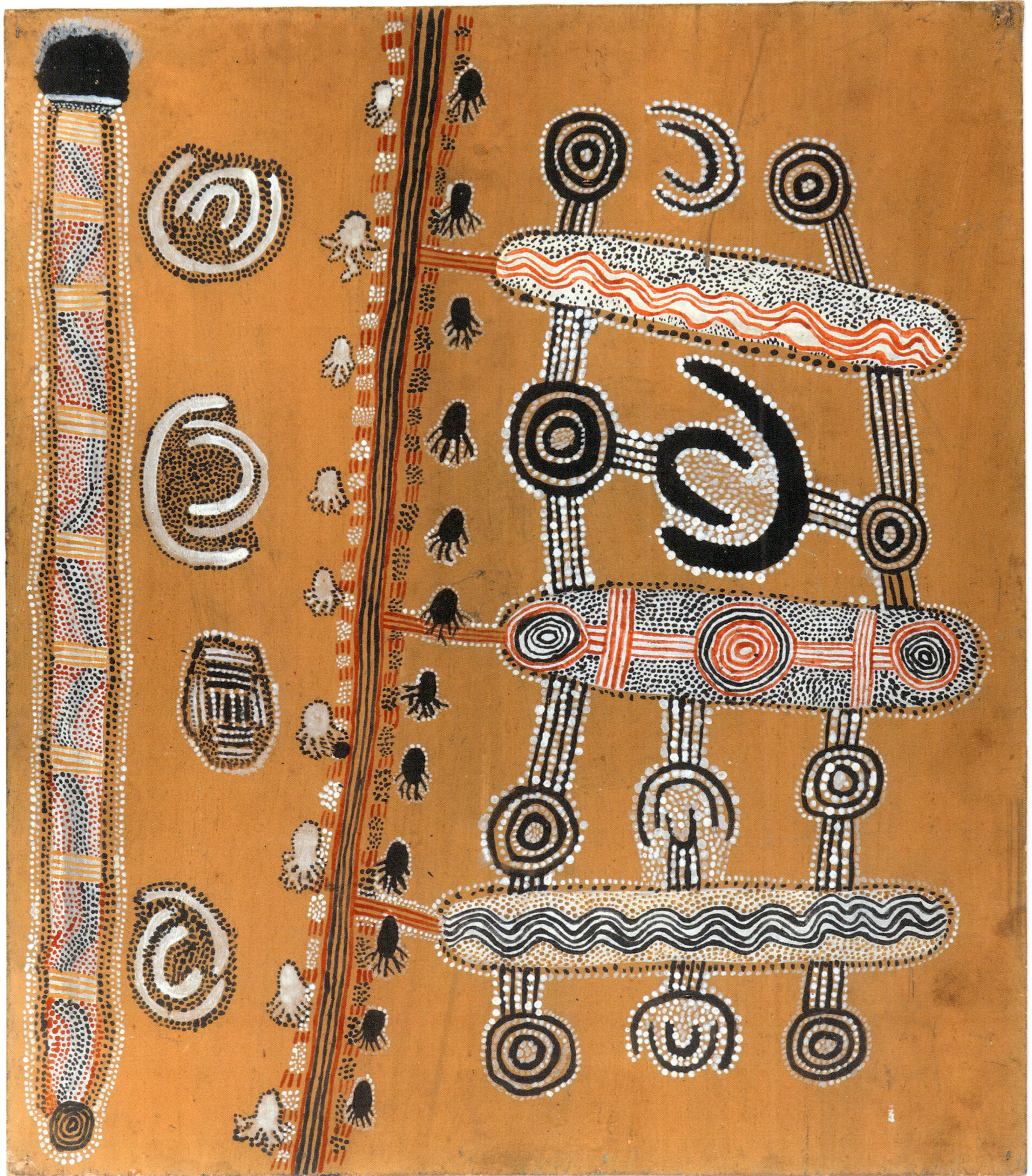

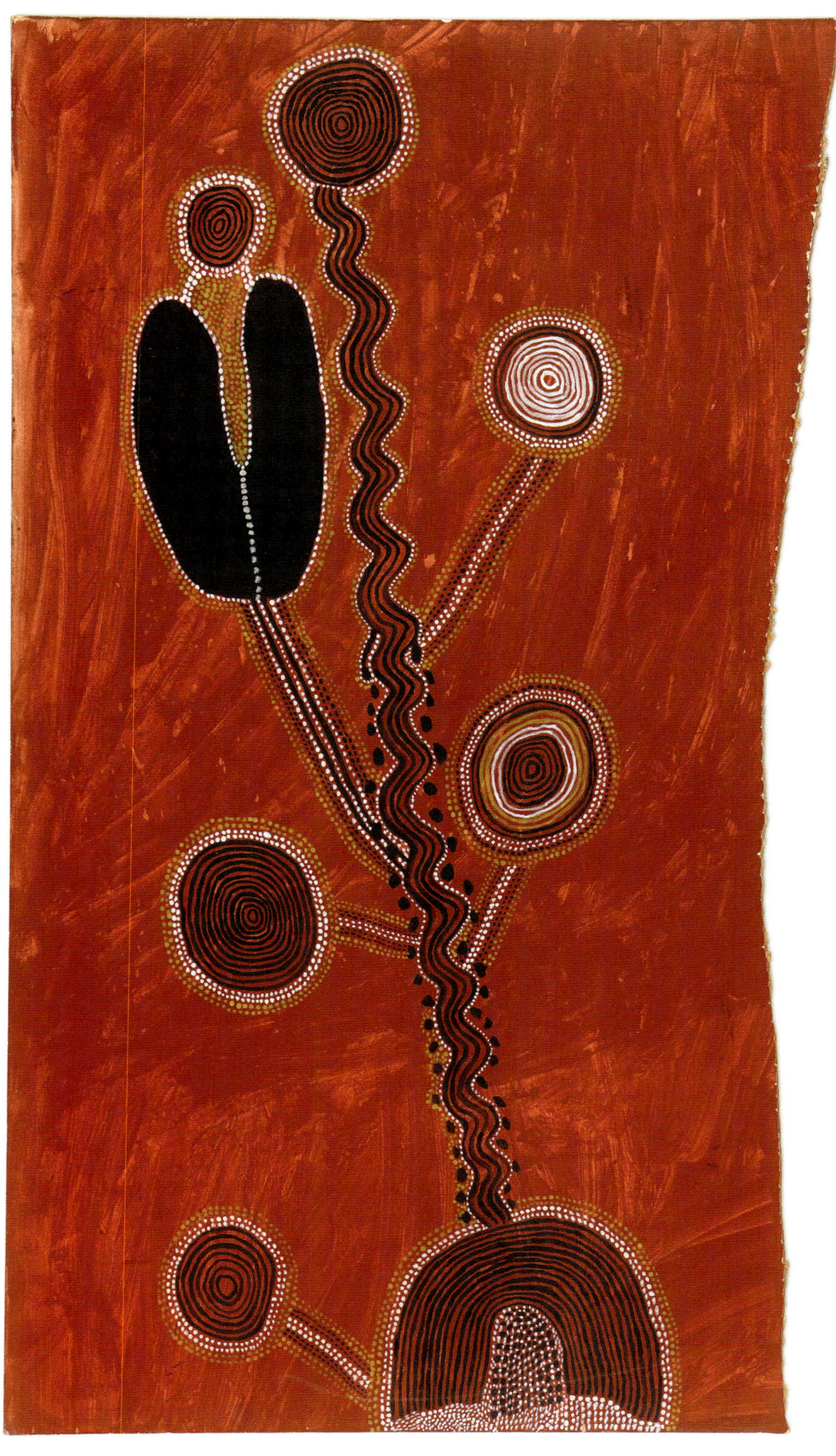

PLATE 47

Uta Uta Tjangala
*Old Man Dreaming at*
*Yumari,* 1973

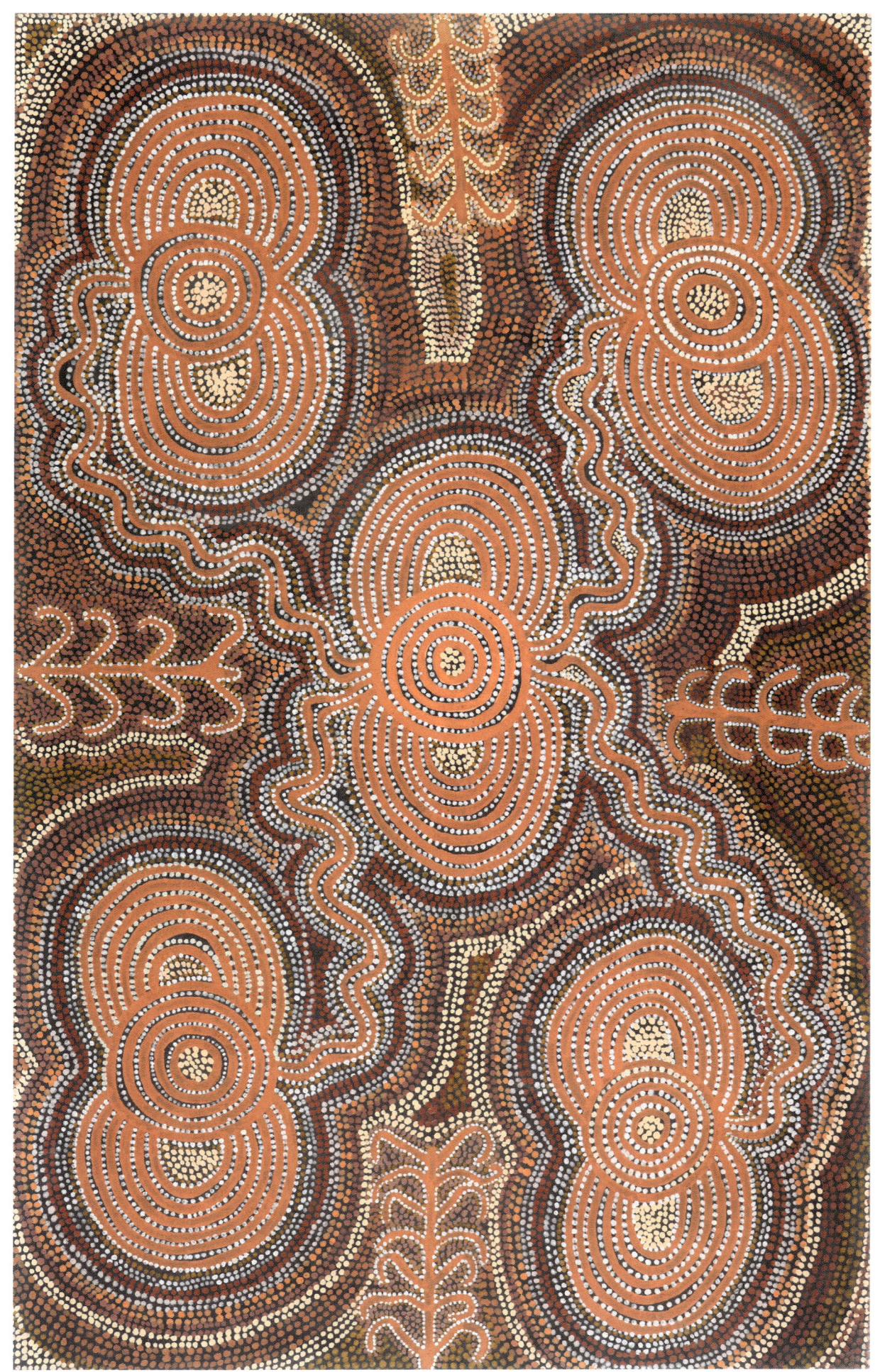

PLATE 48

Charlie Wartuma Tjungurrayi
*Travels of an Old Man to Yumari,*
1980

PLATE 49

Uta Uta Tjangala
*My Country with Sandhills*, 1980

*This is Yumari*. These *tali* [sandhills] are on the south side. *Malu* [red kangaroo] at Yumari traveling west. *Malu* go there, a lot of *malu* there today and wallaby in those hills. The roundels on left of the picture might be Ngurrapalangu and Yumari on the other side. My father was dancing at Yumari, and he was showing the men. They went camping there with the old men. They were dancing overnight, singing the songs and all. They really knew them, *palya* [good].

—MORRIS JACKSON TJAMPITJINPA

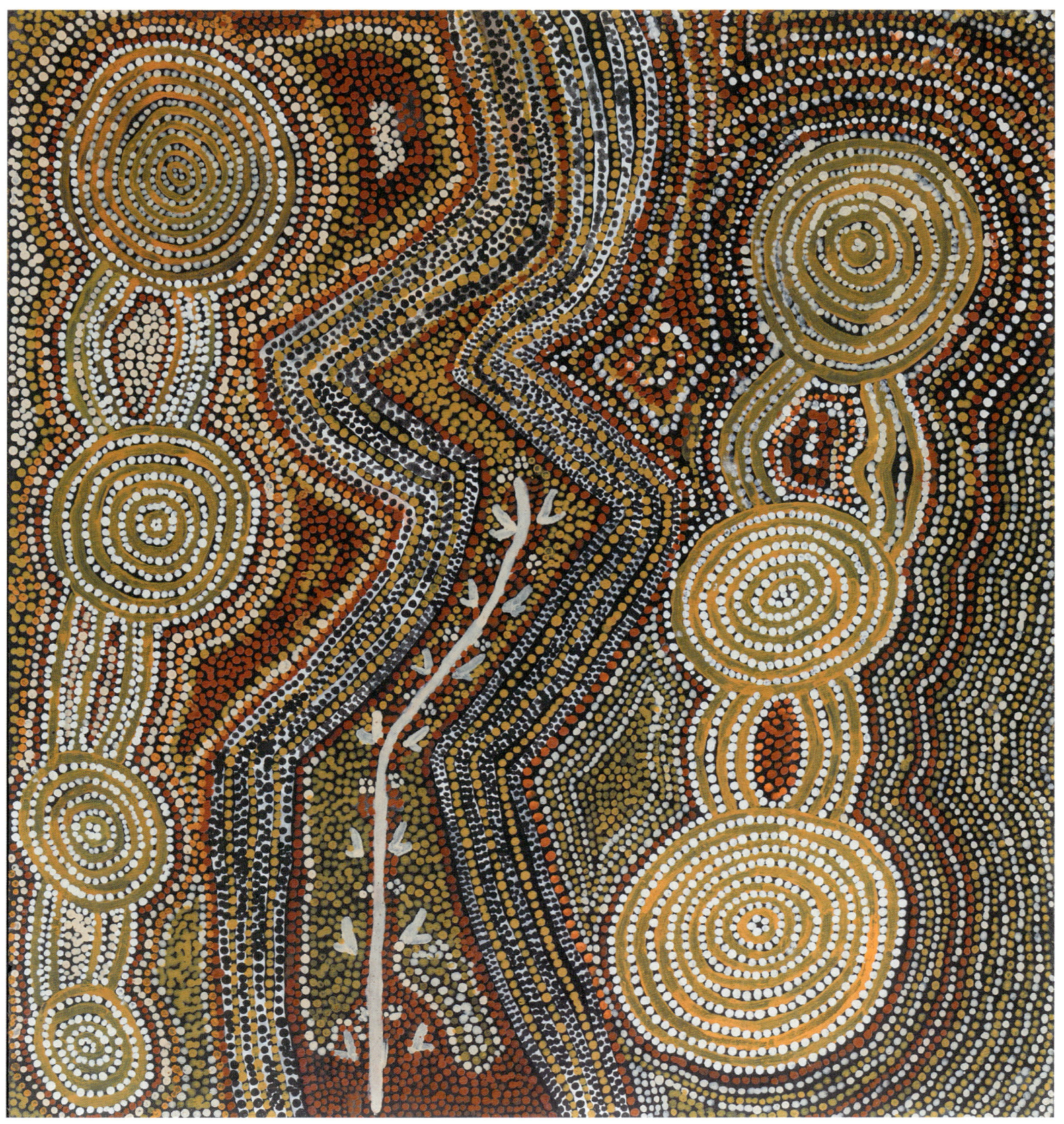

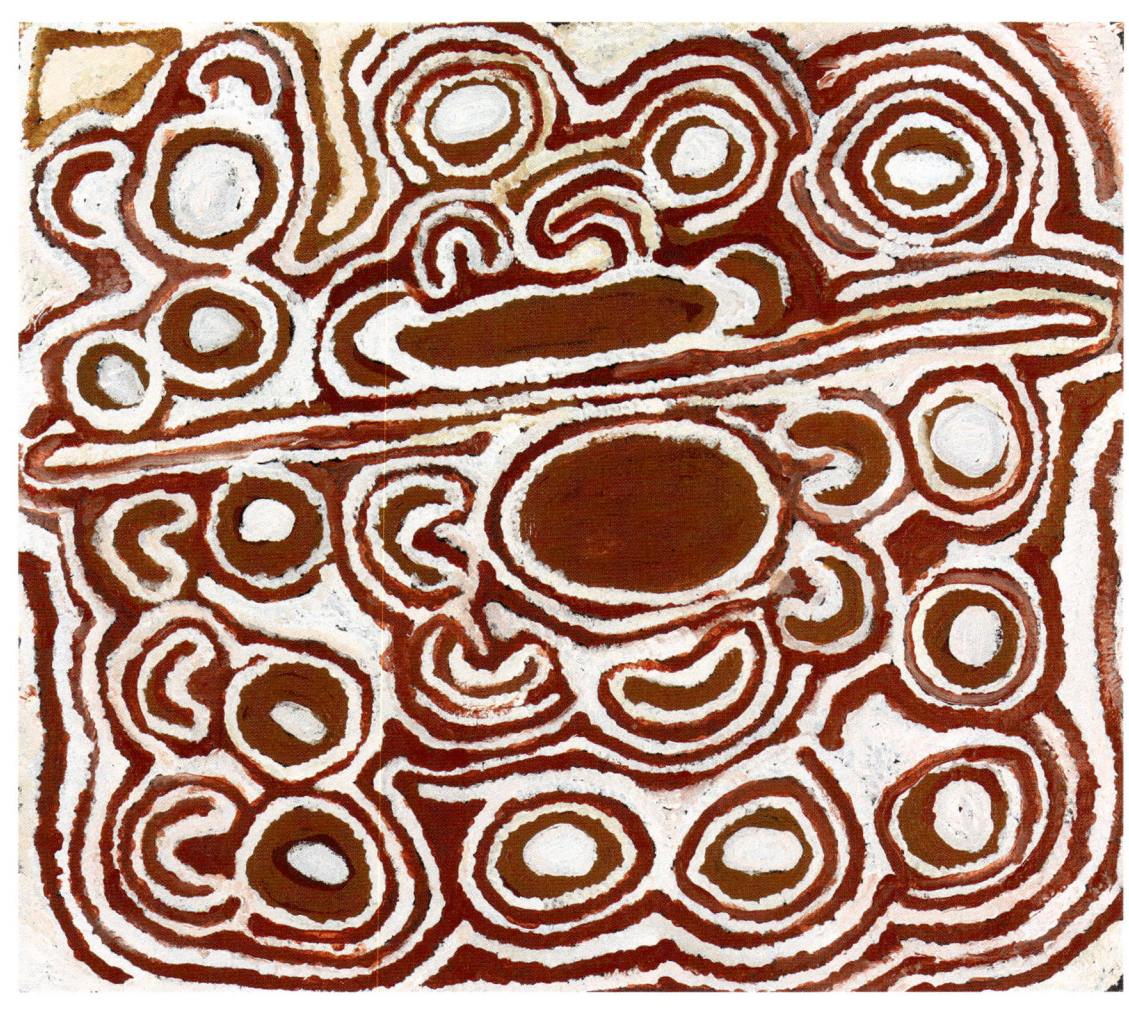

PLATE 50

Tjunkiya Napaltjarri
*Women's Ceremonies at Yumari*, 1996

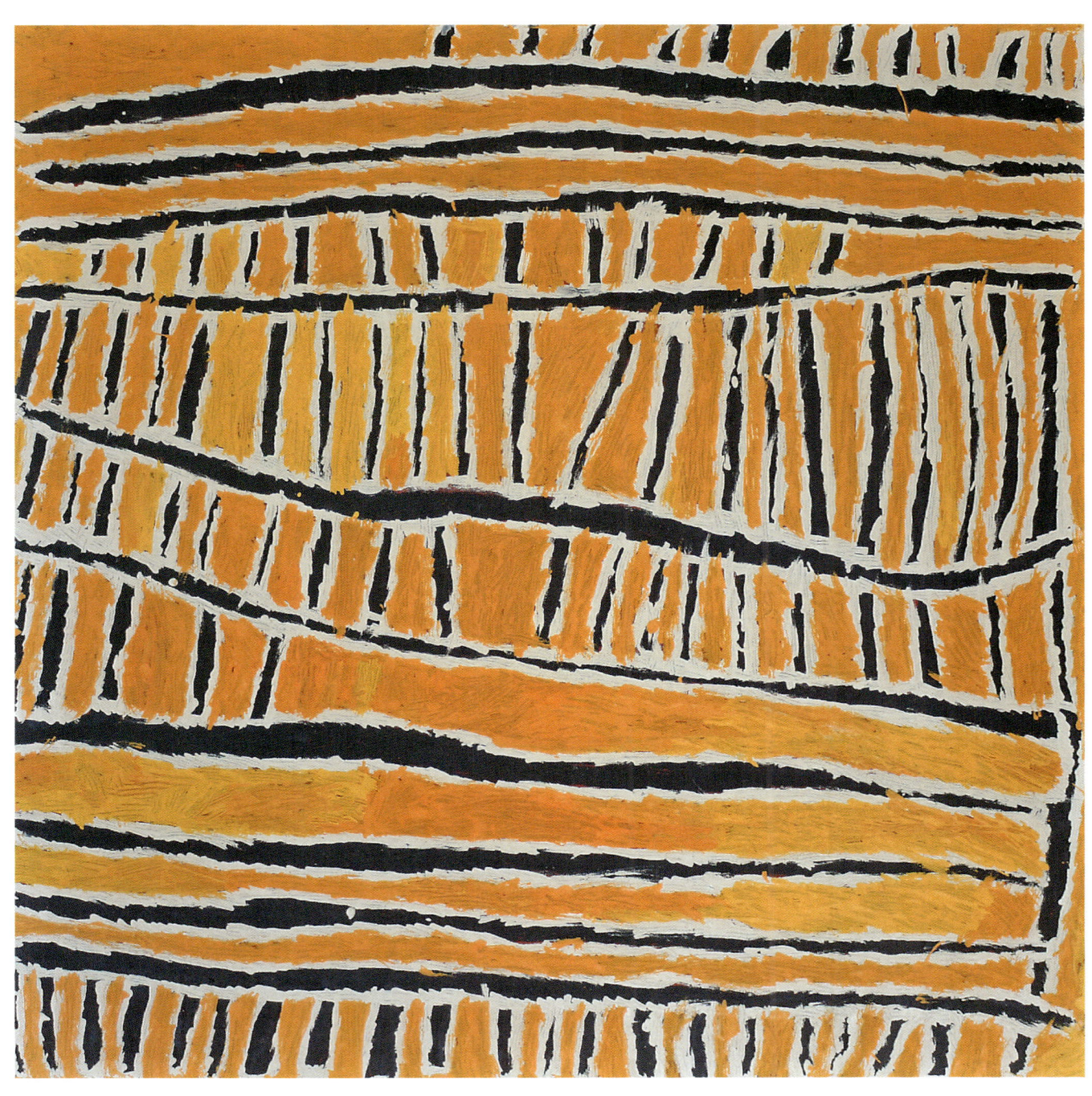

PLATE 51

Tjunkiya Napaltjarri
*Rockhole Site of Yumari*, 2008

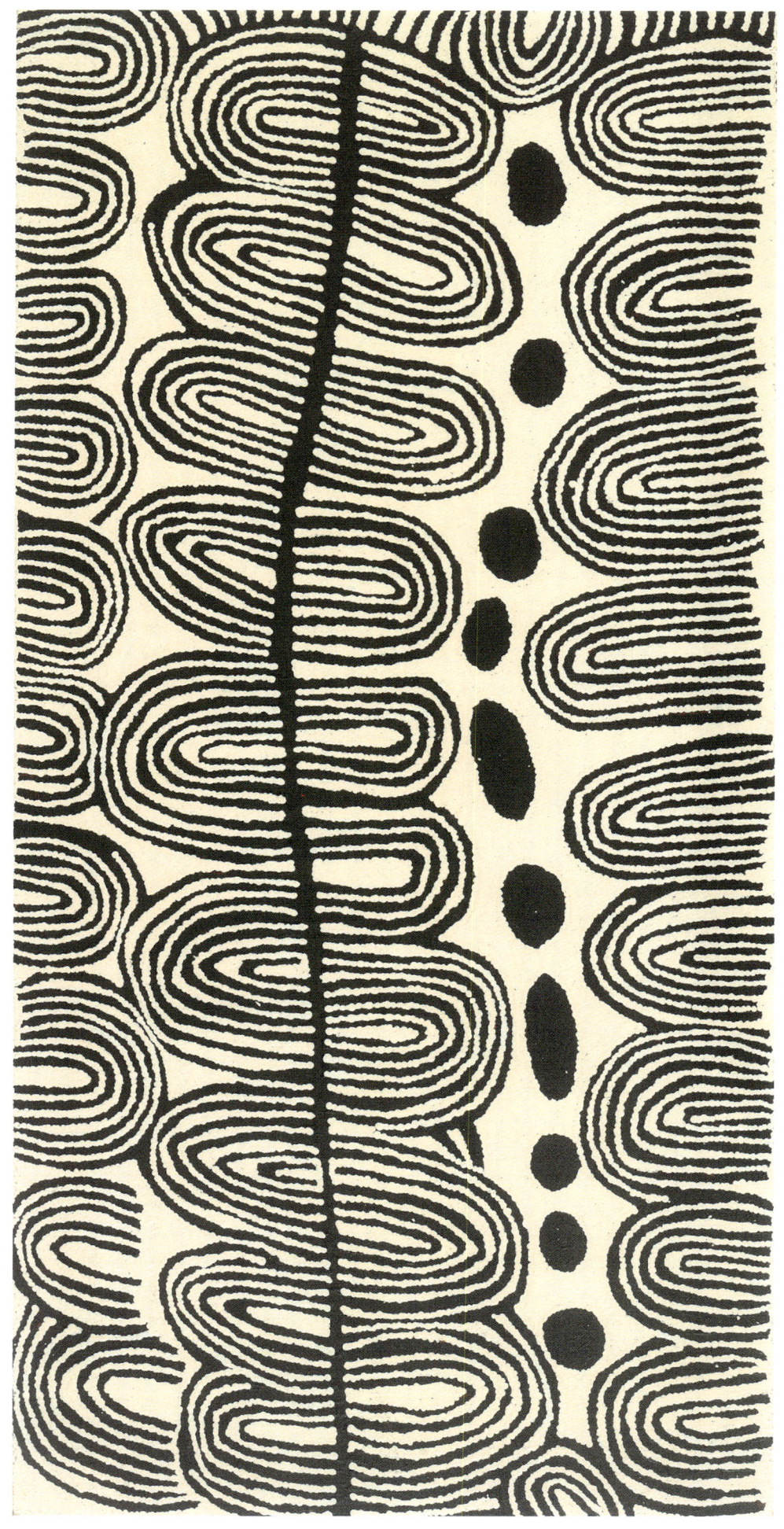

PLATE 52

Yuyuya Nampitjinpa
*Rockhole Site of Yumari*, 2000

Wintjiya Napaltjarri
*Wartunuma Claypan*, 2001

Wartunuma is an ancestral site associated with a species of flying ants of the same name that flew out from a cave there during the Tjukurrpa. The *wartunuma* burrow holes in which they lay their eggs, which hatch after heavy rains, signaling an oncoming period of growth and renewal. Goannas come out from their burrows and get fat on the young flying ants. An important symbol of fertility, their flashing wings and fantastic numbers are indicative of the ancestral presence of this place. The flying ants create flat beds or pavements known as *liinytji*, which are used by men as a platform for ceremony. These black discs can be seen here in Wintjiya Napaltjarri's painting of the site. After mating, the *wartunuma* lose their wings and disperse to create new colonies. Their brief but spectacular life cycle is a metaphor for death and renewal.

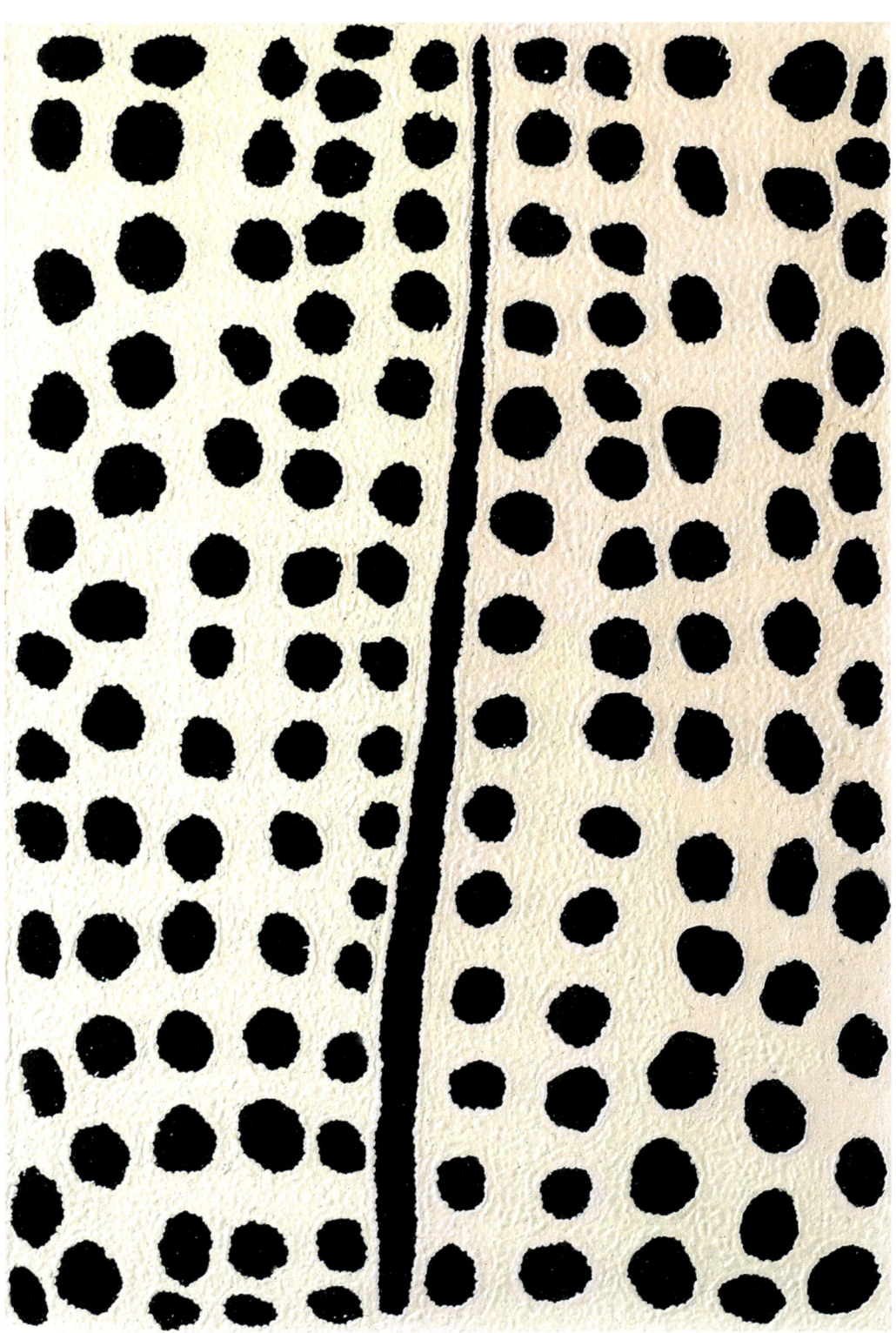

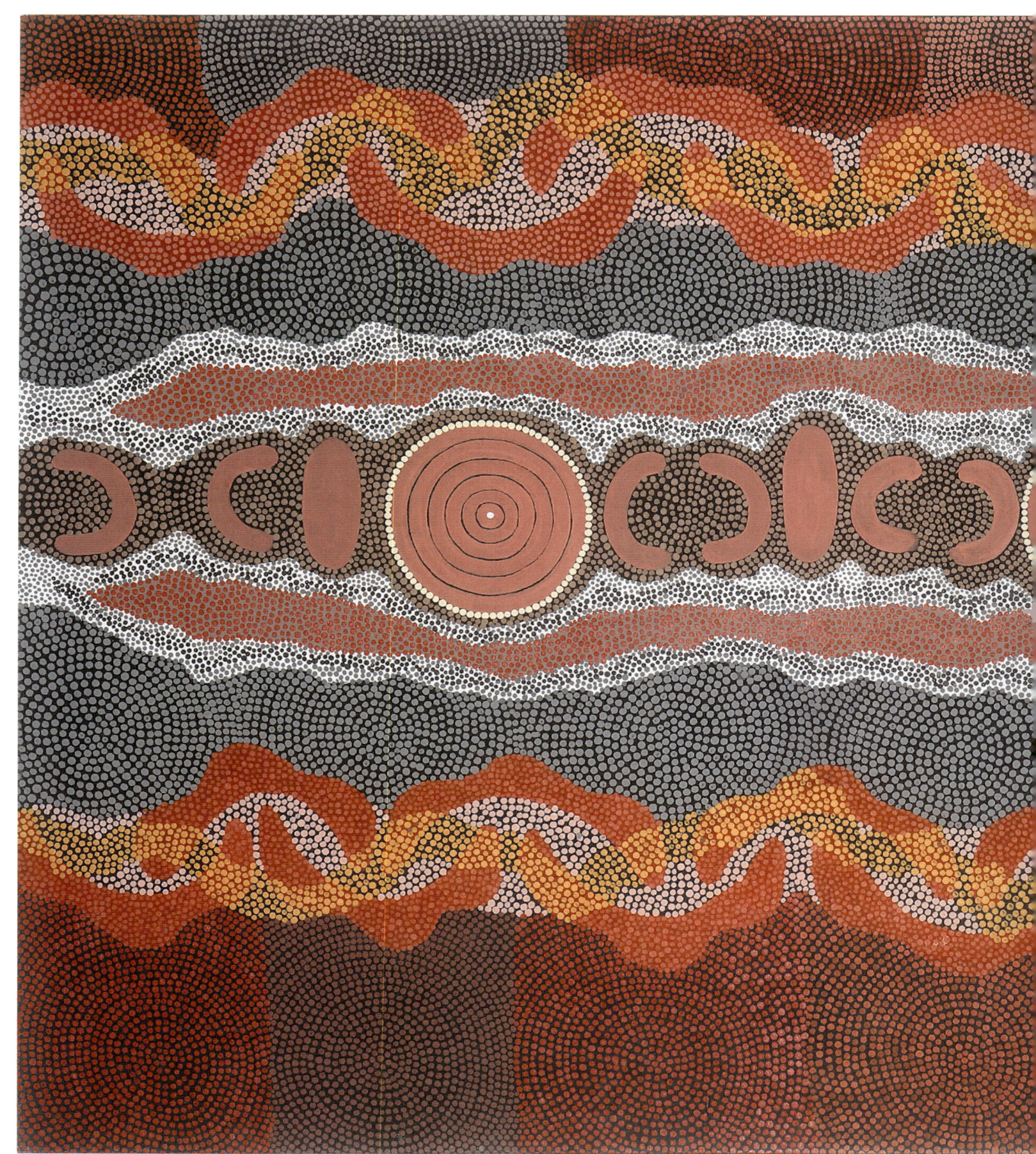

PLATE 54

Pansy Napangardi

*Kungka Kutjarra (Two Women) at Winpirri*, 1988

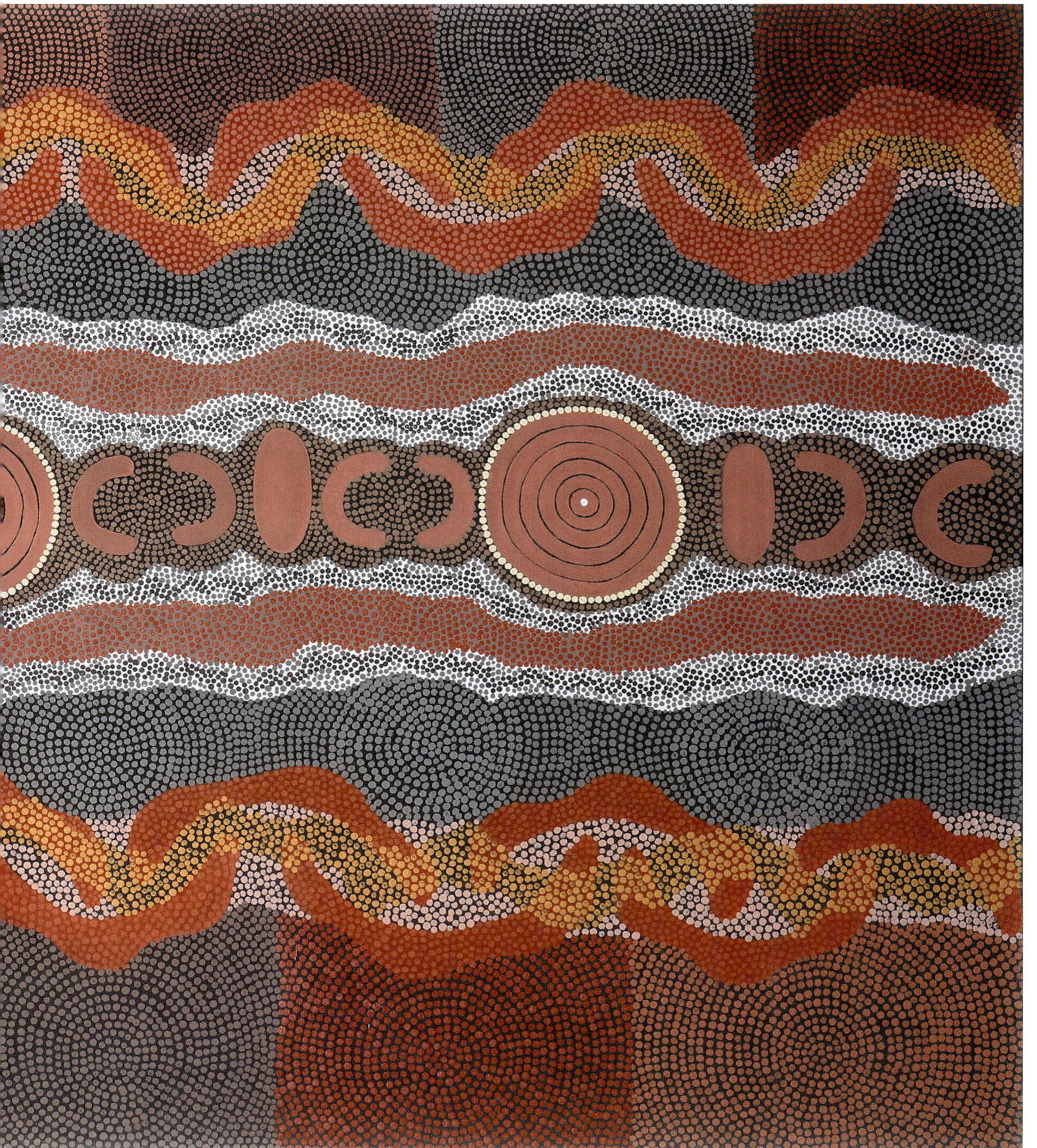

# KUTUNGU

—

# THE SNAKE WOMAN

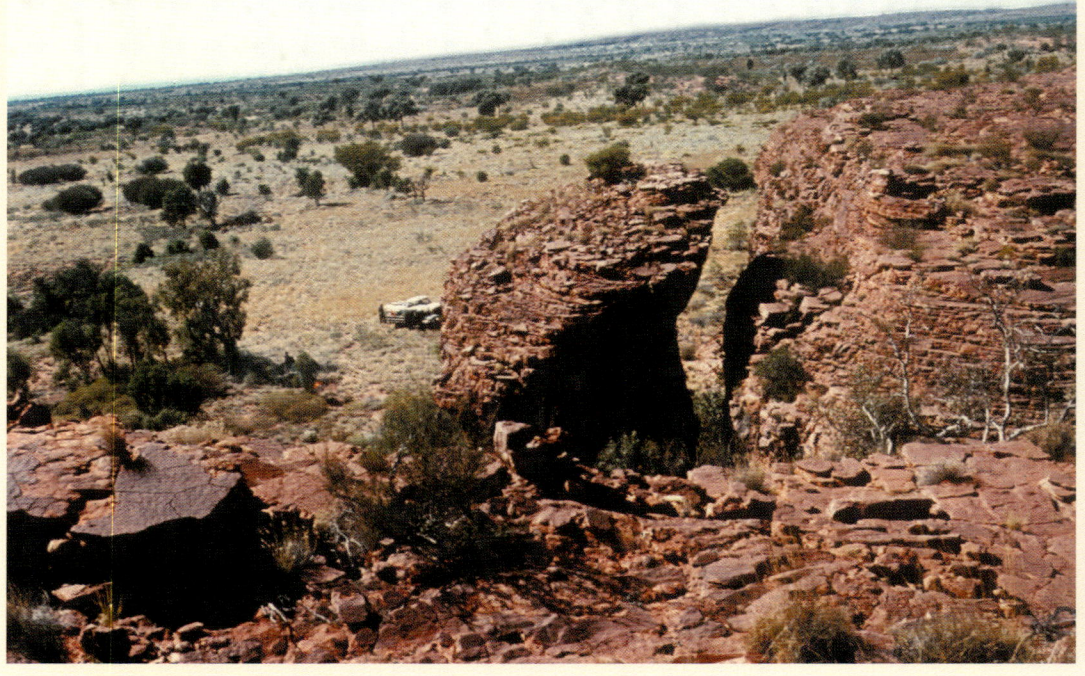

Muruntji, 1975. Photo by Fred Myers.

Kutungu had sharp teeth. She was killing all the women and kids and they turned into round, flat *puli* [stones]. She was round Kiwirrkurra, at Yirututu. Because of the many *munga* [flies] that followed that *mamu* [devil woman] around, the Wati Kutjarra [Goanna men] also came through the area. One was a red one, Tinka Tjukurrpa, sand-goanna man. The other was a black one named Puyunypa Tjukurrpa [a smaller, tree-dwelling goanna]. But there were too many flies following them—everywhere, on their shoulders and *kuru* [in their eyes]—so they ran away and went *yunngu tjarrpangu* [under the ground]. That's why they went into the ground. The Wati Kutjarra used to play jokes and tease Kutungu. At one time, those two Goanna Men climbed up a desert oak that is still there. The put out a *maparnpa* [a magic object drawn from their body] and they flew away.

—BOBBY WEST TJUPURRULA

Kutungu—also known as Walinngi—was an ancestral woman who began her travels from *tjungutjarrpanguru* (where the sun goes down), moving eastward and creating a range of hills south of the Kiwirrkurra road. She hunted, as is common among desert women, with a *wana* (digging stick) and a *piti* (coolamon). Her activities left their record on the land at places such as Papunnga, Ngartannga, Yarrannga, Wanatjalnga and, eventually, at Muruntji.

Many of the narratives involving Kutungu involve violence and death. At Papunnga, she saw a group of people playing on a sandhill and trapped them in a hole. Fanning a fire (*papuntjuninpa* means "to fan"), she smoked the hole, putting the people to death. Later, she dug up their bodies and cooked and ate them. According to Yanatjarri No. III Tjakamarra, Kutungu threw away the skinny ones and ate the fat ones. Next, she traveled to Wanatjalnga, where she saw a *malpuntarri* (quail) nesting on its eggs. Making a wana, she killed the bird, cooked it and ate it along with its eggs.

At Tjintjintjinya, Kutungu made a deep hole, which she is often depicted entering in her snake form (see, for instance, Ronnie Tjampitjinpa's *Tjintjintjin* [1990, plate 59]). Near Muruntji, Kutungu fell asleep and was found by a group of boys, one of whom raped her while she slept. When she awoke, Kutungu noticed a smell from her crotch and realized what had happened. She set out for the boys, tracked them, killed them with her digging stick and cooked and ate them. The distinctive rock formations at Muruntji record this event. As she crawled off, toward Kantawanya, she vomited, leaving a mark in the landscape, and turned into a water snake.

176

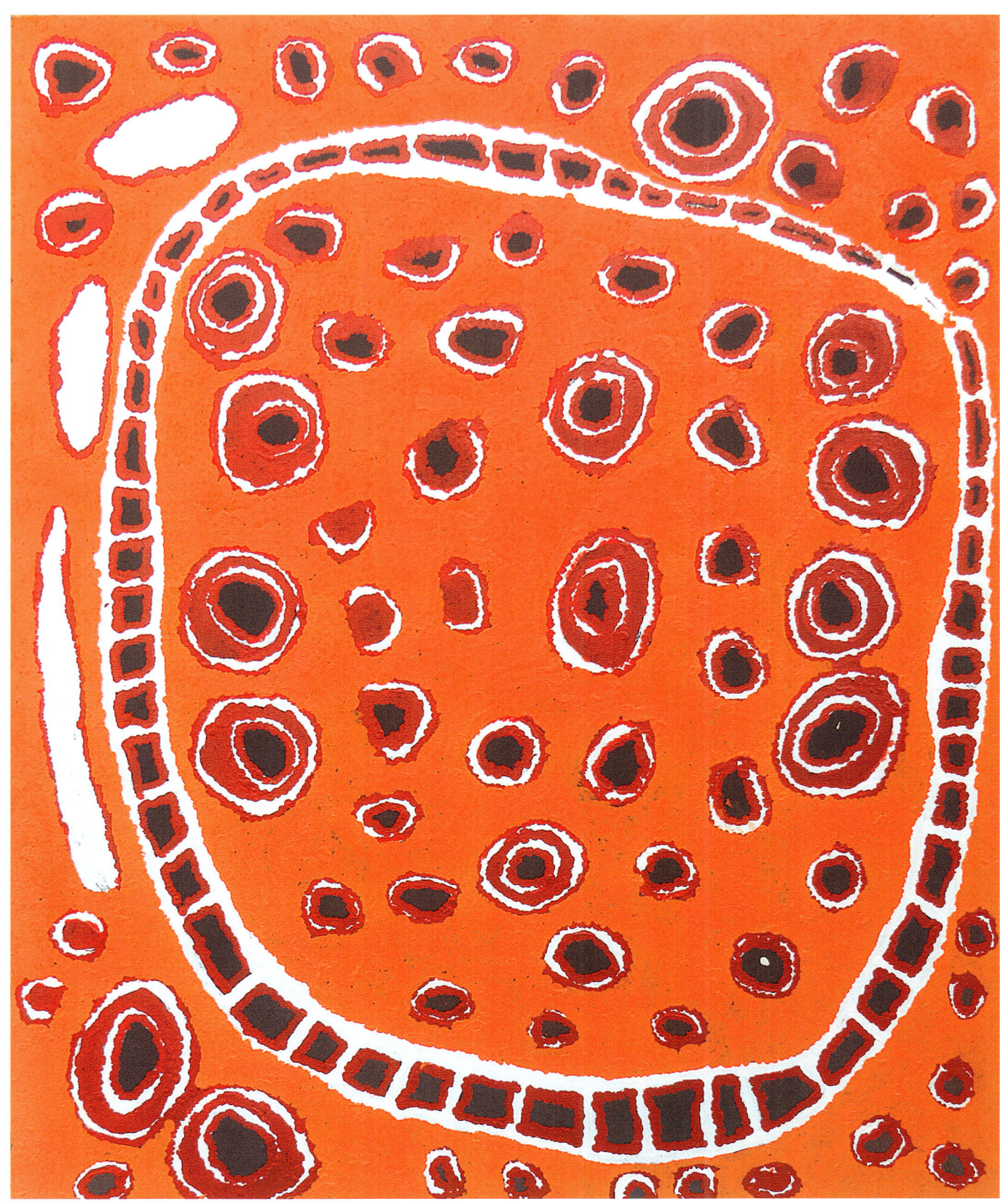

PLATE 55

Inyuwa Nampitjinpa
*Travels of Kutungu from Papunnga
to Muruntji,* 1999

PLATE 56

Yanatjarri No. III Tjakamarra
*Muruntji*, 1988

On September 30, 1988, Yanatjarri No. III Tjakamarra delivered this epic painting to Daphne Williams at Papunya Tula Artists' Walungurru studio. Fred Myers was visiting Walungurru at the time and documented the painting with Yanatjarri. Although titled *Muruntji*, the painting depicts the ancestral travels of two different ancestral women—indicated by the two separate sets of footprints.

At the bottom, Yanatjarri depicts the travels of Kutungu in the artist's Country around Purrungunya, where she encountered two dangerous Wanampi (Water Snakes ancestors). After fleeing the snakes, she made camp bread and seedcake from spinifex grass, normally used for making *kirti* (resin) for spears and other implements. The cake got stuck in her throat—what Yanatjarri referred to as *ngantjarnu* (adhering or making your mouth sticky). It burned her insides, and she ran off defecating black stuff as she ran (presumably from the spinifex resin, which is black).

The woman depicted at the top is a different ancestral Snake woman who traveled from near Kaltukatjara (Docker River) to Kiwirrnga (a waterhole that Kutungu would also visit later in her travels). This women is not dangerous and appears with her hunting implements; the thin white line is her *wana* (digging stick), and two oval shapes are her *wirra* (digging dishes). At Kiwirrnga, the woman "went into the ground," leaving her *wirra* behind, creating hills. The four tasseled forms on the left and right sides of the painting are *mawulyarri*, a possum-tail necklace first spun by this ancestral woman.

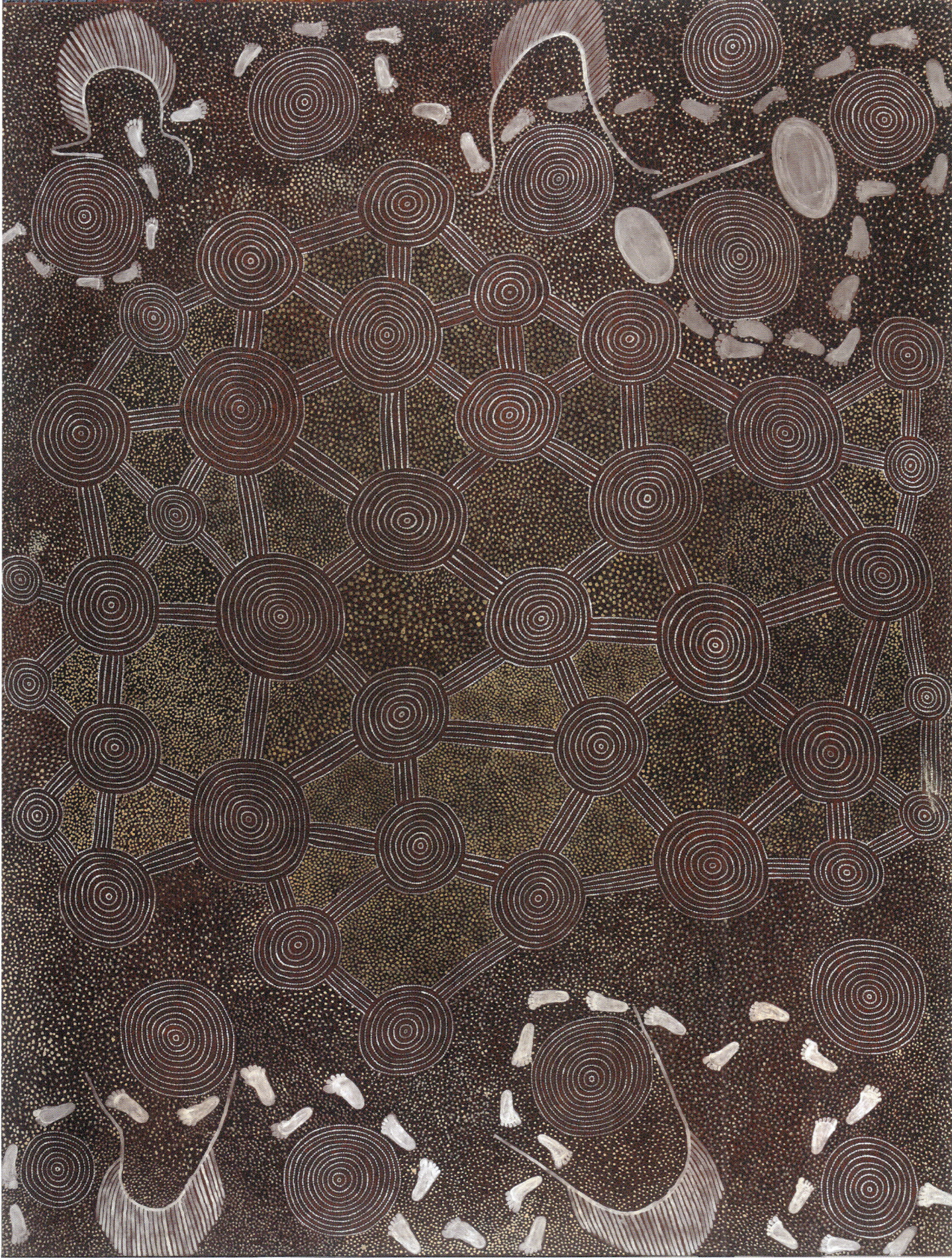

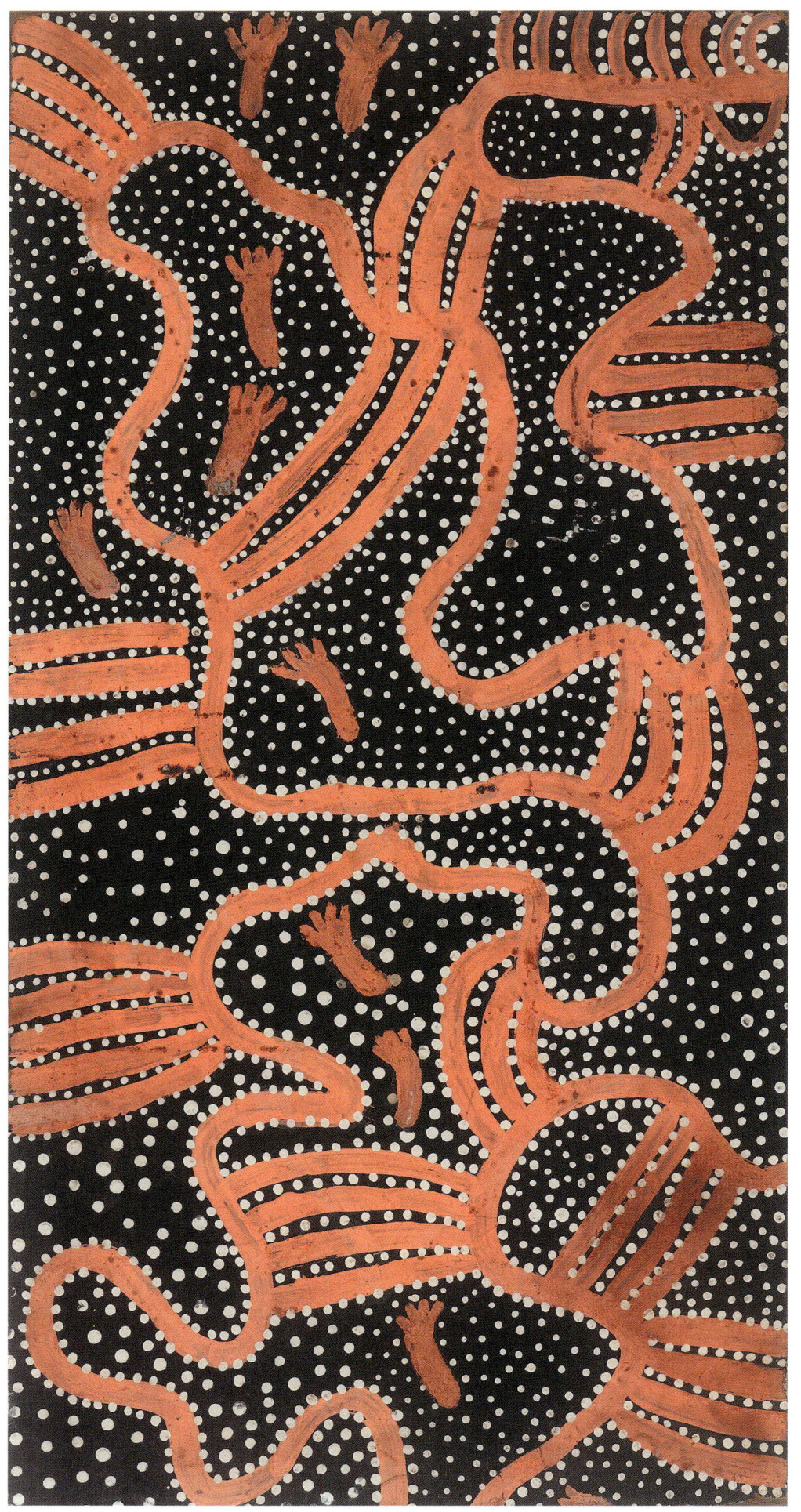

PLATE 57

Charlie Wartuma Tjungurrayi
*Untitled* (probably *The Travels of Kutungu*),
before March 1972

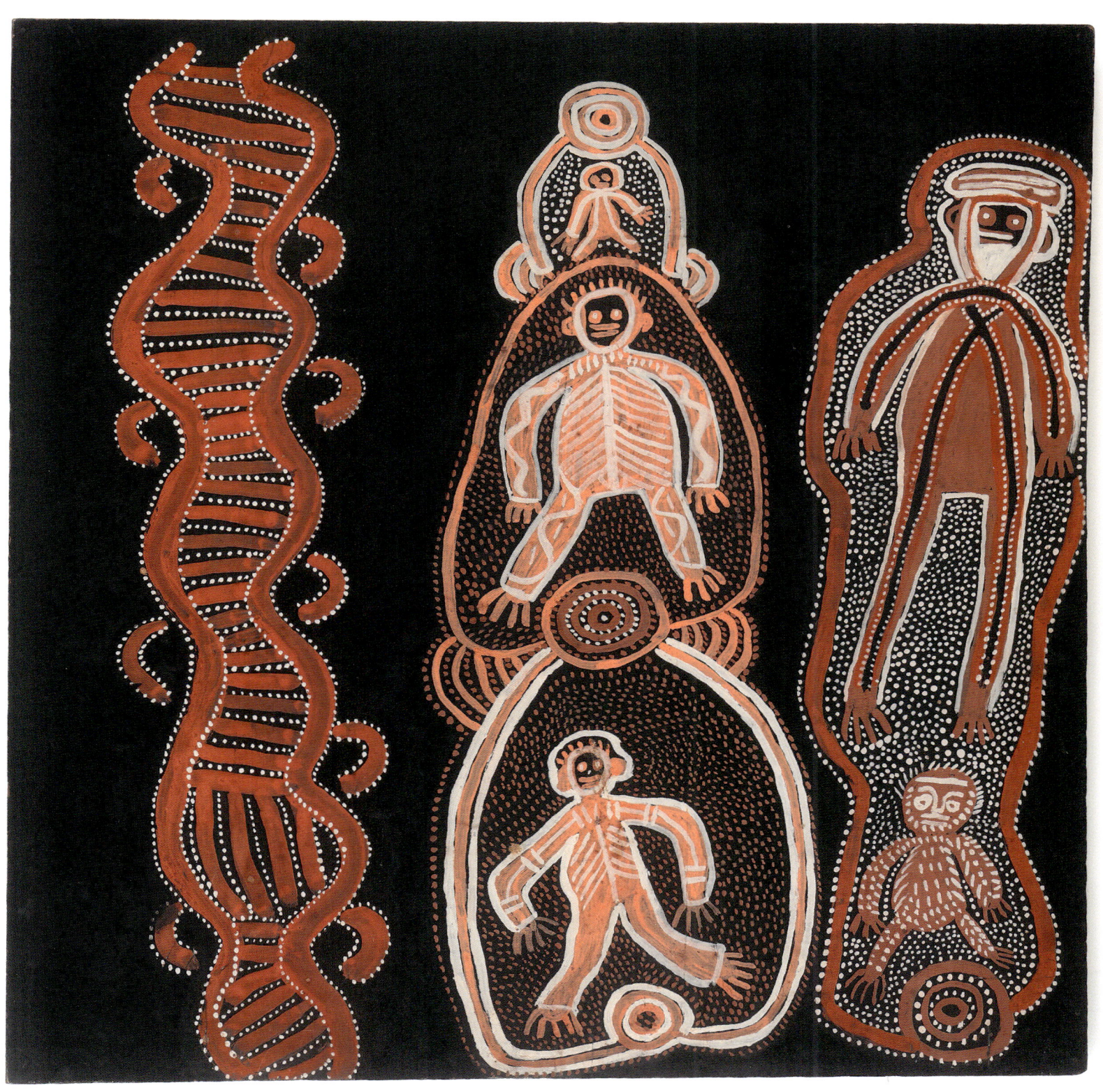

PLATE 58
Mick Namarari Tjapaltjarri
*Muruntji* (formerly *Family Bush Tucker Dreaming*), 1972

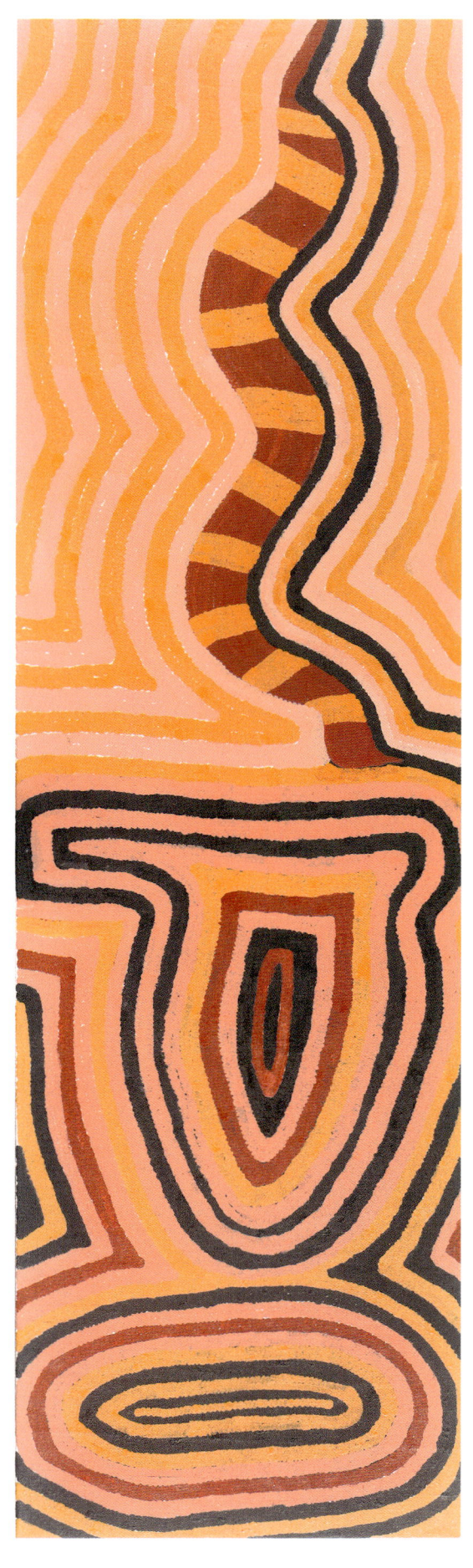

PLATE 59

Ronnie Tjampitjinpa
*Tjintjintjin*, 1990

FACING | PLATE 60

Mick Namarari Tjapaltjarri
*Untitled* (formerly *A Children's Story*), 1972

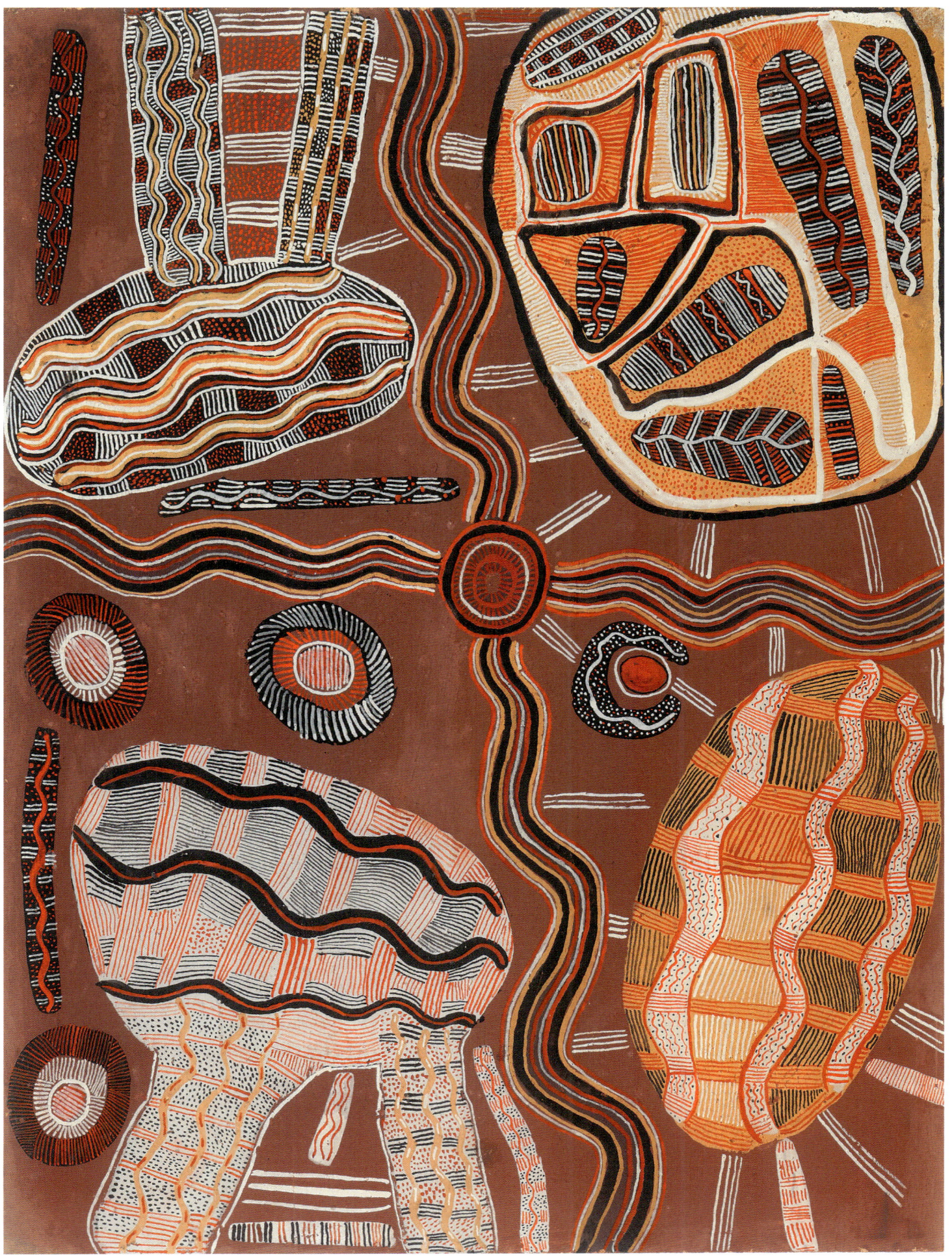

# KUNGKA KUTJARRA

---

# TWO WOMEN DREAMING

There are several Kungka Kutjarra Tjukurrpa (Two Women Dreamings) that cross the Australian desert, narratives that tell of the travels of female ancestral beings. These ancestral women are referred to interchangeably as Kungka Kutjarra and Minyma Kutjarra, the first referring more generically to women of all ages (although often used for younger women), the latter used more specifically for older women.

Both men and women paint versions of the Kungka Kutjarra Tjukurrpa, differing in accordance with their proscribed ceremonial and gender frameworks. In paintings, as well as in ceremonial performances, the Two Women are often associated with their tools: *wana* (digging sticks), *piti* (coolamon), *ngalyipi* (vine fiber) and *manguri* (head-rings for carrying *piti* on their heads). Frequently, the women are described preparing and bringing food for the Tingarri men and their novices in secluded ceremonial camps—as they continue to do in contemporary ceremonial life.

In Pintupi Tjukurrpa narratives and imagery—as in Tatali Nangala's painting *Kungka Kutjarra Tjukurrpa* (*Two Women Dreaming*) (plate 63)—the women depart from the Docker River area, around Wintalkanya, and travel northward in association with, but separately from, the Tingarri men who are also traveling north. At Tjukurlanya, the men and women are joined by another group of Tingarri men coming from the southeast. After a big ceremony, they continue northward.

Pintupi men's paintings identified with Kungka Kutjarra generally involve places and songs associated with the ancestral women's actions, including a dramatic series of interactions in which the women are punished by ceremonial rape for seeing men's sacred objects near the cave site of Mitukatjirri. The women escape and perform their own "love magic" while foraging for food as they head north through the Warman Rocks area of Putjanya and Muni Muni. Finally, they arrive at Walungurru, referred to as Puli Kutjarra (two hills, see pp. 264–65), where they dance and make rockholes and other natural features overseen by women in their ceremonies today. Nearby, the Two Women track Ngintaka, an ancestral perentie lizard from the west. They stab him with their *wana* (digging sticks) at a place called Yunytjunya, which translates as "throat place," referencing the body of Ngintaka, who turned to stone raised high on his front limbs in the characteristic pose of an upstretched lizard.

Several other Two Women narratives run through the Central and Western Deserts. These narratives are distinct and not necessarily connected. For example, Pansy Napangardi's *Kungka Kutjarra (Two Women) at Winpirri* (1988, plate 54) describes the actions of two women pursued by a lustful old man who chases them from Kampurarrnga to Winpirri before they continue their journey south. This songline connects the women to the Yina Tjukurrpa (Old Man Dreaming) depicted in the paintings of Charlie Wartuma Tjungurrayi and Uta Uta Tjangala (plates 45, 47) while creating a songline that connects women from the Central Desert with those of the Anangu Pitjantjatjara Yankunytjatjara Lands some five hundred miles away.

Another narrative connects the women at Kungkayunti (women dancing) in the east with Ngutjulnga in Pintupi country, where the women tried to make fire (by the means known as *ngutjulpungin*, making a fire by rubbing a spear thrower against soft wood). Other songlines of Kungka Kutjarra are danced throughout the Central Desert by Warlpiri women in Yawalyu ceremonies—the most common ceremony celebrating the connection between women and their ancestors.

Minyma Kutjarra carried two *tulku* [sacred objects] looking for *maku* [witchetty grubs], walking around dancing—my Dreaming. They went a long way and they found water, *palurupula ankupai* [those two kept traveling].

—EILEEN NAPALTJARRI

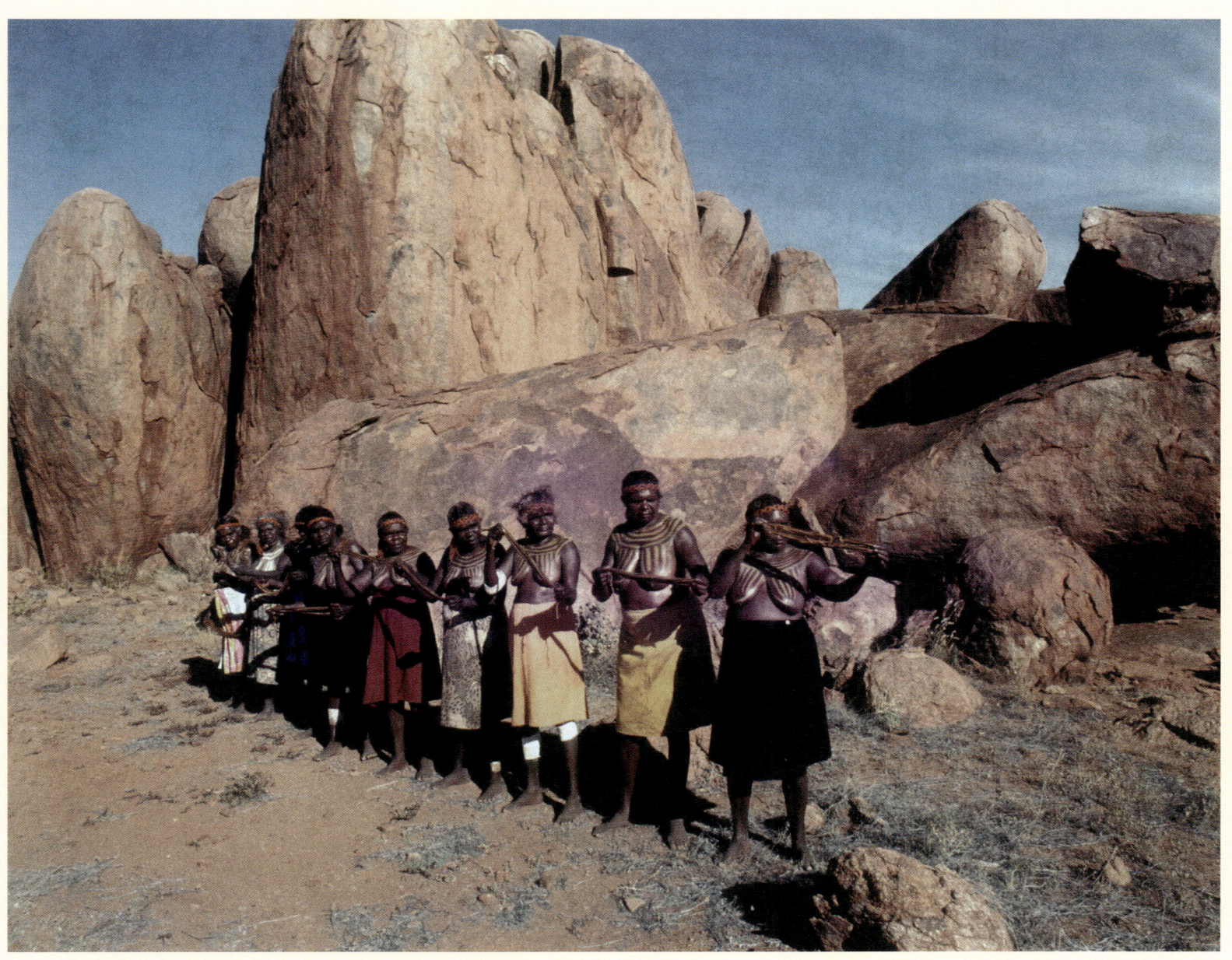

Mantua Napanangka, Nanyuma Napangati, Narpula Scobie Napurrula, Brenda Napaltjarri Maxwell, Kawayi Nampitjinpa, Pantjiya Nungurrayi, Josephine Napurrula, Yuyuya Nampitjinpa and Alice Nampitjinpa at Ngutjulnga, 1994. Photo by Dennis Schulz.

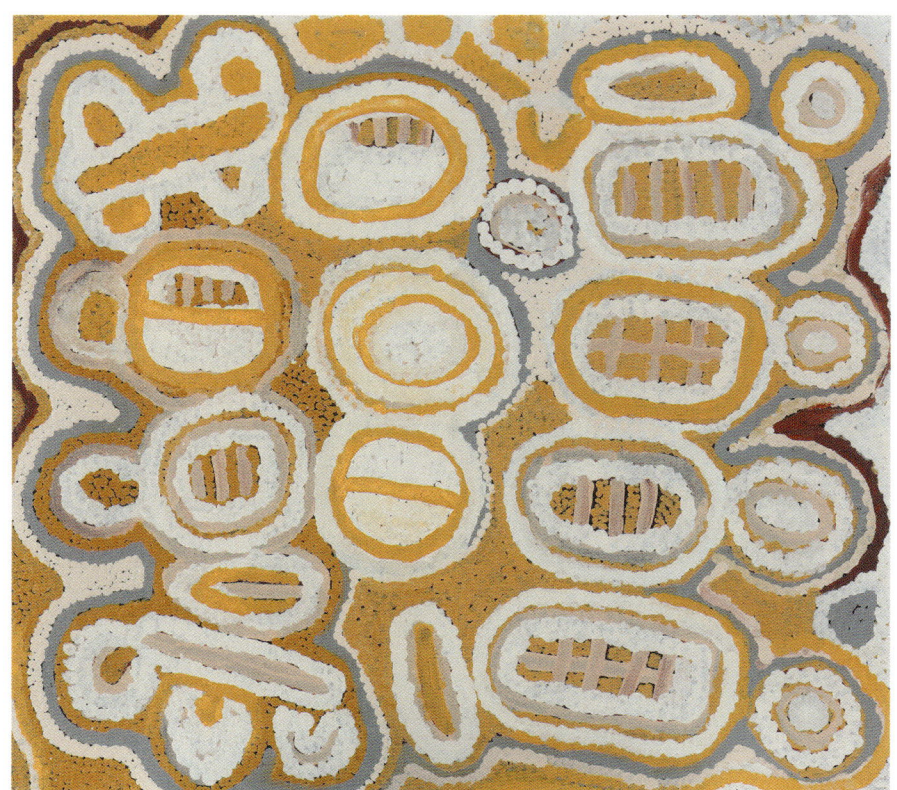

PLATE 61

Nyurapayia Nampitjinpa

*Women at Yulparitja*, 1996

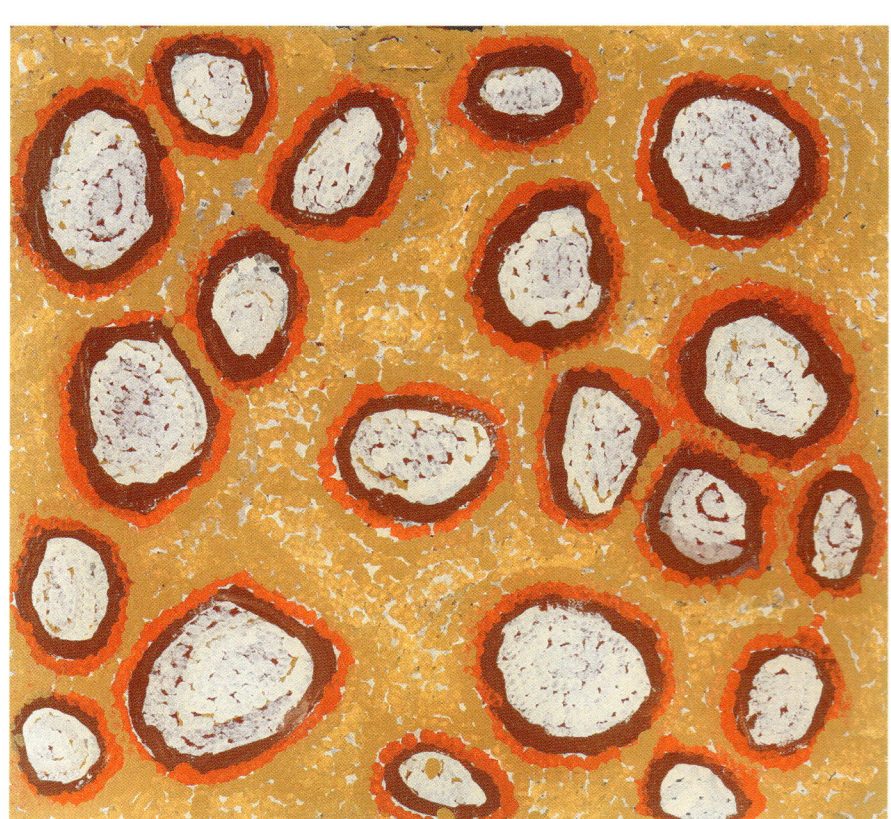

PLATE 62

Inyuwa Nampitjinpa

*Women's Dreaming at Pangkupirri*, 1996

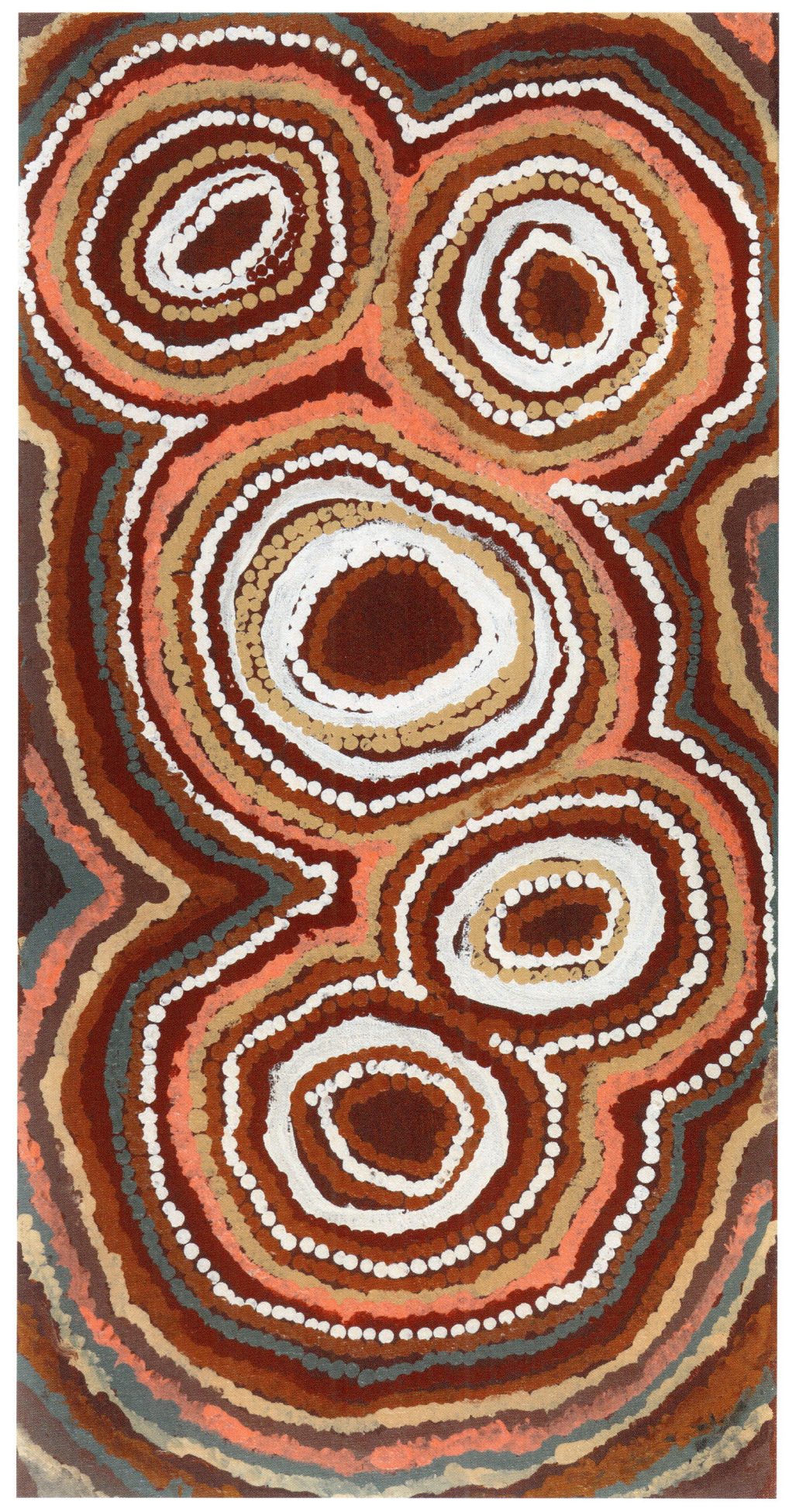

PLATE 63

Tatali Nangala
*Kungka Kutjarra Tjukurrpa*
*(Two Women Dreaming)*, 1996

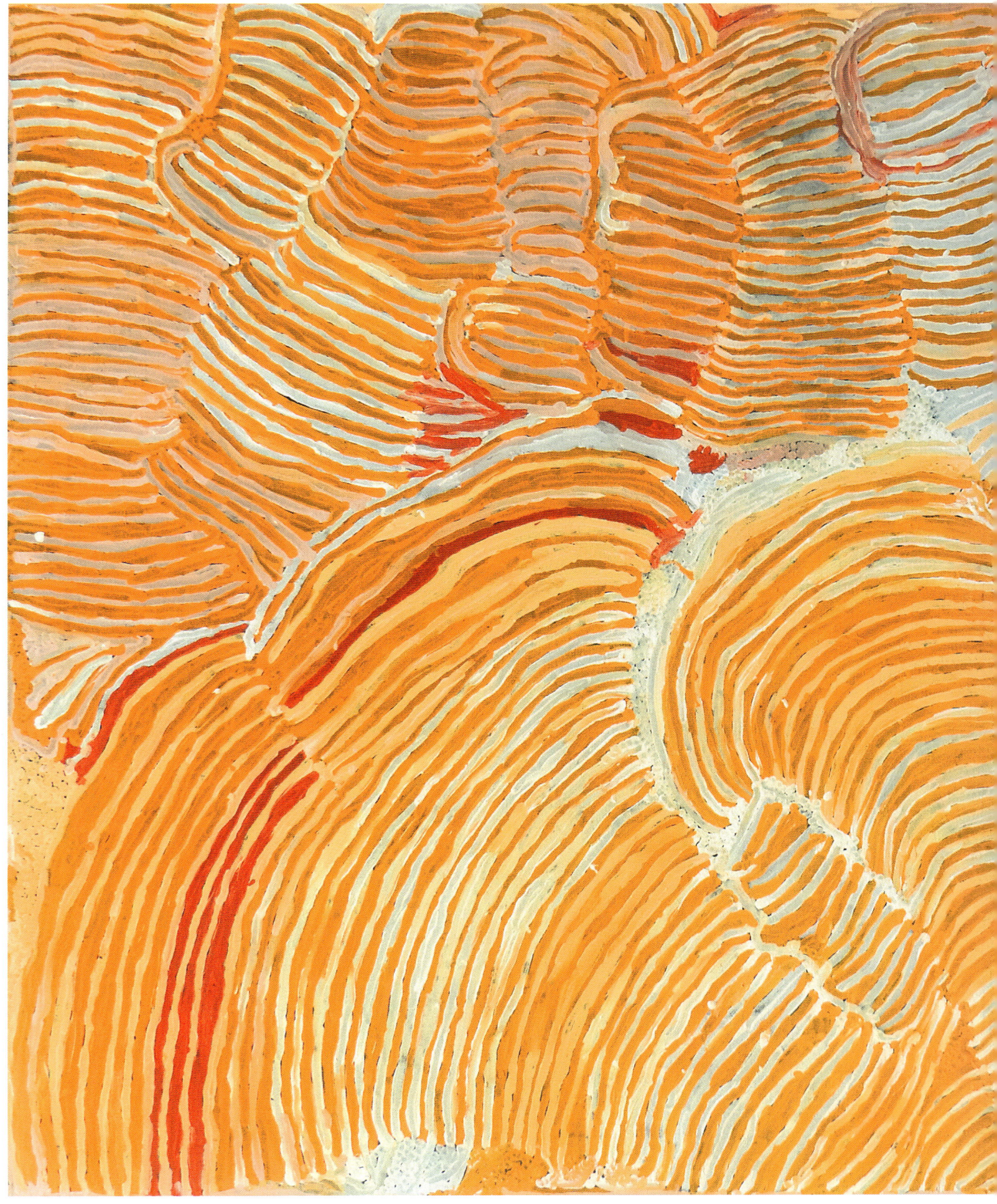

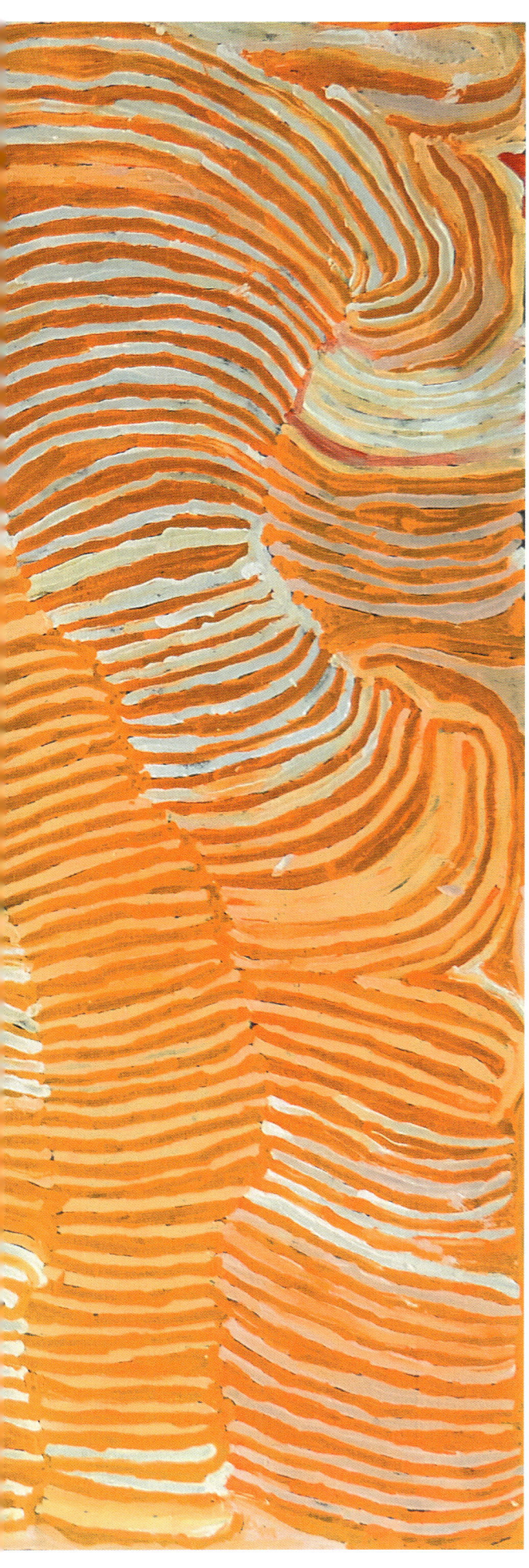

PLATE 64

Makinti Napanangka

*Lupulnga*, 2001

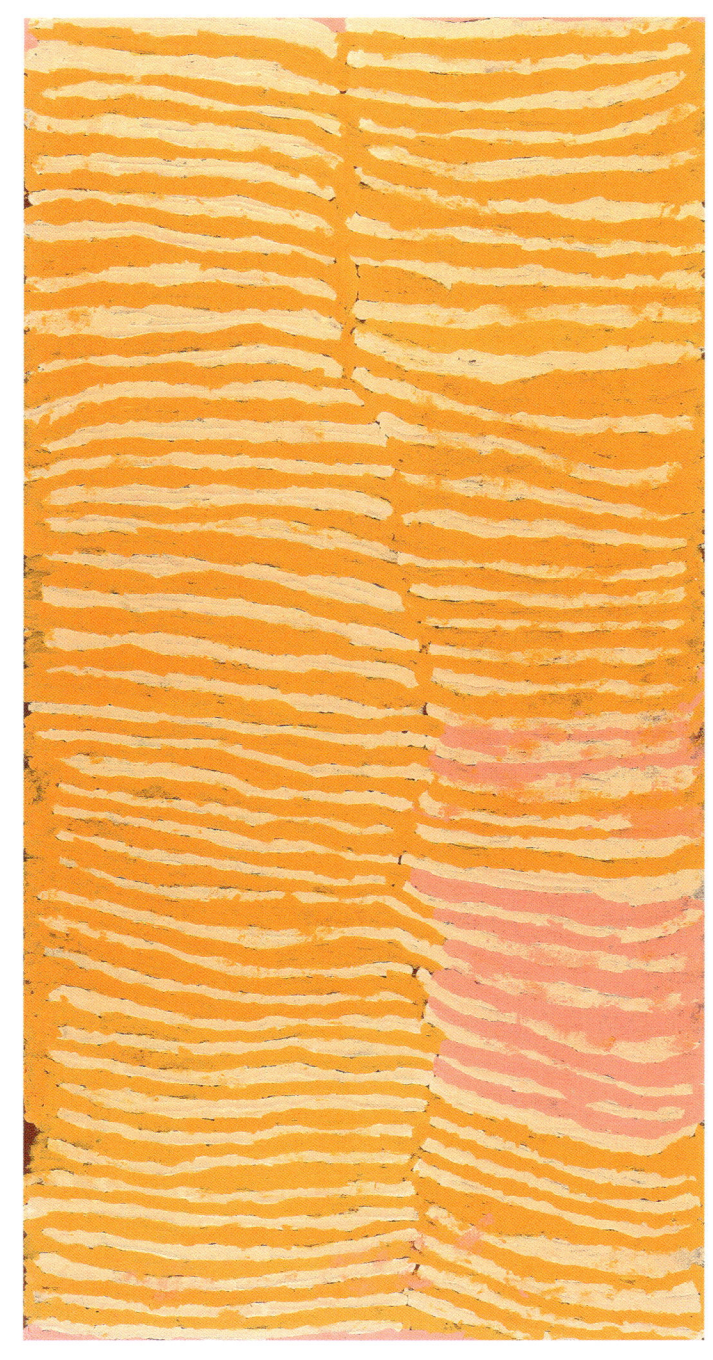

PLATE 65

Makinti Napanangka

*Lupulnga*, 2005

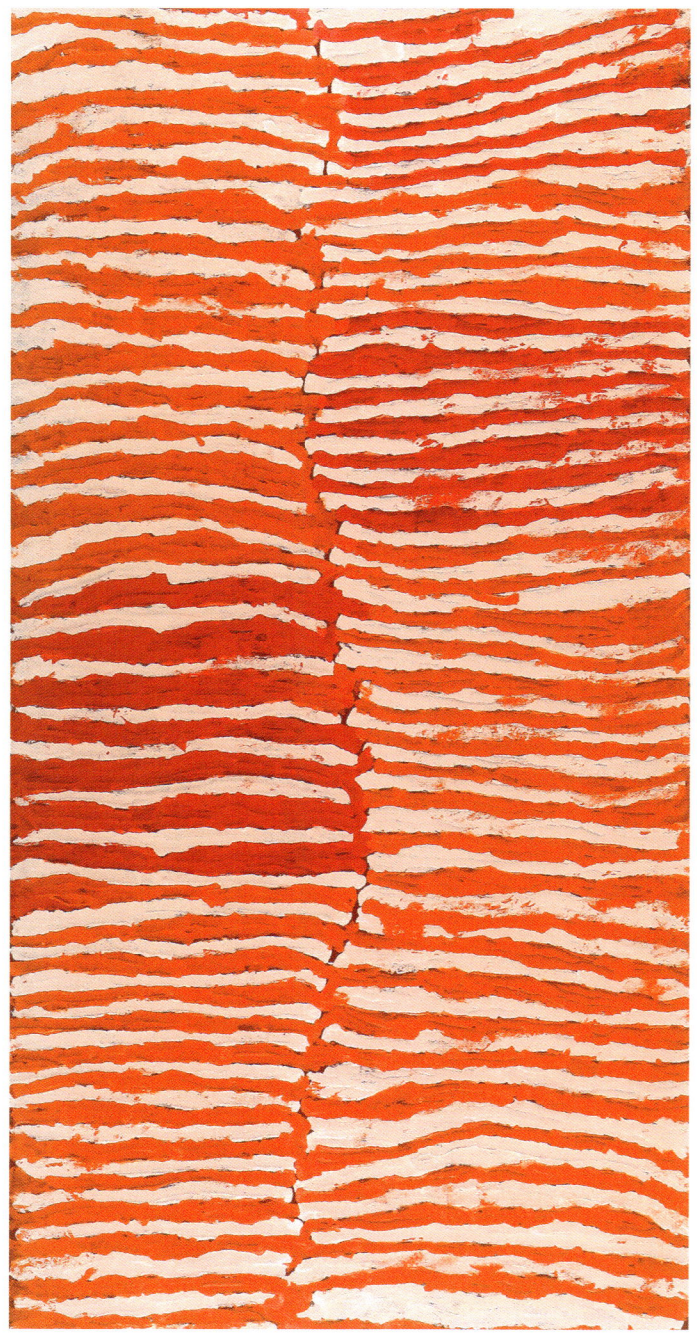

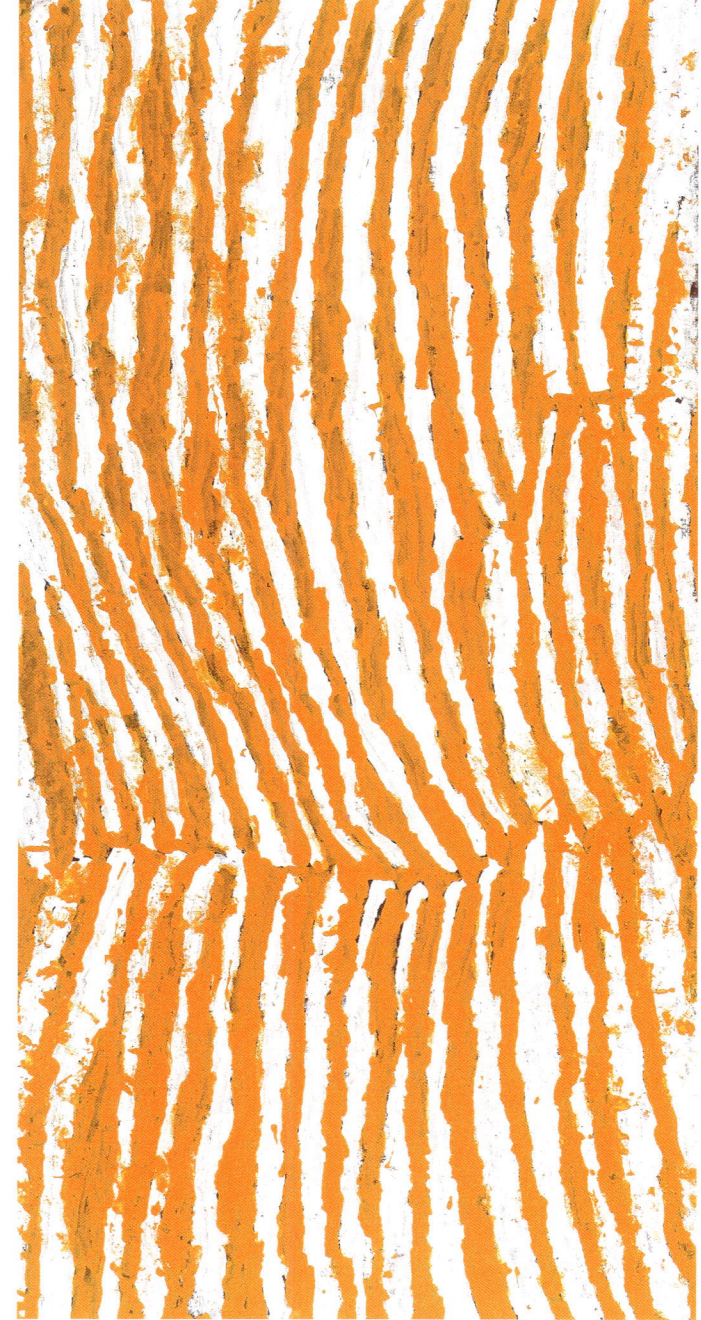

PLATE 66

Makinti Napanangka
*Lupulnga*, 2006

PLATE 67

Makinti Napanangka
*Lupulnga*, 2006

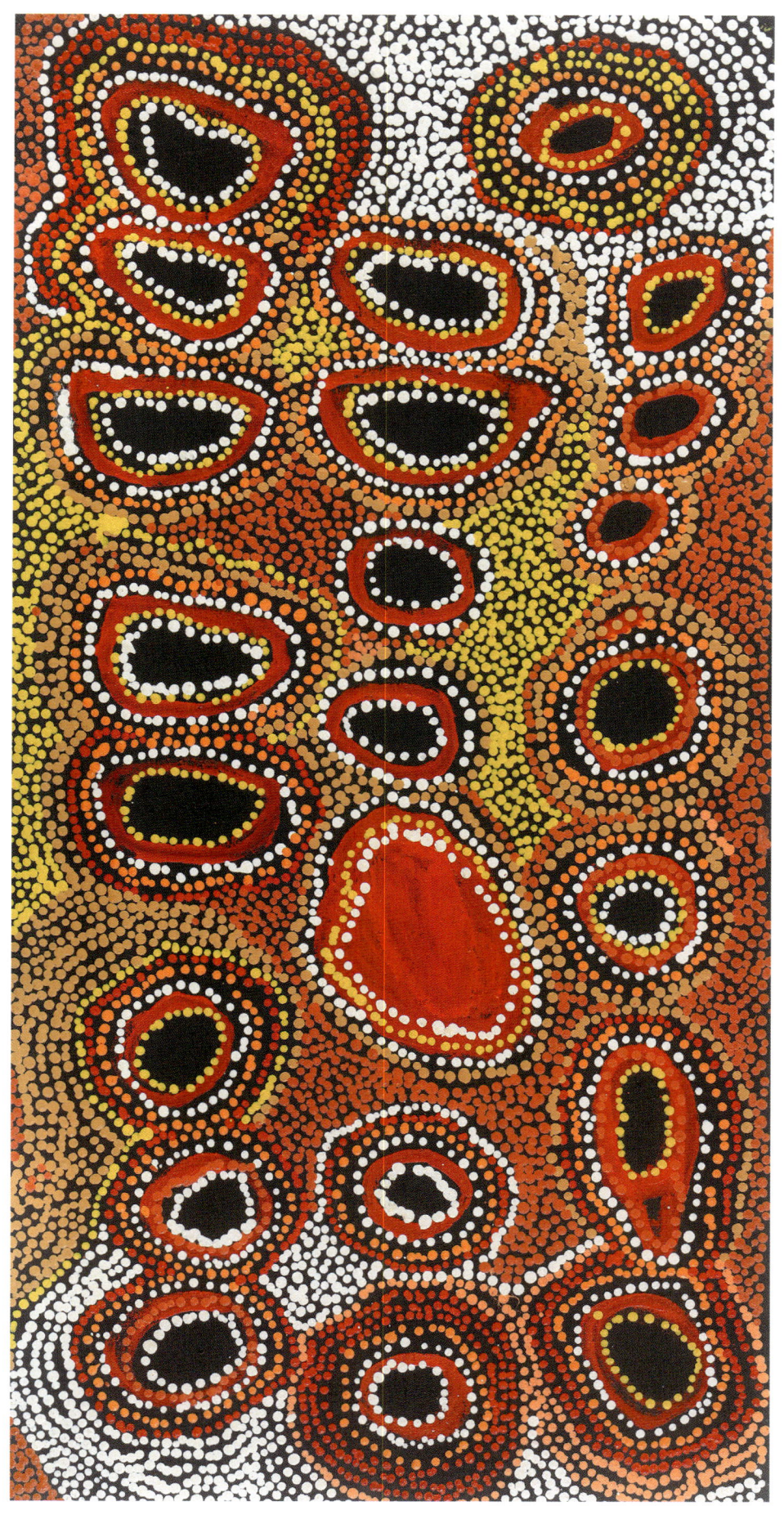

192

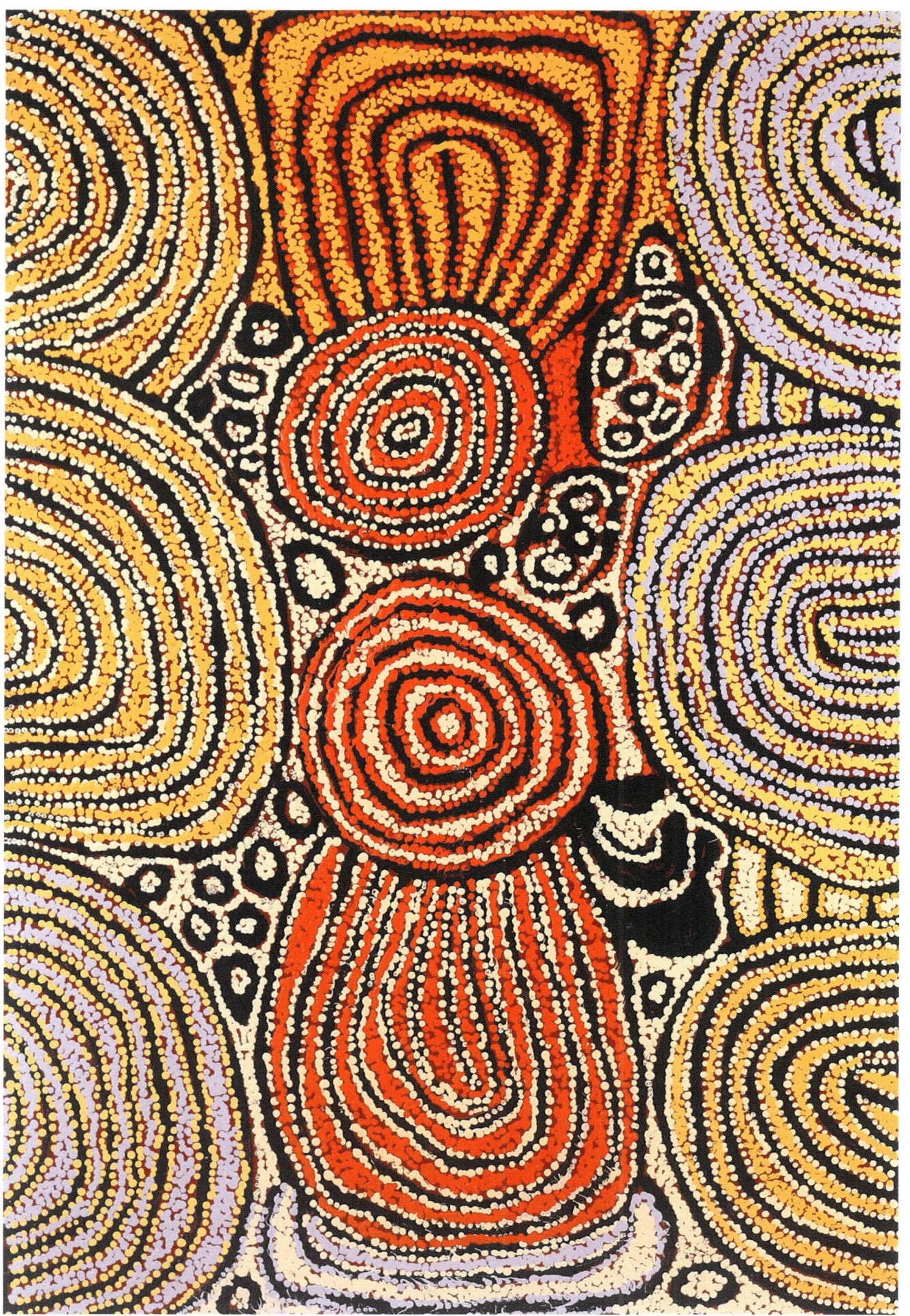

# THE TINGARRI CYCLE

## WHO ARE THE TINGARRI?

The term Tingarri is usually glossed in Pintupi English as "all the men" or "many men," or *punyunyu tjurta* (many novices). While considerable complexities surround the meaning of Tingarri, in the context of Pintupi usage, the word refers to traveling groups of ancestral men who performed ceremonies and created the Country. The men were accompanied by ceremonial novices whom they provided with instruction and guidance. There were also traveling groups of Tingarri women. The adventures of the Tingarri are articulated in song-cycles that form part of the teachings of *punyunyu* today, providing explanations for contemporary customs and cultural practices. These practices are filled with a sense of awe. In shaping the world, the Tingarri cycle explains the most profound aspects of life and death, birth and rebirth, loss and rejuvenation. It is only through the process of ceremonial initiation that the full extent of this wonder is revealed.

Three major geographical lines of named places are described as Tingarri, visited and created in the Tjukurrpa by three distinct groups of traveling people. The groups were made up of novices who had already undergone the basic man-making initiations and who traveled under the guidance and discipline of powerful authoritative "bosses." Secluded from women and the uninitiated, such groups performed and witnessed ceremonies of revelation, as well as hunted, argued and fought, just as contemporary people do. Tingarri narratives and ceremonies are part of ceremonial complexes that demand intergroup cooperation, requiring people to come together in sharing, teaching, performing and revealing the stories, and linking Indigenous groups and people who "share" these Tjukurrpa over large distances.

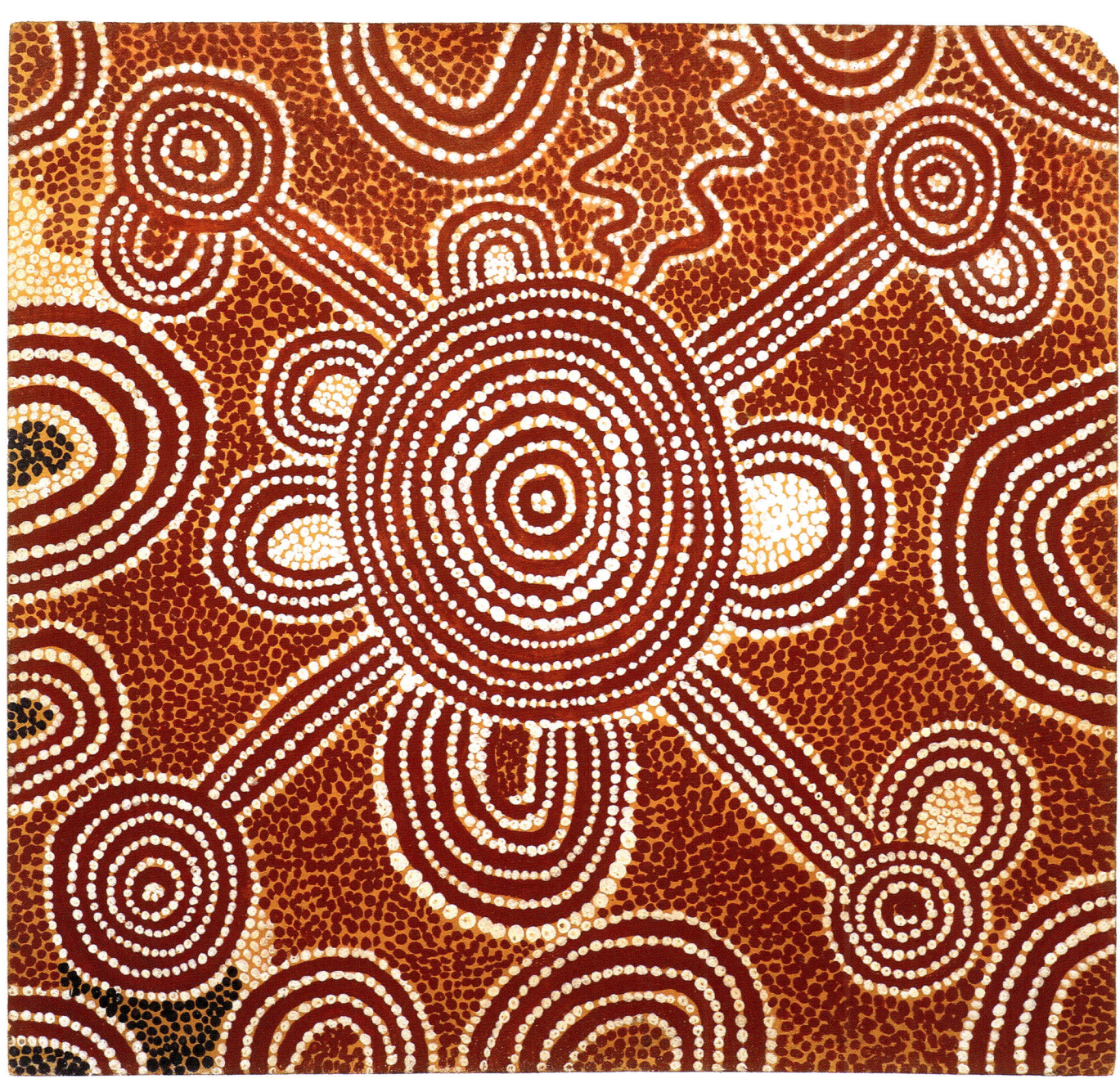

PLATE 70

Shorty Lungkarta Tjungurrayi
*Tingarri Ceremony*, 1975

# Tingarri Ngururrngurrara

## Tingarri in the Middle

The story and travels of Tingarri ngururrngurrara begin with Kuninka (Native Quoll) and his desire for revenge against the Tingarri men from Yawalyurrunya. While walking near Kaakurutintjinya (Lake Macdonald), Kuninka came upon a piece of emu fat and the tracks of the men who had dropped it. They had been hunting in his country, cooking the emu at Tikartika east of the lake, and they hadn't given any to Kuninka, the boss of the country. He became angry because they had sneaked and not shared with him. He told his two sons to get ready, and he set off west to follow the Tingarri men's tracks. He passed the Possum people at the claypans of Yiitjurunya, where the possums were protecting a man who had eloped with a wrong wife from Warlpiri country. Terrifying them with his power, he headed west and then south, to Yawalyurru, where the Tingarri men were underground. He opened their hiding place with his throwing stick, made them come out and sent them on their way—under his authority, as *punyunyu* (novices)—to Kaakurutintjinya. After they stopped around Kulkurtanya (plate 71), where Kuninka told them to wait, the Tingarri men were marched up to Kaakurutintjinya (plates 73, 74, 76) where they were killed with hail and lightning by Kuninka's two sons. Exhausted by this exercise of their powers, the sons died and turned into snakes at the site.

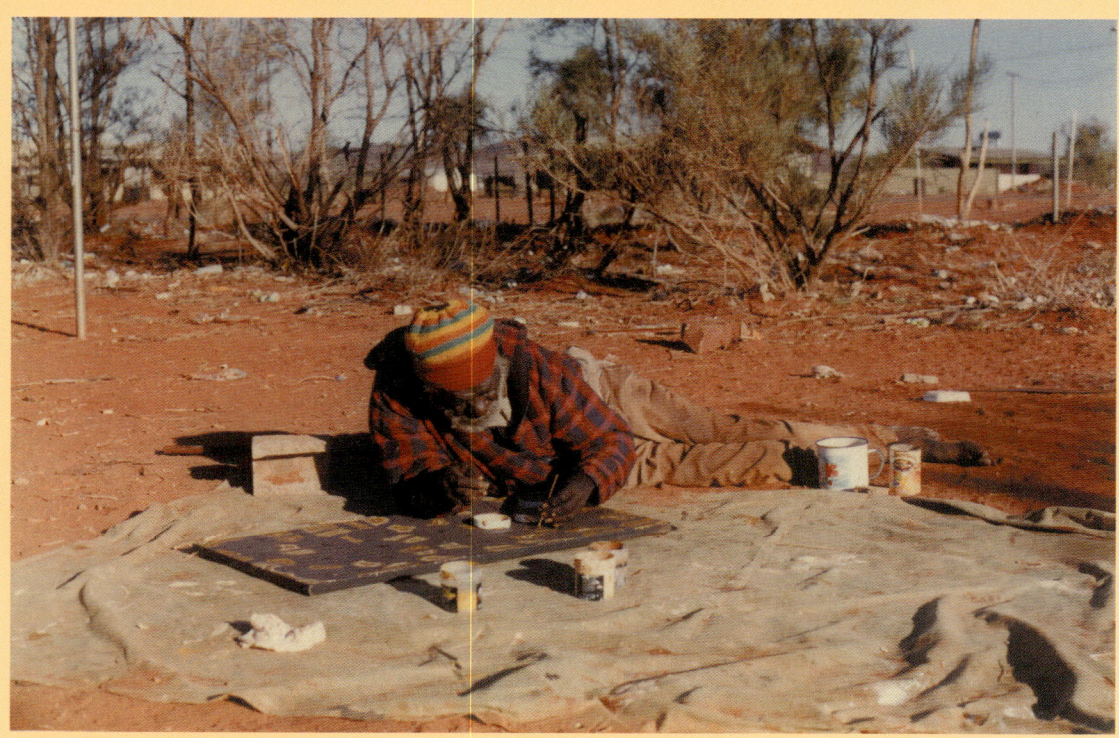

Yala Yala Gibbs Tjugurrayi outside the Papunya Tula Artists Walungurru (Kintore) studio, 1996. Photo by Paul Sweeney.

FACING | PLATE 71

Yanatjarri No. III Tjakamarra
*Artist's Country near Kulkurta*, 1988

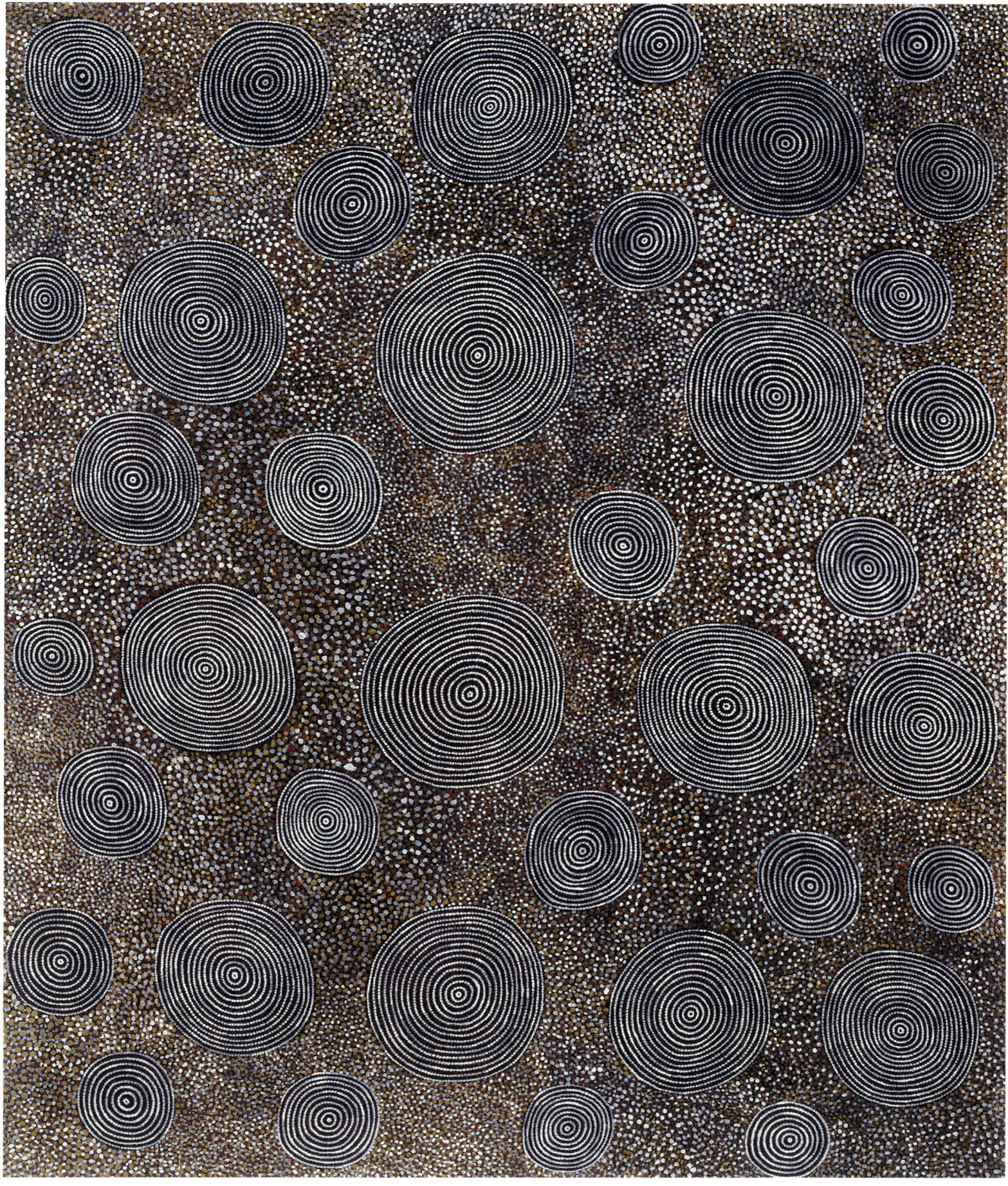

PLATE 72

Simon Tjakamarra
*Tingarri Camp at Pilintjinya*, 1988

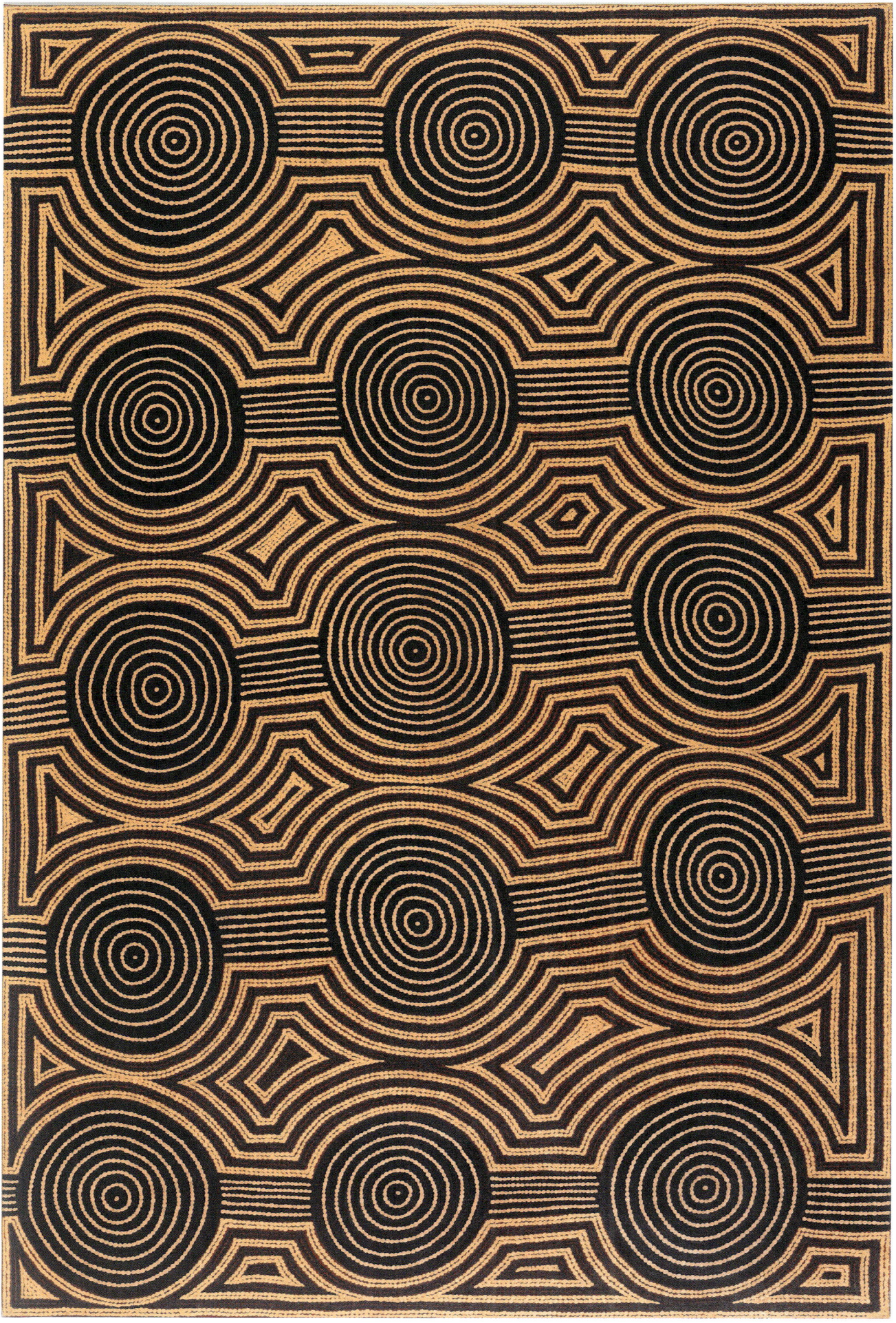

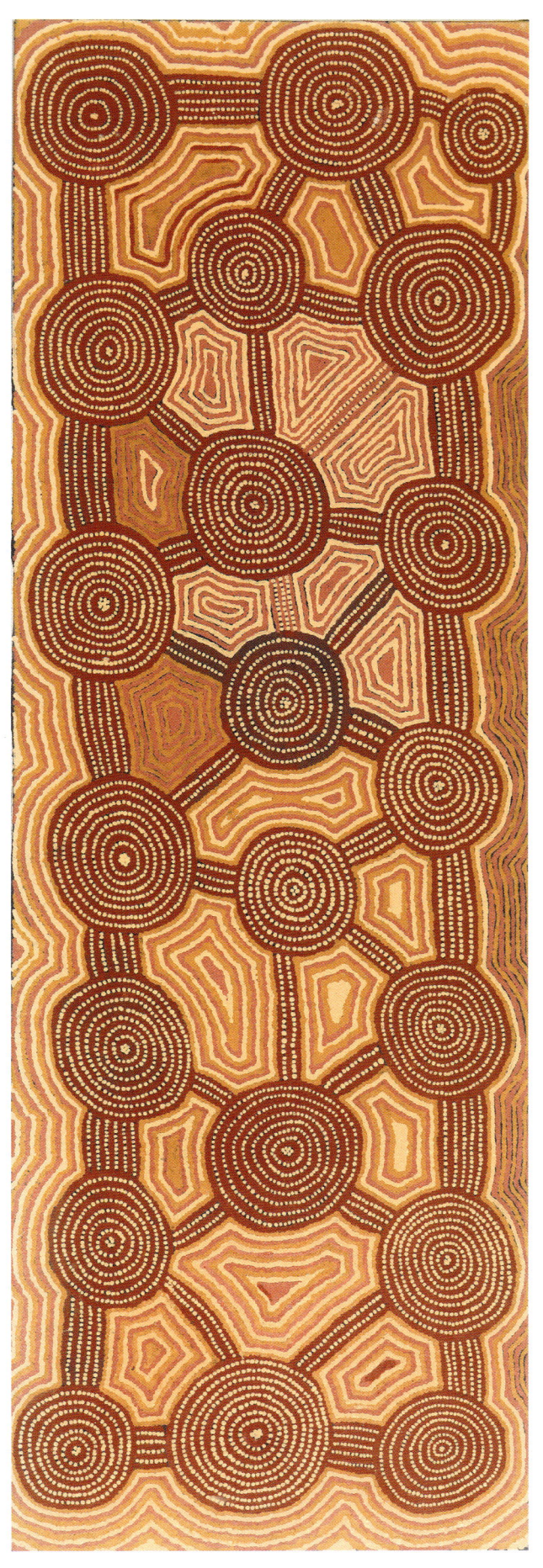

PLATE 73

Yala Yala Gibbs Tjungurrayi
*Two Tingarri Men Traveling to*
*Kaakurutintjinya (Lake Macdonald)*, 1992

FACING | PLATE 74

Yala Yala Gibbs Tjungurrayi
*Kuninka Tjukurrpa at*
*Kaakurutintjinya*, 1988

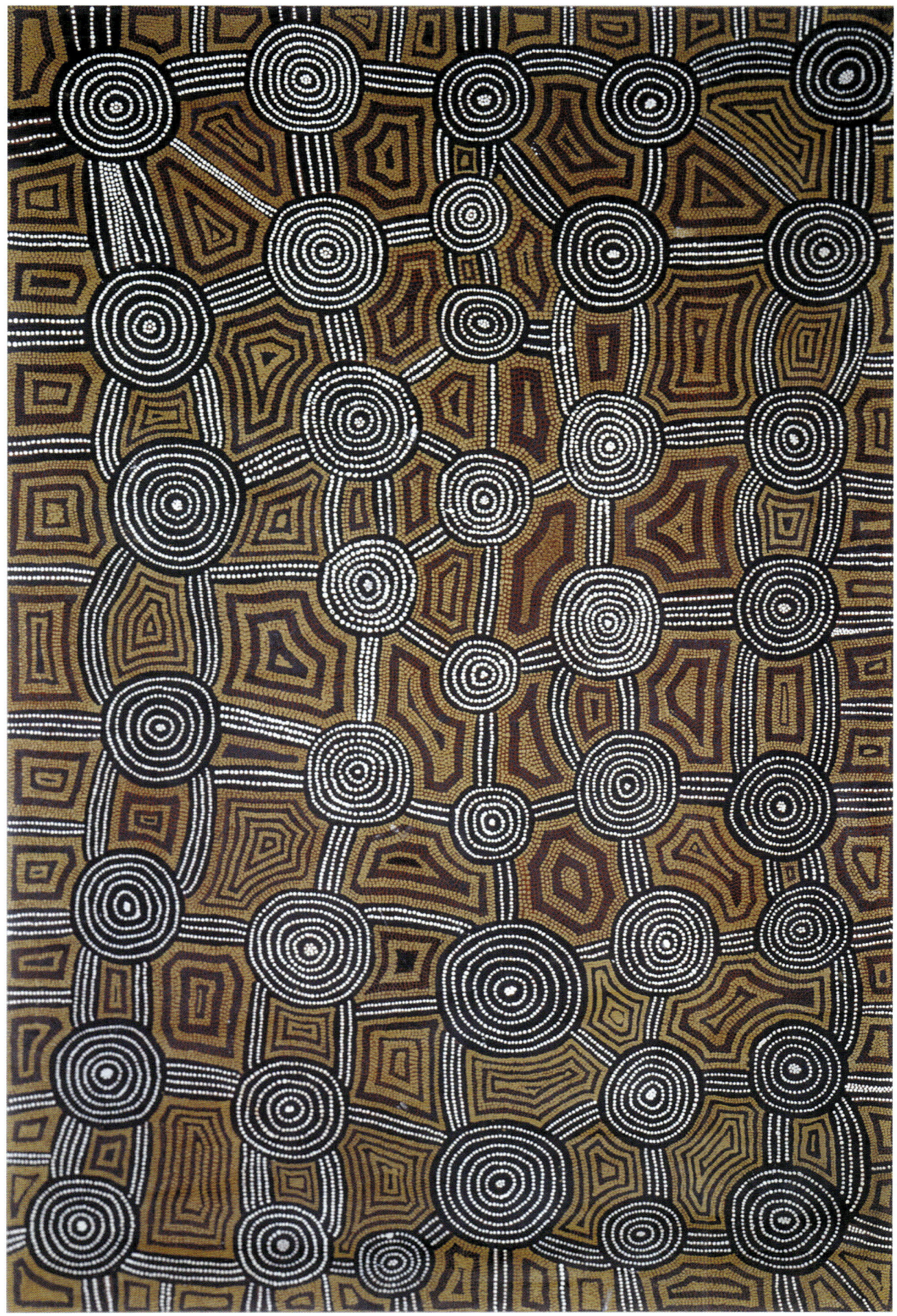

PLATE 75

Willy Tjungurrayi
*Hail at Kaakurutintjinya*, 2001

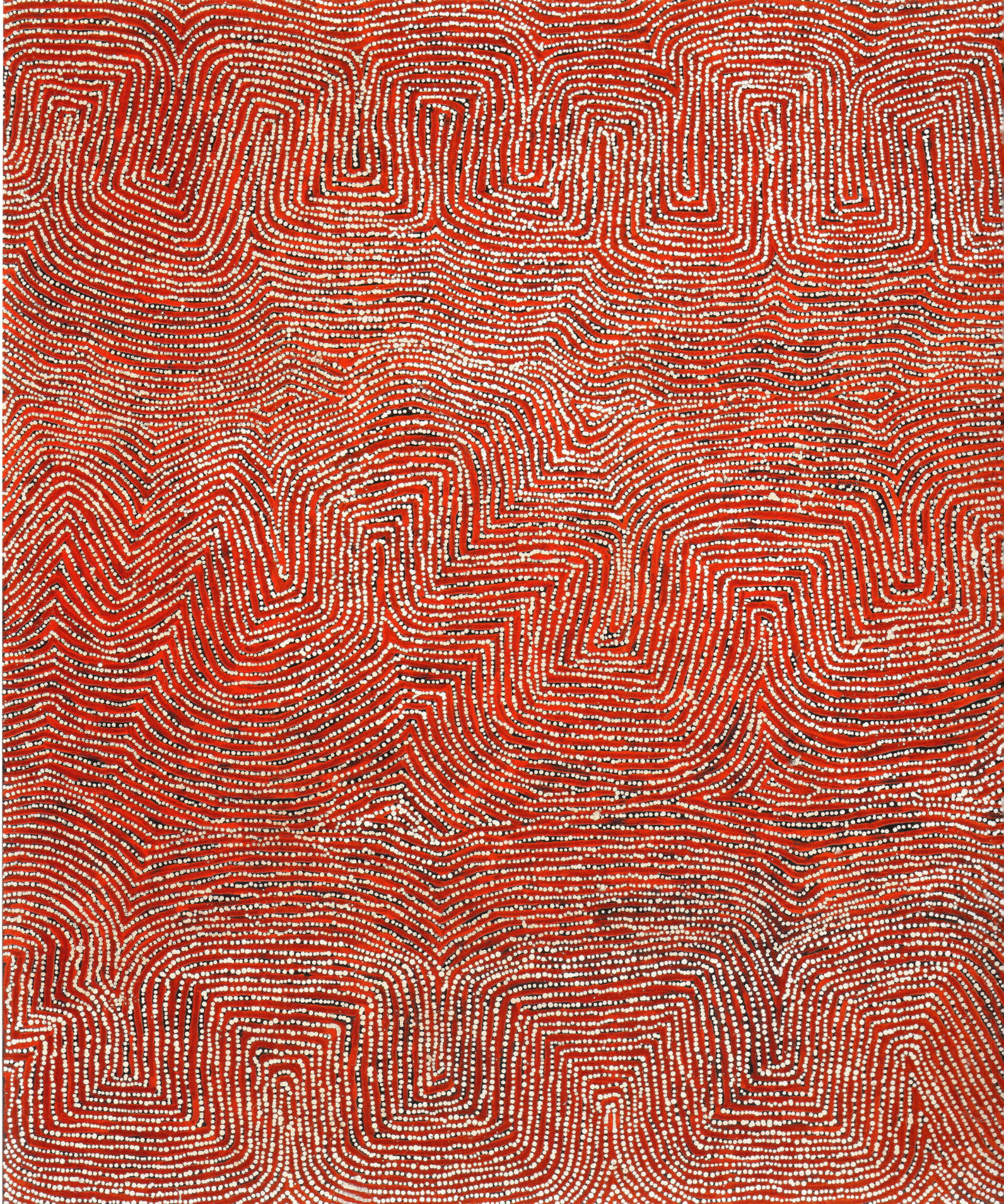

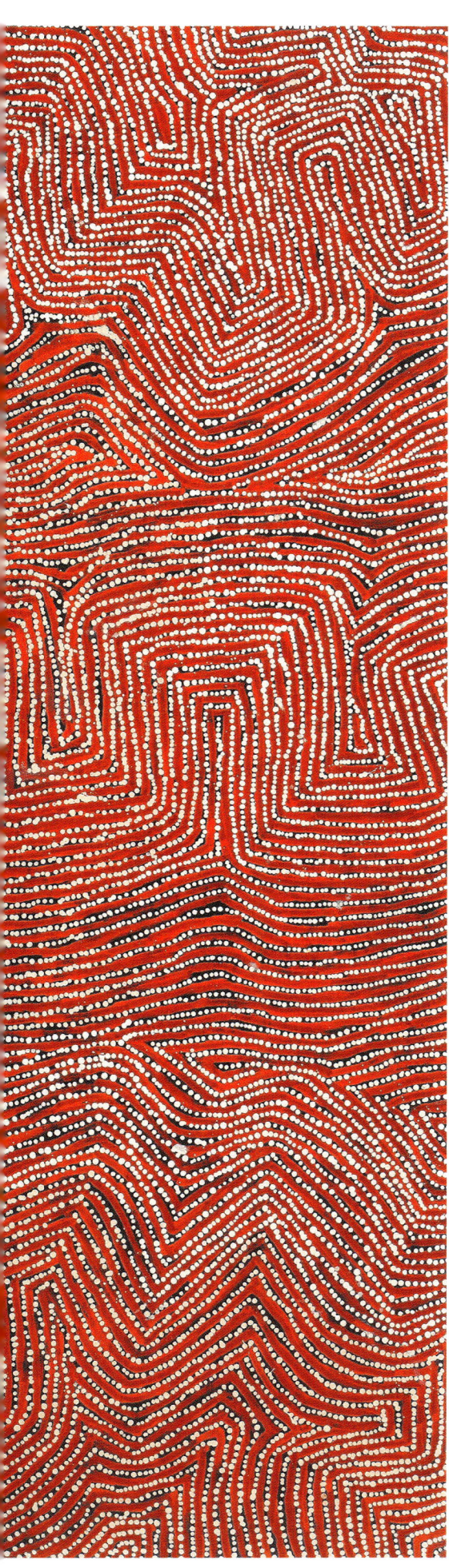

PLATE 76

George Ward Tjungurrayi
*Kaakurutintjinya (Lake Macdonald),*
2003

# Tingarri Yulparirrangurrara

## Tingarri Coming from the South

After Kuninka (the Native Cat ancestor) forced the Tingarri
men at Yawalyurru to leave, he flew further south and
west to Puyulkuranya to direct another Tingarri group eastward toward Kaltukatjara (Docker River) and Tjukurlanya
(plate 77), and from there to Pirrmalnga, Mitukatjirri (plate 78),
Ilingawurrngawurrnga and finally to Pinarinya. At Mitukatjirri,
this group of travelers had a ceremony and then went to
straighten their spears at Ilingawurrngawurrnga (plate 79),
anticipating a fight ahead. Traveling north, they met up
with the Tingarri men coming from the west, at Pinarinya,
where they fought, died and went into the ground at what
is now a permanent water source.

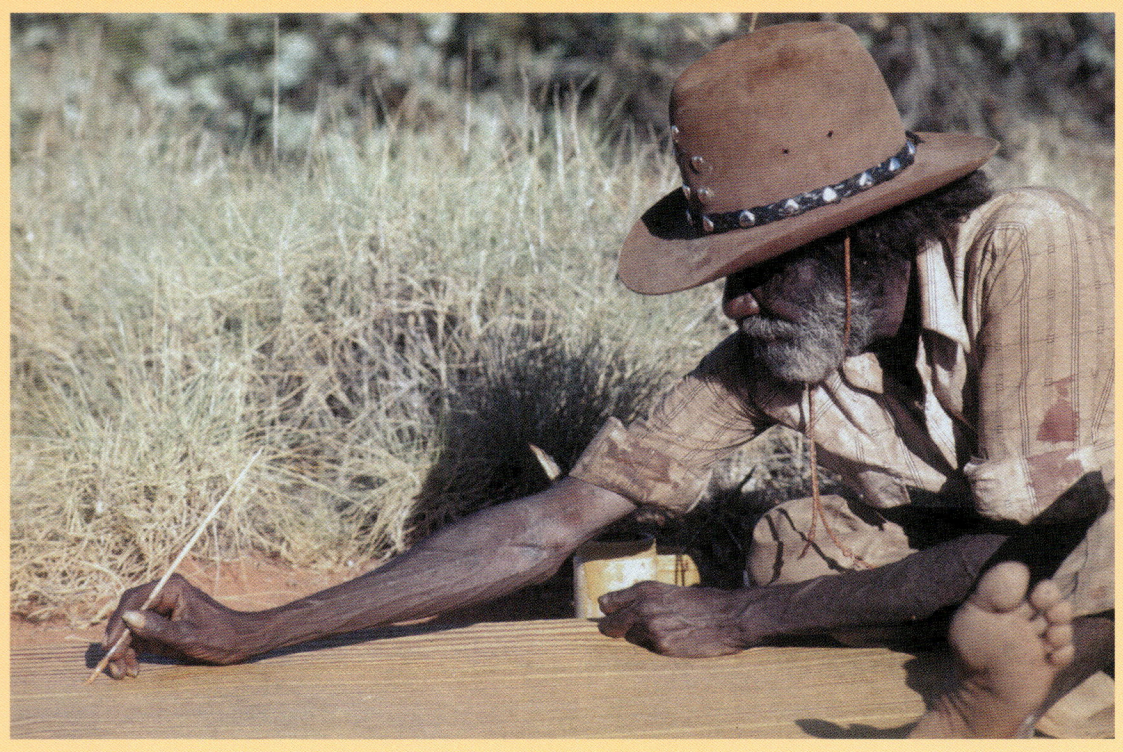

Turkey Tolson Tjupurrula working on
*Straightening Spears at Ilingawurrngawurrnga*
(plate 79) at his outstation near Walungurru
(Kintore), 1993. Photo by Dennis Schulz.

FACING | PLATE 77

John John Bennett Tjapangati
*Travels of the Tingarri Men from Tjukurla to
Mitukatjirri*, 2000

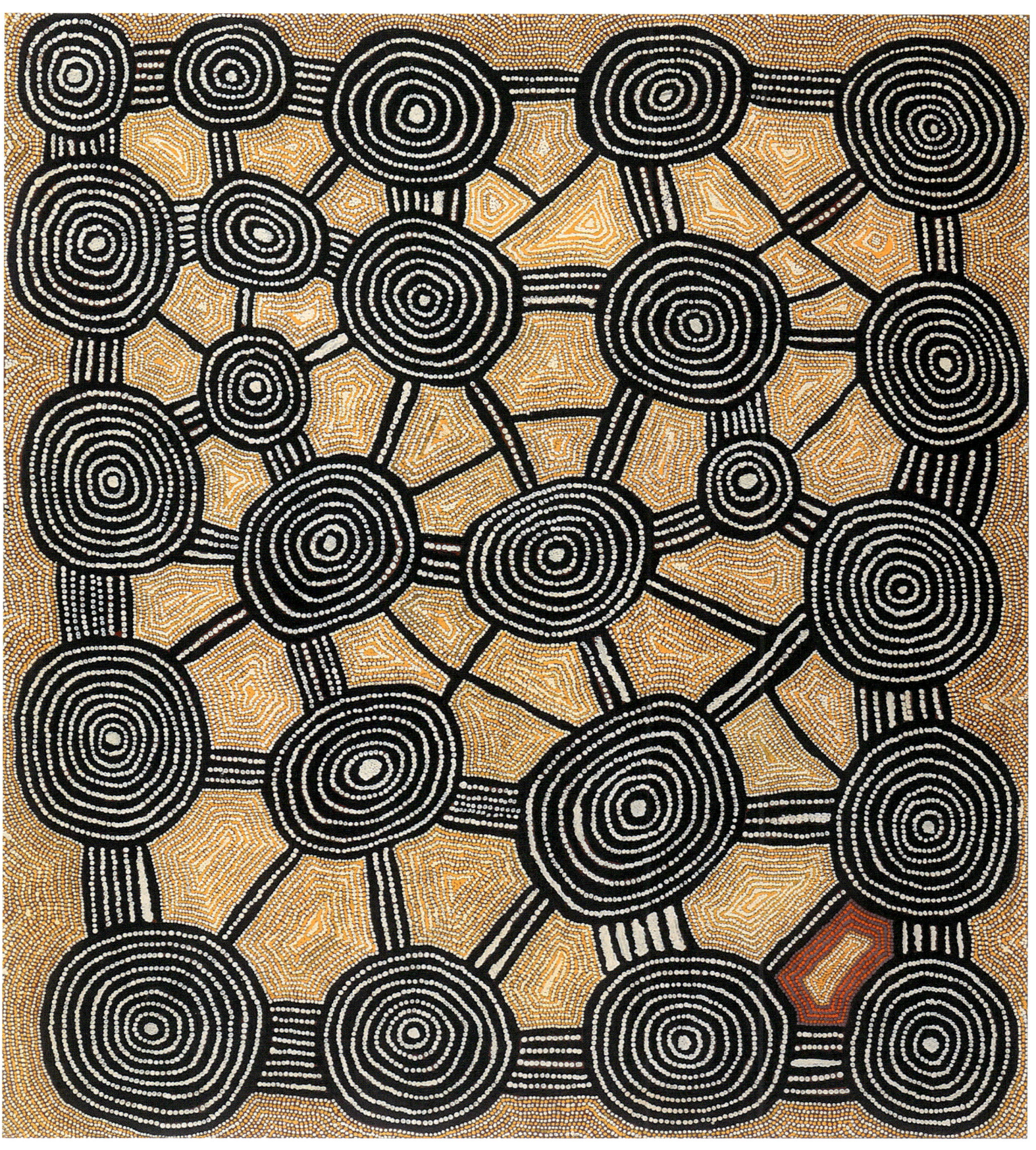

PLATE 78

Mick Namarari Tjapaltjarri
*Mitukatjirri* (formerly *Men's Corroboree*), 1971–72

Previously titled *Men's Corroboree*, this painting is almost certainly
a depiction of the Tingarri Tjukurrpa at one of Mick Namarari
Tjapaltjarri's most important sites, Mitukatjirri, where the Tingarri
men erected sacred objects to reveal to the *punyunyu* (novices) under
their authority. Mick Namarari shared authority over this site with
Turkey Tolson Tjupurrula, who often painted the nearby and related
site of Ilingawurrngawurrnga. Mick Namarari's painting is interesting
for his attempt to depict the interior space of the cave as well as the
larger site itself. The painting of this subject was likely motivated by
the artist's 1972 trip from Papunya with anthropologist Jeremy Long
and filmmaker Roger Sandall. Mick Namarari was one of a group of
men filmed by Sandall performing the ceremony at Mitukatjirri—
a ritual that had not been undertaken in a generation.

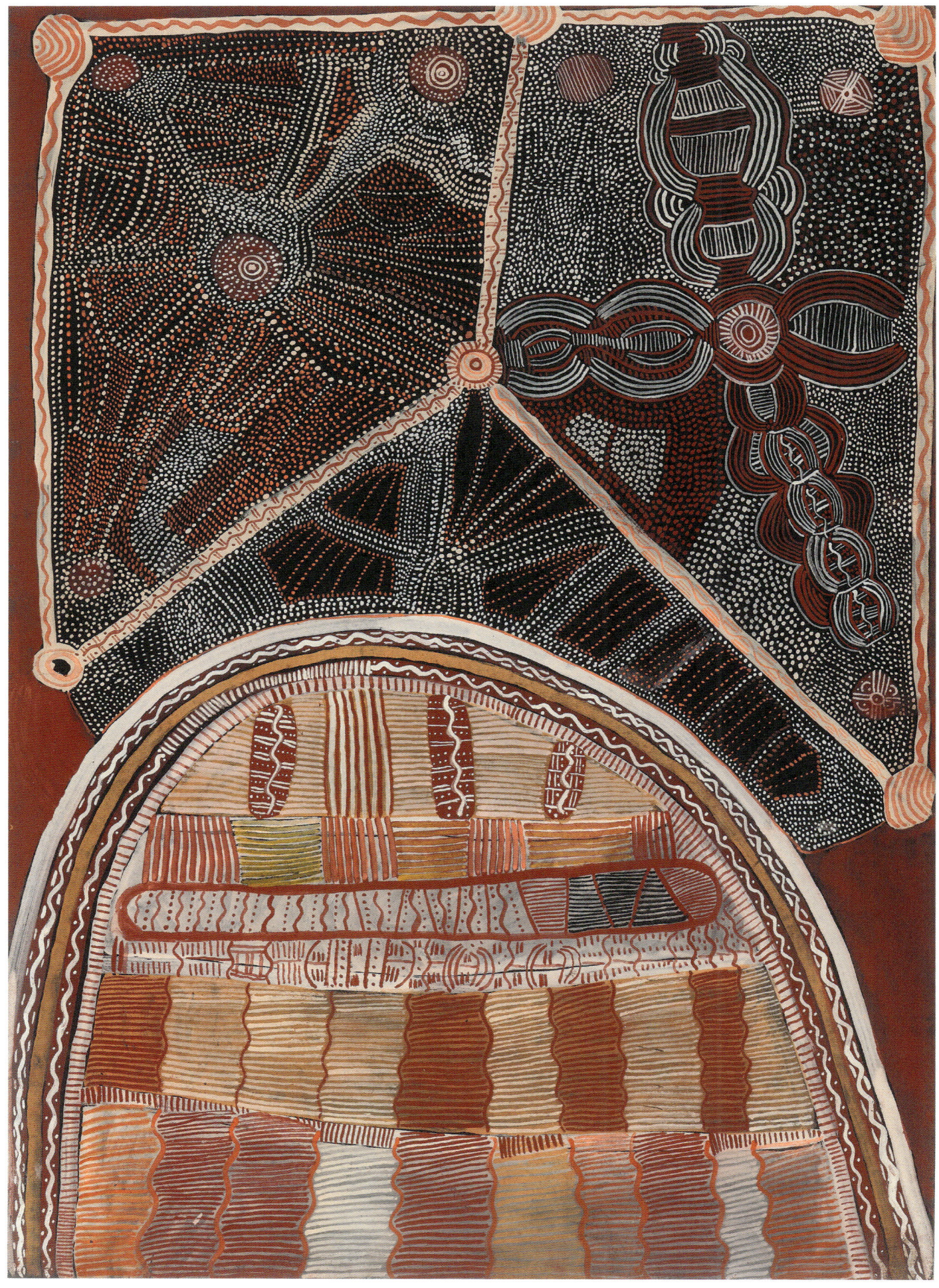

PLATE 79

Turkey Tolson Tjupurrula
*Straightening Spears at*
*Ilingawurrngawurrnga*, 1993

211

# Tingarri Kayilingurrara

## Tingarri Coming from the North

This line of travel connecting places across the northern part of Pintupi country south of Wilkinkarra (Lake Mackay) begins with men coming down from the northwest to meet other groups of men who were living at places near Puntutjarpanya (Jupiter Well). The path they followed was similar to that of the Canning Stock Route, established in 1908. In the north, the men's travels are associated with rain.

They gathered at Ngunyarrmanya (plate 106), where a fire burned and threatened them; although they blocked it by building a huge sandhill, the site is known as Nyaru (burned-out place). From here, these Tingarri traveling men went north and east, toward Karilywarra (plates 87, 88) and the site of the present-day community of Kiwirrkurra, a Tingarri site. Then, turning east in parallel with traveling women, they passed through Ngaminya and Marrapinti to Tjuulnga and Tarkulnga, chasing a Tjilkamarta (Echidna) who tried to steal their sacred objects (plate 98), interacting with various other beings along the way, and leaving their marks on the landscape as named places, reenacted in ceremony and song, until they reached Pinarinya. There, these groups from the north met another group of Tingarri men from the south, led by Kuninka (Native Quoll). They fought and died at Pinarinya and went into the ground, finishing up there in a permanent water.

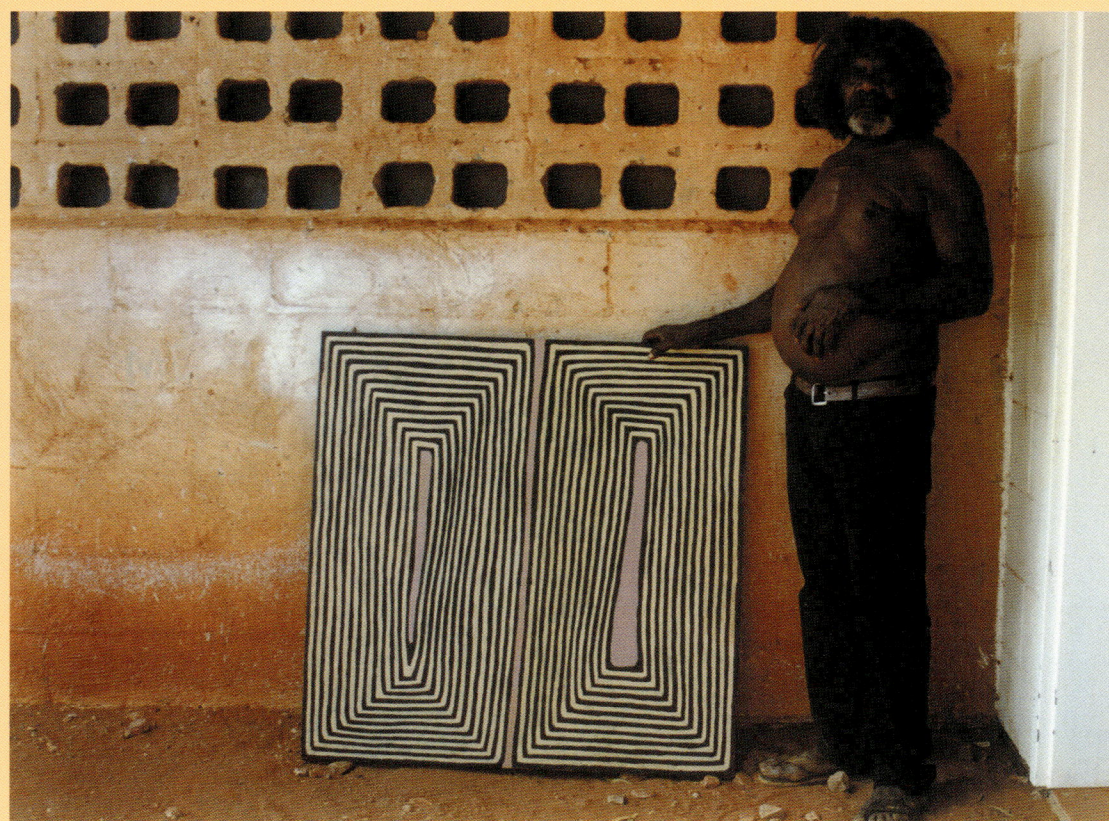

George Tjungurrayi at the Walungurru (Kintore) studio, 1997. Photo by Paul Sweeney.

FACING | PLATE 80

Charlie Ward Tjakamarra
*Two Goanna Ancestral Men*, 2002

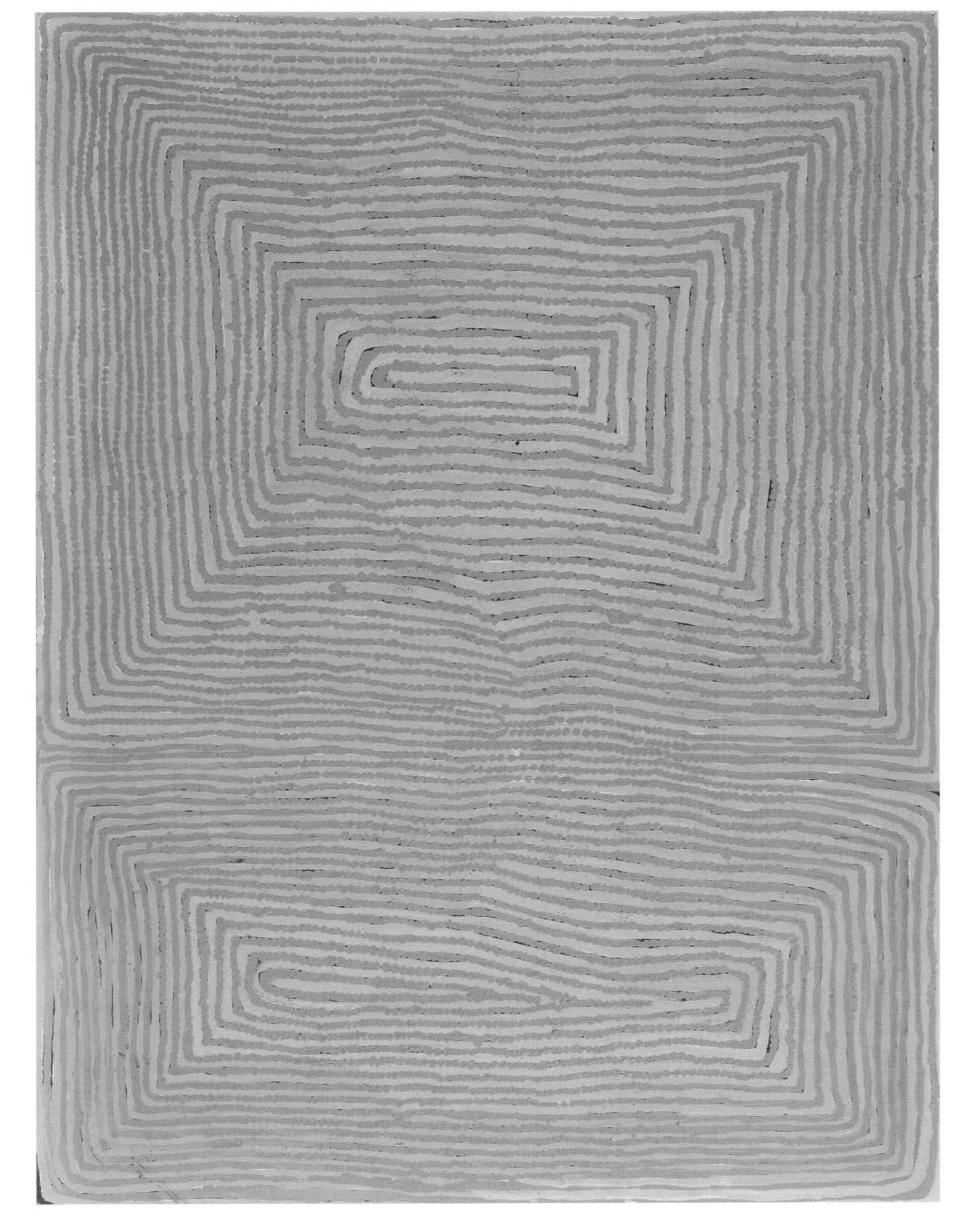

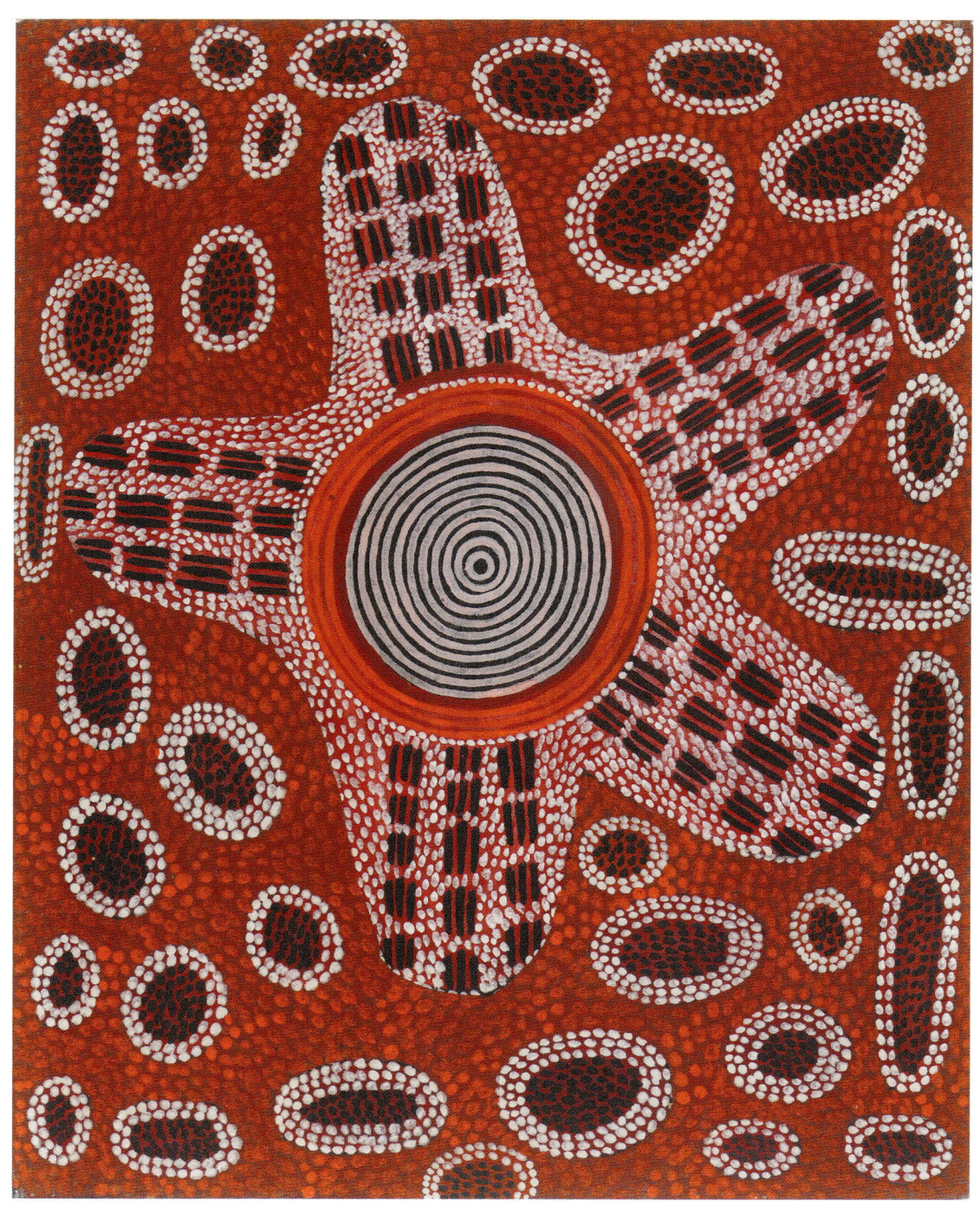

PLATE 81

Yanatjarri No. III Tjakamarra
*Untitled* (possibly *Wati Kutjarra at Pakarangaranya*), 1973

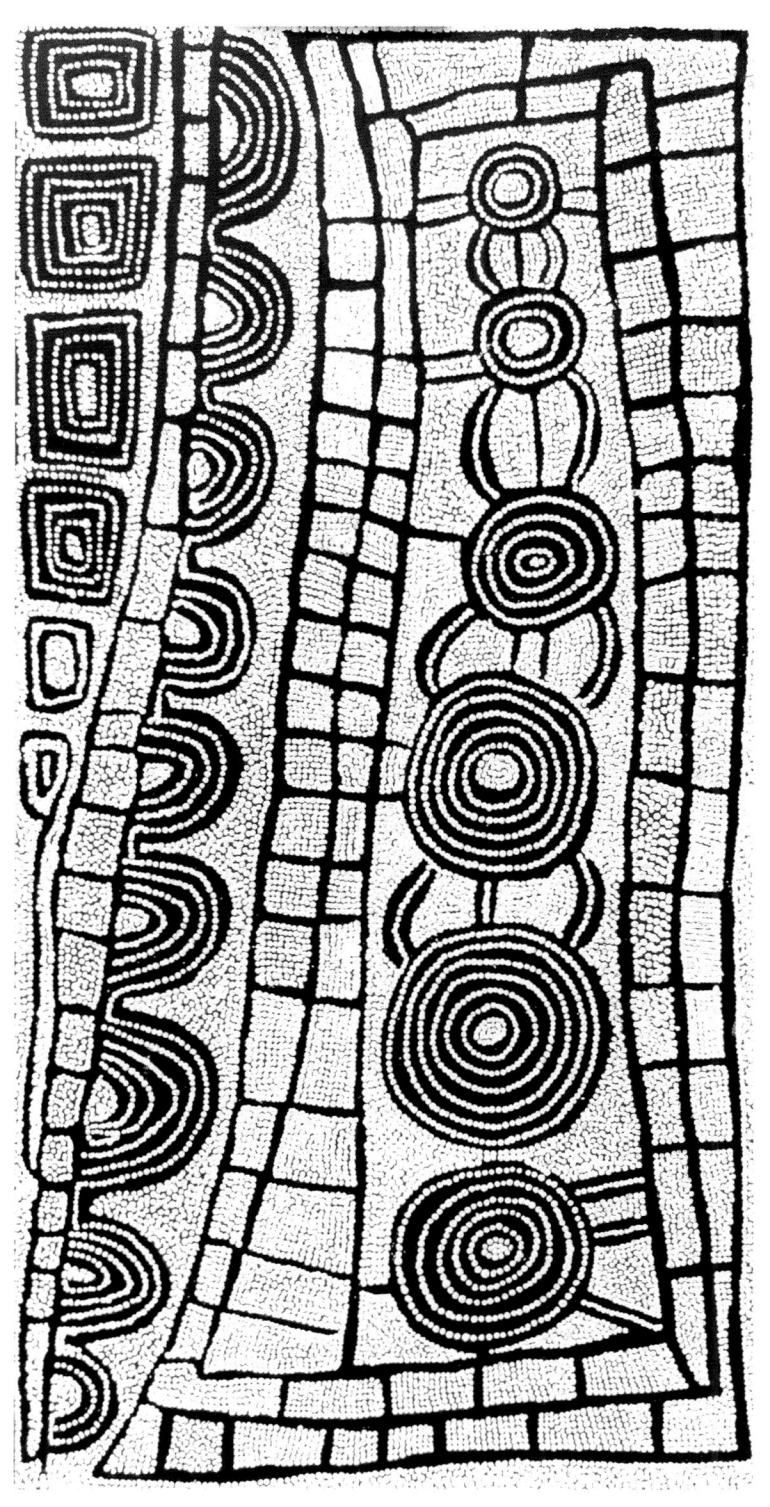

PLATE 82

Patrick Tjungurrayi
*Tjiparitjarra*, 2001

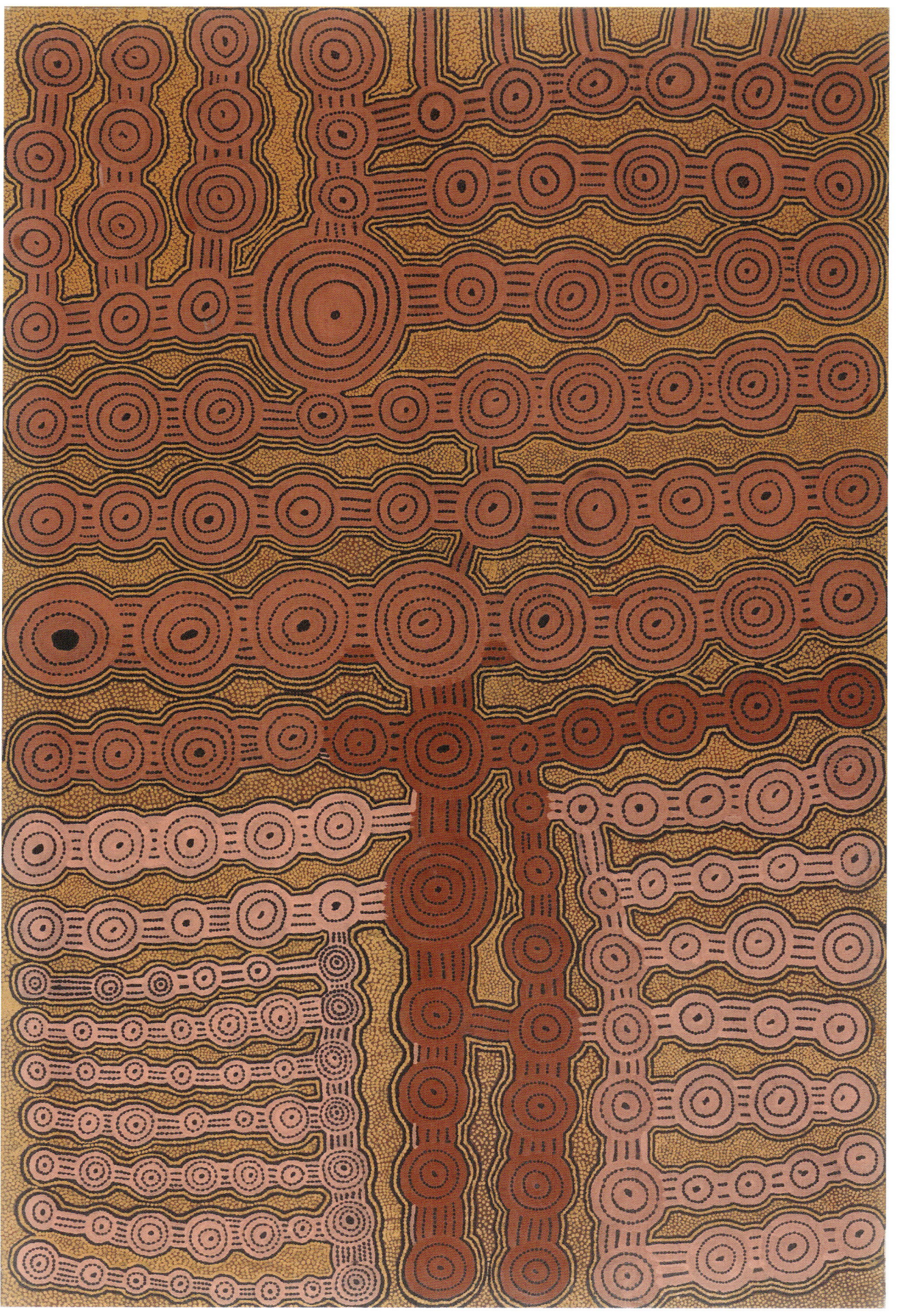

PLATE 83

Dini Campbell
Tjampitjinpa
*Tingarri Cycle at
Minyurlpa near
Jupiter Well*, 1988

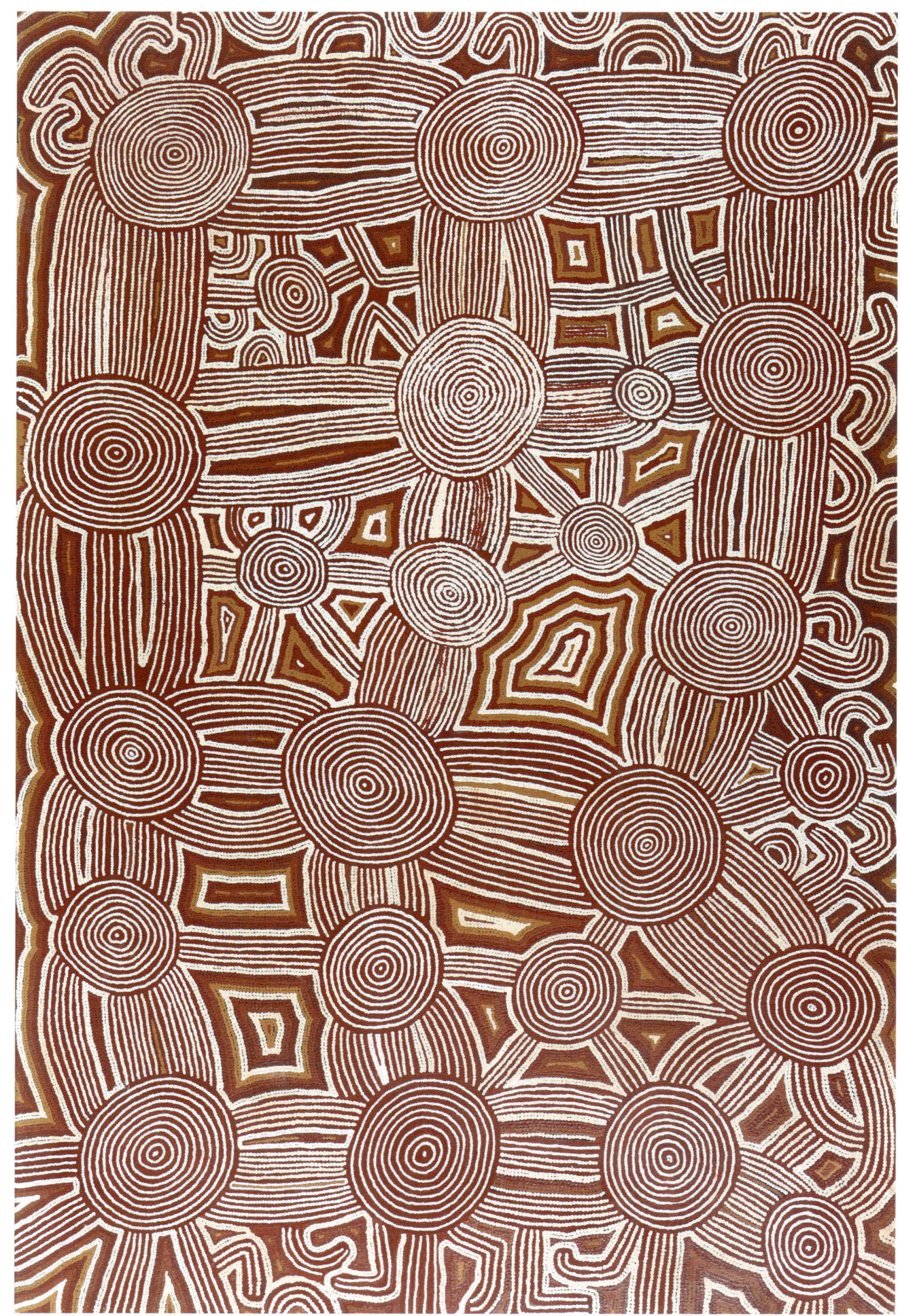

PLATE 84
Fred Ward Tjungurrayi
*Tingarri at Yunarla,*
1989

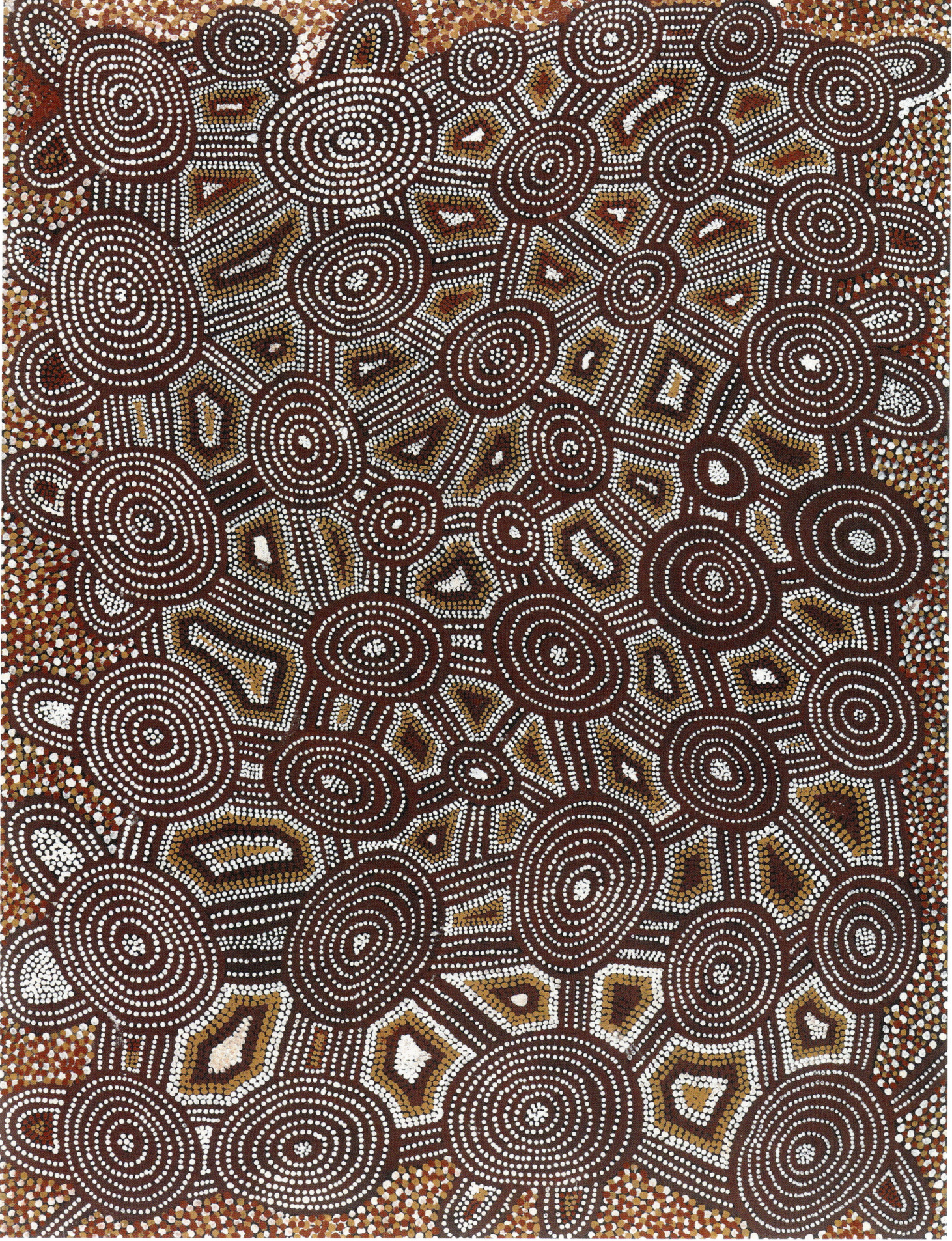

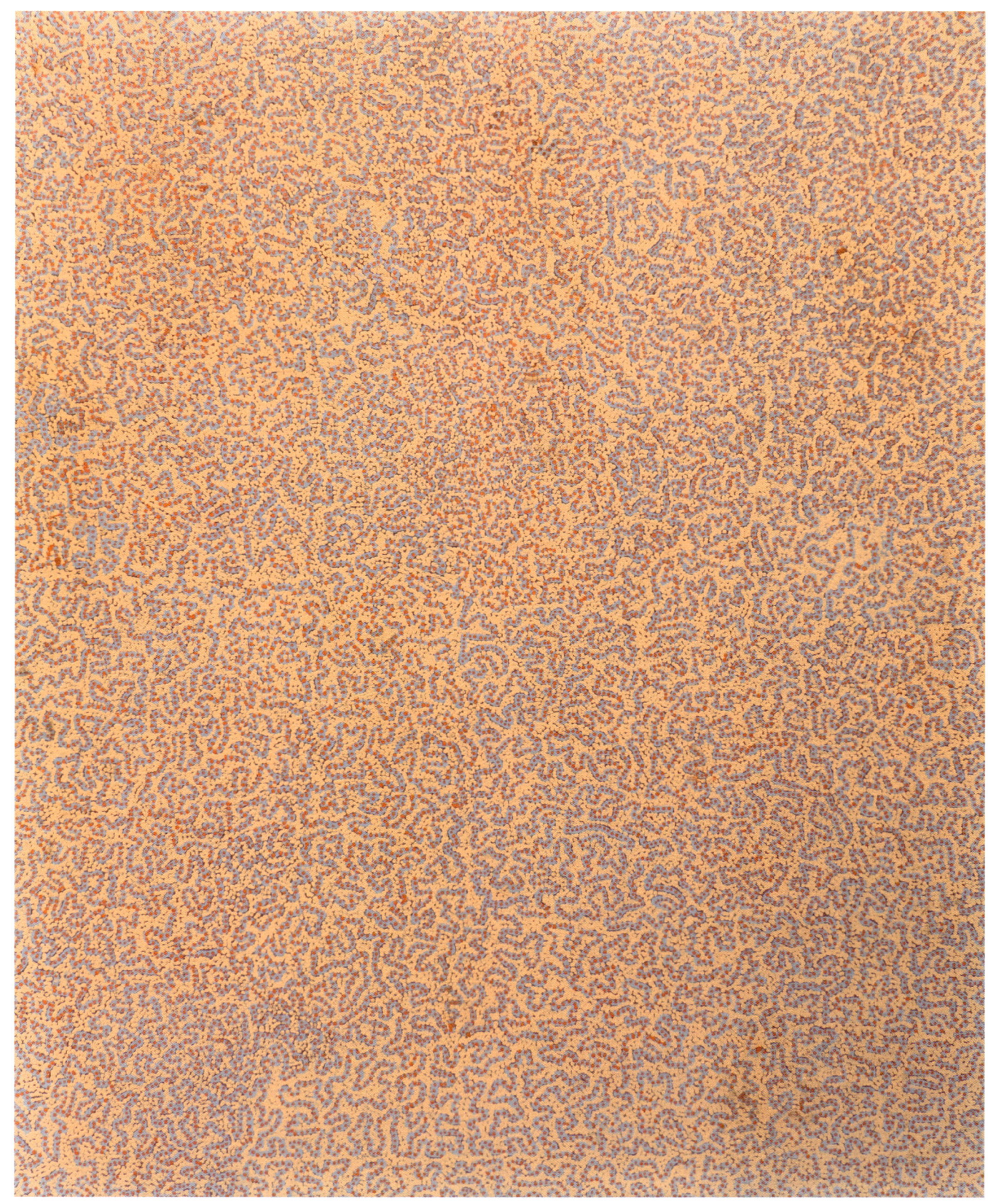

Yanatjarri Tjampitjinpa
*Tingarri at Yunarla*, 1993

PLATE 86

Joseph Jurra Tjapaltjarri
*Yunarla*, 2007

# Karilywarra

A site associated with Kuniya Kutjarra Tjukurrpa (Two Carpet Snake / Rock Python ancestors) who rested there and traveled further to the west before they were killed, Karilywarra in the Pollock Hills area has been an inspiration for both men and women artists. The conception Dreaming site of Freddy West Tjakamarra's father, whose Tjukurrpa incarnation came here with a ceremonial gift of meat, this rockhole and associated claypan have been painted by three celebrated artists: Freddy West, Naata Nungurrayi (plate 88), and her son Kenny Williams Tjampitjinpa (plate 87). Naata's paintings of this place sometimes clearly reference the coiled bodies of the snakes, lying down as they have turned to stone, incorporating the coils into the structure of the painting and sometimes including the publicly accessible concentric circle designs on the rocks said to be left behind by the bodies of the Tjukurrpa figures. Other significant representational strategies emphasize the classical iconographic sign of the wavy line, the tracks of the snakes on the ground or the claypans left by the movement of their bodies across their surfaces.

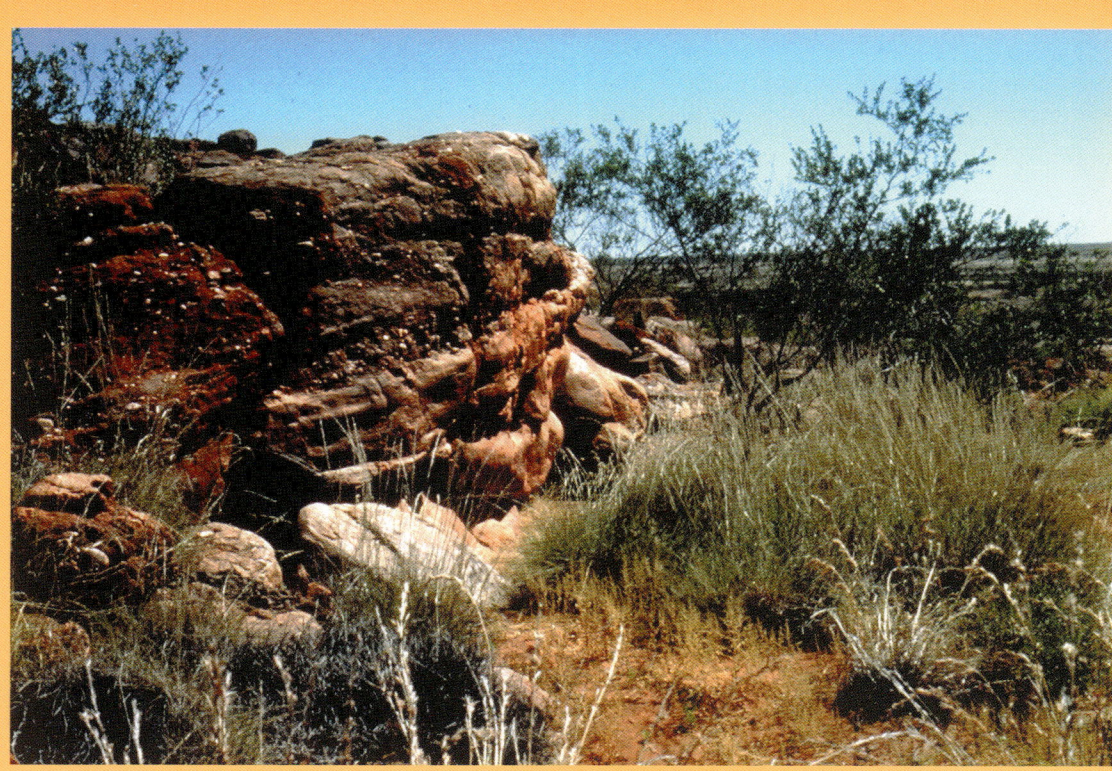

Snake coils at Karilywarra, 1988. Photo by Fred Myers.

FACING | PLATE 87

Kenny Williams Tjampitjinpa
*Hill Site of Karilywarra*, 1988

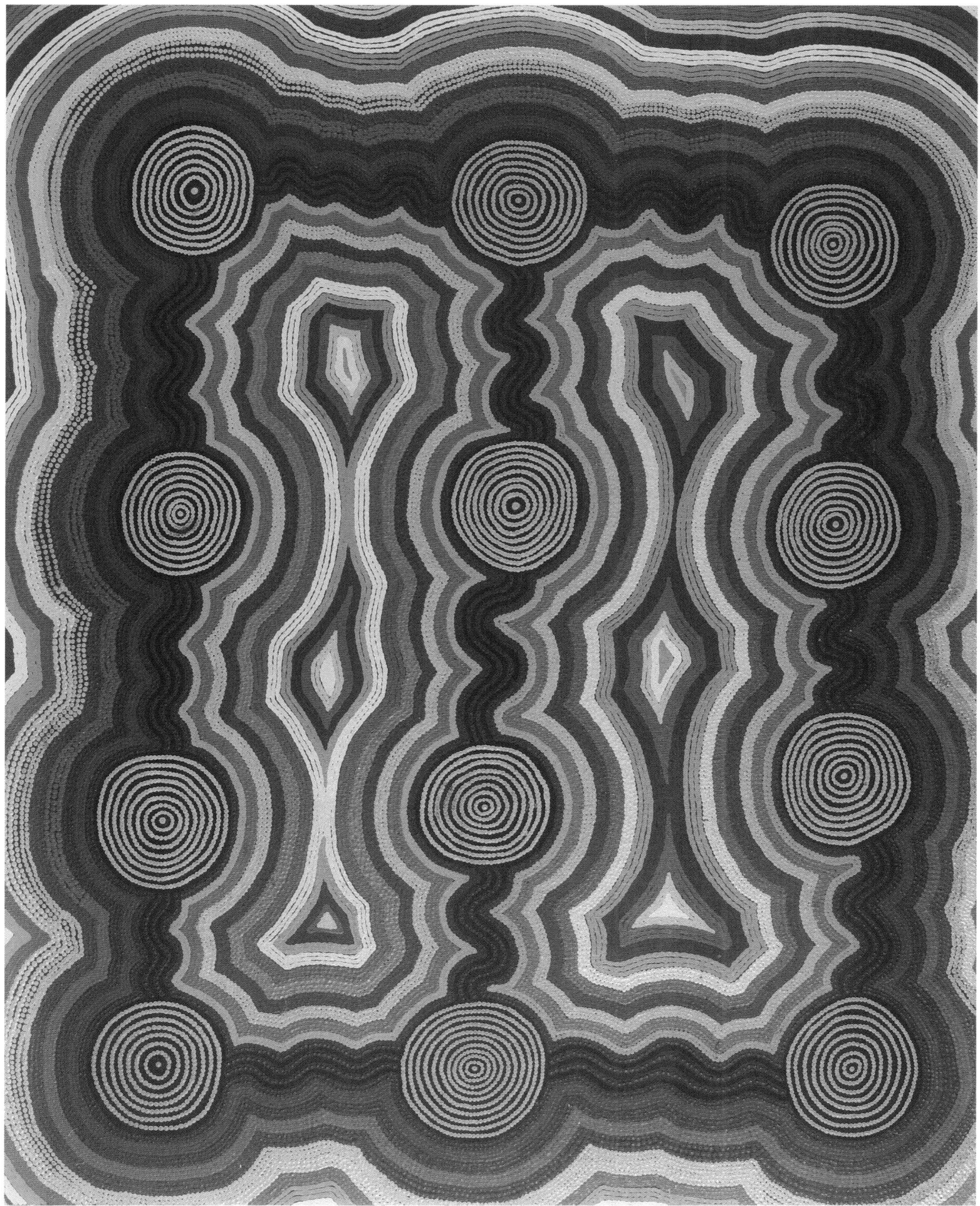

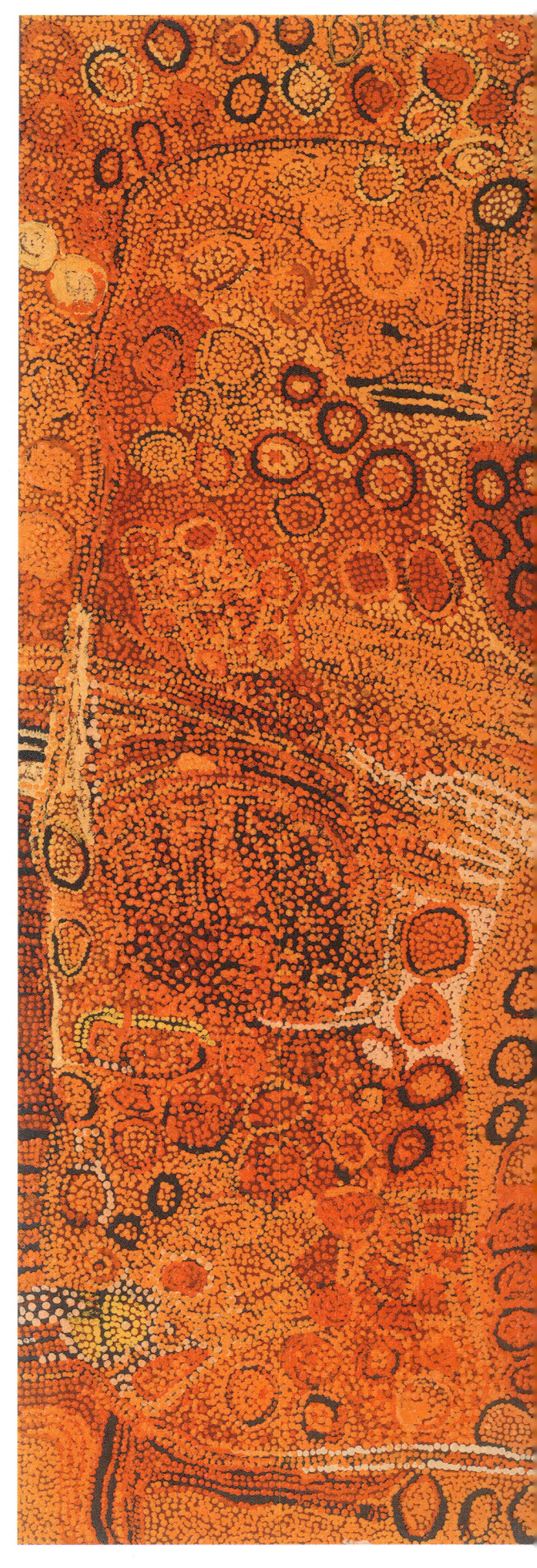

PLATE 88

Naata Nungurrayi
*Karilywarra*, 2010

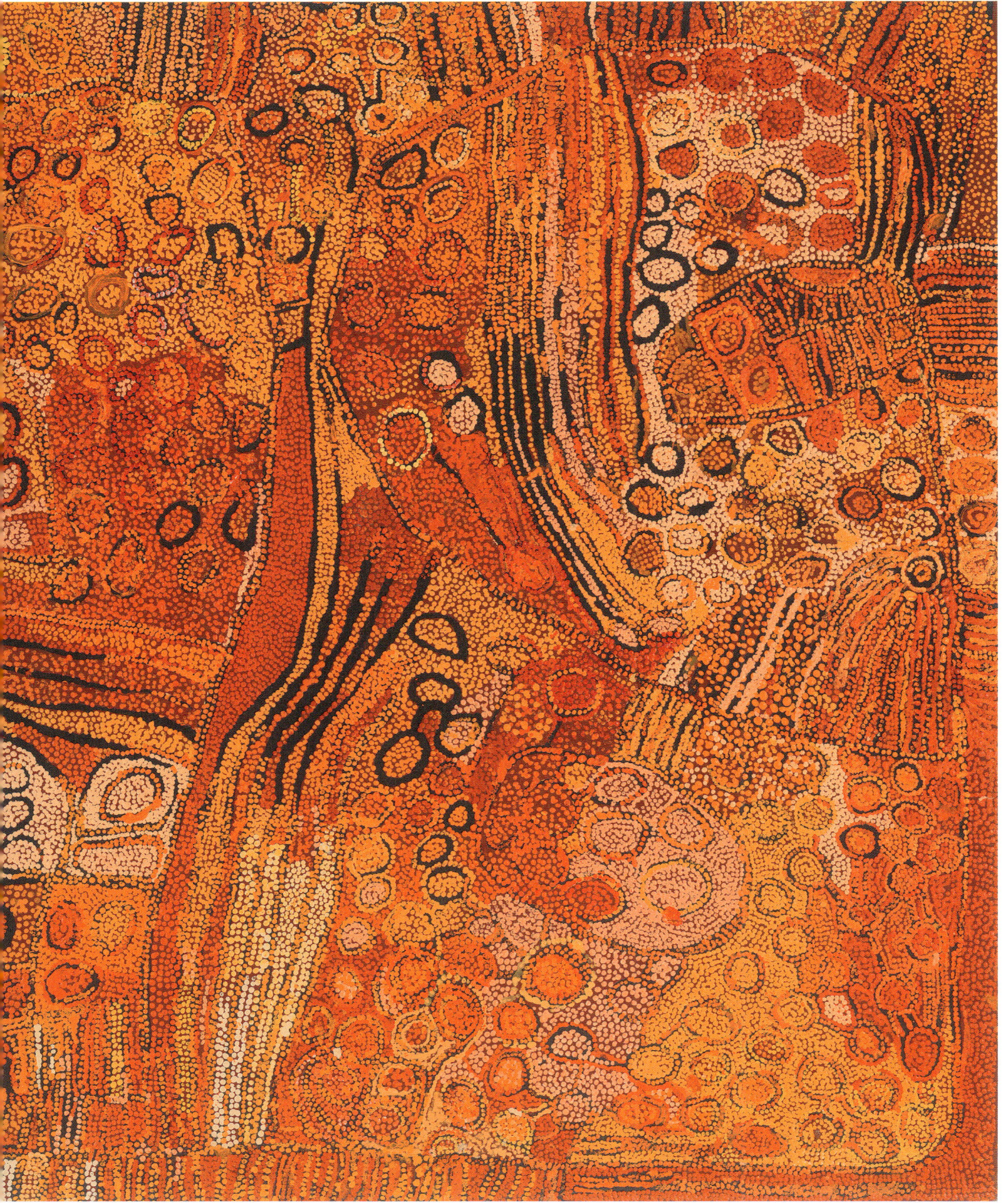

# Marrapinti and Ngaminya

At Marrapinti, a site in the sandhills north and east of Kiwirrkurra, a cave connects to a creek where people used to stay in the rain. The rock formation around the cave is identified with the noses of young women. The Kiwirrkurra Women's Culture and Health Camp recently visited the site, where senior women taught younger ones about women's Law, culture, and traditional skills, such as twining bush sandals and finding *yunarla* (yams).

*Marrapinti* is a common motif for contemporary women painters at Papunya Tula, and can be seen in the works of Doreen Reid Nakamarra (plate 90), Mantua Nangala (plate 119), Nancy Nungurrayi (plate 89), Payu Napaltjarri (plate 118), Walangkura Napanangka (plate 117), Yalti Napangati (plate 116) and Yukultji Napangati (plates 91 and 120).

*Marrapinti* is the Pintupi word for a "nose bone"—usually a kangaroo bone—used in a pierced nasal septum, but it is also the name for a place whose creation is associated with the events for this custom. The custom belongs to what one Pintupi man described as the Kungka Tjukurrpa (Women Dreaming), also known as Kanaputa, that traveled eastward through the Pollock Hills. The songs and story of these women are said to belong to the Tingarri ritual cycle, but there are also versions sung by women. These ancestral women had ceremonies similar to what men have now. They traveled separately, in a distinct line from the men, although they came together at times for ceremonies. That is clear, for example, in a related site south of Marrapinti, where the women pierced their nasal septums while a separate group of Tingarri men were camped in the hills. The women were cooking *walpuru*, a kind of vegetable that is cooked in hot ashes like a yam, though only its protruding "ears" are eaten. The women sing a song relating to the exploding sound of the *walpuru* cooking, while the men sing one whose verses memorialize the piercing of the nasal septum.

From Marrapinti, the ancestral women traveled to Ngaminya, where they pulped the sweet-tasting fruit *kampurarrpa*. Ngaminya is painted by both men and women, such as Bombatu Napangati (plate 123), Nanyuma Napangati (plate 122), Joseph Jurra Tjapaltjarri (plate 92) and Yanatjarri No. III Tjakamarra (plate 56). Joseph Jurra shows women mashing the *kampurarrpa* into balls, referencing both the ancestral women and his own relatives, who continue this practice. The oblong shapes in Yanatjarri's painting represent ceremonial objects associated with these women. After leaving Ngaminya, the women continued along a series of small rocky hills northeast, stopping at the birthing site of Wirrulnga (plate 94) before heading toward Wilkinkarra, as seen in Timmy Payungu Tjapangati's *Tingarri Woman Dreaming at Wilkinkarra* (1987, plate 95).

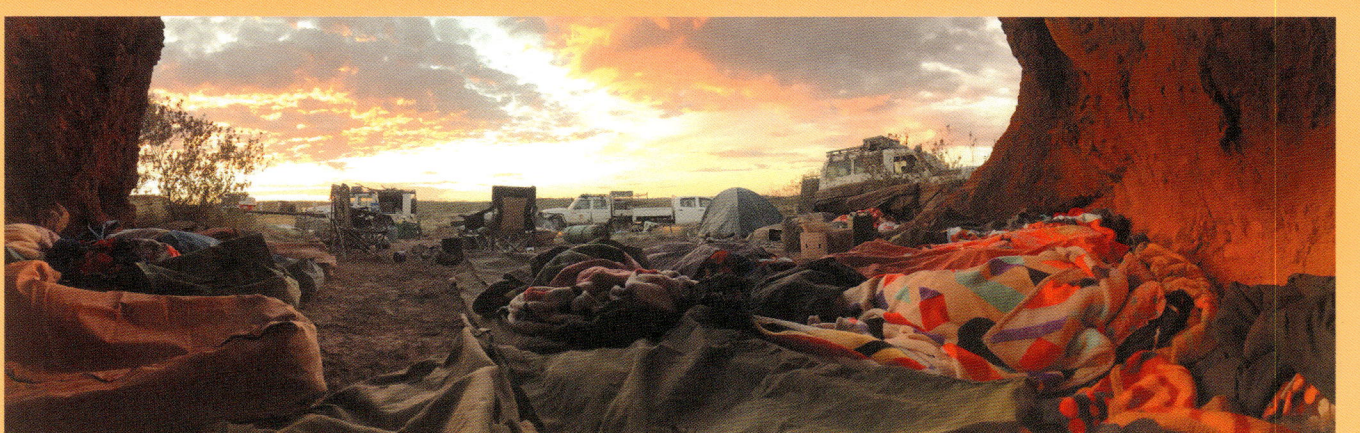

Sunrise in the camp at Marrapinti, May 2021. Photo by Rachel Paltride, courtesy of the Tjamu Tjamu Aborigina Corporation.

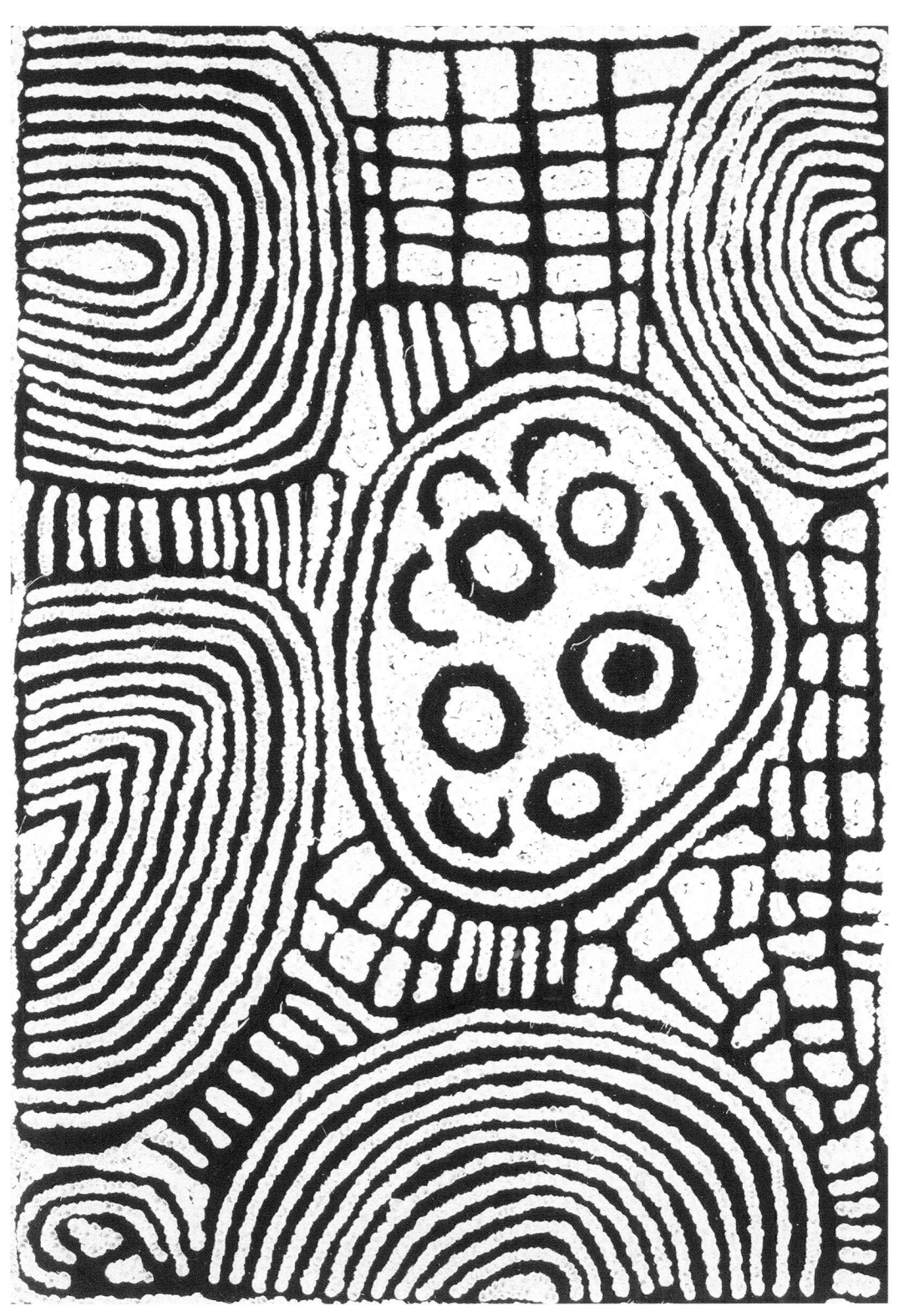

PLATE 89

Nancy Nungurrayi
*Marrapinti Water Soakage,* 2001

PLATE 90

Doreen Reid Nakamarra
*Rockhole Site of Marrapinti,* 2006

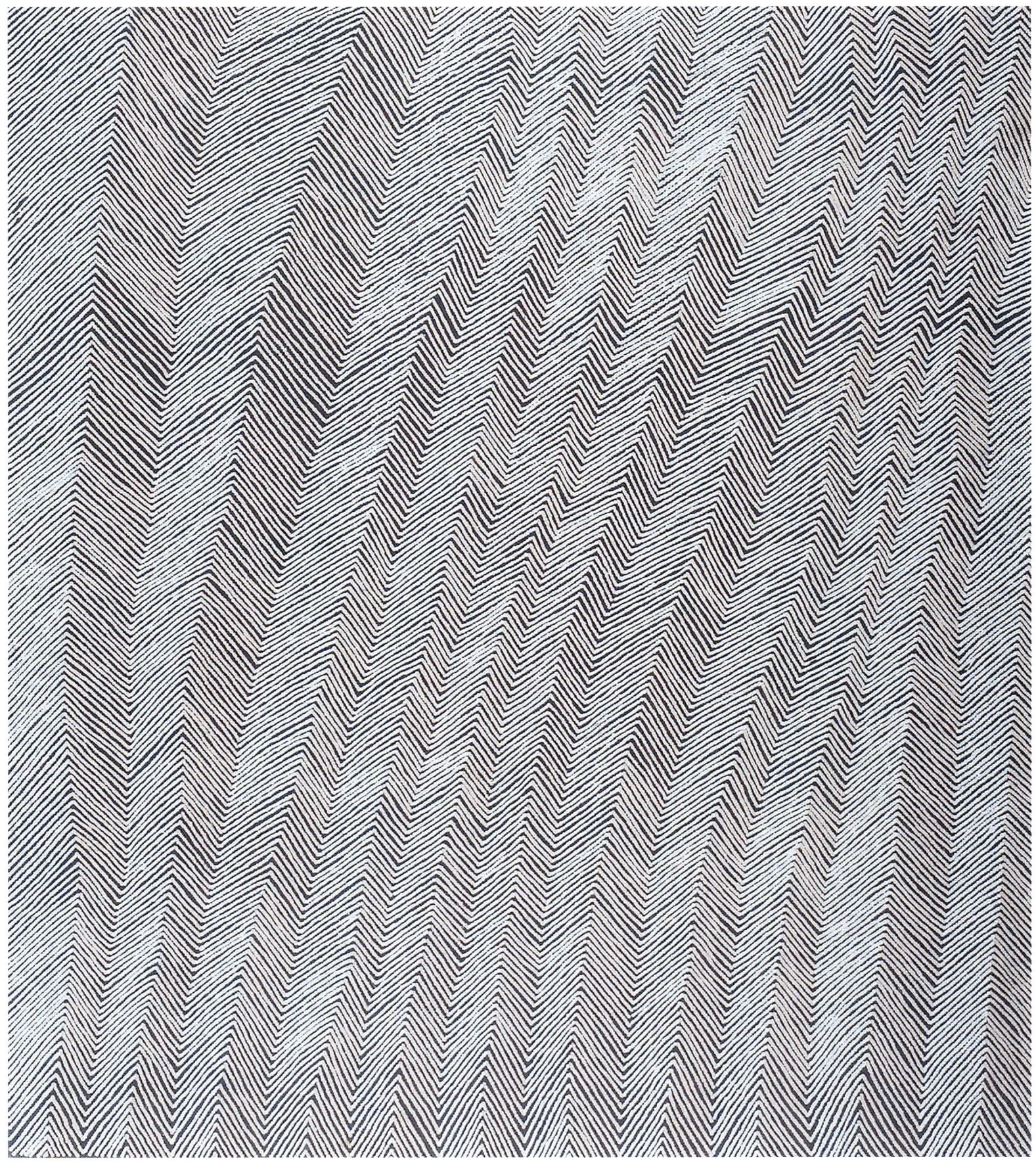

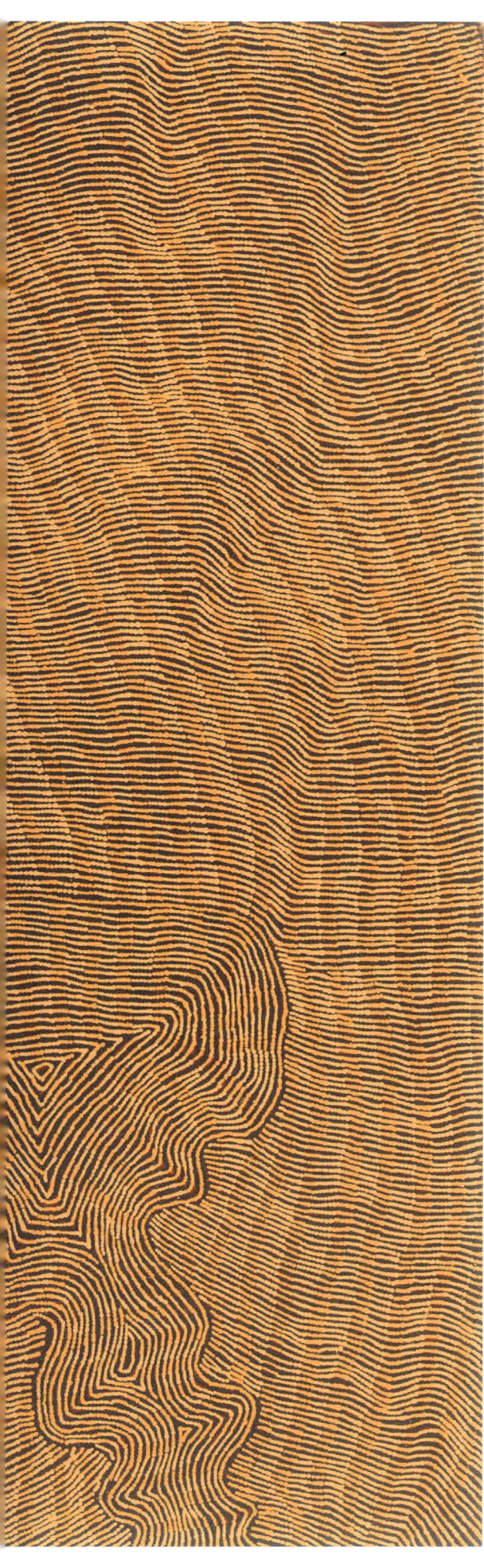

PLATE 91

Yukultji Napangati
*Ancestral Women at Marrapinti*, 2016

229

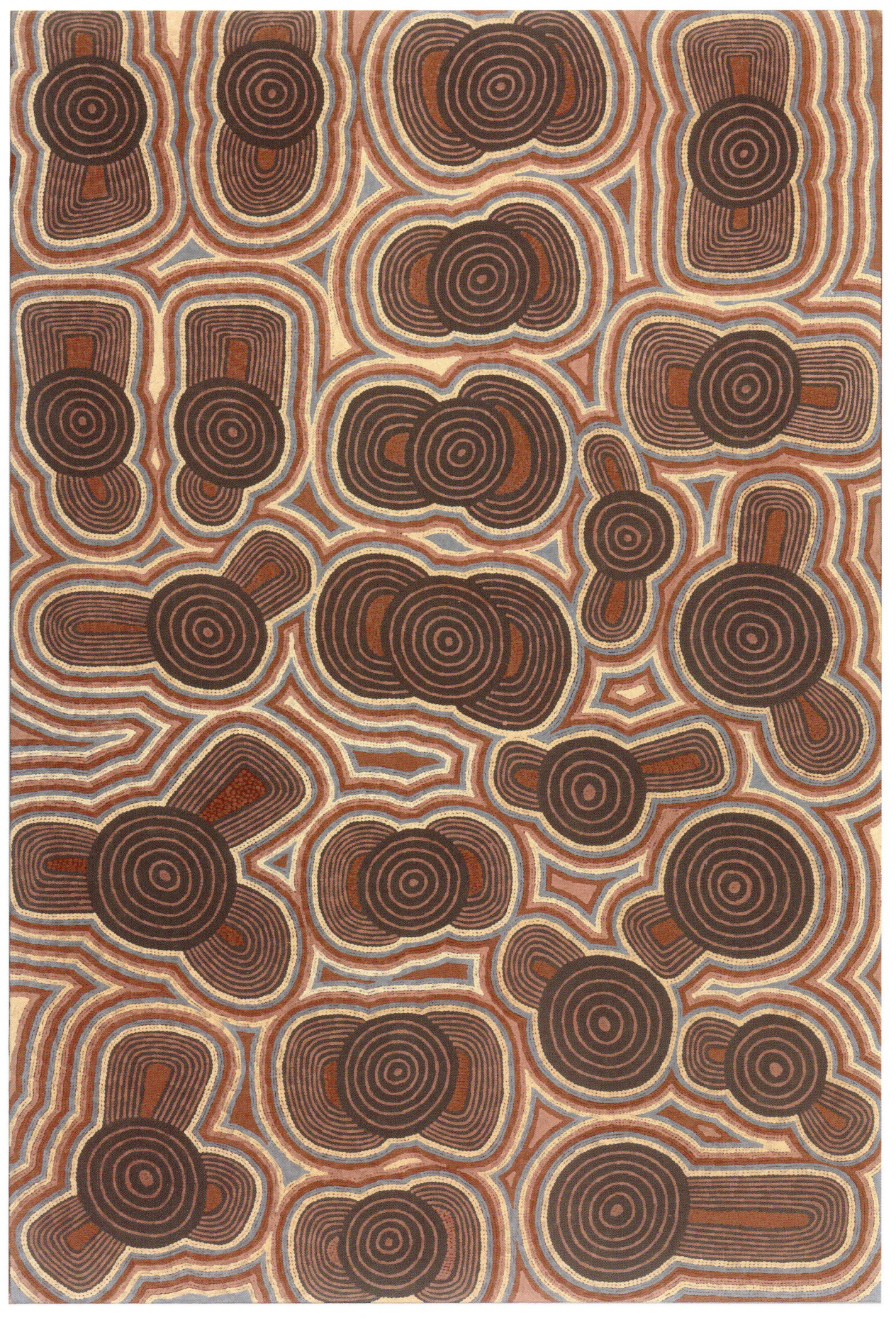

PLATE 92

Joseph Jurra Tjapaltjarri
*Women Pulping Kampurarrpa
at Ngaminya*, 1990

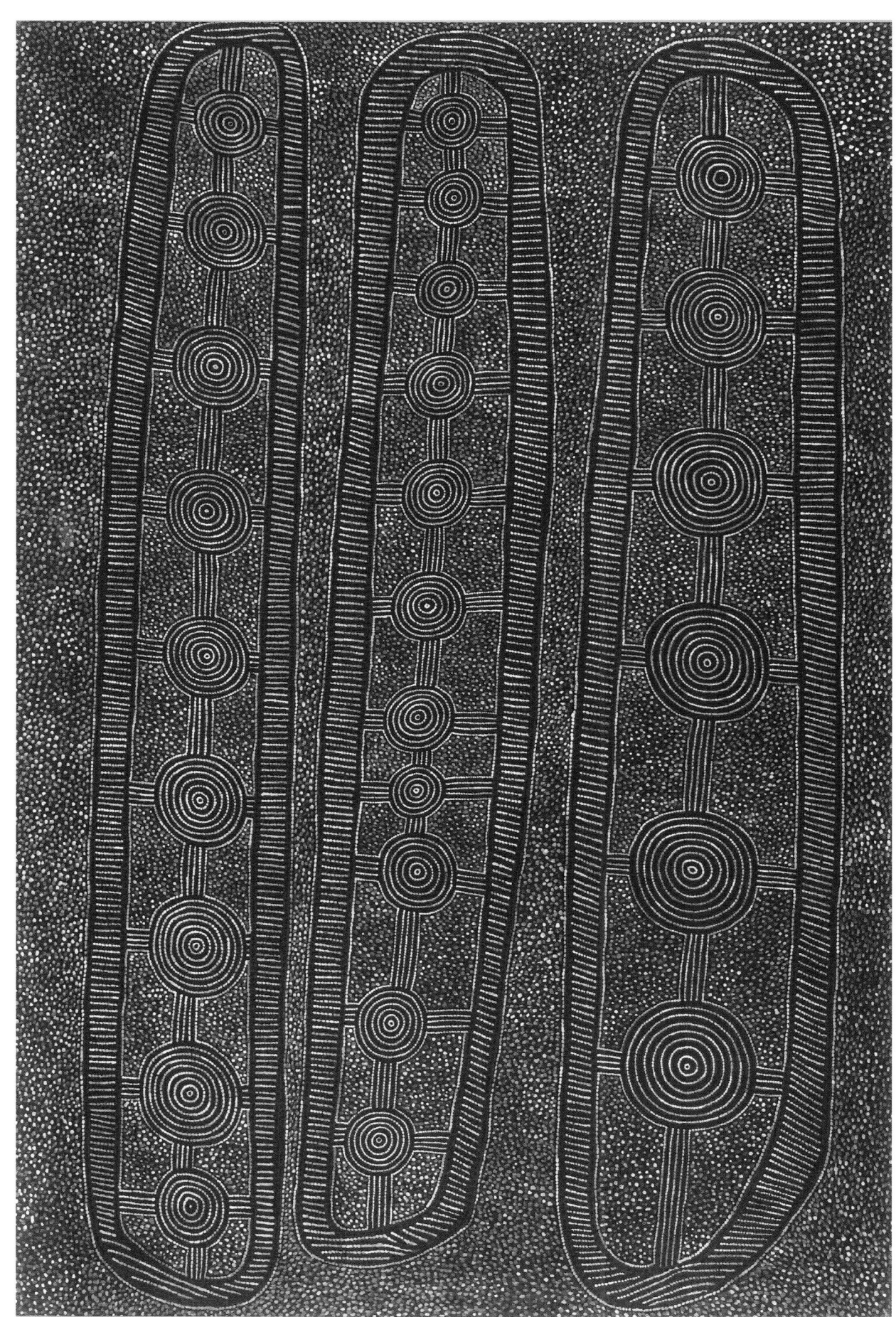

PLATE 93

Yanatjarri No. III Tjakamarra
*Women's Dreaming near*
*Kiwirrkurra*, 1989

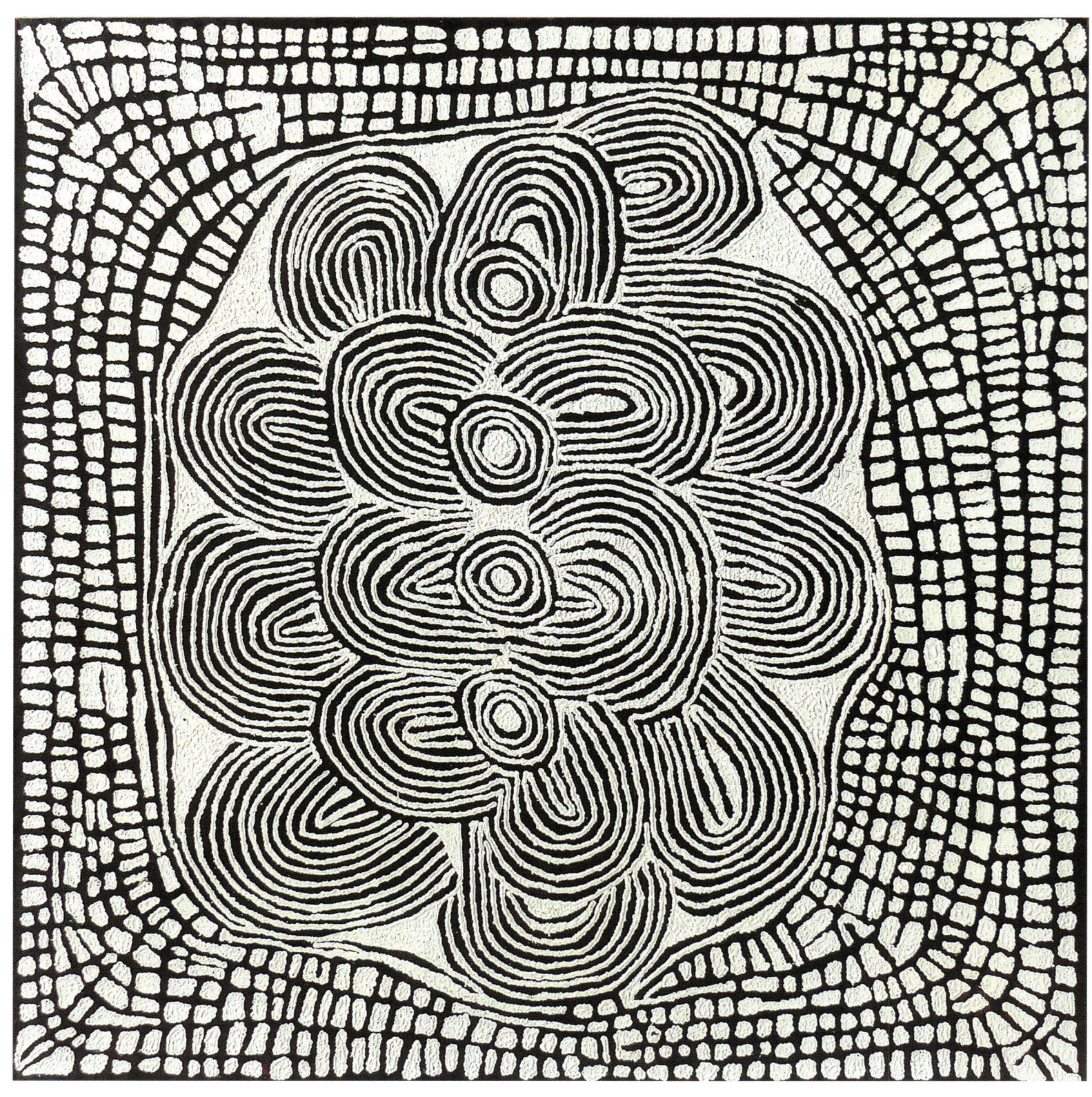

PLATE 94

Ningura Napurrula
*Wirrulnga*, 2001

FACING | PLATE 95

Timmy Payungu Tjapangati
*Tingarri Woman Dreaming at*
*Wilkinkarra*, 1987

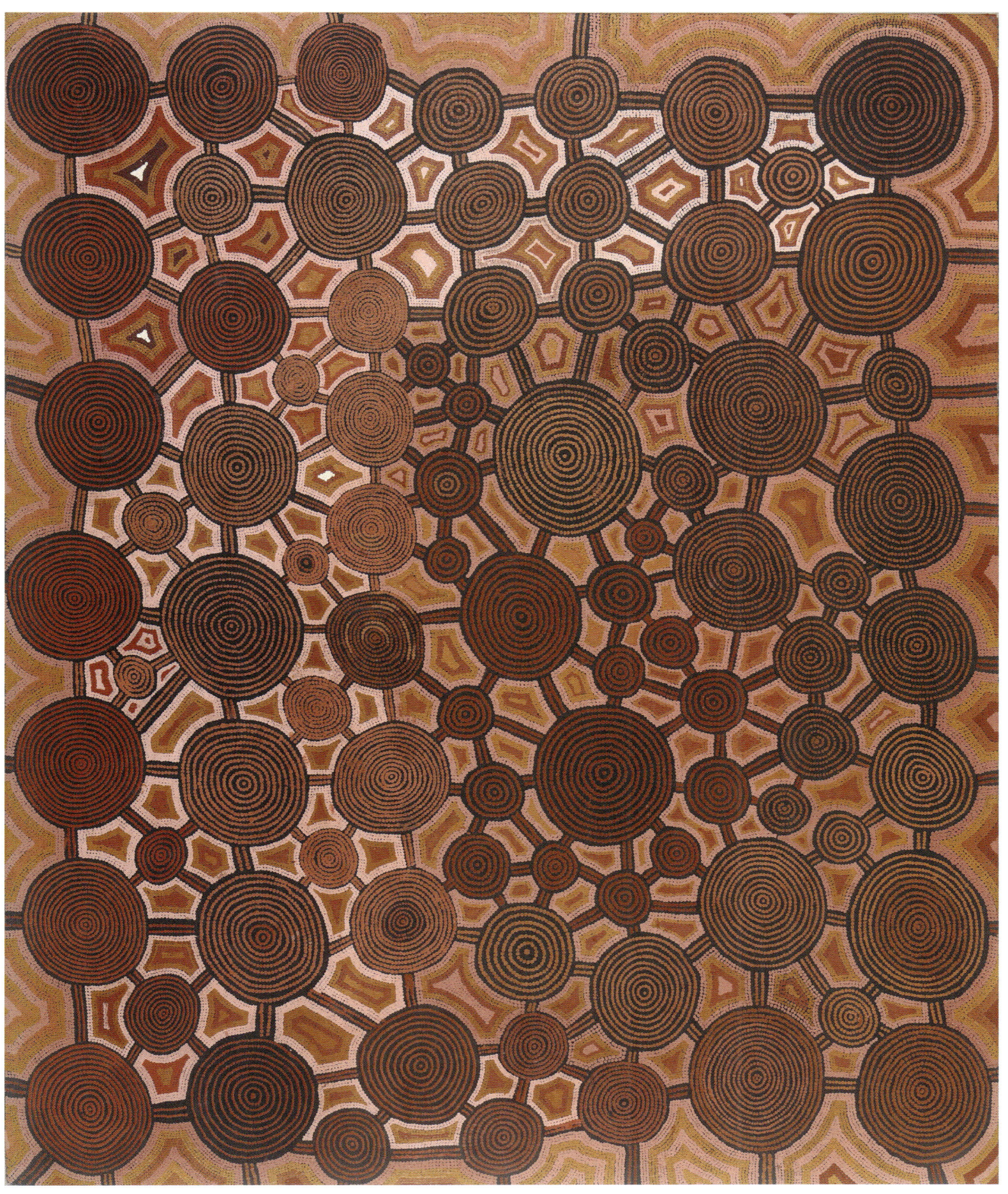

PLATE 96

Uta Uta Tjangala
*Tingarri Men at Warnmanpanya*, 1973

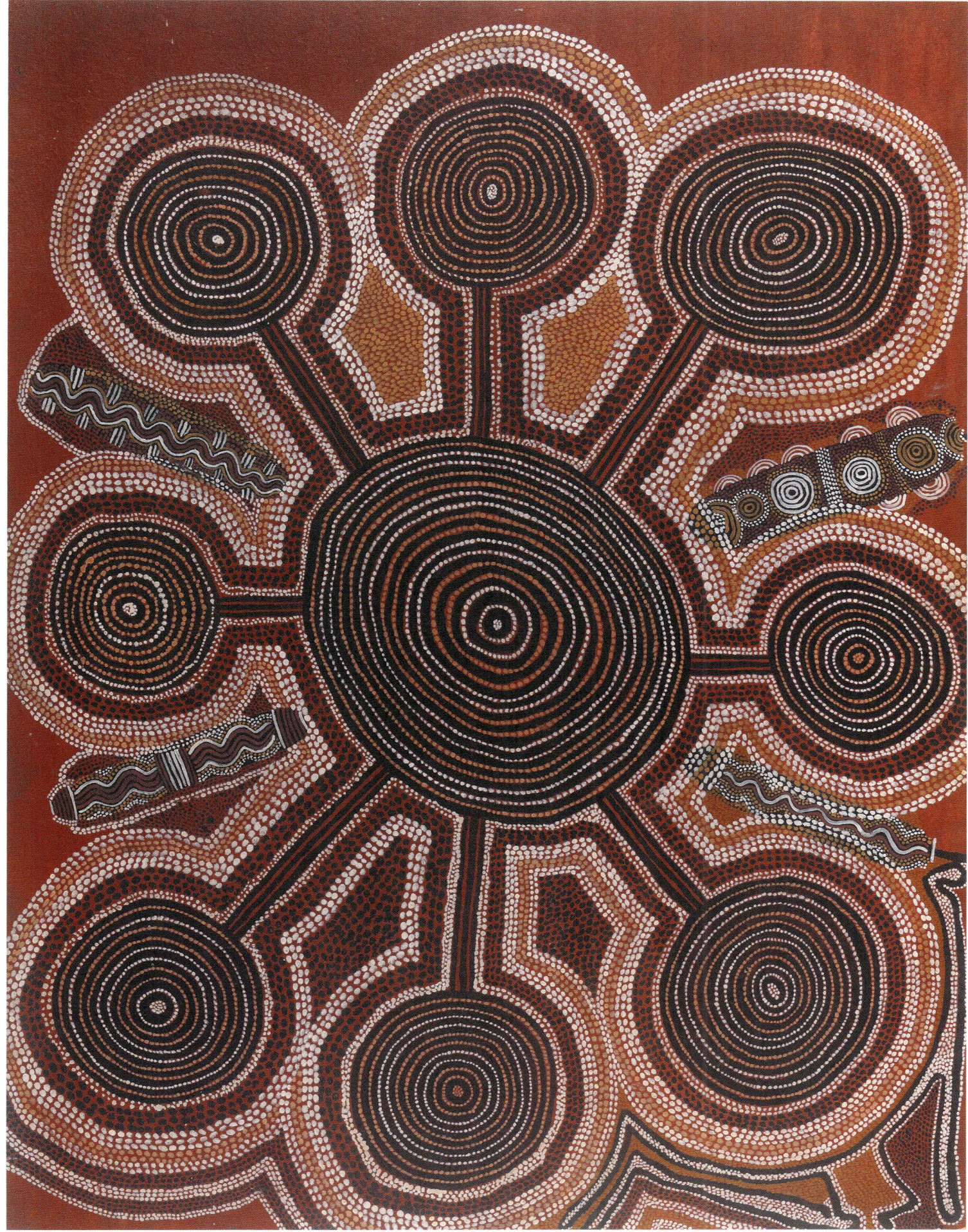

PLATE 97

Freddy West Tjakamarra
*Tingarri Men at Walawala*, 1988

My people went out to Walungurru [Kintore], lived there. From there,
my father, Freddy West Tjakamarra, moved to Kiwirrkurra. He wanted
to go back to traditional country, to Kiwirrkurra. He was from Western
Australia, he was living out there and he wanted to teach young men,
like his sons, Tony and Nicolas, and other young men. He organized a
*punyunyu* [like a university] before he passed away. Others came from
Jigalong, but they were challenged. They were really Law Men, but he
beat them. He was really number one for his song—Tingarri. Some
came from Tjukurla, like Mr. Butler and they put all the young people
in university. Everybody came from Wiluna, Jigalong and Balgo and
did a really big business, and they took them to Yaru Yaru [a major
Tingarri site]. My father wanted to show kids about his country, his
Tjukurrpa that his father gave him to teach the young ones.

This painting is Walawala. There's a carving in the cave and drawings that are still there today. I was there, I saw it. It's got water there
after rain; we've got spring water. He used to paint with circles, it's got
to be proper color, really Tingarri.

—BOBBY WEST TJUPURRULA

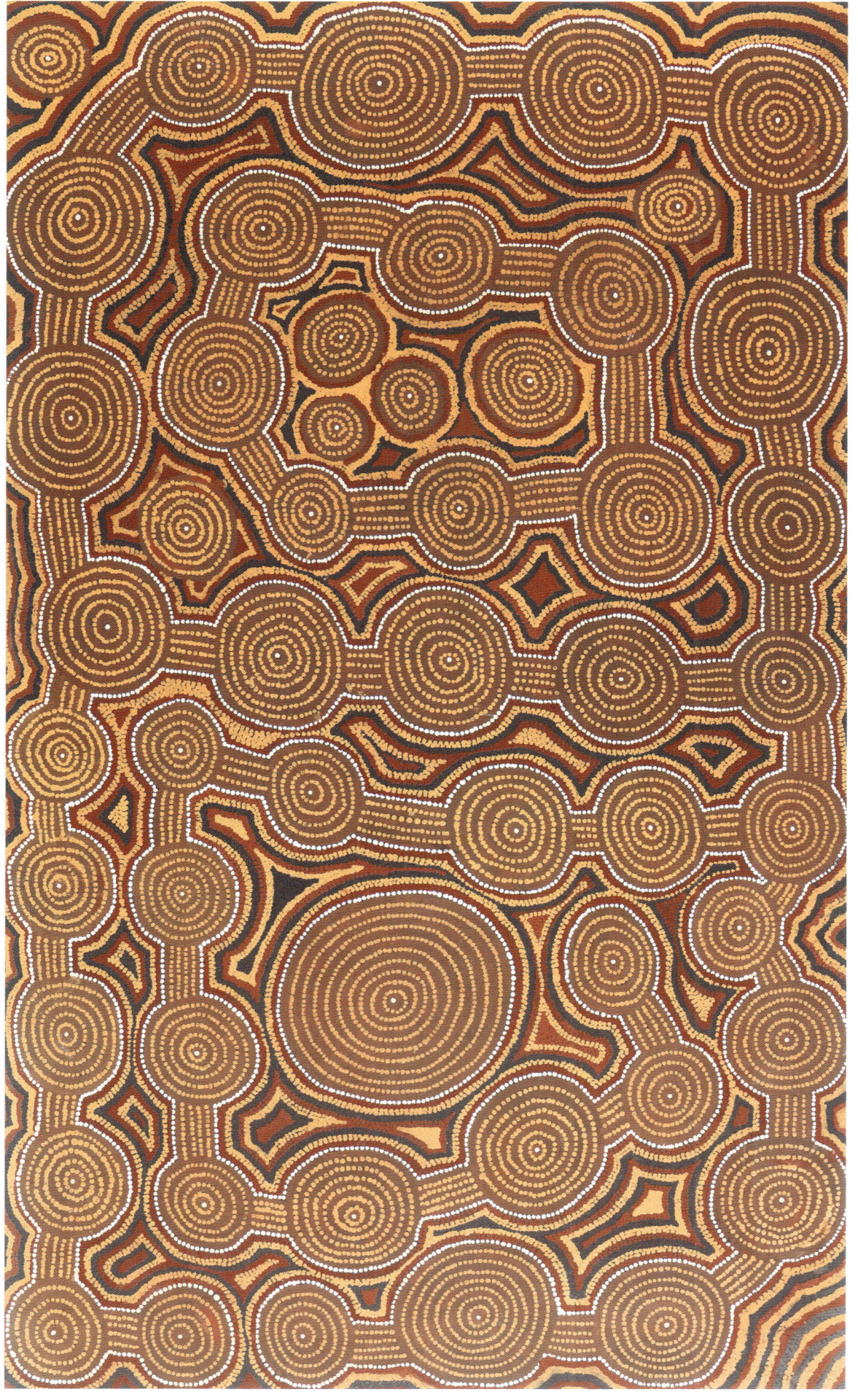

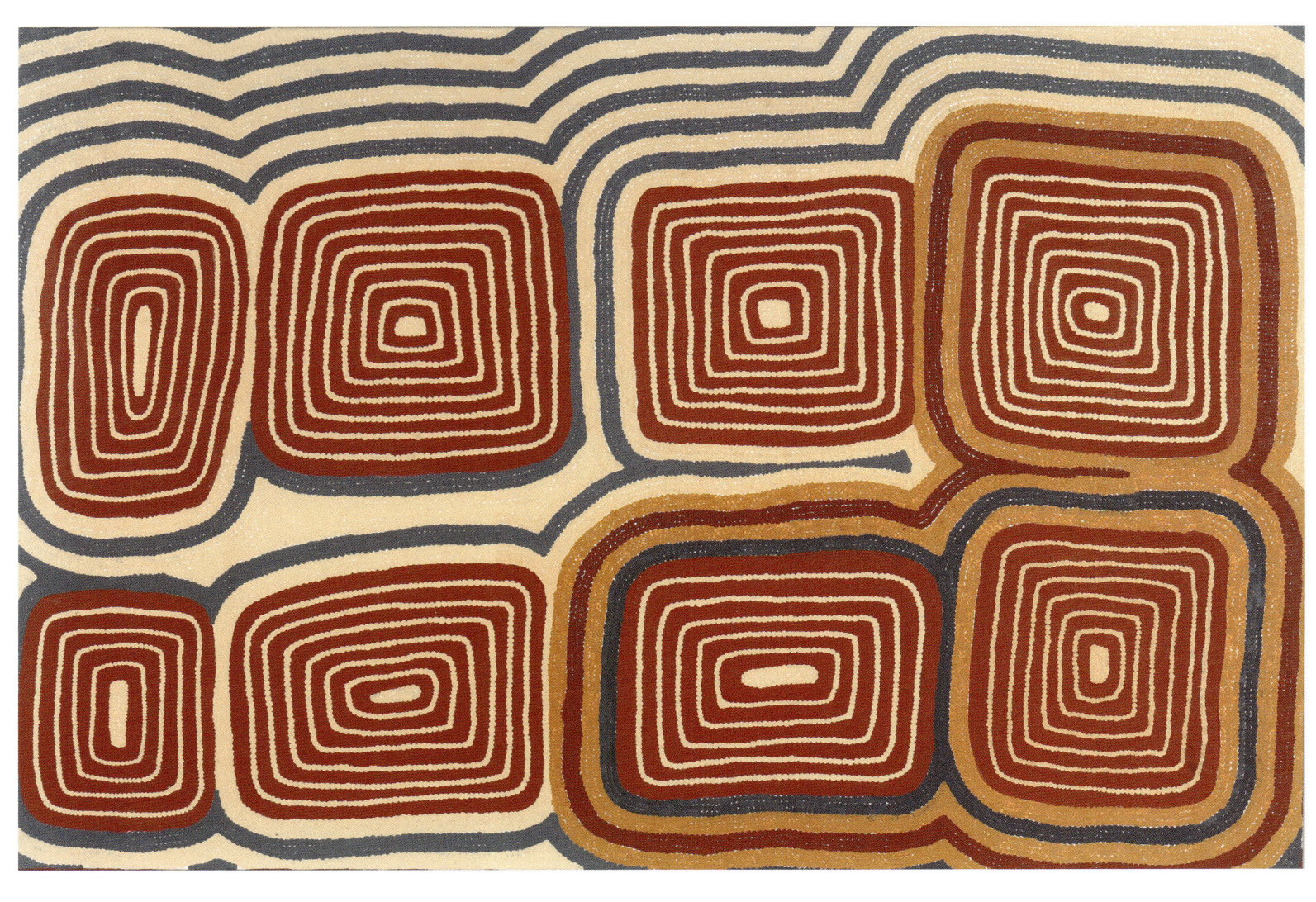

PLATE 98

Ronnie Tjampitjinpa
*Tjilkamata Ancestor Traveling*
*East from Tarkulnga*, 1988

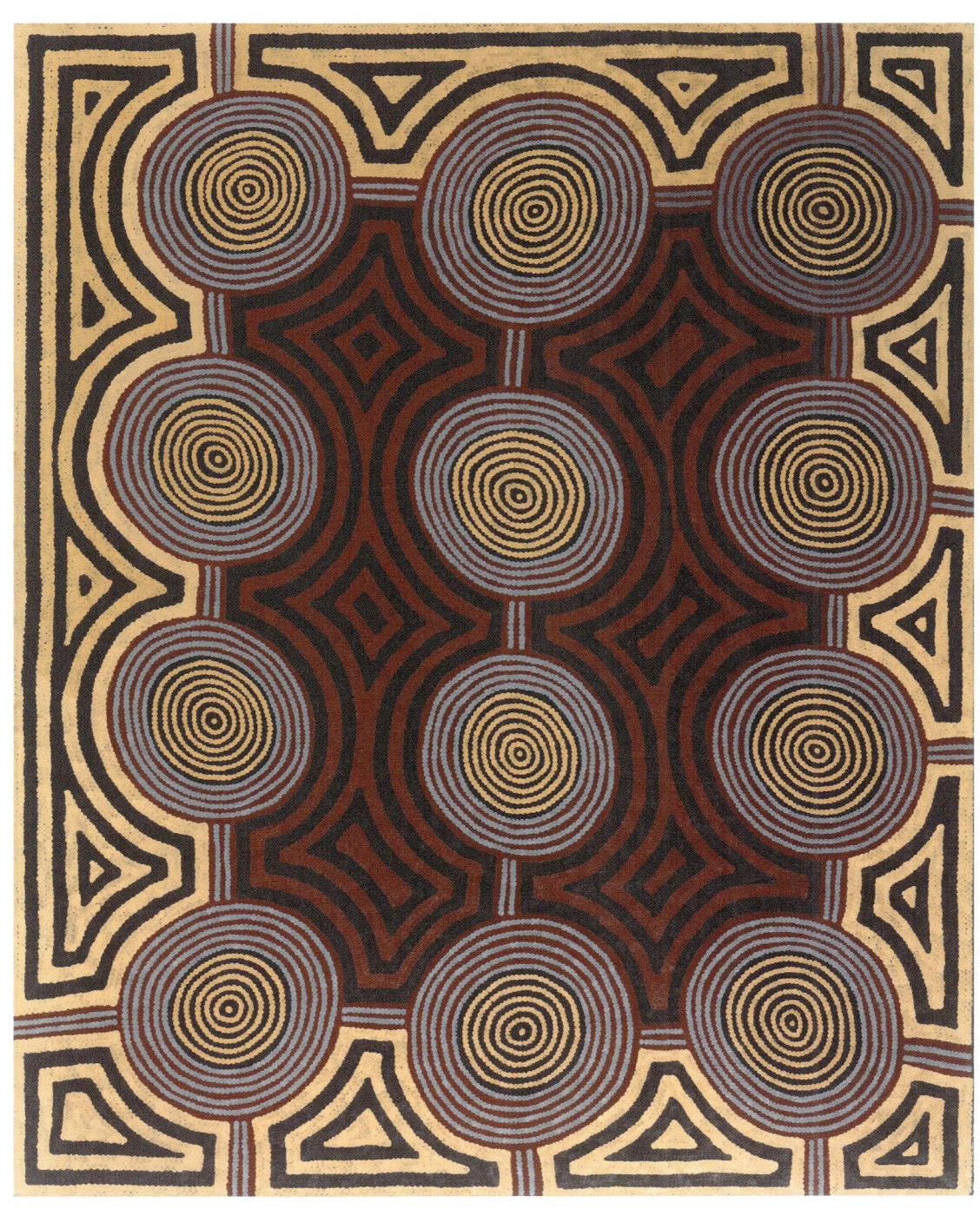

PLATE 99

Ronnie Tjampitjinpa
*Tingarritjarra*, 1989

PLATE 100

Ronnie Tjampitjinpa
*Ralyanya*, 1999

240

# Wilkinkarra

Wilkinkarra refers to the large salt lake in the north side of Pintupi country, also known as Lake Mackay. In addition to its ties to the Pintupi, Wilkinkarra also has Tjukurrpa connections to Kukatja people from Wirrimanu (Balgo) and to some Warlpiri people to the east. Two important ancestral narratives are identified with this area. One, involving a Lirru (King Brown Snake ancestor) comes through Wilkinkarra from Karrinyarra (Central Mount Wedge) in Warlpiri Country, and passes through the area on the way to Nyinmi in the west, leaving salty waters along his path. This poisonous snake is said to have left the depression that forms the lake bed by coiling and uncoiling as it rested and then, burned by fire and thrashing around, created the shape and size of the lake before traveling west. As it traveled, Lirru left salt lakes and claypans as he shed burnt skin before arriving, in weakness, at Nyinmi, where a Bandicoot ancestor bit his head and he died.

Another narrative identifies Wilkinkarra with two old men and a group called the Kanaputa women.[1] The details of this Tjukurrpa vary regionally, as it is told by people from the Wirrimanu or people from the south. The Kanaputa women from the west approached a group of old men who were leading a group of younger initiates, whom they had in hiding. The women asked for meat, which the old men gave them. But then—depending on the version of the story—either seeing the bright red headbands of the young men or noticing a spear head still in the meat, the women realized there were young men present and desired them. The Kanaputa women had intercourse with the young men, angering the jealous elders, who then set fire to the spinifex. The fire engulfed everyone, killing them. But the women, it is said, revived and traveled underground and escaped to head north. Wilkinkarra—the salt lake—formed as a result of the fire and the ashes left behind.

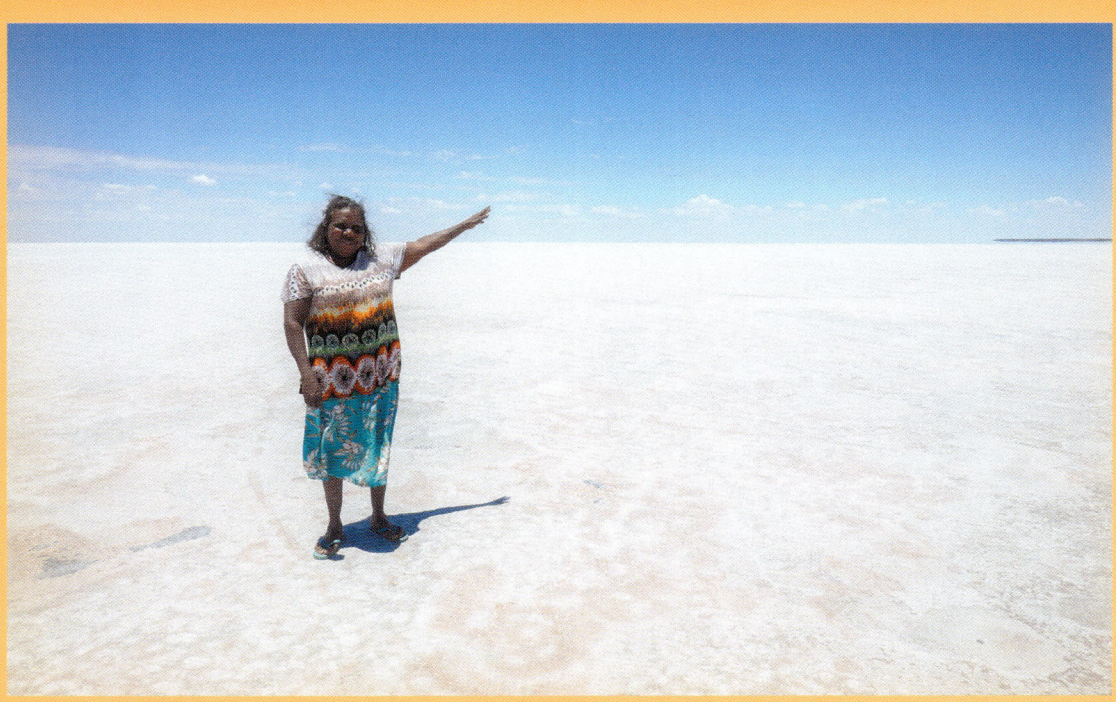

1. The term Kanaputa is widely used and relates to a range of women's Tjukurrpa and ceremonies that are shared by Warlpiri, Kukatja and Pintupi women.

Marlene Nampitjinpa Spencer at Wilkinkarra, 2014. Photo by Matt Frost.

FACING | PLATE 101

Nyilyari Tjapangati
*Wilkinkarra*, 2011

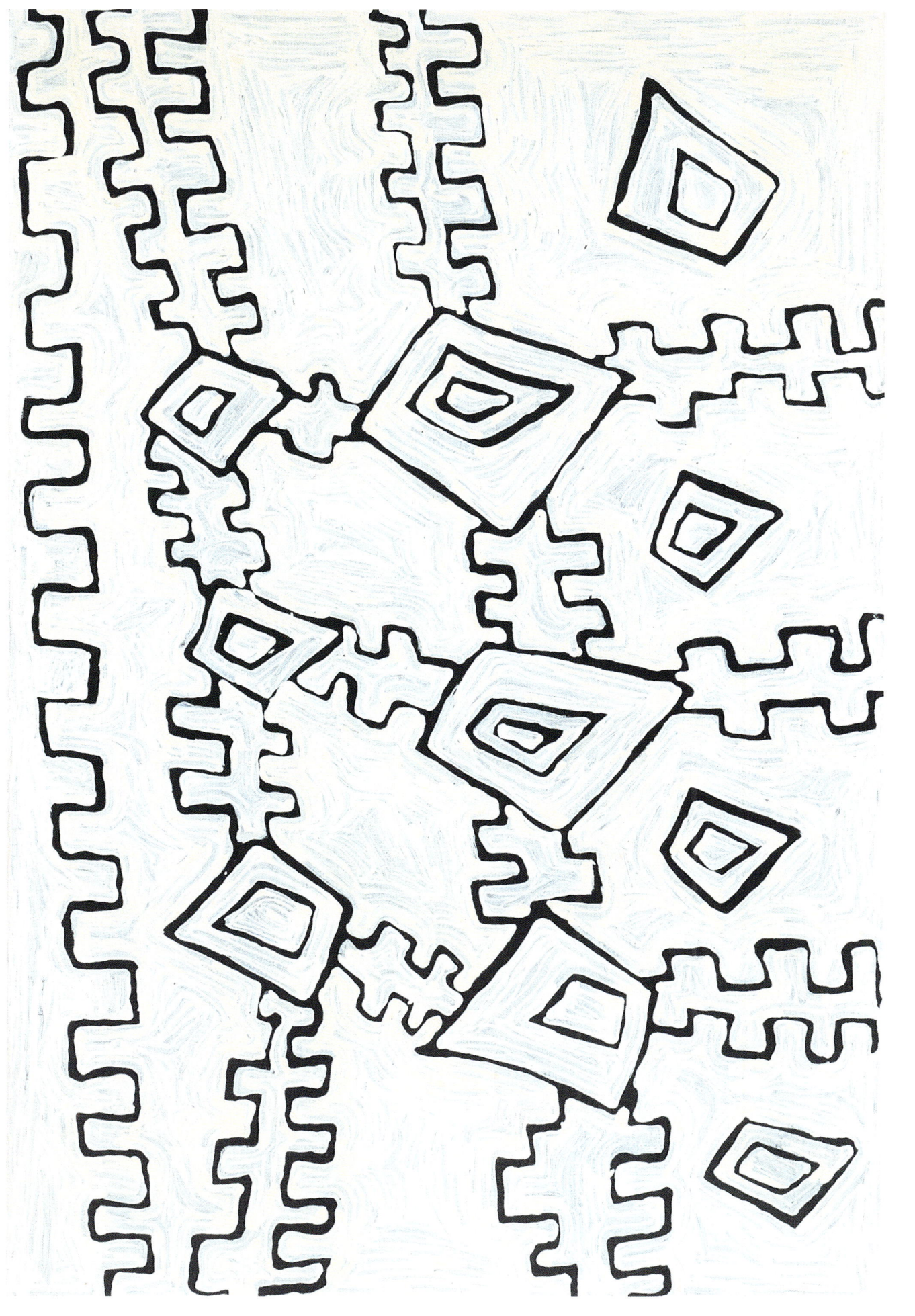

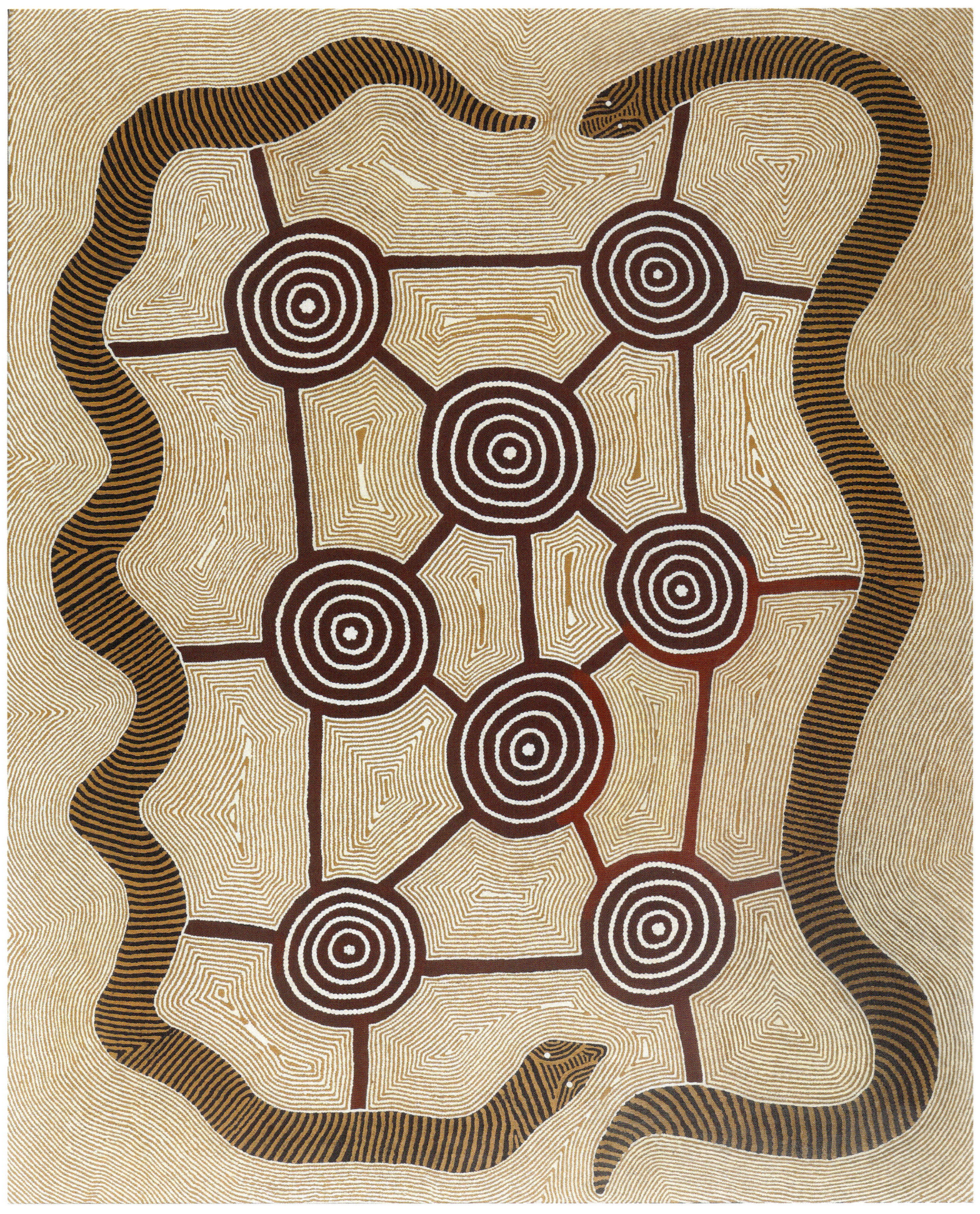

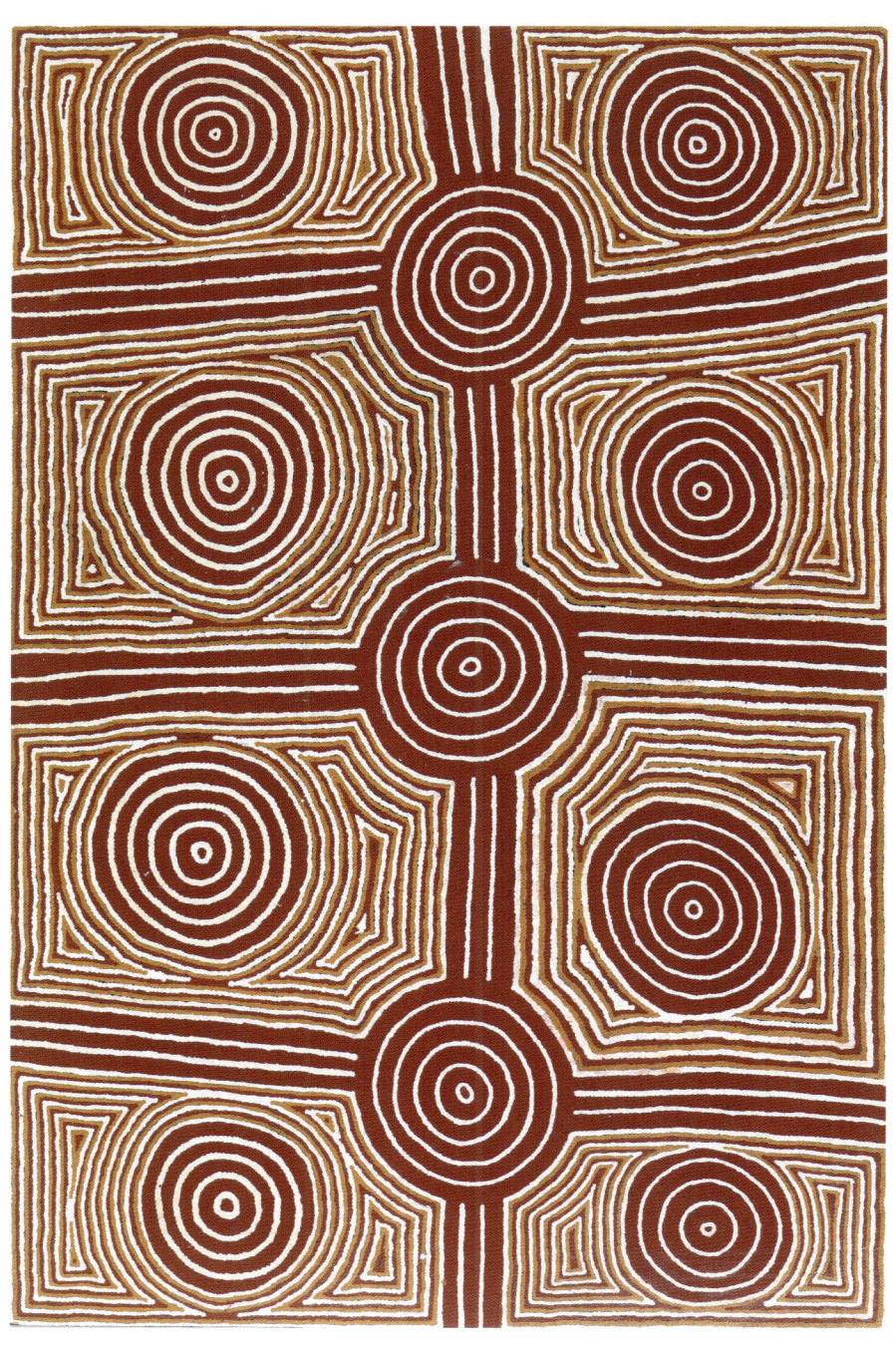

PLATE 104

George Tjungurrayi
*Mamultjunkunya,* 1999

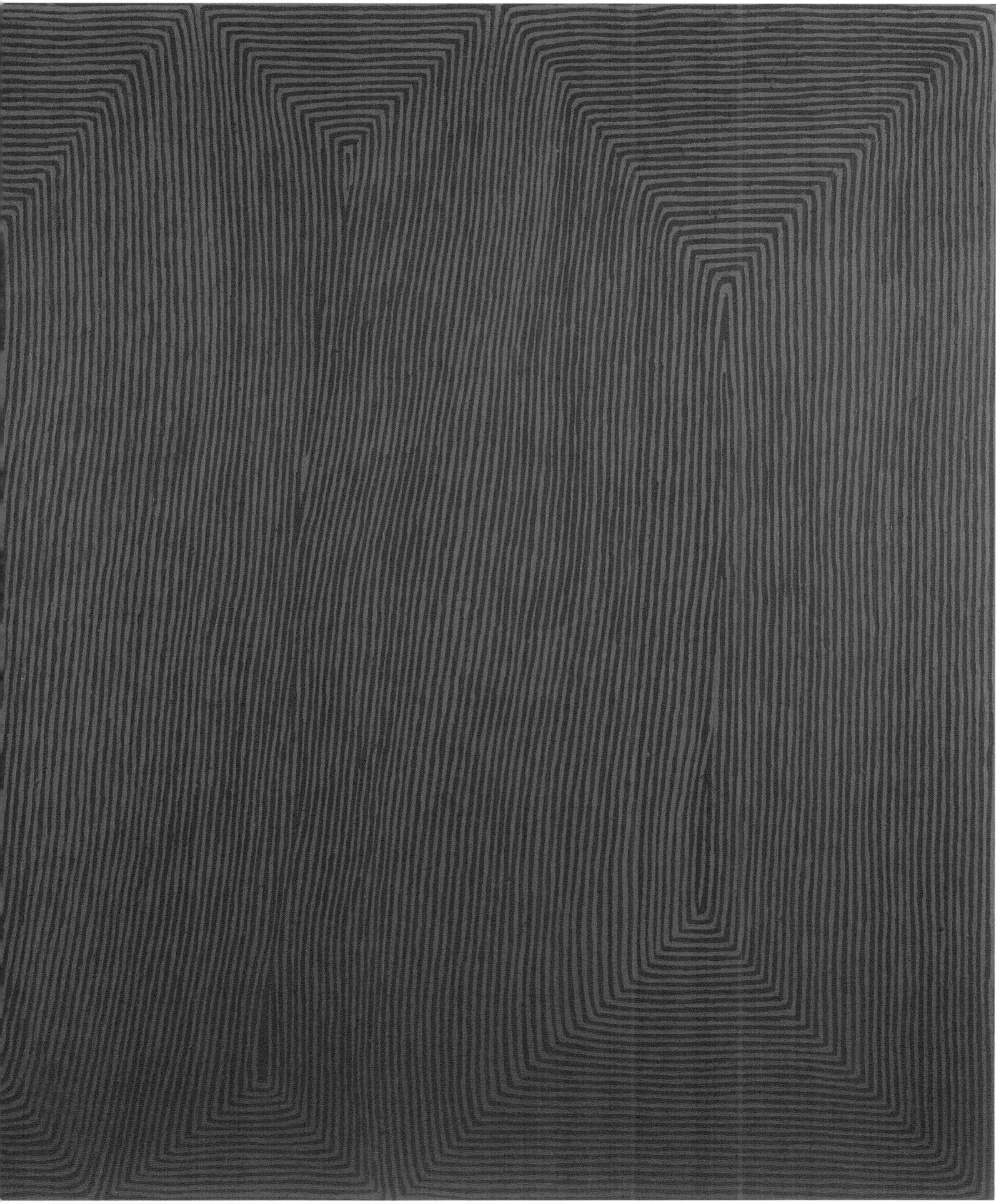

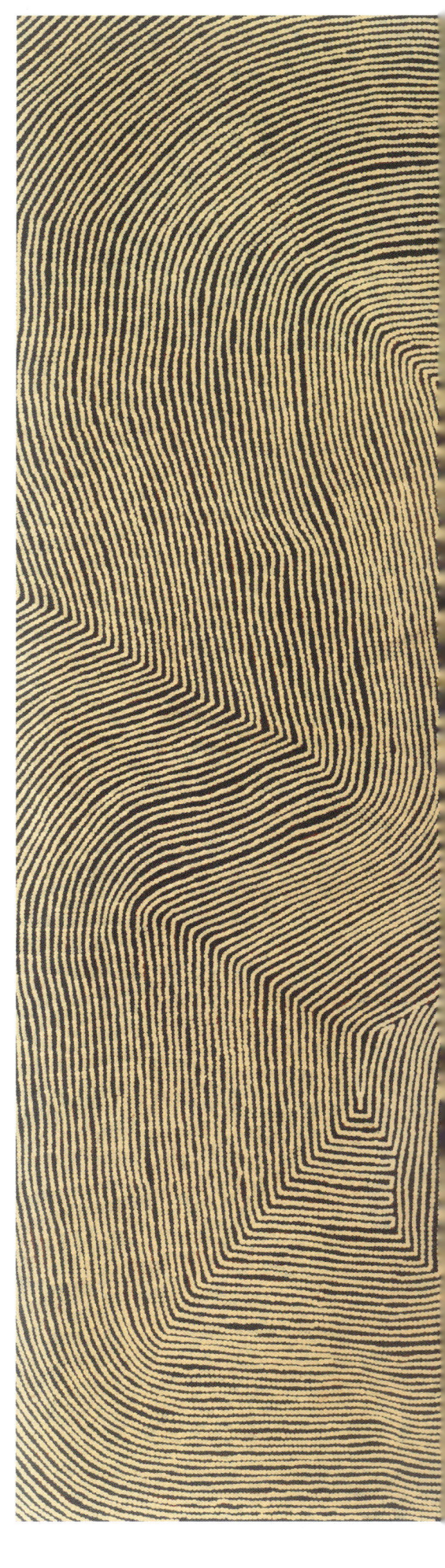

PLATE 105

Warlimpirrnga Tjapaltjarri
*Maruwa*, 2013

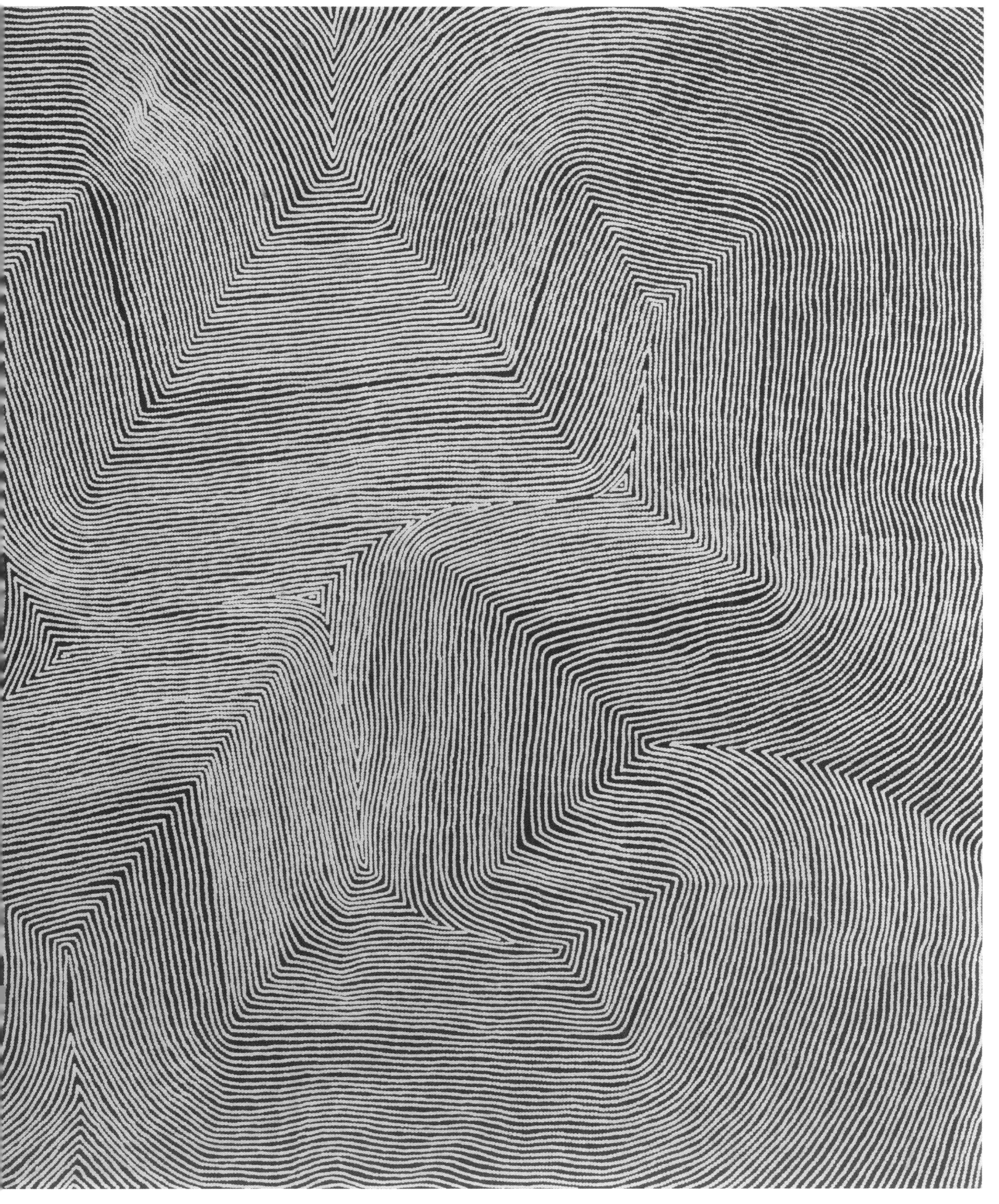

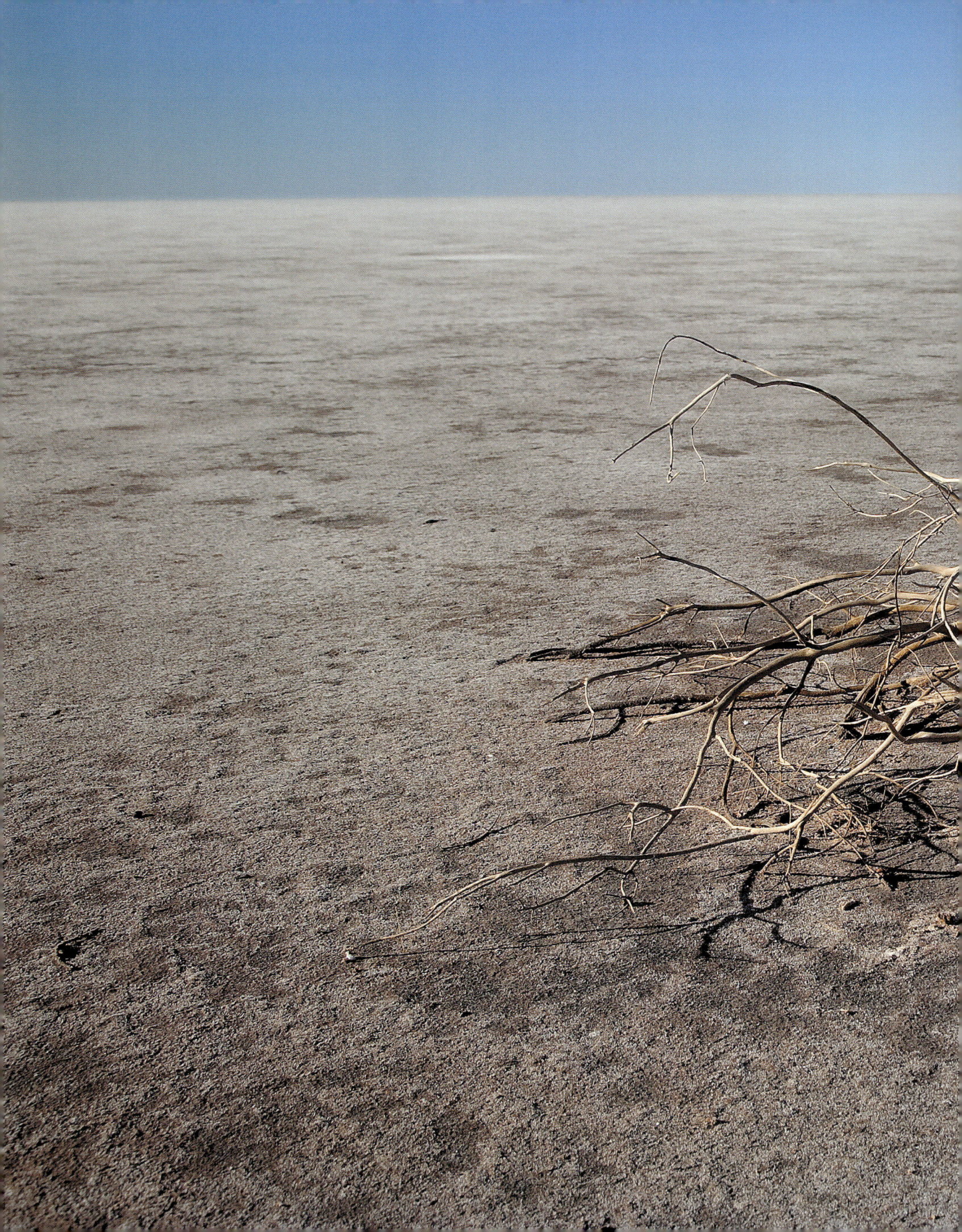

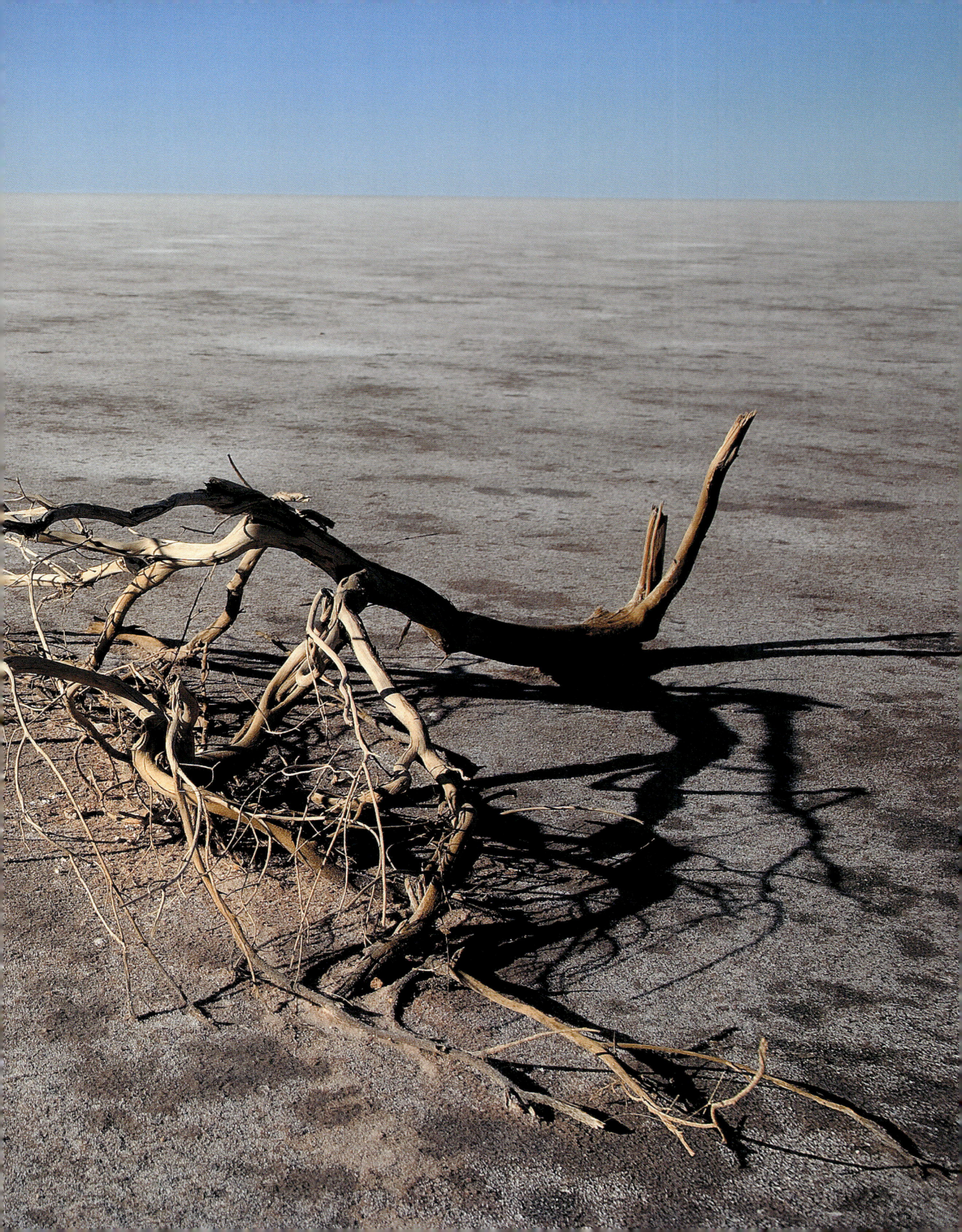

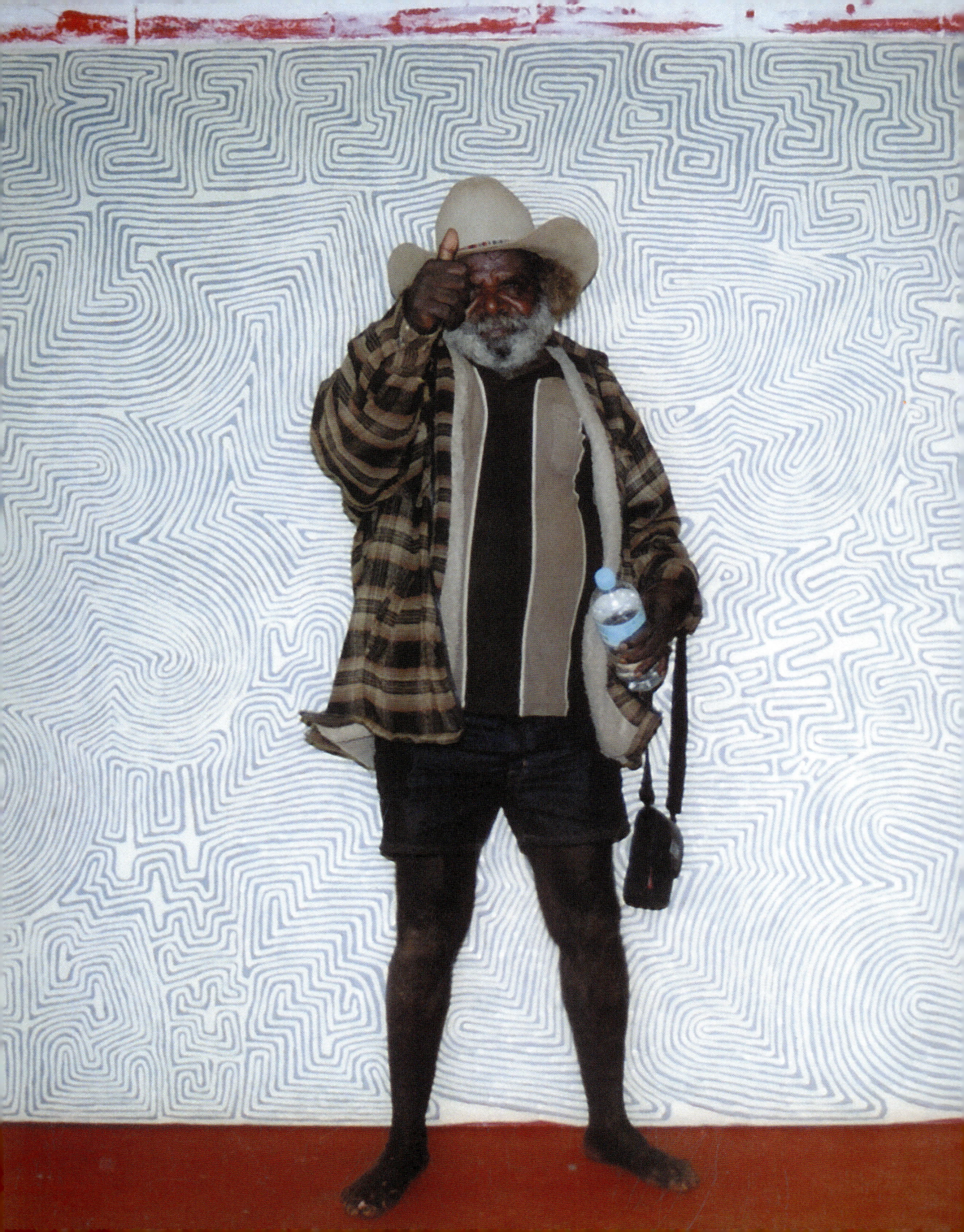

# THE PAPUNYA TULA FIFTIETH ANNIVERSARY SUITE

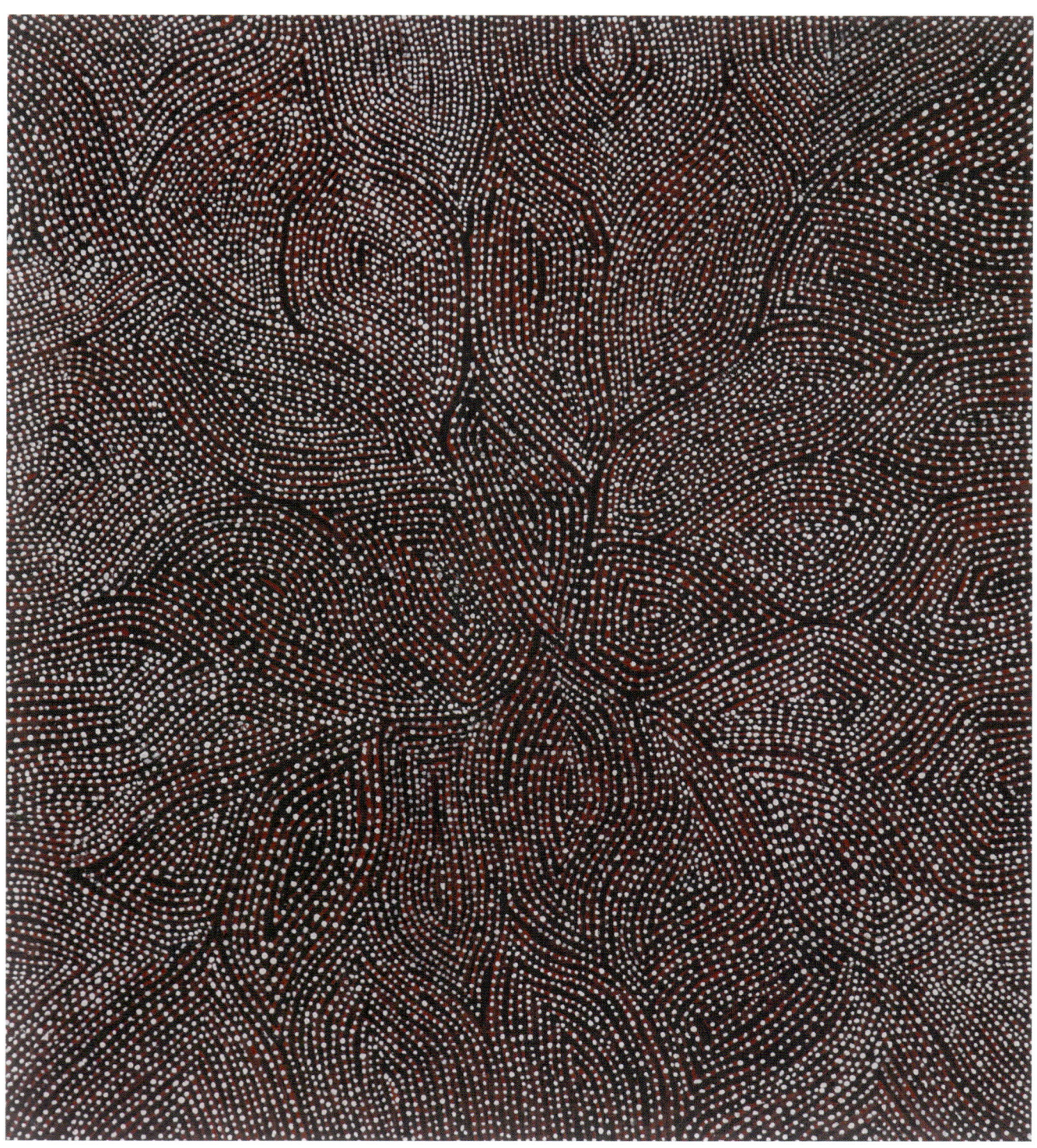

PLATE 106
Richard Yukenbarri Tjakamarra
*Ngunyarrmanya,* 2020

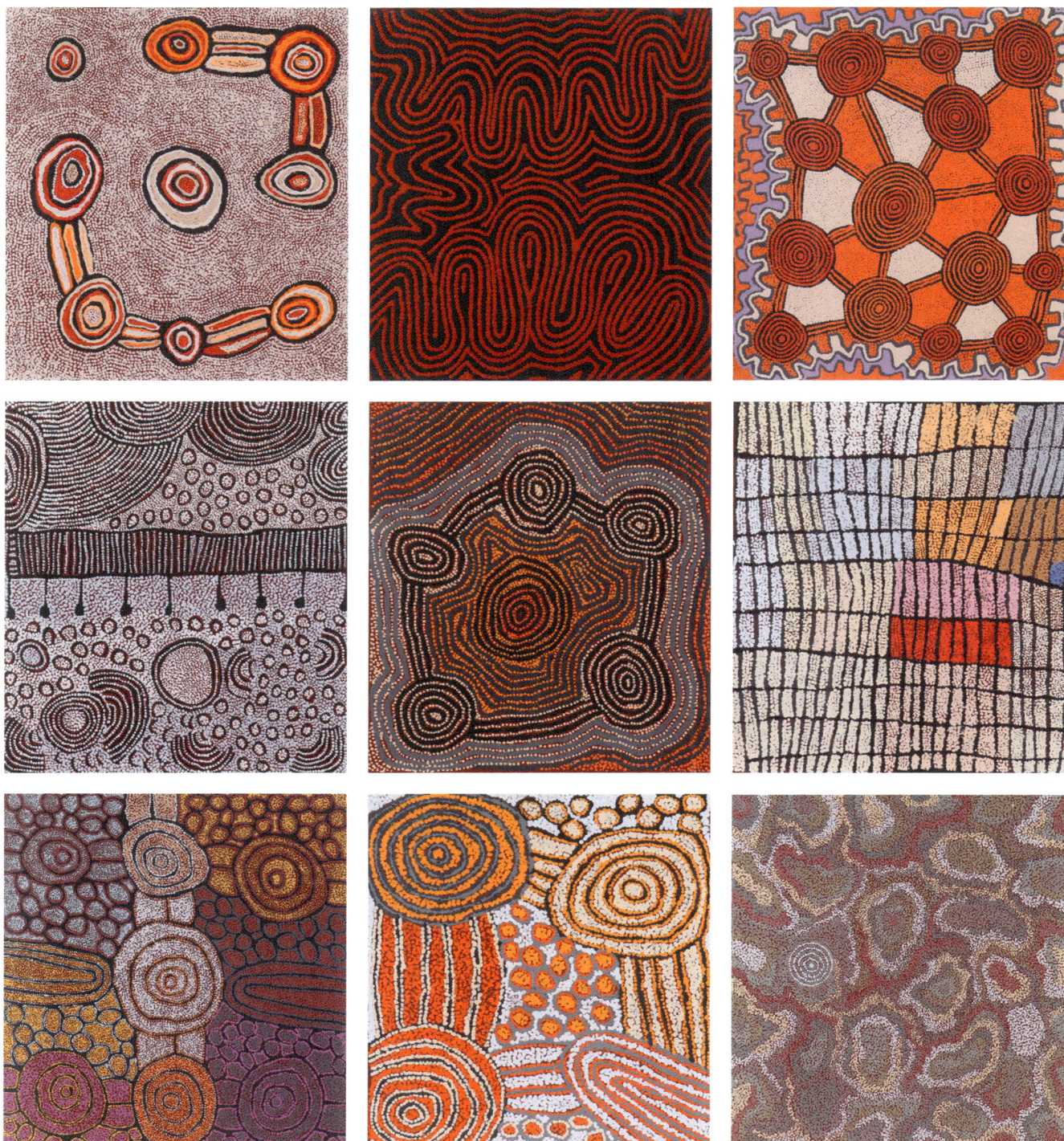

PLATE 107
Lucy Loomoo Nungurrayi
*Maluri*, 2015

PLATE 108
Joan Loomoo Nampitjinpa
*Kingfisher Dreaming at Namalu*, 2002

PLATE 109
Patrick Tjungurrayi
*Ngalkalarra*, 2017

PLATE 110
Yinarupa Nangala
*Mukula*, 2020

PLATE 111
Charlie Tjapangati
*Pirrinya*, 2018

PLATE 112
Josephine Nangala
*Nyinmi*, 2020

PLATE 113
Katherine Nakamarra
*Kutungu at Tjintjintjin*, 2021

PLATE 114
Debra Nakamarra
*Tjintjintjin*, 2020

PLATE 115
John West Tjupurrula
*Palipalintjanya*, 2021

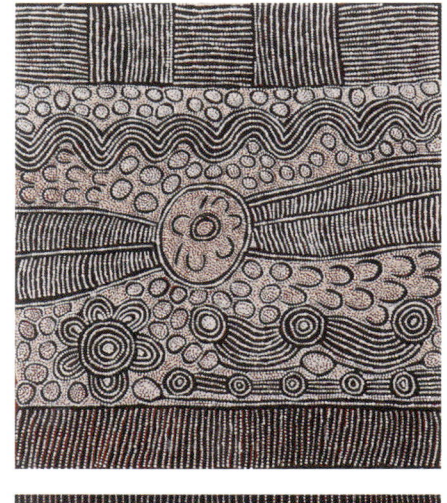
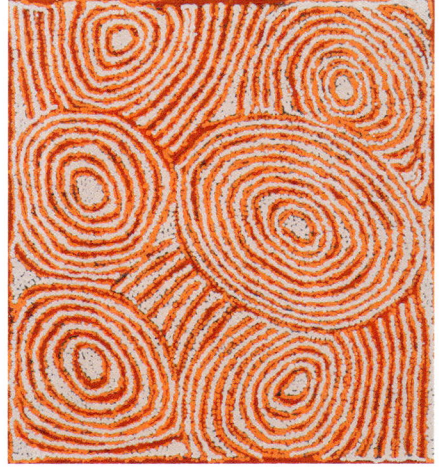
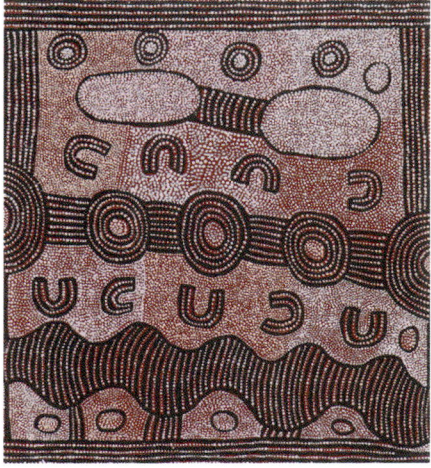

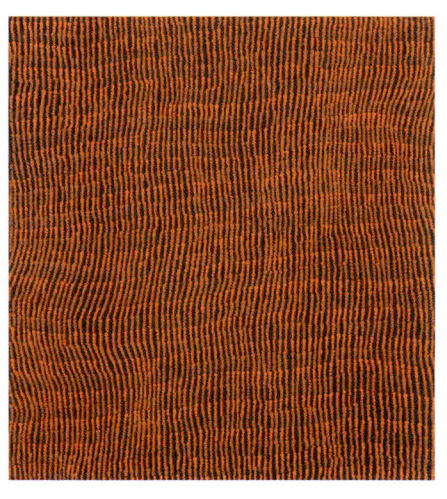
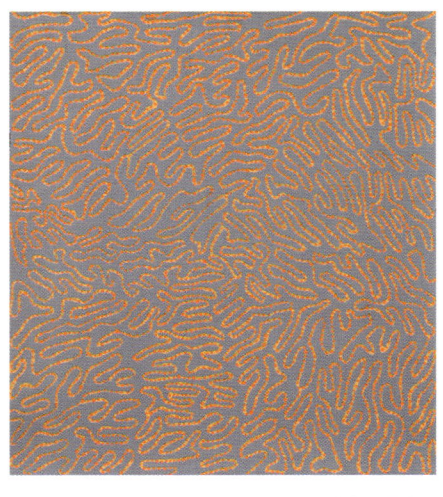
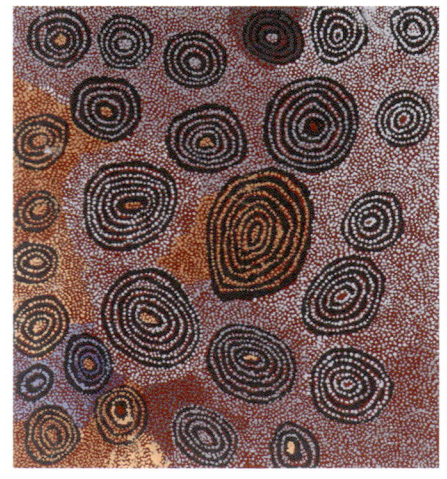

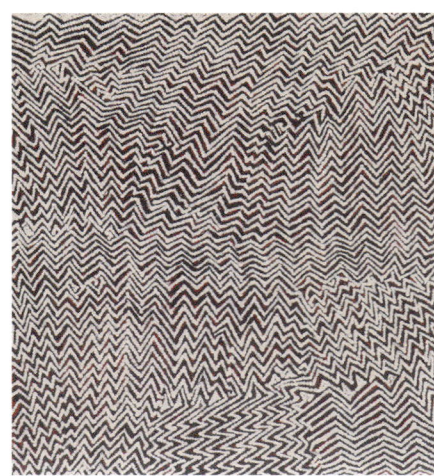

PLATE 116
Yalti Napangati
*Marrapinti*, 2020

PLATE 117
Walangkura Napanangka
(Johnny Yungut's wife)
*Marrapinti*, 2006

PLATE 118
Payu Napaltjarri
*Marrapinti*, 2019

PLATE 119
Mantua Nangala
*Marrapinti*, 2021

PLATE 120
Yukultji Napangati
*Marrapinti*, 2020

PLATE 121
Joseph Jurra Tjapaltjarri
*Yunarla*, 2021

PLATE 122
Nanyuma Napangati
*Ngaminya*, 2020

PLATE 123
Bombatu Napangati
*Ancestral Women at Ngaminya*, 2020

PLATE 124
Bobby West Tjupurrula
*Tarkul*, 2018

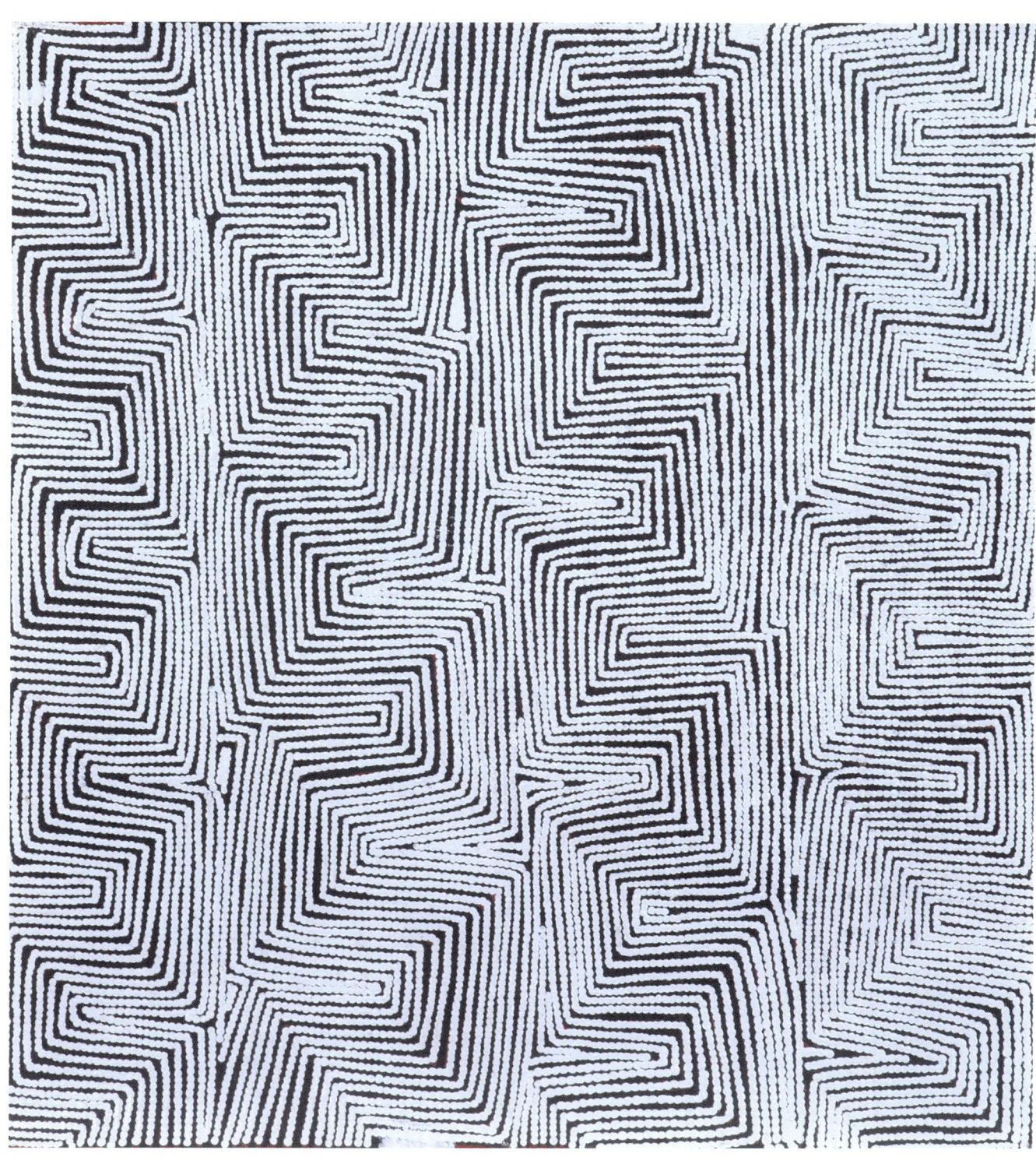

PLATE 125
Ray James Tjangala
*Yunarla*, 2021

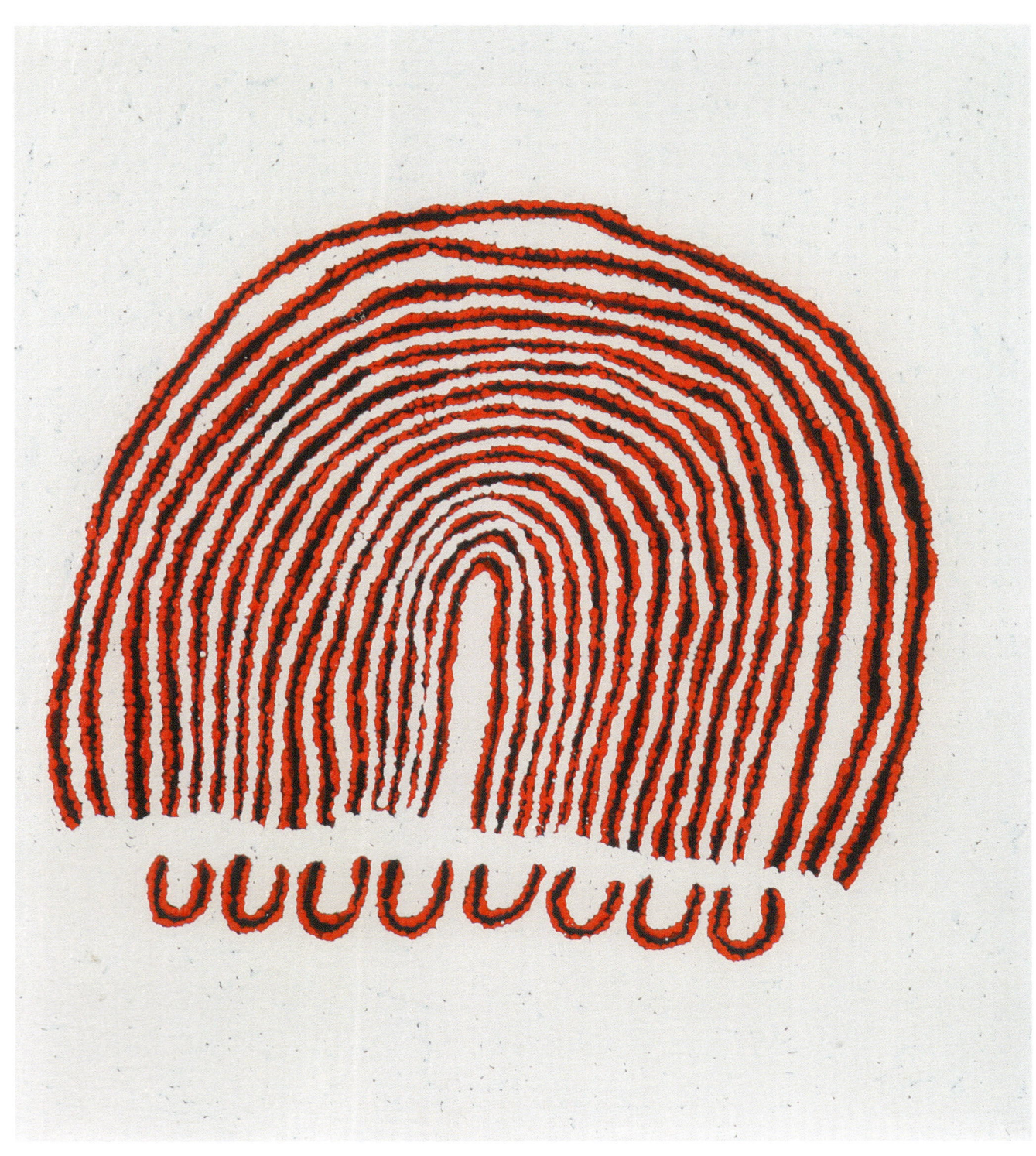

PLATE 126
Yuyuya Nampitjinpa
*Yumari*, 2019

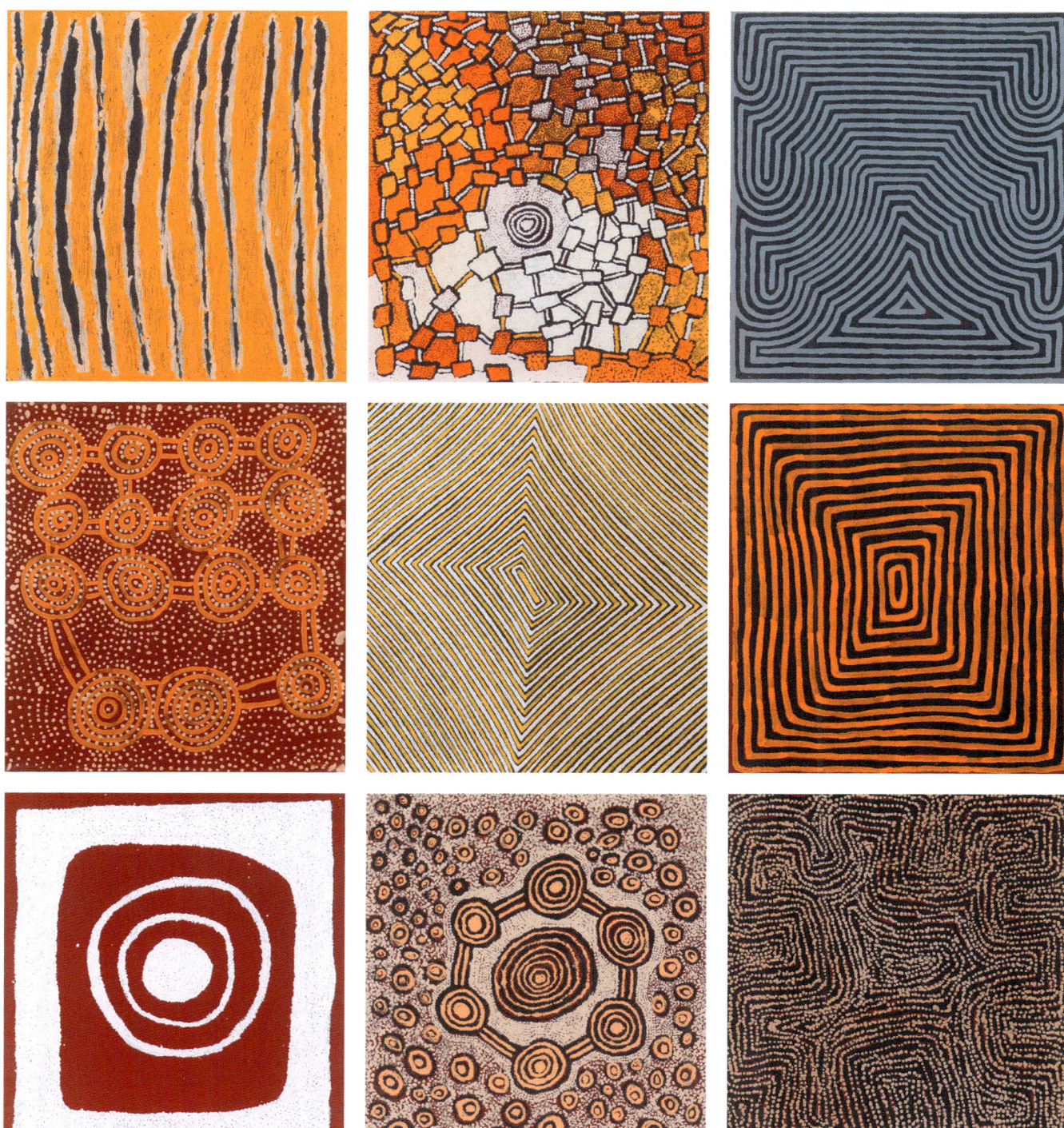

PLATE 127
Tjunkiya Napaltjarri
*Yumari*, 2009

PLATE 128
Edith Nampitjinpa
*Tarkul*, 2019

PLATE 129
Aubrey Tjangala
*Walungurru*, 2020

PLATE 130
Martin Tjampitjinpa
*Muyinnga*, 2004

PLATE 131
Raymond Maxwell Tjampitjinpa
*Kaakurutintjinya*, 2020

PLATE 132
Ronnie Tjampitjinpa
*Walungurru*, 2015

PLATE 133
Morris Gibson Tjapaltjarri
*Kaakurutintjinya*, 2016

PLATE 134
Hilary Tjapaltjarri
*Nyiinkuwakalnga*, 2015

PLATE 135
George Ward Tjungurrayi
*Tingarri at Kalkuritja*, 2012

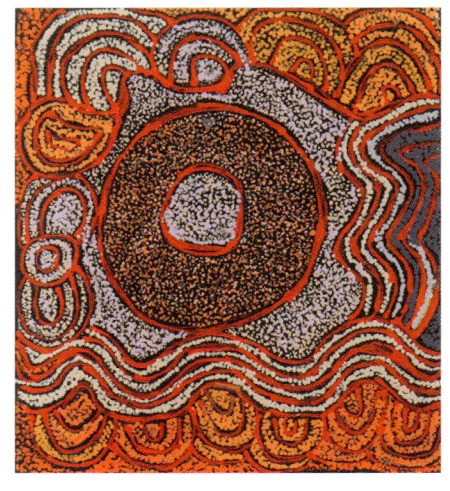
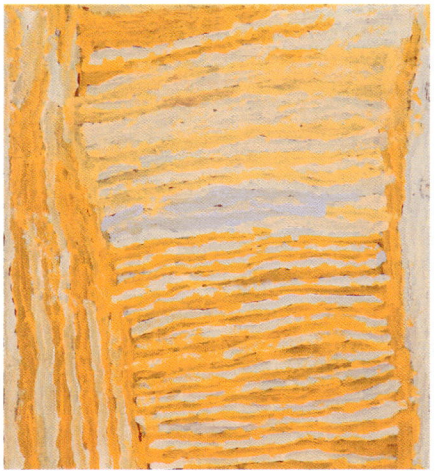
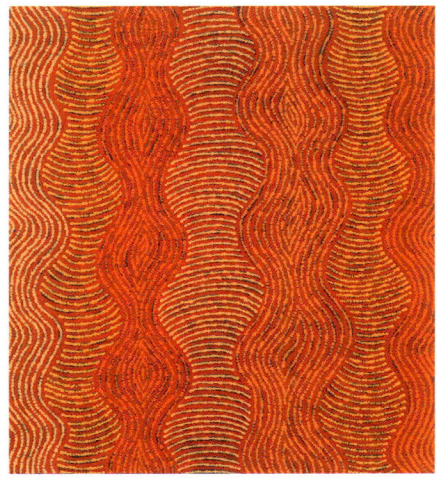
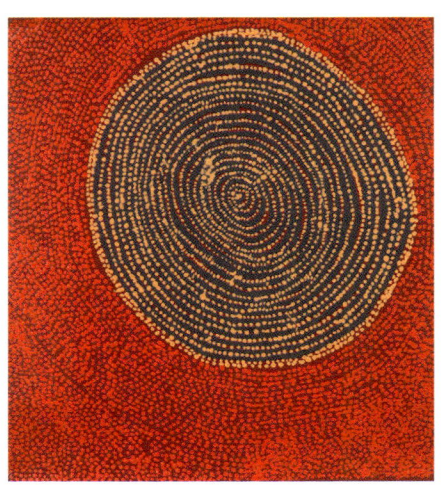
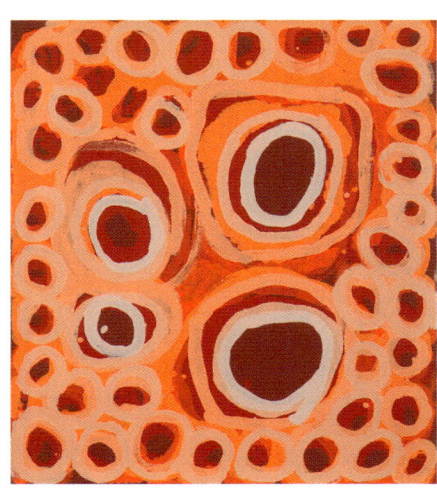
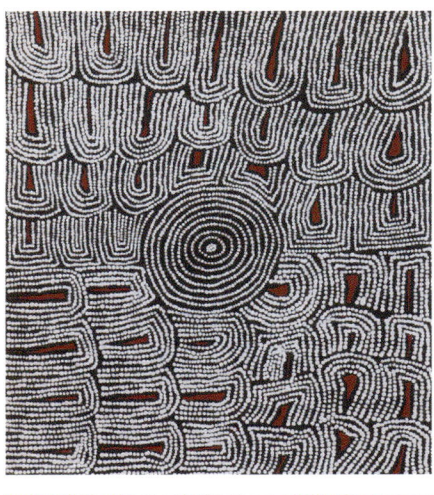
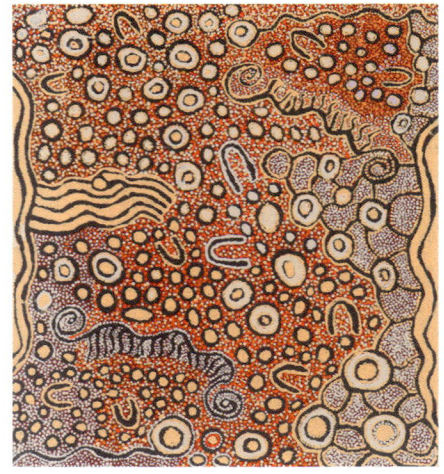
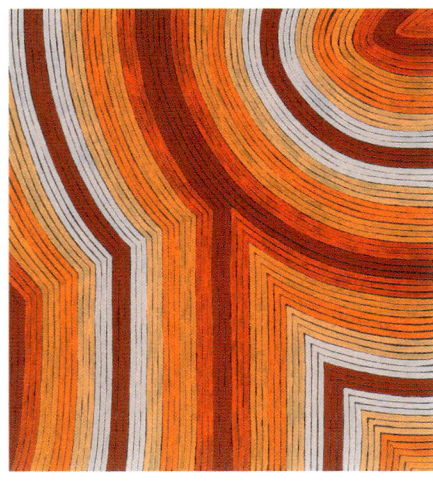
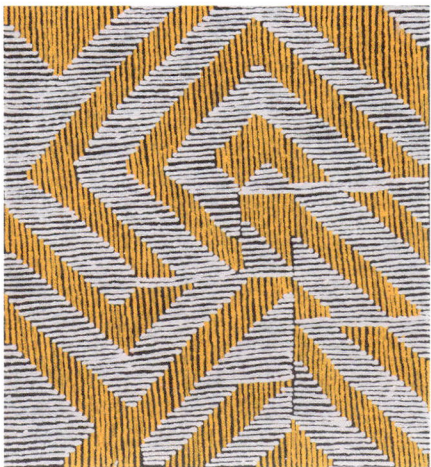

PLATE 136
Jacqueline Reid Nakamarra
*Lupulnga*, 2020

PLATE 137
Makinti Napanangka
*Lupulnga*, 2008

PLATE 138
Patricia Jackson Napanangka
*Lupulnga*, 2020

PLATE 139
Willy Tjungurrayi
*Kirritjinya*, 2016

PLATE 140
Katarra Butler Napaltjarri
*Ancestral Women at Tjukurla*, 2015

PLATE 141
Rosie Nampitjinpa
*Yilpikarri*, 2021

PLATE 142
Rubilee Napurrula
*Yuwalki*, 2020

PLATE 143
Adam Gibbs Tjapaltjarri
*Ngari Tjukurrpa (Honey Ant Dreaming)*
*at Papunya*, 2020

PLATE 144
Elizabeth Marks Nakamarra
*Kalipinypa*, 2021

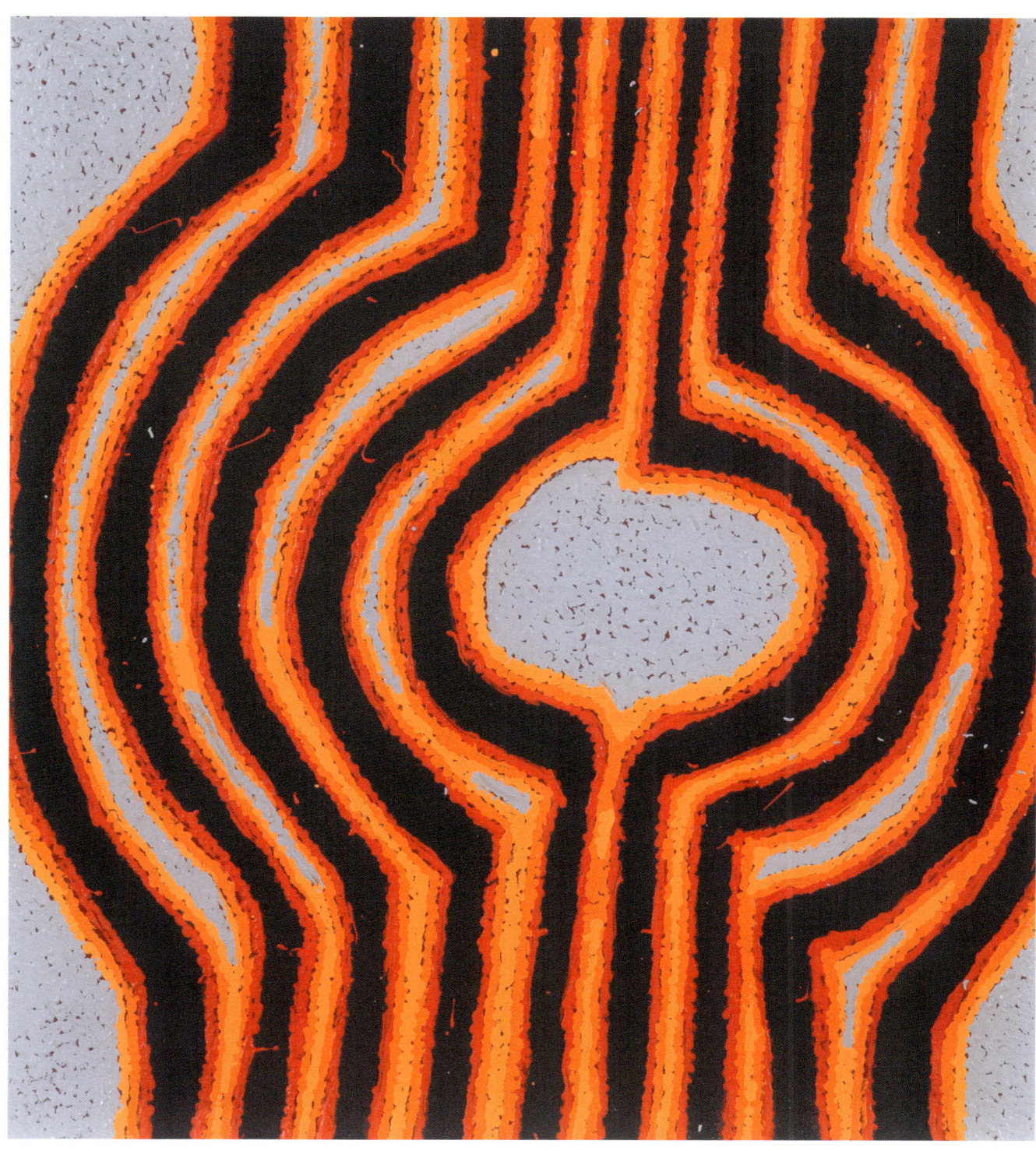

PLATE 145
Eileen Napaltjarri
*Tjitururrnga*, 2020

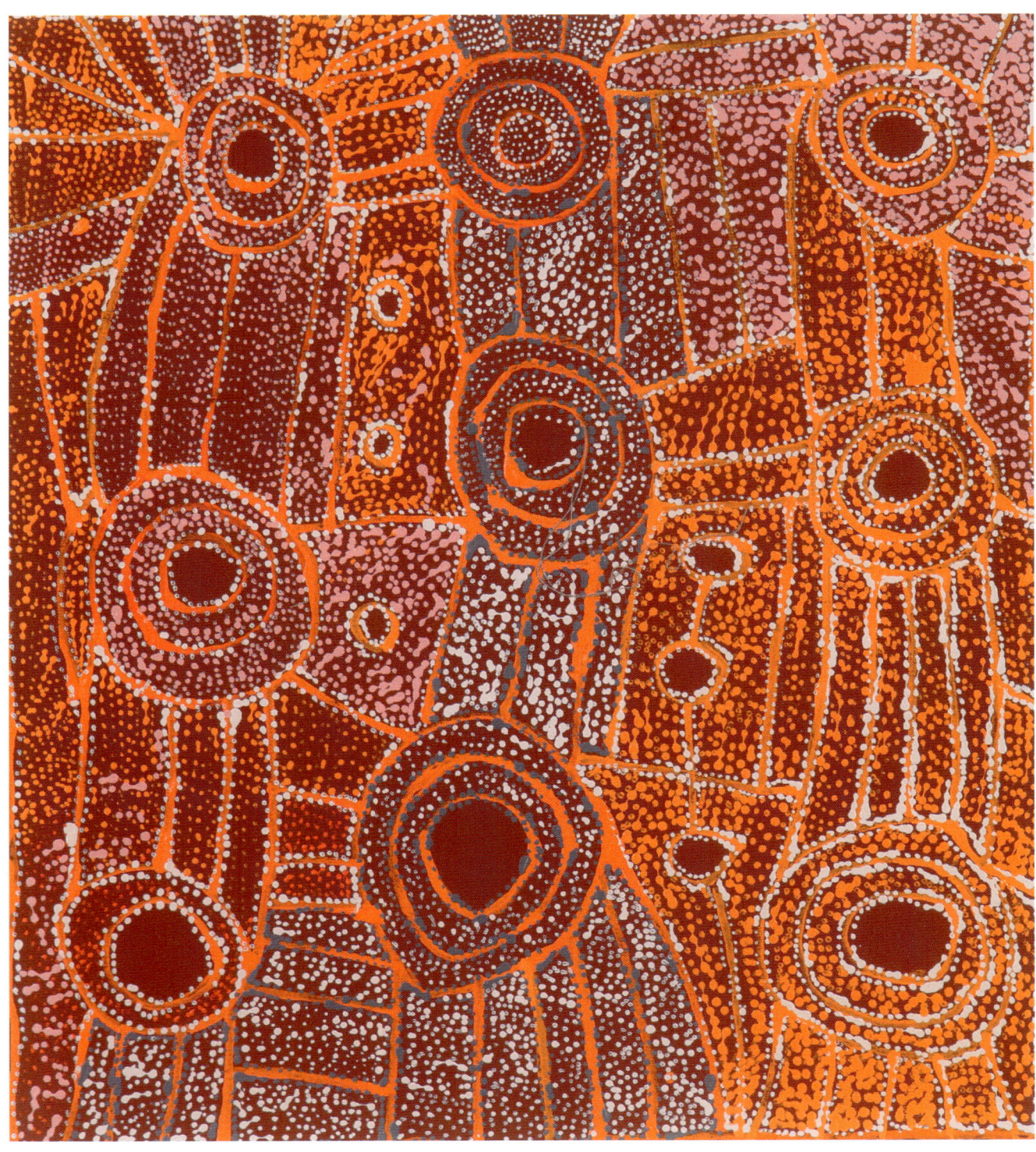

PLATE 146
Mary Napangati
*Tjutalpi*, 2020

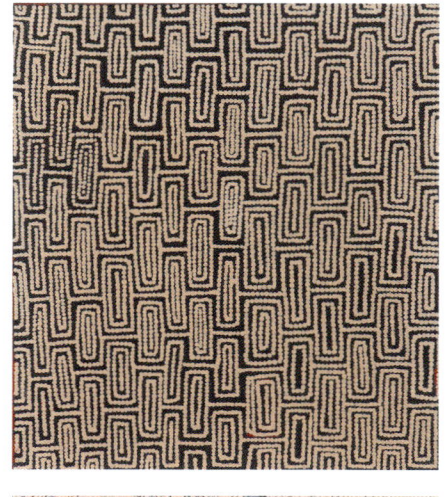
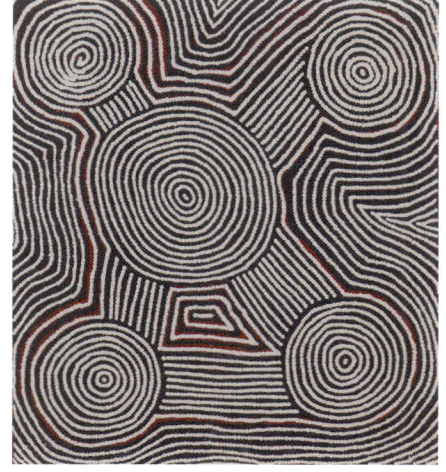
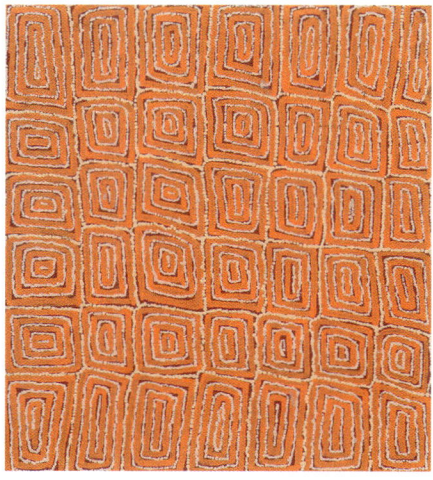
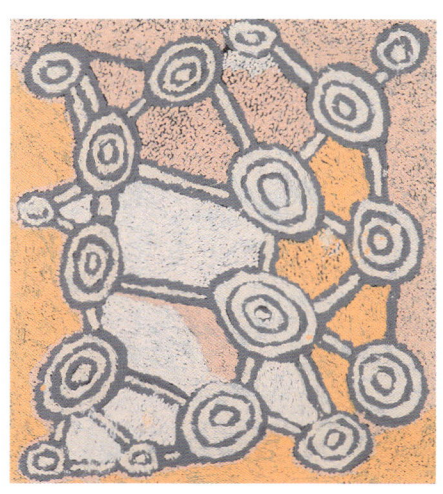
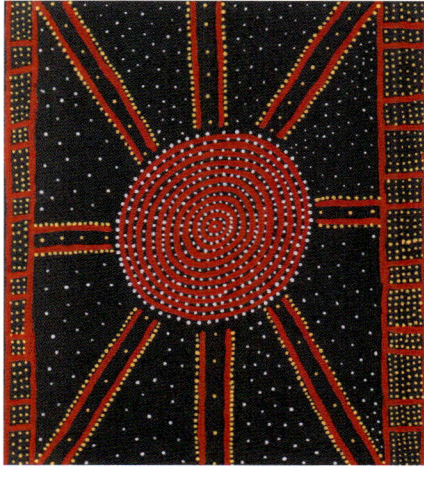
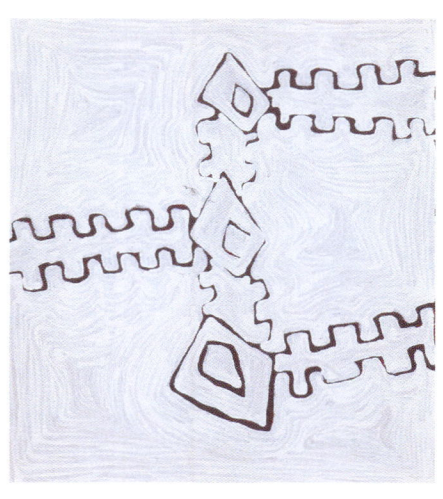
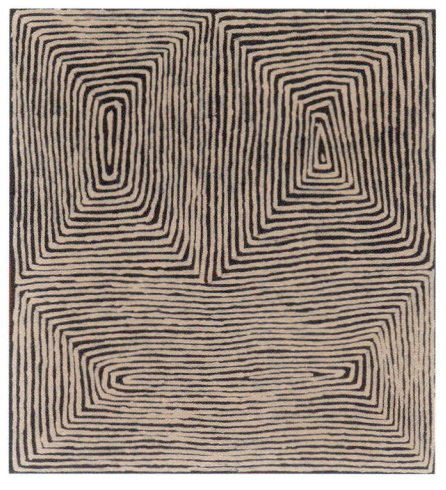
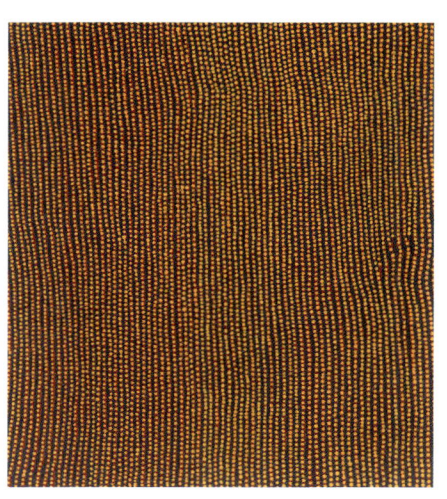
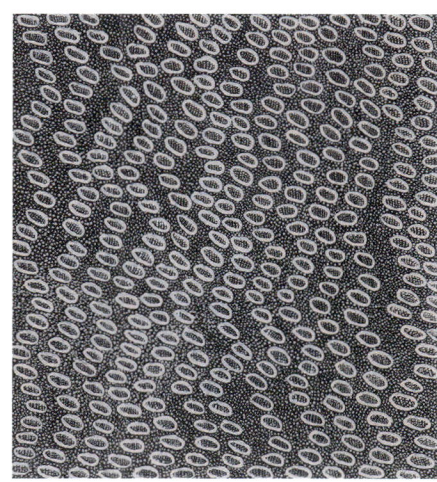

PLATE 147
Angus Tjungurrayi
*Claypan at Murmur*, 2018

PLATE 148
Warlimpirrnga Tjapaltjarri
*Maruwa*, 2016

PLATE 149
Tamayinya Tjapangati
*Wilkinkarra*, 2018

PLATE 150
Johnny Yungut Tjupurrula
*Tjangimanta*, 2011

PLATE 151
Matthew Tjapangati
*Tingarri Men at Murmur*, 2017

PLATE 152
Nyilyari Tjapangati
*Wilkinkarra*, 2017

PLATE 153
George Tjungurrayi
*Kirrimalunya*, 2019

PLATE 154
Florrie Watson Napangati
*Tanyinki*, 2019

PLATE 155
Ngoia Napaltjarri
*Ancestral Women at Wilkinkarra*, 2019

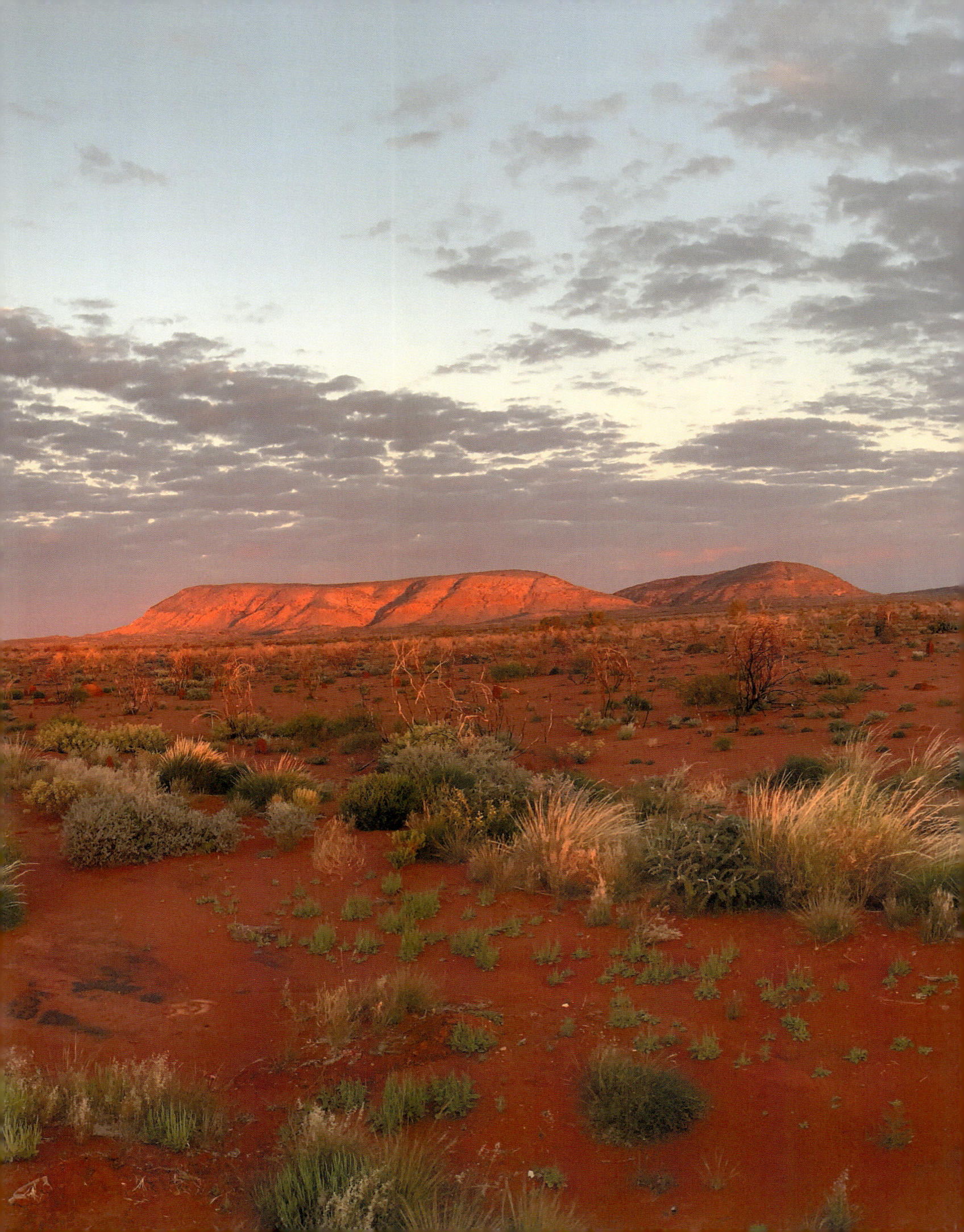

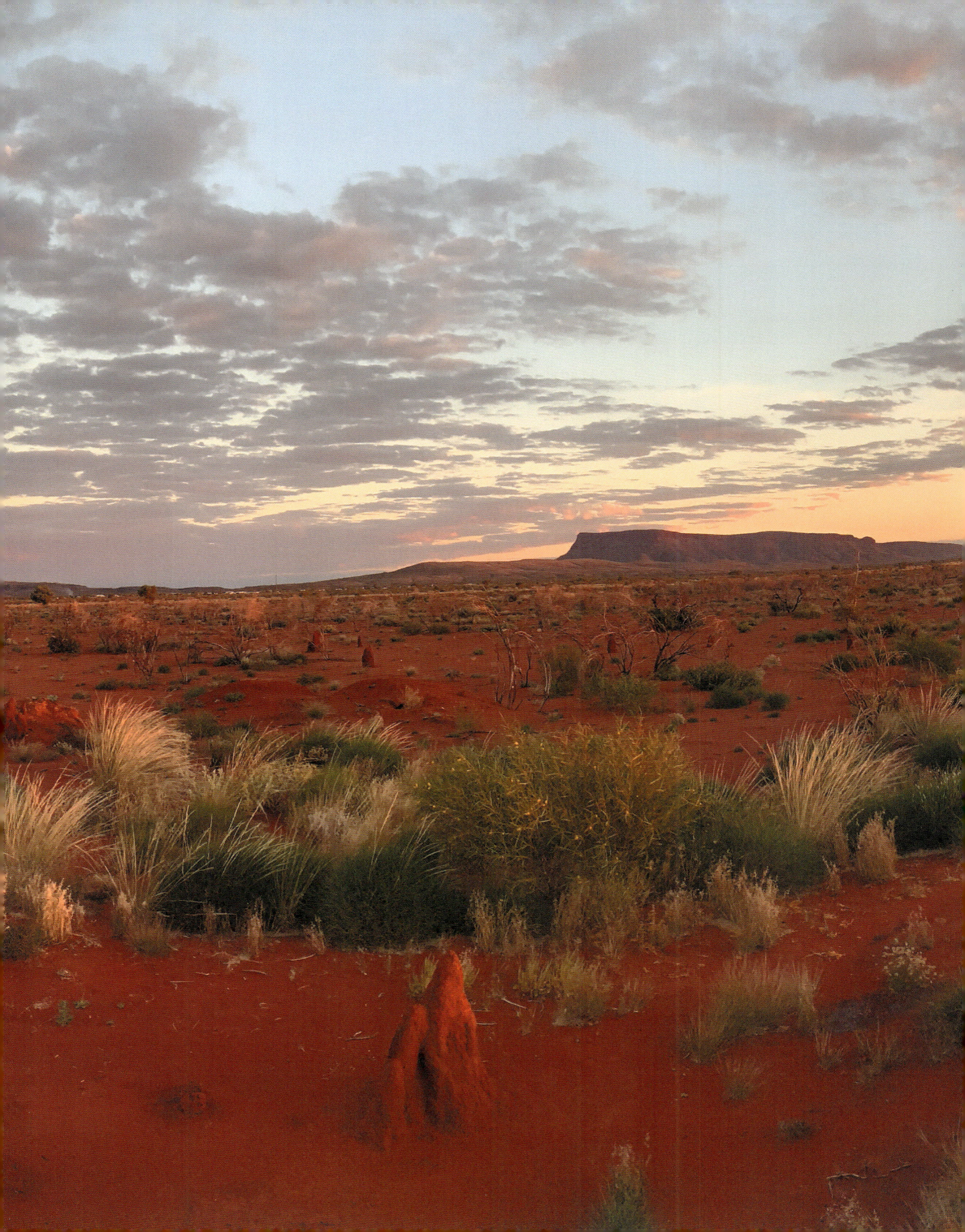

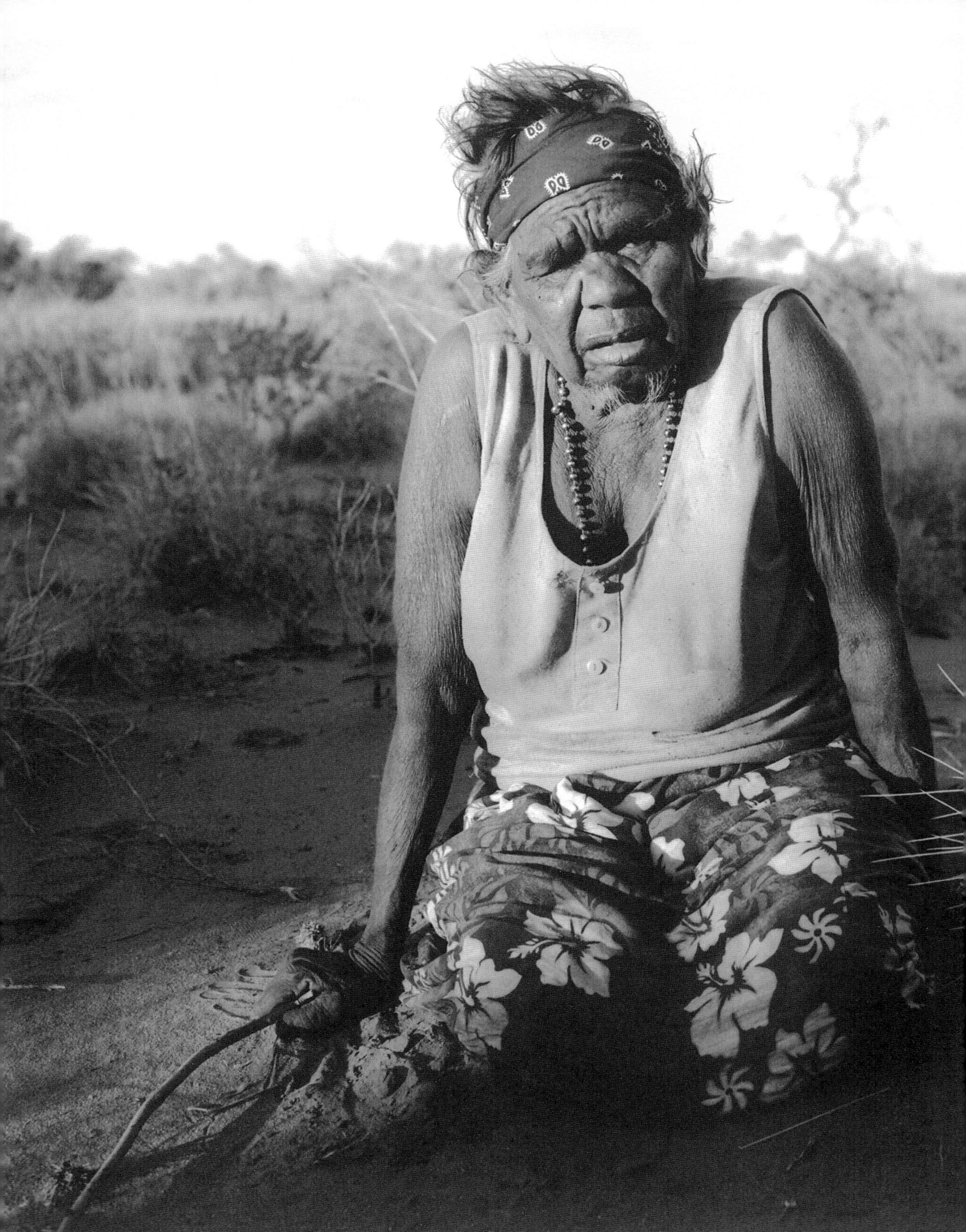

# CHECKLIST

**DEBRA NAKAMARRA**
**Born 1964, Pintupi**

*Tjintjintjin*, 2020
*The Papunya Tula Fiftieth Anniversary Suite*
Synthetic polymer paint on canvas
24 × 21⅝ in. (61 × 55 cm)
Commissioned by Richard Klingler and
Jane Slatter for *Irrititja Kuwarri Tjungu |
Past and Present Together*
Plate 114

**DOREEN REID NAKAMARRA**
**c. 1955–2009, Pintupi**

*Rockhole Site of Marrapinti*, 2006
Synthetic polymer paint on canvas
42¼ × 35¾ in. (107 × 91 cm)
Collection of Stephen and Agatha Luczo
Plate 90

**ELIZABETH MARKS NAKAMARRA**
**Born 1959, Pintupi**

*Kalipinypa*, 2021
*The Papunya Tula Fiftieth Anniversary Suite*
Synthetic polymer paint on canvas
24 × 21⅝ in. (61 × 55 cm)
Commissioned by Richard Klingler and
Jane Slatter for *Irrititja Kuwarri Tjungu |
Past and Present Together*
Plate 144

**JACQUELINE REID NAKAMARRA**
**Born 1958, Pintupi**

*Lupulnga*, 2020
*The Papunya Tula Fiftieth Anniversary Suite*
Synthetic polymer paint on canvas
24 × 21⅝ in. (61 × 55 cm)
Commissioned by Richard Klingler and
Jane Slatter for *Irrititja Kuwarri Tjungu |
Past and Present Together*
Plate 136

**KATHERINE NAKAMARRA**
**Born 1968, Pintupi**

*Kutungu at Tjintjintjin*, 2021
*The Papunya Tula Fiftieth Anniversary Suite*
Synthetic polymer paint on canvas
24 × 21⅝ in. (61 × 55 cm)
Commissioned by Richard Klingler and
Jane Slatter for *Irrititja Kuwarri Tjungu |
Past and Present Together*
Plate 113

**EDITH NAMPITJINPA**
**Born c. 1970, Pintupi**

*Tarkul*, 2019
*The Papunya Tula Fiftieth Anniversary Suite*
Synthetic polymer paint on canvas
24 × 21⅝ in. (61 × 55 cm)
Commissioned by Richard Klingler and
Jane Slatter for *Irrititja Kuwarri Tjungu |
Past and Present Together*
Plate 128

**INYUWA NAMPITJINPA**
**c. 1922–1999, Pintupi**

*Women's Dreaming at Pangkupirri*, 1996
Synthetic polymer paint on canvas
24⅛ × 21⅝ in. (61 × 55 cm)
Kluge-Ruhe Aboriginal Art Collection
Gift of John W. Kluge, 1997
1997.0006.002
Plate 62

*Travels of Kutungu from Papunnga to
Muruntji*, 1999
Synthetic polymer paint on canvas
60 × 48 in. (153 × 122 cm)
Collection of Richard Klingler and Jane
Slatter
Plate 55

**JOAN LOOMOO NAMPITJINPA**
**Born 1971, Kukatja/Pintupi**

*Kingfisher Dreaming at Namalu*, 2002
*The Papunya Tula Fiftieth Anniversary Suite*
Synthetic polymer paint on canvas
24 × 21⅝ in. (61 × 55 cm)
Commissioned by Richard Klingler and
Jane Slatter for *Irrititja Kuwarri Tjungu |
Past and Present Together*
Plate 108

**NYURAPAYIA NAMPITJINPA**
**c. 1930–1998, Pintupi/Pitjantjatjara**

*Women at Yulparitja*, 1996
Synthetic polymer paint on canvas
24 × 21 ⅝ in. (61 × 55 cm)
Kluge-Ruhe Aboriginal Art Collection
Gift of John W. Kluge, 1997
1997.0006.005
Plate 61

**ROSIE NAMPITJINPA**
**Born 1955, Pintupi**

*Yilpikarri*, 2021
*The Papunya Tula Fiftieth Anniversary Suite*
Synthetic polymer paint on canvas
24 × 21⅝ in. (61 × 55 cm)
Commissioned by Richard Klingler and
Jane Slatter for *Irrititja Kuwarri Tjungu |
Past and Present Together*
Plate 141

**YUYUYA NAMPITJINPA**
**Born c. 1946, Pintupi**

*Rockhole Site of Yumari*, 2000
Synthetic polymer paint on canvas
48 × 21⅝ in. (122 × 55 cm)
Collection of Richard Klingler and
Jane Slatter
Plate 52

*Yumari*, 2019
*The Papunya Tula Fiftieth Anniversary Suite*
Synthetic polymer paint on canvas
24 × 21⅝ in. (61 × 55 cm)
Commissioned by Richard Klingler and
Jane Slatter for *Irrititja Kuwarri Tjungu |
Past and Present Together*
Plate 126

### JOSEPHINE NANGALA
**Born c. 1950, Pintupi**

*Nyinmi*, 2020
*The Papunya Tula Fiftieth Anniversary Suite*
Synthetic polymer paint on canvas
24 × 21⅝ in. (61 × 55 cm)
Commissioned by Richard Klingler and
Jane Slatter for *Irrititja Kuwarri Tjungu |
Past and Present Together*
Plate 112

### MANTUA NANGALA
**Born c. 1959, Pintupi**

*Marrapinti*, 2021
*The Papunya Tula Fiftieth Anniversary Suite*
Synthetic polymer paint on canvas
24 × 21⅝ in. (61 × 55 cm)
Commissioned by Richard Klingler and
Jane Slatter for *Irrititja Kuwarri Tjungu |
Past and Present Together*
Plate 119

### NOWEE NANGALA
**c. 1930–1998, Kukatja**

*Kayili*, 1996
Synthetic polymer paint on canvas
35¾ × 18 in. (91 × 46 cm)
Kluge-Ruhe Aboriginal Art Collection
Gift of John W. Kluge, 1997
1997.0006.005
Plate 68

### TATALI NANGALA
**c. 1928–1999, Pintupi**

*Kungka Kutjarra Tjukurrpa (Two Women
Dreaming)*, 1996
Synthetic polymer paint on canvas
24 × 12³⁄₁₆ in. (61 × 31 cm)
Kluge-Ruhe Aboriginal Art Collection
Gift of John W. Kluge, 1997
1997.0006.004
Plate 63

### YINARUPA NANGALA
**Born c. 1961, Pintupi**

*Mukula*, 2020
*The Papunya Tula Fiftieth Anniversary Suite*
Synthetic polymer paint on canvas
24 × 21⅝ in. (61 × 55 cm)
Commissioned by Richard Klingler and
Jane Slatter for *Irrititja Kuwarri Tjungu |
Past and Present Together*
Plate 110

### EILEEN NAPALTJARRI
**Born 1956, Pintupi**

*Tjiturrurrnga*, 2020
*The Papunya Tula Fiftieth Anniversary Suite*
Synthetic polymer paint on canvas
24 × 21⅝ in. (61 × 55 cm)
Commissioned by Richard Klingler and
Jane Slatter for *Irrititja Kuwarri Tjungu |
Past and Present Together*
Plate 145

### KATARRA BUTLER NAPALTJARRI
**Born c. 1946, Pintupi**

*Ancestral Women at Tjukurla*, 2015
*The Papunya Tula Fiftieth Anniversary Suite*
Synthetic polymer paint on canvas
24 × 21⅝ in. (61 × 55 cm)
Commissioned by Richard Klingler and
Jane Slatter for *Irrititja Kuwarri Tjungu |
Past and Present Together*
Plate 140

### NGOIA NAPALTJARRI
**Born c. 1948, Warlpiri/Luritja**

*Ancestral Women at Wilkinkarra*, 2019
*The Papunya Tula Fiftieth Anniversary Suite*
Synthetic polymer paint on canvas
24 × 21⅝ in. (61 × 55 cm)
Commissioned by Richard Klingler and
Jane Slatter for *Irrititja Kuwarri Tjungu |
Past and Present Together*
Plate 155

### PAYU NAPALTJARRI
**Born 1955, Pintupi**

*Marrapinti*, 2019
*The Papunya Tula Fiftieth Anniversary Suite*
Synthetic polymer paint on canvas
21⅝ × 24 in. (55 × 61 cm)
Commissioned by Richard Klingler and
Jane Slatter for *Irrititja Kuwarri Tjungu |
Past and Present Together*
Plate 118

### TJUNKIYA NAPALTJARRI
**c. 1927–2009, Pintupi/Luritja**

*Women's Ceremonies at Yumari*, 1996
Synthetic polymer paint on canvas
21½ × 24 in. (55 × 61 cm)
Kluge-Ruhe Aboriginal Art Collection
Gift of John W. Kluge, 1997
1997.0006.003
Plate 50

*Rockhole Site of Yumari*, 2008
Synthetic polymer paint on canvas
35¹³⁄₁₆ × 35¹³⁄₁₆ in. (91 × 91 cm)
Kluge-Ruhe Aboriginal Art Collection
Promised gift of Greg Castillo
Plate 51

*Yumari*, 2009
*The Papunya Tula Fiftieth Anniversary Suite*
Synthetic polymer paint on canvas
24 × 21⅝ in. (61 × 55 cm)
Commissioned by Richard Klingler and
Jane Slatter for *Irrititja Kuwarri Tjungu |
Past and Present Together*
Plate 127

### WINTJIYA NAPALTJARRI
**c. 1932–2014, Pintupi**

*Wartunuma Claypan*, 2001
Synthetic polymer paint on canvas
35⅞ × 24⅛ in. (91 × 61 cm)
Kluge-Ruhe Aboriginal Art Collection
Museum purchase, 2002
2002.0002.002
Plate 53

### MAKINTI NAPANANGKA
**c. 1922–2011, Ngaatjatjarra**

*Lupulnga*, 2001
Synthetic polymer paint on canvas
60 × 48 in. (153 × 122 cm)
Collection of Richard Klingler and Jane
Slatter
Plate 64

*Lupulnga*, 2005
Synthetic polymer paint on canvas
47¾ × 24 in. (121 × 61 cm)
Kluge-Ruhe Aboriginal Art Collection
Gift of Stephen and Agatha Luczo, 2017
2017.0006.001
Plate 65

*Lupulnga*, 2006
Synthetic polymer paint on canvas
47¾ × 24 in. (121 × 61 cm)
Kluge-Ruhe Aboriginal Art Collection
Gift of Stephen and Agatha Luczo, 2017
2017.0006.002
Plate 66

*Lupulnga*, 2006
Synthetic polymer paint on canvas
47¾ × 24 in. (121 × 61 cm)
Kluge-Ruhe Aboriginal Art Collection
Gift of Stephen and Agatha Luczo, 2017
2017.0006.003
Plate 67

*Lupulnga*, 2008
*The Papunya Tula Fiftieth Anniversary Suite*
Synthetic polymer paint on canvas
24 × 21⅝ in. (61 × 55 cm)
Commissioned by Richard Klingler and
Jane Slatter for *Irrititja Kuwarri Tjungu |*
*Past and Present Together*
Plate 137

**PATRICIA JACKSON NAPANANGKA**
**Born 1983, Pintupi**

*Lupulnga*, 2020
*The Papunya Tula Fiftieth Anniversary Suite*
Synthetic polymer paint on canvas
24 × 21⅝ in. (61 × 55 cm)
Commissioned by Richard Klingler and
Jane Slatter for *Irrititja Kuwarri Tjungu |*
*Past and Present Together*
Plate 138

**WALANGKURA NAPANANGKA**
**(Johnny Yungut's wife), c. 1946–2015,**
**Pintupi**

*Marrapinti*, 2006
*The Papunya Tula Fiftieth Anniversary Suite*
Synthetic polymer paint on canvas
24 × 21⅝ in. (61 × 55 cm)
Commissioned by Richard Klingler and
Jane Slatter for *Irrititja Kuwarri Tjungu |*
*Past and Present Together*
Plate 117

**WALANGKURA NAPANANGKA**
**(Uta Uta's widow), c. 1938–2014, Pintupi**

*Women Making Hairstring at Tjukurla*, 2007
Synthetic polymer paint on canvas
35⅞ × 24⅛ in. (91.12 × 61.28 cm)
Kluge-Ruhe Aboriginal Art Collection
Museum purchase, 2008
2008.0001.001
Plate 69

**PANSY NAPANGARDI**
**Born c. 1940, Luritja/Warlpiri**

*Kungka Kutjarra (Two Women) at*
*Winpirri*, 1988
Synthetic polymer paint on canvas
66⅛ × 35½ in. (167.96 × 90.17 cm)
Kluge-Ruhe Aboriginal Art Collection
Gift of John W. Kluge, 1997
1989.7018.002
Plate 54

*Men's Dreaming at Ilpili*, 1991
Synthetic polymer paint on canvas
53¾ × 35¼ in. (136.53 × 89.54 cm)
Kluge-Ruhe Aboriginal Art Collection
Gift of John W. Kluge, 1997
1991.0036.022
Plate 16

**BOMBATU NAPANGATI**
**Born 1955, Pintupi**

*Ancestral Women at Ngaminya*, 2020
*The Papunya Tula Fiftieth Anniversary Suite*
Synthetic polymer paint on canvas
24 × 21⅝ in. (61 × 55 cm)
Commissioned by Richard Klingler and
Jane Slatter for *Irrititja Kuwarri Tjungu |*
*Past and Present Together*
Plate 123

**FLORRIE WATSON NAPANGATI**
**Born c. 1950, Pintupi**

*Tanyinki*, 2019
*The Papunya Tula Fiftieth Anniversary Suite*
Synthetic polymer paint on canvas
24 × 21⅝ in. (61 × 55 cm)
Commissioned by Richard Klingler and
Jane Slatter for *Irrititja Kuwarri Tjungu |*
*Past and Present Together*
Plate 154

**MARY NAPANGATI**
**Born 1949, Pintupi/Warlpiri**

*Tjutalpi*, 2020
*The Papunya Tula Fiftieth Anniversary Suite*
Synthetic polymer paint on canvas
24 × 21⅝ in. (61 × 55 cm)
Commissioned by Richard Klingler and
Jane Slatter for *Irrititja Kuwarri Tjungu |*
*Past and Present Together*
Plate 146

**NANYUMA NAPANGATI**
**Born c. 1940, Pintupi**

*Ngaminya*, 2020
*The Papunya Tula Fiftieth Anniversary Suite*
Synthetic polymer paint on canvas
24 × 21⅝ in. (61 × 55 cm)
Commissioned by Richard Klingler and
Jane Slatter for *Irrititja Kuwarri Tjungu |*
*Past and Present Together*
Plate 122

**YALTI NAPANGATI**
**Born c. 1969, Pintupi**

*Marrapinti*, 2020
*The Papunya Tula Fiftieth Anniversary Suite*
Synthetic polymer paint on canvas
24 × 21⅝ in. (61 × 55 cm)
Commissioned by Richard Klingler and
Jane Slatter for *Irrititja Kuwarri Tjungu |*
*Past and Present Together*
Plate 116

**YUKULTJI NAPANGATI**
**Born c. 1971, Pintupi**

*Ancestral Women at Marrapinti*, 2016
Synthetic polymer paint on canvas
49⅞ × 61⅞ in. (127 × 157 cm)
Collection of Steve Martin and Anne
Stringfield
Plate 91

*Marrapinti*, 2020
*The Papunya Tula Fiftieth Anniversary Suite*
Synthetic polymer paint on canvas
24 × 21⅝ in. (61 × 55 cm)
Commissioned by Richard Klingler and
Jane Slatter for *Irrititja Kuwarri Tjungu |*
*Past and Present Together*
Plate 120

**NINGURA NAPURRULA**
**c. 1938–2013, Ngaatjatjarra**

*Wirrulnga*, 2001
Synthetic polymer paint on canvas
48 × 48 in. (122 × 122 cm)
Collection of Richard Klingler and
Jane Slatter
Plate 94

**RUBILEE NAPURRULA**
**Born c. 1960, Pintupi**

*Yuwalki*, 2020
*The Papunya Tula Fiftieth Anniversary Suite*
Synthetic polymer paint on canvas
24 × 21⅝ in. (61 × 55 cm)
Commissioned by Richard Klingler and
Jane Slatter for *Irrititja Kuwarri Tjungu |*
*Past and Present Together*
Plate 142

**MICHAEL JAGAMARA NELSON**
**1949–2020, Warlpiri**

*Four Stories at Pikilyi*, 1988
Synthetic polymer paint on canvas
47½ × 71½ in. (120.65 × 181.61 cm)
Kluge-Ruhe Aboriginal Art Collection
Gift of John W. Kluge, 1997
1989.7011.005
Plate 28

*Pikilyi*, 1990
Synthetic polymer paint on canvas
71⅝ × 71⅝ in. (181.93 × 181.93 cm)
Kluge-Ruhe Aboriginal Art Collection
Gift of John W. Kluge, 1997
1990.7014.002
Plate 27

**LUCY LOOMOO NUNGURRAYI**
**1939–2020, Kukatja/Pintupi/Wangkajunka**

*Maluri*, 2015
*The Papunya Tula Fiftieth Anniversary Suite*
Synthetic polymer paint on canvas
24 × 21⅝ in. (61 × 55 cm)
Commissioned by Richard Klingler and
Jane Slatter for *Irrititja Kuwarri Tjungu |*
*Past and Present Together*
Plate 107

**NAATA NUNGURRAYI**
**Born c. 1932, Pintupi**

*Karilywarra*, 2010
Synthetic polymer paint on canvas
48 × 60 in. (122 × 153 cm)
Collection of Steve Martin and
Anne Stringfield
Plate 88

**NANCY NUNGURRAYI**
**c. 1935–2009, Pintupi**

*Marrapinti Water Soakage*, 2001
Synthetic polymer paint on canvas
36 × 24¼ in. (91 × 62 cm)
Kluge-Ruhe Aboriginal Art Collection
Museum Purchase, 2004
2004.0007.001
Plate 89

**CHARLIE WARD TJAKAMARRA**
**c. 1932–2005, Pintupi/Ngaanyatjarra/**
**Pitjantjatjara**

*Two Goanna Ancestral Men*, 2002
Synthetic polymer paint on canvas
47⅞ × 35⅝ in. (122 × 90 cm)
Kluge-Ruhe Aboriginal Art Collection
The Richard Klingler and Jane Slatter
Collection at Kluge-Ruhe, 2019
2019.0018.002
Plate 80

**FREDDY WEST TJAKAMARRA**
**c. 1932–1994, Pintupi**

*Tingarri Men at Walawala*, 1988
Synthetic polymer paint on canvas
58⅞ × 35⅝ in. (150 × 90 cm)
Kluge-Ruhe Aboriginal Art Collection
Gift of John W. Kluge, 1997
1989.7004.008
Plate 97

**JACK LONG PHILLIPUS TJAKAMARRA**
**1932–2020, Ngaliya/Warlpiri**

*Wayuta (Possum Ancestor) at*
*Ngamurunya*, 1973
Synthetic polymer paint on
composition board
22½ × 17 in. (57 × 43 cm)
Kluge-Ruhe Aboriginal Art Collection
Gift of Maria Tussi Kluge, 2012
2012.0002.002
Plate 29

**JOHN TJAKAMARRA**
**c. 1935–2002, Pintupi**

*Pintupi Ceremony*, 1971
Synthetic polymer paint on
composition board
23½ × 12 in. (60 × 31 cm)
Kluge-Ruhe Aboriginal Art Collection
Gift of John W. Kluge, 1997
1993.0008.014
Plate 3

**MICK WALLANGKARRI TJAKAMARRA**
**c. 1905–1996, Kukatja/Ngaliya**

*Honey Ant Travels*, 1971
Synthetic polymer paint on
composition board
8½ × 8½ in. (22 × 22 cm)
Kluge-Ruhe Aboriginal Art Collection
Gift of John W. Kluge, 1997
1993.0008.011
Plate 6

**RICHARD YUKENBARRI TJAKAMARRA**
**Born 1956, Pintupi**

*Ngunyarrmanya*, 2020
*The Papunya Tula Fiftieth Anniversary Suite*
Synthetic polymer paint on canvas
24 × 21⅝ in. (61 × 55 cm)
Commissioned by Richard Klingler and
Jane Slatter for *Irrititja Kuwarri Tjungu |*
*Past and Present Together*
Plate 106

**SIMON TJAKAMARRA**
**c. 1948–1990, Pintupi**

*Tingarri Camp at Pilintjinya*, 1988
Synthetic polymer paint on canvas
71½ × 47¾ in. (182 × 121 cm)
Kluge-Ruhe Aboriginal Art Collection
Gift of John W. Kluge, 1997
1989.7004.014
Plate 72

**TONY TJAKAMARRA**
**Born c. 1950, Pintupi/Warlpiri**

*Tingarri Men at Nyuntjurlnga*, 1990
Synthetic polymer paint on canvas
59⅝ × 48 in. (151 × 122 cm)
Kluge-Ruhe Aboriginal Art Collection
Gift of John W. Kluge, 1997
1991.0006.017
Plate 102

**YANATJARRI NO. III TJAKAMARRA**
**c. 1938–1992, Pintupi/Ngaanyatjarra**

*Untitled (possibly Wati Kutjarra at*
*Pakarangaranya)*, 1973
Synthetic polymer paint on canvas board
30⅛ × 23¹⁵⁄₁₆ in. (77 × 61 cm)
Kluge-Ruhe Aboriginal Art Collection
Gift of John W. and Maria T. Kluge, 2008
2008.0003.015
Plate 81

*Wapintjanya*, 1975
Synthetic polymer paint on canvas board
30 × 24 in. (76 × 61 cm)
Collection of Fred Myers
Plate 30

*Artist's Country near Kulkurta*, 1988
Synthetic polymer paint on canvas
71⅜ × 59¾ in. (181 × 152 cm)
Kluge-Ruhe Aboriginal Art Collection
Gift of John W. Kluge, 1997
1989.7004.016
Plate 71

*Muruntji*, 1988
Synthetic polymer paint on canvas
59⅝ × 48 in. (151 × 122 cm)
Kluge-Ruhe Aboriginal Art Collection
Gift of John W. Kluge, 1997
1989.7018.007
Plate 56

*Women's Dreaming near Kiwirrkurra*, 1989
Synthetic polymer paint on canvas
71½ × 48¹⁄₁₆ in. (182 × 122 cm)
Kluge-Ruhe Aboriginal Art Collection
Gift of John W. Kluge, 1997
1990.7024.001
Plate 93

### DINI CAMPBELL TJAMPITJINPA
#### c. 1942–2000, Pintupi

*Tingarri Cycle at Minyurlpa near Jupiter Well*, 1988
Synthetic polymer paint on canvas
72 × 48⅛ in. (183 × 122 cm)
Kluge-Ruhe Aboriginal Art Collection
Gift of John W. Kluge, 1997
1989.7012.002
Plate 83

### DINNY NOLAN TJAMPITJINPA
#### c. 1928–2012, Warlpiri

*Men's Ceremony*, c. 1974
Synthetic polymer paint on canvas
65 × 19 in. (165 × 48 cm)
Kluge-Ruhe Aboriginal Art Collection
Gift of John W. Kluge, 1997
1991.0021.013
Plate 15

### KAAPA TJAMPITJINPA
#### c. 1926–1989, Anmatyerr/Warlpiri/Arrernte

*Dreaming at Mikantji*, 1975
Synthetic polymer paint on canvas
68⅞ × 80 5/16 in. (175 × 204 cm)
The Embassy of Australia, Washington, DC
Plate 17

### KENNY WILLIAMS TJAMPITJINPA
#### Born c. 1950, Pintupi

*Hill Site of Karilywarra*, 1988
Synthetic polymer paint on canvas
60 × 47⅝ in. (152 × 121 cm)
Kluge-Ruhe Aboriginal Art Collection
Gift of John W. Kluge, 1997
1990.7006.007
Plate 87

### MARTIN TJAMPITJINPA
#### 1963–2007, Pintupi

*Muyinnga*, 2004
*The Papunya Tula Fiftieth Anniversary Suite*
Synthetic polymer paint on canvas
24 × 21⅝ in. (61 × 55 cm)
Commissioned by Richard Klingler and
Jane Slatter for *Irrititja Kuwarri Tjungu |
Past and Present Together*
Plate 130

### MAXIE TJAMPITJINPA
#### c. 1947–1997, Warlpiri

*Bushfire at Warlukurlangu*, 1988
Synthetic polymer paint on canvas
59 × 47½ in. (150 × 121 cm)
Kluge-Ruhe Aboriginal Art Collection
Gift of John W. Kluge, 1997
1989.7008.002
Plate 25

*Evening Bushfire Dreaming*, 1991
Synthetic polymer paint on canvas
47 × 46⅞ in. (119 × 119 cm)
Kluge-Ruhe Aboriginal Art Collection
Gift of John W. Kluge, 1997
1991.0036.023
Plate 26

### RAYMOND MAXWELL TJAMPITJINPA
#### Born 1955, Pintupi

*Kaakurutintjinya*, 2020
*The Papunya Tula Fiftieth Anniversary Suite*
Synthetic polymer paint on canvas
24 × 21⅝ in. (61 × 55 cm)
Commissioned by Richard Klingler and
Jane Slatter for *Irrititja Kuwarri Tjungu |
Past and Present Together*
Plate 131

### RONNIE TJAMPITJINPA
#### Born c. 1943, Pintupi

*Tjilkamata Ancestor Traveling East from Tarkulnga*, 1988
Synthetic polymer paint on canvas
49 × 73 in. (125 × 185 cm)
Kluge-Ruhe Aboriginal Art Collection
Gift of John W. Kluge, 1997
1989.7008.004
Plate 98

*Tingarritjarra*, 1989
Synthetic polymer paint on canvas
59⅝ × 48⅛ in. (151 × 122 cm)
Kluge-Ruhe Aboriginal Art Collection
Gift of John W. Kluge, 1997
1990.7004.001
Plate 99

*Tjintjintjin*, 1990
Synthetic polymer paint on canvas
65⁵⁄₁₆ × 19 in. (166 × 48 cm)
Kluge-Ruhe Aboriginal Art Collection
Gift of John W. Kluge, 1997
1991.0006.003
Plate 59

*Ralyanya*, 1999
Synthetic polymer paint on canvas
48 × 60 in. (122 × 152 cm)
The Collection of James and Elaine
Wolfensohn z"l
Plate 100

*Walungurru*, 2015
*The Papunya Tula Fiftieth Anniversary Suite*
Synthetic polymer paint on canvas
24 × 21⅝ in. (61 × 55 cm)
Commissioned by Richard Klingler and
Jane Slatter for *Irrititja Kuwarri Tjungu |
Past and Present Together*
Plate 132

**WALTER TJAMPITJINPA**
**c. 1912–1981, Pintupi**

*Kalipinypa*, 1972
Synthetic polymer powder paint
on composition board
25¹⁵⁄₁₆ × 16⁹⁄₁₆ in. (66 × 42 cm)
Kluge-Ruhe Aboriginal Art Collection
The Richard Klingler and Jane Slatter
Collection at Kluge-Ruhe, 2020
2020.0009.001
Plate 8

**YANATJARRI TJAMPITJINPA**
**c. 1927–1999, Pintupi**

*Tingarri at Yunarla*, 1993
Synthetic polymer paint on canvas
47¾ × 35⅜ in. (121 × 90 cm)
Kluge-Ruhe Aboriginal Art Collection
Gift of John W. Kluge, 1997
1991.0036.032
Plate 85

**AUBREY TJANGALA**
**Born 1970, Pintupi**

*Walungurru*, 2020
*The Papunya Tula Fiftieth Anniversary Suite*
Synthetic polymer paint on canvas
24 × 21⅝ in. (61 × 55 cm)
Commissioned by Richard Klingler and
Jane Slatter for *Irri̱titja Kuwarri Tjungu |
Past and Present Together*
Plate 129

**RAY JAMES TJANGALA**
**Born c. 1958, Pintupi**

*Yunarla*, 2021
*The Papunya Tula Fiftieth Anniversary Suite*
Synthetic polymer paint on canvas
24 × 21⅝ in. (61 × 55 cm)
Commissioned by Richard Klingler and
Jane Slatter for *Irri̱titja Kuwarri Tjungu |
Past and Present Together*
Plate 125

**UTA UTA TJANGALA**
**c. 1926–1990, Pintupi**

*Tjitji Kutjarra (Two Boys at
Yawarankunya)*, 1971
Synthetic polymer paint on
composition board
25³⁄₁₆ × 19³⁄₁₆ in. (64 × 49 cm)
Kluge-Ruhe Aboriginal Art Collection
Gift of John W. and Maria T. Kluge, 2008
2008.0003.010
Plate 43

*Ngurrapalangunya*, c. 1971–72
Synthetic polymer paint on
composition board
21 × 18¼ in. (53 × 46 cm)
Kluge-Ruhe Aboriginal Art Collection
Gift of John W. and Maria T. Kluge, 2008
2008.0003.004
Plate 46

*Old Man Dreaming at Yumari*, 1973
Synthetic polymer paint on
composition board
28 × 17 in. (71 × 43 cm)
Kluge-Ruhe Aboriginal Art Collection
Gift of John W. and Maria T. Kluge, 2008
2008.0003.006
Plate 47

*Tingarri Men at Warnmanpanya*, 1973
Synthetic polymer paint on
composition board
48³⁄₁₆ × 37 in. (122 × 94 cm)
Kluge-Ruhe Aboriginal Art Collection
Gift of John W. Kluge, 1997
1991.0021.008
Plate 96

*My Country with Sandhills*, 1980
Synthetic polymer paint on canvas board
26 × 23¾ in. (66 × 60 cm)
Kluge-Ruhe Aboriginal Art Collection
Gift of John W. and Maria T. Kluge, 2008
2008.0003.005
Plate 49

**ADAM GIBBS TJAPALTJARRI**
**Born 1967, Pintupi**

*Ngari Tjukurrpa (Honey Ant Dreaming)
at Papunya*, 2020
*The Papunya Tula Fiftieth Anniversary Suite*
Synthetic polymer paint on canvas
21⅝ × 24 in. (61 × 55 cm)
Commissioned by Richard Klingler and
Jane Slatter for *Irri̱titja Kuwarri Tjungu |
Past and Present Together*
Plate 143

**BILL STOCKMAN TJAPALTJARRI**
**c. 1927–2015, Anmatyerr**

*Ngatitjirri Tjukurrpa (Budgerigar
Dreaming)*, 1988
Synthetic polymer paint on canvas
55⅞ × 60⅜ in. (142 × 153 cm)
Kluge-Ruhe Aboriginal Art Collection
Gift of John W. Kluge, 1997
1990.7006.006
Plate 19

**CHARLIE MUTJU EGALIE
TJAPALTJARRI**
**c. 1925–2002, Warlpiri/Luritja**

*Ceremony Dancing*, 1972
Synthetic polymer paint on
composition board
30⅞ × 16⅞ in. (78 × 43 cm)
Kluge-Ruhe Aboriginal Art Collection
Gift of John W. Kluge, 1997
1991.0021.001
Plate 33

*Wallaby Dreaming in the Sandhills at
Tjunti*, 1977
Synthetic polymer paint on canvas board
19⁹⁄₁₆ × 19⅝ in. (50 × 50 cm)
Kluge-Ruhe Aboriginal Art Collection
Gift of John W. and Maria T. Kluge, 2008
2008.0003.003
Plate 32

**CLIFFORD POSSUM TJAPALTJARRI**
**c. 1932–2002, Anmatyerr**

*Paths of the Ancestors*, 1973
Synthetic polymer paint on
composite board
48 × 36 in. (122 × 91 cm)
Collection of Steve Martin and
Anne Stringfield
Plate 21

*Bushfire Dreaming*, c. 1986
Synthetic polymer paint on canvas
67 × 100½ in. (170 × 255 cm)
Kluge-Ruhe Aboriginal Art Collection
Gift of John W. Kluge, 1997
1990.7022.003
Plate 24

*Rain Dreaming at Mount Denison*, 1989
Synthetic polymer paint on canvas
50 × 103½ in. (127 × 263 cm)
Kluge-Ruhe Aboriginal Art Collection
Gift of John W. Kluge, 1997
1989.7012.004
Plate 22

## HILARY TJAPALTJARRI
### c. 1941–2017, Pintupi

*Nyiinkuwakalnga*, 2015
*The Papunya Tula Fiftieth Anniversary Suite*
Synthetic polymer paint on canvas
24 × 21⅝ in. (61 × 55 cm)
Commissioned by Richard Klingler and
Jane Slatter for *Irrititja Kuwarri Tjungu |
Past and Present Together*
Plate 134

## JOSEPH JURRA TJAPALTJARRI
### Born c. 1952, Pintupi

*Women Pulping Kampurarrpa at Ngaminya*,
1990
Synthetic polymer paint on canvas
71¹⁵⁄₁₆ × 47¹⁵⁄₁₆ in. (183 × 122 cm)
Kluge-Ruhe Aboriginal Art Collection
Gift of John W. Kluge, 1997
1990.7014.003
Plate 92

*Yunarla*, 2007
Synthetic polymer paint on canvas
60 × 48 in. (153 × 122 cm)
Collection of Richard Klingler and Jane
Slatter
Plate 86

*Yunarla*, 2021
*The Papunya Tula Fiftieth Anniversary Suite*
Synthetic polymer paint on canvas
24 × 21⅝ in. (61 × 55 cm)
Commissioned by Richard Klingler and
Jane Slatter for *Irrititja Kuwarri Tjungu |
Past and Present Together*
Plate 121

## MICK NAMARARI TJAPALTJARRI
### c. 1927–1998, Pintupi

*Mitukatjirri* (formerly *Men's Corroboree*),
1971–72
Synthetic polymer paint on
composition board
25³⁄₁₆ × 18³⁄₁₆ in. (64 × 46 cm)
Kluge-Ruhe Aboriginal Art Collection
Gift of John W. Kluge, 1997
1991.0021.021
Plate 78

*Muruntji* (formerly *Family Bush Tucker
Dreaming*), 1972
Synthetic polymer paint on
composition board
20⅛ × 20⅛ in. (51 × 51 cm)
Kluge-Ruhe Aboriginal Art Collection
Gift of John W. and Maria T. Kluge, 2008
2008.0003.002
Plate 58

*Untitled* (formerly *A Children's Story*), 1972
Synthetic polymer paint on
composition board
24¼ × 17⅞ in. (62 × 45 cm)
Kluge-Ruhe Aboriginal Art Collection
Gift of Maria Tussi Kluge, 2012
2012.0002.003
Plate 60

*Ceremony at Tjilka*, 1973
Synthetic polymer paint on
composition board
23¹⁵⁄₁₆ × 18 in. (61 × 46 cm)
Kluge-Ruhe Aboriginal Art Collection
Gift of John W. Kluge, 1997
1996.0002.002
Plate 36

*Kangaroo Ancestor at Walukirritji*, 1973
Synthetic polymer paint on
composition board
34 × 23 in. (86 × 58 cm)
Kluge-Ruhe Aboriginal Art Collection
Gift of John W. and Maria T. Kluge, 2008
2008.0003.008
Plate 38

*Family Moon Dreaming*, 1977
Acrylic on composition board
24⅜ × 18⅛ in. (62 × 46 cm)
Kluge-Ruhe Aboriginal Art Collection
Gift of John W. and Maria T. Kluge, 2008
2008.0003.001
Plate 37

*Two Wallabies at Marnpi*, 1989
Synthetic polymer paint on canvas
59¾ × 48 in. (152 × 122 cm)
Kluge-Ruhe Aboriginal Art Collection
Gift of John W. Kluge, 1997
1989.7022.001
Plate 39

*Wallaby Dreaming at Tjunginpa*, 1990
Synthetic polymer paint on canvas
73½ × 60¾ in. (187 × 154 cm)
Kluge-Ruhe Aboriginal Art Collection
Gift of John W. Kluge, 1997
1990.7014.001
Plate 40

## MORRIS GIBSON TJAPALTJARRI
### c. 1957–2017, Pintupi

*Kaakurutintjinya*, 2016
*The Papunya Tula Fiftieth Anniversary Suite*
Synthetic polymer paint on canvas
24 × 21⅝ in. (61 × 55 cm)
Commissioned by Richard Klingler and
Jane Slatter for *Irrititja Kuwarri Tjungu |
Past and Present Together*
Plate 133

## TIM LEURA TJAPALTJARRI
### c. 1929–1984, Anmatyerr

*Yam Spirit Dreaming*, 1972
Synthetic polymer paint on board
27½ × 21¼ in. (70 × 54 cm)
The John and Barbara Wilkerson
Collection
Plate 12

*Honey Ant Dreaming*, 1973
Synthetic polymer paint on
composition board
20 × 13⁵⁄₁₆ in. (51 × 34 cm)
Kluge-Ruhe Aboriginal Art Collection
Gift of John W. Kluge, 1997
1993.0006.006
Plate 7

*Women Sitting around the Fire at
Sunset*, c. 1973–74
Synthetic polymer paint on canvas board
27½ × 24 in. (70 × 61 cm)
Kluge-Ruhe Aboriginal Art Collection
Gift of John W. Kluge, 1997
1993.0006.005
Plate 23

*An Old Person's Dreaming*, 1975
Synthetic polymer paint on
composition board
24½ × 17¾ in. (62 × 45 cm)
Kluge-Ruhe Aboriginal Art Collection
Gift of Maria Tussi Kluge, 2012
2012.0002.001
Plate 14

*Water Dreaming*, 1975
Synthetic polymer paint on
composition board
24½ × 17¾ in. (62 × 45 cm)
Kluge-Ruhe Aboriginal Art Collection
Gift of John W. Kluge, 1997
1993.0008.003
Plate 13

### WARLIMPIRRNGA TJAPALTJARRI
**Born c. 1959, Pintupi**

*Tingarri at Tjulnga*, 1993
Synthetic polymer paint on canvas
53½ × 35⅝ in. (136 × 90 cm)
Kluge-Ruhe Aboriginal Art Collection
Gift of John W. Kluge, 1997
1991.0036.035
Plate 103

*Maruwa*, 2013
Synthetic polymer paint on canvas
60 × 72 in. (153 × 182 cm)
Collection of Steve Martin and Anne
Stringfield
Plate 105

*Maruwa*, 2016
*The Papunya Tula Fiftieth Anniversary Suite*
Synthetic polymer paint on canvas
24 × 21⅝ in. (61 × 55 cm)
Commissioned by Richard Klingler and
Jane Slatter for *Irrititja Kuwarri Tjungu |
Past and Present Together*
Plate 148

### WILLIAM SANDY TJAPALTJARRI
**Born c. 1944, Pitjantjatjara**

*Bush Tucker Dreaming at Wingellina*, 1988
Synthetic polymer paint on canvas
65⅞ × 65¾ in. (167 × 167 cm)
Kluge-Ruhe Aboriginal Art Collection
Gift of John W. Kluge, 1997
1989.7011.006
Plate 42

### CHARLIE TJAPANGATI
**Born c. 1949, Pintupi**

*Pirrinya*, 2018
*The Papunya Tula Fiftieth Anniversary Suite*
Synthetic polymer paint on canvas
24 × 21⅝ in. (61 × 55 cm)
Commissioned by Richard Klingler and
Jane Slatter for *Irrititja Kuwarri Tjungu |
Past and Present Together*
Plate 111

### JOHN JOHN BENNETT TJAPANGATI
**c. 1937–2002, Pintupi**

*Travels of the Tingarri Men from Tjukurla
to Mitukatjirri*, 2000
Synthetic polymer paint on canvas
53⅝ × 47⅞ in. (136 × 122 cm)
Kluge-Ruhe Aboriginal Art Collection
Gift of Stephen and Agatha Luczo, 2017
2017.0006.004
Plate 77

### LIMPI PUTUNGKA TJAPANGATI
**c. 1930–1985, Luritja/Arrernte**

*Yalka and Maku Tjukurrpa (Bush Onion
and Witchetty Grub Dreaming)*, 1980
Synthetic polymer paint on canvas
38½ × 66⅛ in. (98 × 168 cm)
Kluge-Ruhe Aboriginal Art Collection
Gift of John W. Kluge, 1997
1991.0021.017
Plate 41

### MATTHEW TJAPANGATI
**Born c. 1961, Pintupi**

*Tingarri Men at Murmur*, 2017
*The Papunya Tula Fiftieth Anniversary Suite*
Synthetic polymer paint on canvas
24 × 21⅝ in. (61 × 55 cm)
Commissioned by Richard Klingler and
Jane Slatter for *Irrititja Kuwarri Tjungu |
Past and Present Together*
Plate 151

### NYILYARI TJAPANGATI
**Born c. 1965, Pintupi**

*Wilkinkarra*, 2011
Synthetic polymer paint on canvas
35⅝ × 23⅝ in. (91 × 60 cm)
Kluge-Ruhe Aboriginal Art Collection
Gift of Stephen and Agatha Luczo, 2017
2017.0006.005
Plate 101

*Wilkinkarra*, 2017
*The Papunya Tula Fiftieth Anniversary Suite*
Synthetic polymer paint on canvas
24 × 21⅝ in. (61 × 55 cm)
Commissioned by Richard Klingler and
Jane Slatter for *Irrititja Kuwarri Tjungu |
Past and Present Together*
Plate 152

### TAMAYINYA TJAPANGATI
**Born c. 1969, Pintupi**

*Wilkinkarra*, 2018
*The Papunya Tula Fiftieth Anniversary Suite*
Synthetic polymer paint on canvas
24 × 21⅝ in. (61 × 55 cm)
Commissioned by Richard Klingler and
Jane Slatter for *Irrititja Kuwarri Tjungu |
Past and Present Together*
Plate 149

### TIMMY PAYUNGU TJAPANGATI
**c. 1935–2000, Pintupi**

*Tingarri Woman Dreaming at Wilkinkarra*, 1987
Synthetic polymer paint on canvas
71½ × 60 in. (182 × 152 cm)
Kluge-Ruhe Aboriginal Art Collection
Gift of John W. Kluge, 1997
1989.7011.003
Plate 95

### TIMMY PAYUNGU TJAPANGATI (attr.)
**c. 1935–2000, Pintupi**

*Ngapa Tjukurrpa (Storm Dreaming)*, 1971
Synthetic polymer paint on linoleum tile
11¾ × 12 in. (30 × 30 cm).
Kluge-Ruhe Aboriginal Art Collection
Gift of John W. Kluge, 1997
1993.0008.015
Plate 5

### TUTAMA TJAPANGATI (attr.)
**c. 1909–1987, Winanpa/Pintupi**

*Stars at Night Twinkling*, 1971
Synthetic polymer paint on fiber
cement cladding
22¼ × 17¾ in. (57 × 45 cm)
Kluge-Ruhe Aboriginal Art Collection
Gift of John W. Kluge, 1997
1993.0008.00
Plate 2

**ANGUS TJUNGURRAYI**
**Born after 1984, Pintupi**

*Claypan at Murmur*, 2018
*The Papunya Tula Fiftieth Anniversary Suite*
Synthetic polymer paint on canvas
24 × 21⅝ in. (61 × 55 cm)
Commissioned by Richard Klingler and
Jane Slatter for *Irrititja Kuwarri Tjungu |*
*Past and Present Together*
Plate 147

**CHARLIE WARTUMA TJUNGURRAYI**
**c. 1925–1999, Pintupi**

*Frost at Tjitururrnga*, 1971
Synthetic polymer paint on
composition board
11¼ × 11 in. (29 × 28 cm)
Kluge-Ruhe Aboriginal Art Collection
Gift of John W. Kluge, 1997
1996.0002.006
Plate 34

*Untitled* (probably *The Travels of Kutungu*),
before March 1972
Synthetic polymer paint on
composition board
23½ × 12 in. (60 × 30 cm)
Kluge-Ruhe Aboriginal Art Collection
Gift of John W. and Maria T. Kluge, 2008
2008.0003.013
Plate 57

*Untitled* (probably *Tjitururrnga*), 1972
Synthetic polymer paint on
composition board
17¹³⁄₁₆ × 12⅛ in. (45 × 31 cm)
Kluge-Ruhe Aboriginal Art Collection
Gift of Anne M. Chase, 2013
2013.0004.001
Plate 35

*Old Man's Dreaming at*
*Tjurrpungkuntjanya*, 1974
Synthetic polymer paint on
composition board
24¹⁄₁₆ × 18¹⁄₁₆ in. (61 × 46 cm)
Kluge-Ruhe Aboriginal Art Collection
Gift of John W. and Maria T. Kluge, 2008
2008.0003.011
Plate 45

*Travels of an Old Man to Yumari*, 1980
Synthetic polymer paint on canvas
47½ × 30 in. (121 × 76 cm)
Kluge-Ruhe Aboriginal Art Collection
Gift of John W. Kluge, 1997
1991.0021.012
Plate 48

**DON TJUNGURRAYI**
**1939–2020, Warlpiri/Luritja**

*Yantjipirri*, 1985
Synthetic polymer paint on canvas
59⅞ × 71¾ in. (152 × 182 cm)
Kluge-Ruhe Aboriginal Art Collection
Gift of John W. Kluge, 1997
1989.7008.003
Plate 20

**FRED WARD TJUNGURRAYI**
**Born c. 1955, Pintupi**

*Tingarri at Yunarla*, 1989
Synthetic polymer paint on canvas
71⅝ × 47⅝ in. (182 × 121 cm)
Kluge-Ruhe Aboriginal Art Collection
Gift of John W. Kluge, 1997
1990.7014.005
Plate 84

**GEORGE TJUNGURRAYI**
**Born c. 1943, Pintupi**

*Mamultjunkunya*, 1999
Synthetic polymer paint on canvas
60 × 72 in. (153 × 182 cm)
Collection of Richard Klingler and
Jane Slatter
Plate 104

*Kirrimalunya*, 2019
*The Papunya Tula Fiftieth Anniversary Suite*
Synthetic polymer paint on canvas
24 × 21⅝ in. (61 × 55 cm)
Commissioned by Richard Klingler and
Jane Slatter for *Irrititja Kuwarri Tjungu |*
*Past and Present Together*
Plate 153

**GEORGE WARD TJUNGURRAYI**
**Born c. 1945, Pintupi**

*Kaakurutintjinya (Lake Macdonald)*, 2003
Synthetic polymer paint on canvas
60¼ × 72 in. (153.03 × 182.88 cm)
Collection of Stephen and Agatha Luczo
Plate 76

*Tingarri at Kalkuritja*, 2012
*The Papunya Tula Fiftieth Anniversary Suite*
Synthetic polymer paint on canvas
24 × 21⅝ in. (61 × 55 cm)
Commissioned by Richard Klingler and
Jane Slatter for *Irrititja Kuwarri Tjungu |*
*Past and Present Together*
Plate 135

**PADDY CARROLL TJUNGURRAYI**
**c. 1927–2002, Warlpiri/Anmatyerr/Arrernte**

*Pupulu Jukurrpa (Lizard Dreaming) at*
*Tali Tali*, 1990
Synthetic polymer paint on canvas
54 × 34¾ in. (137 × 88 cm)
Kluge-Ruhe Aboriginal Art Collection
Gift of John W. Kluge, 1997
1991.0006.010
Plate 18

**PATRICK TJUNGURRAYI**
**c. 1935–2017, Pintupi/Munkultjarra**

*Tjiparitjarra*, 2001
Synthetic polymer paint on canvas
48 × 24 in. (122 × 61 cm)
Collection of Richard Klingler and
Jane Slatter
Plate 82

*Ngalkalarra*, 2017
*The Papunya Tula Fiftieth Anniversary Suite*
Synthetic polymer paint on canvas
24 × 21⅝ in. (61 × 55 cm)
Commissioned by Richard Klingler and
Jane Slatter for *Irrititja Kuwarri Tjungu |*
*Past and Present Together*
Plate 109

**SHORTY LUNGKARTA TJUNGURRAYI**
**c. 1912–1987, Pintupi**

*Tingarri Ceremony*, 1975
Synthetic polymer paint on
composition board
16¹⁵⁄₁₆ × 16¹⁵⁄₁₆ in. (43.02 × 43.02 cm)
Kluge-Ruhe Aboriginal Art Collection
Gift of John W. Kluge, 1997
1993.0008.010
Plate 70

*Rumiya Tjukurrpa (Goanna Dreaming at Wantarritja)* (formerly *Patterns in the Sand*), 1980
Synthetic polymer paint on composition board
23¹⁵⁄₁₆ × 25¹⁵⁄₁₆ in. (60.8 × 65.88 cm)
Kluge-Ruhe Aboriginal Art Collection
Gift of Maria Tussi Kluge, 2012
2012.0003.001
Plate 44

## WILLY TJUNGURRAYI
### c. 1932–2018, Pintupi/Winanpa

*Hail at Kaakurutintjinya*, 2001
Synthetic polymer paint on canvas
60 × 72 in. (152 × 183 cm)
Collection of Steve Martin and
Ann Stringfield
Plate 75

*Kirritjinya*, 2016
*The Papunya Tula Fiftieth Anniversary Suite*
Synthetic polymer paint on canvas
24 × 21⅝ in. (61 × 55 cm)
Commissioned by Richard Klingler and
Jane Slatter for *Irrititja Kuwarri Tjungu |
Past and Present Together*
Plate 139

## YALA YALA GIBBS TJUNGURRAYI
### c. 1924–1998, Pintupi

*Kuninka Tjukurrpa at Kaakurutintjinya*, 1988
Synthetic polymer paint on canvas
71 × 41½ in. (180.3 × 105.41 cm)
Kluge-Ruhe Aboriginal Art Collection
Gift of John W. Kluge, 1997
1990.7006.005
Plate 74

*Two Tingarri Men Traveling to
Kaakurutintjinya (Lake Macdonald)*, 1992
Synthetic polymer paint on canvas
60³⁄₁₆ × 20⅛ in. (152.88 × 51.12 cm)
Kluge-Ruhe Aboriginal Art Collection
Gift of John W. Kluge, 1997
1991.0036.017
Plate 73

## BOBBY WEST TJUPURRULA
### Born c. 1958, Pintupi

*Tarkul*, 2018
*The Papunya Tula Fiftieth Anniversary Suite*
Synthetic polymer paint on canvas
24 × 21⅝ in. (61 × 55 cm)
Commissioned by Richard Klingler and
Jane Slatter for *Irrititja Kuwarri Tjungu |
Past and Present Together*
Plate 124

## JOHN WEST TJUPURRULA
### Born c. 1968, Pintupi

*Palipalintjanya*, 2021
*The Papunya Tula Fiftieth Anniversary Suite*
Synthetic polymer paint on canvas
24 × 21⅝ in. (61 × 55 cm)
Commissioned by Richard Klingler and
Jane Slatter for *Irrititja Kuwarri Tjungu |
Past and Present Together*
Plate 115

## JOHNNY WARANGKULA TJUPURRULA
### c. 1918–2001, Pintupi

*Yala Tjukurrpa (Desert Yam Dreaming)*,
c. 1971
Synthetic polymer paint on
composition board
20 × 18½ in. (51 × 47 cm)
Kluge-Ruhe Aboriginal Art Collection
Gift of John W. and Maria T. Kluge, 2008
2008.0003.014
Plate 11

*Kalipinypa*, 1972
Synthetic polymer paint on
composition board
31½ × 19 in. (80.01 × 48.26 cm)
Kluge-Ruhe Aboriginal Art Collection
Gift of John W. Kluge, 1997
1993.0006.009
Plate 9

*Water Dreaming at Kalipinypa*, 1972
Synthetic polymer on composition board
31.5 × 29.5 in. (80 × 75 cm)
Collection of John and Barbara Wilkerson
Plate 10

*Tjikarri*, 1974
Synthetic polymer paint on canvas board
29½ × 23½ in. (75 × 60 cm)
Private collection
Plate 31

## JOHNNY YUNGUT TJUPURRULA
### c. 1930–2016, Pintupi

*Tjangimanta*, 2011
*The Papunya Tula Fiftieth Anniversary Suite*
Synthetic polymer paint on canvas
24 × 21⅝ in. (61 × 55 cm)
Commissioned by Richard Klingler and
Jane Slatter for *Irrititja Kuwarri Tjungu |
Past and Present Together*
Plate 150

## TURKEY TOLSON TJUPURRULA
### c. 1943–2001, Pintupi

*Straightening Spears at
Ilingawurrngawurrnga*, 1993
Synthetic polymer paint on canvas
71⅝ × 95⅝ in. (182 × 243 cm)
Kluge-Ruhe Aboriginal Art Collection
Gift of John W. Kluge, 1997
1991.0036.026
Plate 79

## UNIDENTIFIED ARTIST

*Dreaming Story*, 1971
Synthetic polymer paint on board
11¼ × 11 in. (29 × 28 cm)
Kluge-Ruhe Aboriginal Art Collection
Gift of John W. Kluge, 1997
1993.0008.012
Plate 4

## UNIDENTIFIED ARTIST

*Pintupi Design*, 1971
Synthetic polymer paint and natural
pigments on board (two sided)
25¾ × 7½ in. (65 × 19 cm)
Kluge-Ruhe Aboriginal Art Collection
Gift of John W. Kluge, 1997
1993.0008.007
Plate 1

# ADDITIONAL READING

## BOOKS

Amadio, Nadine, and Richard Kimber. *Wildbird Dreaming: Aboriginal Art from the Central Deserts of Australia*. Melbourne: Greenhouse Publications, 1988.

Auckland City Art Gallery. *The Painted Dream: Contemporary Aboriginal Paintings from the Tim and Vivien Johnson Collection*. Auckland: Auckland City Gallery, 1990.

Bardon, Geoffrey. *Aboriginal Art of the Western Desert*. Adelaide: Rigby, 1979.

Bardon, Geoffrey. *Papunya Tula: Art of the Western Desert*. Marleston, SA: Gecko Books, 1991.

Bardon, Geoffrey, and James Bardon. *Papunya: A Place Made after the Story: The Beginnings of the Western Desert Painting Movement*. Carlton, VIC: University of Melbourne Press, 2004.

Benjamin, Roger, ed. *Icons of the Desert: Early Aboriginal Painting from Papunya*. Ithaca, NY: Herbert F. Johnson Museum of Art, Cornell University, 2009.

Brody, Annemarie. *Face of the Centre: Papunya Tula Paintings 1971–84*. Melbourne: National Gallery of Victoria, 1985.

Carty, John, ed. *Patrick Tjungurrayi: Beyond Borders*. Crawley: University of Western Australia Press, 2015.

Crocker, Andrew. *Mr Sandman Bring Me a Dream*. Alice Springs, NT: Aboriginal Artists Agency with Papunya Tula Artists Pty Ltd, 1981.

Johnson, Vivien. *The Art of Clifford Possum*. East Roseville, NSW: Craftsman House, 1994.

Johnson, Vivien. *Lives of the Papunya Tula Artists*. Alice Springs, NT: IAD Press, 2008.

Johnson, Vivien. *Michael Jagamara Nelson*. Roseville, NSW: Craftsman House, 1997.

Johnson, Vivien. *Once Upon a Time in Papunya*. Sydney: University of New South Wales Press, 2010.

Johnson, Vivien, ed. *Papunya Painting: Out of the Desert*. Canberra: National Museum of Australia Press, 2007.

Kimber, Richard. *Friendly Country—Friendly People: An Exhibition of Aboriginal Artworks from the Peoples of the Tanami and Great Sandy Deserts*. Alice Springs, NT: Araluen Arts Centre, 1990.

Mellor, Doreen, and Vincent Megaw. *Twenty-Five Years and Beyond: Papunya Tula Painting*. Adelaide: Flinders University Art Museum, 1999.

Munn, Nancy. *Walbiri Iconography: Graphic Representation and Cultural Symbolism in a Central Australian Society*. Ithaca, NY: Cornell University Press, 1973.

Myers, Fred. *Painting Culture: The Making of an Aboriginal High Art*. Durham, NC: Duke University Press, 2002.

Myers, Fred. *Pintupi Country, Pintupi Self: Sentiment, Place, and Politics among Western Desert Aborigines*. Washington, DC: Smithsonian Institution Press, 1986.

O'Halloran, Alec. *The Master from Marnpi: Mick Namarari Tjapaltjarri*. Sydney: LifeDesign, Australia, 2018.

Papunya Tula Artists. *Nganana Tjungurringanyi Tjukurrpa Nintintjakitja: We Are Here Sharing Our Dreaming*. Alice Springs, NT, New York and Sun Valley, ID: Papunya Tula Artists, NYU Steinhardt and Harvey Art Projects, 2009.

Perkins, Hetti, and Hannah Fink. *Papunya Tula: Genesis and Genius*. Sydney: Art Gallery of New South Wales, 2000.

Ryan, Judith. *Mythscapes: Aboriginal Art of the Desert from the National Gallery of Victoria*. Melbourne: National Gallery of Victoria, 1989.

Ryan, Judith, and Philip Batty. *Tjukurrtjanu: Origins of Western Desert Art*. Melbourne: National Gallery of Victoria, 2011.

Scholes, Luke, ed. *Tjungunutja: From Having Come Together*. Darwin: Museum and Art Gallery of the Northern Territory, 2017.

Weber, John. *Papunya Tula: Contemporary Paintings from Australia's Western Desert*. New York. John Weber Gallery, 1989.

Williamson, Stephen. *Unique Perspectives: Papunya Tula Artists and the Alice Springs Community*. Alice Springs, NT: Araluen Art Centre and Papunya Tula Artists, 2012.

## FILM AND TELEVISION

*Art + Soul*. Directed by Warwick Thornton. Australian Broadcasting Corporation, 2010.

*Mr. Patterns*. Directed by Catriona McKenzie. Film Australia, 2004.

*Remembering Yayayi*. Directed by Pip Devenson, Ian Dunlop and Fred Myers. Documentary Educational Resources, 2014.

*The World about Us*. Season 11, episode 9, "The Desert Dreamers." Produced by the British Broadcasting Company. Aired April 2, 1977, on BBC Two.

# CONTRIBUTORS

**JOHN KEAN** is an independent writer, producer and curator. He is an honorary associate of the Museum Victoria, where he was a producer for fifteen years. From 1977 to 1979, he was the art adviser at Papunya Tula Artists.

**STEVE MARTIN** is an American actor, comedian, writer, producer, musician and art collector. Over his distinguished career, he has earned five Grammy Awards, a Primetime Emmy Award and an Honorary Academy Award.

**FRED MYERS** is the Silver Professor of Anthropology at New York University and author of the books *Pintupi Country, Pintupi Self: Sentiment, Place, and Politics among Western Desert Aborigines* (Smithsonian Institution, 1986) and *Painting Culture: The Making of an Aboriginal High Art* (Duke University Press, 2002).

**ELIZABETH MARKS NAKAMARRA** was born at Papunya in 1959 and raised by Turkey Tolson Tjupurrula. She was married to Mick Namarari Tjapaltjarri and began painting after his death in 1998.

**NARLIE NELSON NAKAMARRA** is the eldest daughter of renowned Papunya Tula artist Johnny Warangkula Tjupurrula, from whom she learned the stories of Kalipinypa, the subject of most of her paintings.

**EILEEN NAPALTJARRI** is the daughter of the artists Charlie Wartuma Tjungurrayi and Tatali Nangala. She has painted for Papunya Tula Artists since 1996, and her works are held in numerous public collections, including the National Gallery of Australia and the Hood Museum of Art, Dartmouth.

**CHARLOTTE PHILLIPUS NAPURRULA** is an acclaimed Warlpiri/ Luritja artist who lives and works at Papunya. She is the daughter of Jack Long Phillipus Tjakamarra, one of the founders of Papunya Tula Artists.

**PUNATA STOCKMAN NUNGURRAYI** is the daughter of Bill Stockman Tjapaltjarri and Yintinaka Nampitjinpa. Along with her mother, Punata assisted her father with his paintings before becoming an artist in her own right.

**RACHEL PALTRIDGE** is the coordinator of the Kiwirrkurra Indigenous Protected Area. She has worked on conservation projects with the people of the Western Deserts since the 1990s, focusing on projects that integrate traditional Indigenous knowledge with scientific methods and technologies.

**HETTI PERKINS** is a member of the Arrernte and Kalkadoon communities. From 1989 to 2011 she was the senior curator of Aboriginal and Torres Strait Islander art at the Art Gallery of New South Wales (AGNSW), where she curated the exhibition *Papunya Tula: Genesis and Genius* (2000). In 2010, she curated the project *Art + Soul*, which became an exhibition at the AGNSW, a book and a television documentary.

**CARA PINCHBECK** is a member of the Kamilaroi community of northern New South Wales. She is the senior curator of Aboriginal and Torres Strait Islander art at the Art Gallery of New South Wales, where her exhibitions and publications include *Yirrkala Drawings* (2013), *When Silence Falls* (2015), *Art from Milingimbi: Taking Memories Back* (2016) and *Noŋgirrŋa Marawili: From My Heart and Mind* (2018).

**MARGO SMITH** is director of the Kluge-Ruhe Aboriginal Art Collection of the University of Virginia. In 2015, she was appointed an Honorary Member of the Order of Australia.

**HENRY SKERRITT** is curator of the Indigenous arts of Australia at the Kluge-Ruhe Aboriginal Art Collection of the University of Virginia. His exhibitions and publications include *No Boundaries: Contemporary Aboriginal Australian Abstract Painting* (Nevada Museum of Art, 2014) and *Marking the Infinite: Women Artists from Aboriginal Australia* (Nevada Museum of Art, 2016).

**MARINA STROCCHI** is an internationally exhibited painter and printmaker whose work is held in many national collections. She was the founding manager of Ikuntji Artists and, in 1994, facilitated the Minyma Tjukurrpa Kintore / Haasts Bluff Painting Project catalyzed the women's painting movement at Papunya Tula.

**PAUL SWEENEY** is the manager of Papunya Tula Artists, a position he has held since 2003. Prior to this he worked in the roles of assistant manager and field officer during his twenty-six years at the company.

**MORRIS JACKSON TJAMPITJINPA** is the son of Uta Uta Tjangala and served as a consultant on the 2017 exhibition *Tjungunutja (From Having Come Together)* at the Museum and Art Gallery of the Northern Territory.

**JOSEPH JURRA TJAPALTJARRI** is an internationally recognized artist and former chairperson of Papunya Tula Artists. He learned to paint assisting Charlie Wartuma Tjungurrayi before beginning in his own right in 1986, and he has traveled to Europe and the United States to represent the company.

**BOBBY WEST TJUPURRULA** is the son of founding Papunya Tula artist Freddy West Tjakamarra. He served as chairman of the Kiwirrkurra Council for over a decade during the 1990s and has been a long-term board member and chairperson of Papunya Tula Artists.

**JODIE NAPURRULA WARD** is a young leader and ranger from Kiwirrkurra Community who is passionate about two-way science and helping to pass on traditional knowledge from the Elders to the younger generation. She is the eldest daughter of the renowned artist Yukultji Napangati.

Published in 2021 by the Kluge-Ruhe Aboriginal Art Collection of the University of Virginia and distributed by the University of Virginia Press.

Kluge-Ruhe Aboriginal Art Collection of
the University of Virginia
400 Worrell Drive
Charlottesville, VA 22911-8691
Tel: +1-434-244-0234
E-mail: kluge-ruhe@virginia.edu
kluge-ruhe.org

University of Virginia Press
P.O. Box 400318, Charlottesville, VA 22904-4318
Tel: +1-434-924-3468
E-mail: vapress@virginia.edu
upress.virginia.edu

ISBN: 978-1-7353-2692-4

Library of Congress Control Number: 2021913876

Edited by Kristin Swan
Designed by Lindsay Starr

Printed in Dulles, VA, by Integrated Books International

Front cover: Unidentified artist, *Pintupi Design*, 1971 (detail, plate 1, front).

Back cover: Unidentified artist, *Pintupi Design*, 1971 (detail, plate 1, back).

NEXT PAGE

Makinti Napanangka leaving the Papunya Tula Artists studio at Walungurru (Kintore), 1996. Photo by Paul Sweeney.

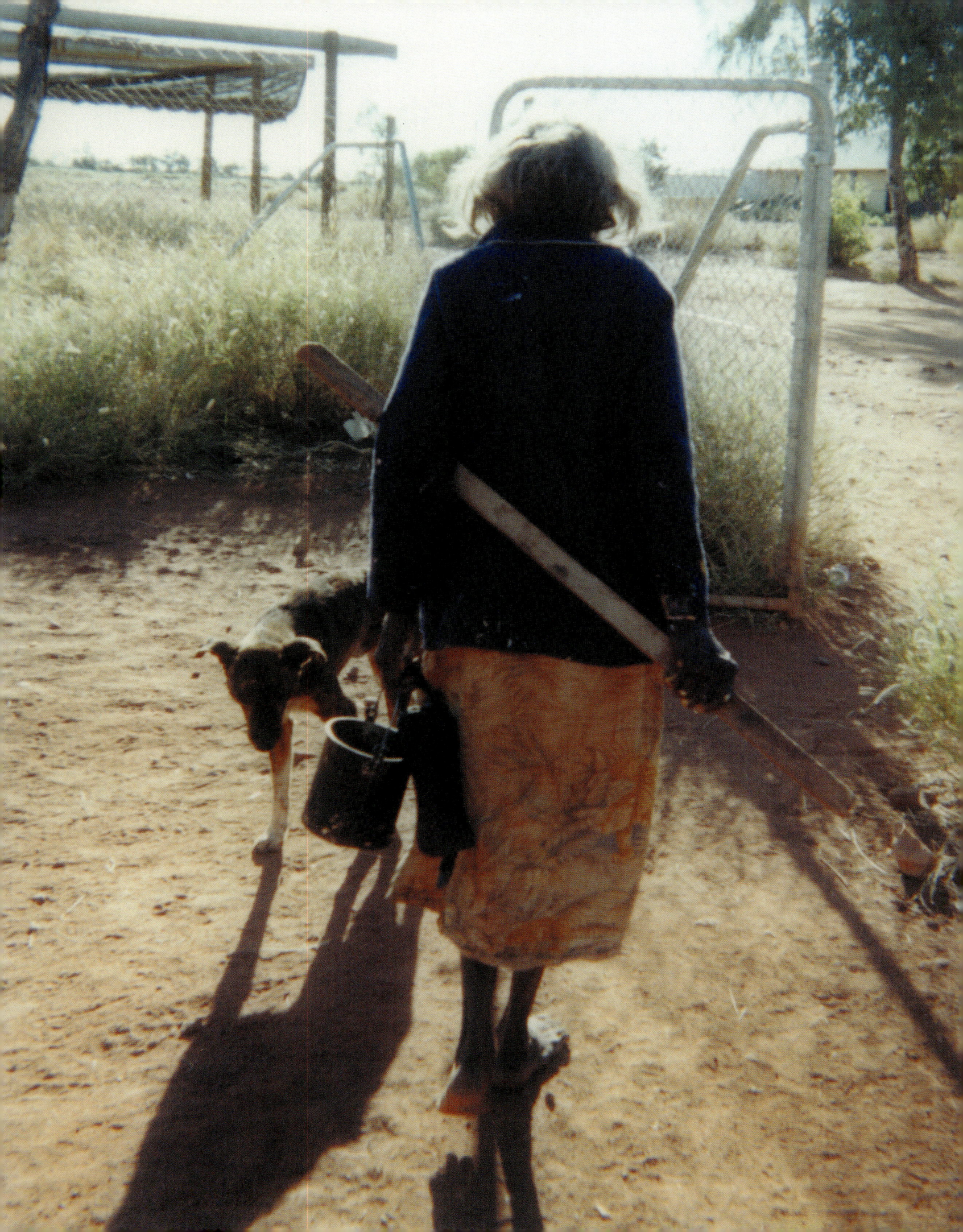